Corporation Finance

Dr. Marshall's Course

Finance 237

Authors
Laurence Booth • Pamela Peterson Drake • W. Sean Cleary

Instructor
Dr. James N. Marshall

Muhlenberg College

ISBN 9781119307167

Printed in the United States of America 10 9 8 7 6 5 4 3 2 1

List of Titles

Corporate Finance
by Laurence Booth, W. Sean Cleary, and Pamela Peterson Drake
Copyright © 2014, ISBN: 978-0-470-44464-1

Table of Contents

CORPORATE FINANCE

FINANCIAL MANAGEMENT IN A GLOBAL ENVIRONMENT

CORPORATE FINANCE

FINANCIAL MANAGEMENT IN A GLOBAL ENVIRONMENT

Laurence Booth, DBA
University of Toronto

W. Sean Cleary, PhD, CFA
Saint Mary's University

Pamela Peterson Drake, PhD, CFA
James Madison University

VICE PRESIDENT & EXECUTIVE PUBLISHER	George Hoffman
EXECUTIVE EDITOR	Joel Hollenbeck
SENIOR PRODUCT DESIGNER	Allison Morris
EDITORIAL OPERATIONS MANAGER	Yana Mermel
CONTENT EDITOR	Jennifer Manias
ASSISTANT EDITOR	Courtney Luzzi
ASSOCIATE DIRECTOR OF MARKETING	Amy Scholz
SENIOR MARKETING MANAGER	Jesse Cruz
SENIOR CONTENT MANAGER	Dorothy Sinclair
SENIOR PRODUCTION EDITOR	Erin Bascom
DESIGN DIRECTOR	Harry Nolan
PHOTO DEPARTMENT MANAGER	Hilary Newman
SENIOR EDITORIAL ASSISTANT	Erica Horowitz
MARKETING ASSISTANT	Justine Kay
SENIOR MEDIA SPECIALIST	Elena Santa Maria
PRODUCTION MANAGEMENT SERVICES	Bruce Hobart/Laserwords Maine
TEXT AND COVER DESIGNER	Madelyn Lesure
COVER PHOTO	© Stefan Siems/Getty Images, Inc.

Credit for author photos: Carole Booth, Sean Cleary, Katie Landis.
Repeated icon photos: (magnifying glass and spreadsheet) Joe Belanger/iStockphoto; (calculator) Jeremiah Thompson/iStockphoto

This book was set in Times Ten LT Std 10/12 by Laserwords and printed and bound by RRD/Jefferson City. The cover was printed by RRD/Jefferson City.

This book is printed on acid free paper. ∞

Founded in 1807, John Wiley & Sons, Inc. has been a valued source of knowledge and understanding for more than 200 years, helping people around the world meet their needs and fulfill their aspirations. Our company is built on a foundation of principles that include responsibility to the communities we serve and where we live and work. In 2008, we launched a Corporate Citizenship Initiative, a global effort to address the environmental, social, economic, and ethical challenges we face in our business. Among the issues we are addressing are carbon impact, paper specifications and procurement, ethical conduct within our business and among our vendors, and community and charitable support. For more information, please visit our website: www.wiley.com/go/citizenship.

Library of Congress Cataloging-in-Publication Data
Booth, Laurence D.
  Corporate finance / Laurence Booth, W. Sean Cleary, Pamela Peterson Drake.
    p. cm.
  Includes index.
  ISBN 978-0-470-44464-1 (cloth)
  1. Corporations—Finance. I. Cleary, W. Sean (William Sean), 1962- II. Peterson Drake, Pamela, 1954-
III. Title.
  HG4026.B646 2013
  658.15—dc23
                                                                                                            2012026781

978-0-470-44464-1   (Main Book ISBN)
978-1-118-12936-4   (Binder-Ready Version ISBN)

Printed in the United States of America
10 9 8 7 6 5 4 3 2 1

Laurence Booth, D.B.A., M.B.A., M.A. (Indiana University); B.S. (London School of Economics) holds the CIT chair in structured finance at the Rotman School of Management at the University of Toronto. He has published over fifty articles in academic journals, as well as major textbooks for McGraw-Hill, *International Business*, with Alan Rugman and Don Lecraw, and John Wiley & Sons, *Introduction to Corporate Finance,* 2nd edition, with Sean Cleary.

At the University of Toronto since 1978, Laurence Booth has taught graduate courses in business finance, international financial management, corporate financing, mergers and acquisitions, financial management, and financial theory, as well as short executive programs on the money & foreign exchange markets, business valuation, mergers and acquisitions, and financial strategy. He is a frequent expert financial witness on financial management topics such as the cost of capital, financial structure and the importance of bond ratings.

W. Sean Cleary, Ph.D. (University of Toronto) M.B.A. (Saint Mary's University), B.Ed. (Saint Francis Xavier University), B.A. (Acadia University), CFA, is the BMO Professor of Finance and Director of the Master of Finance, Queen's School of Business, Queen's University.

In addition to numerous articles in various academic journals, he is coauthor of *Introduction to Corporate Finance*, John Wiley & Sons Canada Limited (2007, 2010). He is the Canadian author of the first three editions of the textbook, *Investments: Analysis and Management*, with Charles P. Jones, also published by John Wiley & Sons Canada Limited (1999, 2004, 2008). He coauthored the textbook, *Finance in a Canadian Setting* (6th edition), with Peter Lusztig and Bernard Schwab, published in 2001 by John Wiley & Sons Canada Limited. He is also the author of *The Canadian Securities Exam Fast Track Study Guide*, also published by John Wiley & Sons Canada Limited.

Sean Cleary has taught numerous university finance courses, including capital markets, financial institutions, investments, introductory finance, corporate finance, and mergers and acquisitions.

Pamela Peterson Drake, Ph.D. (University of North Carolina), B.S. (Miami University), CFA, is the J. Gray Ferguson Professor of Finance and Department Head, Department of Finance and Business Law in the College of Business at James Madison University.

In addition to authoring or coauthoring articles in academic journals, Pamela Peterson Drake has written a number of books with Frank Fabozzi, including *Analysis of Financial Statements*, *Basics of Finance*, *Capital Budgeting*, and *Financial Management and Analysis*, all published by John Wiley & Sons. She is also author or coauthor for numerous readings that are part of the CFA curriculum, as well as the monographs published by the CFA Institute, *Real Options*, with Don Chance, and *Company Performance and Measures of Value Added*, with David R. Peterson.

Pamela Peterson Drake has been at James Madison University since 2007 and teaches courses in financial management, financial analysis, analysis of financial policy, analytical methods, and spreadsheet skills. She taught financial management and quantitative methods previously at Florida State University (1981–2004) and Florida Atlantic University (2004–2007).

In this text, we have tried to address the basic question: What do students need to know about the principles of finance? Though not everyone who picks up this book is a finance major or is destined for a finance career, finance is ubiquitous; you can find it throughout any business enterprise.

What are the key ingredients to finance? Accounting, economics, and mathematics.

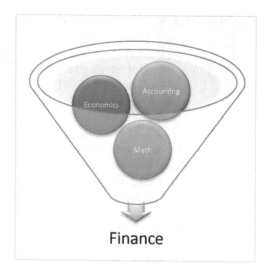

Finance

- Financial managers use accounting information, combined with market information, to make decisions.
- Financial decision making requires economic reasoning and the principles of both micro- and macroeconomics.
- Financial calculations at this level use algebra and well-disguised calculus.

The Structure of This Book

In a nutshell, this book begins with the building blocks of financial management:

Setting the stage for the environment in which decisions are made, in Part 1 we introduce students to financial intermediation (Chapter 1) and financial markets (Chapter 2). We introduce students to financial analysis in Part 2 by first reviewing the financial statements (Chapter 3) and then focusing on how to use these financial statements to evaluate the financial performance and condition of a business enterprise (Chapter 4).

In part 3 we introduce the student to financial mathematics (Chapter 5) and then apply this to bonds (Chapter 6) and equity (Chapter 7). Recognizing that financial decision making of an enterprise is not made in a vacuum, but rather in the context of financial markets, in Part 4 we discuss the concepts and theories of the pricing of assets (Chapter 8), followed by a discussion of the theories of how assets are priced (Chapter 9).

We build on this foundation with applications that involve long-term investment and financing decisions:

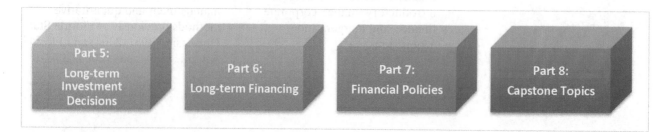

In Part 5 we detail the methods of evaluating long-term investments (a.k.a. capital budgeting; Chapter 10), followed by a discussion of and demonstration of the tools we use to make capital budgeting decisions (Chapter 11). Financial decisions involve not only the investment decisions—that is, what to do with funds to help the enterprise grow—but also how a company finances these investments, as we discuss in Part 6. In part 7 we discuss raising

vi

money using debt instruments (Chapter 12) and using equity securities (Chapter 13). We also detail the costs of financing (Chapter 14), which affect investment choices.

A discussion of financing instruments is not complete without a discussion of the factors that affect the company's choice of how to finance its investments (Chapter 15). Because any dividend paid to owners is a use of funds that could have been employed for investment purposes, we discuss the theories and reasons why companies pay dividends (Chapter 16).

We present a number of aspects of financial management decision making that affect both investments and financing in Part 8, including financial planning (Chapter 17), risk management (Chapter 18), working capital management (Chapter 19), leasing (Chapter 20), and mergers and acquisitions (Chapter 21). A module on Global Financial Management is also available online.

Focus

Our focus in this book is on decision making for a business enterprise, whether that enterprise is a small business, a publicly traded corporation, or a limited liability company. We also recognize that decisions of an enterprise are rarely restricted to a specific locale, so we have tried to take a global view of financial decision making. Though the original edition of this book was written for a Canadian readership, the present book is neither Canadian-centric nor U.S.-centric; rather, we attempt to explain decision making without regard to the country of the enterprise. Though a few topics are U.S. specific, such as taxes, these few topics can be viewed as representative of what an enterprise faces, regardless of whether the enterprise is located in India, Japan, China, the United States, or elsewhere.

Pedagogy

Throughout this book, we have tried to address different learning styles so that all students may be successful. To that end, we provide a number of pedagogical features:

Learning Outcomes correspond directly to the sections in the chapter and to specific end of chapter questions and problems.

Learning Outcomes

After reading this chapter, you should be able to:

LO 5.1 Describe and compare the principles of compound interest and simple interest, and apply these principles to solve present value and future value problems involving a single sum.

LO 5.2 Identify and apply the appropriate method of valuing different patterns of cash flows, including the ordinary annuity, annuity due, deferred annuity, and perpetuity.

A **running glossary** allows for a quick review of key terms. A comprehensive glossary with extended definitions is available at the back of the book.

simple interest interest paid or received on only the initial investment

principal amount loaned or the amount of the investment

Summary boxes to help put together the pieces.

SUMMARIZING

The equation for the future value, $FV_n = PV_0(1 + i)^n$, has four values, and if we know any three of them we can solve for the last one. We can solve four different types of finance problems using this equation:

1. *Future value problems*: How much will I have in w years at $x\%$ if I invest $\$y$?
2. *Present value problems*: What is the value today of receiving $\$z$ in w years if the interest rate is $x\%$?
3. *Determining the interest rate*: What rate of return will I earn if I invest $\$y$ today for w years and get $\$z$?
4. *Determining the number of periods*: How long do I have to wait to get $\$z$ if I invest $\$y$ today at $x\%$?

It's Greek to Me | FINANCE in the News

Sovereign debt is indebtedness issued by a national government. For example, the Treasury bills and bonds issued by the U.S. government are part of the sovereign debt of the U.S. One of the fallouts of the 2007–2008 crisis is the downgrading of sovereign debt. Greece, with its long history of budget problems, was the first to fall. Its debt was downgraded in 2009, in 2010, in 2011, and then again in 2012. The rating of Greece's debt from Moody's fell from A1 to C in this three-year period. To put this in perspective, the rating of Greece's debt went from "High economic, financial or institutional strength" to "One shock away from default, and/or material concerns about the willingness to pay."[28] The upshot of the downgrade is that the debt is considered riskier, and therefore, the cost of raising capital

increases. By 2012, the yield on 10-year Greek debt was over 3,300 basis points (that is, 33%) higher than other European sovereign debt, and the debt was, effectively, in default.[29] Other countries followed suit, with Portugal and Spain following close behind Greece.

Like any business, an economic slowdown such as the one that followed the global crisis affects the countries that have the weakest economies. Factors considered important in rating sovereign debt include gross domestic product, government policies in dealing with budgets, policies of the central bank, and unemployment.[30] The challenge is that once the debt is downgraded, the cost of raising new capital is greater, and the country will have difficulty raising capital to finance its operations.

Special topic boxes provide context, examples, and illustrations of the material in terms of Ethics (the good, the bad, and the ugly), Finance in the News (good and bad), Global Perspectives (it's a small world after all, isn't it?), and Lessons Learned (learning from the past).

Boxed examples that are illustrations of the calculations, both in terms of the math and with the use of calculators to solve the problems. We also provide additional examples on the book's web site in case the reader needs more.

PROBLEM   EXAMPLE 5.1

Suppose someone invests $10,000 today for a five-year term and receives 3% annual sim-   **Simple Interest**
ple interest on the investment. How much would the investor have after five years?

Solution

Annual interest = $10,000 × 0.03 = $300 per year.

Or

$$FV_5 = \$10,000 + [5 \times \$10,000 \times 0.03] = \$10,000 + 1,500 = \$11,500$$

Year	Beginning amount	Ending amount
1	$10,000	$10,300
2	10,300	10,600
3	10,600	10,900
4	10,900	11,200
5	11,200	11,500

The interest earned is $300 every year, regardless of the beginning amount, because interest is earned on only the original investment. Interest is *not* earned on any earned interest.

---

1. At what frequency of compounding is the effective annual rate equal to the annual   *Concept Review*
   percentage rate? Explain your answer.   *Questions*

2. The Truth-in-Lending law in the U.S. requires lenders to disclose the APR for any
   loan transaction. Does the APR overstate or understate the true cost of a loan?
   Explain.

Concept review questions at the end of each section, are designed to get the reader to think critically about the material in the section.

SUMMARY

- By applying the process of compounding or discount at an appropriate rate of return, we can calculate economically equivalent values through time. For example, we can calculate the future value five years from now of an amount today. We can also determine the equivalent present value or future value for a series of cash flows.

- Annuities represent a special type of cash flow stream that involve equal payments at the same interval, with the same interest rate being applied throughout the period. We see that these kinds of cash flow streams are commonplace in finance applications (e.g., loan payments) and that there are relatively simple formulas that enable us to determine the present value or future value of such cash flows.

- It is possible to convert a stated rate (that is, the annual percentage rate) into an effective rate, which is important because compounding often takes place at other than annual intervals and the annual percentage rate understates the true, effective rate.

- Time value of money principles may be applied to a number of situations, including the personal finance decisions related to saving for retirement and home mortgage problems.

Chapter summaries in bullet points, provide a quick review of the key concepts developed in the chapter.

End of Chapter Pedagogy

Multiple choice questions provide a quick test of the reader's comprehension of the chapter material. Answers are provided at the back of the book.

Multiple Choice

1. If you invest $1,000 today in an account that pays 5% interest, compounded annually, the balance in the account at the end of ten years, if you make no withdrawals, is *closest* to:
   A. $613.91   B. $1,000.00   C. $1,500.00   D. $1,628.89

2. Which of the following has the largest future value if € 1,000 is invested today?
   A. Ten years, with a simple annual interest rate of 8%
   B. Five years, with a simple annual interest rate of 12%
   C. Nine years, with a compound annual interest rate of 7%
   D. Eight years, with a compound annual interest rate of 8%

Practice Problems and Questions

5.1 Time Is Money

11. What is simple interest?

12. Explain how you would calculate the interest-on-interest on an investment.

Questions and Problems enable the reader to master the chapter material.

Cases provide in-depth analyses and application of the material in the chapter.

> **Case**
>
> **Case 5.1 Saving for retirement, considering different scenarios**
>
> Suppose you are advising a client, Arturo, who is planning for his retirement and wants to have $1 million by the time he retires at age sixty. And suppose you want to lay out alternative savings plans for different return scenarios:
>
> **Scenario 1:** *Steady state*
> Earns 8% on all funds invested.
> **Scenario 2:** *Declining returns*
> Earns 8% each year for the first five years, 6% for the next five years, and 4% thereafter.
> **Scenario 3:** *Increasing returns*
> Earns 8% each year for the first five years, 10% for the next five years, and 12% thereafter.
> **Scenario 4:** *Varying returns*
> Earns 8% each year for the first five years, 6% for the next five years, and 10% thereafter.

Robust Instructor and Student Resources

We have worked to develop myriad tools for teaching and learning corporate finance.

For the instructor

The book's *Companion Web Site*—www.wiley.com/college/booth—contains additional examples, explanations, and tools.

The *Instructors' Manual* includes teaching notes, solutions to end-of-chapter problems, solutions to concept questions, and discussion questions for the special topic boxes.

The *Test Bank* includes multiple choice, short answer, and practice problems, all with complete solutions. All these questions and problems are classified by the level of difficulty and the learning outcome. The *Computerized Test Bank* allows instructors to modify and add questions and customize exams.

PowerPoint Presentations provide highlights for each chapter. For chapters that include calculations, we provide worked out problems that are similar, but not identical, to those in the book.

For the student

We provide a number of resources on the book's *Companion Web Site*—www.wiley.com/college/booth—that supplement the book and the in-class experience, including:

Practice Quizzing: multiple-choice quizzes with instant feedback for additional practice;

Spreadsheet Templates for all worked-out examples in the book.

WileyPLUS

WileyPlus is an innovative, research-based online environment for effective teaching and learning.

WileyPlus builds students' confidence because it takes the guesswork out of studying by providing students with a clear road map: what to do, how to do it, if they did it right. This interactive approach focuses on:

Confidence Research shows that students experience a great deal of anxiety over studying. That's why we provide a structured learning environment that helps students focus on what to do, along with the support of immediate resources.

Motivation To increase and sustain motivation throughout the semester, *WileyPLUS* helps students learn how to do it at a pace that's right for them. Our integrated resources—available 24/7—function like a personal tutor, directly addressing each student's demonstrated needs with specific problem-solving techniques.

Success *WileyPLUS* helps to ensure that each study session has a positive outcome by putting students in control. Through instant feedback and study objective reports, students know if they did it right, and where to focus next, so they achieve the strongest results.

With *WileyPLUS*, our efficacy research shows that students improve their outcomes by as much as one letter grade. *WileyPLUS* helps students take more initiative, so you'll have greater impact on their achievement in the classroom and beyond.

What do students receive with *WileyPLUS*?

- The complete digital textbook, saving students up to 60% off the cost of a printed text.

- Question assistance, including links to relevant sections in the online digital textbook.

- Immediate feedback and proof of progress, 24/7.

- Integrated, multimedia resources—including animated problems, flash cards, pre-requisite course reviews (accounting, economics, algebra, and statistics), problem-solving videos, and much more—that provide multiple study paths and encourage more active learning.

What do instructors receive with *WileyPLUS*?

- Reliable resources that reinforce course goals inside and outside the classroom.

- The ability to easily identify those students who are falling behind.

- Media-rich course materials and assessment content including—Instructor's Manual, Solutions Manual, Test Bank, Computerized Test Bank, PowerPoint®Slides, Pre- and Post-Lecture Quizzes, and much more.

www.wileyplus.com. Learn More.

Acknowledgments

A large-scale textbook project such as this one is not the work of just the authors; rather, it is a combined effort of many people whom we wish to acknowledge. We would first like to thank our many reviewers, listed here and several others who wish to remain anonymous, who took the time to read and evaluate the draft manuscripts. Without their many helpful comments, suggestions, and feedback, this textbook would not be what it is today.

Alexander Amati, *Rutgers University*; Alan Blaylock, *Murray State University*; Carol Boyer, *Long Island University*; Ed Boyer, *Temple University*; Susan J. Crain, *Missouri State University*; Julie Dahlquist, *University of Texas, San Antonio*; Michael Ferguson, *University of Cincinnati;* Eric Fricke, *California State University, East Bay*; Partha Gangopadhyay, *Saint Cloud State University*; Aparna Gupta, *Rensselaer Polytechnic Institute*; Eric Hayden, *University of Massachusetts, Boston*; Suzanne Hayes, *University of Nebraska, Kearney*; Michael B. Imerman, *Rutgers University*; Burhan Kawosa, *Wright State University*; Dongmin Ke, *Kean University*; Jiro Edouard Kondo, *Northwestern University*; Vladimir Kotomin, *University of Wisconsin–Eau Claire*; Gregory LaBlanc, *University of California, Berkeley*; Mark J. Laplante, *University of Georgia*; Malek K. Lashgari, *University of Hartford*; Richard L. B. LeCompte, *Wichita State University*; Bingxuan Lin, *University of Rhode Island*; Scott W. Lowe, CPA, CMA; William Mahnic, *Case Western Reserve University*; Stefano Mazzotta, *Kennesaw State University*; Hassan Moussawi, *Wayne State University*; David Offenberg, *Loyola Marymount University*; Hyuna Park, *Minnesota State University, Mankato*; Vedapuri Sunder Raghavan, *Embry-Riddle Aeronautical University*; Joshua Rauh, *Chicago Graduate School of Business*; Carolyn Reichert, *University of Texas, Dallas*; Manuel Chu Rubio, *UPC–Laureate International*; Harley E. Ryan, Jr., *Georgia State University*; Ronald F. Singer, *University of Houston*; Jan Strockis, *Santa Clara University*; John Strong, *College of William and Mary*; Dr. C. R. Krishna Swamy, *Western Michigan University*; James Teague, *University of Pittsburgh, Johnstown*; and Alan M. Weatherford, *California Polytechnic State University*.

In addition, several participated in Focus Groups:

Riza Emekter, *Robert Morris University*; Eric Fricke, *California State University, East Bay*; Suzanne Hayes, *University of Nebraska, Kearney*; Dongmin Ke, *Kean University*; and Carolyn Reichert, *University of Texas, Dallas*.

And, served on the Corporate Finance Advisory Board:

Francisca M. Beer, *California State University, San Bernardino*; Susan J. Crain, *Missouri State University*; Praveen Kumar Das, *University of Louisiana*; Amadeu DaSilva, *California State University, Fullerton*; Erik Devos, *The University of Texas at El Paso*; Tom G. Geurts, *The George Washington University*; Beverly Hadaway, *The University of Texas at Austin*; Karen L. Hamilton, *Georgia Southern University*; James D. Keys, *Florida International University*; Lan Liu, *California State University, Sacramento*; Suzan Puhl Murphy, *The University of Tennessee, Knoxville*; G. Michael Phillips, *California State University, Northridge*; Christopher R. Pope, *University of Georgia*; Helen Saar, *University of Hawaii, Manoa*; Mark Stohs, *California State University, Fullerton*; Devrim Yaman, *Western Michigan University*; Jasmine Yur-Austin, *California State University, Long Beach*; and Kermit C. Zieg, *Florida Institute of Technology*.

We have to acknowledge and thank Peg Monahan-Pashall for her assistance in developing the manuscript. We would also like to thank our team at Wiley, especially Joel Hollenbeck, Executive Editor, and Jennifer Manias, Content Editor, for their thoughtful direction. In addition, George Hoffman, Publisher; Erica Horowitz, Editorial Assistant; Madelyn Lesure, Senior Designer; Jesse Cruz, Senior Marketing Manager; Allison Morris, Senior Product Designer; Erin Bascom, Senior Production Editor; and Bruce Hobart at Laserwords were ever-helpful during the making of this book.

PART 1

THE FINANCIAL ENVIRONMENT

"Remember that time is money. He that can earn ten shillings a day by his labour and goes abroad or sits idle one-half of that day, though he spends but sixpence during his diversion or idleness, ought not to reckon that the only expense; he has really spent, or rather thrown away, five shillings besides.

Remember that credit is money. If a man lets his money lie in my hands after it is due, he gives me the interest, or so much as I can make of it during that time. This amounts to a considerable sum where a man has good and large credit and makes good use of it.

Remember that money is of the prolific, generating nature. Money can beget money, and its offspring can beget more, and so on. Five shillings turned is six; turned again it is seven and three pence, and so on till it becomes a hundred pounds. The more there is of it the more it produces every turning, so that the profits rise quicker and quicker. He that kills a breeding sow destroys all her offspring to the thousandth generation. He that murders a crown destroys all that might have produced even scores of pounds."

Benjamin Franklin, "Advice to a Young Tradesman," *Poor Richard's Almanack*, 1738

1

AN INTRODUCTION TO FINANCE

© Kyu Oh/iStockphoto

From the letter to shareholders of Berkshire Hathaway, from Warren Buffett, accompanying the Berkshire Hathaway 2008 Annual Report which followed the U.S. Government's response to the financial crisis and problems in financial markets:

Whatever the downsides may be, strong and immediate action by government was essential last year if the financial system was to avoid a total breakdown. Had one occurred, the consequences for every area of our economy would have been cataclysmic. Like it or not, the inhabitants of Wall Street, Main Street and the various Side Streets of America were all in the same boat.

Amid this bad news, however, never forget that our country has faced far worse travails in the past. In the 20th Century alone, we dealt with two great wars (one of which we initially appeared to be losing); a dozen or so panics and recessions; virulent inflation that led to a 21½% prime rate in 1980; and the Great Depression of the 1930s, when unemployment ranged between 15% and 25% for many years. America has had no shortage of challenges.

Without fail, however, we've overcome them. In the face of those obstacles—and many others—the real standard of living for Americans improved nearly *seven*-fold during the 1900s, while the Dow Jones Industrials rose from 66 to 11,497. Compare the record of this period with the dozens of centuries during which humans secured only tiny gains, if any, in how they lived. Though the path has not been smooth, our economic system has worked extraordinarily well over time. It has unleashed human potential as no other system has, and it will continue to do so. America's best days lie ahead.

Learning Outcomes

After reading this chapter, you should be able to:

LO 1.1 Define finance and explain the types of decisions made in finance.

LO 1.2 Identify the basic types of financial instruments and explain how they are traded.

LO 1.3 Explain the significance of the global financial system and the global economy to business entities and a country's economy.

Chapter Preview Often, the first finance course that business students take is a finance principles course that focuses on financial management. Yet financial management cannot be taught in isolation; it is simply one part of finance, which includes securities and securities markets, financial institutions, and the economy. Moreover, events in 2007 and 2008 remind us that all these parts are inter-related and that finance is a truly global field.

2

1.1　WHAT IS FINANCE?

Finance, in its broadest terms, is the allocation of funds between those with more funds than they need and those who need the funds. More specifically, finance deals with the "how" and "under what terms" of this allocation.[1]

You may recognize in this definition a similarity between finance and economics. Economics deals with the allocation of scarce resources in an economy, whereas finance focuses on how resources are allocated and by what channels, as well as the terms of the allocation. In many ways, we can view finance as applied economics. For example, the scope of financial decision making within a business entity includes managing investments— whether these assets are production machinery, buildings, or inventory—and deciding how to finance the short-term and long-term needs of the business.

As you learn more about finance, you will notice that financial managers use accounting information in decision making. Accounting captures the company's financial condition and performance over a fiscal period (generally a year or a quarter), so it is capturing what has happened in the past. Finance is forward looking, and financial managers must make decisions about investments and financing now that may have consequences in both the short term and the long term. To formulate those projections, however, financial managers often look at historical financial statements to gauge past performance, growth rates in various accounts, relationships among different accounts, and so on. Therefore, financial managers must be able to read and interpret financial statements.

finance study of how and under what terms funds are allocated between those with excess funds and those who need funds

The Three Primary Areas of Finance

Finance is a broad field, which we can break down into three areas, as we describe in Figure 1-1. **Business finance**, also referred to as **corporate finance** and **financial management**, deals with the financing decision making within a business entity, whether this be a sole proprietorship, a corporation, a partnership, or a limited liability company. The types of decisions that a financial manager faces in a business entity include decisions regarding long-term investments, how the business is financed, and where and when to borrow to meet seasonal needs. A **financial institution** is an entity that serves as an intermediary in the financial system and includes banks, credit unions, and financing companies. Financial managers in these entities manage financial products and services and operate in a highly regulated environment. **Investments** deals with financial markets and securities, including stocks, bonds, and options. Decision making in investment firms includes portfolio choices, making markets in securities, and analyzing alternative investments. Investment firms are regulated and operate in markets that are, for the most part, highly monitored.

business finance or **corporate finance** or **financial management** financing decision making within a business entity

financial institution entity that serves as an intermediary in the financial system, and includes banks, credit unions, and financing companies

investments deals with financial markets and securities, including stocks, bonds, and options

FIGURE 1-1　**The Three Areas of Finance**

---

[1] In economics, providers of funds are often referred to as "surplus agents" or "lenders" and users of funds as "borrowers" or "deficit agents."

Our focus in this book is business finance. However, business finance shares the same foundation as the study of financial institutions and investments. Specifically, this foundation comprises:

- financial statements analysis;
- the time value of money and other valuation financial mathematics; and
- portfolio theory and asset pricing.

Along with the foundation material, an underlying theme in all areas is the global nature of financial decision making. We have long operated in an environment in which there are linkages among many countries, especially with respect to financial markets and the exporting and importing of goods and services. Financial managers in all three areas of finance face issues related to currency fluctuations, regulatory environments that differ among countries, different accounting standards, import and export fees and limitations, and a flow of funds that crosses borders with ease. Financial managers in the U.S. seldom operate solely in the U.S.; many businesses rely on outsourcing some of their production or services, import raw materials, and sell goods overseas. Therefore, financial managers must think globally in their decision making.

In this chapter, we review briefly financial instruments and markets, as well as the overall regulatory system for financial institutions and markets. By introducing you to financial markets and financial instruments, you will be able to follow the financial news during your study of financial management. We also introduce you to many of the players in the financial system, both in the U.S. and globally.

It is important that financial managers understand not only the role of business entities in the financial system, but also how the financial system affects their decisions. We also provide an overview of the 2007–2008 financial crisis and its reverberation for years that followed and discuss the lessons learned for the financial management of a business enterprise.

The Role of Financial Intermediaries

financial system environment in which households provide funds to businesses and government

financial intermediary entity that transforms the nature of securities in a market

market intermediary entity that facilitates the working of markets and helps provide direct intermediation but does not change the nature of the transaction; also called a *broker*

The **financial system** of any country provides an environment in which households provide funds to businesses and government, as we show in Figure 1-2. The basic financial flow is facilitated or intermediated through the financial system, which comprises financial intermediaries and market intermediaries. A **financial intermediary** transforms the nature of the securities they issue and invest in, whereas a **market intermediary** simply makes the markets work better.

Financial intermediaries include investment banks, commercial banks, insurance companies, and mutual funds, whereas market intermediaries include brokers, brokerage firms, and exchanges, such as the NYSE Euronext and the CME Group.[2] The whole package of institutions is the financial system.

FIGURE 1-2 **The Financial System**

---

[2] The NYSE Euronext is the holding company that combined the New York Stock Exchange and Euronext to create a linkage between the world's largest equities exchanges. The CME Group is the world's largest futures and options exchange.

In a financial system, parties transfer money from those with a surplus to those who need it. This transfer occurs through **intermediation**, which is the process of bringing these parties together. If we think of how this intermediation may occur, one obvious way is for individuals to borrow directly from friends, relatives, and acquaintances.[3] Another is to borrow from a specialized financial institution, such as Bank of America or BB&T. These are two extremes in terms of the transfer of money from lenders to borrowers. In the first case, borrowers obtain funds directly from individuals, whereas in the second, they borrow indirectly from individuals who have first deposited their savings, which is lending their savings to a financial institution. The financial institution, in turn, lends funds to the ultimate borrowers, such as a homeowner who needs a mortgage.

> **intermediation** transfer of funds from lenders to borrowers

We illustrate these two patterns of intermediation in Figure 1-3 using three basic channels. The first channel is intermediation, where the lender provides money directly to the ultimate borrower without any help from a specialist. This is a nonmarket transaction because the borrower and lender negotiate the exchange directly. An example would be a relative lending you money to buy a car.

The second channel also represents direct intermediation between the lender and borrower, but in this case, some help is needed because no one individual can lend the full amount needed or because the borrower is not aware of the available lenders. As a result, the borrower needs help to find suitable lenders, which is what market intermediaries do. A **market intermediary** or **intermediary** is simply an entity that facilitates the working of markets and helps the direct intermediation process.

Typically, we refer to market intermediary as a **broker**. The real estate market has real estate and mortgage brokers, who help with the sale and financing of houses. The insurance market has insurance brokers, who facilitate the sale of insurance, and the stock market has stockbrokers, who facilitate the sale of financial securities, particularly shares. In each case, market intermediaries help to make the market work; their responsibilities are to assist with the transaction and bring borrowers and lenders together, but they do not change the nature of the transaction itself. The most important financial markets in U.S. are the stock markets, including the New York Stock Exchange and the NASDAQ, which support a variety of market intermediaries, from stockbrokers who advise clients, through traders who buy and sell securities, to investment bankers who help companies raise capital. In each case, their raison d'être is to make markets work.

> **broker** a market intermediary, who facilitates exchanges in a market

The third savings channel is completely different. It represents financial intermediation, in which the financial institution or financial intermediary lends the money to the ultimate borrowers, yet raises the money itself by borrowing directly from other individuals. In this case, the ultimate lenders have only an indirect claim on the ultimate borrowers; their direct claim is on the financial institution. The difference between a financial intermediary and a market intermediary is that a financial intermediary changes the nature of the transaction, whereas the market intermediary does not.

FIGURE 1-3 **Channels of Savings**

---

[3] In small business, this is often referred to as financing through the 3 Fs: family, friends, and fools.

1. What is finance?

2. What are the three areas of finance?

3. What differentiates market intermediaries from financial intermediaries?

1.2   FINANCIAL INSTRUMENTS AND MARKETS

Now that we have the big picture of how a financial system works, we can focus on the instruments and institutional arrangements that are used to transfer these funds in a financial system.

Financial Instruments

financial instrument
legal agreement that
represents an ownership
interest, a debt
obligation, or other claim
on assets or income

security negotiable
financial instrument that is
evidence of indebtedness
or ownership

A **financial instrument** is any legal agreement that represents an ownership interest, a debt obligation, or other claim on assets or income. A **security** is a negotiable financial instrument that is evidence of indebtedness or ownership. Securities include the following:

*   Debt obligations, such as a bond or a note with a fixed term for repayment and interest to compensate the lender for the use of the funds

*   Equity interests, such as common stock, which represent the ownership interest that the provider of funds has in the user of funds

*   Hybrid securities, such as a convertible bond, that has characteristics of both equity and debt

Exchanging funds for securities opens up an opportunity to be creative in developing securities to facilitate the flow of funds, but additional risk may accompany this creativity and complexity. As a result, the study of finance requires an understanding of economics, securities, law, markets, and the institutions that facilitate and monitor the exchange of funds.

debt instrument legal
obligation to repay
borrowed funds at a
specified maturity date
and to provide interim
interest payments

creditor a party lending
funds through a loan
arrangement

Financial assets are formal legal documents that set out the rights and obligations of all the parties involved. The two major categories of financial securities are debt and equity. A **debt instrument** represents legal obligations to repay borrowed funds at a specified maturity date and provide interim interest payments as specified in the agreement. The party lending the funds is the **creditor** of the borrower. Some of the most common examples of debt instruments are short-term borrowing, such as bank loans, commercial paper, bankers' acceptances, and U.S. Treasury bills (T-bills), and long-term borrowings, including mortgage loans, municipal bonds, and corporate bonds:[4]

Short-term debt

Bank loan	A loan made by a financial institution
Commercial paper	A loan issued by a business or governmental entity
Bankers' acceptance	A credit instrument that is issued by a business and guaranteed by a bank
U.S. Treasury bill	A short-term indebtedness of the U.S. government

---

[4] We will cover each of these later in this text. Bank loans are self-explanatory. Commercial paper is a promissory note with a maturity generally less than one year, usually used for short-term financing by large, creditworthy companies. Bankers' acceptances are short-term financing typically used in import/export transactions.

Long-term debt

Mortgage loan	A loan that is backed by specific collateral, such as a home in the case of a home mortgage
Municipal bond	An indebtedness issued by a state or local government
Corporate bond	An indebtedness issued by a corporation

The key is that debt instruments compensate the lender with interest, whether this interest is explicit or implicit.

A debt instrument may be backed or secured with collateral, or it may be unsecured. **Collateral** is the borrower's pledge of specific property, which may be a building, aircraft, or any other identifiable, tangible asset. If the borrower does not pay what is owed on the debt, the lender in a secured debt can take possession of the collateral or force its sale to recover funds. If debt is not secured, it is backed by the "full faith and credit" of the issuer.[5] We refer to this debt that is unsecured as a **debenture**.

A **bond** is a debt instrument that takes the form of a security that investors can buy and sell. The owner of the bond is the creditor of the bond issuer. A bond typically has a fixed maturity of more than ten years, pays interest (which is referred to as a coupon), and repays the loan at maturity. A **note** is similar to a bond, but with a maturity in the range of one to ten years. In common usage, however, the term "bond" is often used interchangeably with the term "note."

One type of municipal bond is the **general obligation bond**, which is backed by the full faith and credit of the issuer, much like U.S. Treasury bonds. Another type of municipal bond is the **revenue bond**, which is backed by a specific revenue stream of the issuing entity, such as the payments for electricity by customers of a city-owned electric utility. Still another type of municipal bond is the **assessment bond**, which is backed by the property taxes that are assessed by the local government. An advantage of investing in municipal debt is that the interest earned on this investment is exempt from federal income tax and, depending on the state, may be exempt from state income tax.

An **equity instrument** or **equity security** represents an ownership stake in a company. The most common form of equity is **common stock**. Common stock represents the residual ownership of a corporation; the common stock owners are last in line, in terms of seniority of claims on the company, but they also reap the benefits from the company's earnings and appreciation in value. Common stock owners generally also have voting rights, with the ability to elect members of the company's Board of Directors. Companies also issue another form of ownership, **preferred stock**, which usually entitles the owner to fixed dividend payments that must be made before any dividends are paid to common shareholders.

Aside from the debt versus equity distinction, financial instruments can be categorized in several additional ways. One way is to distinguish between nonmarketable and marketable financial assets. The most familiar forms of nonmarketable assets are savings accounts or demand deposits with financial institutions, such as commercial banks. These funds are available on demand, which guarantees the liquidity of these investments.

Marketable securities are those that can be traded among market participants. They are typically categorized not only according to whether they are debt or equity securities, but also by their "term to maturity," or time until the obligation must be repaid. A **money market security** is a short-term (i.e., maturity of less than one year) security; examples include debt instruments such as T-bills, commercial paper, and bankers' acceptances. A **capital market security** is a security with a maturity greater than one year and includes notes, bonds, and debentures, as well as equity securities, which represent ownership in a company and generally have no maturity date.

general obligation bond debt security backed by the general credit of the issuer

revenue bond debt obligation backed by a specific revenue stream

assessment bond security backed by the property taxes of a government entity

equity instrument or **equity security** ownership stake in a company

preferred stock equity security that usually entitles the owner to fixed dividend payments that must be made before any dividends are paid to common shareholders

money market security short-term debt instrument

capital market security debt security with a maturity of greater than one year

---

[5] Full faith and credit refers to the unconditional requirement to repay the borrowed funds and any interest owed.

As we mentioned earlier, governments raise new financing via the debt markets. They sell Treasury bills as a source of short-term financing, and they issue notes and bonds for long-term financing. Businesses raise short-term financing in the form of debt through loans, or by issuing commercial paper, bankers' acceptances, and so on. They raise long-term financing in the form of debt (i.e., through loans, by issuing bonds, or by using other long-term debt instruments) or in the form of equity (i.e., by issuing common shares or preferred shares).

Financial Markets

We now we provide a brief description of the financial markets that permit the issue and trading of financial instruments. It is important to recognize that financial markets play a critical role in any open economy by facilitating the transfer of funds from lenders or investors to borrowers. In addition, if markets are efficient, such funds will be allocated to those with the most productive use for them.

For discussion purposes we begin by distinguishing between primary and secondary markets. In a **primary market** issuers issue new securities in return for cash from investors. In the case of a debt obligation, the issuer is the borrower and the investor is the lender. For example, when the government sells new issues of T-bills or bonds, or when a company sells new common shares to the public, these are primary market transactions; new securities are created, and the borrowing entity raises monies it can spend. When a company goes public, selling equity interests to investors for the first time, we refer to the offering as an **initial public offering (IPO).** We show the initial public offering activity in the U.S. in Figure 1-4. The IPO activity tends to move along with the market, with more offerings in periods of strong economic activity and fewer during economic downturns.

Primary markets are the key to the wealth creation process because they enable money to be transferred to those who can make the best use of it in terms of developing new real assets like houses and factories. We provide a graph of the issuance of debt and equity by U.S. corporations from 1990 through 2010 in Figure 1-5. In this graph we show straight corporate debt (the typical notes and bonds) as well as convertible debt, which investors can exchange for the stock of the issuing company. We also include both the common and the preferred stock issuances in Figure 1-5.

primary market market that involves the issue of new securities by the borrower in return for cash from investors (or lenders)

initial public offering (IPO) first sale of equity interests to the public

FIGURE 1-4 Initial Public Offerings by U.S. Corporations, 1990–2010
Source of data: *Securities Industry and Financial Markets Association*

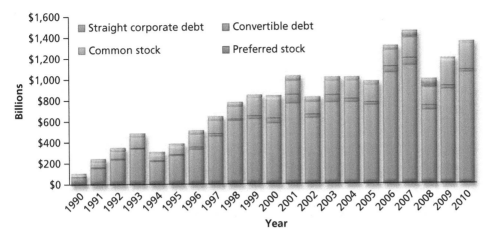

FIGURE 1-5 Debt and Equity Issuance by Corporations, 1990–2010
Source of data: *Securities Industry and Financial Markets Association*

Primary markets, however, will not work properly without a well-functioning **secondary market**. A secondary market provides trading (or market) environments that permit investors to buy and sell existing securities. This service is critical to the functioning of the primary markets because governments and companies would not be able to raise financing if investors were unable to sell their investments when necessary. Consider how reluctant an investor would be to buy a 20-year corporate bond worth $1,000 or $1,000 worth of a company's common shares if she was unable to sell the securities in the event she had to raise money in a hurry or because she became nervous about the company's future prospects.

There are two major types of secondary markets, although the distinction between them has becoming increasingly blurred over the past few years: (1) **exchange market** or **auction market**; and (2) **dealer market** or **over-the-counter (OTC) market**. Exchanges have been referred to as auction markets because they involve a bidding process that takes place in a specific location (i.e., similar to an auction). Investors (both buyers and sellers) are represented at these markets by brokers. In contrast, OTC or dealer markets do not have a physical location, but rather consist of a network of dealers who trade directly with one another. The distinction has become blurred in recent years because trading on most of the major exchanges in the world has become fully computerized, making the physical location of the exchanges of little consequence. At the same time, OTC markets have become increasingly automated, reducing the amount of direct haggling between dealers.

Money market instruments trade in dealer markets. They tend to be very large and are typically issued in sizes of $100,000 or more. As a result, money market trading is dominated by governments, financial institutions, and large corporations. Long-term debt instruments, such as bonds, are also traded primarily through dealer markets, though some are traded on exchanges.

Equity securities in general, and common shares in particular, represent the major financial security issued by corporations and comprise a proportionate ownership in a company. Unlike debt securities, which are normally paid back and result in constant refinancing activity, common shares are generally issued once and then stay outstanding indefinitely.[6] As a result, secondary market trading in equity securities is many times the size of the primary market, whereas for debt securities it is the opposite.

We often compare stocks by referring to their **market capitalization**. A company's market capitalization is the product of the market price of a share and the number of shares outstanding. For example, as of December 2010, the market capitalization of

secondary market trading (or market) environment that permits investors to buy and sell existing securities

exchange market or **auction market** secondary market that involves a bidding process that takes place in a specific location

dealer market or **over-the-counter (OTC) market** secondary market that does not have a physical location and consists of a network of dealers who trade directly with one another

---

[6] There are occasional share repurchases, but relative to the continuous retirement of debt, the amounts are generally insignificant.

FIGURE 1-6 S&P 500 January 1950 Through March 2011

Source of data: *Yahoo! Finance*

General Electric was $17.50 × 10.65 million shares = $186 billion. In comparison, the market capitalization of Procter & Gamble Co. was $178 billion, Google was $189 billion, Motorola was $20 billion, and that of Yahoo! was $21 billion.

We can gauge the performance of stock markets by looking at specific indexes. For example, the S&P 500 is an index of 500 large, representative stocks. We plot this index over time in Figure 1-6. We can see the effect of the 2007–2008 financial crisis: The S&P 500 Index peaked in May 2007 and then got caught in the tailspin of the worldwide decline in equity markets as the U.S. banking system verged on collapse, recovering in 2009.

In addition to the primary and secondary markets there are also the third and fourth markets. The **third market** refers to the trading of securities that are listed on organized exchanges in the OTC market. Historically, this market has been particularly important for "block trades," which are extremely large transactions involving at least 10,000 shares or $100,000. Finally, the **fourth market** refers to trades that are made directly between investors (usually large institutions), without the involvement of brokers or dealers. The fourth market operates through the use of privately owned automated systems, with one of the most widely recognized systems being Instinet.[7]

third market trading of securities that are listed on organized exchanges in the OTC market

fourth market trading of securities directly between investors without the involvement of brokers or dealers

[7] Instinet is owned and operated by Instinet, LLC, which is owned by Nomura Holdings.

Equity Markets | GLOBAL PERSPECTIVE

The NYSE Euronext market in the U.S. is the world's largest equity market in terms of the value of the stocks listed with the exchange, as of November 2011:

Exchange	Market capitalization in billions of U.S. dollars
NYSE Euronext (US)	$11,233
NASDAQ OMX	3,855
London Stock Exchange	3,301
Tokyo Stock Exchange Group	3,287
NYSE Euronext (Europe)	2,509
Shanghai Stock Exchange	2,452
Hong Kong Exchanges	2,184
TMX Group	1,953
BM&FBOVESPA	1,256
Bombay SE	1,087

Source: World Federation of Exchanges, www.world-exchanges.org/statistics

The NYSE Euronext U.S. market's listings comprise 1790 domestic companies and 521 foreign companies. This contrasts with the Tokyo SE Group, which has 2,272 domestic listed companies and only twelve foreign listed companies, and with the Shanghai Stock Exchange, with 929 domestic but no foreign companies among its listings.

Regulation

Most economies operate with a central bank that oversees financial institutions and the economy's money supply. In the U.S., the central bank is the Federal Reserve System.[8] The **Federal Reserve System (the Fed)** consists of the Board of Governors and twelve districts banks, as we show in Figure 1-7. A financial institution may become a member of this system by becoming a nationally chartered bank or by being a state-chartered bank that voluntarily joins the system. As a member of the system, a financial institution can borrow from the Fed; the Fed becomes a lender of last resort.

Federal Reserve System (the Fed) central bank of the U.S., consisting of the Board of Governors and twelve district banks

The Board of Governors of the Federal Reserve System comprises seven members who are appointed by the president, and confirmed by the Senate, to 14-year terms. From these seven members, the chairman and the vice chairman of supervision are appointed

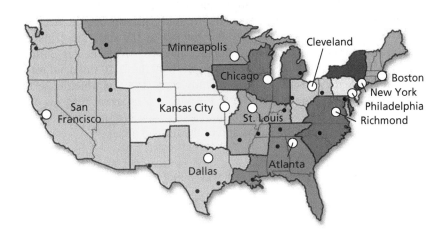

FIGURE 1-7 The Twelve Districts in the U.S. Federal Reserve System

Source: *www.federalreserveonline.org*

[8] The Federal Reserve System was established with the Federal Reserve Act of 1913.

by the president and confirmed by the Senate for four-year terms. The chairman of the Board of Governors, the most visible member of this board, reports to Congress on the board's monetary objectives and meets with the secretary of the treasury. The vice chairman of supervision position is relatively new, with this member charged with overseeing the supervision and regulation of entities within the Federal Reserve's jurisdiction, as well as making policy recommendations for the Federal Reserve.[9]

The primary responsibility of the Board of Governors is to determine monetary policy, which it does through the **Federal Open Market Committee (FOMC)**. The FOMC consists of the seven members of the Board of Governors and the five Federal Reserve Bank presidents.

The Board of Governors establishes the reserve requirements of federally chartered banks, shares responsibility with the district banks regarding discount rate policy, sets margin requirements, participates in the payment system, and supervises and regulates the banks in the system.

The Banking Act of 1933, more familiarly known as the Glass-Steagall Act, gave the Fed the power to regulate the maximum interest rate that banks provide on deposits. The purpose of this power was to regulate competition among banks because it was believed that excessive competition led to the Great Depression of the 1930s. Over the years, the Fed has been given the power, among other things, to:

- establish margin requirements, which affect the extent that stock is purchased with borrowed funds;[10]
- require disclosures regarding consumer lending;[11] and
- assess reserve requirements of member banks and nondepository institutions.[12]

The responsibilities of the Fed in the financial industry are significant. Each time there is a financial crisis, the powers of the Fed are enhanced to deal with the new threat. For example, following the savings and loans crisis of the 1980s, in which 747 financial institutions failed, the Financial Institutions Reform, Recovery, and Enforcement Act of 1989 was passed. It created additional supervisory bodies (the Office of Thrift Supervision and the Federal Housing Finance Board) and regulations for the savings and loan industry. Following the 2007–2008 financial crisis, Congress gave the Board of Governors of the Federal Reserve greater responsibility to regulate nonbank financial companies that are deemed systematically important and to establish risk-based capital, liquidity, and leverage requirements.[13]

Historically, insurance was regulated at the state level. The National Association of Insurance Commissioners (NAIC) has worked with various state agencies to develop uniform evaluation standards of insurance companies, which has brought some degree of consistency in their regulation. For example, the NAIC developed the Insurance Regulatory Information System (IRIS) ratios, which are used to assess the financial solvency of an insurance company. Because insurance is regulated at the state level, insurance companies create state-based subsidiaries to operate in each state. The regulation of insurance companies, however, is changing. For example, with the 2010 financial reforms, some insurance companies may qualify as systemically important, in which case they would also be regulated by the Federal Reserve.[14] Further, the financial reforms establish the **Federal Insurance Office (FIO)**. Though the FIO is merely monitoring and advisory in nature at this time, its role may be expanded in the future.

Federal Open Market Committee (FOMC) twelve-member committee that affects the monetary policy of the U.S.

Federal Insurance Office (FIO) federal agency responsible for monitoring and advising regulators about insurance companies' risk and solvency

---

[9] This position was created in 2010 by the Dodd-Frank Wall Street Reform and Consumer Protection Act.

[10] Regulations G, T, U and X.

[11] Regulation W, the Truth-in-Lending Act, Equal Credit Opportunity Act, the Fair Credit Billing Act, and the Community Reinvestment Act.

[12] Depository Institutions Deregulation and Monetary Control Act of 1980.

[13] In the most recent legislation, the Dodd-Frank Wall Street Reform and Consumer Protection Act, signed into law July 2010 [Public Law 111-203 H. R. 4173], systemically important nonbank companies are those with $50 billion or more in assets.

[14] A financial services company with $50 billion or more of assets may be deemed "systemically important."

The **Securities and Exchange Commission (SEC)** bears the responsibility of ensuring that financial markets are fair, orderly, and efficient. In addition, the SEC is tasked with encouraging capital flows from investors to businesses, but also with protecting investors. We list the major laws that regulate securities markets and securities transactions in Table 1-1, for which the SEC has primary responsibility. The first five laws in this table—Securities Act of 1933, the Securities Exchange Act of 1934, the Trust Indenture Act of 1939, the Investment Company Act of 1940, and the Investment Advisers Act of 1940—pertain to the regulation of securities, securities trading, investment managers, brokers, and dealers. The Sarbanes-Oxley (SOX) Act, passed into law in 2002 as a reaction to the scandal involving Enron, deals with financial management issues, including disclosures, corporate governance, and the accounting profession. The Dodd-Frank Wall Street Reform and Consumer Protection Act deals with wide-reaching changes in the structure of financial regulation.

The SEC has the responsibility of oversight of **self-regulatory organizations (SROs)**. The largest such SRO is the **Financial Industry Regulatory Authority (FINRA)**. FINRA was created in 2007 from the merger of the National Association of Security Dealers (NASD) and some functions of the New York Stock Exchange. FINRA registers brokers and brokerage firms, enforces securities laws among the registered brokers and firms, and regulates the NASDAQ stock market, the American Stock Exchange, the International Stock Exchange, and the Chicago Climate Exchange.

The regulatory power of the SEC was expanded in the 2010 financial reforms to include enhancing investor protections, regulating hedge funds, and expanding its regulation of credit rating agencies, among other things.

Securities and Exchange Commission (SEC) U.S. agency responsible for ensuring that financial markets are fair, orderly, and efficient

self-regulatory organization (SRO) organization that oversees and monitors its members and member organizations

Financial Industry Regulatory Authority (FINRA) self-regulatory organization that monitors and regulates brokerage firms, brokers, and market intermediaries

TABLE 1-1 Highlights of Selected U.S. Securities Laws

Law	*Purpose*
Securities Act of 1933	Requires disclosure of specific information about securities offered to the public, and prohibits misrepresentations and fraud in the sale of securities.
Securities Exchange Act of 1934	Created the Securities and Exchange Commission, giving the SEC the power and responsibility to regulate and oversee brokerage firms, agents, and self-regulatory organizations. Requires periodic reporting by companies with publicly traded securities.
Trust Indenture Act of 1939	Regulates the provisions of indentures for bonds, debentures, and notes sold to the public.
Investment Company Act of 1940	Regulates investment companies, such as mutual funds.
Investment Advisers Act of 1940	Regulates investment advisers, and specifies who must register with the SEC.
Sarbanes-Oxley Act of 2002	Increases disclosure requirements of publicly traded companies, creates oversight boards for independent public accountants, requires specific corporate governance provisions, and holds the chief executive officer and the chief financial officer accountable for a public company's disclosures.
Dodd-Frank Wall Street Reform and Consumer Protection Act of 2010	Increases oversight responsibility and regulation of hedge funds, credit-rating agencies, and brokers and dealers, among other things.

Deregulation of the Financial Services Industry

The Banking Act of 1933 and the Bank Holding Company Act of 1956 created barriers between different financial service businesses: banking, insurance, and securities.[15] The Financial Services Modernization (FSM) Act, more commonly referred to as the Gramm-Leach-Bliley (GLB) Act, was signed into law in 1999 and changed the shape of the financial services sector.[16] Many companies took advantage of the deregulation aspects of this act, entering into other financial services that were previously restricted because the changes permitted commercial banks, investment banks, and insurance companies to enter each other's markets.

One of the consequences of the Gramm-Leach-Bliley Act was the merging of companies within and across the different financial sectors. Large financial services mergers include J.P. Morgan & Co. and Chase Manhattan in 2000, Bank of America and Fleet Boston Financial in 2003, Travelers' Property Casualty and St. Paul Companies in 2003, JPMorgan Chase & Co. and Bank One in 2004, Wachovia and SouthTrust Corporation in 2004, and Bank of America Corporation and MBNA in 2006. The result? Fewer, but larger firms; the largest banking institutions became even more substantial, raising the issue of whether these institutions were too big to fail. In other words, if these institutions were so large that their failure would jeopardize the economy, then they were too big to be allowed to fail, necessitating some form of government or regulatory action to prevent or mitigate their failure.

The financial crisis of 2007–2008 resulted in a wave of mergers to avoid failures of certain institutions. Consider the institutions that we list in Table 1-2 as the largest financial institutions in terms of revenue in 2010. Bank of America grew from $113 billion in revenues in 2008 to $134 in 2010, mostly by virtue of its acquisition of Merrill Lynch in January 2010.[17] Other notable mergers resulting from the financial crisis include Wells Fargo's acquisition of Wachovia, PNC Bank's acquisition of National City, and JPMorgan Chase's acquisition of Washington Mutual.[18]

TABLE 1-2   Largest Financial Service Firms, 2010

United States

Rank	Company	2010 Revenues in billions of U.S. dollars
1	Fannie Mae	$154
2	General Electric	152
3	Berkshire Hathaway	136
4	Bank of America	134
5	JPMorgan Chase	115

Globally

Rank	Company	2010 Revenues in billions of U.S. dollars	Home country
1	Japan Post Holdings	$204	Japan
2	AXA	162	France
3	Fannie Mae	154	U.S.
4	General Electric	152	U.S.
5	ING Group	147	Netherlands

Source: *Insurance Information Institute Fact Book 2012*

[15] The Banking Act of 1933, commonly known as the Glass-Steagall Act [June 16, 1933, Ch 89 §20, 48 Stat. 188; Aug 23, 1935, Ch 614, Title III, § 302, 49 Stat. 707].

[16] U. S. Public Law No. 106-102, signed into law November 12, 1999.

[17] Bank of America acquired Countrywide Financial in mid-2008.

[18] Jonathan Rich and Thomas G. Scriven, "Bank Consolidation Caused by the Financial Crisis: How Should the Antitrust Division Review 'Shotgun Marriages,'" *The Antitrust Source*, www.antitrustsource.com, December 2008.

Concept Review Questions

1. What are the main differences between debt and equity securities?

2. What distinguishes primary and secondary markets?

3. What is the role of the Securities and Exchange Commission?

1.3 THE GLOBAL FINANCIAL CRISIS

The financial crisis of 2007–2008 was a significant event that affected businesses and economies around the world. To understand the crisis, it is important to first appreciate the linkages that exist among the global economies. After we emphasize the global linkages in the financial system, we explore the major events of this crisis and for a period following. After our overview of the events, we examine some of the challenges that this crisis presented to financial managers.

The Global Financial Community

In addition to domestic financial markets, global financial markets represent important sources of funds for borrowers and provide investors with significant alternatives. Indeed, U.S. debt and equity markets represent only a small proportion of the total global marketplace. Therefore, it makes sense for U.S. investors to borrow and invest abroad, which has become easier to do in today's global business environment as investment barriers are relaxed.

In Table 1-3 we illustrate the importance of global markets to U.S. investors and vice versa. As you can see in this table, the investment in the United States by non-U.S. investors exceeds the investment that U.S. investors have outside the United States in each year. More important, the extent that U.S. assets are owned outside the United States and foreign assets are owned by U.S. investors illustrates the interconnection of the economies. A **financial derivative** in this table is an investment whose value is based on some other investment, such as options (securities that give the investor the right to buy or sell a stock) and interest-rate swaps (agreements to exchange sets of cash flows, e.g., fixed interest for floating interest). We break out financial derivatives separately to give you an idea of the importance of these types of securities when compared to all other securities. The variations that we may see from year-to-year investments are likely caused by the performance of U.S. and non-U.S. markets, fluctuations in currency exchange rates, and

financial derivative investment whose value is based on some other investment

TABLE 1-3 U.S. Investors' International Investments, Second Quarter 2010 and 2011

Positive values indicate inflows to the U.S. and negative values indicate outflows from the U.S.

(in millions)	Second quarter 2010	Second quarter 2011
U.S.-owned assets abroad, excluding financial derivatives	–$175,174	–$343,848
Foreign-owned assets in the U.S., excluding financial derivatives	188,526	486,470
Net position	$13,352	$142,622
Financial derivatives, net	$9,980	$3,220

Source: *U.S. Bureau of Economic Analysis, Balance of Payments, Table 1, "U.S. International Transactions."*

changes in the economies throughout the world. The bottom line of this analysis is that there is substantial investment in the U.S. by non-U.S. investors, and there is also substantial investment outside the U.S. by U.S. investors.

The world's money markets and bond markets are very global in nature, with the U.S. markets representing the largest and most active debt markets in the world; global debt markets are primarily dealer markets. The United States also possesses the largest equity markets in the world. The **NYSE Euronext** is the world's largest stock market with a market capitalization at the end of January 2011 of $15.1 trillion. In total, as of January 2011, there were 7,803 companies listed on the NYSE Euronext, 2,452 of which were listed on the New York Stock Exchange (NYSE).[19]

The second-largest and most important stock market in the United States is the NASDAQ Stock Market, or, simply, the NASDAQ. The NASDAQ is the second-largest stock market in the world, based on its market capitalization of $3.6 trillion. In fact, the NASDAQ has more listed companies than the NYSE, with approximately 3,200; the average number of shares traded per day (2 billion) is close to the figure for the NYSE.[20] However, larger companies tend to list on the NYSE, which is why its market capitalization far exceeds that of the NASDAQ.

Securities exchanges around the world have been consolidating. In 2007, the NYSE and Euronext merged, creating the first truly global securities exchange. On January 16, 2009, the American Stock Exchange was phased out after its acquisition by the NYSE and became the NYSE's trading platform for options, closed-end funds, and exchange traded funds (ETFs).[21,22] Consequently, even though there are almost 200 stock exchanges around the world, the industry is rapidly consolidating.

The globalization of the equity markets means that linkages between the markets are getting tighter. Never has this been better demonstrated than by the events of 2007 and 2008, when a crisis in the U.S. banking sector turned into the first global financial meltdown and recession. The events also reinforce the fact that the financial decisions of a company are not made in a vacuum.

The Foundation for the Crisis

In addition to the globalization of financial investments and instruments, a number of other factors set the stage for the global crisis. But first we need to explain one of the simplest financial products, a mortgage, before we can understand the sources of problems in the financial crisis.

A **mortgage** is a debt obligation that is secured by specific property. The mortgages at the heart of the crisis are primarily home mortgages, where the collateral is the individual borrower's home. Normally, to qualify for a mortgage, the bank requires a down payment from the borrower and lends the balance with a loan secured on the value of the house. However, house prices in the U.S. started to increase quite dramatically as the U.S. recovered from a serious recession in 2002. The increase was fueled by economic expansion, low mortgage rates, and a series of financial innovations that in retrospect reduced the checks in the mortgage lending process.[23] These factors, combined with loose regulation by the U.S. banking authorities, meant that credit was easily available.

The increased activity in the real estate market, combined with real estate speculation, heated up some housing markets in the U.S., such as Las Vegas, Los Angeles, and Miami. As you can see in Figure 1-8, home prices began rising in the early 2000s, peaking in late 2006.

[19] Source: NYSE Euronext *Fact Book*, 2010-current.
[20] Source: NASDAQ website at www.nasdaq.com.
[21] An ETF is a security that tracks an index, a commodity, or a portfolio of assets that is traded just like common stock.
[22] And in 2011, the NYSE Euronext and Deutsche Börse plan to merge, though as of the end of 2011 this merger had not gone through because of antitrust concerns.
[23] The annual growth in gross domestic product was over 3% in both 2004 and 2005.

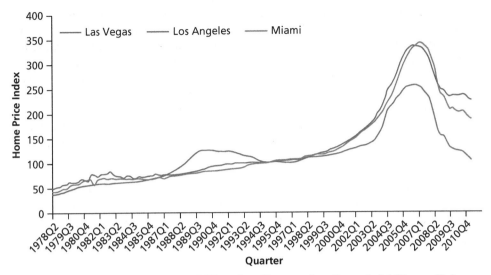

FIGURE 1-8 **Office of Federal Housing Enterprise Oversight Home Price Index, Second Quarter 1978 Through Third Quarter 2011 for Selected Metropolitan Statistical Areas**

Source: *Federal Housing Finance Agency (FHFA), HPI index.*

The annual rate of growth of home prices in these three markets during the period 2004–2006 averaged over 15% per year, much higher than the typical home value increase in a year. You can see the home-price bubble and the decline in values in these three markets after 2007.

The Financial Crisis

One of the challenges in understanding and dealing with the financial crisis of 2007–2008 is that there is no one single cause of the crisis, but rather many that occurred to create the perfect storm. One of the most visible causes of the crisis was the housing bubble, but others include lax lending standards, a push for the **government-sponsored entities (GSEs)** of Freddie Mac and Fannie Mae to purchase lower quality loans for resale as securities, the insatiable appetite of investors for high-return, high-risk securities that were backed by mortgages, and rampant fraud in mortgage origination.

In any discussion of the financial crisis, you will hear reference to securitization. **Securitization** is the process of converting loans into securities. In the case of mortgages, the mortgage originator (the party lending the funds to the borrower) sells mortgages to a party that pools them together and then sells securities that have rights to the cash flows of the mortgages. The party pooling the mortgages may be a GSE, such as Freddie Mac. This security is a **mortgage-backed security**, secured by the mortgages in the pool. Sounds simple? Not really, because predicting whether borrowers will default on a loan and predicting whether borrowers will pay off a loan early (e.g., refinancing) is not easy. And, as many learned, even the best prediction models did not consider the defaults in the magnitude that occurred.

government-sponsored entity (GSEs) financial service corporations that are created by the government to perform a service, such as buying mortgages

securitization pooling of loans, and then creating and selling securities that have rights to specific cash flows from this pool

mortgage-backed securities claims on the cash flows of a pool of mortgages

The beginning of the crisis: Early 2007

You would think that in an overheated housing market lenders would be more cautious in their lending. However, in the U.S. this did not happen as banks and other financial institutions often loaned in excess of 100% of the value of a house with very little documentation in NINJA loans: no income, no job, no assets.[24] Mortgages were originated for some borrowers who had poor credit histories and who could not otherwise qualify for

---

[24] Another nickname for these loans is "liar loans" because of the lack of information on the borrower's income or assets.

subprime mortgage home loan to a borrower with poor credit who would not otherwise qualify for a conventional mortgage

a conventional mortgage; we refer to this type of mortgage as a **subprime mortgage**. By 2006 the U.S. subprime market was exploding. Why would lenders lend money when documentation was deficient or when the borrower was a high credit risk? Because mortgage originators received fees based on the mortgages originated, not the quality of these mortgages. Further, there were ready buyers of these mortgages, which encouraged more production by originators. Loan originators sold these loans to dealers, who repackaged them into securities through securitization.

Everything might have been fine if home prices had continued to increase, but with the supply of homes outpacing demand, supply and demand principles dominated, and the housing market collapsed. Lenders started to catch on that credit was too generous, and financing started to contract. By summer 2007 U.S. house prices began to fall, as you can see in Figure 1-8. Loans made with a high ratio of loan to the value of the home—the **loan-to-value ratio**—were soon problematic, as the value of the home became much lower than the amount owed. In other words, these loans were "underwater," which provided the incentive for some homeowners to simply walk away from the home—and the loan.[25]

loan-to-value ratio ratio of the amount of a loan to the value of the collateral used as security on the loan

The crisis is heating up: Mid-2007

With U.S. house prices in hot markets off by an average of 40%, even prime U.S. mortgage loans were now greater than the value of the houses they were secured against. The result was an increase in late payments and defaults, followed by large losses for the banks that made the loans. These problems were magnified by the securitization of loans. Many loan originators went out of business, leaving behind mortgaged-backed securities with defaults and a declining value of the collateral. For example, New Century Financial Corporation, one of the largest originators of subprime mortgages, filed for bankruptcy in April 2007. Following this, Countrywide Financial Corporation, another large originator, became financially distressed, and American Home Mortgage Investment Corporation filed for bankruptcy in August 2007.

In addition to the mortgage originators, investment firms with significant investments in mortgage-backed securities began to disclose problems.[26] The first major sign of this involved Bear Stearns, an investment bank, and its liquidation in July of 2007 of two hedge funds that invested heavily in mortgage-backed securities. In addition, the major banking institutions of Citigroup, Bank of America, and JPMorgan Chase attempted to raise capital in October 2007 to support special-purpose vehicles that were used in securitizations.[27]

Early 2008

There were several acquisitions intended to stem the failures among financial institutions. For example, in January of 2008, Bank of America acquired Countrywide Financial, and JPMorgan Chase acquired Bear Stearns in March 2008. These acquisitions were problematic because the acquired firms had substantial stakes in mortgage-backed securities and, hence, large realized and unrealized losses in these securities.

The Economic Stimulus Act of 2008 was signed into law in February 2008 to help generate consumer spending, and the FOMC took actions to stabilize the economy. In addition, the Federal Reserve Board took several steps to provide liquidity to the markets, establishing the Term Securities Lending Facility (TSLF) and the Primary Dealer Credit Facility.

Mid-to-late 2008

systemic risk uncertainty that affects the larger economy

The problems related to lax lending standards and the securitization of subprime loans, accompanied by high default rates, led to systemic risk for the economy. **Systemic risk** is risk that affects the larger economy, and because the effects ripple throughout the

[25] Homeowners who walked away from their mortgages and home would mail the keys to the lender; hence the term "jingle mail" applied to these cases.

[26] Around this time, accounting rules went into effect that required valuation of these investments using some form of index rather than a company's own estimate of their value.

[27] In December 2007, these firms announced that this was not needed.

It's Greek to Me | FINANCE in the News

Sovereign debt is indebtedness issued by a national government. For example, the Treasury bills and bonds issued by the U.S. government are part of the sovereign debt of the U.S. One of the fallouts of the 2007–2008 crisis is the downgrading of sovereign debt. Greece, with its long history of budget problems, was the first to fall. Its debt was downgraded in 2009, in 2010, in 2011, and then again in 2012. The rating of Greece's debt from Moody's fell from A1 to C in this three-year period. To put this in perspective, the rating of Greece's debt went from "High economic, financial or institutional strength" to "One shock away from default, and/or material concerns about the willingness to pay."[28] The upshot of the downgrade is that the debt is considered riskier, and therefore, the cost of raising capital increases. By 2012, the yield on 10-year Greek debt was over 3,300 basis points (that is, 33%) higher than other European sovereign debt, and the debt was, effectively, in default.[29] Other countries followed suit, with Portugal and Spain following close behind Greece.

Like any business, an economic slowdown such as the one that followed the global crisis affects the countries that have the weakest economies. Factors considered important in rating sovereign debt include gross domestic product, government policies in dealing with budgets, policies of the central bank, and unemployment.[30] The challenge is that once the debt is downgraded, the cost of raising new capital is greater, and the country will have difficulty raising capital to finance its operations.

---

economy, it cannot be diversified away. The systemic risk arising from the mortgage/housing crisis was pervasive in the financial system.

September 2008 marked the beginning of a credit crunch in the U.S. and other countries. A **credit crunch**, which we also refer to as a **credit squeeze**, is the lack of available loans for businesses; lenders stop or slow down lending and tighten credit standards, making it difficult for businesses to obtain funds, no matter the cost. A credit crunch is most significant for small businesses that cannot access capital markets to issue bonds or stock, but instead depend on bank lending to meet their liquidity needs.[31]

credit crunch or **credit squeeze** lack of available loans for businesses

The culmination of the severe liquidity crisis and the economic downturn resulted in restructuring in the financial system. Several large financial institutions failed in 2008, including IndyMac Bank in July, Integrity Bank in August, and Lehman Brothers Holdings Incorporated and Washington Mutual Bank in September. When Lehman Brothers was allowed to fail in the biggest ever bankruptcy at that time, it triggered a massive loss of confidence in the banking sector and desperate efforts by the U.S. government to shore up its banks.

To avoid failures, several acquisitions were arranged by the Federal Reserve, in which financially healthy institutions acquired unhealthy institutions. Examples include Bank of America's acquisition of Merrill Lynch, in a deal initiated in September, and Wells Fargo & Co.'s acquisition of Wachovia in October. In addition, Fannie Mae and Freddie Mac were placed in government conservatorship in September of 2008, and the U.S. Treasury put into place an agreement to purchase the preferred stock of the GSEs and to provide needed liquidity.

The stocks of several financial institutions, as well as nonfinancial firms, fell dramatically during the financial crisis, and it was believed that this was exaggerated by short selling pressure. Short selling, in a nutshell, is the sale of borrowed shares, with the expectation that the shares would be purchased at a later date at a lower price and the borrowed shares returned.[32] The Securities and Exchange Commission banned short selling the stock of GSEs in July 2008 and all financial stocks in September 2008.

---

[28] Moody's Investor Service, "Sovereign Bond Ratings," September, 2008, p. 4.

[29] Marcus Bensasson, "Greek debt rating cut three steps to B1 by Moody's on rising default risk," *Bloomberg*, March 7, 2011.

[30] Moody's Investors Service, "2010 in Perspective and Global Macro Risk Scenarios 2011–2012: Curbing Contagion," February 4, 2011.

[31] *Federal Reserve Bank of San Francisco Economic Letter*, Federal Reserve Bank of San Francisco, 2009–09; March 6, 2009.

[32] This uses the old adage "Buy low, sell high," but the selling is done first.

Troubled Asset Relief Program (TARP) U.S. government program to infuse capital in the financial system by purchasing assets and equity from troubled financial institutions

To address the lack of liquidity in the capital markets, several actions were taken. The most significant was the $700 billion **Troubled Asset Relief Program (TARP)**, created by Congress in October 2008.[33] A component of the TARP was the $250 billion Capital Repurchase Program, in which the U.S. Treasury acquired preferred stock of banks, providing needed funds. In addition, the Federal Reserve Board established several programs to inject funds into the financial system, including the Commercial Paper Funding Facility (CPFF) to purchase commercial paper from high-quality issuers. Actions were also taken to shore up individual companies, including providing $85 billion to American International Group (AIG) through certain transactions.[34] In addition to banks, the insurance companies Lincoln National, Hartford Financial Services, and Genworth Financial, as well as auto companies General Motors and Chrysler, received loans through the TARP program.

Early 2009

The Federal Reserve Bank of New York began buying fixed-rate mortgage-backed securities guaranteed by Fannie Mae, Freddie Mac, and Ginnie Mae as a means of adding liquidity to the financial system.[35] In addition, Congress passed the American Recovery and Reinvestment Act of 2009 in February, with the intent of stimulating the economy with government spending and some tax cuts. Further, the U.S. Treasury and the Fed announced an additional program, the **Term Asset-Backed Securities Loan Facility (TALF)** to lend funds to owners of specific AAA-rated asset-backed securities, specifically to investors of high-quality loans backed by student loans, auto loans, credit card loans, and Small Business Administration–backed loans.

Term Asset-Backed Securities Loan Facility (TALF) U.S. government program to inject capital in the financial system by lending funds to investors of specific high-quality asset-backed securities

stress test scenario-based evaluation of a company's solvency, where the scenario is the worst-case scenario

Federal regulators performed stress tests on large bank holding companies, addressing the issue of whether banks would have adequate capital under severe economic conditions. A **stress test** is a scenario-based evaluation of a company's solvency, where the scenario is the worst-case scenario of an economic depression. Of the nineteen companies examined, nine were found to have adequate capital; those not meeting the standards were required to develop a plan to enhance their capital.

Several banks began repaying TARP funds in June of 2009, including State Street Bank, Goldman Sachs, Morgan Stanley, Capital One Financial, American Express, and BB&T. Despite receiving TARP funds, however, General Motors filed for bankruptcy in June of 2009, and CIT Group Inc., a lender to small and medium-sized businesses, filed for bankruptcy in November 2009.

Developments in 2010 and 2011

Financial institutions continued to repay TARP funds in 2010, and most of the troubled financial institutions that were not acquired or liquidated began to show profitability. Of the $475 billion of funds authorized in the TARP program, $389 billion had been disbursed by November of 2010, and $122 billion was outstanding as of October 2011.[36] The U.S. had recouped $13.5 billion of its investment in General Motors (GM) when GM had an initial public offering in November of 2010.

The most important development from the financial crisis was the impetus for reform in the financial industry, which began with the Dodd-Frank Wall Street Reform and Consumer Protection Act of 2010. We discuss this act later in this chapter.

---

[33] October 3, 2008, Emergency Economic Stabilization Act of 2008 (Public Law 110–343).

[34] These transactions involved borrowing securities from AIG in exchange for cash. The total authorized assistance, in the form of debt and equity, was $123.948 billion, and the assistance outstanding in July 2011 was $85.011 billion. General Accounting Office, Troubled Asset Relief Program: *The Government's Exposure to AIG Following the Company's Recapitalization*, July 2011.

[35] Ginnie Mae is a "sister" of Freddie and Fannie. Ginnie Mae guarantees the principal and interest on Federal Housing Administration insured mortgages and Department of Veterans Affairs–guaranteed mortgages.

[36] Troubled Assets Relief Program (TARP), Month 105(a) Report, November 2010, U.S. Department of the Treasury. The TARP program ceased making new investments in October 2010.

Subprime Loans and More | ETHICS

It's a Bull Market for Financial Fraud

Imagine landing your dream home. Your credit is a bit shaky, but you manage to get a subprime loan with an adjustable rate mortgage. A few years later the interest rates jump, and you can no longer afford to pay. You see an ad for a business that's willing to help—it'll pay your mortgage for a modest monthly fee while you get back on your feet. But here's the heartbreak: it's a scam. The con artists just take your money and run . . .

It's just one of the latest schemes and frauds we're seeing these days across the financial services industry, our senior criminal investigators said during a briefing Tuesday with the news media in Washington.

These scams—which include plenty of shenanigans with mortgages and subprime loans—are costing the nation tens of billions of dollars a year.

"Greed is definitely not good for our economy right now," said our top criminal investigative exec Ken Kaiser following the briefing. "It's hurting homeowners. It's hurting honest businesses. And it's hurting investors and markets around the world."

All good reasons why we're squarely focused on cracking down on the largest of these financial crimes, launching proactive initiatives and shifting resources as trends emerge, all the while working hand-in-hand with a host of government and private sector partners.

Among the specifics discussed at the briefing:
Subprime mortgage loans:

- We're investigating 14 corporations involved in subprime lending as part of our Subprime Mortgage Industry Fraud Initiative launched last year.

- The companies come from across the financial services industry, from mortgage lenders to investment banks that bundle loans into securities sold to investors. We're also looking at insider trading by some executives.

Traditional mortgage fraud:

- We have more than 1,200 cases open today (up about 40% from last year), mostly involving fraud for profit, where groups of straw buyers, realtors, etc. rig schemes to buy properties that are flipped or allowed to go into foreclosure.

- Hotspots include California, Texas, Arizona, Florida, Ohio, Michigan, and Utah.

- Suspicious activity reports that we review for potential mortgage fraud have grown from 3,000 in fiscal year 2003 to 48,000 in fiscal year 2007. This year, we're on pace to receive more than 60,000 such reports.

- A recent case: In November, the owners of a long-time Minnesota homebuilder called Parish Marketing—along with a bank officer, a closing agent, and others—pled guilty to a $100 million mortgage scheme involving some 200 homes.

- Right now, we're seeing no links to organized crime syndicates, street gangs, or terrorist groups in our cases.

Source: Federal Bureau of Investigation, January 31, 2008, www.fbi.gov

What Is to Come

The U.S. financial markets and institutions are currently undergoing changes, with some of these changes yet to come. Until 2008 the U.S. was unique in having five very powerful investment banks that dominated the market intermediary function in the U.S. markets; no more. Lehman Brothers was allowed to fail in September of 2008, Merrill Lynch was acquired by Bank of America, Morgan Stanley required a capital injection from Asian investors and has become a bank so as to receive protection from the U.S. Federal Reserve Board, Bear Stearns was sold to J.P. Morgan in 2008, and Goldman Sachs converted to a bank holding company in September of 2008 to have access to the government's emergency lending facilities.

Among the elite U.S. commercial banks there is similar wreckage: Citibank received $65 billion in emergency funds from the U.S. government to stay solvent as well as getting special insurance to cover $306 billion in toxic subprime-related mortgages, and Bank of America has $109 billion in similar bad loan insurance with $45 billion in emergency funds. Almost every major U.S. bank accepted special financial support from the U.S. government through TARP, as the government realized that allowing more banks to fail would lead to the complete collapse of the U.S. financial system.

During and following the financial crisis of 2007–2008, many banks failed. However, we should put this in perspective. The number of banks failing during this recent financial crisis is far fewer than in prior economic downturns. As you can see in Figure 1-9, the consolidation of the industry due to deregulation in the 1990s has resulted in larger failures in terms of losses. Comparing 1989 with 2009, we see that even before we worry about adjusting for inflation, the losses during 1989 exceed those of 2009, though the average size of the loss per institution has increased significantly:[37]

	1989			*2009*		
	Number of failed institutions	**Losses in millions**	**Average loss per institution in millions**	**Number of failed institutions**	**Losses in millions**	**Average loss per institution in millions**
Commercial banks	206	$5,909	$29	126	$24,390	$203
Savings institutions	328	$47,514	$145	22	$12,967	$648

Source of data: *Federal Deposit Insurance Corporation, Failures and Assistance Transactions.*

In the banking crisis of the 1980s, Continental Illinois National Bank failed in May 1984. This failure raised two key issues: (1) Was regulatory oversight sufficient to evaluate and monitor a bank's risk, and (2) Was Continental Illinois National Bank, the seventh largest bank at the time, "too big to fail"?[38] A failure of a large financial institution could have significant effects on the rest of the economy. The Continental failure encouraged changes in the insurance program, but until the recent financial crisis, the changes had not been tested.[39] The failures of financial institutions in 2008 and 2009 raised, once again, the question of whether a financial institution could be "too big to fail."[40]

FIGURE 1-9 Bank and Savings Institution Failures 1934 Through 2011
Source: *Federal Deposit Insurance Corporation.*

---

[37] If we consider inflation, the $53.4 billion of losses in 1989 is equivalent, on an inflation-adjusted basis, to $92.4 billion in 2009 dollars, far exceeding the total losses in 2009 of $37.3 billion. The number of failures rose to 157 in 2010, but then fell to 92 in 2011. However, the failures in 2010 were of smaller institutions, with total losses of $19,931 million.

[38] "Continental Illinois and Too Big to Fail," Federal Deposit Insurance Corporation, *Histories of the Eighties— Lessons for the Future*, Chapter 7.

[39] Federal Deposit Insurance Corporation Improvement Act of 1991 (FDICIA).

[40] The Dodd-Frank Wall Street and Consumer Protection Act instituted a process of evaluating institutions that may be "too big to fail."

Stock markets reacted to the economic crisis, not just in the U.S., but throughout the world. For example, on September 15, 2008, the day Lehman Brothers filed for bankruptcy, all major world markets reacted, either in anticipation or as soon as the news was released, as we show in Table 1-4. On September 16, 2008, the U.S. Treasury and the Federal Open Market Committee took several actions, including a ban on short selling, to calm the markets, which helped the U.S. markets recover slightly.

Beginning in October 2008, the world moved into a serious recession. Recall that there is one big financial market, and all parts of it are interconnected to a greater or lesser degree. Events in the U.S. mortgage market have washed like a tsunami throughout the world and caused problems in corporate and government financing, as several countries from Iceland to Hungary have required emergency international loans to keep their economies afloat.

The regulatory structure in the U.S. financial system is undergoing changes to address the problems that created significant systemic risk. A major step in this reform was the passage of the Dodd-Frank Wall Street Reform and Consumer Protection Act of 2010, which was passed in mid-2010.[41] This is a wide-reaching act that altered the regulatory landscape in the U.S. financial system and set the stage for further changes. Among other things, the act:

- creates the Financial Stability Oversight Council, which provides a formal system of coordination among key regulators.
- creates criteria and standards for systemically important financial companies.
- provides for the orderly liquidation of financial companies that are insolvent.
- limits proprietary trading (Volcker Rule).

TABLE 1-4 Market Losses Around the World: September 15, 2008

		Percentage change	
Index or Average	Country	September 15, 2008	September 16, 2008
Sao Paulo Bovespa	Brazil	–7.59%	1.68%
S&P/TSX Composite	Canada	–4.04%	–0.22%
DAX	Germany	–2.74%	–1.63%
Hang Seng	Hong Kong	closed	–5.44%
Bombay Sensex	India	–3.35%	–0.09%
RTS Index	Russia	–4.78%	–11.47%
Johannesburg All Share	South Africa	–1.96%	–2.59%
Kospi	South Korea	closed	–6.10%
IBEX35	Spain	–4.50%	0.11%
FTSE 100	United Kingdom	–3.92%	–3.43%
Dow Jones Industrial Average	United States	–4.42%	1.30%
S&P 500 Index	United States	–4.71%	1.75%
Wilshire 500	United States	–4.55%	1.75%

Source of data: *Wall Street Journal Historical Data.*

[41] Dodd-Frank Wall Street Reform and Consumer Protection Act (H.R. 4173, Public Law No. 111-203, signed into law July 21, 2010).

- regulates derivatives, including swaps.
- regulates hedge funds, which previously operated without any required disclosures.
- enhances regulation of securities, including credit rating agencies and securitizations.
- creates the Bureau of Consumer Financial Protection, which deals with consumer financial products and services.

Consider the Financial Stability Oversight Council, which is responsible for monitoring the stability of the U.S. financial system. Under this act, the council comprises 15 members. The voting members of this council are:

- the U.S. Treasury Secretary
- the Chairman of the Federal Reserve Board
- the Chairman of the Office of the Comptroller of the Currency (OCC)
- the Chairman of the Bureau of Consumer Financial Protection
- the Chairman of the Securities Exchange Commission
- the Chairman of the Federal Depositor Insurance Commission
- the Chairman of the Commodity Futures Trading Commission
- the Director of the Federal Housing Finance Agency
- the Chairman of National Credit Union Administration
- an independent member with expertise in insurance

In addition to these members, there are five nonvoting members, two representing the Office of Financial Research and the Federal Insurance Office, one state insurance commissioner, one state banking supervisor, and one state securities commissioner. It is expected that by formally coordinating efforts, the council will be in a position to identify threats to the financial system, promote market discipline, and respond to risks that may arise.

Lessons for Financial Managers

The financial crisis presented many challenges and many lessons for financial managers. The economic downturn, coupled with a credit crunch, made the financial manager's job more difficult. Among these lessons:

1. ***Financial risk management is important.*** Financial managers need to identify, assess, and manage risks; companies must develop an assessment of how much risk they are willing to take (that is, their risk appetite), and risk management must be an essential part of a company's strategy.

2. ***Companies that rely on securitizing their assets should be prepared for the associated risks.*** Securitization of assets is performed by many companies, not just banks and, for example, has been a source of cash flow for companies that sell their receivables through these transactions. For instance, Harley-Davidson Financial Services securitized the loans made on the purchases of Harley-Davidson motorcycles; when the securitization market dried up and the company could no longer securitize the loans, it could not turn the loans into cash, but rather had to retain and maintain them.

3. ***Reliance on bank financing for short-term needs is problematic during a credit crunch.*** Many companies that relied on lines of credit from banks or issuing commercial paper to meet seasonal needs found that they could not get financing during severe times. For example, the commercial paper market was disrupted in September 2008 with Lehman Brothers' bankruptcy; in December 2008, the outstanding commercial paper was half of what is was at the end of 2007.[42]

---

[42] The U.S. Treasury and the Federal Reserve stepped in during October of 2008 to support the commercial paper market through the Money Market Investor Funding Facility, Richard G. Anderson and Charles S. Gascon, "The Commercial Paper Market, the Fed, and the 2007–2009 Financial Crisis," *Federal Reserve Bank of St. Louis Review*, November/December, 91, no. 6, 589–612.

4. ***Executive compensation should be tied to some measure of risk, not just earnings.*** Many financial institutions tied compensation to earnings, without regard to the risk associated with the expansion of the entity into other, riskier lines of business. The focus on earnings may have inadvertently encouraged excessive risk taking.

The financial management challenges that occurred during the financial crisis have reshaped financial decision making. For example, companies at the end of 2010 were sitting with a great deal of cash; interest rates in general were at historical lows, and capital markets had recovered, making it a great time to borrow. However, the uncertainties regarding the economic recovery and taxes, coupled with the recent experience with the credit crunch, have made many financial managers cautious and have, as a result, stifled the capital expenditures that are key to economic recovery.

The Benefit of Being Nimble | LESSONS LEARNED

The interest rates that companies pay on their borrowing fell during 2010 to record lows that hadn't been seen since the 1960s:

Interest rates of AAA rated corporate bonds: 1950 through 2010

Source of data: Board of Governors of the Federal Reserve System, Moody's Seasoned AAA Corporate Bond yield, Series, H.15.

These low rates encouraged many corporations to issue new debt, even those with lots of cash on hand. Why issue debt when you don't need to? The cost of debt capital is relatively cheap, and they can raise the new capital now instead of when their current debt matures, when interest rates are expected to rise.[43]

Case in point: Johnson & Johnson typically has around 15 percent of its assets in cash and marketable securities.

In its fiscal year 2010, Johnson had almost 27 percent of its assets in cash and marketable securities, thanks to its offering of $550 million in notes in August 2010. The vast majority of Johnson & Johnson's investment in cash and marketable securities is invested in government securities and obligations: $22.3 billion of its $27.7 billion in cash and marketable securities.[44]

1. Why are global financial markets so important to U.S. investors?

2. What was the role of subprime mortgages in the 2007–2008 financial crisis?

Concept Review Questions

---

[43] Robert McNatt, "Credit FAQ: Why Do Companies Issue Debt When They Don't Seem to Need the Money?," Standard & Poor's, October 20, 2010.

[44] Johnson & Johnson 2010 10-K filing with the Securities and Exchange Commission.

SUMMARY

- Finance as a subject area is the study of the flow of funds from those with funds to those who need funds. Financial decision making encompasses investment and financing decisions, which may be short-term or long-term decisions.

- A business may borrow funds, either through borrowing or selling equity interests in the business. Borrowing includes loans from banks, issuing commercial paper, or issuing notes or bonds. Borrowing requires repayment of the debt, as well as interest on the debt. Management may sell ownership stakes in the company, which are represented by shares of stock. These shares may be common stock or preferred stock.

- The financial system is global, with parties crossing borders to raise and invest funds. No better example of the globalization of the financial system is available than the 2007–2008 financial crisis, where linkages among the markets were evident as the U.S. economy faltered, along with economies around the world.

QUESTIONS AND PROBLEMS

Multiple Choice

1. An equity security represents:
   A. a debt obligation.   B. an ownership interest.

2. Which of the following transactions takes place in the primary market? An investor:
   A. selling a corporate bond.
   B. selling a U.S. Treasury bill.
   C. buying shares of stock through a broker.
   D. buying shares of an initial public offering.

3. Which of the following transactions takes place in the secondary market? An investor:
   A. selling a share of stock through a broker.
   B. buying shares of an initial public offering.
   C. buying a U.S. Treasury bill through the government auction.

4. Which of the following is considered a money market security?
   A. Common stock   B. Preferred stock   C. U.S. Treasury bills   D. U.S. Treasury notes

5. Regulators' stress tests on banks examine banks' capital adequacy under the:
   A. best-case economic scenario.   B. worst-case economic scenario.   C. most-likely economic scenario.

6. Which of the following is not a government program designed to assist financial institutions during the financial crisis of 2007–2008?
   A. Troubled Asset Relief Program
   B. Troubled Asset-Backed Securities Fund
   C. Term Asset-Backed Securities Loan Facility

7. The Financial Industry Regulatory Authority is best described as a:
   A. dealer market.
   B. government regulator.
   C. self-regulatory organization.
   D. government-sponsored entity.

8. Which of the following is not considered a debt obligation?
   A. Note   B. Debenture   C. Preferred stock   D. General obligation bond

9. A mortgage is best described as a:
   A. debenture.   B. secured debt.   C. equity instrument.

10. Systemic risk is best described as risk that:
    A. affects the entire economy.
    B. moves along with the risk of the market.
    C. is confined to one sector of the economy.
    D. affects only one geographical area of the country.

Practice Questions and Problems

1.1 What Is Finance?

11. List the primary areas of finance.

12. Why is it important for a financial manager to understand accounting and financial statements?

13. What is the role of a market intermediary?

14. What is an example of a financial intermediary?

1.2 Financial Instruments and Markets

15. What is meant by the description of a transaction as occurring in the primary market?

16. Provide three examples of a debt obligation.

17. What distinguishes a note from a bond?

18. Why are the owners of common stock referred to as the residual owners of a corporation?

19. What are secondary market transactions, and how do secondary markets facilitate the primary markets?

20. Who regulates the securities markets in the U.S.?

21. For each of the following companies, calculate the market capitalization:

		Number of shares outstanding	Market price per share
A.	Company A	1,000,000	$5
B.	Company B	10,000,000	$10
C.	Company C	5,000,000	$20
D.	Company D	3,500,000	$25
E.	Company E	300,000,000	$13

22. Classify each of the following transactions as occurring in either the primary market or the secondary market:

	Primary	*Secondary*
A. An investor buys 1,000 shares of Google through her broker at E-trade in November 2004.		
B. An investor sells 10,000 shares of General Motors common stock in December 2010 through his broker, Charles Schwab.		
C. Cirrus Logic, a publicly traded company, buys $20 million of its own shares in the open market from January 2009 through November 2010.		
D. General Motors goes public, offering 478 million shares in November 2010.		
E. Google goes public with an offering of 19.6 million shares in August 2004.		
F. Prudential Financial, which is already a publicly traded company, makes a public offering of 18 million shares in November 2010.		

23. Classify each of the following as either a money market security or a capital market security:

	Money market security	*Capital market security*
A. 90-day Treasury bill		
B. 20-year debenture		
C. 30-year bond		
D. Common stock of Microsoft		
E. Commercial paper		
F. 5-year Treasury note		
G. General obligation bond		

24. Consider the following information for a company:

Common shares outstanding	5 million shares
Book value per share of common stock	$3.50
Market value per share of common stock	$8.00
Total assets	$20 million

   What is this company's market capitalization?

25. HCA Holdings had its first day as a publicly traded company on March 10, 2011. The stock closed at a price of $31.02, with 64.6 million shares traded on this day. There are 515 million shares of common stock outstanding after this offering.

   A. What type of transaction took place on March 10, 2011?

   B. What is the market capitalization of HCA, based on the price of a share at the end of trading March 10, 2011?

1.3 The Global Financial Crisis

26. What is meant by the term "subprime mortgage"?

27. Suppose a company has accounts receivable from its customers. Explain the process of securitizing these receivables by diagramming the process of converting them into securities.

28. What are the societal and ethical issues involved with originating mortgages for individuals with poor credit?

CAREERS IN FINANCE

Every manager should be a financial manager, in the sense that the concepts, principles, and analysis techniques discussed in this textbook are important for all managers within a company. However, when we think of finance jobs, we generally distinguish between jobs in corporate finance (i.e., working within the finance function of a nonfinancial company) and finance jobs within a financial service firm, such as JPMorgan Chase, Bank of America, Barclays, Goldman Sachs, and Manulife Financial Corporation.

1A.1 FINANCIAL OFFICERS

In Figure 1A-1 we provide the basic functional breakdown of the finance function within a nonfinancial corporation. The top person is generally designated as the **chief financial officer (CFO)**, or in more traditional companies, the **senior vice-president of finance**. Under the CFO are the two main finance jobs: the **treasurer** and the **controller**. Although the breakdown of responsibilities varies from company to company, typically the treasurer's responsibilities are primarily financial decision making, whereas the controller's responsibilities lie in accounting and financial reporting. Because accounting information is the primary information for financial decision making and reporting, anyone interested in working in a treasurer or controller capacity must have a strong accounting background.

The treasurer has the pure finance job in a company. The treasurer's basic function is to manage the company's funds. To do this, the treasurer has to manage the company's cash and decide whom to extend credit to: cash and credit management. The treasurer must then pay the bills and make sure that cash is available when needed. This means forecasting the company's future cash position, determining its capital expenditure plans, and arranging both debt and equity financing. If the company has a pension plan, the treasurer is also responsible for managing these financial assets the same way as a portfolio manager in a mutual fund would manage them. Finally, the treasurer is responsible for risk management. Traditionally, this has meant arranging adequate insurance and making

chief financial officer (CFO) top financial manager in a company

senior vice-president of finance in some companies functions as the CFO

treasurer one of the two main finance jobs in a nonfinancial company; focuses on the finance side: forecasting, pension management, capital budgeting, cash management, credit management, financing, risk management

controller one of the two main finance jobs in a nonfinancial company; focuses on the accounting side: compliance, tax management, systems/MIS, internal audit, accounting, and budgeting

Chief Financial Officer

Treasurer

Forecasting
Pension
Management
Capital Budgeting
Cash Management
Credit Management
Financing Risk
Management

Controller

Compliance Tax
Management
Systems/MIS
Internal
Audit Accounting
Budgeting

FIGURE 1A-1 Finance in a Nonfinancial Company

sure the company was covered if a fire burned down the building. However, over the past 30 years, many new techniques have emerged to manage financial risks, such as the risk of serious exchange rate or interest rate movements. These new techniques of financial risk management are the responsibility of the treasurer.

The controller is responsible for compliance. This entails making sure that the company meets its statutory legal responsibilities with securities commissions and other regulatory bodies, makes its tax payments to the government, fulfills its responsibility to prepare and file financial statements, and ensures that its internal control systems eliminate fraud so that the financial statements fairly represent the company's financial position. As part of this financial system, the controller is normally responsible for the management information system (MIS) because its main purpose is to collect the data required for internal audits and to prepare the company's financial statements. Finally, the system that produces the financial statements is the same system that generates budgets and targets for the upcoming year.

From this brief description of the controller's functions, it follows that finance jobs in the controller's department require training in financial accounting, management accounting, taxes, MIS, and control systems. These are all regarded as "finance" in nonfinancial companies.

The important thing about finance jobs within a nonfinancial company is that the jobs are very broad and require a strong dose of accounting and knowledge developed in other courses in a business school as well as finance. This is still true, but to a lesser extent, for the finance jobs within a financial intermediary such as a bank or an insurance company.

1A.2   ENTRY-LEVEL AND MIDCAREER FINANCIAL POSITIONS

analyst entry-level job in a financial institution

associate second-level job in a financial institution; it requires an MBA or a professional designation (e.g., CFA)

account manager financial professional who manages a bank's relationships with companies, extending credit, helping to manage receivables and cash, and directing them to the bank's more specialized services

banking associate financial professional who generates reports on companies, prepares industry reports, and performs background checks on credit applicants

Generally, in the major financial institutions, a common entry-level position is as an **analyst**, who most often has an undergraduate degree.[45] The next step is **associate**, which normally requires an MBA or a professional designation, such as certified public accountant (CPA), certified management accountant (CMA), or chartered financial analyst (CFA), before being promoted to manager.

In the traditional commercial banking, or business lending side, positions include

account manager	Manages the bank's relationships with companies by extending credit, helping to manage their receivables and cash, and directing them to the bank's more specialized services, such as foreign exchanges services, mergers and acquisitions, and specialized credit
banking associate	Generates reports on companies, prepares industry reports, and performs the background checks (due diligence) needed before extending credit.

The investment banking side of the major bank holding companies has three major types of jobs, either in sales or trading, or in "pure" investment banking. The investment banking side of the business is structured as a separate business segment, which is referred to as an investment dealer or investment banks. The pure investment dealer activities reflect the division of the business into corporate financing and mergers and acquisitions (M&A). These are the advisory functions that mirror the corporate finance jobs in a nonfinancial company.

---

[45] Analysts are not unique to financial institutions, and you will find analyst positions in corporations, commercial banks, investment banks, and rating agencies, among others.

Corporate financing employees, whether analysts, associates, or managers, advise clients and help them access the capital markets to raise capital, either through borrowing or issuing new equity. Although a company may raise capital relatively infrequently, investment dealers constantly advise their clients on what is available in the capital market. In mergers and acquisitions, investment dealers advise their clients on suitable candidates for acquisition or on how to defend themselves against a hostile acquisition. This often involves restructuring operations, selling off divisions (divestitures), or changing the company's financial structure.

Investment dealers, whether in corporate financing or M&A, derive part of their expertise from their knowledge of what is happening in the financial markets. Positions with an investment dealer include

security analyst	monitors the valuations of the companies he or she follows and makes recommendations to buy and sell a company's shares.
sales and trading	executes trades on behalf of their clients and conducts proprietary trading for the dealer itself using the investment bank's own capital.
retail broker and **private banker**	helps their clients manage their personal wealth.

Insurance companies and pension funds have significant long-term investments. As a result, they employ buy side analysts to do research on which particular investments to buy or sell. Several positions support these decisions, including

financial analyst or **investment analyst**	conducts detailed analyses of individual investments and makes recommendations on overall financial strategy.
portfolio manager	manages an investment portfolio.
fixed income trader or **equity trader**	implements investment strategies involving the buying or selling of fixed income or equity securities.

The final major group with a significant number of finance jobs is the management consulting and accounting companies. In their consulting practices, these companies need to analyze the financial health of a company, and often their advice contains a corporate finance element. Many of the smaller deals that do not involve significant capital market access are structured by accounting and consulting companies. A finance professional in these organizations is typically referred to as a **corporate finance associate** or **consultant**, and he or she advises on restructuring, small-scale M&A, and corporate financing.

security analyst financial professional who monitors the valuations of the companies and makes recommendations to buy and sell a company's shares

sales and trading activity that involves executing trades on behalf of the clients and conducting proprietary trading for the dealer itself by using the bank's own capital

retail broker and **private banker** financial professional who helps clients, usually people who have small to medium-sized accounts, manage their personal wealth

financial analyst and **investment analyst** finance professional who performs research, conducts detailed analyses of individual investments, and makes recommendations on overall financial strategy

portfolio manager professional in charge of the overall management of a portfolio

fixed income or **equity trader** finance professional who implements investment strategies and either buys or sells the securities of companies

corporate finance associate or **consultant** finance professional who advises on restructuring, small-scale M&A, and corporate financing

1A.3 PROFESSIONAL DESIGNATIONS

There are numerous professional designations that someone in a finance career may want to obtain. Most of these designations require a great deal of self-study, testing, and demonstrated work experience in the field. Though there are too many to list here, we include the most common designations by field in Table 1A-1, along with the web site address if you wish to find additional information.

In addition to the professional designations that we list in Table 1A-2, financial professionals who are involved in the securities business must register with FINRA, the self-regulatory organization for the securities profession and markets, and qualify by passing exams appropriate for the type of securities involved. These exams are referred to as series, and they relate to specific product responsibilities.

TABLE 1A-1 Professional Designations in Finance Careers

Designation		Focus	Website
CFA	Chartered Financial Analyst	Investment management and research	www.cfainstitute.org
CFE	Certified Fraud Examiner	Fraud detection and prevention	www.acfe.com
CFP	Certified Financial Planner	Financial planning for individuals	www.cfp.net
ChFC	Chartered Financial Consultant	Financial planning	www.theamericancollege.edu
CIA	Certified Internal Auditor	Internal auditing of for-profit and non-profit entities	www.theiia.org
CMA	Certified Management Accountant	Financial management and accounting	www.imanet.org
CPA	Certified Public Accountant	Public accounting	www.aicpa.org
FRM	Financial Risk Manager	Risk management and analysis	www.garp.org

TABLE 1A-2 Registrations Required in the U.S. Securities Business

Series	Examination
4	Registered Options Principal
6	Investment Company Products/Variable Contracts Limited Representative
7	General Securities Representative
9 and 10	General Securities Sales Supervisor
11	Assistant Representative—Order Processing
14	Compliance Officer
22	Direct Participation Programs Limited Representative
23	General Securities Principal—Sales Supervisor Module
24	General Securities Principal
26	Investment Company Products/Variable Contracts Limited Principal
27	Financial and Operations Principal
28	Introducing Broker/Dealer Financial and Operations Principal
39	Direct Participation Programs Limited Principal
42	Registered Options Representative
51	Municipal Fund Securities Principal
52	Municipal Securities Representative
55	Equity Trader Limited Representative
53	Municipal Securities Principal
62	Corporate Securities Limited Representative
63	Uniform Securities Agent State Law Examination
65	Uniform Investment Adviser Law Examination
66	Uniform Combined State Law Examination
72	Government Securities Limited Representative
79	Limited Representative—Investment Banking
82	Limited Representative—Private Securities Offerings Representative
86 and 87	Research Analyst

Source: *FINRA, www.finra.org.*

CHAPTER 2

FINANCIAL MANAGEMENT

© malerapaso/iStockphoto

Social Responsibility? These days, businesses are being called upon more than ever to act in a manner that is socially, economically, and environmentally responsible.

Being a good corporate citizen, however, can put a company at odds with its fundamental obligation, which is to maximize the value of the entity for its owners. Consider Green Mountain Coffee Roasters, Inc., which was ranked as the number one company in the U.S. each year 2003 through 2007 by *Business Ethics*, and number 39 in 2010 in the Corporate Responsibility rankings of companies in the Russell 1000 index.* This ranking is an assessment of a company's business ethics, based on its community service, governance, diversity, employee relations, environment, product, and human rights. The company attributes its position as a leader in social and environmental responsibility to its view of "profit as a means to achieve a higher purpose."**

Learning Outcomes

After reading this chapter, you should be able to:

LO 2.1 List the advantages and disadvantages of the primary forms of a business organization.

LO 2.2 Describe the ultimate objective of a company and explain why this is a logical objective.

LO 2.3 List and describe agency costs and how they may affect owners' wealth.

LO 2.4 Discuss the primary types of decisions made by business entities regarding the financial management of assets, as well as the associated financing decisions.

Chapter Preview We discuss the role of the form of business in decision making in this chapter and provide the background necessary to analyze how a business's investment and financing decisions are made. In the process, we examine the goals of the corporation and how its internal affairs are organized.

Corporate Responsibility Magazine, www.thecro.com.
**Green Mountain Coffee, About Our Company, www.gmcr.com.

33

2.1 FORMS OF BUSINESS ORGANIZATIONS

The business sector makes investment decisions that are intended to increase its ability to produce goods and services in the future—that is, to generate future growth in consumption and wealth. But the business sector comprises different forms of business entities, including proprietorships, partnerships, and corporations. If you were to count the number of businesses in the U.S., you would find that sole proprietorships are the largest group. On the other hand, if you were to add up all the revenues generated by business entities, you would find that corporations contribute by far the largest share of revenues.

In the U.S., as in most countries, businesses can be organized in different ways. The major forms of business organizations are the:

1. sole proprietorship;
2. partnership;
3. limited liability company; and
4. corporation.

We discuss each of these next.

Sole Proprietorships

sole proprietorship
business owned and operated by one person

A **sole proprietorship** is a business owned and operated by one person. Starting a proprietorship is as simple as drumming up business. Many important businesses have been started by someone trying to meet a market need, whether it's the neighbor's child who starts a lemonade stand one hot summer day or the teenager who cleans up yards to earn spending money. These people have both started sole proprietorships, in which one person begins working on his or her own rather than for someone else. If these examples seem trivial, think about Bill Gates and Paul Allen (Microsoft Corporation), who started out working on personal computers in their parents' garages.

The big advantage of a sole proprietorship is that setting one up is easy—no paperwork is involved, and the owner needs only to start doing business. Of course, if the business begins to grow, the owner might want to register a business name or web site, or even patent a particular business process to keep imitators away or at least make them pay a royalty. However, the critical thing is that the business is almost inseparable from the owner; if that lemonade turns out to be bad, or if part of that yard isn't cleaned up, the business owner is personally liable. This isn't a big factor for most very small businesses, but if that web page inadvertently damages a client by directing traffic elsewhere, the owner is personally liable. More to the point, the owner can be sued for damages. If the owner has other assets, he or she could lose them or, in extreme cases, be forced into bankruptcy and lose everything because of a bad decision made in the sole proprietorship. This accountability is **unlimited liability** because an owner is liable not only to the extent of what is invested in the business but also for any other assets owned.

unlimited liability
responsibility for obligations of a business that extends beyond the original investment, including personal assets

Aside from the liability issue, there are financial implications to sole proprietorships. The sources of funds available for sole proprietorships are the same ones that are available to individuals. No complicated finance options are available—owners borrow from relatives and friends or, depending on their credit rating, from the bank, through either a loan or a credit card.[1] If businesses create some revenue, owners can use one of the many government programs designed to stimulate small businesses.

If a business grows and the owner wants to sell it, it can be problematic. All the contacts and relationships are personal and belong to the owner because legally the

---

[1] This is known as the three Fs: friends, fools, and family.

owner and the business are one in the same. Selling a profitable window-cleaning business may mean visiting every contact and explaining that someone new is taking over the business and will be serving them in the future. The fact is, there is no continuity in a sole proprietorship, which makes it difficult to sell and, of course, the business dies with the owner.

Because a sole proprietorship is legally inseparable from the individual, the owner has to report the income on his or her annual individual income tax return. Sole proprietors have to keep the same accounting records as big businesses do and report the income after deducting all reasonable expenses. However, the net income is simply added to any regular salary income and taxed at ordinary tax rates.

Advantages and Disadvantages to the Sole Proprietorship Form of Business

Advantages	*Disadvantages*
1. Easy to form.	1. Unlimited liability.
2. Business income is taxed once, at the individual's personal level.	2. Lack of continuity.
	3. Limited access to additional funds.

SUMMARIZING

Partnerships

Suppose you are designing a new web page and need some help from a friend. The two of you start working together. After a while, it becomes a solid relationship, and you always work together on jobs for clients. This relationship is a **partnership**, rather than a sole proprietorship. This partnership can be formalized by having a lawyer create a partnership agreement, which establishes how decisions are made, such as how each partner can buy out the other in the event that one wants to dissolve the partnership. If the partnership grows, then the owners also need to document how new partners enter and what their attendant obligations are, as well as how others can cash out.

partnership business owned and operated by two or more people

The partnership agreement further stipulates how the partnership's income is allocated among the partners. Individuals have to be careful with partnerships because a legal agreement is not required to be considered a partner. Sometimes a partnership can be implied by the actions of a group of people working together. This becomes a problem when a disaffected party sues everyone associated with a business, even people who are not formal partners.

Similar to sole proprietorships, the income of the partnership is taxed at the individual partner level. The partnership income is allocated according to the terms of the partnership agreement and included in the individual partners' taxable income, whether or not it is distributed.

Also similar to the sole proprietorship, continuity is a potential problem because if a partner no longer exists or if a partner wishes to exit the partnership, the partnership agreement must be rewritten. In a partnership with many partners, this may become quite burdensome to manage.

Partnerships' access to capital is somewhat easier to obtain than that of sole proprietorships, though instead of relying on one individual's personal assets the partnership relies on the personal assets of all the partners. The business's access to capital is limited, however, because raising capital beyond the partners' contributions and local banks may be challenging, especially in some economic environments. And because a partnership is owned 100% by its partners, bringing in additional owners would not be possible unless the partnership agreement is rewritten.

Nevertheless, some very big companies began operations as traditional partnerships, most of which were in the professional services area, such as accounting companies, investment banks, doctors' offices, engineering firms, and dentists' offices. Such companies needed more than one person to deliver a full range of services, yet "society" judged it important to hold each member individually responsible for his or her own actions and for those of his or her colleagues. But, over time, the increasing complexity of partnership operations—for example, in the accounting and investment banking areas—weakened this argument. With hundreds of partners in a company, imagine how difficult it would be to justify making all the partners responsible for the actions of one rogue partner. As a result, the importance of traditional partnerships has diminished.

Partnerships are still significant for smaller companies because they maintain the integration of partnership income with other income for each partner. However, newer partnership models have emerged that maintain this tax treatment while removing the unlimited personal liability. The two main partnership forms are the **general partnership** and the **limited liability partnership (LLP)**, which we often refer to as simply a **limited partnership**, though all partnerships have at least one general partner. In a general partnership, the partners share the management and income of the business. In an LLP, there is at least one general partner who manages the business, but there may be any number of limited partners, who are passive investors. These limited partners have limited liability in the event of a lawsuit against the company, yet each partner's income is still included as ordinary income and filed by using an individual tax return. As long as the limited partners are not active in the business, they have the advantage of **limited liability**; the most they can lose is their initial investment. The general partner, conversely, has unlimited liability as the operator of the business. In practice, however, many general partners are corporations (discussed later) and indirectly benefit from limited liability.[2]

We observe large partnerships in oil and gas exploration. In some countries, limited partnership interests can be traded publicly on the exchanges, in which case it is referred to as a **master limited partnership**. In the U.S., large master limited partnerships, such as Kinder Morgan Energy Partners (KMP) and Enterprise Products Partners (EPD), have ownership units that trade on the New York Stock Exchange, with market capitalizations of $22 billion and $34.7 billion, respectively, in 2011. The largest Canadian natural gas distribution company in Quebec is Gaz Métro Limited Partnership (GZM) with 2009 revenues of CAD $603 million and profit of CAD $222.6 million.[3]

general partnership
form of business in which all partners share in the management and the profits of the business, and the income and losses from the business are reflected on the individual owners' tax returns

limited partnership or **limited liability partnership (LLP)** form of business in which there are both general and limited partners, with general partners making management decisions and having unlimited liability, and the limited partners being passive investors with limited liability

master limited partnership form of business in which there are general and limited partners, with limited partner interests traded in the public market

SUMMARIZING

Advantages and Disadvantages to the Partnership Form of Business

Advantages	*Disadvantages*
1. Easy to form.	1. Unlimited liability for general partners.
2. Business income is taxed once, at the individual partners' level.	2. Lack of continuity.
	3. Limited access to additional funds.

[2] Limited partnerships had been used as tax shelters and for this reason they are scrutinized by tax authorities to make sure they are not a vehicle for tax avoidance; however, there are legitimate reasons to set up a limited partnership.

[3] CAD indicates Canadian dollars. The CAD before the dollar sign lets you know that this is not U.S. dollars, which we would designate as USD.

Corporations

A **corporation** is easy to recognize because it has Inc. for incorporated, Ltd. for limited, or, in Europe, PLC for private limited corporation or AG for Aktiengesellschaft, after its name. In each case, the abbreviations or initials indicate that the owners have the benefit of **limited liability**: the maximum that owners can lose is their investment—that is, they cannot be forced to invest more in the company to make up for any losses the company incurs. Unlike a partnership or sole proprietorship, a business that operates as a corporation separates personal assets from any malfeasance or failure at the corporate level. Although the courts have occasionally "pierced the corporate veil" and extended that liability, it is very rare and happens only in cases involving significant public policy concerns.

A corporation is usually formed by filing articles of incorporation and receiving a certificate of incorporation from the state. The articles of incorporation indicate the most basic information about the company, such as its mailing address, name, line of business, number of shares issued, names and addresses of the officers of the company, and so on. The critical feature is that the corporation is a *distinct legal entity*. For this reason the corporation is entitled to sign contracts in its own name, file its own tax returns, borrow money, make investments, and sue and be sued—all in its own name.

As a distinct legal entity, the corporation has significant advantages over a partnership or a sole proprietorship. For one it is *immortal*. This indefinite life means that unlike people, corporations can borrow by using debt that will be paid off in 40, and even 100, years' time. Individuals, with finite lives, would have difficulty getting these terms from a bank. It also means that transferring and selling assets is relatively easy because all the contracts go with the company, and the share ownership is simply transferred. Therefore, there is no issue of continuity that we see with sole proprietorships and partnerships.

One of the most difficult aspects of corporations is the issue of control. In partnerships and sole proprietorships, the owners run the business. In corporations, the owners are the owners of the ownership interests—that is, the shareholders—who elect members of the board of directors, who in turn hire and monitor the company's management. For smaller companies, the separation of management and ownership isn't a problem, but for larger companies, it becomes a serious concern. This division is the fundamental problem of the governance structure of large companies. We will discuss governance in detail later because it is integral to the role of mergers and acquisitions and to understanding valuation.

Every company has a set of bylaws that indicate how it is to be run. Some of the content of the bylaws is determined by corporate law, but some is discretionary and up to the company. Some may be very broad, such as Berkshire Hathaway's bylaw 4.1:

> The Board of Directors shall consist of one or more members, the number thereof to be determined from time to time by resolution of the Board of Directors.[4]

or very specific, such as Ford Motor Company's Section 5, (2) power to determine working capital levels:

> (2) To fix, and from time to time to vary, the amount of working capital of the Company, and to set aside from time to time out of net profits, current or accumulated, or surplus of the Company such amount or amounts as they in their discretion may deem necessary and proper as, or as a safeguard to the maintenance of, working capital, as a reserve for contingencies, as a reserve for repairs, maintenance, or rehabilitation, or as a reserve for revaluation of profits of the Company or for such other proper purpose as may in the opinion of the directors be in the best interests of the Company; ...[5]

corporation business organized as a separate legal entity under corporation law, with ownership divided into transferable shares

limited liability limit on the financial responsibility of owners of a business entity to the amount of their investment

---

[4] 4.1 *By-Laws of Berkshire Hathaway Inc*, as amended through April 29, 1991.
[5] *By-Laws of Ford Motor Company*, As Amended Through October 30, 2001, Article III, Section 5, subsection (2).

What is not discretionary is the requirement that the company have a board of directors whose responsibility is to represent the owners and manage the operating and financial affairs of the company. These directors are elected by the owners.[6]

In theory, the members of the board of directors are elected by the shareholders and act in shareholders' best interests. Their statutory responsibilities are determined by the law of the state in which the corporation is incorporated and, if the corporation's stock is publicly traded, the rules of the exchange on which it trades and the relevant securities law.

Essentially, this legal requirement means that members of the board of directors must exercise the normal standards of professionalism expected of people in their position. This standard is known as the "due diligence" standard, and as long as it is met, members of the board of directors cannot be sued for negligence. The scandal surrounding Enron Corporation inspired the passage of the Sarbanes-Oxley Act of 2002.[7] This act enhanced the responsibilities of the board of directors, holding the members of the board of directors responsible for attesting to the internal controls of the company, as well as the company's quarterly and annual reports.

flow-through taxation income flows directly to the owners as taxable income and is not taxed at the business entity level

Another challenge to the corporate form is the issue of taxation. Sole proprietorships and partnerships have **flow-through taxation**. This means that the income flows to the owners' tax return and is therefore taxed only once. Under Subchapter C of the Internal Revenue Code, corporations do not have the benefit of flow-through taxation; rather, corporate income may be taxed twice or more.[8] To see how this works, consider a corporation that has $10 million of income and pays this entire amount to shareholders in the form of dividends. If the corporation's income tax rate is 35% and the individual shareholders have a tax rate of 38%, what is the effective tax on this income after it passes through both layers of taxation?

(in millions)

Corporate income before taxes	$10.000
Tax at 35%	3.500
Income after tax	$6.500
Dividend income of individuals	$6.500
Tax at 38%	2.470
Income after tax	$4.030

Total taxes paid are $3.50 + 2.47 = $5.97 million. This means that the effective tax on the $10 million of corporate income tax is $5.97 ÷ $10 = 59.7%. What if the corporation pays only half of its income in dividends? The effective rate would be 47.35%:

(in millions)

Corporate income before taxes	$10.000
Tax at 35%	3.500
Income after tax	$6.500
Dividend income of individuals	$3.250
Tax at 38%	1.235
Income after tax	$2.015

---

[6] In the United States, directors can only be removed for cause before the end of their term of appointment. This means that it is technically possible to own 51% of the company and yet not be able to immediately remove the board of directors and control the company. In Canada, in contrast, the owners may remove a director during his or her tenure.

[7] Public law 107–204, signed into law July 30, 2002. Enron Corporation met its demise in 2001 when accounting fraud was revealed, among other things.

[8] Title 26 U.S. Code, Subchapter C.

We can capture this in a formula, using t_c to represent the corporate tax rate, t_i to represent the individual tax rate, and *DPO* to represent the portion of dividends paid to owners:

$$\text{Effective tax rate on corporate income} = t_c + [(1 - t_c) \; DPO \; t_i] \qquad (2\text{-}1)$$

In the last example,

$$\text{Effective tax rate on corporate income} = 0.35 + [(1 - 0.35) \times 0.5 \times 0.38] = 0.4735 \text{ or } 47.35\%$$

Let's compare the taxation of a corporation with that of a partnership. Consider two companies, Company P, organized as a partnership, and Company C, organized as a corporation. Suppose that both companies have $100,000 of income and distribute all this income after tax to their owners. If corporate income is taxed at a rate of 35% and individual income is taxed at the rate of 30%, what is the difference in taxes paid on company income for each company?

	Company P	*Company C*
Taxable income	$100,000	$100,000
Taxes paid by the company	0	35,000
Income distributed to owners	$100,000	$65,000
Taxes paid by owners	30,000	19,500
Income to owners after taxes	$70,000	$45,500
Total taxes paid on company income	$30,000	$54,500
Effective tax rate on company income	30%	54.5%

The taxes paid on Company C's income are much higher than those of Company P: 54.5% compared to 30%. Taking this a step further, if any of Company C's shareholders are corporations, there may be additional layers of taxes paid on the income, depending on the relationship between the two corporations.[9] As you can see in this example, the flow-through taxation provides an advantage to the sole proprietorship and partnership forms of business when compared to the corporate form.

PROBLEM	EXAMPLE 2.1

ABC Corporation and DEF partnership are in the same line of business, and each has $1 million of income before taxes for the most recent fiscal year. Both companies pay out a quarter of income after tax to owners. ABC is subject to a corporation income tax of 40%, and all individuals are subject to a 30% tax on income. What is the effective rate of tax for each company's income, considering the taxes of the business and the owners?

The Benefit of Flow-Through Taxation

Solution

For ABC, the effective rate of tax is $0.40 + [0.60 \times 0.30 \times 0.25] = 44.5\%$
For DEF, the effective rate of tax is 30%

---

[9] We will discuss this in more detail in a later chapter, but basically if a corporation owns 100% of another corporation, the income will not be taxed again. However, if a corporation owns less than 100% of another corporation, some of the corporate income may be taxed.

SUMMARIZING

Advantages and Disadvantages to the Corporate Form of Business

Advantages	Disadvantages
1. Limited liability.	1. Income taxed at the corporate level and at the owners' level, when distributed.
2. Unlimited life.	2. Separation of owners and management.
3. Access to capital.	

Limited Liability Companies

limited liability company (LLC) business organized as a separate legal entity in which owners have limited liability, but the income is passed through to the owners for tax purposes

A **limited liability company (LLC)** is a company that embodies some of the best features of both the partnership and corporate forms of business. Similar to a corporation, the owners have limited liability. This means that creditors of the LLC cannot look to the owners of the LLC to pay off the company's debts. Like a corporation, the most that the owners of an LLC may lose is the amount of their investment.[10]

Similar to a partnership, the LLC has flow-through taxation.[11] That is, the owners report their share of the LLC's income on their individual tax return. If the owner is a corporation, then this income flows to the owner's own corporate tax return. The owners of an LLC are referred to as members, and there can be just one member or any number of members. And a member can be an individual, a partnership, a corporation, or even another LLC.

LLCs are regulated by state law, and these laws vary slightly among states. States restrict certain types of businesses from using the LLC form of business if viewed in the public interest. For example, insurance companies, banks, law offices, and nonprofit organizations are generally prohibited from becoming LLCs.

SUMMARIZING

Advantages and Disadvantages to the Limited Liability Company Form of Business

Advantages	Disadvantages
1. Limited liability for the owners.	1. Separation of owners and management.
2. Unlimited life.	2. Access to capital.
3. Income taxed only at the owners' level.	

Subchapter S Corporations

Sub S corporation corporation that elects to be taxed as a partnership

Corporations that meet specific requirements may elect annually to be treated as a partnership for tax purposes. A corporation electing such treatment is often referred to as a **Subchapter S corporation** or, simply, **Sub S corporation**, because the treatment is

---

[10] Of course, there are exceptions to this limited liability in the case where the individual owner commits fraud or directly injures someone. In addition, as in the case of a corporation, if the owners treat the business as an extension of their own personal affairs, instead of as a separate, legal entity, the limited liability protection may not apply.

[11] There is a limitation on the deductibility of losses, which can be a disadvantage to this form of business.

spelled out in Subchapter S of the Internal Revenue Code. Sub S is not a separate form of business, but rather is an annual election made by corporations on their tax returns. Even so, the term "Sub S" has crept into the nomenclature as equivalent to a form of business. We distinguish the Sub S corporation from a corporation that does not elect special treatment by referring to the later as a **C corporation**.

> **C corporation** business taxed as a corporation according to Subsection C of the Internal Revenue Code

So how does a Sub S compare with an LLC? Let's consider their basic characteristics:

Characteristic	*Sub S*	*LLC*
Taxation	Pass-through	Pass-through
Ownership	Maximum of 75 shareholders	No maximum
Liability	Limited liability	Limited liability
Life	Perpetual	Limited

The Sub S status was once popular with small corporations, allowing them to avoid the double taxation that befalls corporations. However, with the widespread acceptance of limited liability companies, which accomplish this same tax treatment without such an election, the LLC is often viewed as a preferred form of business.

Forms of Business | GLOBAL PERSPECTIVE

The primary forms of business in the United States can be found in most other countries, as you can see in this table:

Form of business in the United States

Country	General partnership	Limited partnership	Corporation	Limited liability company
Germany	Offene Handelsgesellschaft (oHG)	Kommanditgesellschaft (KG)	Aktiengesellschaft (AG)	Gesellschaft mit beschränkter Haftung (GmbH)
Japan	Gomei Kaisha	Goshi Kaisha	Kabushiki Kaisha (KK)	Godo Kaisha (LLC)
France	Société en nom collectif	Société en commandite simple	Societe anonyme (SA)	Société à responsabilité limitée
United Kingdom	Unlimited company	Limited partnership	Public limited company (PLC)	Limited company (Ltd.)
Sweden	Handelsbolag (HB)	Kommanditbolag (KB)	Publikt aktiebolag (AB)	*no equivalent*

Prevalence

What are the most popular forms of business? Consider the statistics from the Internal Revenue Service, as we show in Figure 2-1. The most common form of business, in terms of number of businesses, is the sole proprietorship. However, if we consider the revenues, corporations have the largest share. In other words, although there are fewer corporations, the corporations are quite large relative to partnerships and sole proprietorships.

The IRS classifies limited liability companies as partnerships because the tax treatment is the same. The limited liability company form of business represents 59% of the number of partnerships and 54% of the revenues of partnerships.[12]

---

[12] This is in contrast to the proportions we observed in the 1980s, when LLCs were not an option, and the general partnership was the most prevalent form of partnerships in terms of both the number of businesses and the revenues.

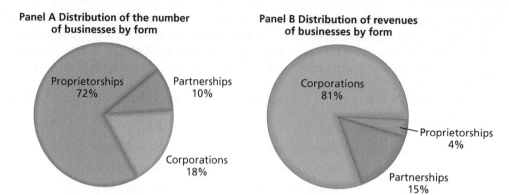

FIGURE 2-1 **Distribution of Number of Businesses and Revenues of Business by Form**

Source of data: *Statistics of Income, Internal Revenue Service, U.S. Department of the Treasury, using data from 2008 tax returns (the most recent data available).*

Concept Review Questions

1. Describe the main advantages and disadvantages of sole proprietorships and partnerships.

2. Explain why a business may be formed as an LLC instead of as a partnership.

3. What are the main advantages and disadvantages of the corporation structure?

2.2 THE GOALS OF THE BUSINESS ENTERPRISE

You might remember from your economics course that the goal of the company is to maximize its economic profits, where economic profits are the difference between revenues and expenses. These expenses are similar to the expenses we consider for accounting purposes, but also include the opportunity costs of the funds the business uses. Opportunity costs, basically, represent what could have been earned on funds if invested elsewhere.

Stakeholders

stakeholder any party affected by the decisions and actions of an entity

A **stakeholder** of a business is a party that is affected by the decisions and operations of the business entity. Stakeholders include not only the owners, but also the creditors, the employees, the suppliers, and the customers. We can also extend the concept of stakeholders to include the community in which the business operates. We illustrate the role of the business in relation to its stakeholders in Figure 2-2.

As you can see in Figure 2-2 the company is, essentially, an input–output mechanism. It takes inputs, such as raw materials, labor, and supplies, and transforms them into something more useful to society when it produces goods or services. For all companies, this activity is regulated both by implicit societal pressures to be "good" and by laws passed by government to prevent companies from doing things it regards as "bad." For example, minimum wage and employment laws prevent companies from using underage labor or paying wages that are too low. Similarly, laws on environmental protection, packaging of goods, and so on ensure that the company operates according to what is in consumers' interests.

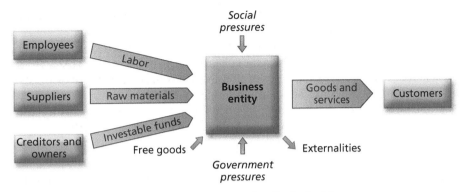

FIGURE 2-2 The Business Entity and Its Stakeholders

The Goal of the Business Enterprise

Recall that the goal of the management of a company is to enhance the owners' wealth. Apart from obeying the law, for sole proprietorships and partnerships, this is the end of the story; those companies are then run in the interests of their owners. Normally, this means that the management of companies enhances the owners' welfare by making decisions that maximize the value of the owners' interest. The value today of the owners' interest is the present value of all current and future cash flows to owners.[13]

Profit in this context refers to **economic profit**, not what is reported in a company's financial statements. The primary difference between economic profit and accounting profit is that the former includes a deduction of the opportunity cost of funds, whereas the latter does not. We discuss the relation between economic profits and wealth in more detail later in the context of valuation.

When the company's goal is applied to publicly traded companies, the goal of the company is to maximize the market value of the equity interest or, alternatively, *maximize shareholder value*: the company should take resources and create products that society values more highly than it values the inputs.

Note that there are two points in Figure 2-2 that we have not discussed: the existence of free goods and externalities. *Free goods* are goods or services that the company doesn't pay for. As a result, the company creates value without taking into account these other valuable resources and may make decisions that are not in the public's best interests. For example, consider the use of water. Should companies be allowed to use water without paying for it? Water is something that in some areas is in abundance, and it would be relatively easy to set up a plant to export water to, say, the U.S. southwest, which is largely a desert. In fact, it is possible to reverse the flow of water down the Mackenzie Valley, moving it down the Colorado River to Arizona and California, instead of having it go to the Arctic. This was an issue in the Free Trade Agreement (FTA) between the United States and Canada: Would the United States have the right to Canadian water, and would refusing a request be a violation of trade under the FTA? Clearly, large-scale diversion of water entails a cost not captured in the rates the public pays for water, and to charge this lower rate for large-scale water diversion is almost certainly not in the best interests of Canada, even though it may be in the best interests of people sponsoring the idea.

Externalities are costs or benefits from some decision to an entity or an individual who was not party to the decision. Examples of positive externalities (that is, those that create benefits) include a homeowner who paints his home and therefore enhances the value of other homes in the neighborhood, research that provides cures not originally intended, and education, which contributes to a more highly skilled workforce and hence a healthier economy. Examples of negative externalities (that is, those that create costs to

economic profit
difference between revenue and expenses, after considering the opportunity cost of funds

---

[13] The present value of the current and future profits is what someone would be willing to pay now to receive these future cash flows, considering the time value of money and the uncertainty of these future cash flows.

others) include air pollution, ground water contamination from fertilizer, and plastic bags that do not decay quickly in landfills.

The bottom line of both free goods and externalities is that these elements are generally not incorporated in decision making, even though there are benefits or costs arising from these. Why should this matter? When managers of a business maximize the value of owners' wealth, free goods and externalities are not considered in the decision making. Should they be?

The maximization of owners' value has been widely accepted, not just by academic theorists but also by regulators. Economist Milton Friedman argued that[14]

> there is one and only one social responsibility of business—to use its resources and engage in activities designed to increase its profits so long as it stays within the rules of the game, which is to say, engages in open and free competition without deception or fraud.

A company has a duty to do the right thing as enshrined in law and the contracts that it signs with employees, for example. The company should operate legally and in compliance with its contractual responsibilities, in the interests of its owners, by creating value for them. But is a company's management obligated to consider, for example, the social and environmental impact of each decision? Should financial managers of a corporation focus on shareholders or, more broadly, stakeholders? Milton Friedman would argue that as long as there is competition, the focus on the most efficient allocation of resources through owners' wealth maximization provides for the maximum benefit for all stakeholders. If, on the other hand, there were monopolies, the maximization of owners' wealth would not be consistent with an efficient allocation of resources because monopolistic owners would raise prices, and there would not necessarily be an incentive for the owners to produce the quantity of goods required by society.

LESSONS LEARNED | Economic Value Added

Economic value added, or simply economic profit, is the difference between revenues and expenses, where expenses include the cost of the capital used by the business. Stern Stewart & Co. trademarked the acronym EVA in the 1990s and promoted EVA as a tool to help nonfinance executives understand profitability in the economic sense.

Companies that focus on earnings-per-share tend to emphasize short-term gains and growth, rather than a long-term focus and value. For example, General Motors' bonus system, prior to its demise in 2009, was based on earnings per share. Although that alone was not the cause of GM's problems, it does illustrate a focus on the short term instead of the long term. As an example, GM exchanged lower wages for its unions for better retirement benefits, which resulted in lower operating costs, but higher debt obligations in terms of pension liabilities.

Economic value added is consistent with shareholder wealth maximization because it uses the cost of the company's capital as the hurdle in evaluating a company's or division's performance in a period. Calculating economic value added requires first calculating the net operating profits after taxes (NOPAT), and then subtracting the cost of capital in dollar terms. The cost of capital is the cost of using long-term sources of funds, whether they are debt or equity.

For example, if a company has a cost of capital of 7% and uses $10 million of capital (that is, interest-bearing debt plus equity), its cost of capital in dollar terms is 7% × $10 million = $0.7 million. If the company has NOPAT of $1 million, its economic profit or economic value added is $0.3 million.

Although economic value added is a useful tool for evaluating performance in a given period, it is not useful extended for multiple periods, such as when we evaluate a capital project. Another potential problem with using economic profit as a measure of performance is that it is short-sighted, which can tempt managers to make decisions that would affect this period's operating earnings, and hence economic profit, instead of taking the long view, which would maximize shareholder wealth.

Some companies promote the use of economic value added as a management tool that has improved the management of the company and enhanced shareholder wealth, but the use of economic value added is not a guarantee of success. Measuring economic value added is one of many tools that managers can use to evaluate performance.

---

[14] Milton Friedman, "The Social Responsibility of Business Is to Increase Profits," *New York Times Magazine,* September 13, 1970, p. 33.

1. What is the primary goal of the corporation?

2. Who are the stakeholders for a company such as McDonald's?

2.3 THE ROLE OF MANAGEMENT AND AGENCY ISSUES

When making decisions within a business enterprise, it is necessary to have a goal in mind; otherwise, decision making would be quite random. But what should this goal be? If the managers and owners are the same people, as in small companies, the goal is most often to maximize the owners' wealth. Even some very large companies have a controlling shareholder to make certain that managers act in the shareholders' best interests.

For most large corporations, however, shareholders are widely dispersed, and there is most often a separation of the decision making of the company from the ownership of the company. And although managers have a responsibility to make decisions that will benefit shareholders, the interests of managers and shareholders do not necessarily coincide.

The Agency Relationship and Agency Costs

Managers are employees and as such are *agents* working on behalf of the shareholders. We refer to this relationship as **agency relationship**. And despite the fact that managers have a duty to shareholders, there is always the possibility that managers will act in their own self-interest. This is the classic **agency problem** associated with the separation of ownership from management.

The costs associated with the agency problem are referred to as **agency costs**. There are different types of agency costs: some direct, such as costs associated with producing financial statements and annual reports for investors and shareholders, and some indirect, such as the cost of making suboptimal investments and providing stock options to motivate managers.

Suppose you hire the son of a friend to clean up your yard. You could sit on the back porch and watch him to make sure he does a good job. However, this monitoring of his work is expensive for you; after all, you probably hired him because your time is valuable and you have other things to do. Monitoring him defeats the purpose. Instead, you can compensate him to try to meet your objectives. Suppose you pay him $10 an hour and think the job will take four hours. What might happen when you come back after four hours? If he does not expect repeat business (and therefore his reputation is not at stake), he'll probably be only partly finished because with a cost-plus contract, his incentive is to stretch out the job. Conversely, if you agree on a fixed fee, say $40, you'll probably come back after four hours and discover that he left two hours earlier. Then you'll have to check everything because he's probably taken shortcuts. In this case, his personal incentive is to finish early. What you want to do is align his interests with yours so you don't have to monitor and check his behavior.

Like your interests and those of your friend's son, the interests of managers and shareholders are usually fundamentally different. For example, shareholders tend to have a short-term interest in the company and hold the shares and other securities of many entities in a large investment portfolio. If they see the managers acting contrary to what they would like, rather than trying to remove management through a costly proxy fight at the annual general meeting, they will merely sell their shares and go elsewhere.[15] It is simply too costly for most shareholders to try to remove management in a large corporation; however, this is not to say that it doesn't happen. U.S. fund manager Tweedy Browne

agency relationship relationship that occurs when managers work on behalf of the shareholders

agency problem issue or conflict that arises due to potential divergence of interest between managers, shareholders, and creditors

[15] A proxy fight involves a party accumulating the votes of shareholders so as to be their representative when voting the shares on a particular issue, such as a takeover or obtaining seats on the board of directors.

Company LLC waged an expensive war to remove Conrad Black from Hollinger International Inc., a U.S. publishing company, and eventually succeeded. In this case the fund manager was angered by what was perceived as corporate wrongdoing: Conrad Black was found guilty of using company funds for his personal benefit, among other things.[16]

Aligning Managers' and Owners' Interests

Managers don't necessarily pursue the best interests of the shareholders because their investment in the corporation goes much deeper than that of a typical shareholder: Their careers are inextricably bound up with the company, and that goes beyond any stockholdings. For this very reason, managers tend to be more conservative in their decisions than would seem justified by the shareholder approach.

The different perspectives of managers and shareholders are evident in terms of performance measurement. For example, when being appraised, managers want to be judged relative to accounting numbers, such as profits and return on investment (ROI), because they can control these numbers to some extent.[17] In contrast, shareholders are interested in stock market performance because they want managers to create shareholder value. Similarly, in investment analysis, which involves selecting long-term projects, managers want to choose the internal rate of return (IRR) of the best project, relative to other divisions of the company or past performance, because, again, this is what they control.[18] In contrast, shareholders are interested in what they can do with the money, which can be measured by comparing the return on a project with the company's weighted average cost of capital. The **weighted average cost of capital (WACC)** is the marginal cost of funds, calculated as the weighted average of the marginal costs of the different sources of capital (that is, debt, preferred equity, and common equity).[19] If the company can't meet the shareholders' criteria, it should give the money to the shareholders so they can invest elsewhere.

FINANCE in the News | General Electric Sheds Light on Its Smooth Earnings

General Electric, a U.S.-based company with a market capitalization of over $175 billion, has reported smooth earnings growth to its shareholders from 1994 through 2004, meeting or exceeding analysts' expectations. However, this ability to smooth earnings and meet analysts' expectations has not come without a cost: In August of 2009, the Securities and Exchange Commission (SEC) fined General Electric $50 million for violating generally accepted accounting standards. Specifically, GE was able to manipulate its reported earnings by using several different accounting tricks during 2002 and 2003 fiscal years:

1. Reporting sales of locomotives that were not true sales.
2. Avoiding losses on some transactions by using unacceptable accounting (pertaining to its interest rate derivatives).

3. Improper application of accounting principles in accounting for a commercial paper funding program.
4. Improper changes for sales of aircraft engines' spare parts.

The pressure to meet or exceed analysts' forecasts—or to ensure making bonus targets—may encourage companies' management to manage or manipulate its reported financial statements. The reality is that companies most likely cannot always produce a pattern of smooth earnings over time and may not be able to meet or exceed analysts' forecasts each period.

Sources: U.S. Securities and Exchange Commission, Litigation Release No. 21166, August 4, 2009, and "Accounting Tricks Catch Up with GE," by Dan Fisher, *Forbes*, August 4, 2009.

---

[16] U.S. Securities and Exchange Commission v. Conrad M. Black, F. David Radler and Hollinger, Inc., Civil Action No. 04c7377.

[17] The return on investment is the ratio of the profit to the amount of the investment. We look closer at this and other performance metrics in later chapters.

[18] The internal rate of return is the return that a particular investment or set of investments is expected to provide. We discuss IRR in later chapters.

[19] We discuss WACC in detail later.

Shareholders and managers also differ in their approach to risk and financing. Shareholders take a portfolio approach because they hold many assets. This allows them to reduce risk by diversifying (that is, invest in assets whose returns are not perfectly in synch with one another), whereas managers may see their careers totally tied up with the company and tend to act more conservatively. This approach is carried over to financing, where many managers follow a "pecking order": They want to retain earnings first, rather than pay them out in dividends, then use bank debt, and finally issue new equity only as a last resort. In contrast, the shareholders want the company to use debt, then use retained earnings and new equity. Debt financing is attractive from a shareholders' perspective because the corporation can deduct the interest for tax purposes, making debt a much lower cost source of funds. But greater debt results in more risk.

The challenge is to design compensation schemes that encourage managers to act in the best interest of shareholders. The elements that are typically included are salary, bonus, and options. We list the five highest paid executives in the U.S. for fiscal year 2010 in Table 2-1, with a breakdown of their compensation by salary, bonus, shares of stock, options, and other. Notice that in all cases, the salary compensation is relatively low compared with the total package. This is likely the result of the limitation of $1 million per executive for the deductibility of compensation for tax purposes.[20] Annual bonuses are generally somewhat larger, but the largest component, by far, is share compensation. This comes in two forms: grants of restricted stock awarded under incentive plans, and stock options, for which if the company's stock price goes above a certain level, the executive gets the right to buy the stock at a fixed lower price, referred to as the exercise or strike price.

The idea behind share incentive plans is simply to affiliate the best interests of CEOs and senior managers with those of shareholders. Often, shares are granted based on reaching certain objectives, such as revenue targets or investment returns. In such cases, the manager has an incentive to get the share price up as high as possible. In the same way, if an executive is given the right to buy shares at a price of $50 when they are selling for $40, then the executive has incentive to get the share price over $50 to trigger the option. If the share price never reaches $50, the options are worthless. Grants of stock and stock options aim to achieve the basic objective of aligning the interests of shareholders and managers.

It is doubtful that share compensation schemes successfully meet their objectives, but sometimes it does happen. For example, Michael L. Bennett, CEO of Terra Industries, earned on average $3.5 million in compensation over the fiscal periods from 2003 through 2008, but shareholders earned an average of 64% per year. Similarly, the CEO of Amazon.com,

TABLE 2-1 CEO Compensation

| | | | | *(in millions)* | | |
CEO	Company	Salary	Bonus	Shares/ Options	Other	Total
Lawrence J. Ellison	Oracle	$1.00	10.78	$543.75	$1.45	$556.98
Ray R. Irani	Occidental Petroleum	1.30	3.63	184.39	33.32	222.64
John B. Hess	Hess	1.50	3.50	112.92	36.66	154.58
Michael D. Walford	Ultra Petroleum	0.60	1.75	113.48	1.1	116.93
Mark G. Papa	EOG Resources	0.94	1.00	69.67	18.86	90.47
William R. Berkley	WR Berkley	1.00	8.50	72.56	5.42	84.48
Matthew K. Rose	Burlington Santa Fe	1.18	1.68	45.06	20.70	68.62
Paul J. Evanson	Allegheny Energy	1.12	1.23	42.63	22.28	67.26
Hugh Grant	Monsanto	1.29	3.33	50.67	9.32	64.60
Robert W. Lane	Deere & Co.	1.44	3.59	41.04	15.24	61.30

Source: *"Special Report: CEO Compensation," Forbes.com, edited by Scott DeCarlo and Brian Zajac, April 22, 2009.*

[20] Anything over $1 million must be tied to performance to be tax deductible.

Jeffrey P. Bezos, earned an average annual compensation of $1 million, and the shareholders earned an annual return of 21%.[21]

Problems with aligning management's interests with shareholders' include the following:

1. Few companies require executives to own the stock after exercising an option, so often the shares obtained with an option exercise are sold immediately.

2. Some companies reprice the options if the stock's price is far under the original exercise price, setting the exercise price much below the original price.

3. It is challenging to establish a plan that compensates executives for making long-term strategy and investment decisions today that take the long-run view of maximizing owners' equity.

It would be nice to think that the senior management group would suffer losses along with their shareholders. But that is not always the case. For example, Kenneth D. Lewis, CEO of Bank of America, earned an average of $29.7 million for the six years 2003–2008, but the average annual stock return for the same period was –16%. As another example, Jeffrey R. Immelt, CEO of General Electric, enjoyed an average annual compensation of $14.4 million, but the shareholders of GE earned an average annual stock return during the same period of –11%.[22]

corporate governance
set of processes and procedures established to manage the organization in the best interests of its owners

Compensation structure is one component in the broader structure of corporate governance. **Corporate governance** is the set of processes and procedures established to manage the organization in the best interests of its owners. In addition to the compensation structure, corporate governance includes the composition and processes of the compensation committee of the company's board of directors, the composition of the committee that selects and oversees the work of the independent auditor, and the transparency of financial reporting.

The compensation committees of the board of directors that design compensation systems were not always completely independent of the CEOs who received the compensation, but this changed with the Sarbanes-Oxley Act of 2002 (SOX Act).[23] As a result of the SOX Act, publicly traded companies in the U.S. must now have compensation committees that comprise independent directors.

The important point to remember is that the interests of managers and shareholders are not aligned if, on the downside, managers do not suffer along with the shareholders. In fact, managers have an incentive to use short-sighted measures to pump up the share price so they can exercise their options or share grants. For the managers, this is a "heads they win, tails they don't lose" strategy.

One final wrinkle in the use of executive stock options is the fraud by management of many U.S. companies. The U.S. Securities and Exchange Commission investigated 74 companies for "backdating" executive stock options grants.[24] The fraud was that senior managers would get the compensation committee to award them stock options and then date them to an earlier period when the company's stock price was low.[25] Effectively, this meant that on the approval date (with the help of this backdating), the stock was already worth a large amount of money, so there was little incentive value to the grant. Companies charged by the SEC with backdating include Monster Worldwide, Converse Technology, Research in Motion, and UnitedHealth Group.

---

[21] "Special Report: CEO Compensation," Forbes.com, edited by Scott DeCarlo and Brian Zajac, April 22, 2009.
[22] "Special Report: CEO Compensation," Forbes.com, edited by Scott DeCarlo and Brian Zajac, April 22, 2009.
[23] Public Law 107-204, 116 Stat 745, enacted July 30, 2002. The compensation committees of the board of directors are supposed to be made up of outside directors to avoid this conflict of interest. Compensation committees must now comprise only independent members of the Board of Directors.
[24] David Henry, "How the Options Mess Got So Ugly and Expensive," *Business Week*, September 11, 2006.
[25] This type of fraud was more difficult in some other countries because the rules on reporting executive stock options are much tighter than in the United States.

Though companies are free to specify the exercise price of an option, the dating of the option has implications for tax purposes:

- If an option is granted when the stock's price is above the exercise price, there is no compensation for tax purposes at the time of the grant.
- If an option is granted when the stock's price is below the exercise price, there is a tax-deductible compensation for the company and taxable income to the employee.

One problem with backdating is that it involves altering official company documents, such as board of directors' meeting minutes. Another problem is a benefit to the employee at the expense of the employer: by backdating the option-grant date, the company is helping the employee who receives such an option to avoid taxes on the grant—while at the same time not getting a tax deduction for this compensation for the company. In March 2007, Research In Motion admitted to having backdated options, and Jim Balsillie resigned as chairman of the board of directors. This demonstrates some of the problems in designing incentive schemes where the people for whom incentives are provided are in charge of the program.

If compensation schemes have largely been used to reward management, rather than to provide managers with incentive to act like shareholders, where does this leave the goal of the company?[26] Luckily, it does not affect the goal of the company because of a more powerful control: the threat of acquisition. Poor management translates into poor stock market performance and a share price that is less than its intrinsic value. If a company owns assets with an intrinsic value of $50 a share and is selling them for $25 because management is incompetent, and $25 reflects the value of the profits they are generating, then more efficient managers can afford to bid for the company to turn it around for a profit. This is termed the *market for corporate control* because it is based on teams of managers competing for the right to manage corporate assets.

The most important task for regulators and governments is to ensure that the assets in the economy are managed as efficiently as possible so that the economy is as healthy as possible. This requires that the most successful managers be given the chance to manage assets. In turn, this means that hostile takeovers should be encouraged, and managers should be prevented from mounting defensive measures that simply entrench their ability to mismanage corporate assets. We examine mergers and acquisitions later, but for now, remember that this is the reason that finance people believe the best defense against a takeover is a high stock price. Ultimately, the market for corporate control, not managerial incentives, ascertains that shareholder value creation is the company's objective.

1. Describe the nature of the basic owner–manager agency relationship.

2. Define agency costs and describe both types.

3. How have management compensation schemes been designed to better align owner–manager interests? How well have these schemes performed in this regard?

Concept Review Questions

2.4   FINANCIAL MANAGEMENT

The combination of the real asset decisions and financial asset acquisition decisions represents acquisition or investment decisions. Generally, we talk about investment decisions in terms of financial management. **Financial management** is the management of the financial resources of a business or government entity, where financial resources include both the investments of the entity, but also how the entity finances these assets.

financial management
management of the financial resources of a business or government entity, where financial resources include both the investments of the entity, but also how the entity finances these assets

---

[26] Does $75 million really provide managers with that much more incentive than, say, $10 million? Or, alternatively, how many millions does it take to motivate management?

Investment Decisions

We refer to the framework for analyzing long-term investment or asset decisions as **capital budgeting** or **capital expenditure analysis,** and these decisions are some of the most important that a company can make. These long-term investments include building a new plant, introducing a new product, and acquiring another company. Without capital investments, the company will not continue as a going concern.

Evaluating capital budgets requires analyzing the future incremental cash flows that a project is expected to generate, considering the project's cost of capital. In most cases, a capital investment requires a substantial outlay at the beginning, but the investment is expected to generate incremental cash flows for a number of periods into the future. The incremental cash flows are how much the cash flows of the business are expected to change when the capital investment is made. The cost of capital is the return that providers of capital—that is, creditors and owners—require with their investment in the company. The project's cost of capital reflects the cost of funds, considering the risk of the project.

Long-term investments make up only 16% of total assets, on average, for U.S. business entities.[27] However, if we break this down by industry, we get a different picture: the investment of companies' assets varies by industry. For example, in the air, rail, and water transportation industry, 72% of the companies' assets are invested in plant, property, and equipment, whereas in the food manufacturing industry only 14% of the companies' assets are invested in plant assets.[28] In contrast, air, rail, and water transport companies have very little investment in operating assets, such as cash, inventory, and accounts receivable, compared to, say, gasoline retail stores, which have over 30% of their investments in these assets.

The investment in plant, property, and equipment is an investment in long-lived assets that are expected to provide benefits in the long term. The investments in **operating assets,** which are short-lived or current assets, support these long-term investments and are necessary for day-to-day operations of the business. We often refer to these operating assets as the company's **working capital** because they are put to work to support the long-term investments of the company and consist of cash, inventory, and accounts receivable. The amount of working capital a company needs is determined, in large part, by the company's line of business. For example, for the fiscal year ending January 31, 2011, Wal-Mart Stores had $51.9 billion of current assets, which is 29% of its total assets. As a retailer, Wal-Mart has substantial amount of inventory on hand at any point in time. In contrast, Darden Restaurants had only 13% of its assets in current assets, and CSX Corporation, a railway company, had only 11% of its assets in current assets. We compare the asset compositions of CSX, a railroad company, Wal-Mart Stores, and Darden Restaurants in Figure 2-3.

operating assets short-lived assets that support the company's long-term investments

working capital current, operating assets of a company; also known as operating assets

Financing Decisions

The financing decisions of a company involve the management of short-term obligations, such as bank loans, and long-term financing, which may be debt and/or equity. The management of short-term obligations requires understanding the needs of the company throughout the year for short-term borrowing and trade credit. There are many forms of short-term financing, and the financial manager must evaluate the cost of each available type.

An important decision of a company regards its capital structure. A company's **capital structure** is the mix of debt and equity that the company uses to finance its business. **Debt capital** consists of interest-bearing debt obligations, which may be notes or bonds, whereas **equity capital** consists of stock issues and retained earnings and is the ownership interest

debt capital interest-bearing obligations of an enterprise

equity capital ownership interest of an enterprise

[27] U.S. Internal Revenue Service, www.irs.gov
[28] Based on Statistics of Income, Internal Revenue Service, www.irs.gov, with the most recent available data for calendar year 2006.

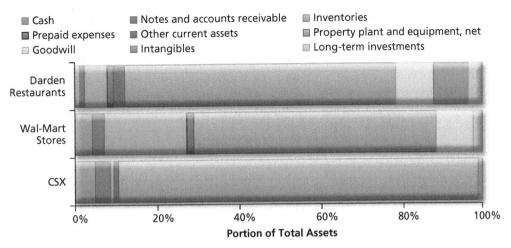

FIGURE 2-3   Asset Composition for CSX, Wal-Mart Stores, and Darden Restaurants

Source of data: *10-K filings of CSX (fiscal year ending 12/31/2011), Wal-Mart Stores (fiscal year ending 1/31/2011), and Darden Restaurants (fiscal year ending 5/29/2011).*

in a business enterprise. Because debt obligates the company to pay interest and repay the principal amount of the loan—whereas no such obligation exists with stock—using debt introduces some risk. Therefore, the capital structure decision affects the **financial risk** of a company: the more debt capital, relative to equity capital, the greater the company's financial risk.

So what do the liabilities and equity look like? We provide the composition of the capital of CSX, Wal-Mart Stores, and Darden Restaurants in Figure 2-4. Just as companies wait for others to pay them, they are also waiting to pay others, which gives rise to accounts payable (one of the major accounts included in short-term liabilities of Wal-Mart) for the customer side of the transaction.

The balance of short-term liabilities, long-term liabilities, and equity differs among industries. Some of this is due to customary practices, such as extending customers credit, and some is due to the business risk of the industry, which may permit a company to take on more risk in the form of larger long-term obligations relative to equity interests.

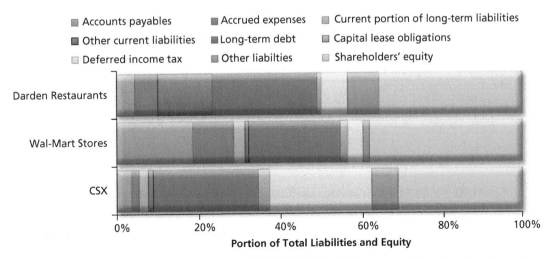

FIGURE 2-4   Capital Composition for CSX, Wal-Mart Stores, and Darden Restaurants

Source of data: *10-K filings of CSX (fiscal year ending 12/31/2011), Wal-Mart Stores (fiscal year ending 1/31/2011), and Darden Restaurants (fiscal year ending 5/29/2011).*

These relative amounts of liabilities and equity raise the following basic questions in corporate financing:

financing sources of money for a company, including using debt or equity, retaining earnings or issuing equity, going public, using bank debt or bonds, and using the short-term money market or borrowing from a bank

corporate finance financial management of assets and financing decisions in a corporate enterprise

1. How does a company decide between raising money through debt or through equity?
2. In terms of equity, how does a company raise the equity: through retaining earnings or through issuing new equity?
3. Why does a company decide to go public and issue shares to the general public versus remaining a nontraded private company?
4. If a company decides to issue debt, what determines whether it is bank debt or bonds issued to the public debt market?
5. What determines whether a company accesses the short-term money market versus borrowing from a bank?

These basic questions represent the core of liability management for corporations, which we refer to as their corporate **financing** decisions. Taken together, the financial management of assets and corporate financing decisions represent the area of **corporate finance**.

Concept Review Questions

1. Describe the two key decision areas with respect to the financial management of assets.

2. What are some of the key corporate financing decisions made by companies?

ETHICS | The Cost of Fraud

Under Section 304 of the Sarbanes-Oxley Act of 2002, when a company's management commits fraud, reporting greater profits than actually earned, any bonuses based on the exaggerated profits must be paid back to the company.[29] This is the case whether the manager conspired to commit the fraud or not. This "clawback" provision is designed to protect shareholders from paying bonuses that were not truly earned.

A case in point is Beazer Homes. The Securities and Exchange Commission (SEC) brought a case against Beazer Homes for their fiscal year 2006 financial statements. The company's senior vice-president and chief accounting officer, Michael Rand, was charged with violating Generally Accepted Accounting Principles in the scheme to exaggerate profits to meet analysts'

expectations. One of the techniques used was "cookie jar accounting," which is a scheme to save recognition of income or expenses for specific years rather than when they should be recognized based on generally accepted accounting principles (GAAP). Following charges by the SEC, Beazer Homes' financial statements for fiscal year 2006 (and other years) were restated in 2008.

Beazer Homes' CEO and president did not repay bonuses that he received in 2006, even though he had signed statements that attested to the financial reports' accuracy and was involved in the company's accounting. The CEO received a bonus of $7.1 million in 2006 and realized profits on the sale of his stock of $7.3 million. The SEC brought an action against the CEO in March of 2011 to compel repayment of the bonuses.[30]

SUMMARY

- There are many different ways of organizing businesses, including the sole proprietorship, partnership, corporate, and limited liability company forms of business.

- Considerations in evaluating the form of business enterprise include liability, taxation, control, and continuity.

[29] Public Law 107–204.

[30] Securities and Exchange Commission v. Ian J. McCarthy, United States District Court for the Northern District of Georgia Atlanta Division, Civil Action, March 3, 2011.

- The management of a company should make decisions that maximize owners' wealth, though this is not always the case. When the managers are also the owners, it is a simple situation. In large corporations, in which there is separation between management and owners, motivating management to act in the owners' best interest is challenging.

- Agency costs may arise because managers may not act in the best interests of shareholders or because they must be induced to act optimally.

- The primary decisions made by corporations involve the financial management of the company's real and financial assets, as well as the associated corporate financing decisions.

FORMULAS

(2-1)   Effective tax rate on corporate income $= t_c + [(1 - t_c) \, \text{DPO} \, t_i]$

QUESTIONS AND PROBLEMS

Multiple Choice

1. Which of the following businesses is least likely to be operated as a partnership?

   A. Steel foundry   B. Dentist's office   C. Accounting firm   D. Physician's office

2. Which of the following statements is true?

   A. The ownership of limited liability partnerships cannot be traded publicly.
   B. In the limited and general partnership form, the general partner has limited liability.
   C. In the limited and general partnership form, the limited partners are passive investors.

3. Which of the following forms of business organization have owners with limited liability?

   A. Corporation   B. Sole proprietorship   C. General partnership

4. Income is taxed at only one level, the owners' individual income, for all but which of the following forms of business?

   A. Corporation   B. Partnership   C. Sole proprietorship   D. Limited liability company

5. Limited liability companies are specific to the United States.

   A. True   B. False

6. Which of the following are characteristics of a sole proprietorship?

Liability	Life
A. Limited	Limited
B. Limited	Perpetual
C. Unlimited	Limited
D. Unlimited	Perpetual

7. Which of the following are characteristics of a corporation?

Liability	Life
A. Limited	Limited
B. Limited	Perpetual
C. Unlimited	Limited
D. Unlimited	Perpetual

8. Which of the following best describes the taxation of corporations?
   A. Taxed once, as owners' income
   B. Taxed twice: once as corporate income, and again as owners' income
   C. Taxed twice: once as corporate income, and again as owners' income only if distributed

9. The interests of shareholders and managers are properly aligned if managers receive stock options.
   A. True   B. False

10. Which of the following is the primary concern from the point of view of a company's shareholders?
    A. Minimize risk
    B. Market value of equity
    C. Maximize earnings per share
    D. Maximize accounting return on investment

Practice Questions and Problems

2.1   Forms of Business Enterprise

11. List and describe briefly the four major forms of a business organization.

12. State the main differences between corporations and partnerships.

13. Describe what is meant by flow-through taxation.

14. What would be the advantage, if any, of forming a business as a corporation and electing Subchapter S status, rather than forming the business as a limited liability company?

15. Complete the following table, calculating the effective tax on corporate income:

	Dividend Payout	Corporate Tax Rate	Shareholders' Tax on Dividend Income	Effective Tax on Corporate Income
A.	40%	45%	15%	
B.	20%	40%	0%	
C.	25%	35%	15%	
D.	25%	40%	15%	

16. Consider a corporation that has $5 million of taxable income for the year and is subject to a 40% tax on corporate income. And suppose the corporation pays 25% of its income after tax to its shareholders.
    A. If its shareholders are taxed at a rate of 32%, what is the effective rate of tax on this corporation's income?
    B. If this corporation was a partnership instead, what would be the effective rate of tax on this income?

17. Consider a corporation that pays all its earnings to owners as dividends and has a tax rate of 36%.
    A. How much of the corporation's income is taxed at the corporate level?
    B. If the corporation's shareholders are taxed at a rate of 40% on dividend income, what is the effective tax rate on this corporation's income, considering the taxation at both the corporate and the individual levels?
    C. If the shareholders of this corporation have a tax rate of 20% on any dividends instead of 32%, what is the amount of tax at the individual owner level?

2.2   The Goals of the Business Enterprise

18. What is the goal of the management of a business entity?

19. What is a stakeholder?

20. Why does a company focus on the value of equity rather than earnings in making long-term decisions?

21. Is shareholder wealth maximization consistent with the efficient allocation of resources? Explain.

2.3 The Role of Management and Agency Issues

22. What are agency costs?

23. Provide an example of the conflicts of interest between shareholders and managers.

24. What measures can be taken to reduce agency costs?

25. Why would a bonus system that rewards managers based on earnings per share be problematic?

26. Why do corporations use stock options in executive compensation?

27. How do the owners of a corporation, which may have thousands of owners, monitor the management of the corporation?

2.4 Financial Management

28. What is meant by the term *capital structure*? How does capital structure relate to a company's financial risk?

29. What does a financial manager consider in evaluating an investment in a capital project?

30. Classify each of the following as either a financing decision or an investment decision:

Decision	Investment	Financing
Buying a new plant	☐	☐
Acquiring another company	☐	☐
Issuing a bond	☐	☐
A corporation buying back its own stock	☐	☐
Borrowing from a bank	☐	☐

31. Consider the information on three corporations for fiscal year 2010:

(in millions)	Hewlett-Packard	Boeing	Verizon
Line of business	Manufactures and sells computers and computer equipment	Manufactures and sells aircraft	Telecommunications provider
Current assets	$51,404	$40,572	$22,348
Total assets	$119,933	$68,565	$220,005

Calculate the proportion of assets that are invested in current assets for each company, and explain why these proportions differ from one another.

Cases

Case 2.1 The Tex Tech Company

When you hired Dan to manage your business, the Tex Tech Company, you agreed to pay him a bonus of 10% of profits at the end of each year. There are now two projects available for investment by Tex Tech, but it can only take on one of them: Project A will generate profits of $50,000 per year, and the detailed financial calculations show that it will increase the value of the company by $123,100. Project B will generate profits of $40,000 per year, but will increase the company's value by $125,500.

    A. Which project is Dan likely to choose, and why?

    B. Which project would you, the owner of the company, prefer?

    C. By what means can the owners of the company encourage Dan to focus on owners' wealth maximization?

Case 2.2 To Invest or Not to Invest

As the CFO of your company, it falls to you to make the final decision on large expenditures. Recently, your controller has proposed purchasing a new computer system at a cost of $50,000. He believes the system will deliver savings of $60,000 in the accounting department and could be useful to other departments as well. Your treasurer takes a decidedly different view of the proposal. She claims that the company will have to borrow money to buy the computer system, and this will cost $10,000 in interest. As well, she is concerned that the amount of savings promised by the controller won't materialize.

    A. What factors should you consider in this decision?

    B. Based on these facts, should you purchase the computer system? Justify your decision.

PART 3

THE BASICS OF VALUATION

In finance, the time value of money is an essential building block for valuing stocks, bonds, or any other asset. In this section, we develop the basic discounted cash flow model that is the workhorse of finance. We start with the basic principles and math of the time value of money and then apply the basic discounting framework to valuing bonds and equities. In the process, we develop a model for valuing equities and discuss how equity valuation is related to fundamentals.

139

CHAPTER 5

THE TIME VALUE OF MONEY

© Masterfile

What does the Credit Card Act of 2009 do for you? The Credit Card Accountability Responsibility and Disclosure Act of 2009, or Credit Card Act of 2009, changed the landscape for credit card companies and consumers with new credit card rules, rules that seek to protect consumers from abuses from credit card companies.[1] These rules also reduce sources of income that these companies sought to offset the risks of default on these debt obligations.

These rules include the following:

1. Credit card marketing to those under twenty-one years of age is restricted, and colleges are required to disclose any contracts with credit card companies that involve selling student and alumni contact information.

2. Credit card companies cannot raise the interest rate on existing balances but only on future purchases, if sufficient notice has been provided. This negates the previous practice of raising the interest rate on existing balances, a practice that spun many credit card debtors into a financial down-spiral.

3. Credit card bills must include a disclosure about how long it would take a person to pay off the balance of the account if only the minimum payments are made. Also disclosed is the amount that would have to be paid each month to have everything paid off within three years.

4. A ban has been placed on universal default, a practice of credit card companies declaring an account in default if the credit card customer has been in default with another obligation. However, universal default can be applied on future purchases if there is sufficient notice.

5. A ban on over-the-limit fees has been placed, except when the credit card holder has agreed to these fees in advance.

6. If a credit card customer has different balances with different interest rates, payments are now allocated in the manner that minimizes cost to the customer, rather than at the credit card company's discretion.

7. Gift cards cannot expire in less than five years, and inactivity fees cannot be imposed within the first twelve months.

These rules, among others, may be effective in encouraging consumers to reduce debt. Consider the disclosure rules on paying off the balance. Suppose you have a balance of $5,000, with the following terms:

• Minimum payment due is 3% of balance

• Interest rate is 15% per year

Unless you have a really clear understanding of the time value of money, you may not have a good idea of how long it will take you to pay off your balance if you make the minimum payment. Under the new rules, your credit card bill will tell you the following:

• It will take fourteen and a half years to pay off the balance if you make only the minimum payment of $150 each month.

• You can pay off the balance in three years if you make a payment of $173.33 each month.

This example may encourage you to pay more than the minimum.

[1] Public-Law 111-24, 123 STAT. 1734, May 22, 2009.

140

Learning Outcomes

After reading this chapter, you should be able to:

LO 5.1 Describe and compare the principles of compound interest and simple interest, and apply these principles to solve present value and future value problems involving a single sum.

LO 5.2 Identify and apply the appropriate method of valuing different patterns of cash flows, including the ordinary annuity, annuity due, deferred annuity, and perpetuity.

LO 5.3 Calculate and compare annual percentage rates and effective annual rates for both discrete and continuous compounding.

LO 5.4 Apply the time value of money mathematics to solve loan and retirement problems.

Chapter Preview We introduced you to the study of finance in Part 1 and examined the importance of company financial statements in Part 2. In Part 3, we discuss the basic valuation process and apply it to financial securities. This valuation process relies heavily on discounting future expected cash flows, one of the tools discussed in this chapter. To understand finance, you need to have a solid foundation in the tools that we present in this chapter, including the math of translating a value from one period to another, time-lines to sort out the various cash flows and values, and identifying the sensitivity of values, both present and future, to interest rates and time.

In this chapter, we introduce you to everyday problems, such as taking out a loan, setting up a series of payments, and valuing them. The ideas in this chapter are important for all types of financial problems: determining payments for a home mortgage, buying versus leasing a new car, appropriately valuing a bond or stock, determining whether a company should expand production or abandon a product line, and deciding how much a company should be willing to pay for another company. Although each situation involves unique circumstances that will be covered in subsequent chapters, the basic framework used to evaluate these problems is the same and relies on material covered in this chapter.

5.1 TIME IS MONEY

In this chapter, we are concerned with the time value of money. The **time value of money** is the concept that money today is more valuable than the same quantity of money in the future. For example, $1 today is worth more than $1 to be received next year or ten years from now. As we saw in Chapters 1 and 2, the financial system is designed to transfer savings from lenders to borrowers so that savers have money to spend in the future. Money, in this sense, represents our ability to buy goods and services; that is, it operates as a medium of exchange and has no value in and of itself. A **medium of exchange** is any instrument that facilitates the exchange of goods or services. Of course, an investor could simply store the money (that is, stash it under the mattress) and spend it in the future; a dollar today is always worth at least a dollar in the future.[2] However, this option ignores the fact that the saver has other uses for that money, which we refer to as an "opportunity cost" or an "alternative use." This results in the time value of money.

A **loan** is a contract in which the borrower uses the funds of the lender, and in exchange the borrower not only repays the amount borrowed but also pays the lender compensation for use of the funds in the form of interest. **Interest** is compensation for the time value of money: In the case of a loan, the borrower is expected to repay an amount loaned plus interest to compensate the lender who did not have the use of the funds during the term of the loan.

The opportunity cost of money is the return that is expected when it is invested in something of similar risk. For this reason, we also refer to the interest rate as the price of money. It helps us analyze the problem of determining the value of money received at different times. Suppose, for example, a person has three choices: receiving $20,000 today,

time value of money idea that money invested today has more value than the same amount invested later

medium of exchange something that provides a way to buy goods and services but has no value in and of itself

loan contract in which the borrower uses the funds of the lender, and, in exchange, repays the amount borrowed plus compensation for the use of the funds

interest compensation for the time value of money

---

[2] This ignores the fact that what we are really concerned about is what that dollar will buy in terms of goods and services, that is, its purchasing power. We discuss this later in the chapter.

141

$31,000 in five years, or $3,000 per year indefinitely. Making a choice from these different options requires knowing how to value the dollars received at different times; that is, we need to adjust for the time value of money.

To make a decision, we need to know the interest rate. We will use i as a standard notation throughout this textbook for the market interest rate.[3] We will also refer to this market interest rate by several other names later in the textbook, such as the **required rate of return** or **discount rate**. The reason for these different names will become clear later, but in all cases, we are looking at the investor's opportunity cost, that is, what he or she can do with the money being invested. However, first we have to make some basic distinctions in terms of how this interest rate is earned and distinguish between simple interest and compound interest.

required rate of return or discount rate market interest rate or the investor's opportunity cost

Simple Interest

simple interest interest paid or received on only the initial investment

principal amount loaned or the amount of the investment

Simple interest is interest paid or received on only the initial investment (the **principal**). In practice, only a limited number of applications use simple interest, but we introduce it first to contrast it with compound interest, which is the typical type of interest.

Suppose you deposit $100 in an account that pays 5% per year, using simple interest. If you leave your money in this account for three years, what will the balance be in the account? With simple interest, the interest is based on the principal amount, which is $100 in this case. Therefore, the interest is $100 \times 0.05 = $5 each year in this example. This means that at the end of three years, there is $100 + $5 + $5 + $5 = $100 + (3 \times $100 \times 0.05) = $115 in the account.

Because the same amount of interest is earned each year with simple interest, we can use the following equation to find the value of the investment at any point in time:

$$FV_n = PV_0 + (n \times PV_0 \times i) \tag{5-1}$$

where FV_n is the future value at the end of n periods, PV_0 is the principal amount today (period 0), n is the number of periods, and i is the interest rate per period.

Consider another example. Suppose you invest $1,000 today for five years in an account that pays 6% interest. Note that $PV_0 \times i$ = interest, so in applying this equation to this problem means that:

PV = $1,000

$n = 5$

$i = 6\%$

The value in year 5 is $1,000 + (5 \times $60) = $1,300. The basic point of simple interest is that to get the future value of an investment, we calculate the annual interest (in our case $60), multiply this by the number of years of the investment, and add it to the starting principal.

Compound Interest

compound interest arrangement in which interest is earned on the principal amount invested *and* on any accrued interest

Compound interest is interest that is earned on the principal amount invested *and* on any accrued interest. Compound interest can result in dramatic growth in the value of an investment over time. This growth is directly related to the number of periods as well as to the level of interest or return earned. Because most financial transactions involve compound interest, you should assume compound interest applies unless explicitly told that the transaction is simple interest.

---

[3] Other common notations for the interest rate are k and r. We use i when we discuss the time value of money because i is the notation used in popular financial calculators.

EXAMPLE 5.1

Simple Interest

PROBLEM

Suppose someone invests $10,000 today for a five-year term and receives 3% annual simple interest on the investment. How much would the investor have after five years?

Solution

Annual interest = $10,000 × 0.03 = $300 per year.

Or

$$FV_5 = \$10,000 + [5 \times \$10,000 \times 0.03] = \$10,000 + 1,500 = \$11,500$$

Year	Beginning amount	Ending amount
1	$10,000	$10,300
2	10,300	10,600
3	10,600	10,900
4	10,900	11,200
5	11,200	11,500

The interest earned is $300 every year, regardless of the beginning amount, because interest is earned on only the original investment. Interest is *not* earned on any earned interest.

We calculate a future value of a lump sum when interest is compounded by considering interest not only on the principal amount but also on any accumulated interest. Consider an example of how compound interest works. Suppose you deposit $100 in an account that pays 5% interest per year. What is the balance in the account at the end of two years (that is, the future value or FV_2) if interest is compound interest? The answer is $110.25:

$$FV_1 = \$100 + (\$100 \times 0.05) = \$105$$
$$FV_2 = \$105 + (\$105 \times 0.05) = \$110.25$$

Unlike simple interest, the amount of compound interest earned increases every year; the interest rate is applied to the principal plus interest earned, so the value of the investment increases. As a result, the interest received each successive year is greater than that of the previous year because of **compounding**.

Let us look at the first two years of interest by using a little algebra. For the first year, everything is the same as with simple interest; that is, the amount at the end of the first year, which we represent as FV_1, is the starting principal (that is, PV_0) plus the interest, or:

compounding increase in value over time due to interest on both the principal amount and any interest earned up to that point in time

$$FV_1 = PV_0(1 + i)$$
$$FV_1 = \$1,000 + (\$1,000 \times 0.10)$$
$$FV_1 = \$1,000 \times (1 + 0.10)$$
$$FV_1 = \$1,100$$

where PV_0 = the present value today (i.e., at time 0). We used a bit of algebra to restate the future value as the principal multiplied by 1 plus the interest rate.

For the second year, the full $1,100 is reinvested; that is, we do not take the $100 of interest out and spend it. As a result, we have the following:

$$FV_2 = \$1,100 + (\$1,100 \times 0.10) = \$1,210 = \$1,100 \times (1 + 0.10)$$

using the notation

$$FV_2 = PV_1(1 + i) = PV_0(1 + i)^2$$

In this case, \$1,100 is invested at the beginning of the second year, and it earns 10% percent interest. The interest earned in the second year is \$110: the \$100 interest on the starting principal plus \$10 interest earned on the \$100 of interest reinvested at the end of the first year. We can rearrange all this using algebra to get the formula for the future value at the end of the second year. This is the starting principal, multiplied by 1 plus the interest rate squared. As we increase the number of periods, we get the general formula:

$$FV_n = PV_0(1 + i)^n \qquad (5\text{-}2)$$

where FV_n is the future value at time n.

compound factor or **future value interest factor** amount that reflects the interest rate and the number of periods, which, when multiplied by a current or present value, results in the equivalent future value

We refer to this equation as the basic *compounding equation*, and the last term $(1 + i)^n$ as the **compound factor** or **future value interest factor**. Applying this equation to our example of investing \$1,000 for five years at 10%, we get:

$$FV_5 = \$1,000 (1 + 0.10)^5 = \$1,000 \times 1.61051 = \$1,610.51$$

This is \$110.51 more than we would receive for the investment earning simple interest. We show the growth in the \$1,000 over the five years in Figure 5-1. As you can see in this figure, the principal remains constant, the interest on the principal grows at a rate of \$100 per year, and the interest-on-interest grows each year. The **interest-on-interest** is the amount of value attributed to the fact that interest is paid on previously earned interest.[4]

interest-on-interest interest earned on previously accumulated interest

We illustrate what happens with the two types of interest over time in Figure 5-2. Note that for the first few years, the difference between compound and simple interests is minimal, but over time, the difference gets bigger and bigger. You can also see that the value grows in a straight line with simple interest, growing by \$100 each year, whereas the future value with compound interest grows at a rate of 10% per year, which means that the line representing the future values is convex.

You can also solve this example using a financial calculator. Most financial calculators have one set of keys dedicated to the time value of money calculations. Your task is to type in the given values and input them into the calculator's registers by striking the appropriate time value of money key associated with the value. You repeat this process for each of the known values, and then, once you have input all the given values, you strike

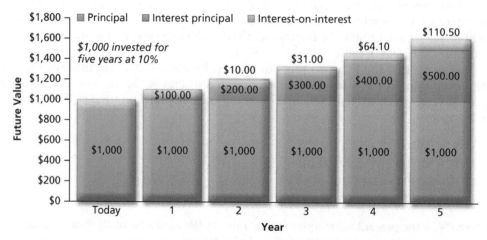

FIGURE 5-1 Growth of Value Over Time with Compound Interest

[4] The easy way to determine interest on interest in any problem is to calculate the future value with compound interest and the future value with simple interest and then take the difference. This difference is the interest-on-interest.

FIGURE 5-2 Simple Versus Compound Interest

the key corresponding to the unknown value; the answer then appears in the display window.

If you are using a financial calculator to perform the calculation using basic mathematics, you use the interest rate in a decimal form. However, if you are using the time value of money functions within a financial calculator, you use the interest rate expressed as a whole number; that is, 10% is 10, 5% is 5, and so forth.

Here is something that trips up a lot of people when they first use a financial calculator: The present value must be typed in as a negative number. You enter the PV with a negative sign (on most financial calculators) to reflect the fact that investors must pay money now to get money in the future. Alternatively, we could have left it positive, which would produce a negative sign in front of the FV, which we could simply ignore.[5]

PROBLEM	EXAMPLE 5.2

PROBLEM

Suppose you invest $10,000 today for a five-year term and receive 5% annual compound interest.

EXAMPLE 5.2

Compound Interest

A. How much would you have after five years?

B. How much interest-on-interest would you earn during the five years?

Solution

A. Annual interest is earned on the original $10,000 (principal) *plus* on accrued interest. Therefore, the investor would have $12,762.82 at the end of five years:

Year	Beginning amount	Compound interest	Ending amount
1	$10,000.00	$10,000.00 × 0.05 = $500.00	$10,500.00
2	$10,500.00	$10,500.00 × 0.05 = $525.00	$11,025.00
3	$11,025.00	$11,025.00 × 0.05 = $551.25	$11,576.25
4	$11,576.25	$11,576.25 × 0.05 = $578.81	$12,155.06
5	$12,155.06	$12,155.06 × 0.05 = $607.75	$12,762.82

B. The future value with compound interest is $12,762.82. If interest were simple interest only, the future value would be $10,000 + 2,500 = $12,500. Therefore, the interest-on-interest is $12,762.82 − 12,500 = $262.82

---

[5] This is because of the way the manufacturers have programmed the calculator. If do not input the PV as a negative number, inaccuracies may not occur in simple problems, but you may get an error message or incorrect answers in other, more complex problems.

For our example of investing $1,000 for five years at 10%, we input the three known values (PV, i and n) and solve for the one unknown, which is the future value five years from now. We represent these inputs as the following inputs:

PV = $1,000
$i = 10\%$
$n = 5$

We represent these inputs generically in the remainder of this chapter and throughout the remainder of this text because this sets you up for a variety of calculators and spreadsheets.

Remember, when you enter these values into your calculator or spreadsheet, you enter the present value as a negative number without the comma and currency symbol and you enter the interest rate without the percentage sign and as a whole number (for example, "10") in the financial calculator, and in decimal form (for instance, "0.10") in the spreadsheet. For example, in most financial calculators the inputs for this problem would be the following:[6]

1000 +/- PV 10 I/YR 5 n FV

USING A SPREADSHEET TO SOLVE FOR THE FUTURE VALUE

We can use the FV function in Excel to calculate the future value:

= FV(RATE, NPER, PMT, PV, type)

where   RATE = interest rate (expressed as a decimal)
        NPER = number of periods
        PMT = the payment amount, which is zero is in this case
        PV = present value
        type = 0 if it is an ordinary annuity, 1 if it is annuity due.[7]

Note the key difference between the financial calculator function and the spreadsheet function: The interest rate is in decimal form in the spreadsheet, but not with the financial calculator. If we want to determine the future value of $1,000 in five years with 10% interest, we would enter the following in the appropriate cell:

= FV(0.10, 5, 0, –1000, 0)

This yields 1,610.51.

Another difference between the spreadsheet and the calculator function is that you cannot leave out an element in the spreadsheet function unless it is the optional "type." For example, if the problem does not have a regular payment (that is PMT), and you do not type this in as the third argument in parentheses, the function will interpret the PV you entered as the PMT and the type as the PV, giving you an answer to a completely different problem.

---

[6] Before you begin any calculation using the time value of money in a financial calculator, be sure to clear the calculator's registers (that is, where the data are stored internally); otherwise, old data may be stored. For example, there is no payment (i.e., PMT) in this example. If you had calculated a problem with a payment before this one, you would still have that payment stored in the calculator, and it would be included in this next calculation. To be on the safe side, clear your financial calculator prior to every calculation. Check the owners' manual for the procedure for clearing the registers.

[7] We will explain what the difference is shortly; for now, our examples involve ordinary annuities.

CALCULATOR TOOLS: COMPOUNDING WITH A FINANCIAL CALCULATOR

When calculating a future value, you have the present value, the interest rate, and the number of periods, and you need to determine the future value. In other words, you have three values, and your task is to solve for the one unknown value. Therefore:

PV = 1000
i = 10%
n = 5

and you need to solve for FV.

The actual keystrokes for common financial calculators are the following:

HP10B	**TI BAII**	**HP12C**	**TI83/84**
1000 +/– PV	1000 +/– PV	1000 CHS PV	*Using TVM Solver App:*
10 I/YR	10 I/YR	10 i	N = 5
5 N	5 N	5 n	i = 10
FV	FV	FV	PV = –1000
			PMT = 0
			FV = *Solve*
			P/Y = 1
			C/Y = 1

Warning Financial calculators are programmed such that any value entered into a registry (i.e., a storage location in the calculator's memory) will remain unless written over or explicitly cleared. For example, if you enter 1000 +/– PV 10 I/YR 5 N in one problem, and then 2000 +/– PV 12 I/YR in the next, the 5 will remain in the number of periods registry. This can be handy in some applications or result in errors if not intended.

You can use either of two approaches to avoid this problem:

1. Type a zero value for any unused variable
2. Clear the calculator before each problem

The best approach depends on both the calculator and what you feel comfortable with. The process of clearing the calculator registries varies by model, so check your manual.

For the calculators that we present in this chapter, you clear by using the following keystrokes:

HP10B	**TI BAII**	**HP12C**	**TI83/84**
■ CLEAR ALL	2nd CLR TVM	f FIN	*Enter 0 in display*

Let us now extend the time horizon in our example of investing $1,000 at 10%. Investing $1,000 for fifty years at an annual interest rate of 10% produces $117,390.85. Note the difference between this amount and the future value of the same $1,000 invested for fifty years, but earning simple interest: ($1,000 + [50 × $100]) = $6,000. You can see the difference that compounding makes over this fifty-year span in Figure 5-3. What is the difference between the two future values after fifty years? You would get $111,390.85, which is the interest-on-interest.

You might be tempted to ask whether a fifty-year term is realistic. It is for many investments. Consider someone who begins investing for retirement in his or her early twenties.

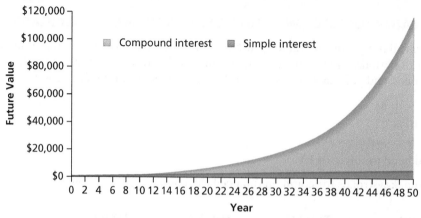

FIGURE 5-3 **Simple Versus Compound Interest Over Fifty Years**

Those early investments could earn compound returns for forty years or more before the individual retires. Further, assuming the individual does not withdraw all of the retirement savings on his or her retirement day (which would have severe tax consequences) and assuming that this person lives another twenty to twenty-five years after retirement, some investment dollars may remain untouched for more than fifty years.

LESSONS LEARNED

Behold the Miracle of Compounding

Compound interest has been called the eighth wonder of the world. And with good reason. It magically turns a little bit of money, invested wisely, into a whole lot of cash. Even Albert Einstein—a bit of a smarty pants—is said to have called it one of the greatest mathematical concepts of our time.

But you don't need to be a genius to harness the power of compounding. Even the most average of Joes can use it to make money. Trust me. This is *so* much easier than the theory of relativity.

Here's the gist: When you save or invest, your money earns interest or appreciates. The next year, you earn interest on your original money *and* the interest from the first year. In the third year, you earn interest on your original money and the interest from the first *two* years. And so on. It's like a snowball—roll it down a snowy hill and it'll build on itself to get bigger and bigger. Before you know it . . . avalanche!

Harness the power

Here are three steps to help you make the power of compound interest or compound earnings work for you. And when I say "work FOR you," I mean it. Once you set up an account, you don't have to do much else. Just sit back and wait for the money to roll in.

1. **Start young.** When you're in your twenties and thirties, your best friend is TIME. Start rolling your snowball at the top of the hill and you'll have a much bigger mass at the bottom than someone who started halfway down.

    Consider this: Amy, a 22-year-old college graduate, saves $300 per month into an account earning 10% per year for six years. (That's the average annual return of the stock market over time.) Then at age 28, she starts a family and decides to stay home with the children full time. By then, Amy had kicked in $21,600 of her own money. But even if she doesn't contribute another cent *ever*, her money would grow to a million bucks by the time she turned 65.

    Compare that to Jason, who put off saving until he was 31. He's still young enough that becoming a millionaire is within reach, but it will be tougher. Jason would have to contribute the same $300 a month for the next 34 years to earn $1 million by age 65. Although Amy invested less money out-of-pocket — $21,600 over six years vs. Jason's $126,000 over 34 years — her money had more time to grow, or compound. . . . Bottom line: Getting rich is easier and more painless the earlier you start.

2. **Remember that a little goes a long way.** Don't think you have enough money to start investing? You can get into a good mutual fund for as little as $50 a month.

    Let's say a 20-year-old stashes $50 a month into a fund earning 10% annually. He'd have $528,000 by age 65. Not bad for practically starting with pocket change!

    A little bit can make a difference elsewhere in compounding, too. For example, if our 20-year-old earned 9% annually instead of 10%, he would amass only $373,000 in the same period of time. That seemingly small 1% difference in performance resulted in 29% less money over the long haul.

3. **Leave it alone.** The prospect of making a lot of money without doing anything sounds good on paper. But, admittedly, in practice, it can be maddening. Every time you receive your account statement, you watch your balance s-l-o-w-l-y inch up—or even drop. How on earth are you ever going to get rich at this pace?

Investing is a lot like Heinz ketchup: Good things come to those who wait. You must be patient for compounding to work its awesome power. Remember that as your money earns more, it'll earn even *more*. You certainly won't get rich overnight this way. But you will get rich if you start young, invest wisely and leave it alone.

Source: "Behold the Miracle of Compounding," by Erin Burt, *Kiplingers*, November 8, 2007, www.kiplinger.com/columns/starting/archive/2007/st1107.htm.

In Table 5-1, we provide some evidence regarding the power of compound returns, where we show the future values that would have resulted from investing $1,000 at the beginning of different points in time and what it would be worth today. The dramatic difference in ending values results from differences in the rate of return: If you invested $1,000 at the beginning of 1930 at 1% per year, you would only have $2,217 at the end of 2009. If, instead, you invested $1,000 earning 10% per year, you would have over $2 million at the end of 2009. Now you can see why finance professionals struggle to increase

PROBLEM

Suppose you deposit $10,000 in an account that pays 5% compound interest. At the end of three years, if you have never made any withdrawals:

A. How much will you have in the account at the end of three years?

B. How much interest-on-interest did you earn in your account at the end of three years?

EXAMPLE 5.3

Interest-on-Interest

Solution

A. $FV = \$10,000 (1 + 0.05)^3 = \$11,576.25$

B. $FV_{Simple} = \$10,000 + (\$10,000 \times 0.05 \times 3) = \$11,500$

Interest-on-interest = $\$11,576.25 - 11,500 = \$76.25$

TABLE 5-1 Ending Wealth of $1,000 Invested for Different Investment Periods at Different Rates

Invested at the beginning of:	Results in a value at the end of 2009, if invested at:			
	1% per year	4% per year	7% per year	10% per year
1930	$2,217	$23,050	$224,234	$2,048,400
1940	$2,007	$15,572	$113,989	$789,747
1950	$1,817	$10,520	$57,946	$304,482
1960	$1,645	$7,107	$29,457	$117,391
1970	$1,489	$4,801	$14,974	$45,259
1980	$1,348	$3,243	$7,612	$17,449
1990	$1,220	$2,191	$3,870	$6,727
2000	$1,105	$1,480	$1,967	$2,594

basis point one one-hundredths of 1 percent

the returns on their investments even by very small amounts. In fact, it is normal to keep track of returns down to one-hundredth of 1%, which is a **basis point**.[8]

Earning just a few basis points more on one investment causes the future value of the portfolio to compound that much faster. For example, if you invested at the beginning of 1930 and could have earned fifty basis points more than the 7% we show in this table, you would have a value of $325,595 at the end of 2009 instead of $224,234; the fifty basis points produces over $100,000 more wealth over that period.[9]

Until now, we have assumed that the interest rate remains the same each period. There is always the possibility that interest rates earned on investments or paid on obligations may change over time. Though the interest may change, the mathematics do not; we simply cannot use shortcuts, calculator functions, or spreadsheet functions to perform the math. Consider an investment of $20,000 in which you expect to earn 3% the first year, 4% the second year, and 5% the third year. How much is the investment worth in three years? It is worth $22,495.20:

$$FV_3 = \$20,000 \times (1 + 0.03) \times (1 + 0.04) \times (1 + 0.05) = \$22,495.20$$

How much of this investment is interest on the principal, and how much is interest-on-interest? We can use the same approach as we did previously to break down the future value into principal, interest on the principal, and interest-on-interest components:

Year	Beginning value	Interest rate	Interest on the principal	Interest-on-interest	Balance at the end of the year
1	$20,000.00	3%	$600.00	$0.00	$20,600.00
2	$20,600.00	4%	$800.00	$24.00	$21,424.00
3	$21,424.00	5%	$1,000.00	$71.20	$22,495.20

The interest-on-interest is the product of the interest rate for the period and any accumulated interest. Let us consider Year 2 in this example. The interest on the principal amount is $20,000 × 0.04 = $800; the interest-on-interest is $600 × 0.04 = $24. For the third year, the interest-on-interest is ($600 + 800 + 24) × 0.05 = $71.20. The interest-on-interest over this three year period is $24 + 71.20 = $95.20. Another way of calculating this is to compare the

---

EXAMPLE 5.4

Compounding with Different Rates of Return

PROBLEM

Consider depositing €1,000 in an account that is expected to pay 5% interest for the first three years and 2% for the following three years.[10] What will be the balance in the account six years from now if there are no withdrawals from the account?

Solution

$$FV_6 = €1,000 (1 + 0.05)^3 (1 + 0.02)^3 = €1,000 \times 1.157625 \times 1.061208 = €1,228.48$$

---

[8] Therefore, if an interest rate changes from 5% to 6%, we say that the interest rate has changed by 100 basis points.

[9] Why worry about such a long period? Remember that while you may be currently thinking short term, many financial instruments exist—and are valued—for the long run.

[10] You will notice that the monetary units do not matter. The time value of money mathematics apply whether we are using U.S. or Canadian dollars ($), euro (€), Japanese yen (¥), British pounds (£), or any other currency.

Islamic Law and Interest | GLOBAL PERSPECTIVE

Islamic law promotes a faith-based financial system that forbids interest, or *riba*, on transactions but permits profits from investments, *mudharabah*, that are shared between the parties to the transaction. The prohibition of interest, the sharing of profits, and the prohibition on speculation result in differences between the Islamic financial system and the traditional European and U.S. systems.

Consider the following:

- A simple savings account, in the U.S. system, results in periodic interest being provided to the depositor in exchange for the bank having the use of the funds.

In the Islamic financial system, the bank cannot pay interest, but the bank may provide a gratuity, a *hibah*, in gratitude for the depositor leaving the funds in the hands of the bank.

- A loan in the U.S. system results in the borrower paying the amount borrowed plus interest. In the Islamic system, the borrower does not pay interest for a loan (a *qard*) but can provide a gratuity to the bank.

Source: Shanmugam, Bala, and Zaha Rina Zahari, *A Primer on Islamic Finance*, CFA Institute, December 2009.

---

future value with compound interest, the $22,495.20, with the value with simple interest, $20,000 + 600 + 800 + 1,000 = $22,400: $22,495.20 - 22,400 = $95.20.

Discounting

So far, we have been concerned with finding future values, but there is a problem with comparing future values: There are many of them! We could choose an arbitrary common period to make the comparisons, which would solve this problem. The obvious choice is to compare the values at the current time; so, instead of calculating future values, we determine present values. We refer to this process as **discounting**. We will explain it with a simple example.

discounting calculating the present value of a future value, considering the time value of money

Suppose an investor estimates that she needs $1 million to live comfortably when she retires in forty years. How much does she have to invest today, assuming a 10% interest rate on the investment?

First, start with what we already know: the future value formula from Equation 5-2:

$$FV_n = PV_0(1 + i)^n$$

where $(1 + i)^n$ is the compound factor. With a starting present value, we multiply by the compound factor to get the future value. Turning this around, we can divide the future value by the compound factor to arrive at the present value, or, rearranging Equation 5-2 and solving for PV_0,

$$PV_0 = \frac{FV_n}{(1 + i)^n} = FV_n \times \left(\frac{1}{(1 + i)^n}\right) \tag{5-3}$$

This is the basic discounting equation, and the last term, $1 \div (1 + i)^n$, is the **discount factor**.

So, let us return to our example. With

discount factor value that, when multiplied by the future value, results in the present value of this future value

FV = $1,000,000

$i = 0.10$

$n = 40$

we arrive at the present value of $22,094.93:

$$PV_0 = \$1,000,000 \times \frac{1}{1.10^{40}}$$

$$PV_0 = \$1,000,000 \times \frac{1}{45.259256}$$

$$PV_0 = \$1,000,000 \times 0.02209493$$

$$PV_0 = \$22,094.93$$

Therefore, an investment of $22,094.93 today, earning a 10% return per year, has a future value of $1 million in forty years. With a 10% market interest rate, $22,094.94 today and $1 million in forty years' time are worth the same:

$$FV = \$22,094.94 \times 1.10^{40} = \$22,094.94 \times 45.25926 = \$1,000,000$$

Now you know why we call this process *discounting*. If people do not want to pay the full price for something, they ask for a discount, that is, they ask for something off the price. In the same way, $1 million in forty years is not worth $1 million today, so you discount, or take something off, to get it to its true value. Discounting future values to find their present value is the same process, except that when we know the market interest rate, we can use Equation 5-3 to calculate the value today.

EXAMPLE 5.5

Solving for a Present Value

PROBLEM

Suppose you are considering an investment that promises $50,000 in three years. If you determine that the appropriate discount rate for this investment, considering its risk, is 15%, what is this investment worth to you today?

Solution

Using the formula:

$$PV_0 = \frac{\$50,000}{(1 + 0.15)^3} = \frac{\$50,000}{1.520875} = \$32,875.81$$

Using a financial calculator:

    FV = 50000
    $n = 3$
    $i = 15$
    Solve for PV.

Using a spreadsheet function:

    = PV(0.15,3,0,50000)

Note the following important points from the previous examples:

- Discount factors are always less than 1 (as long as $i \geq 0$). This means that future dollars are worth less than the same dollars today, or PV > FV.
- Discount factors are the reciprocals of their corresponding compound factors, and vice versa. In other words, discounting is compounding in reverse.

Compounding and Discounting with Continuous Compounding

discrete compounding compound interest in which interest is paid at specified intervals of time, such as quarterly or annually

continuously compounded interest or continuous compounding interest is instantaneous, compounded an infinite number of times

Until now, we have used **discrete compounding**; that is, interest is compounded a fixed number of times. There are many applications in finance in which interest is compounded continuously. **Continuously compounded interest** or, simply, **continuous compounding**, means that interest is instantaneous, or compounded an infinite number of times. Though this may seem like an abstract concept, continuously compounded interest is the basis for many financial transactions (such as interest on credit card balances).

Consider a lump sum of $10,000 deposited in an account for six years. If interest is compounded annually, at the end of five years you will have:

$$FV_5 = \$10,000 \ (1 + 0.05)^6 = \$13,400.96$$

If, however, interest is calculated quarterly, the rate per period is 1.25% and there are 4 × 6 = 24 periods. The result is:

$$FV_5 = \$10,000 \ (1 + {}^{0.05}\!/_4)^{24} = \$13,473.51$$

Therefore, the inputs for your calculator's calculation are:[11]

PV = $10,000
$i = 1.25\%$
$n = 24$

If interest is compounded daily:

$$FV_5 = \$10,000 \ (1 + {}^{0.05}\!/_{365})^{2,190} = \$13,498.31$$

If interest is compounded continuously, we have to resort to using Euler's e, which is a mathematical constant (approximately 2.71828):[12]

$$FV_5 = \$10,000 \ e^{0.05 \times 6} = \$10,000 \ e^{0.3} = \$13,498.59$$

where e is the unique Euler constant. You can find this constant on your calculator (usually represented as e) and in a spreadsheet program (usually indicated as EXP). You will notice that as the frequency of compounding increases, the future value increases as well. The limit to this increase is the continuously compounded value.

Discounting works in a similar manner. Suppose you have a goal of having $20,000 in an account at the end of four years. If you make a deposit today in an account earning 6%

---

[11] You could also adjust the payments per period (often designated as P/YR) and input the 5% rate and the number of periods. We do recommend this approach because many students forget to change the payments per period back to P/YR = 1, which would result in errors in subsequent calculations. The simplest method is to convert i and n and then enter these values in the calculator.

[12] Euler's e is a really cool number because it is used in many ways in mathematics and in finance. Euler's e is (1) the inverse of the natural logarithm, (2) the base of the natural logarithm, (3) a function that is equal to its own derivative, and (4) an irrational number (with so many digits that there are contests for memorizing or programming the decimal digits). There is even a book written about it: *e: The Story of a Number*, by Eli Manor [Princeton University Press (1998)].

interest, how much would you have to deposit as a lump sum today to meet your goal? It will depend on the frequency of compounding:

Frequency of compounding	Present value
Annual	$PV_0 = \dfrac{\$20,000}{(1 + 0.06)^4} = \$15,841.87$
Quarterly	$PV_0 = \dfrac{\$20,000}{(1 + 0.015)^{16}} = \$15,760.62$
Daily	$PV_0 = \dfrac{\$20,000}{(1 + 0.00016438)^{1,460}} = \$15,732.87$
Continuous	$PV_0 = \dfrac{\$20,000}{e^{0.06 \times 4}} = \$15,732.56$

As you can see, the more frequent the compounding, the smaller is the present value.

Determining the Interest Rate

Let us look at the basic valuation equation again:

$$FV_n = PV_0(1 + i)^n$$

We have used this equation to solve for future values (FV) and present values (PV), but note that we can solve for two other values: (1) the interest rate, i, and (2) the period, n. If both the present and future values are known, and we know either the interest rate or the period, we can solve for the last unknown.

For example, suppose you want to find out the interest rate necessary for your investment to double in value in six years:

PV = $1

FV = $2

$n = 6$

And then solve for i:

$$\$2 = \$1(1 + i)^6$$

Rearranging and solving for i produces an interest rate of 12.246%:

$$\frac{\$2}{\$1} = (1 + i)^6 \rightarrow \sqrt[6]{\frac{\$2}{\$1}} = (1 + i) \rightarrow i = \sqrt[6]{\frac{\$2}{\$1}} - 1 = 12.246\%$$

In other words, you can double your money in six years if you can earn 12.246% on your investment.

Let us apply this to a company's dividends per share. International Business Machines (IBM) paid $0.51 in dividends per share during 2000. In 2011, IBM paid $2.90 in dividends. What is the growth rate of IBM's dividends? We know the following:

PV = $0.51 *The starting value of dividends*

FV = $2.90 *The ending value of dividends*

$n = 11$ *The number of periods since 2000*

Solving for i, we have the rate of growth in dividends, which is 17.117%.

Determining the Number of Periods

Now consider another example, this time solving for the number of periods. How long does it take to triple your money if the interest rate is 3% per year? The known values are:

PROBLEM

EXAMPLE 5.6

Solving for the Interest Rate

What would the annual interest rate have to be so that your investment at the end of twenty years:

1) doubled?
2) tripled?
3) quadrupled?

Solution

Formula	Calculator	Spreadsheet	Answer
1) $2 = 1(1 + i)^{20}$ $i = \sqrt[20]{\dfrac{\$2}{\$1}} - 1$	PV = −1; FV = 2; n = 20	=RATE(20,0,−1,2)	3.526%
2) $3 = 1(1 + i)^{20}$ $i = \sqrt[20]{\dfrac{\$3}{\$1}} - 1$	PV = −1; FV = 3; n = 20	=RATE(20,0,−1,3)	5.647%
3) $4 = 1(1 + i)^{20}$ $i = \sqrt[20]{\dfrac{\$4}{\$1}} - 1$	PV = −1; FV = 4; n = 20	=RATE(20,0,−1,4)	7.177%

PV = $1
FV = $3
i = 3%

and the unknown value, the one you solve for is n:

$$\$3 = \$1(1 + 0.03)^n$$

Rearranging and solving for i:[13]

$$\frac{\$3}{\$1} = (1 + 0.03)^n$$

Taking the natural logs of both sides and then solving for n, we find that n is 37.16676:

$$\ln 3 - \ln 1 = n \ln (1.03)$$

$$n = \frac{\ln 3 - \ln 1}{\ln(1.03)} = \frac{1.0986 - 0}{0.029559} = 37.16676$$

$$n = 38$$

Therefore, if you can earn 3% per year on your investment, you will triple your money in 38 years.[14]

When solving for the interest rate or solving for the number of periods, you can use mathematics, as we just did, or use a financial calculator or spreadsheet. It is very important when you use a calculator or spreadsheet that you change the sign on the present value when you enter it. If you do not, the calculator cannot compute a solution.

---

[13] In this calculation, we take a natural log of a value. While we will not go into all the painful details on what logarithms and base e mean, we can tell you that this allows us to make this equation easier to solve by using the properties of logarithms to bring the exponent n into a linear equation and thus solve for n. How do you take a natural log of something? You probably have a key on your calculator that is labeled "LN" or "ln."

[14] Why not round down to thirty-seven years? Because at thirty-seven years, we have not tripled the money; however, by the time interest is compounded the thirty-eighth time (remember, this is discrete interest), we have tripled the money.

EXAMPLE 5.7

**Solving for
the Number
of Periods**

PROBLEM

If you can earn 5% on your investment, how long does it take, rounding up to the next
whole compounding period, for your money to:

1. double?
2. triple?
3. quadruple?

Solution

	Formula		Calculator	Spreadsheet	Answer
1)	$n = \dfrac{Ln\ 2}{Ln\ 1.05}$	$= \dfrac{0.693147}{0.048790}$	$PV = -1; FV=2; i = 5$	=NPER(0.05,0,–1,2)	14.2067
2)	$n = \dfrac{Ln\ 3}{Ln\ 1.05}$	$= \dfrac{1.098612}{0.048790}$	$PV = -1; FV=3; i = 5$	=NPER(0.05,0,–1,3)	22.5171
3)	$n = \dfrac{Ln\ 4}{Ln\ 1.05}$	$= \dfrac{1.386294}{0.048790}$	$PV = -1; FV=4; i = 5$	=NPER(0.05,0,–1,4)	28.4134

SUMMARIZING

The equation for the future value, $FV_n = PV_0(1 + i)^n$, has four values, and if we know
any three of them we can solve for the last one. We can solve four different types of
finance problems using this equation:

1. *Future value problems*: How much will I have in w years at x% if I invest $y?
2. *Present value problems*: What is the value today of receiving $z in w years if the
   interest rate is x%?
3. *Determining the interest rate*: What rate of return will I earn if I invest $y today
   for w years and get $z?
4. *Determining the number of periods:* How long do I have to wait to get $z if I
   invest $y today at x%?

*Concept Review
Questions*

1. You are given a choice of receiving $1,000 today or $1,000 one year from today.
   Are you indifferent to the difference between the two choices? Why, or why not?

2. Suppose you are considering lending someone $10,000. If your opportunity cost
   of funds is 5%, what interest rate should you charge for this loan? Explain your
   reasoning.

3. An investor wants to calculate the average annual return on an investment. She
   identified the amount invested and the value of the investment at the end of
   the investment period. She then calculated the percentage change in the value
   of the investment from the beginning to the end of the investment period and
   divided this by the number of years to arrive at the average annual return on the
   investment. Is this the correct approach? Explain.

5.2 ANNUITIES AND PERPETUITIES

So far, what we have examined are single-sum problems because we were looking at a single investment today and a single payoff in the future or looking at the value today of a future lump sum. In principle, we can solve almost any problem by using the techniques we have discussed because, for example, valuing a series of receipts in the future can be done by valuing each one individually. However, special formulas exist for standard problems in finance, for which the receipts or payments are the same each period.

Ordinary Annuities

Up to this point, we have dealt with PV and FV concepts as they apply to only two cash flows—one today (i.e., the PV) and one in the future (i.e., the FV). In practice, we often need to compare different series of receipts or payments that occur through time. An **annuity** is a series of payments or receipts, which we will simply call **cash flows**, over some period that are for the same amount and paid over the same interval; that is, for example, they are paid annually, monthly, or weekly. Annuities are common in finance: The one you may be familiar with is a personal loan or mortgage payment. This involves identical payments made at regular intervals based on a single interest rate for a loan.

annuity regular payments from an investment that are for the same amount and are paid at regular intervals of time

cash flows actual cash generated from an investment

An **ordinary annuity** involves *end-of-period* payments. We have the same values as in our earlier discussion: FV, PV, *n*, and *i*. However, now we have another term, PMT, for the regular annuity payment or receipt. The example below demonstrates how to determine the FV and PV of an ordinary annuity.

ordinary annuity equal payments from an investment over a fixed number of years, with the payments made at the end of each period

Suppose someone plans to invest $1,000 at the end of each year for the next five years and expects to earn 13% per year. How much will the investor have after five years? How much would the investor need to deposit today to obtain the same results?

We can first depict the series of payments in a timeline, which shows when the cash flows occur:

Timelines are very useful in finance, and you may want to develop the habit of displaying the data in a problem in a timeline to avoid any confusion about the timing of cash flows. For example, from the diagram above, we can see that by the end of Year 5, the first deposit of $1,000 will earn a return for four years because there are four years from the end of Year 1 to the end of the problem in Year 5. In contrast, the second payment will earn a return for only three years, the third for only two, the fourth for one year, and the final payment will not earn a return at all.

Future value of an ordinary annuity

Suppose we want to calculate the future value of this series of cash flows, with an interest rate of 13%. Using this information, we could view this as a five-part problem in which we have to find the future value of each of the five payments:

$$FV_5 = \left(\$1,000 \times (1.13)^4\right) + \left(\$1,000 \times (1.13)^3\right) + \left(\$1,000 \times (1.13)^2\right)$$
$$+ \left(\$1,000 \times (1.13)^1\right) + \left(\$1,000 \times (1.13)^0\right)$$
$$FV_5 = (\$1,000 \times 1.63047) + (\$1,000 \times 1.44290) + (\$1,000 \times 1.27690)$$
$$+ (\$1,000 \times 1.130) + (\$1,000 \times 1)$$
$$FV_5 = \$1,000 \times 6.48027 = \$6,480.27$$

The investor would have \$6,480.27 after five years, as we depict in the timeline:

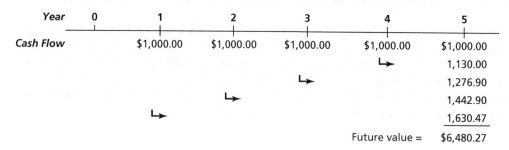

When we have to solve a problem that involves valuing a series of even cash flows, we can always do this the long way: determining the future value of each of the cash flows and then summing these future values. This approach is fine in the case of a five-period annuity, but it would be tedious in the case of, say, a twenty-five-year, monthly-payment mortgage with 300 payments.

Fortunately, there is a much quicker way (even without the use of a financial calculator or a spreadsheet). If we look closely at our solution, we can see that we are multiplying \$1,000 by the sum of five compound factors based on a 13% return (i.e., the compound factor for $i = 13\%$, with $n = 4, 3, 2, 1$, and 0, respectively).

The formula for the future value of an ordinary annuity is:

$$FV_n = PMT \sum_{t=1}^{N} (1 + i)^{N-t} = PMT \left[\frac{(1 + i)^N - 1}{i} \right] \tag{5-4}$$

future value annuity factor sum of the individual periods' future value compound factors that, when multiplied by the amount of an annuity, provides the future value of the annuity

where PMT is the end-of-period annuity payment and N is the number of payments. The term in brackets is the **future value annuity factor**. The advantage of Equation 5-4 is that it involves only one factor and it can be easily solved by using a simple calculator. How could you arrive at the future value annuity factor without this formula, but by using a financial calculator? Simply provide a PMT of 1 and then enter i and N; when you solve for FV, this will be the future value annuity factor.

Using this equation, we can solve for the future value as follows:

$$FV_5 = PMT \sum_{t=1}^{5} (1 + 0.13)^{5-t} = \$1,000 \left[\frac{(1 + 0.13)^5 - 1}{0.13} \right]$$
$$= \$1,000 \times 6.48027 = \$6,480.27$$

We can derive the future value annuity factor for five years at 13% using a simple calculator.[15] Note that the sum of the compound factors for the N periods is equal to the future value annuity factor for N payments, that is:

$$\text{Future value annuity factor} = \sum_{t=1}^{N} (1 + i)^{N-t} = \left[\frac{(1 + i)^N - 1}{i} \right]$$

In our example,

Year	Cash flow at end of year	Future value interest factor	Future value, end of fifth year
1	\$1,000	1.63047	\$1,630.47
2	\$1,000	1.44290	\$1,442.90
3	\$1,000	1.27690	\$1,276.90
4	\$1,000	1.13000	\$1,130.00
5	\$1,000	1.00000	\$1,000.00
Future value annuity factor = 6.48027			FV = \$6,480.27

[15] Simply substitute 1 for the PMT: $i = 13, n = 5$, PMT $= 1$, and solve for FV.

Of course, we could also use a financial calculator or a spreadsheet:[16]

Financial Calculator	**Spreadsheet**
PMT = –$1,000	=FV(0.13,5,–1000,0)
$i = 13$	
$n = 5$	
PV = 0	
Solve for FV.	

Present value of an ordinary annuity

The present value of an ordinary annuity is the discounted value of the series of cash flows, with the first cash flow occurring one period from today. Consider the example of a series of five cash flows of $1,000 to be received at the end of each year if the interest rate is 13%. What is the present value of this series? Taking a closer look, we can solve for the present value by viewing this as a five-part problem for which we have to find the present value of each of the five annual payments:

$$PV_0 = \frac{\$1,000}{1.13^5} + \frac{\$1,000}{1.13^4} + \frac{\$1,000}{1.13^3} + \frac{\$1,000}{1.13^2} + \frac{\$1,000}{1.13^1} = \$3,517.24$$

Or each cash flow is multiplied by the appropriate corresponding discount factor and then summed:

$$PV_0 = (\$1,000 \times 0.54276) + (\$1,000 \times 0.61332) + (\$1,000 \times 0.69305)$$
$$+ (\$1,000 \times 0.78315) + (\$1,000 \times 0.88496) = \$3,517.24$$

Or multiply the periodic cash flow by the **present value annuity factor**, which is the sum of the individual discount factors:

$$PV_0 = \$1,000 \times 3.51724 = \$3,517.24$$

present value annuity factor sum of the discount factors that, when multiplied by the amount of an annuity payment, results in the present value of the annuity

Using a timeline, you can see that we discount the first cash flow one period and the last cash flow five periods:

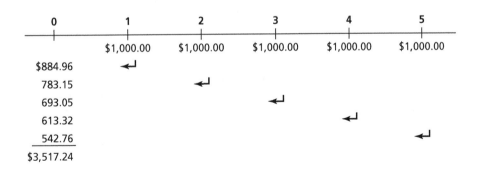

---

[16] You will notice that we use "N" to indicate the number of payments in an annuity, but refer to the "n" in the calculator calculations. This is because the number of payments and number of periods share the same key in the financial calculator.

As before, note that we are using the long way, by multiplying $1,000 by the sum of the relevant five discount factors, which add to 3.51724. Fortunately, the formula for determining the PV of ordinary annuities will do this for us:

$$PV_0 = PMT\sum_{t=1}^{N}\frac{1}{(1+i)^t} = PMT\left[\frac{1 - \dfrac{1}{(1+i)^N}}{i}\right] \tag{5-5}$$

To further demonstrate the relationship between the discount factors and the present value annuity factor, examine the problem in a table format:

Year	Cash flow at end of year	Discount factor	Present value, today
1	$1,000	0.88496	$884.96
2	$1,000	0.78315	783.15
3	$1,000	0.69305	693.05
4	$1,000	0.61332	613.32
5	$1,000	0.54276	542.76
		Present value annuity factor = 3.51724	PV = $3,517.24

By using this equation to solve this example, we arrive at:

$$PV_0 = \$1,000\left[\frac{1 - \dfrac{1}{(1.13)^5}}{0.13}\right] = \$1,000 \times 3.51724 = \$3,517.24$$

Using a calculator or spreadsheet:

Using a financial calculator
PMT = $1,000
$i = 13\%$
$n = 5$
FV = 0

Solve for PV.

Using a spreadsheet
=PV(0.13,5, −1000,0)

Note: You can either change the sign on the PMT to negative or change the sign on the PV once it is calculated.

From this example, we can see that:

$3,517.24 today = $1,000 at the end of each of the next five years = $6,480.27 five years from today

Annuities Due

lessor person or company that leases out an item

lessee person or company that leases an item, paying a periodic amount in exchange for the use of the item

Sometimes, annuities are structured such that the cash flows are paid at the beginning of a period rather than at the end. For example, leasing arrangements are usually set up like this, with the **lessee** (the one borrowing) making an immediate payment on taking possession of the equipment, such as a car, to the **lessor** (the one lending). Such an annuity is an **annuity due**. Let us look at an example to see how to evaluate these cash flows.

annuity due annuity for which the payments are made at the beginning of each period

Consider a problem similar to the annuity problem that we just looked at, except that now the payments are made at the beginning rather than at the end of each year. How much will the investor have after five years? How much would the investor have to deposit today to have the same results?

We begin as before by depicting the data in a timeline:

Note that as before, we have five cash flows of $1,000 each. However, each cash flow appears one period *earlier*, and thus each receives an *extra* period of interest at the rate of 13%.

Future value of an annuity due

We can solve for the future value of an annuity due in much the same way as we solved for the future value of an ordinary annuity, but we adjust for the additional compounding that each cash flow receives. Using the "brute force approach," we can find the future value of each of the five payments:

$$
\begin{aligned}
FV_5 &= \$10,00(1.13)^5 + \$1,000(1.13)^4 + \$1,000(1.13)^3 \\
&\quad + \$1,000(1.13)^2 + \$1,000(1.13)^1 \\
&= (\$1,000 \times 1.84244) + (\$1,000 \times 1.63047) + (\$1,000 \times 1.44290) \\
&\quad + (\$1,000 \times 1.27690) + (\$1,000 \times 1.1300) \\
&= \$1,000 \times 7.32271 \\
&= \$7,322.71
\end{aligned}
$$

We illustrate this same compounding in a timeline:

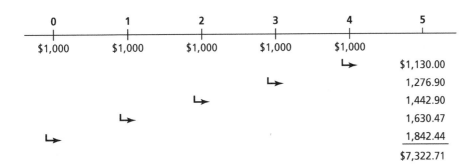

Note that because each flow gets one extra period of compounding at 13%, the net result is that we multiply our answer to the ordinary annuity by 1.13. In other words, the FV (annuity due) = [FV (ordinary annuity)](1 + i):

$$
FV_{5,annuity\ due} = FV_{5,ordinary\ annuity} \times (1 + i) = \$6,480.27 \times 1.13 = \$7,322.71
$$

Therefore, we can alter Equation 5-4 to find the FV of an annuity due as follows:

$$
FV_n = PMT \sum_{t=1}^{N}(1 + i)^t = PMT\left[\frac{(1 + i)^N - 1}{i}\right](1 + i) \tag{5-6}
$$

However, we can now solve the example as follows:

$$FV_5 = PMT\left[\frac{(1 + 0.13)^5 - 1}{0.13}\right](1 + 0.13) = \$1{,}000 \times 6.48027 \times 1.13 = \$7{,}322.71$$

In other words, the value of the annuity due of $7,322.71 is 1.13 times larger than the value of the ordinary annuity that we calculated earlier of $6,480.27. Using a table format and identifying the individual compound factors, we see that the future value of this annuity is the sum of the individual future values, which is also equal to the product of the period cash flow and the sum of the compound factors:

Year	Cash flow at the beginning of the year	Compound factor	Future value
1	$1,000	1.84244	$1,842.44
2	$1,000	1.63047	1,630.47
3	$1,000	1.44290	1,442.90
4	$1,000	1.27690	1,276.90
5	$1,000	1.13000	1,130.00
	Future value annuity due factor = 7.32271		FV =$7,322.71

Using a financial calculator, we first put the calculator in the "Begin," "BEG," "Due" mode, depending on the calculator model, and then:

PMT = $1,000

$i = 13\%$

$n = 5$

Using a spreadsheet function, you indicate the timing of the cash flows using the fifth argument in the function with a "1." The spreadsheet entry is:

$$= FV(0.13, 5, -1000, 0, 1)$$

Present value of an annuity due

As before, to solve for the present value, we could view this as a five-part problem for which we have to find the present value of each of the five payments.

$$PV_0 = \frac{\$1{,}000}{(1 + 0.13)^4} + \frac{\$1{,}000}{(1 + 0.13)^3} + \frac{\$1{,}000}{(1 + 0.13)^2} + \frac{\$1{,}000}{(1 + 0.13)^1}$$

$$+ \frac{\$1{,}000}{(1 + 0.13)^0} = \$3{,}974.48$$

We can also represent in a timeline, noting that the cash flow at the beginning of, say, Year 2 is the same as the cash flow at the end of Year 1:

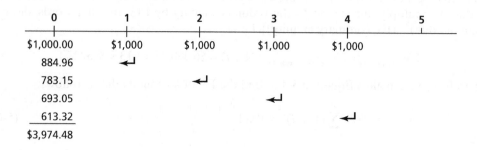

Or we can use a table format:

Year	Cash Flow at the Beginning of the Year	Discount Factor	Present Value
1	$1,000	1.00000	$1,000.00
2	$1,000	0.88496	884.96
3	$1,000	0.78315	783.15
4	$1,000	0.69305	693.05
5	$1,000	0.61332	613.32
		3.97448	$3,974.48

Note that we could also multiply our answer to the ordinary annuity valuation by 1.13, that is, $(1 + i)$:

$$PV_0 = \$1,000 \times 3.51724 \times 1.13 = \$3,974.48$$

Accordingly, we can modify Equation 5-5 to arrive at the formula for determining the PV of an annuity due:

$$PV_0 = PMT \sum_{t=1}^{N} \frac{1}{(1 + i)^{N-t}} = PMT \left[\frac{1 - \dfrac{1}{(1 + i)^N}}{i} \right] (1 + i) \qquad (5\text{-}7)$$

Using this to solve for the present value, we get:

$$PV_0 = \$1,000 \left[\frac{1 - \dfrac{1}{(1.13)^5}}{0.13} \right] (1.13) = (\$1,000 \times 3.51724 \times 1.13) = \$3,974.48$$

Deferred Annuities

A **deferred annuity** is simply an annuity that begins two or more periods from the present. These annuities occur when a series of payments or receipts are delayed into the future. The classic example is saving for retirement: When you think about how much you need for your retirement, you usually start with figuring out how much you need to live on each year, and then you back into what you need to have saved by the time you retire. This is a deferred annuity.

deferred annuity annuity that begins two or more periods from the present

Let us start with a very basic example. Suppose you are promised a series of four payments of $1,000 each that begins three years from now, and the appropriate discount rate is 4%. There are three ways to solve this problem:

The long way

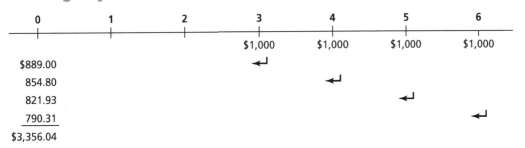

As a discounted ordinary annuity

Using this method, you discount the four $1,000 cash flows as an ordinary annuity. This provides you with a value as of the end of the second period (Remember: The present value of an ordinary annuity is one period before the first cash flow). Discounting this value for two periods provides you with the value today.

As a discounted annuity due

This method is similar to Method 2, but because of the timing of the valuation, there is one more discount period. Why? Because when you discount the four payments as an annuity due, you get a value coinciding with the first cash flow, which is at the end of the third period.

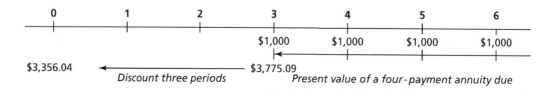

As you can see, you get to the same place using each of the three methods. Which is easier? For very simple problems, it is really a matter of personal choice. For problems involving many more cash flows? Most likely, Method 2 is easier because you can use the built-in calculator or spreadsheet annuity function and, if you are using a financial calculator, you do not have to change any settings on the calculator.

Perpetuities

perpetuity annuity that provides periodic payments forever

A **perpetuity** is a special annuity that goes on forever, so N goes to infinity in the annuity equation. In this case, Equation 5-5 reduces to:[17]

$$PV_0 = \frac{PMT}{i} \qquad (5\text{-}8)$$

Perpetuities are easy to value because all we do is divide the cash payment or receipt by the interest rate. Consider an investment that promises to pay $2 each year, forever. If the discount rate is 8%, the present value of this investment is $2 ÷ 0.08 = $25.

There is only a small difference in the present value of the cash streams between a perpetuity and an annuity with many payments. For example, the difference between $2 in perpetuity and a fifty-period ordinary annuity of $2 each year is $25 − 24.47 = $0.53. This tells us that the PV of the cash flows of $2 per year from Year 51 to infinity (that is, ∞) is only $0.53. This is a very important result and is the driving force behind many financial innovations because it means that cash flows far into the future are of very little value because of the discounting involved in the time value of money.

---

[17] If N is infinity, then $PV_0 = PMT \sum_{t=1}^{\infty} \frac{1}{(1+i)^t}$ which reduces to $PMT ÷ i$.

PROBLEM

Consider an annuity of $3,000, with cash flows occurring at the end of each period and an interest rate of 12%.

A. If the cash flows occur for thirty years, what is the present value of this annuity?
B. If the cash flows occur each period, forever, what is the present value of this stream of cash flows?

Solution

A. $PV_0 = \$3,000 \left[\dfrac{1 - \dfrac{1}{(1.12)^{30}}}{0.12} \right] = \$3,000 \times 8.05518 = \$24,165.55$

B. $PV_0 = \dfrac{\$3,000}{0.12} = \$25,000$

EXAMPLE 5.8

Annuities and Perpetuities

Determining the Number of Periods or the Interest Rate

When we focused on the value of a single sum, whether compounding or discounting, we could solve for the number of periods given a future value, a present value, and an interest rate. We could also solve for the interest rate or return given a future value, a present value, and the number of periods. We can do the same for an annuity or a perpetuity, although using formulas in some cases becomes a bit burdensome. To overcome this, we can rely on financial calculators and spreadsheets to do the heavy lifting in solving these types of problems.

Consider solving for an interest rate, given the present value, the number of payments, and the amount of the payment. This is a common application when the loan terms are disclosed and the borrower wants to know the cost of the loan based on these terms. The general setup for the problem features the present value annuity formula:

$$PV_0 = PMT \sum_{t=1}^{N} \frac{1}{(1 + i)^t}$$

If $10,000 is borrowed, the present value is $10,000. If the payments are $2,000 each, and there are six payments, then:

$$\$10,000 = \$2,000 \sum_{t=1}^{6} \frac{1}{(1 + i)^t}$$

There is no direct solution to the problem; the best we can do is determine that the present value annuity factor is equal to $10,000 ÷ $2,000 = 5. We could use the trial-and-error method to eventually find the interest rate, i, but this becomes quite tedious. Instead, using a calculator:

PV = $10,000

PMT = $2,000

$n = 6$

Solve for i.

You should note that the present value and the payment must have different signs when entered into the calculator, or the program will not be able to determine a solution. Using a spreadsheet function, RATE,

$$= \text{RATE(number of periods, payment, present value, future value)}$$

or

$$= \text{RATE}(6,2000,-10000,0,0)$$

The rate is 5.472%.[18]

We solve for the number of payments in a similar manner. Suppose Company X can borrow $100 million and determines that it can pay this back in semi-annual payments of $4 million each. If the annual rate of interest on this borrowing is 5% but the rate per semi-annual payment is 2.5%, how many payments need to be made by Company X? We again use:

$$PV_0 = PMT \sum_{t=1}^{n} \frac{1}{(1 + i)^t}$$

Substituting the known values for PV_0, PMT, and i:

$$\$100 = \$4 \sum_{t=1}^{N} \frac{1}{(1 + 0.025)^t}$$

Using a financial calculator or a spreadsheet, we can calculate the number of payments as 39.7217:

Financial calculator	*Spreadsheet*
PV = $100	= NPER(0.025,4,−100,0)
i = 2.5%	
PMT = 4	
Solve for n.	

Because these are semi-annual payments, it will take forty payments (with the last payment not quite $4 million) to repay the loan.

EXAMPLE 5.9

Ordinary Annuities and Annuities Due

PROBLEM

Consider two series of cash flows:

Series A: Beginning today, produces a cash flow of $2,000 each month for sixty months.

Series B: Beginning one month from today, produces a cash flow of $2,050 each month for fifty-nine months.

If the discount rate appropriate for both series is 0.5% per month, which series is more valuable today?

Solution

Series B has a larger present value, so it is more valuable today.

---

[18] Be sure to place a zero in the fourth argument because there is future value.

Series A: Present value of a sixty-payment annuity due:

$$PV_0 = \$2,000 \sum_{t=1}^{60} \frac{1}{(1 + 0.005)^{60-t}} = \$2,000$$

$$\left[\frac{1 - \dfrac{1}{(1 + 0.005)^n}}{0.005} \right] (1 + 0.005) = \$103,968.38$$

or a fifty-nine-payment ordinary annuity plus one payment:

$$PV_0 = \left[\$2,000 \sum_{t=1}^{59} \frac{1}{(1 + 0.005)^t} \right] + \$2,000 = \$103,968.38$$

Series B: Present value of an ordinary annuity

$$PV_0 = \left[\$2,050 \sum_{t=1}^{59} \frac{1}{(1 + 0.005)^t} \right] = \$104,517.59$$

SUMMARIZING

Ordinary annuity: The first cash flow occurs one period from today.

Example: Three-payment ordinary annuity

Annuity due: The first cash flow occurs today.

Example: Three-payment annuity due

Deferred annuity: The first cash flow occurs beyond one period from today.

Example: Three-payment deferred annuity, with the first payment deferred one period

Perpetuity: The first cash flow occurs one period from today, and continues *ad infinitum.*

FINANCE in the News | Structured Settlements

In resolving legal claims, such as injuries from an accident, a prevailing party may accept either a lump-sum payment or a series of payments. When the claimant elects to receive a periodic stream (i.e., an annuity), this is referred to as a *structured settlement*. These payments, in most cases, are tax-free cash flows.

Since the 1970s, specialized companies have been making offers to claimants who may prefer to receive a lump-sum cash payment today in exchange for the annuity. From the point of view of the claimant selling the annuity to these companies, the decision involves comparing the present value of the annuity with the offered lump sum. Because the implicit interest on the annuity payments is not taxed but earnings on any invested lump sum are taxed, receiving the annuity is generally more attractive than receiving the lump sum. However, the claimant's individual situation or age may make the lump sum more attractive.

From the point of view of the structured settlement company, the decision is slightly more complex because

the federal government has a punitive tax on the difference between the undiscounted value of the annuity and the amount paid for the annuity at a 40% rate. This tax occurs if the sale of the annuity to the company is not approved by the respective state court.[19] Therefore, from the perspective of the structured settlement company, the decision regarding a transfer that is not approved involves comparing the undiscounted value of the annuity with the lump sum offered for the rights to the structured settlement, after subtracting the 40% excise tax. In other words, if the transfer is not approved by the state court, there is no incentive to transfer. If the state court approves the transfer (considering what is best for the recipient), the decision involves comparing the present value of the annuity with the lump sum offered to the claimant.

Sources: Internal Revenue Service Form 8876 *Excise Tax on Structured Settlement Factoring Transactions*, and Allen, Brad, "How to Evaluate Structured Settlement Buyout Offers," *Fox Business News*, www.foxbusiness.com, June 29, 2010.

Concept Review Questions

1. What is the mathematical relation between an ordinary annuity and an annuity due?

2. When you use a financial calculator or a spreadsheet to calculate the future value of an annuity, at what point in time is the resultant FV for the ordinary annuity? for the annuity due?

3. When solving for the number periods of a lump sum or an ordinary annuity, some perfectionists insist on rounding up the number of periods to the next whole period. What is the basis of the reasoning for this?

5.3 NOMINAL AND EFFECTIVE RATES

So far, we have assumed that payments are made annually and that interest is compounded annually, so we have been able to use quoted rates to solve each problem. In practice, in many situations payments are made (or received) at intervals other than annually (e.g., quarterly, monthly), and compounding often occurs more frequently than annually. We need to be sure that we use the appropriate effective interest rate.

annual percentage rate (APR) or stated rate or nominal rate stated rate of interest, calculated as the product of the interest rate per compounding period and the number of compounding periods

APR Versus EAR: Discrete Compounding

The **annual percentage rate (APR)** is the rate stated for an annual period, assuming no compounding of interest within the year. We often refer to the APR as the **nominal rate** or **stated rate**. Because this rate does not consider compounding, it understates the

[19] Internal Revenue Code Section 5891.

true, effective rate of interest. The **effective annual rate (EAR)** for a period is the rate at which a dollar invested grows over that period. It is usually stated in percentage terms based on an annual period. To determine effective rates, we first recognize that the annual rates of financial institutions will equal the effective annual rate only when compounding is done on an annual basis. We will use some examples to illustrate the process for determining effective rates.

Suppose that an account earns 4% interest per year, compounded quarterly. This means that there is $4\% \div 4 = 1\%$ interest every three months. If you deposit \$1 in this account today and leave it in the account for five years, you will have \$1.22 at the end of twenty quarters, or five years:

$$FV_5 = \$1(1 + 0.01)^{20} = \$1.22$$

If you have \$1 today and \$1.22 at the end of five years, you have, effectively, earned 4.06% per year. How did we know this? We took the given values and solved for the annual rate: $PV = \$1; FV = \$1.22; n = 5 \rightarrow$ solve for i.

PROBLEM

Suppose you invest \$1,000 today for one year at a quoted annual rate of 16% compounded annually.

1. What is the FV at the end of the year?
2. If interest is compounded quarterly, what is the effective annual rate?

Solution

1. $FV_1 = 1,000(1.16)^1 = \$1,160.$

   This means that each \$1 grows to \$1.16 by the end of the period, so we can say that the "effective" annual interest rate is 16%.

2. When the rate is quoted at 16%, and compounding is done quarterly, the appropriate adjustment (by convention) is to charge $16\% \div 4 = 4\%$ per quarter, so we have

   $$FV = \$1,000(1.04)^4 = \$1,170$$
   $$EAR = \$1,170 \div \$1,000 - 1 = 17\% \text{ or } (1 + 0.04)^4 - 1 = 17\%$$

EXAMPLE 5.10

Effective Versus Annual Percentage Rates

We can use the following equation to determine the effective annual rate for any given compounding interval:

$$EAR = \left(1 + \frac{APR}{m}\right)^m - 1 \tag{5-9}$$

where EAR is the effective annual rate, APR is the quoted rate, and m is the number of compounding intervals per year.

If the APR is 4% and interest is compounded quarterly, the EAR is 4.06%:

$$EAR = (1 + {}^{0.04}/_4)^4 - 1 = 4.06\%$$

If we leave \$1 in an account that pays interest at the rate of 4%, compounded quarterly, we can determine the future value in five years as:

$$FV_5 = \$1(1 + 0.0406)^5 = \$1.22$$

Or, equivalently,

$$FV_5 = \$1(1 + 0.01)^{20} = \$1.22$$

You can, of course, solve effective interest rate problems using a calculator or a spreadsheet. If interest is compounded more frequently than once per year, you have two, equivalent approaches to solving for a value:

Approach 1 Convert the APR into an equivalent rate per period, and adjust the number of periods, and then solve appropriately.

Approach 2 Solve for the effective annual rate and then use this rate to determine the value.

Solving for the future value, $FV = \$1,000 \times (1 + 0.01)^{20} = \$1,000 \times 1.22019 = \$1,220.19$. Consider investing $1,000 for five years in an account that has an APR of 4% and interest is compounded quarterly. What will be in the account at the end of five years?

Approach 1: *Convert the APR into usable inputs*

$PV = \$1,000$

$i = 4\% \div 4 = 1\%$

$n = 5 \times 4 = 20$

Solving for the future value, $FV = \$1,000 (1 + 0.01)^{20} = \$1,220.19$

Approach 2: *Calculate and then use the effective annual rate*

$PV = \$1,000$

$i = (1 + 0.01)^4 - 1 = 0.040604$ or 4.0604%

$n = 5$

Solving for the future value, $FV = \$1,000(1 + 0.040604)^5 = \$1,220.19$.

As you can see, we end up with the same future value, regardless of the approach.

Let us combine what you know about annuities with what you know about effective annual rates. Suppose that you borrow $10 million and will repay this loan with monthly payments of $0.3 million per month. We calculate the monthly interest rate by solving for i using the trial-and-error method:

$$\$10 = \$0.3 \sum_{t=1}^{60} \frac{1}{(1 + i)^t}$$

Using a calculator:

$PV = \$10$

$FV = \$0$

$PMT = \$0.3$

$N = 60$

Or, using a spreadsheet,

$$=\text{RATE}(60,0.3,-10,0).$$

This produces a monthly rate of 2.175%. However, to enhance comparability with other borrowing arrangements, we should place this rate on an annual basis. The equivalent APR is $2.175\% \times 12 = 26.1\%$. The effective annual rate is:

$$EAR = (1 + 0.02175)^{12} - 1 = 29.46\%$$

This is a common type of problem in consumer finance: We know the amount borrowed, what the payments are, and how many payments there will be. While the APR is provided in the fine print, we usually have to calculate the effective rate on our own.

APR Versus EAR: Continuous Compounding

When compounding is conducted on a continuous basis, we use the following equation to determine the effective annual rate for a given quoted rate:

$$EAR = e^{APR} - 1 \qquad (5\text{-}10)$$

where, once again, e is the unique Euler number (approximately 2.718). For example, if an investment has an APR of 5% and interest is compounded continuously:

$$EAR = e^x - 1 = e^{0.05} - 1 = 5.127\%$$

Using a calculator, we click on the key for Euler's "e" (recall that this is often indicated as e^x), enter the exponent in decimal form, and then subtract one:

$$EAR = e^x - 1$$

Suppose you want to calculate the future value of $10 million invested five years at 6% interest, compounded continuously. The future value is:

$FV_5 = \$10 \text{ million } e^{0.05 \times 6}$

$FV_5 = \$10 \text{ million} \times e^{0.3}$

$FV_5 = \$10 \text{ million} \times 1.349859$

$FV_5 = \$13.49859 \text{ million}$

We calculate the present value with continuous compounding in a similar manner. Suppose you want to find today's value of $1,000 three years from now, with 5% interest, compounded continuously:

$$PV_0 = \frac{FV_3}{e^{i \times n}} = \frac{\$1,000}{1.161834} = \$860.7080$$

You perform this calculation in the calculator using the math function, e^x.

USING A SPREADSHEET FOR CONTINUOUS COMPOUNDING

Suppose you want to calculate the EAR in a spreadsheet for an APR of 5%. Using the spreadsheet function EXP and using "^–1" to invert $e^{i \times n}$, you enter:

$$=EXP(0.05)-1$$

which is 5.127%.

Applying this to a present value problem, calculating the present value of $1,000 to be received at the end of three years with an APR of 5%, continuously compounded:

$$=1000 * (EXP(3*0.05)^\wedge -1)$$

which is $860.7080. The "^" indicates an exponent. Taking something to the power of –1 is the same as taking the inverse.

A few observations about EAR and APR:

- If interest is compounded annually, the EAR is equal to the APR.
- If interest is compounded more frequently than once per year, the effective rate is higher than the quoted rate.
- The more frequent the compounding within a year, the greater is the difference between the EAR and the APR.
- The limit is continuous compounding: The largest difference between the EAR and the APR is when interest is compounded continuously.

EXAMPLE 5.11

Effective Annual Rates for Various Compounding Frequencies

PROBLEM

What are the effective annual rates for the following quoted rates?

A. 12%, compounded annually
B. 12%, compounded semi-annually
C. 12%, quarterly
D. 12%, monthly
E. 12%, daily
F. 12%, continuously

Solution

	Formula	*Calculator*	*Spreadsheet*	*Answer*
A.	$EAR = \left(1 + \dfrac{0.12}{1}\right)^{1} - 1$			12%
B.	$EAR = \left(1 + \dfrac{0.12}{2}\right)^{2} - 1$	NOM=12 P/PYR=2 *Solve for EFF*	=EFFECT(0.12,2)	12.36%
C.	$EAR = \left(1 + \dfrac{0.12}{4}\right)^{4} - 1$	NOM=12 P/PYR=4 *Solve for EFF*	=EFFECT(0.12,4)	12.55%
D.	$EAR = \left(1 + \dfrac{0.12}{12}\right)^{12} - 1$	NOM=12 P/PYR=12 *Solve for EFF*	=EFFECT(0.12,12)	12.68%
E.	$EAR = \left(1 + \dfrac{0.12}{365}\right)^{365} - 1$	NOM=12 P/PYR=365 *Solve for EFF*	=EFFECT(0.12,365)	12.747%
F.	$EAR = e^{0.12} - 1$	EXP or *e* 0.12 −1	=exp(.12)−1	12.75%

ETHICS | The Cost of Small Consumer Loans

Some borrowers do not have access to conventional loans from banks and instead resort to other loan arrangements, such as payday loans, car title loans, and refund anticipation loans. While these loans are easy to get, there is a very high cost to them. The Consumer Federation of America summarized the cost of unconventional loans:

- A payday loan is a loan for a week or two, until the borrower gets paid. The borrower writes a post-dated check for the amount borrowed plus interest and fees, which is then cashed by the lender at the loan due date. Payday loans may cost more than 500% in financing costs.

- Car title loans require you to hand over your car title if you do not repay the loan. Car title lending costs have an effective interest rate around 300%.

- Refund anticipated loans are generally related to anticipated tax refunds. The borrower borrows the expected amount of the refund, less commission and fees, and the lender receives the anticipated refund. Refund anticipation loans have effective interest of over 500%.

The Federal Deposit Insurance Company (FDIC) initiated a pilot program in February 2008 to encourage banks to make small loans that are affordable. After one year of this program, involving thirty-one banks, $18.5 million had been loaned through the 16,000 loans.

The new consumer protection agency, created by the Wall Street Reform and Consumer Financial Protection Act of 2010, is charged with overseeing the many forms of consumer lending arrangements, which may provide some degree of uniformity among states regarding payday loans, car title loans, and tax refund anticipation loans.

Sources: Consumer Federation of America, "Research Findings Illustrate the High Risk of High-Cost Short-term Loans for Consumers," February 18, 2009; FDIC Press Release, PR-52-2007: "FDIC Issues Final Guidelines on Affordable Small-Dollar Loans"; and "The FDIC's Small-Dollar Loan Pilot Program: A Case Study after One Year," FDIC Quarterly, 2009, Vol. 3, No. 2.

Concept Review Questions

1. At what frequency of compounding is the effective annual rate equal to the annual percentage rate? Explain your answer.

2. The Truth-in-Lending law in the U.S. requires lenders to disclose the APR for any loan transaction. Does the APR overstate or understate the true cost of a loan? Explain.

5.4 APPLICATIONS

Next, we apply some of the time value of money mathematics to a few examples to demonstrate the basic principles.

Comparing Alternative Savings Plans

Let us consider an example of two investors and the role of compound interest. Each investor follows one of two different investing approaches. Assume each investor earns a 5% annual return.

Investor A: Invests early

Investor A begins investing $2,302.37 per year (at year end) for six years, and then she makes no further contributions. She makes her first payment on her twenty-second birthday and therefore makes her last payment on her twenty-seventh birthday. Note that she invests the same amount each year, so this is an example of an annuity. How much money will she have when she turns sixty-five?

We perceive this as a two-part problem, which we can solve in several ways. One way to solve this is to estimate the future value of the payments as of the last payment and then compound this balance until Investor A turns sixty-five. To do this, we first estimate the future value of the six $2,302.37 payments at the end of six years, or at Investor A's twenty-seventh birthday:

Age	Investor A deposit	Investor A balance in account
22	$2,302.37	$2,302.37
23	$2,302.37	$4,719.86
24	$2,302.37	$7,258.22
25	$2,302.37	$9,923.50
26	$2,302.37	$12,722.04
27	$2,302.37	$15,660.51

Or

$$FV_{27} = PMT\left[\frac{(1 + i)^n - 1}{i}\right] = \$2,302.37\left[\frac{(1.05)^6 - 1}{0.05}\right]$$
$$= \$2,302.37 \times 6.8019 = \$15,660.51$$

Note that the first payment is made on Investor A's twenty-second birthday. Therefore, there have been six payments by the time of her twenty-seventh birthday: five that have earned interest, one that was just made on her twenty-seventh birthday that has not yet earned interest.

We estimate the future value of the accumulated savings after thirty-seven years (i.e., from Investor A's twenty-seventh birthday to her sixty-fifth birthday):

$$FV_{65} = PV_{27}(1 + i)^n = \$15,660.51 \times (1.05)^{38} = \$15,660.51 \times 6.3855 = \$100,000$$

In other words, Investor A will have \$100,000 saved by her sixty-fifth birthday.

Investor B: Delayed savings

At age twenty-two, Investor B postpones investing until he reaches age thirty-six, then he invests \$1,505.14 per year, starting on his thirty-sixth birthday, for thirty years, with his last payment on his sixty-fifth birthday. How much will he have when he turns sixty-five?

In the case of Investor B, the periodic payment is \$1,500, and there are thirty such payments:

$$FV_{65} = PMT\left[\frac{(1 + i)^n - 1}{i}\right] = \$1,505.14\left[\frac{(1.12)^{30} - 1}{0.12}\right] = \$1,505.14 \times 66.4388$$
$$= \$100,000$$

In other words, Investor B arrives at the same balance on his sixty-fifth birthday, but he got there by making thirty payments.

Investor A versus Investor B

In this example, we show how the compounding effect is magnified as the time horizon increases. You can see the difference in the accumulation of funds for the investors in Figure 5-4. By starting earlier, Investor A sets aside less than Investor B does but achieves the same result.

FIGURE 5-4   **The Balance in the Investment Accounts for Investor A and Investor B**

Loans and Mortgages

One common and important application of annuity concepts is with respect to loan or **mortgage** arrangements. Typically, these arrangements involve "blended" payments for equal amounts that include both an interest component and a principal repayment component. The loan payments are designed to **amortize** the loan, which means paying off a loan over time such that each payment made on the loan consists of principal repayment and interest.[20] In many amortized loans, the principal balance at the end of the loan term is zero. However, in some loans, a lump sum remains at the end of the loan term. We refer to this amount as the *balloon payment*.

Because these loans involve equal payments at regular intervals, based on one fixed interest rate specified when the loan is made, the payments can be viewed as annuities. Therefore, we can determine the amount of the payment, the effective period interest rate, and so on, by using Equation 5-5 and recognizing that the PV equals the amount of the loan.

The process of determining the interest and principal portions of each payment is **amortization**. An **amortization schedule** is a spreadsheet that details how much of each payment is interest and how much is principal, as well as how much of the loan balance remains outstanding after each payment. This is of importance to businesses and individuals, as the interest portion is a deductible expense for tax purposes. We calculate the interest portion by applying the effective period interest rate to the principal outstanding at the beginning of each period. The remaining portion of the payment reduces the amount of principal outstanding.

Consider an example of a three-year $5,000 loan with a 9.701% annual interest rate. To complete an amortization schedule, we first solve for amount of the payment, given:

PV = $5,000

$n = 3$

$i = 9.701\%$

Solving for the PMT using the formula, we find that the periodic payment is $2,000:

$$PMT = \frac{PV_0}{\left[\dfrac{1 - \dfrac{1}{(1 + i)^n}}{i}\right]} = \frac{5,000}{\left[\dfrac{1 - \dfrac{1}{(1.09701)^3}}{0.09701}\right]} = \frac{\$5,000}{2.5} = \$2,000$$

Using a financial calculator, and remembering to input the present value as a negative value,

FV = $0

PV = $5,000

$n = 3$

$i = 9.701\%$

Solve for PMT.

Using a spreadsheet function, PMT, we enter the interest rate, the number of payments, and the amount of the loan:

=PMT(0.09701,3,5000,0)

We can determine the loan amortization schedule based on the payment, the interest rate, the number of payments, and the amount of the loan. The loan is a simple annual

> **mortgage** loan, usually for real estate, that involves level, periodic payments consisting of interest and principal repayment over a specified payment period
>
> **amortize** determine the repayment of a loan in which regular payments consist of both interest and principal
>
> **amortization** process of determining how much of each payment is interest and principal repayment
>
> **amortization schedule** breakdown of each payment of an amortized loan into interest and principal components

---

[20] There are, of course, balloon loans, in which a specified lump sum is paid at the end of the loan period. In this case, a portion of the loan is amortized, and a portion of the loan is repaid as a lump sum at the end of the loan period.

payment loan, so the cost of the loan is the annual interest rate multiplied by the outstanding balance. For the first period, this is 9.07% multiplied by $5,000 or $453.50.

Payment	[1] Beginning principal	[2] Payment	[3] Interest $i \times [1]$	[4] Principal reduction $[2] - [3]$	[5] Ending principal $[1] - [4]$
1	$5,000.00	$2,000.00	$485.05	$1,514.95	$3,485.05
2	$3,485.05	$2,000.00	$338.08	$1,661.92	$1,823.13
3	$1,823.13	$2,000.00	$176.86	$1,823.14	− $0.01

This is the first charge on the loan payments; the residual, which is $1,514.95 in the first year, goes to reduce the amount of the loan. For the next year, the outstanding balance on the loan is now $3,485.05, and the interest of the loan goes down to $338.08, even though the payment is the same amount, $2,000. You can see this in Figure 5-5. As a result, the amount going toward the repayment of the loan increases to $1,661.92 with the second payment and to $1,823.14 with the third payment.

We can calculate the remaining loan balance, with P representing the number of payments that have been made, using:

$$\text{Remaining principal balance} = \frac{\text{Principal}\left[(1 + i)^N - (1 + i)^P\right]}{(1 + i)^N} \qquad (5\text{-}11)$$

So, after the first two payments are made, the remaining loan balance is:

$$\text{Remaining principal balance} = \frac{\$5,000\left[(1 + 0.09701)^3 - (1 + 0.09701)^2\right]}{(1 + 0.09701)^3 - 1} = \$1,823.14$$

In practice, loan repayments are often not made on an annual basis, with many calling for quarterly, monthly, or even weekly repayments. For these arrangements, we need to convert the quoted annual rates into effective period rates that correspond to the frequency of payments; in other words, we need to divide the APR by the number of payments in an annual period to determine i, and then n represents the number of payments over the life of the loan.

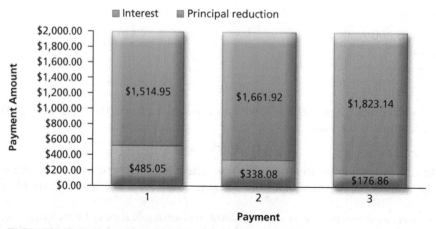

FIGURE 5-5 Interest and Principal Repayment in an Amortized Three-Year Loan of $5,000 with Interest of 9.701%

SPREADSHEET APPLICATIONS: AMORTIZING LOANS

Instead of working through the math ourselves, we could use some spreadsheet functions to determine the interest and principal paid with each payment:

=IPMT(i, payment number, number of periods, amount of loan)

=PPMT(i, payment number, number of periods, amount of loan)

For example, the interest paid with the second payment is:

=IPMT(0.097,A3,3,−5000)

and the principal paid with the second payment is:

=PPMT(0.097,A3,3,−5000)

The amortization formulas in the spreadsheet are therefore:[21]

	A	B	C	D	E	F
		Beginning				Ending
1	Period	principal	Payment	Interest	Principal reduction	Principal
2	1	5000	=PMT(0.1,3,−B2,0)	=IPMT(0.1,A2,3,−B2)	=PPMT(0.1,A2,3,−B2,0)	=B2−E2
3	2	=F2	=PMT(0.1,3,−B2,0)	=IPMT(0.1,A3,3,−B2)	=PPMT(0.1,A3,3,−B2,0)	=B3−E3
4	3	=F3	=PMT(0.1,3,−B2,0)	=IPMT(0.1,A4,3,−B2)	=PPMT(0.1,A4,3,−B2,0)	=B4−E4

Mortgages represent an example of a loan that requires that payments be made more frequently than annually. In fact, mortgage payments must be made at least monthly, but some may offer the opportunity to make biweekly or weekly payments.[22] The amortization of a mortgage is similar to the previous example.

Consider a mortgage of $200,000 that is to be repaid over 360 months. If the annual percentage rate on this mortgage is 6%, what are the monthly mortgage payments? The given information is the following:

PV = $200,000

$i = 6\% \div 12 = 0.5\%$

$n = 360$

Solving for the payment, using a financial calculator or spreadsheet, provides the answer $1,199.10.

Constructing an amortization schedule, we need to consider that unlike the simple annual payment loan, for which the cost of the loan is the annual interest cost, the cost here is the monthly interest rate of 6% ÷ 12 = 0.5% because we have a monthly amortization schedule. It is this monthly rate applied to the outstanding balance that determines how much of the mortgage's monthly payments represent the cost of the loan. As is clear from the amortization schedule, very little of the early payments go toward reducing the principal—most of the early payments are for interest. This is true for all long-term loans because, by definition, the repayment of the loan is being done over a long period. As time passes, the interest cost of the fixed payments continues to decrease, and the payment of principal correspondingly increases. The reason for this is simply that the interest rate is

---

[21] The $ next to the cell reference indicates that this is a fixed or absolute reference, so if you were to copy the function (e.g., PMT), it would still refer to the same cell for the principal amount of the loan—and would not change as other relative references change.

[22] As an example of further complications, consider mortgages in Canada. In Canada, mortgages are complicated by the fact that compounding is done on a semi-annual basis, even though payments are made at least monthly.

the cost of borrowing money, and this cost, based on the declining amount of principal that is owed, is subtracted first from the monthly payment—and what is left is used to repay some of the principal amount of the loan. But no matter what, the sum of the interest and principal payments is the amount of the payment.

We amortize this mortgage monthly, using the monthly payment of $1,199.10 and the monthly interest rate of 0.5% for the first five months:

	[1]	*[2]*	*[3]*	*[4]*	*[5]*
				Principal reduction	*Ending principal*
	Beginning		*Interest*		
Period	*principal*	*Payment*	*i × [1]*	*[2] – [3]*	*[1] – [4]*
1	$200,000.00	$1,199.10	$1,000.00	$199.10	$199,800.90
2	$199,800.90	$1,199.10	$999.00	$200.10	$199,600.80
3	$199,600.80	$1,199.10	$998.00	$201.10	$199,399.71
4	$199,399.71	$1,199.10	$997.00	$202.10	$199,197.61
5	$199,197.61	$1,199.10	$995.99	$203.11	$198,994.50

One question common to a mortgagee—that is, the borrower—would be how much of the loan would be retired after a certain time. We can solve this problem in the same method that we used for the last example, focusing on the ending principal, as compared with the original amount of the loan. In the case of any amortized loan, a high proportion of each of the early payments goes toward interest rather than principal reduction. You can see how the principal remaining on the mortgage falls more rapidly over time in Figure 5-6.[23]

balloon payment
payment that represents repayment of some amount of the principal of loan above and beyond what is paid as part of the amortized loan payments

Now let us see what happens if we introduce a balloon payment. A **balloon payment** is a payment that represents repayment of some amount of the principal of loan above and beyond what is paid as part of the amortized loan payments.

Suppose we have a 6% loan of $200,000 for thirty years, with monthly payments, and with a balloon payment of $50,000 at the end of thirty years. What is the monthly payment on this loan? The inputs are similar to our last example, but now we have a future value of $50,000 to consider:

PV = $200,000

FV = $50,000

$i = 6\% \div 12 = 0.5\%$

$n = 360$

The payment in this case is $1,149.326, less than the $1,199.10, with no balloon payment. You can see the difference in the rate of the loan repayment between the loans without

FIGURE 5-6 Principal Remaining on a Mortgage with Loan of $200,000, with Payments of $1,199.10, an Apr of 6%, and 360 Payments

[23] The balance remaining on the loan at any point in time is simply the present value of the remaining payments.

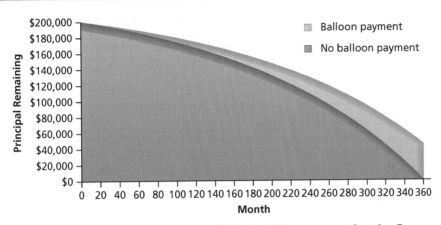

FIGURE 5-7 **Comparison of the Principal Repayment for the Loan of $200,000 at 6% for 360 Months, without and with a Balloon Payment of $50,000 at the End of the Loan Term**

and with the balloon payment in Figure 5-7. For a closer look, you can see the difference in amortization by examining the first six months of payments:

	No balloon payment payment is $1,199.10 per month			Balloon payment payment is $1,149.15 per month		
Month	Interest	Principal repayment	Remaining principal balance	Interest	Principal repayment	Remaining principal balance
1	$1,000	$199	$199,801	$1,000	$149	$199,851
2	$999	$200	$199,601	$999	$150	$199,701
3	$998	$201	$199,400	$999	$151	$199,550
4	$997	$202	$199,198	$998	$152	$199,398
5	$996	$203	$198,994	$997	$152	$199,246
6	$995	$204	$198,790	$996	$153	$199,093

Saving for Retirement

You are advising a client who plans on retiring thirty-five years from today. On retirement, the client wishes to have sufficient savings in his account to guarantee $48,000 each year for twenty years, with his retirement withdrawals beginning one year from his retirement date, for a total of twenty withdrawals. You estimate that at the time of his retirement, your client can sell his business for $200,000. You expect that interest rates will be relatively stable at 8% a year for the next thirty-five years. Thereafter, you expect interest rates to decline to 6%, forever. Suppose your client wishes to make equal, annual deposits at the end of each of the next thirty-five years, how much should he deposit each year to meet his stated objective?

We can visualize the problem using a timeline, using 0 to represent today, D to represent deposits, W to represent withdrawals, and B to represent the proceeds from the sale of the business:

Determine how much the client needs after thirty-five years

At this time, the client wants a twenty-year ordinary annuity of $48,000 because he will be drawing down funds beginning one year from retirement, at a 6% interest rate. In other words, find the PV of a twenty-year annuity, with $i = 6\%$.

$$PV_{35} = \$48,000 \left[\frac{1 - \dfrac{1}{(1.06)^{20}}}{0.06} \right] = \$48,000 \times 11.46992122 = \$550,556.22$$

Using a financial calculator:

   $FV = 0$
   $PMT = 48,000$
   $i = 6$
   $n = 20$
   Solve for PV.

Using a spreadsheet:

$$=PV(0.06,20,48000,0,0)$$

Your client needs to have $550,556.22 in savings thirty-five years from now so that he can begin to make withdrawals starting thirty-six years from today.[24]

Determine the amount of the periodic savings

In Step 1, it was determined that the client needs $550,556.22 saved thirty-five years from today so that he will have the $48,000 per year that he requires. Subtract the $200,000 you expect the client to get for his business, leaving the amount needed through his investments: $550,556.22 – 200,000 = $350,556.22.

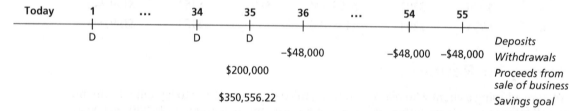

Determine the required year-end payments over the next 35 years

Once you determine the savings goal thirty-five years into the future, now you need to calculate the payment necessary to get there. Using the present value of an annuity formula, substituting the known values and solving for PMT, the payment is $2,034.37:

$$PMT = \frac{\$350,556.22}{\left[\dfrac{(1.08)^{35} - 1}{0.08} \right]} = \frac{\$350,556.22}{172.3168037} = \$2,034.37$$

[24] Why do we concern ourselves with thirty-five years from now when the first withdrawal is thirty-six years from now? We calculated the ordinary annuity of $48,000 per year for twenty years. This gave us a present value that is one year before the first cash flow (the assumption built into the math for an ordinary annuity). We could have alternatively calculated the present value of the annuity due as of thirty-six years from today, but then we would have to discount this one period to thirty-five years from now to line it up in time with the $200,000 of proceeds from the sale of the business.

Using a financial calculator:

PV = 0

FV = 350,556.22

$i = 8$

$n = 35$

Solve for PMT.

Using a spreadsheet:

$$=PMT(0.08,35,0,350556.22,0)$$

Therefore, we can represent the cash flows in the timeline:

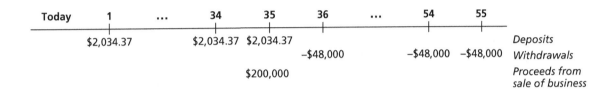

We can see the effects of savings, the business proceeds, and the withdrawals in Figure 5-8. In this figure, we see that the balance in savings:

- grows from both the deposits and the interest on the deposits;
- spikes upward when the business proceeds are received; and
- declines each year after Year 36 by less than the withdrawn amount because of the interest earned on the funds remaining in savings.

Note that this retirement problem appears complicated at first but is quite manageable if you break it down into steps. Timelines are very useful for this purpose because they help us visualize what information we have and what is needed to solve the problem. If you are able to solve these problems, then you have a good understanding of the basic concepts involving the time value of money.

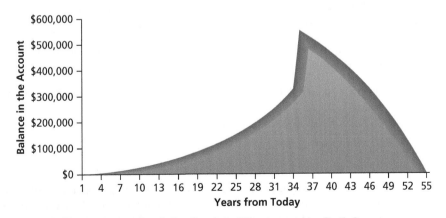

FIGURE 5-8 Growth of the Savings Necessary to Satisfy Retirement Needs

LESSONS LEARNED | I-O Mortgages

Leading up to the Housing Bubble that burst in 2007 and 2008, a popular form of mortgage was the interest-only mortgage, or I-O mortgage. This mortgage required the borrower to pay only the interest for a certain period, typically somewhere in the range of three to ten years, and then the payments were adjusted to pay off the loan, amortized for the remainder of the term of the mortgage.

Consider a $200,000 I-O mortgage that has an annual rate of 5% and requires monthly payments. The payments are I-O for the first ten years, and then the loan is amortized over Years 11 through 30.

The I-O mortgage requires payments of $833 for each month for the first ten years, and $1,319.91 thereafter. A comparable thirty-year, fully amortized mortgage requires a payment of $1,073.64. The payment of interest only means that there is no build-up of equity in the home, as there would be for the fully amortized mortgage: At the end of ten years, there is no equity in the case of an I-O mortgage but $37,316 for the traditional mortgage.

The sudden increase in the mortgage payments once the I-O period is over, combined with the lack of built-up equity, contributed to some of the woes of homeowners as the housing bubble burst.

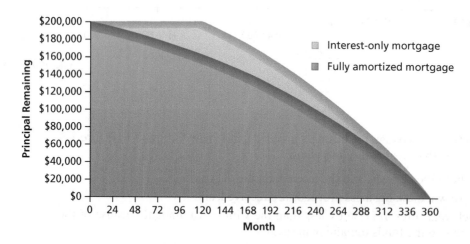

Sources: FDIC, "Interest-Only Mortgage Payments and Option-Payment ARMs," www.fdic.gov/consumers/consumer/interest-only/index. html; Guttentag, Jack, "Interest-only Loans: Not Magic, Usually Not Smart," moneycentral.msn.com/content/banking/homefinancing /p118084.asp; and Bernanke, Ben S. "Monetary Policy and the Housing Bubble," speech to the Annual Meeting of the American Economic Association, January 3, 2010.

Concept Review Questions

1. What are the basic calculation steps for determining how much of a given loan payment is toward interest and how much is toward principal?

2. How do you calculate the amount of principal remaining on a loan at any given point in time during the loan?

3. If a loan is amortized, what is the balance of the loan outstanding after the last payment is made?

SUMMARY

- By applying the process of compounding or discount at an appropriate rate of return, we can calculate economically equivalent values through time. For example, we can calculate the future value five years from now of an amount today. We can also determine the equivalent present value or future value for a series of cash flows.

- Annuities represent a special type of cash flow stream that involve equal payments at the same interval, with the same interest rate being applied throughout the period. We see that these kinds of cash flow streams are commonplace in finance applications (e.g., loan payments) and that there are relatively simple formulas that enable us to determine the present value or future value of such cash flows.

- It is possible to convert a stated rate (that is, the annual percentage rate) into an effective rate, which is important because compounding often takes place at other than annual intervals and the annual percentage rate understates the true, effective rate.

- Time value of money principles may be applied to a number of situations, including the personal finance decisions related to saving for retirement and home mortgage problems.

FORMULAS/EQUATIONS

(5-1) $FV_n = PV_0 + (n \times PV_0 \times i)$

(5-2) $FV_n = PV_0(1 + i)^n$

(5-3) $PV_0 = \dfrac{FV_n}{(1 + i)^n} = FV_n \times \left(\dfrac{1}{(1 + i)^n}\right)$

(5-4) $FV_n = PMT\left[\dfrac{(1 + i)^N - 1}{i}\right]$

(5-5) $PV_0 = PMT\left[\dfrac{1 - \dfrac{1}{(1 + i)^N}}{i}\right]$

(5-6) $FV_n = PMT\left[\dfrac{(1 + i)^N - 1}{i}\right](1 + i)$

(5-7) $PV_0 = PMT\left[\dfrac{1 - \dfrac{1}{(1 + i)^N}}{i}\right](1 + i)$

(5-8) $PV_0 = \dfrac{PMT}{i}$

(5-9) $EAR = \left(1 + \dfrac{APR}{m}\right)^m - 1$

(5-10) $EAR = e^{APR} - 1$

(5-11) Remaining principal balance
$$= \dfrac{Principal\left[(1 + i)^N - (1 + i)^P\right]}{(1 + i)^N - 1}$$

QUESTIONS AND PROBLEMS

Multiple Choice

1. If you invest $1,000 today in an account that pays 5% interest, compounded annually, the balance in the account at the end of ten years, if you make no withdrawals, is *closest* to:

    A. $613.91   B. $1,000.00   C. $1,500.00   D. $1,628.89

2. Which of the following has the largest future value if €1,000 is invested today?

    A. Ten years, with a simple annual interest rate of 8%

    B. Five years, with a simple annual interest rate of 12%

    C. Nine years, with a compound annual interest rate of 7%

    D. Eight years, with a compound annual interest rate of 8%

3. Suppose you deposit $10,000 in an account that pays interest of 4% per year, compounded annually. After five years, the interest paid on interest is *closest* to:

    A. $166.53   B. $200.00   C. $2,000.00   D. $2,166.53

4. Suppose an investor wants to have ¥10 million to retire forty-five years from now. The amount that she would have to invest today with an annual rate of return equal to 15% is closest to:

    A. ¥16,140   B. ¥18,561   C. ¥21,345

5. Maggie deposits £10,000 today and is promised £17,000 in eight years. The implied annual rate of return is *closest* to:

   A. 4.36%   B. 6.07%   C. 6.86%   D. 7.88%

6. To triple $1 million, HFund invested today by using an annual rate of return of 9%. The length of time it will take HFund to achieve its goal is *closest* to:

   A. 8.04 years   B. 12.75 years   C. 16.09 years

7. Jan plans to invest an equal amount of $2,000 in an equity fund every year end, beginning this year. The expected annual return on the fund is 10%. She plans to invest for twenty years. The amount she expects to have at the end of twenty years is *closest* to:

   A. $13,455   B. $102,318   C. $114,550

8. Which of the following credit terms has the highest effective annual rate?

   A. 9¾%, compounded daily
   B. 9.9%, compounded monthly
   C. 9.7%, compounded continuously
   D. 9.8%, compounded every other day

9. The present value of a perpetuity with an annual year-end payment of €1,500 and expected annual rate of return equal to 12% is *closest* to:

   A. €11,400   B. €12,500   C. €13,500   D. €14,000

10. Consider a mortgage loan of $200,000, to be amortized over thirty years with monthly payments. If the annual percentage rate on this mortgage is 6%, the amount of principal and interest in the second month's mortgage payment is closest to:

    A. Principal repayment is $199.10, and interest paid is $1,000.
    B. Principal repayment is $200.10, and interest paid is $999.00.
    C. Principal repayment is $2,529.78, and interest paid is $12,000.
    D. Principal repayment is $2,497.78, and interest paid is $11,848.21.

Practice Problems and Questions

5.1 Time Is Money

11. What is simple interest?

12. Explain how you would calculate the interest-on-interest on an investment.

13. What is the present value of $200,000, discounted five years at 9%?

14. What is the future value of $200,000, compounded five years at 9%?

15. What is the future value of £1,000 invested thirty years at:

    A. 8%, compounded annually?
    B. 8%, compounded quarterly?
    C. 8%, compounded continuously?

16. Consider a company that invests $100,000 in an investment that is expected to earn 4% interest per year, which is reinvested in the investment.

    A. What is the value of this investment at the end of four years?
    B. Using the time-line below, complete the timeline by indicating the value of the investment at the end of each year in the appropriate box:

17. Suppose you invest $10,000 today and your investment earns interest at 6% for each of the first two years and 5% for the next two years.

A. What is your investment worth four years from today?

B. Diagram the value of this investment using the following timeline, inserting the value of the investment at the end of each year in the appropriate box:

C. What is the amount of interest that you have earned on your investment each year?

D. What is the amount of interest-on-interest that you earn on your investment over the life of the investment?

18. Complete the following table:

	Present Value	Number of Periods	Interest Rate per Year	Future Value
A.	$100	5	6%	
B.	$1,000	5	6%	
C.	$500	2	2%	
D.	$2,000	10	1.50%	
E.	$3,000	4	4%	

19. Complete the following table:

	Future Value	Number of Periods	Discount Rate per Year	Present Value
A.	$100	5	6%	
B.	$1,000	5	6%	
C.	$500	2	2%	
D.	$2,000	10	1.50%	
E.	$3,000	4	4%	

20. Complete the following table:

	Present Value	Future Value	Number of Periods	Interest Rate per Year
A.	$100	$200	5	
B.	$100	$300		6%
C.	€1,000		5	10%
D.		$30,000	6	7%
E.	$6,000		3	3%

21. An investment adviser promises that you will triple your money in 10 years with Investment A. A comparable investment, Investment B, has a return of 12% per year. Which investment has the highest return?

22. How many years will it take for an investment to double in value if the rate of return is 9%, and compounding occurs:

A. annually?   B. quarterly?

23. How many years will it take for a balance in a savings account to triple if the interest on the account is 5% a year, compounded continuously?

24. Suppose a company invests $1 million today, and expects this investment to grow in value at the rate of 8% for the first two years, 9% for the next two years, and 7% for the two years after that.

   A. What is this investment expected to be worth in six years?

   B. Calculate and graph the growth in the value of the investment for the six years.

5.2   Annuities and Perpetuities

25. What distinguishes an annuity due from an ordinary annuity?

26. Suppose you have a client who would like a plan for saving for her retirement. She would like to begin saving an amount each year, starting in five years, to provide for her retirement that she plans in thirty years. Her goal is to save $2 million thirty years from today and then live off of her savings for the twenty years after her retirement.

   A. Draw a timeline for this client.

   B. How would you determine how much she needs to save each year to meet her goal? Explain your method.

   C. How would you determine how much she would have to spend each year in retirement? Explain your method.

27. Of the present value of an ordinary annuity and the present value of an annuity due, which has the same number of discount periods as payments?

28. Consider an ordinary annuity consisting of five annual payments of $1,000 each.

   A. As long as the interest rate is greater than or equal to 0%, what is the largest that the present value can be?

   B. As long as the interest rate is greater than or equal to 0%, what is the smallest that the future value can be?

   C. Explain your reasoning for each.

29. Without performing a calculation, select and explain your selection for which of the following will be the larger value for a given number of periods, periodic amount, and interest rate:

- Present value of the ordinary annuity
- Present value of the annuity due
- Future value of the ordinary annuity
- Future value of the annuity due

30. For each of the following, match the loan type with the financial math approach to analyze the problem:

Loan Arrangement	Financial Math Approach
A. Lottery winnings, paid in twenty annual instalments, beginning when the winning ticket is turned in.	1. Present value of an ordinary annuity
B. Mortgage payments, made at the end of each month for thirty years.	2. Present value of an annuity due
	3. Future value of an ordinary annuity
C. Three-year subscription to a magazine, paid as a lump sum at the beginning of the three years.	4. Future value of an annuity due
	5. Present value of a lump-sum
D. Parents set aside $10 at the end of month to save $60,000 for their child's college education.	6. Future value of a lump-sum
E. Rent of $450 per month, paid at the beginning of each month.	

31. Consider an ordinary annuity of $100 per year, for four years. Assume that the appropriate interest rate for valuing this annuity is 7%.

   A. Complete the following timeline, indicating the following:
   - Cash flows
   - Present value of the annuity
   - Future value of the annuity

   B. What is the relationship (mathematically) between the present and future values?

32. Complete the following table:

	Payment per Year	Number of Years	Interest Rate per Year	Future Value
A.	$100	5	3%	
B.	$500	6	4%	
C.	$1,000	10	8%	
D.	$450	12	3%	
E.	$10,000	4	4%	

33. Complete the following table:

	Payment per Year	Number of Years	Interest Rate per Year	Present Value
A.	$200	10	3%	
B.	$200	4	4%	
C.	$250	5	10%	
D.	$30,000	3	5%	
E.	$2,100	10	4%	

34. A magazine publisher offers its customers three options on subscriptions:

   Option 1: $50 today for three years.

   Option 2: A two-year rate of $38 paid immediately, followed by a one-year rate of $17 paid at the beginning of the third year.

   Option 3: $17 paid at the beginning of each of the three years.

   A. From the perspective of the company, which option is best if the company's opportunity cost of funds is 8%? Explain.

   B. From the perspective of the subscriber, which option is best in terms of minimizing the cost of subscription if the subscriber's opportunity cost of funds is 5%? Explain.

5.3 Nominal and Effective Rates

35. Under what circumstances, if any, will the annual percentage rate on a loan arrangement be equal to the loan's effective annual rate?

36. If you are a manager at a bank and want to calculate the advertised APR for what the bank is willing to pay, on an effective annual rate basis, how would you go about calculating this APR? Explain your method.

37. Complete the following table:

	Annual Percentage Rate (APR)	Compounding Frequency	Effective Annual Rate (EAR)
Bank V	12%	monthly	
Bank W	5%	semi-annual	
Bank X	8%	continuous	
Bank Y	10%	semi-annual	
Bank Z	5%	quarterly	

38. A credit card company advertises interest rates of 15% on unpaid balances. If interest is compounded daily, what is the effective interest rate that the credit card company charges?

39. Bank A pays 7.25% interest compounded semi-annually, Bank B pays 7.20% compounded quarterly, and Bank C pays 7.15% compounded monthly. Which bank pays the highest effective annual rate on its certificates of deposit?

40. Calculate the effective annual rates for the following:
    A. 24%, compounded daily
    B. 24%, compounded quarterly
    C. 24%, compounded every four months
    D. 24%, compounded semi-annually
    E. 24%, compounded continuously

41. The return on a stock for the most recent quarter was 2%. Suppose this stock is expected to earn 2% each quarter for the rest of the year.
    A. What is the return, stated in terms of an annual percentage rate?
    B. What is the return, stated in terms of an effective annual rate?

42. The Big-Bank would like to pay, effectively, 3% per year, on its preferred checking accounts. What APR must Big-Bank advertise for this account if the interest is compounded monthly? continuously?

5.4   Applications

43. Google, Inc., traded at $100.01 per share on September 3, 2004. On September 3, 2010, Google stock traded at $470.03 per share. What is the average annual return on this stock over this period if Google did not pay dividends? *[Hint: The share price in 2004 is the present value; the share price in 2010 is the future value.]*

44. Roger has his eye on a new car that will cost $20,000. He has $15,000 in his savings account, earning interest at a rate of 0.5% per month.
    A. How long will it be before he can buy the car?
    B. How long will it be before Roger can buy the car if, in addition to savings, he can save $250 per month?

45. Consider a $200,000 10-year loan with an interest rate of 12%, compounded monthly. Payments on the loan are made monthly.
    A. What is the monthly payment required for this loan?
    B. What is the outstanding loan amount after six months.

46. The Athens Company has been awarded a settlement in a lawsuit that that will pay $2.5 million one year from now. However, the company really needs the money today and has decided to take out a loan. If the bank charges an interest rate of 8%, how much can the Athens Company borrow so that the settlement will just pay off the loan?

47. Johann started a small business and was too busy to consider saving for retirement. He sold the business for $600,000, and these proceeds will comprise his retirement savings. If he can invest this total sum and earn 10% per year, how much will his investment be worth in five years? In ten years?

48. Knox Villas has been forced to borrow money to get through the tough economy this year. If the loan is for $2 million at an interest rate of 7%, with payments of interest and principal each year, how much must Knox Villas pay each year if the loan is to be paid off in three years, with end-of-year, equal payments?

49. Jack is 28 years old now and plans to retire in thirty-five years. He works in a local bank and has an annual income of $45,000. His expected annual expenditure is $36,000, and the rest of his income will be invested at the beginning of each of the next thirty-five years (with the first payment on his twenty-ninth birthday) at an expected annual rate of return of 5%. What amount will Jack have saved when he retires if he never gets a raise?

50. Shawna just turned twenty-one years old and currently has no investments. She plans to invest €5,500 at the end of each of the next eight years, starting with her twenty-second birthday. The rate of return on her investment is 4%, continuously compounded.
    A. What will be the balance in her investment account when she makes the last of the eight payments?
    B. Suppose she has an alternative investment, but with similar risk, that can produce a return of 4.2%, compounded annually. Which investment plan should she select?

51. After a summer of travelling (and not working), a student finds himself $1,500 short for this year's tuition fees. His parents have agreed to loan him the money at a simple interest rate of 6%.
    A. How much interest will he owe his parents after one year?
    B. How much will he owe, in total, if he waits to pay for three years?

52. Public corporations have no fixed lifespan; as such, they are often viewed as entities that will pay dividends to their shareholders in perpetuity. Suppose KashKow Inc. pays a dividend of $2 per share every year.
    A. If the discount rate is 12%, what is the present value of all the future dividends?
    B. KashKow Inc. has just declared that its dividend next year will be $3 per share. That rate of payment will continue for an additional four years, after which, the dividends will fall back to their usual $2 per share. What is the present value of all the future dividends?

53. On the advice of a friend, Gilda invests $20,000 in a mutual fund that has earned 10% per year, on average, in recent years. Your own investment research turned up another interesting mutual fund that you recommend to Gilda, which has had an average annual return fifty basis points greater than the one her friend recommended. If she had taken your advice, how much more would her investment be worth after:
    A. one year?
    B. five years?
    C. ten years?

54. To start a new retail guitar business, Keith Richards has three opportunities to borrow the needed $25,000 of funds.
    A. The Local Bank asks him to repay the loan in five equal, end-of-year installments of $6,935.24. What is the bank's effective annual interest rate on the loan transaction?
    B. The Business Development Bank is willing to loan Keith the $25,000 he needs to start his new business. The loan will require monthly payments of $556.11 over five years. What is the effective annual rate on this loan?
    C. The Balloon Bank is willing to offer Keith a loan that has five equal end-of-year installments of $5,000 and a balloon payment of $13,000 along with the last payment. What is the effective annual rate on this loan?
    D. Which is the better deal for Keith, and why?

55. Consider a $50 million loan that is amortized over four years, with end-of-year payments of $19.4 million each.
    A. What is the effective rate of interest on this loan?

B. Complete the amortization table, with table entries in millions of dollars:

Year	Beginning-of-Year Loan Balance	Payment	Interest	Principal Repayment	End-of-Year Loan Balance
1	$50.000				
2					
3					
4					$0.000

56. The fund manager can choose between two investments that have the same cost today. Both investments will ultimately pay $1,300 but at different times, as shown in the table below. If the fund manager does not choose one of these investments, she could leave the funds in a bank account paying 5% per year.

Year	Investment A	Investment B
1	$0	$200
2	$500	$400
3	$800	$700

A. Which investment should she choose?

B. If the cost of each investment is $1,000, should the fund manager invest in one of them, or simply leave the money in the bank account? Would her decision change if the investments instead cost $1,200 each?

C. Suppose the investments cost $1,000. Determine the rate of return on each. If the fund manager can only choose one of them, which should it be?

57. The following calculation explanation was abstracted from a web site, showing how the total interest on a mortgage is calculated:[25]

"Using your principal and interest (P&I) payment, multiply it by 360 payments, which is thirty years of payments.

Example: $100,000 loan for thirty years at a 5% interest rate will create a $536.82 monthly payment. (This amount does not include taxes or homeowners insurance.) Multiply $536.82 by 360 months. It equals $193,255.20.

Subtract the loan amount from the total you arrive at in Step 1. In the example above, you would subtract $100,000 from $193,255.20, ending with $93,255.20. This represents the amount of interest that is paid over a thirty-year amortized loan, which is commonly how mortgage principal and interest (P&I) is paid."

A. Verify these calculations. Are they correct?

B. Create an amortization table in a spreadsheet for this mortgage, for all 360 months, using the following headings:

Payment	Interest	Principal Repayment	Principal Balance Remaining

C. Do these calculations consider the time value of money? Explain.

58. Suppose you deposit $100,000 in an account today. And suppose you can earn 4% interest per year on the principal amount and earn 2% interest on any interest earned on interest.

A. Create a worksheet using a spreadsheet program to calculate how much will you have in the account at the end of five years.

---

[25] Joey Campbell, "How to Calculate Interest Paid Over the Life of a Mortgage," *eHow Money*, www.ehow.com/how_6216640_calculate-paid-over-life-mortgage.html, accessed July 17, 2011.

B. Graph the balance in the account, separating the interest earned on the principal from the interest earned on interest.

Cases

Case 5.1 Saving for Retirement, Considering Different Scenarios

Suppose you are advising a client, Arturo, who is planning for his retirement and wants to have $1 million by the time he retires at age sixty. And suppose you want to lay out alternative savings plans for different return scenarios:

Scenario 1: Steady state
Earns 8% on all funds invested.

Scenario 2: Declining returns
Earns 8% each year for the first five years, 6% for the next five years, and 4% thereafter.

Scenario 3: Increasing returns
Earns 8% each year for the first five years, 10% for the next five years, and 12% thereafter.

Scenario 4: Varying returns
Earns 8% each year for the first five years, 6% for the next five years, and 10% thereafter.

Address the following requirements:

1. Using a spreadsheet program, calculate and graph the balance in savings up to Arturo's sixtieth birthday if he saves $3,000 each year, starting on his twenty-first birthday, under each scenario. His last deposit is on his sixtieth birthday.

2. Suppose your client estimates that once he turns eighty years old, he will need only $48,000 per year for nursing home costs; to simplify, assume payable at the end of the year. Assume that once he retires on his sixtieth birthday, he shifts all of his investments to CDs with a fixed interest rate of 3% per year.

   A. If Arturo plans to live until his ninetieth birthday and leave nothing in his estate, how much is available under each scenario to withdraw from his savings each year starting at his sixty-first birthday until he enters the nursing home? His last withdrawal before the nursing home is on his eightieth birthday.

   B. Calculate and graph the balance in Arturo's savings up through his ninetieth year under each scenario.

Case 5.2 Evaluating an Investment

The Bridgewater Gazebo Company is evaluating a new line of outdoor living outbuildings to add to its successful gazebo line. The expanded manufacturing facilities would cost $1.2 million, but they expect to be able to generate cash flows from this new line that would justify this cost. The current estimates from the project manager, expecting that nearby competitors, such as Yoder Buildings, will enter this line within five years, are the following:

Year	End of Year Cash Flows
1	$100,000
2	$500,000
3	$300,000
4	$300,000
5	$100,000
6 and beyond	$50,000

The discount rate that Bridgewater Gazebo uses to evaluate future cash flows is 8%. *[Hint: The cash flows for Year 6 and beyond are a perpetuity.]*

A. What is the present value of the cash flows on this new line?

B. Should Bridgewater Gazebo enter this line of business? Explain your recommendation.

C. What would be your recommendation if Bridgewater Gazebo used 10% to discount its future cash flows?

D. What would be your recommendation if Bridgewater Gazebo used 12% to discount its future cash flows?

CHAPTER 6

DEBT VALUATION AND INTEREST RATES

At the end of 2010, corporations had over $7.5 trillion of debt outstanding. Because common stock never matures, yet bonds do, many corporations must issue bonds frequently. In 2010, corporations issued four times more debt than equity:

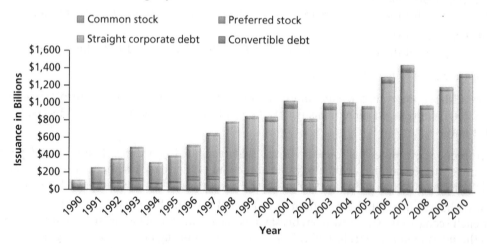

We can see the effect of the credit crunch in 2008 on debt issuance. In 2007, corporations issued over $1.1 trillion of straight corporate debt, whereas in 2008 corporations issued a little over $0.7 trillion in debt. However, the recovery, along with record lower interest rates, encouraged corporate borrowing in both 2009 and 2010.

Source of data: *Securities Industry and Financial Markets Association.*

Learning Outcomes

After reading this chapter, you should be able to:

LO 6.1 Explain the basic features of different types of debt obligations.

LO 6.2 Value debt when given an appropriate discount rate, and explain and demonstrate how bond prices change over time.

LO 6.3 Calculate the yield on a straight bond, a zero-coupon bond, and a callable bond.

LO 6.4 Describe the various government securities, and calculate the value and the yield on Treasury bills.

LO 6.5 List and briefly describe the factors affecting yields on debt securities.

192

Chapter Preview We introduced the basic time value of money concepts in an earlier chapter, and in this chapter we discuss debt securities, which provide investors with predetermined future cash flows. As such, the analysis of bonds provides an important application of compounding and discounting.

6.1   THE BASICS OF BONDS

A **debt** is a promise by the borrower to repay the amount borrowed, plus interest. Interest on the debt may be periodic, such as paid every six months, or it may all be paid at the debt's maturity along with the principal repayment. We often refer to long-term debt instruments that promise fixed payments to their investors generically as bonds, but to be accurate, we should really use specific terms, depending on the maturity of the debt instrument. A short-term debt obligation with an initial maturity less than 1 year is a **bill** or **paper**; a debt obligation with a maturity between 1 and 7 years is a **note**; and a debt obligation with a term longer than 7 years is a **bond**. Because we value these instruments in the same manner (that is, discounting promised cash flows), we often simply refer to these debt obligations as bonds in our discussion.

The bond market is an important part of the capital market and a major source of financing for companies, as well as for governments and financial institutions. For example, over $1 trillion of bonds were issued in U.S. markets in 2010 by corporations, but only $240 billion in common stock were issued in the same year.[1] Understanding the topics covered in this chapter will deepen your knowledge of how to apply the tools of valuation as well as your familiarity with financial securities.

The key feature of a bond is that the borrower typically agrees to pay the lender a regular series of cash payments, and to repay the full principal amount—that is, the amount borrowed—by the maturity date. We often refer to the borrower as the **issuer** of the bond and the lender or creditor as the **bondholder**. These promises are stipulated in the bond contract and are a fixed contractual commitment. Though many payment structures are possible, the traditional bond provides for identical payments at regular intervals (usually semi-annually or annually), with the full principal to be repaid at the stated maturity date.

We refer to the interest payment as a **coupon** because at one time bonds literally had coupons attached to them, and the investor had to cut the coupon from the bond certificate and send it for payment.[2] Today, almost all bonds are registered, and the payments are made electronically into individual bank accounts, providing a record of who has paid and who has received the interest. Unlike an amortized loan, such as a mortgage, the principal amount of the bond is paid at maturity.[3]

As we have noted, the typical bond is the debt obligation in which the issuer pays interest periodically and then pays the principal amount at maturity along with the last interest payment. We refer to this type of bond as a **straight bond** or a **straight coupon bond**. However, for some bonds the issuer does not commit to paying interest, but rather the bond is sold at discount from its face value. A bond that pays no interest is a **zero-coupon bond** or **zero-coupon note** (or **zero**), which is issued at a discount and repays the face value at the maturity date. The return earned on a zero-coupon bond or note represents the difference between the purchase price and the redemption price. The lower the price paid for the bond, the higher the return. Zero-coupon notes and bonds were initially

debt promise by the borrower to repay the amount borrowed, plus interest

bill or **paper** short-term debt instruments with an initial maturity of less than 1 year

note debt instruments with initial maturities between 1 and 7 years

bond long-term debt instrument in which the borrower promises repayment, usually with interest, with an initial maturity longer than 7 years

issuer party that receives funds in exchange for a security, such as a bond

bondholder party that lends funds by buying a bond issued by another party

coupon interest payment from a note or bond

straight bond or **straight coupon bond** debt obligation that commits the issuer to pay a fixed amount of interest periodically, and then repay the principal amount at maturity

zero-coupon bond or **zero-coupon note** (or **zero**) debt obligation issued at a discount from its face value, pays no coupons, and repays the face value at the maturity date

---

[1] It is true, however, that retained earnings (and, hence, equity) is a major source of funds for corporation. But in terms of investment banking activity in raising capital for corporations, more than four times the amount of bonds are issued compared to equity. This is due, in part, to the fact that equity never matures, yet bonds mature and corporations therefore refinance by issuing additional bonds.

[2] The coupons were attached to the bond and could be mailed in by whoever had the bond. Such bonds were called *bearer bonds* and are still widely used in parts of the world where personal tax rates are high.

[3] In general, when the principal payment is made in one lump sum at maturity, it is called a bullet payment or balloon payment.

where PMT is the periodic interest payments and FV is the principal repayment

FIGURE 6-1 The Cash Flow Pattern for a Traditional Coupon-Paying Bond

created by financial intermediaries who purchased traditional bonds, "stripped" the cash flows (both the interest and the principal repayment components) from them, and sold the cash flows separately. Today, most zeroes are created this way; however, some are also initially issued as zero-coupon securities.[4]

Bonds are referred to as fixed income securities because the interest payments and the principal repayment are often specified or fixed at the time the bond is issued. In most cases the bond purchaser knows the amount and timing of the future cash payments to be received, barring default by the issuer. However, if the buyer decides to sell the bond before maturity, the price received depends on the level of interest rates at that time.

We depict the typical pattern of cash payments for a semi-annual pay bond using a timeline in Figure 6-1. In the case of a semi-annual pay bond, interest is paid at the end of every six months. We represent the periodic interest or coupon as PMT, and the face value of the bond as FV.

Two things are obvious from Figure 6-1. First, the structure of the payments differs from that of the loan or mortgage because those involve payments consisting of both interest and principal components. In contrast, a typical bond has interest payments throughout its life and a principal repayment at maturity. You can see this in Figure 6-2, where we compare the interest paid on a $1 million loan: If the loan is amortized, you see the pattern in Panel A, and if the loan is a bond, you see the pattern in Panel B. In the case of the amortized loan, principal is paid off over time, whereas in the case of the bond the principal is paid off at the bond's maturity.

Second, we can view a bond as two separate components: an annuity consisting of the identical and regular interest payments, plus a lump-sum principal payment at maturity. In this way, valuing a traditional bond becomes a straightforward application of the time value of money concepts.[5]

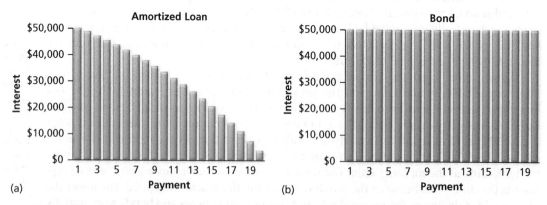

FIGURE 6-2 Comparison of Interest on a 20-Year, $1 Million Amortized Loan and a Bond, both with Annual Payments and 5 Percent Interest

---

[4] Zeroes are very popular with financial institutions, which often use them for hedging purposes with respect to their outstanding liabilities. Zeroes are ideally suited for this purpose because, unlike traditional bonds, there are no issues with respect to reinvesting interest payments that are received before maturity.

[5] A coupon bond can be stripped into its coupon and principal components, and these two cash flow streams can be sold separately: The principal portion becomes a zero-coupon bond, whereas the coupon portion becomes an interest-only (IO) security.

Bond Terminology

Before discussing how to value bonds, we introduce some of the terminology and institutional features attached to different types of bonds. Most bonds are sold to a number of investors, and someone must make sure that the payments are made on time. This problem is solved by including all relevant details for a particular bond issue in a **bond indenture**, or **indenture agreement**, that is held and administered by a trust company. This is a legal document that specifies the payment requirements, all other salient matters relating to the issue (such as any assets that might serve as security or **collateral** for the bond), any protective provisions, and other additional features. The trust company then makes sure that these covenant provisions are observed by the issuer.

The **par value** (or **face value** or **maturity value**) represents the amount that is paid at maturity for traditional bonds. The par value of most bonds is $1,000, though bond prices are typically quoted based on a par value of 100. In other words, if the price of a bond is quoted at 99.583, a $1,000 par value bond would be selling for $995.83. The time remaining to the maturity date is the **term to maturity** of the bond. The regular **interest payment** (or **coupon**) is determined by multiplying the **coupon rate** (which is stated on an annual basis) by the par value of the bond. For example, a bond with a coupon rate of 6 percent and a par value of $1,000 would pay coupons of $60 if they are paid annually, or $30 every six months if they are paid semi-annually. Most U.S. corporate bonds pay interest semi-annually; that is, every six months.

Security and Protective Provisions

Though the term is used loosely to encompass many types of debt securities, technically bonds are debt obligations secured by real assets. A bond secured by real property is a **mortgage bond**, and a bond secured by a pledge of other financial assets, such as common shares, bonds, or Treasury bills, is a **collateral trust bond**.

An **equipment trust certificate** is secured by equipment, such as the rolling stock of a railway (that is, vehicles, such as train cars, that move along the railway); the assets pledged as security are owned by investors through a lease agreement with the railway until the loan has been retired. The certificates have serial numbers that dictate their maturity date, with a certain amount maturing every year.

However, not all bonds are secured by real property. For example, a **debenture** is a debt obligation that is not secured by specific asset, but rather is secured by a general claim on the company's unencumbered assets, that is, those assets that have not been pledged as security for other debt obligations. Government bonds are debentures because no specific security is pledged as collateral; however, they are referred to as bonds as a matter of convention.

The indenture agreement is the contract between the issuer of the bond and the bondholders. This agreement not only details the payment schedule and amounts, but also may contain covenants that protect the investor. A **protective covenant** is any clause in the bond indenture that restricts the actions of the issuer. A **negative covenant** prohibits certain actions; for example, a company may be restricted from making a dividend payment larger than a certain amount or prevented from pledging its assets to another lender. A **positive covenant** specifies actions that the company agrees to undertake, for example, to provide quarterly financial statements or maintain certain working capital levels.

Credit Ratings

Credit-rating firms perform detailed analyses of bond issuers and issues to determine the likelihood that the issuer will make the payments of interest and principal repayments on a debt obligation when promised. In the U.S., these firms are known as

---

bond indenture or **indenture agreement** legal document that specifies the payment requirements and all other salient matters relating to a particular bond issue, held and administered by a trust company

collateral assets that can serve as security for the bond in case of default

par value or **face value** or **maturity value** amount paid at maturity for traditional bonds

term to maturity time remaining to the maturity date

interest payment or **coupon** amount paid on a bond at regular intervals

coupon rate percentage of a bond or note's face value that is paid in interest each year

mortgage bond debt instrument that is secured by real assets

collateral trust bond bond secured by a pledge of other financial assets, such as common shares, bonds, or Treasury bills

equipment trust certificate type of debt instrument secured by equipment, such as the rolling stock of a railway

debenture debt instrument secured by a general claim on the issuer's unencumbered assets

protective covenant clause in a bond indenture that restrict the actions of the issuer; covenants can be positive or negative

negative covenant clause in a bond indenture that prohibits certain actions by the issuer

positive covenant clause in a bond indenture that requires specific actions by the issuer

Nationally Recognized Statistical Rating Organizations (NRSROs) credit rating firms that are registered with the U.S. Securities and Exchange Commission

Nationally Recognized Statistical Rating Organizations (NRSROs) and are registered with the Securities and Exchange Commission.[6] The largest NRSROs are Standard & Poor's (S&P), Moody's, and Fitch, but thanks to changes in the regulation of NRSROs, the field has widened and includes DBRS, Ltd.; A. M. Best Company, Inc.; and Kroll Bond Rating Agency, among others. The issuer of a debt obligation contracts with one or more of these NRSROs for a rating based on the creditworthiness of the issuer, tempered by the features of the debt obligation. For example, it is possible for two debt obligations of the same issuer to have different ratings if the issues have different features (e.g., seniority, collateral).

debt rating evaluation by professional debt-rating services after detailed analyses of bond issuers to determine their ability to make the required interest and principal payments

The NRSRO assigns a **debt rating** to a debt obligation to reflect its judgment regarding the issuer's ability to satisfy the promised obligations (that is, interest and principal) when promised. NRSROs use a classification system starting with the highest-rated debt, AAA or Aaa, and then lesser ratings are AA or Aa, A, BBB or Baa, and so on. We provide the debt-rating categories for S&P and Moody's in Figure 6-3.[7]

investment-grade debt debt obligation with a credit rating of AAA, AA, A or BBB (or Aaa, Aa, A, Baa)

Investment-grade debt is debt with a rating at or above BBB (Standard & Poor's and Fitch Ratings), Baa (Moody's), or higher; in other words, investment-grade debt comprises the top four major classes. **Speculative debt** has a credit rating below investment grade; if a rated bond is not investment grade, then it is speculative. Other names for speculative debt include **high-yield debt**, **junk bond**, or **low-grade debt**.

speculative debt or **high-yield debt** or **junk bond** or **low-grade debt** debt that is not investment grade; debt rated below BBB or Baa

These ratings may be modified to indicate the relative ranking within a category, either using numbers or other symbols in addition to the letters (e.g., A1 or A+). This is particularly useful in distinguishing debt in classifications in which there are a large number of debt obligations.

Why have an issue evaluated by a credit-rating firm? Because many investors either want to have or are required to have a third-party assessment of the creditworthiness of the debt. For example, many pension funds are restricted to investing in investment-grade debt. Is all debt rated? No, some issuers will place an issue directly with an investor and need not have the issue rated if the investor does not require it.

FIGURE 6-3 **Debt-Rating Categories for Standard & Poor's and Moody's**

Source: *Standard & Poor's, www.standardandpoors.com; Moody's, www.moodys.com.*

[6] As of this writing, there were ten NRSROs.
[7] Rating systems are similar for other rating agencies, such as Fitch. For example, S&P uses AAA for the top-rated bonds, whereas Moody's uses Aaa.

SEC Rules Take Aim at Credit Rating Agencies | ETHICS

As evidenced in the hearings on credit rating agencies in the 2007–2008 financial crisis, there were some problems in the process of credit rating that may have exacerbated the financial crisis:[8]

- An inherent conflict of interest when issuers can "shop" for ratings among the different credit rating agencies.
- A problem when the rating agencies provided advice to those parties creating some structured finance instruments (e.g., mortgage-backed securities) regarding how to ensure that the instruments received the best rating. Hence, the agencies were acting like both the referee and the goalie.

- The mathematical models used by Moody's and S&P for some types of debt had inappropriate assumptions, hence resulting in mislabeling the creditworthiness of some instruments.
- Competition among rating agencies and significant volume of activity created pressures for the rating analysts to "play ball" (that is, give a good rating or be kept from future rating activity).

In response to the problems identified during the subprime crisis in 2007–2008, the Securities and Exchange Commission was charged with the responsibility to improve the credit rating system.[9]

Additional Bond Features

A bond is a contract, and what is in that contract varies from one bond to another. Unlike common shares, each bond contract has to be reviewed separately because they differ from one another. Without recognizing this, the differences can come back to haunt investors years after the bond has been issued.

So far, we have focused our discussion on traditional or regular coupon-paying bonds that provide for full principal repayment at the maturity date. Because bonds can be customized to the needs of the issuer or the investor, we observe many combinations of various features. We describe a few of the features that fall into three groups:

1. Sinking fund and purchase fund provisions
2. Embedded options
3. Floating-rate bonds

Sinking fund and purchase fund provisions

A **sinking fund provision** requires the issuer to set money aside each year so that funds are available at maturity to pay off the debt. Provisions are made in two ways. In the first, the company repurchases a certain amount of debt each year, through a **sinking fund call**, so that the amount of debt decreases. In the second, the company puts funds into a sinking fund trust to buy other bonds, usually government bonds, so that money is available at maturity to pay off the debt. Sinking fund provisions benefit the issuer because the issuer is able to avoid paying the entire face value of the issue at the maturity date.

Bonds with a sinking fund are not always beneficial to investors because in some sinking fund arrangements it may be specified that the bonds will be randomly called based on their serial number and repaid. Therefore, there is a risk that the investor's holding period for the bond will be shortened by the sinking fund call. Further, the bonds are normally called at par value, and the investors may suffer a loss if the bonds are worth more at the time of the repurchase. Finally, as the amount of the issue declines, there may be a loss in liquidity in terms of these bonds trading in the market, resulting in the bonds

sinking fund provision
requirement that the issuer set aside funds each year to be used to pay off the debt at maturity

sinking fund call
repurchase of bonds that have a sinking fund provision permitting the issuer to buy back the bonds

---

[8] *Wall Street and the Financial Crisis: The Role of Credit Rating Agencies*, Permanent Subcommittee on Investigations, U.S. Senate Committee on Homeland Security & Governmental Affairs, April 23, 2010.
[9] At this writing, the SEC has only proposed rules regarding changes, such as increased transparency, training of analysts, and enhancing competition among credit rating agencies.

purchase fund provisions requirements that the repurchase of a certain amount of debt can occur only if it can be repurchased at or below a given price

callable bond debt obligation that gives the issuer the option to repurchase outstanding bonds at predetermined prices at specified times

call price price, generally at a premium over par, at which an issuer can repurchase a bond

putable bond or **retractable bond** debt obligation that allows the bondholder to sell the bonds back to the issuer at predetermined prices at specified times earlier than the maturity date

extendible bond debt obligation that allows the bondholder to extend the bonds' maturity dates

becoming less attractive. These disadvantages are offset, at least in part, by the lowered risk of default as less of the bond issue is outstanding.

A **purchase fund provision** is similar to a sinking fund provision, but requires the borrower to repurchase a certain amount of debt only if it can be bought back from the bondholders at or below a given price. These provisions are generally advantageous to bondholders because they provide some liquidity and downward price support for the market price of the debt instruments.

Embedded options

Issuers of bonds may include any number of embedded options with a debt instrument. These options may provide the issuer more flexibility, the investor more flexibility, or simply make a bond more attractive to investors and, hence, lower the return required by investors.

A **callable bond** gives the issuer the option to "call" or repurchase outstanding bonds at a predetermined **call price** (generally at a premium over par) at specified times. There can be a single call price or a schedule of call prices. These types of bonds create an additional risk for the bondholder because the bond could be called away when interest rates are falling, and hence the bondholder's reinvestment opportunities are lower as well.

Conversely, a **putable bond**, also referred to as a **retractable bond,** allows the bondholder to sell (or "put") the bond back to the issuer at predetermined prices at specified times earlier than the maturity date. In this way, the maturity of the bond is retracted or shortened. In contrast, an **extendible bond** allows the bondholder to extend the maturity date of the bond. In effect, put and retractable features provide bondholders with the flexibility of changing the maturity of the bonds to their advantage.

LESSONS LEARNED | Poison Puts

In the 1980s, there were a number of leveraged buyouts (LBOs) in which a publicly traded company was taken private by an investment group, with this buyout financed significantly by debt. The case of notoriety is that of RJR Nabisco. RJR Nabisco announced that it was going private in a leveraged buyout (LBO) in October 1988. Because the LBO meant that the company was taking on more debt, the existing debt became riskier, and the value of RJR's existing debt fell by almost 20 percent on the announcement of the LBO. In addition, the value of the debt of other large companies fell also on fears that a similar fate awaited these other companies.

In a response to this and a few other cases, investors demanded the ability to sell their bonds back to the company in the event of a merger, a takeover, going private, or a major recapitalization. These putable bonds are sometimes referred to as poison puts because selling bonds back the issuer at face value during one of these events may jeopardize the event—which, to some, is the basic idea of poison puts.

Sources: Burroughs, Bryan, and John Helyar, *Barbarians at the Gate: The Fall of RJR Nabisco,* Harper & Row, Publishers, New York (1991), and Mohan, Nancy, and Carl R. Chen, "A Review of the RJR Nabisco Buyout," *Journal of Applied Corporate Finance,* Summer 1990, Volume 3.2 (2005), pp. 102–108.

convertible bond or **convertible note** debt obligation that can be converted into common shares at a predetermined conversion price at the investor's option

A **convertible bond** or **convertible note** is a debt obligation that can be converted into common shares or other securities of the issuer at a predetermined exchange rate. In this case, the investor has the option to continue to hold the bonds or to exchange the bonds. Companies often issue convertible bonds to make debt issues more attractive to investors, hence lowering the return that investors demand on these securities. These securities are attractive to investors because the investors can benefit from any appreciation of the stock of the company, while at the same time collecting interest. For example, Ford Motor Company issued $2.875 billion of convertible notes in November 2009. Such notes have a fixed coupon rate of 4.25 percent, they mature in 2016, and the issuer has the option to settle any exchange in either stock or an equivalent amount of cash.[10] The exchange

[10] These notes are referred to as 4.25% Senior Notes Convertible, CUSIP 345370CNB.

rate, or conversion rate, is 107.5269 shares per $1,000 note. Therefore, if Ford's common stock price is above $1,000 ÷ 107.5269 = $9.30, investors in these notes can either wait to convert their notes, hoping the price increases even more while they collect interest, or exchange the notes and make a profit.[11]

Convertible bonds are almost always callable, which then gives the issuer the ability to force a conversion at a point in time.[12] If the company calls the bond when it is attractive to the investor to convert it, the investor is faced with a dilemma: have the bond called away at the call price or convert it into shares.

Floating-rate bonds

A **floating-rate bond** (**floater**) has a coupon that adjusts, with the coupon rate tied to some variable short-term rate, such as the U.S. Treasury bill rate or the LIBOR, although many variations exist.[13] Floaters differ significantly from traditional fixed-coupon bonds because the coupons on floaters increase as interest rates increase and vice versa. Therefore, floaters provide protection against rising interest rates and tend to trade near their par value.

For example, in 2004 Caterpillar Financial Services issued floating-rate demand notes that mature April 15, 2019.[14] The coupon rate is variable, changing periodically to be at least equal to a recent 7-day average yield on money market funds. The result of this floating is that the price of the bond is generally very close to 100.

> **floating-rate bond (floater)** debt obligation that has adjustable coupons that are usually tied to some variable short-term rate

1. In what ways are bonds different from mortgages?

2. Describe the call, conversion, and put features of bonds. Which ones give the issuer more flexibility? Which ones are most attractive to investors?

Concept Review Questions

Issuing Debt in Different Currencies | GLOBAL PERSPECTIVE

Many U.S. companies issue debt denominated in currencies other than the U.S. dollar. For example, Procter & Gamble had $19.647 billion of long-term debt obligations at the end of their 2010 fiscal year. Of this debt:

Currency	Fair Value (in billions)
U.S. dollar	$9.704
Euro	8.061
Japanese Yen	1.129
British Pound Sterling	0.753
Total	$19.647

Procter & Gamble has issued bonds in different currencies at the same time. For example, in 2007 the company issued three types of bonds: 10-year bonds denominated in Euros, 20-year bonds denominated in Euros, and 30-year bonds denominated in U.S. dollars.

Source: Procter & Gamble 2010 10-K filing.

[11] Ford's stock price rose above $9.30 in December 2009 and remained above this price until at least the end of 2011. As of the end of 2011, only $883 million of this issue has not been converted by bondholders, and the bonds are trading around 139.

[12] Convertible bonds may be issued with a feature that allows conversion once the bonds have been called, or they may be issued with a feature that prohibits conversion once a call has been announced. Forcing conversion can only occur if bonds or notes allow conversion at call.

[13] London Interbank Offering Rate (LIBOR) is an average of rates that banks would charge to their best customers.

[14] These are medium-term notes issued by the financing subsidiary of Caterpillar [CUSIP 14911QTQ4].

6.2 BOND VALUATION

yield to maturity (YTM)
or market rate of
interest discount rate
used to value the cash
flows of a debt obligation

We are now ready to examine how to value a bond. Once investors know the face value, the term to maturity, and the coupon rate, they know both the amount and the timing of all the future promised payments on a bond. The value of a bond is determined by discounting these future payments by using an appropriate discount rate, often referred to as the **yield to maturity (YTM)** or **market rate of interest**. This market rate of interest is a function of market conditions, that is, other market interest rates, as well as of issue and issuer specific factors.

Valuing Straight Bonds

The value of a straight bond is the present value of the future cash flows on the bond, which consist of interest payments and the par value repaid at maturity. We can use the following equation to value the bond:

$$\frac{\text{Value of a}}{\text{bond today}} = \frac{\text{Present value of}}{\text{coupon payments}} + \frac{\text{Present value of}}{\text{maturity value}}$$

or,

$$PV_0 = \left(\sum_{t=1}^{N} \frac{PMT_t}{(1 + r_b)^t} \right) + \frac{FV_N}{(1 + r_b)^N} \qquad (6\text{-}1)$$

where PV_0 = bond value;

PMT_t = periodic interest (or coupon) payments;

r_b = bond discount rate (or market rate);

N = number of periods remaining to maturity;

FV_N = face (par) value of the bond.

Valuing a straight coupon bond is an example of applying time value of money concepts. Equation 6-1 should look familiar: It is simply the combination of the formulas for the present value of an annuity and the present value of a lump sum. We discount the interest as an ordinary annuity, and we discount the par value as a lump sum. In terms of notation that we have used previously, the coupon payments are the payments, PMT, that occur at regular intervals of time throughout the life of the bond.

Most U.S. bonds pay coupons semi-annually, although many non-U.S. bonds are annual-pay bonds. The valuation process is not different for semi-annual pay bonds and annual-pay bonds, but we must make the appropriate adjustments when dealing with semi-annual periods rather than annual ones. Specifically, we must divide the annual coupon payments by two to determine the amount of semi-annual coupons and multiply the number of years to maturity by two to obtain the number of semi-annual periods to maturity. Finally, we need a semi-annual discount rate because that coincides with the frequency of payments. For bonds, as a matter of convention, the appropriate adjustment is to divide the yield to maturity, which is the market bond yield, by two to obtain the six-month market yield.[15]

Consider a semi-annual bond with a face value of $1,000, matures in 5 years, has a coupon rate of 6.5 percent, and is priced to yield 5 percent. The inputs are:

PMT_t = ($1,000 × 0.065) ÷ 2 = $32.50

r_b = 0.05 ÷ 2 = 0.025 or 2.5%

N = 5 × 2 = 10 six-month periods

FV = $1,000

---

[15] Notice that this implies the bond yields are not effective rates, but rather are analogous to annual percentage rates.

We use the phrase "priced to yield" because we are saying that if you buy the bond at this price, whatever it turns out to be, you will have a return on your investment equal to the yield to maturity. Of course, there is an assumption underlying the math: When you receive the coupon payment, you will reinvest it in a similar-yielding investment.

We can solve this as the sum of the parts (that is, the present value of the FV, plus the present value of the annuity of PMT_t),

$$PV = \left(\sum_{t=1}^{10}\frac{\$32.50}{(1+0.025)^t}\right) + \frac{\$1,000}{(1+0.025)^{10}}$$

$$= \frac{PV \text{ of an}}{annuity} + \frac{PV \text{ of a}}{lump\text{-}sum}$$

$$= \$284.44 + 781.20$$

$$= \$1,065.64$$

or, simply use a financial calculator or spreadsheet to solve this in one calculation:

HP10B		TI BAII		HP12C		TI83/84	Spreadsheet
32.5	PMT	32.5	PMT	32.5	PMT	N = 10	=PV(0.025,10,32.5,1000)
2.5	I/YR	2.5	I/Y	2.5	i	I% = 2.5	
10	N	10	N	10	n	PV = Solve	
1000	FV	1000	FV	1000	FV	PMT = 32.5	
PV		CPT	PV	PV		FV = 1000	
						P/Y = 1	
						C/Y = 1	

What if this same bond was priced to yield 8 percent (that is, its yield to maturity is 8 percent)? In this case, the bond would sell for less than its face value of $1,000. Using the sum of the pieces,

$$PV = \left(\sum_{t=1}^{10}\frac{\$32.50}{(1+0.04)^t}\right) + \frac{\$1,000}{(1+0.04)^{10}}$$

$$= \$263.60 + 675.56$$

$$= \$939.17$$

or, simply use a financial calculator or spreadsheet to solve this in one calculation:

HP10B		TI BAII		HP12C		TI83/84	Spreadsheet
32.5	PMT	32.5	PMT	32.5	PMT	N = 10	=PV(0.04,10,32.5,1000)
4	I/YR	4	I/Y	4	i	I% = 4	
10	N	10	N	10	n	PV = Solve	
1000	FV	1000	FV	1000	FV	PMT = 32.5	
PV		CPT	PV	PV		FV = 1000	
						P/Y = 1	
						C/Y = 1	

What if this same bond were priced to yield 6.5 percent?

$$PV = \left(\sum_{t=1}^{10}\frac{\$32.50}{(1+0.0325)^t}\right) + \frac{\$1,000}{(1+0.0325)^{10}}$$

$$= \$273.73 + 726.27$$

$$= \$1,000$$

or, simply use a financial calculator or spreadsheet to solve this in one calculation:

HP10B		TI BAII		HP12C		TI83/84	Spreadsheet
32.5	PMT	32.5	PMT	32.5	PMT	N = 10	=PV(0.04,10,32.5,1000)
3.25	I/YR	3.25	I/Y	3.25	i	I% = 3.25	
10	N	10	N	10	n	PV = *Solve*	
1000	FV	1000	FV	1000	FV	PMT = 32.5	
PV		CPT	PV	PV		FV = 1000	
						P/Y = 1	
						C/Y = 1	

What this means is that if an investor bought the bond at its par value of $1,000 and held it to maturity, he or she would earn a return equal to the coupon rate of 6.5 percent if the investor reinvested each coupon to provide a return of 6.5 percent. To see this, let's assume that each cash flow is reinvested at 6.5 percent (3.25 percent each six-month period) until maturity:

Year	Six-month Period	Cash Flow	Number of Periods of Compounding	Future Value of Cash Flow
	1	$32.50	9	$43.34
1	2	32.50	8	41.98
	3	32.50	7	40.65
2	4	32.50	6	39.38
	5	32.50	5	38.14
3	6	32.50	4	36.94
	7	32.50	3	35.77
4	8	32.50	2	34.65
	9	32.50	1	33.56
5	10	1,032.50	0	1,032.50
			Total future value =	$1,376.89

Therefore,

$$FV = \$1,376.89$$
$$PV = \$1,000$$
$$N = 10$$

When we solve for i, $i = 3.25\%$, and the yield is 2×3.25 percent = 6.5 percent. In other words, the person would invest $1,000 and get a 6.5 percent return on that investment per year; that is, $65 in interest each year, any interest on reinvested interest, and then receive $1,000 back at maturity. Thus, when market rates equal the coupon rate, bonds trade at par.[16]

SUMMARIZING

Element		Calculator
Coupon payment ÷ 2	=	PMT
Number of years to maturity × 2	=	N
Yield to maturity ÷ 2	=	i
Face value	=	FV

[16] Bonds are often issued at (or very close to) par by setting the coupon rate equal to the market rate at the time of issue.

Bond prices are typically quoted in terms of value per $100 of face value. For example, if a $1,000 face value bond sells at $990, its bond quote is 99. As another example, if a $500 face value bond sells for $495, its bond quote is $495 ÷ $500 = 99. Using bond quotes, we eliminate the need to know a bond's face value.

Consider the bond that matures in 5 years, has a coupon rate of 6.5 percent, and is priced to yield 8 percent. What is the appropriate quote for this bond?

	Using Dollar Amounts, Assuming a $1,000 Face Value	Stating Monetary Amounts as a Percentage of Face Value
Coupon	$32.50	3.25
N	10	10
FV	$1000	100
i	4%	4%

You will notice that the only inputs changing are the coupon and the future value. In equation form, the value of the bond is:

$$PV_0 = \left(\sum_{t=1}^{10} \frac{3.25}{(1 + 0.04)^t} \right) + \frac{100}{(1 + 0.04)^{10}} = 93.9$$

The quote of 93.9, therefore, is stating the price as a percentage of face value. If the face value is $1,000, the value of the bond is $939.

SPREADSHEET TOOLS: VALUING A BOND

There are two ways that you can value a bond using spreadsheet functions. The first, the simplest, is to use the PV function, which calculates the present value of specified periodic cash flows (the PMTs) and the present value of a lump sum (the FV). For example if you want to calculate the value of a bond that has a coupon rate of 8 percent (paid semi-annually), 5 years to maturity, a face value of $1,000, and is priced to yield 10 percent:

$$=PV(r_b, N, PMT, FV)$$

$$=PV(0.05, 10, 40, 1000)$$

This returns a value that is negative, –922.78, so we then multiply the result by –1 to arrive at the present value of $922.78.

Another way to calculate the value of the bond is to use the PRICE function, which provides the value per $100 face value. The PRICE function requires a settlement date (that is, the day you want the price of the bond), maturity date, the coupon rate, the yield, the redemption value (that is, the face value), and the frequency of interest payments within a year:

= PRICE (settlement date, maturity date, coupon rate, yield to maturity, redemption value, frequency)

Because we are not provided the detailed dates of a bond in most of our problems, we can use spreadsheet functions to help us. The function NOW() provides today's date. If we use NOW() * (365 * N), with N as the number of years, we can arrive at the maturity date N years from today. This way we do not have to know the precise maturity date of a bond to value it. However, to be more precise, we would want to adjust for leap years.

In our example, =PRICE(NOW(), NOW()+(365*5),0.08,0.10,100,2)

This provides us 92.281 (the bond quote in terms of per $100 face value), which we then multiply by 10 to get the value of $922.81.

premium amount by which a bond's value is above its face value

discount amount by which a bond's value is below its face value

When a 6.5 percent coupon bond yields 5 percent, the bond is selling at a **premium** from its face value. That is, when investors demand a 5 percent return and the bond provides a coupon greater than that, the bond's price will be bid upward until buying at the market price provides the investor with a market yield of 5 percent. When the 6.5 percent coupon bond is yielding 8 percent, it is selling at a **discount** from its par value. Because the future payments are fixed, the only way to get a return higher than the coupon rate on this bond is to pay less than the par value for it. The preceding examples illustrate the most important property of fixed income investments, such as bonds: *If interest rates increase, the market prices of bonds decline and vice versa.*

EXAMPLE 6.1
Bond Valuation

PROBLEM

Determine the value of a 15-year semi-annual pay bond with a coupon rate of 5 percent, when the appropriate market rate is 6 percent.

Solution

Assuming $1,000 par value:

$$PV = \sum_{t=1}^{30} \frac{\$25}{(1 + 0.03)^t} + \frac{\$1,000}{(1 + 0.03)^{10}} = \$901.9978$$

Using a financial calculator

Assuming a $1,000 Face Value		*Using Bond Quote Terms*	
FV	1000	FV	100
PMT	25	PMT	2.5
i	3	i	3
N	30	N	30
Solve for PV		*Solve for PV*	

Using a spreadsheet

Using the PV function, =PV(0.03,30,25,1000) or =PV(0.03,30,2.5,100)

Consider a bond that has a 5 percent coupon that matures in 15 years. If the yield is less than 5 percent, the bond trades at a premium. If the yield is greater than 5 percent, the bond trades at a discount, as you can see when we look at yields to maturity ranging from 0% to 10% in the table at the top of the next page.

You can also see this inverse relationship between yields and bond values in Figure 6-4, in which we depict the bond price-yield curve for this bond for yields from 0% to 20%. You can see that the relationship between market rates and bond price is not linear; the curve representing this relationship is convex.[17]

The shape of this curve shows two additional factors in the relationship between bond prices and market rates. First, for a given change in interest rates, bond prices increase more when rates decrease than they will decrease when rates increase. Note, for example, that the curve is steeper to the left of any point than it is to the right, so the impact of decreasing interest rates is different from the effect of increasing ones. Second, the curve is steeper for lower interest rates, which means that a given change in interest rates will have a much greater impact on bond prices when rates are lower than if they are higher.

---

[17] A curve is convex if all lines connecting any two points on the curve lie above the line. The convexity is evident if we look at the bond pricing equation, in which the discount rate is raised to powers other than one.

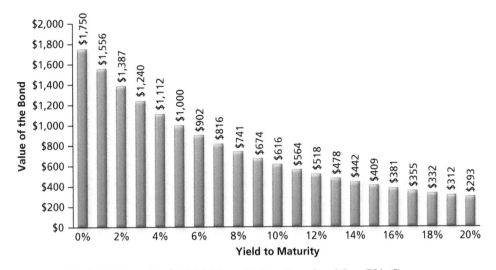

FIGURE 6-4 Value of a $1,000 Face Value Bond, with a 5% Coupon Maturing in 15 Years, for Different Yields to Maturity

Yield to Maturity	Discount Rate Per Period	Number of Periods	Coupon Payment	Future Value	Present Value	
i × 2	i	N	PMT	FV	PV	
0%	0.0%	30	$25	$1,000	$1,500.00	
1%	0.5%	30	$25	$1,000	$1,379.75	
2%	1.0%	30	$25	$1,000	$1,270.68	Premium
3%	1.5%	30	$25	$1,000	$1,171.69	
4%	2.0%	30	$25	$1,000	$1,081.76	
5%	2.5%	30	$25	$1,000	$1,000.00	← At par
6%	3.0%	30	$25	$1,000	$925.61	
7%	3.5%	30	$25	$1,000	$857.88	
8%	4.0%	30	$25	$1,000	$796.15	Discount
9%	4.5%	30	$25	$1,000	$739.84	
10%	5.0%	30	$25	$1,000	$688.44	

The second-most important property of bonds is that *the longer the time to maturity, the more sensitive the bond price is to changes in market rates.* Intuitively, this makes sense because the longer the term to maturity, the longer the investor has locked in fixed payments based on the bond's coupon rate. When market rates rise above this rate, the bond price will fall more because the coupon rate is unattractive relative to prevailing rates for a longer period. The longer an investor is locked in, the greater the disadvantage and the more the bond price will fall to adjust. Similarly, when rates fall below the coupon rate, the longer an investor is locked in, the greater the attractiveness of the higher coupon.[18]

Consider a bond that has a $1,000 face value and a 7 percent coupon, paid semi-annually. And let's compare the bond with two different maturities: 5 years and 20 years. If the yield to maturity of both bonds is 6 percent, the value of the bonds is $1,042.65 and $1,115.57, respectively. But if the yield to maturity changes from 6 percent, which bond's price is more sensitive to this change?

---

[18] What determines when all the adjusting is done? When the bond price has reached a level such that if the investor buys it at the price and holds it until maturity, the investor will earn the market yield at the time of the purchase of the bond.

Yield to Maturity	5 Years to Maturity	20 Years to Maturity
5 percent	$1,087.52	$1,251.03
6 percent	$1,042.65	$1,115.57
7 percent	$1,000.00	$1,000.00

EXAMPLE 6.2

Estimating Prices for Bonds with Different Terms to Maturity

PROBLEM

Consider the semi-annual pay $1,000 par value 5 percent bond, with market rates at 6 percent. Calculate the value on this bond assuming that the term to maturity is:

1. 5 years.
2. 30 years.

Solution

1. 5 years. $PV = \sum_{t=1}^{10} \dfrac{\$25}{(1 + 0.03)^t} + \dfrac{\$1,000}{(1 + 0.03)^{10}} = \$957.349$

Using a financial calculator

Given information:

FV	1000
PMT	25
i	3
N	10

Solve for PV

Using a spreadsheet

Using the PV function,

$$=PV(0.03,10,25,1000).$$

2. 30 years. $PV = \sum_{t=1}^{60} \dfrac{\$25}{(1 + 0.03)^t} + \dfrac{\$1,000}{(1 + 0.03)^{10}} = \$861.622$

Using a financial calculator

Given information:

FV	1000
PMT	25
i	3
N	60

Solve for PV

Using a spreadsheet

Using the PV function,

$$=PV(0.03,60,25,1000).$$

And therefore,

Percentage Change in Price if Yields Change from 6 Percent to:	5 Years to Maturity	20 Years to Maturity
5 percent	4.303%	12.142%
7 percent	−4.091%	−10.360%

As you can see, the 20-year maturity bond's price is more sensitive to changes in the yield than the 5-year bond.

The sensitivity of bond values to interest rates is directly related to interest rate levels and to the term to maturity. It is also related to the level of the coupon rate associated with the bond, though this factor is much less important than either interest rate levels or the term to maturity. In particular, bond values are more sensitive to changes in interest rates for bonds with lower coupon rates than they are for higher-coupon-paying bonds. This is intuitive, if we recall that the compounding or discounting effect is accentuated with time, which suggests that a change in the discount rate has the greatest impact on the most distant cash flows, including the par value to be received at maturity in the case of bonds. For bonds that pay lower coupons, the principal repayment, which occurs at the maturity date, represents a higher proportion of the total payments to be received by the bondholder. As a result, their prices fluctuate more for a given change in interest rates than will otherwise identical higher-coupon-paying bonds.

PROBLEM

EXAMPLE 6.3

Estimating Prices for Bonds with Different Coupon Rates

Consider two bonds that have 15 years remaining to maturity, one with a 5 percent coupon rate, and the other with a 7 percent coupon rate.

1. What is the value of these two bonds if the yield to maturity is:
   a. 5 percent?
   b. 7 percent?

2. Which bond's value is more sensitive to the change in the yield from 5 percent to 7 percent?

Solution

5% COUPON BOND

1a. at 5% the value of the bond is $1,000:

$$PV_0 = \sum_{t=1}^{30} \frac{\$25}{(1 + 0.025)^t} + \frac{\$1,000}{(1 + 0.025)^{10}} = \$1,000$$

Using a financial calculator

Given information:

FV 1000
PMT 25
i 2.5
N 30
Solve for PV

7% COUPON BOND

1a. at 5% the value of the bond is $1,209.30:

$$PV_0 = \sum_{t=1}^{30} \frac{\$35}{(1 + 0.025)^t} + \frac{\$1,000}{(1 + 0.025)^{10}} = \$1,209.30$$

Using a financial calculator

Given information:

FV 1000
PMT 35
i 2.5
N 30
Solve for PV

Using a spreadsheet
Using the PV function, =PV(0.025,30,25,1000).

1b. at 7%, the value of the bond is $816.08

$$PV_0 = \sum_{t=1}^{30} \frac{\$25}{(1 + 0.035)^t} + \frac{\$1,000}{(1 + 0.035)^{10}} = \$816.08$$

Using a financial calculator
Given information:

FV   1000
PMT 25
i   3.5
N   30
Solve for PV

Using a spreadsheet
Using the PV function, =PV(0.035,30,25,1000).

Using a spreadsheet
Using the PV function, =PV(0.025,30,35,1000).

1b. at 7%, the value of the bond is $1,000

$$PV_0 = \sum_{t=1}^{30} \frac{\$35}{(1 + 0.035)^t} + \frac{\$1,000}{(1 + 0.035)^{10}} = \$1,000$$

Using a financial calculator
Given information:

FV   1000
PMT 35
i   3.5
N   30
Solve for PV

Using a spreadsheet
Using the PV function, =PV(0.035,30,35,1000).

2. The bond with the 5 percent coupon has a value more sensitive to the change in yield.

The percentage change in the price of the first bond:

$$\% \text{ change} = \frac{\$1,000 - 816.08}{\$1,000} = -18.39\%$$

The percentage change in the price of the second bond:

$$\% \text{ change} = \frac{\$1,209.30 - 1000.00}{\$1,209.30} = -17.31\%$$

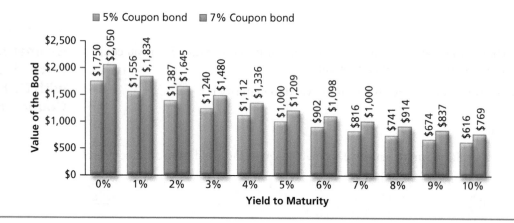

The sensitivity of bond prices to changes in interest rates is **interest rate risk**. All else constant, longer-term bonds with lower coupon rates and with lower market yields have greater interest rate risk than will shorter-term, higher coupon bonds with higher market yields. An important measure of interest rate risk, **duration**, incorporates all these factors into a single measure. Duration is the sensitivity of a bond's value to a change in interest rates; the greater the sensitivity, the greater the duration. The calculation of duration is beyond the scope of this book, but you already have an idea of what contributes to the sensitivity to interest rates, based on the examples and graphs so far:[19]

interest rate risk sensitivity of bond prices to changes in interest rates

duration measure of interest rate risk that incorporates several factors

*   The lower the market yields, the higher the duration (compare the slope of the graph of bond values for lower yields versus higher yields; the slope [and, hence, sensitivity] is greater at lower yields).

[19] Duration is a measure of the time-weighted cash flows of a bond: The sooner the cash flows are received, the lower the duration.

- The longer the maturity, the higher the duration (compare the sensitivity to a yield change in the example of 5-year and 20-year maturity bonds).
- The lower the coupon, the higher the duration (compare the example bonds with 5 percent and 7 percent coupons; the bond with the 5 percent coupon has a greater sensitivity for the yield change).

Valuing Zero-Coupon Bonds

Zero-coupon bonds are easy to evaluate by using a variation of Equation 6-1 in which we drop the first term because there are no interest payments to discount. This leaves us with Equation 6-2:

$$PV_0 = \frac{FV_N}{(1 + r_b)^N} \tag{6-2}$$

Remember that, by convention, we value these bonds assuming semi-annual discounting periods and convert our quoted yield to a semi-annual yield; therefore, the number of periods should also be expressed in terms of semi-annual periods. Although that may seem odd because there are no coupons to reinvest every six months, we do this so that the yields on zeroes are comparable to those of coupon bonds.

Consider a zero-coupon bond that has 5 years remaining to maturity. If the bond is priced to yield 6 percent, the value of the bond, using bond quote terms, is:

$$PV_0 = \frac{100}{(1 + 0.03)^{10}} = 74.409$$

Using a calculator, the inputs are:

FV = 100
i = 3%
N = 10

and you solve for the present value. We provide the value of this zero-coupon bond for different yields to maturity in Figure 6-5. As you can see, there is a curvilinear relationship between the value of the bond and the yield to maturity, which we also found with the coupon bonds.

Notice in the equation and in Figure 6-5 that the value of a zero increases as yields fall and decreases as yields increase, just as is the case for a regular coupon-paying bond. In fact, the market prices of zeroes are even more sensitive to interest rate changes because

FIGURE 6-5 Value of a Zero-Coupon Bond with 5 Years Remaining to Maturity

FIGURE 6-6 **Value of a Zero-Coupon Bond and a Coupon Bond at Different Yields, Both with 5 Years to Maturity**

they make no coupon payments at all. You can see this by comparing the zero-coupon bond that matures in 5 years with a similar bond, but with a coupon rate of 6 percent. If the yield to maturity is 6 percent, the zero-coupon bond has a value of 74, whereas the coupon bond has a value of 100. If the rate goes from 6 percent to 7 percent, the zero-coupon bond's value falls to 71, a drop of 4.73 percent, whereas the coupon bond's value falls to 96, a drop of 4.16 percent. We show this in Figure 6-6, comparing the values of the zero-coupon bond with that of a similar maturity 6% coupon bond.

EXAMPLE 6.4

Valuing a Zero-Coupon Bond

PROBLEM

Determine the value of a 15-year zero-coupon bond with a face value of $1,000 and a market yield of 5 percent.

Solution

$$PV_0 = \frac{\$1,000}{(1 + 0.025)^{30}} = \$476.7427$$

Solution using a financial calculator

Given information:

FV	1000
PMT	0
i	2.5
N	30

Solve for PV

Solution using a spreadsheet

Using the PV function, =PV(0.025,30,0,1000)

A bond quote may differ from the actual prices investors pay for bonds whenever bonds are sold at a date other than the date of a coupon payment. Up until now, we have made an assumption that we are valuing the bond on the coupon date; that is, the owner of the bond has just received a coupon payment, and we have not figured this most recent coupon into the valuation of the bond.

In reality, bonds can trade at any time in the bond's life, so any bond transaction will consider the interest that accrues to bondholders between such payment dates. For example, an investor who held a bond for 45 days since the last coupon has "earned" 45 days of interest, even though he will not receive those 45 days of interest if he sells it now because coupons are paid semi-annually—in fact, the bond purchaser will receive the entire coupon payment on the next scheduled coupon payment date. Based on the convention of a 360-day year (and, therefore, a 180-day coupon period), the seller is due $45 \div (360 \div 2) = 25$ percent of the period's coupon, and the buyer receives the rest; therefore, the price that the buyer must pay is the bond's value as of the most recent coupon, plus the accrued interest (the 25 percent of the coupon in our example). This amount is the **cash price** of the bond. The cash price is often referred to as the **dirty price**, and the price quote of the bond without the accrued interest (that is, as of the most recent coupon) is the **clean price**.

cash price or **dirty price** the actual price paid for a debt obligation that considers the amount of accrued interest on the security

clean price bond quote that does not consider the accrued interest

---

PROBLEM

Consider a $1,000 face value bond with a coupon rate of 5 percent and priced to yield 4 percent. If there were 5 years remaining to maturity as of the most recent coupon payment date, and the bond is sold 30 days into the next coupon period, what is the accrued interest that buyer must pay the seller as part of the bond's price?

Solution

Accrued interest $= (30 \div 180) \times 0.04 \times \$1,000 = \$6.67$

EXAMPLE 6.5

Accrued Interest

---

1. What two time value of money formulas do we need to value a bond?

2. When market interest rates are above the coupon rate on a bond, is it a premium or discount bond?

3. If market interest rates increase, what happens to bond prices? Why?

Concept Review Questions

6.3 BOND YIELDS

Up until now, we have provided the market interest rate, the yield that is needed to value a bond today. However, different types of yields are actually associated with bonds: the yield to maturity, the yield to call, and the current yield.

Yield to Maturity

The discount rate that we use to evaluate bonds is the yield to maturity (YTM). It is the yield that an investor would realize if he or she bought the bond at the current price, held it to maturity, received all the promised payments on their scheduled dates, and reinvested all the cash flows received at this yield. Given the value of a bond and all the details regarding the amount and timing of interest and principal repayments, we can estimate the bond's YTM using Equation 6-1:

$$P_0 = \left(\sum_{t=1}^{N} \frac{PMT_t}{(1 + r_b)^t} \right) + \frac{FV_N}{(1 + r_b)^N}$$

The yield to maturity is r_b if the bond pays annual coupons and is $r_b \times 2$ if the bond pays semi-annual coupons. The challenge is that when we use Equation 6-1 to solve for r_b, we do not find a direct solution. Instead, we must iterate—that is, choose a different value of r_b—until we find a yield that equates the present value with the value of the future flows (interest and principal). Choosing too high a rate will cause the right-hand side of 6-1 to be smaller than the left-hand side; choosing too low a rate will cause the right-hand side of 6-1 to be larger than the left-hand side.

internal rate of return (IRR) return implicit in a set of cash flows, assuming reinvestment of cash flows in a similar-yielding investment

For a bond that pays interest annually, the YTM is r_b; for bonds that pay interest semi-annually, the YTM is $r_b \times 2$. The yield to maturity is an **internal rate of return (IRR)**. An internal rate of return is an investment's effective return, considering the investment's cash flows and any interest earned on reinvesting these cash flows. Implicit in the math of the bond valuation formula (Equation 6-1) is that when the investor receives the cash flows (the PMT), these are reinvested in a security with a similar yield.

The YTM therefore represents the return on the bond, assuming:

1. the bond is held to maturity, and
2. all cash flows—that is, the interest—can be reinvested in similar yielding investments.

Unfortunately, solving for r_b in Equation 6-1 and, hence, the YTM, is difficult because of the various powers involved in the equation, making it impossible to find the algebraic solution. We must therefore resort to using a financial calculator, a spreadsheet program, or time-consuming trial and error.[20,21]

Consider a semi-annual bond that has a face value of $1,000, matures in 5 years, and has a coupon rate of 6.5 percent. If the bond has a current market value of $980, what is the bond's yield to maturity? Assuming that the bond has semi-annual interest, which we assume unless specified otherwise,

PMT = ($1,000 × 0.065) ÷ 2 = $32.50
N = 5 × 2 = 10 six-month periods
FV = $1,000
PV = $980

Solving this would require a trial-and-error approach—solving for the YTM that causes the right-hand side of this equation to be equal to the left-hand side, $980:

$$\$980 = \left(\sum_{t=1}^{10} \frac{\$32.50}{(1 + r_b)^t} \right) + \frac{\$1,000}{(1 + r_b)^{10}}$$

The six-month rate is 3.49 percent, so the yield to maturity is 6.98 percent. Better yet, we can use a financial calculator or spreadsheet to solve this:

HP10B		TI BAII		HP12C		TI83/84	Spreadsheet
32.5	PMT	32.5	PMT	32.5	PMT	N = 10	=RATE(10, 32.5, −980, 1000)*2
10	N	10	N	10	n	I% = Solve × 2	
1000	FV	1000	FV	1000	FV	PV = −980	
980	+/−	980	+/−	980	CHS PV	PMT = 32.5	
	PV		PV	i		FV = 1000	
I/YR		CPT	I/Y	× 2		P/Y = 1	
× 2		× 2				C/Y = 1	

---

[20] Old-fashioned bond tables, which show yields corresponding to various prices, coupon rates, and maturity dates are also available.

[21] An approximation formula does exist, but it can be off by a significant amount sometimes, especially for longer-term bonds that are trading at prices that are quite different from their par value.

PROBLEM

Estimate the YTM on a 20-year 6 percent bond that pays semi-annual coupons and is selling for $1,030.

Solution

$$\$1,030 = \left[\sum_{t=1}^{40} \frac{\$30}{(1 + r_b)} \right] + \frac{\$1,000}{(1 + r_b)^{40}}$$

$r_b = 2.8729\%$ Therefore, YTM = 5.7457%

Using a financial calculator

Given:

PV	−1030
FV	1000
N	40
PMT	30

Solve for i, then multiply by 2

Using a spreadsheet program

Using the RATE function,   =RATE(N,PMT,PV,FV): =RATE(40,30,-1030,1000)*2

Using the YIELD function,   =YIELD(NOW( ),NOW()+(20*365),0.06,1030,1000,2,1)

EXAMPLE 6.6

Estimating the Yield to Maturity on a Semi-Annual-Pay Bond

It is relatively straightforward to solve for the yield on a zero if we are given the price of the bond. In particular, we can rearrange Equation 6-1 to determine an exact solution for the semi-annual yields to maturity, as shown in Equation 6-3. This value is then doubled to find the annual YTM.[22]

$$YTM = \left(\sqrt[N]{\frac{FV_N}{PV_0}} - 1 \right) \times 2 \qquad (6\text{-}3)$$

For example, suppose a zero-coupon bond that matures in six years is issued at 78. What is this bond's yield to maturity? The inputs are:

FV = 100

PV = 78

N = 6 × 2 = 12

Solving for the YTM,

$$YTM = \left(\sqrt[12]{\frac{100}{78}} - 1 \right) \times 2 = \left[\left(\frac{100}{78} \right)^{\frac{1}{12}} - 1 \right] \times 2 = 4.1842\%$$

---

[22] Notice that this differs from the coupon-paying bonds, for which there was no finite solution for YTM. Another way of representing this equation, which is closest to how you would solve this using a calculator, is

$$r_b = \left[\left(FV_N / PV_0 \right)^{1/N} - 1 \right] \times 2.$$

EXAMPLE 6.7

Estimating the Yield to Maturity on a Zero-Coupon Bond

PROBLEM

Determine the YTM on a 10-year zero-coupon bond that is presently quoted at 56.

Solution

$$\text{YTM} = \left(\left[\frac{100}{56} \right]^{\frac{1}{20}} - 1 \right) \times 2 = 0.058831 \text{ or } 5.8831\%$$

Using a financial calculator

Given information:

FV	100
PV	56
PMT	0
N	20

Solve for i, then multiply by 2. Don't forget to enter the PV as a negative value in your calculator.

Using a spreadsheet

Using the RATE function, =RATE(20,0,−56,100)*2

LESSONS LEARNED | The Yield to Maturity as an Internal Yield

Consider a semi-annual bond that has 3 years to maturity, a coupon rate of 6 percent, and a price of 90. Therefore:

$N = 6$
$PMT = 3$
$FV = 100$
$PV = 90$

Solving for i, $i = 4.9682\%$. Therefore, the yield to maturity is 9.9363%.

Now let's see what happens in terms of cash flows and reinvestment, as we calculate the future value of each cash flow as of the bond's maturity:

Six-Month Period	Cash Flow	Future Value of Cash Flow, Reinvested at 4.9682%
0	−$90	
1	3	$3.8231 ←$3 × (1 + 0.049682)^5
2	3	3.6421
3	3	3.4697
4	3	3.3055
5	3	3.1490
6	103	103.0000
		$120.3894

Investing $90 in this bond will result in $120.3894 in value at the end of six periods or 3 years. Given this information:

$PV = 90$
$FV = 120.3894$
$N = 6$

We solve for i: $i = 4.9682\%$ and YTM $= 4.9682\% \times 2 = 9.9363\%$

Bond Quotes | FINANCE in the News

Investors can find bond prices from FINRA, which provides quoted prices on corporate, government, and municipal bonds.[23] Consider a selection of the bonds issued by IBM and outstanding as of July 2009. Per FINRA, we see the following as of July 3, 2009:

Symbol	Coupon	Maturity	Callable	Moody's	S&P	Fitch	Price	Yield
IBM.KG	5.70	09/14/2017	Yes	A1	A+	A+	106.300	4.760
IBM.LA	7.63	10/15/2018	Yes	A1	A+	A+	119.913	4.922
IBM.GT	8.38	11/01/2019	No	A1	A+	A+	125.206	5.186
IBM.GW	7.00	10/30/2025	Yes	A1	A+	A+	112.536	5.799
IBM.KY	8.00	10/15/2038	Yes	A1	A+	A+	131.130	5.781

The price is that of the last sale, stated in bond quote terms (that is, as a percentage of face value). The yield is the yield to maturity on the bond based on this last trade.

We can interpret the quote for IBM's 5.7 bond maturity 2017, with the symbol of IBM.KG, as the following:

- The bond has a coupon of 5.7 percent, but because the market yield of 4.76 percent is less than the coupon rate, the bond trades at a premium from its face value.
- If you own $100,000 of face value of these bonds, the value of your bonds is 106.3 × $100,000, or $106,300.
- The bond is callable, which means that if certain conditions are met, IBM can buy the bond from the investor.
- The bond is rated A1, A+, and A+ by the three agencies, which means that this is an investment grade bond.

Yield to Call

We mentioned earlier that bonds often have flexible maturity dates because some bonds are callable by the issuer, and for some, the maturity can be retracted or extended by the investor. This means that we can calculate the yield to maturity for these different dates. Suppose, for example, that the bond in the previous example was callable after five years at par.[24] This means that it is quite possible that the bond will not be outstanding for 20 years, because it may be called after 5 years. This yield, which is associated with a bond's first call date, is called its **yield to call** (**YTC**). We can estimate it in the same way as we estimated the yield to maturity by using Equation 6-1, except that we replace the time to maturity (N) with the time to first call (M), and we replace the face value (FV) with the call price (CP). This gives us the following equation:

yield to call (YTC) return on a callable bond, assuming that the bond is called away before maturity

$$PV_0 = \left(\sum_{t=1}^{M} \frac{PMT_t}{(1 + r_b)} \right) + \frac{CP_t}{(1 + r_b)^M} \tag{6-4}$$

Bonds are callable at a specified price (the call price), but there is often a schedule of call prices associated with a given callable bond. The call price is usually stated as a percentage of par value. Therefore, a call price of 105 indicates that a $1,000 face value bond is callable at $1,050; a call price of 110 indicates that a $1,000 face value bond is callable at $1,100. Generally, we evaluate the YTC based on the bond's first available call.

Consider a semi-annual pay bond with 10 years remaining to maturity, a 6 percent coupon rate, and a face value of $1,000, that is priced to yield 5 percent. If the bond is callable in 2 years at 110, what is the bond's yield to call? First, we need to solve for the current price (PV) based on the yield to maturity of 5 percent:

PMT_t = ($1,000 × 0.06) ÷ 2 = $30
r_b = 0.05 ÷ 2 = 0.025 or 2.5%
N = 10 × 2 = 20 six-month periods
FV = $1,000

---

[23] FINRA is the Financial Industry Regulatory Authority, www.finra.org.
[24] In practice, many callable bonds may have more than one call date.

Solving for PV, the current value of the bond is $1,077.95.

Solving for the yield to call requires using trial and error to solve for YTC in the following:

$$\$1{,}077.95 = \left(\sum_{t=1}^{4}\frac{\$30.00}{(1+\text{YTC})^t}\right) + \frac{\$1{,}000}{(1+\text{YTC})^4}$$

Or,

$$\text{PMT}_t = (\$1{,}000 \times 0.06) \div 2 = \$30.00$$
$$\text{N} = 2 \times 2 = 4 \text{ six-month periods}$$
$$\text{FV} = \$1{,}100$$
$$\text{PV} = \$1{,}077.95$$

Better yet, we can use a financial calculator or spreadsheet to solve this:

HP10B		TI BAII		HP12C		TI83/84	Spreadsheet
30	PMT	30	PMT	30	PMT	N = 4	=RATE(4,30,−1077.95,1100)*2
4	N	4	N	4	n	I% = Solve × 2	
1100	FV	1100	FV	1100	FV	PV = −1077/95	
1077.95	+/− PV	1077.95	+/− PV	1077.95	CHS PV	PMT = 30	
I/YR		CPT	I/Y	i		FV = 1100	
× 2		× 2		× 2		P/Y = 1	
						C/Y = 1	

The yield to call is 6.54 percent.

If the call price is above its current market price, it is unlikely that the bond would be called back by the issuer, so the bond will sell based on its YTM rather than its YTC. It would trade at a price based on its YTC if it was likely that the bond would be called, which would occur if the bond were trading above its call price and, correspondingly, if the YTC < YTM. Generally, a callable bond trades at a value that reflects the lower of YTC and YTM.

EXAMPLE 6.8

Estimating the Yield to Call

PROBLEM

Estimate the YTC on a 20-year 6 percent semi-annual pay bond that is callable in 5 years at a call price of $1,050, if the bond pays semi-annual coupons and is selling for $1,030.

Solution

$$\$1{,}030 = \left[\sum_{t=1}^{10}\frac{\$30}{(1+r_b)}\right] + \frac{\$1{,}050}{(1+r_b)^{10}}$$

$$r_b = 3.0814\% \qquad \text{Therefore, YTC} = 6.1627\%$$

Using a financial calculator

Given:

PV	−1030
FV	1050
N	10
PMT	30

Solve for i, then multiply by 2

Using a spreadsheet program

Using the RATE function, =RATE(N,PMT,PV,FV): =RATE(10,30,−1030,1050)*2

Current Yield

The **current yield** (**CY**) is the ratio of the annual coupon interest divided by the current market price. As such, it is not a true measure of the return to a bondholder because it disregards the bond's purchase price relative to all the future cash flows and uses just the next year's interest payment. The current yield is also sometimes referred to as the flat or cash yield. We calculate this rate using Equation 6-5:

$$CY = \frac{\text{Annual interest}}{\text{Current market price}} \tag{6-5}$$

You will notice when working problems involving bonds that the current yield usually does not equal the coupon rate or the YTM. This will be the case, unless the bond is trading at its face value and all three rates—coupon rate, YTM, and CY—are equal. It is clear that whenever bonds trade at a premium, the CY will be less than the coupon rate but greater than the YTM, and whenever they trade at a discount, the CY will be greater than the coupon rate but less than the YTM, as shown here:

current yield (CY): the ratio of the annual coupon interest divided by the current market price

Price-Yield Relationships

Bond Price	Relationship
Par	Coupon rate = CY = YTM
Discount	Coupon rate < CY < YTM
Premium	Coupon rate > CY > YTM

1. When calculating a yield to call, what is different from the calculation of a yield to maturity on the same bond?

2. Is the yield to call always greater than the yield to maturity?

Concept Review Questions

6.4 GOVERNMENT DEBT OBLIGATIONS

We refer to a debt obligation of a national government as a **Treasury security** and refer to these obligations as **sovereign debt**.

Treasury security debt obligation of a national government

sovereign debt obligation of a national government that is denominated in a currency other than that of the issuing government

Sovereign Debt

National governments issue debt obligations that, in theory, are considered to be risk free because the government can print money or raise revenues through taxes to meet the cash flow obligations of this sovereign debt. We say "in theory" because there have been situations in which this debt has been viewed as not risk free; Venezuela, Russia, Argentina, the Ukraine, and Belize, among other nations, have defaulted on their debt. In some cases the debt is restructured, allowing the nation to repay the debt under more favorable terms.[25]

---

[25] Of course, there is the case of Ecuador in 2008; the government decided simply not to pay its debts on the basis of moral grounds, though the country could likely have paid its debts.

Sovereign debt ratings are similar to those of corporate debt ratings in terms of a ratings scheme, but as you would expect, the factors are different. Sovereign debt ratings consider:

- fiscal performance.
- debt burden.
- external liquidity and international investment position.
- institutional effectiveness.
- political risks.
- monetary flexibility.
- economic structure.
- growth prospects.

Consider the case of Greece (Hellenic Republic), which is part of the European Union. Its debt credit rating has deteriorated over time, as the economic conditions in the country have worsened:[26]

Date	Debt Rating
March 26, 1997	A–
March 13, 2001	A
June 10, 2003	A+
November 17, 2004	A
January 14, 2009	A–
December 16, 2009	BBB+
April 27, 2010	BB+
March 29, 2011	BB–
May 9, 2011	B
June 13, 2011	CCC
July 27, 2011	CC
February 27, 2012	D
May 2, 2012	CCC

These credit ratings reflect the burgeoning debt, relative to the country's gross domestic product; for example, the ratio of debt to GDP climbed from 94 percent in 1999 to 142.8 percent in 2010. In addition, GDP growth went from positive 1 percent in 2008 to negative 2 and 4.5 percent in 2009 and 2010, respectively. Greece is part of the European Union, and as such cannot print more money and must seek assistance from the European Central Bank. Therefore, it has limited flexibility in dealing with its economic woes.

The credit ratings of countries are not all AAA; rather, they reflect the varying economic conditions. For example, you can see that downgrades that reflect the worsening conditions in the European Union:

Country	Rating as of June 30, 2011	Rating as of January 13, 2012
Germany	AAA	AAA
Iceland	BBB–	BBB–
India	BBB–	BBB–

---

[26] Standard & Poor's *Sovereign Rating and Country T&C Assessment Histories,* July 5, 2011; Standard & Poor's *Sovereign Government Rating Methodology and Assumptions,* June 30, 2011; "Ratings on Greece Raised to 'CCC' From Selective Default following Completion of Debt Exchange; Outlook Stable," Standard & Poor's, May 2, 2012. The rating "D" in this case is selective default, which means that it applies to specific obligations, but not all.

Country	Rating as of June 30, 2011	Rating as of January 13, 2012
Israel	AA–	AA–
Italy	A+	BBB+
Japan	AA–	AA–
Mexico	A	A–
People's Republic of China	AA–	AA–
Russian Federation	BBB+	BBB+
Sweden	AAA	AAA
United Kingdom	AAA	AAA
United States	AAA	AA+

The U.S. was not immune to the effects of the economy and its spending on its ratings. On August 5, 2011, Standard & Poor's lowered the rating on the debt of the United States from AAA, which the U.S. had had since 1917, to AA–. This downgrade followed a rancorous debate over the debt ceiling, the budget, and deficit spending.[27,28]

U.S. Treasury Obligations

Obligations of the U.S. government include short-term securities, which we refer to as Treasury bills (or T-bills), medium-term debt that we refer to as notes, and long-term debt (bonds). Treasury securities also include Treasury Inflation Protected Securities (TIPS), which protect the investor against the effects of inflation. You can see the amount of this debt outstanding in each year 1996 through 2010 in Figure 6-7 and can see how the debt of the U.S. came to a crisis in mid-2011. In addition to the marketable U.S. Treasury securities in Figure 6-7 of $8.85 trillion at the end of 2010, the U.S. government indebtedness

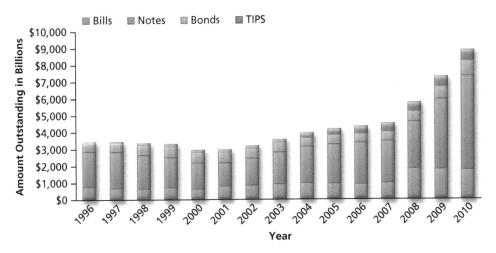

FIGURE 6-7   **U.S. Treasury Securities Outstanding**
Source of data: *Securities Industry and Financial Markets Association, SIFMA.*

[27] Congress passed the *Budget Control Act of 2011* [Public Law 112-25 S. 365], and the bill was signed into law on August 2, 2011, to increase the debt limit, attempting to avert a credit downgrade or default on the debt. Standard & Poor's downgraded the U.S. debt within one week of this bill being signed into law. This debt crisis brought to the forefront the issue of how much debt the federal government should or could bear.
[28] At the time of this writing, both Moody's and Fitch Ratings rated the U.S. as AAA. However, both agencies had put the U.S. on a "negative watch," which means that conditions are present that may result in a downgrade.

includes U.S. intragovernmental holdings of $4.6 trillion, which, together, came close to hitting the debt limit of $14.29 trillion by mid-2011.[29]

Treasury bills

A **Treasury bill (T-bill)** is a short-term government debt obligation that matures in 1 year or less. The available maturities are 4 weeks, 13 weeks, 26 weeks, and 52 weeks. Partly because of this short term to maturity, they do not make regular interest payments but rather are sold at a discount from their par (or face) value, which is paid on the maturity date. The discount rate, which is the difference between the face value and the price of the bill, is determined through the U.S. Treasury's auction when the bills are first issued. The interest earned is the difference between the purchase price and the face value.

Treasury securities, including bills, are sold through auctions. Bidding in a government securities auction consists of competitive and noncompetitive bids. The competitive bids comprise 35 percent of an offering, in which the bidder specifies the yield that is acceptable. The noncompetitive bids accept the rate that results from the competitive bids. The rate set by the auction process is the result of a Dutch auction. In a **Dutch auction**, bidders submit the rate and amount that they are willing to buy. The Treasury then determines the rate at which it can sell the amount of securities, accepting all bids at or below the clearing rate. For example, suppose the Treasury wants to sell $50 million of securities and receives the following bids:

Bidder	*Rate*	*Quantity in Millions*
1	4.5%	$25
2	4.8%	$10
3	5.0%	$15
4	5.5%	$20
5	6.0%	$25

The rate in this case would be set to 5% because at that rate the Treasury would sell the $25 + 10 + 15 = $50 million in securities. Bidders 1, 2, and 3 would receive a rate of 5%, and bidders 4 and 5 would be left out.

Similar to bonds, T-bills can be priced by estimating the present value of the expected future payment (i.e., the par value that is to be repaid at maturity). The value of a T-bill today, P, is the discounted face value, using the annualized rate adjusted to the proportion of the year. In the equation for the valuation of a bill, r_{BEY} is the bond equivalent yield, FV is the face value, and n = the term to maturity expressed as number of days:

$$P = \frac{FV}{1 + \left(r_{BEY} \times \dfrac{n}{365} \right)} \tag{6-6}$$

As evident from its name, the **bond equivalent yield** is the yield on the bill annualized in a manner similar to that of bonds. The logic of this equation is that the present value of the T-bill is the face value, F, divided by 1 plus the rate of interest, where the rate of interest is based on both the bond equivalent yield and the proportion of the year. Therefore, if the bond equivalent yield is 5 percent and the maturity is 90 days, the present value of this bond for each $1 face value is:

$$P = \frac{FV}{1 + \left(0.05 \times \dfrac{90}{365} \right)} = \frac{\$1}{1.01233} = \$0.9878$$

---

[29] The debt ceiling was raised by $500 billion in the *Budget Control Act of 2011*, with further increases conditional on Congressional approval and spending cuts. The debt ceiling was raised again in January of 2012, this time to $16.4 trillion.

EXAMPLE 6.9

Determining the Price of a T-Bill

PROBLEM

Calculate the value of a 91-day T-bill with a face value of $10,000 that has a quoted yield of 4.20 percent.

Solution

$$P = \frac{FV}{1 + \left(0.042 \times \frac{91}{365}\right)} = \frac{\$10,000}{1.010471233} = \$9,896.37$$

Similar to bonds, T-bill prices are usually quoted on the basis of $100 of par value, so the price quote for this T-bill is 98.78.

Rearranging Equation 6-6, we can determine the yield on T-bills using the following equation:

$$r_{BEY} = \frac{FV - P}{P} \times \frac{365}{n} \tag{6-7}$$

In the United States, yields on T-bills are also usually quoted based on the **bank discount yield**. The differences arise because of the use of face value instead of price in the denominator of the first term and because 360 days is used instead of 365 days to annualize the rate. The resulting equation is given where r_{BDY} = the bank discount yield:

bank discount yield method of stating interest rates that compares the discount with the face value of the security, annualized by 360 divided by the maturity of the security

$$r_{BDY} = \frac{FV - P}{FV} \times \frac{360}{n} \tag{6-8}$$

Suppose a T-bill with 90 days to maturity has a quoted price of 98.78. The bank discount yield for this T-bill is:

$$r_{BDY} = \frac{100 - 98.78}{100} \times \frac{360}{90} = 0.0122 \times 4 = 4.88\%$$

EXAMPLE 6.10

Estimating the Yield on a T-Bill

PROBLEM

Estimate the bond equivalent yield, as well as the discount yield, on a 182-day T-bill that is presently quoted at 98.20.

Solution

$$r_{BEY} = \frac{100 - 98.2}{98.2} \times \frac{365}{182} = 0.01833 \times 2.0055 = 0.03676 \text{ or } 3.676\%$$

$$r_{BDY} = \frac{100 - 98.2}{100} \times \frac{360}{182} = 0.01800 \times 1.97802 = 0.03560 \text{ or } 3.560\%$$

Therefore, the bond equivalent yield is 3.676%, and the discount yield is 3.56%

In addition to the traditional Treasury bills, the U.S. Treasury will also sell a **cash management bill**, which has a variable rate and is not available at every Treasury auction.[30] These bills are issued as needed by the Treasury to meet temporary cash shortfalls of the U.S. government for such uses as paying scheduled Social Security retirement

cash management bills short-term obligations of the U.S. government issued to meet temporary cash needs of the government

[30] These bills have been used since 1975.

U.S. Treasury note
obligation of the U.S. government that has a maturity of 2, 3, 5, 7, or 10 years and pays interest semi-annually

U.S. Treasury bond
obligation of the U.S. government that has a maturity of 30 years and that pays interest semi-annually

I Savings bond debt obligation of the U.S. Treasury that protects the investor against inflation

EE/E Savings bond debt obligation of the U.S. Treasury with a maturity of 20 or 30 years, with a fixed interest rate and interest accrued and paid at maturity

Treasury Inflation Protected Securities (TIPS) bonds issued by the U.S. government that provide investors with protection against inflation

benefits and have maturities that range from a few days to six months.[31] Like the T-bills, these bills are sold at a discount from their face value.

Treasury notes and bonds

A **U.S. Treasury note** has an original maturity of 2, 3, 5, 7, or 10 years, and a **U.S. Treasury bond** has an original maturity of 20 or 30 years. Both notes and bonds pay interest semi-annually. The only distinction between notes and bonds is therefore the maturity. The interest rates on Treasury notes and bonds are determined when these notes and bonds are sold in the Treasury auction. The interest rate is determined at the auction, and this rate becomes the fixed rate until the security matures. The interest earned on U.S. Treasury bonds is taxable for federal income tax purposes, but is not taxed at the state and local level.

In addition to these notes and bonds, the U.S. Treasury also sells bonds as a means for individuals' savings. These savings bonds include the **I Savings bond** and the **EE/E Savings bond**. The I Savings bonds protect against inflation, whereas the EE/E Savings Bonds are 30-year bonds with a fixed interest rate. The interest paid on the savings bonds is not paid to the bondholder as earned; rather, the interest is accrued and paid upon maturity.

The U.S. government also sells **Treasury Inflation-Protected Securities (TIPS)**, which provide investors with protection against inflation by providing a specific real yield. These securities have maturities of 5, 10, or 30 years. Protection from inflation is achieved by pegging the face value to the rate of inflation (as measured by the CPI) and paying interest at the coupon rate applied against the adjusted principal.[32] At maturity, the investor receives the greater of the original principal or the inflation-adjusted principal. The primary difference between the I Savings bond and the TIPS is that the TIPS are marketable (that is, they can be sold among investors), whereas the I Savings bonds are not marketable.[33]

FINANCE in the News | A Point of No Return

In the midst of the financial crisis in 2008, some U.S. Treasury bills had rates that were actually negative at some point during the trading day, Tuesday, December 9, 2008, but ended the trading day at 0.01 percent. In other words, if you bought a Treasury bill when rates were negative, you paid the government for the privilege of owning the bill. Negative rates occurred again in November 2009.

The negative rates in 2008 are blamed on the panic from the Lehman Brothers collapse, but the negative rates in 2009 are explained by the strong demand for bills (especially by banks wanting to spruce up their balance sheets), but insufficient supply, which drove prices up—and yields down.

The U.S. experienced negative Treasury bills once again on the same day as the stock markets fell over 4 percent (August 4, 2011), as investors sold stocks and bought Treasury securities as a "flight to safety." And on December 9, 2008, there was a time during the day when Treasury bill rates were negative, but the day ended with 4-week bills closing at a rate of 0.01 percent and 6-month bills closing at 0.0742 percent.

Sources: U.S. Treasury; Liz Capo McCormick, "Money Market Rates Fall Below Zero as Treasury Bills Retain Haven Demand," *Bloomberg*, August 4, 2011; Daniel Kruger and Cordell Eddings, "Treasury Bills Trade at Negative Rates as Haven Demand Surges," *Bloomberg*, December 9, 2008.

Concept Review Questions

1. How does the formula for determining the price of a T-bill resemble the formula for determining the price of a zero-coupon bond? Why is this so?

2. How does the U.S. bank discount yield differ from U.S. bond equivalent yield?

---

[31] U.S. Government Accountability Office, Debt Management: Treasury Has Refined Its Use of Cash Management Bills, but Should Explore Options That May Reduce Cost Further, GAO-06-269, March 2006.

[32] For example, for 100 of principal, an inflation rate of 2 percent would result in an adjusted principal of $100 \times 1.02 = 102$.

[33] The I Savings bonds can be redeemed after twelve months, with a penalty.

6.5 INTEREST RATES

Interest rates are usually quoted on an annual percentage basis. As we discussed earlier, the interest rate is the price of money, which is determined by the laws of supply and demand, as for any other commodity. In the case of interest rates, it is the supply and demand for loanable funds. All else constant, as the demand for loanable funds decreases, so does the price, and as a result interest rates increase; conversely, interest rates decrease as the supply of loanable funds increases. The interest rate that we have been discussing so far is the **nominal interest rate** because this is the rate charged for lending today's dollars in return for getting dollars back in the future, without taking into account the purchasing power of those future dollars.

nominal interest rate rate charged for lending today's dollars in return for getting dollars back in the future, without taking into account the purchasing power of those future dollars

Base Interest Rates

We refer to the base rate as the **risk-free rate** (**r**$_f$), which is the compensation for the time value of money. We will discuss risk at length shortly, but the term risk-free, although conventional, is a bit of a misnomer; what it actually refers to is **default free**: Investors know exactly how many dollars they will get back on their investment. It is common to use the yield on short-term government Treasury bills (T-bills), which are discussed in greater detail later in this chapter, as a proxy for this risk-free rate. Federal government T-bill yields are generally considered risk-free because they possess no risk of default, but the U.S. government debt crisis in 2011 has brought attention to the possibility that there may be some risk of default. Further, government T-bills have very little interest rate risk because their term to maturity is very short.

risk-free rate (r$_f$) compensation for the time value of money

default free no risk of nonpayment

As a result, we have the following *approximate* relationship:

$$r_f = \text{Real rate} + \text{Expected inflation}$$

This relationship is an approximation of the direct relationship between inflation and interest rates that is often referred to as the "Fisher relationship," after Irving Fisher. Using this relationship, if the risk-free rate of interest is 3 percent and the expected inflation rate is 1.8 percent, the real rate is 3 percent – 1.8 percent = 1.2 percent.

What the Fisher effect means is that investors attempt to protect themselves from the loss in purchasing power caused by inflation by increasing their required nominal yield. As a result, interest rates will be low when expected inflation is low and high when expected inflation is high. More precisely, the Fischer relationship is the following:

$$r_f = [(1 + \text{Real rate})(1 + \text{Expected inflation})] - 1 \qquad (6\text{-}9)$$

Applying a bit of algebra, we see that the risk-free rate is not only the sum of the real rate and the expected inflation rate, but also the cross-product term, real rate × expected inflation:

$$r_f = 1 + \text{Real rate} + \text{Expected inflation} + (\text{Real rate} \times \text{Expected inflation})$$

We often see the approximation simply because the cross-product term (the rightmost term) is generally so small when inflation rates are low.

We show the annual rate of change in the consumer price index (CPI), the yield on a 3-month U.S. Treasury bill, and the yield on a 10-year U.S. Treasury bond in Figure 6-8. The level of nominal interest rates generally tracks the increase in inflation throughout the 1960s, until inflation peaked at more than 12 percent in 1973. Since then, interest rates have generally declined with the rate of inflation. As we just discussed, one measure of the real rate is the difference between the ongoing expected inflation rate and the level of nominal interest rates. This difference was much larger from 1981 until recently than it was in the 1960s because the capital market persistently failed to take into account the inflationary pressures in the economy at that time. Interest rates were at historical lows

FIGURE 6-8   Interest Rates and Inflation, January 1960–July 2011

Source of data: *Federal Reserve Bank of St. Louis, FRED II.*

EXAMPLE 6.11

Real Rate of Return

PROBLEM

If T-bill rates are presently 4.5 percent and the expected level of inflation is 2.0 percent, estimate the real rate of return.

Solution

Using the Fisher relationship of $r_f = [(1 + \text{Real rate})(1 + \text{Expected inflation})] - 1$, and inserting the known values:

$$0.045 = [(1 + \text{Real rate}) \times (1 + 0.02)] - 1$$

Rearranging to solve for the real rate:

$$\text{Real rate} = (1.045 \div 1.02) - 1 = 2.451\%$$

---

in 2008, with deflation (that is, negative inflation) occurring in some periods, especially in late-2008.

The Term Structure of Interest Rates

So far, we have discussed the major factors affecting the base level of interest rates or r_f, which we proxy as the yield on short-term government T-bills. The yields on other debt instruments will differ from r_f for several reasons. One important factor affecting debt yields is related to its term to maturity. This is obvious if we look at bond quotes, where we can see various yield levels for bonds with different maturity dates, even though the bonds were issued by the same entity.

The relationship between interest rates and the term to maturity on underlying debt instruments is the **term structure of interest rates**. In Figure 6-9 we provide a graphical representation of this relationship, the **yield curve**. The curve is based on debt instruments that are from the same issuer, or else default risk, as well as other risk factors, will affect the difference in yields, in addition to maturity differentials. Therefore, the yield curve is almost always constructed by using sovereign debt issues because they possess the same default risk and levels of liquidity, as well as similar issue characteristics; in Figure 6-9, for example, we have graphed the U.S. term structure using the federal government debt obligations. In addition, the government tends to have a large number of issues outstanding at any given time; therefore, we can construct a yield curve with rate estimates for a wide variety of maturities.

One of the yield curves we depict in Figure 6-9 is for July 1, 2009. This yield curve is slightly upward sloping, with longer maturity securities that have higher yields than the shorter-term securities; that is, although long-term government bonds are virtually free from default risk in the same manner as short-term government T-bills are, long-term bonds typically yield more than medium-term bonds, which generally yield more than T-bills.

Although yield curves are usually upward sloping, they can assume a wide variety of shapes, as we show using March 1, 2007, yields in Figure 6-9. The downward-sloping (or inverted) yield curve for 2007 is less common, with short-term rates exceeding long-term rates. These "inverted" yield curves are unusual, and some market participants believe they indicate that short-term rates will fall. In fact, the inverted yield curve precedes the economic recession of 2008. Another, less common shape, is the relatively flat yield curve, which indicates that long- and short-term rates are very similar.

Several theories that attempt to account for the various shapes and movements of the yield curve incorporate liquidity, investor preferences, and supply and demand. We describe the most popular theories in Appendix 6A (available online).

term structure of interest rates relationship between interest rates and the term to maturity on underlying debt instruments

yield curve graphical representation of the term structure of interest rates, based on debt instruments that are from the same issuer

Yield Premiums

In addition to differences in terms to maturity, the yield on bonds will differ from the risk-free rate because of additional risks or features associated with these instruments. The difference between any two interest rates is the **spread**. The spread is often quoted in

spread difference in yields, generally expressed in basis points

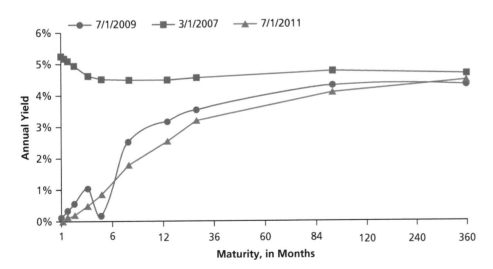

FIGURE 6-9   U.S. Government Yield Curve

Source of data: *U.S. Treasury, www.treasury.gov.*

terms of a **basis point (bp)**, where one basis point is 1/100th of a percent. Therefore, if the yields on two investments are 4 percent and 5 percent, respectively, the spread is 100 basis points, or 100 bps. One of the most commonly referenced spreads is between the yield on a security and the yield on a similar maturity Treasury security. In other words, investors expect extra compensation for assuming additional risks, and therefore they require higher returns. We can express this relationship using the following equation:

$$r_b = r_f + \text{Risk premium} \qquad (6\text{-}10)$$

> **risk premium** difference in yield that compensates the investor for the assumption of additional risks

> **default risk** uncertainty associated with the bond issuer and its ability to pay

We have already discussed the maturity yield differential, and we now turn our attention to the last term in Equation 6-10. The **risk premium** compensates the investor for the assumption of additional risks, which may include some or all of the following: (1) default or credit risk, (2) liquidity, and (3) issue-specific features. We discuss each of these in turn.

The most obvious difference in yield arises because of the different levels of **default risk** associated with the bond issuer. In other words, bondholders require higher yields to compensate them for the possibility that the borrower may default on the promised debt payments. For example, if we consider three bond issues that have similar coupon rates and mature on or about the same date, we can observe that their yields differ when they are from different issuers, which reflects different levels of default risk. Consider a snapshot of yields on the following bonds as of August 2, 2011:[34]

Issuer	CUSIP	Rating	Maturity	Coupon Rate	Yield to Maturity
Procter & Gamble	742718DA4	Aa3	08/15/2014	4.95%	0.741%
Coventry Health Care Inc.	222862AH7	Ba1	08/15/2014	6.30%	3.239%
Springleaf Finance Corp.	02639EMM3	B3	08/15/2014	5.75%	8.250%
Procter & Gamble	742718DF3	Aa3	03/05/2037	5.55%	4.311%
News America	652482BN9	Baa1	03/01/2037	6.15%	5.929%
American Stores Co. LLC	030096AH4	B2	05/01/2037	7.50%	9.733%

You should notice a few things from this snapshot:

- The lower the bond rating, the higher the yield to maturity. Compare the bonds maturing August 15, 2014. Procter & Gamble's bond's yield is less than those of Coventry and Springleaf. This difference in yields reflects the default risk.
- The longer the maturity, the higher the yield. This is because the yield curve on this date is upward sloping. Compare the two similar-rated Procter & Gamble bonds: the shorter-maturity bond has a lower yield.

Most of the differences in yields for bonds of the same term to maturity we observed as we move from government bonds to corporate bonds are due to differences in the default risk associated with the issuers. We refer to this difference as the **default spread**.

> **default spread** difference in yields attributed to the difference in default risk of the securities

> **liquidity premium** additional yield offered on bonds that are less liquid than others

A portion of the spread between corporate yields and Treasury yields for similar maturity bonds is also due to the fact that government bonds trade more actively than most investment-grade corporate bonds, which trade more actively than junk bonds. In other words, some bonds are more liquid than others; they are easier to buy and sell, and the required price concessions are lower. Bonds that are less liquid may have to offer investors a higher yield to compensate them for this illiquidity. This additional yield is referred to as the **liquidity premium**.

[34] The CUSIP is a unique identifier for the bond: the first six characters identify the issuer and the last three characters identify the specific security issue of that issuer. Hence, the identifiers for the Procter & Gamble bonds differ only with the last three characters (DA4 v. DF3).

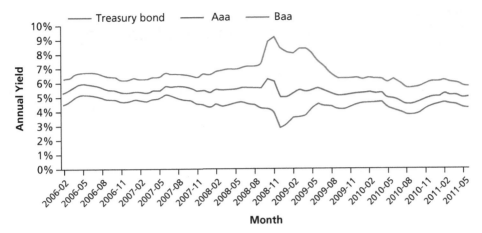

FIGURE 6-10 **Yield for U.S. Treasury Bonds and Aaa and Baa Corporate Bonds, February 2006 through July 2011**

Source of data: *Federal Reserve Bank of St. Louis, FRED II.*

An **issue-specific premium** arises when bonds have features that cause them to be more or less attractive to investors, relative to straight (option-free) bonds. For example, as discussed previously, the call feature is detrimental to bondholders. The reason is that these bonds are likely to be called by the issuer when interest rates are low (so that they can be refinanced at lower rates), which is exactly when the market prices of these bonds are increasing. As a result, investors will not pay as much for a callable bond as they would for an otherwise identical noncallable bond (i.e., they will demand a higher return). Conversely, retractable bonds permit investors to sell the bonds back to the issuer at predetermined prices when interest rates rise (and bond prices fall), which provides protection against rising rates. Similarly, extendible bonds will only be extended by investors if the coupon rates on such bonds are competitive; if rates increased, the investors would choose not to extend and could invest in other bonds that offer higher coupon rates. Therefore, extendible and retractable bonds, as well as convertible bonds, offer investors an additional privilege, and so they will trade at higher prices than otherwise identical straight bonds (i.e., they will provide a lower return).

All three of these factors are embedded in the corporate spread over equivalent maturity U.S. government bonds. In practice, it is very difficult to separate these three components of the corporate spread. In Figure 6-10, we graph the historic rates among Aaa corporate, Baa corporate, and the equivalent maturity U.S. government bonds.

The spread between Aaa and Baa rates was around 150–170 bps in 2006, but this spread widened in late 2008 and 2009 to over 500 bps in some months. Similarly, the spread between the U.S. government bonds and Aaa bonds was less than 100 bps in 2006, but widened to 200 bps in later 2008. In other words, the default spreads widened as the economy entered into the 2008 recession. This is generally the case: Default spreads widen in economic downturns. In fact, the credit spreads began to widen six months prior to the recession. The spreads between the yields of AAA-rated bonds and Treasuries began increasing in June 2008 and peaked in November 2008 at 325 basis points, coinciding with the collapse of Lehman Brothers.[35,36] At that same time, the spread between the yields on BAA rated bonds and Treasuries was 634 basis points. The spreads narrowed again in mid-2009 through mid-2011.

issue-specific premium additional yield, relative to straight, option-free bonds, required by investors when bonds have features that cause them to be more or less attractive to investors

---

[35] A basis point is 1/100th of a percent.

[36] We discussed the 2007–08 financial crisis in Chapter 1. One of the key events was the collapse of Lehman Brothers.

LESSONS LEARNED | Credit Spreads and the Economy

Corporate bond yields change along with the changing economy. Not only do credit spreads, the difference between corporate bond yields and Treasury yields, increase in a recession, but also the spread between yields on corporate bonds that have different credit risk increases, as indicated by the spread between yields on AAA rated bonds and BAA rated bonds. We can see these characteristics when examining the credit spreads leading up to and beyond the recession that began in December 2007:

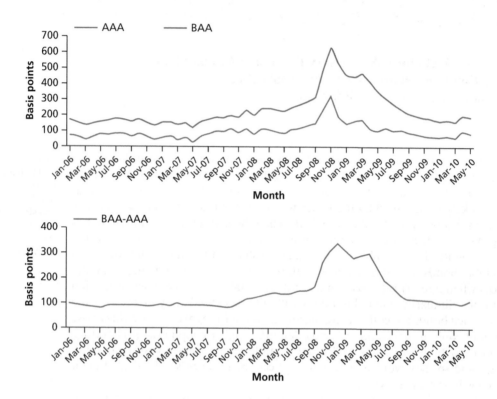

In fact, the credit spreads began to widen six months prior to the recession. The spreads between the yields of AAA rated bonds and Treasuries began increasing in June 2008 and peaked in November 2008 at 325 basis points, coinciding with the collapse of Lehman Brothers.[37,38] At that same time, the spread between the yields on BAA rated bonds and Treasuries was 634 basis points. The spread between yields on AAA and BAA rated bonds began increasing in October 2007 and then peaked in the month following the start of the recession, December 2008, at 338 basis points. The spreads narrowed again during the recovery period in 2010.

Source of data: *Federal Reserve Bank of St. Louis, FRED II.*

Concept Review Questions

1. How does the expected rate of inflation affect nominal interest rates?

2. What is the relationship between the default spread and the economic environment?

SUMMARY

- The traditional coupon-paying bond has a series of cash payments of interest every six months, with the principal repayment at maturity. However, bonds may also have features such as sinking funds, embedded options, and floating rates. In addition, some bonds do not pay interest and, hence, are priced at a discount from their face value.

- We value debt obligations as we do any stream of cash flows. The key for bond valuation is that we understand the timing of the bond's cash flows and the appropriate discount rate.

- One of the most important factors affecting bond prices is the level of interest rates. There is an inverse relation between the yield on a bond and its value.

- Treasury securities include short-term securities, notes, and bonds. The short-term securities, Treasury bills, are priced at a discount because these securities do not bear interest.

FORMULAS/EQUATIONS

(6-1) $\quad PV_0 = \left(\sum_{t=1}^{N} \dfrac{PMT_t}{(1 + r_b)^t} \right) + \dfrac{FV_N}{(1 + r_b)^N}$

(6-2) $\quad PV_0 = \dfrac{FV_N}{(1 + r_b)^N}$

(6-3) $\quad YTM = \left(\sqrt[N]{\dfrac{FV_N}{PV_0}} - 1 \right) \times 2$

(6-4) $\quad PV_0 = \left(\sum_{t=1}^{M} \dfrac{PMT_t}{(1 + r_b)^t} \right) + \dfrac{CP_M}{(1 + r_b)^M}$

(6-5) $\quad CY = \dfrac{\text{Annual interest}}{\text{Current market price}}$

(6-6) $\quad P = \dfrac{FV}{1 + \left(r_{BEY} \times \dfrac{n}{365} \right)}$

(6-7) $\quad r_{BEY} = \dfrac{FV - P}{P} \times \dfrac{365}{n}$

(6-8) $\quad r_{BDY} = \dfrac{FV - P}{FV} \times \dfrac{360}{n}$

(6-9) $\quad r_f = [(1 + \text{Real rate})(1 + \text{Expected inflation})] - 1$

(6-10) $\quad r_b = r_f + \text{Risk premium}$

QUESTIONS AND PROBLEMS

Multiple Choice

1. Which of the following statements concerning bonds is most likely *incorrect*?
   A. Periodic payments on bonds involve payments that include principal and interest.
   B. Bondholders are paid a series of fixed periodic amounts before the maturity date.
   C. The bond indenture is a legal document, specifying payment requirements and so on.
   D. Bonds have a fixed maturity date at which time the issuer repays the full principal amount.

2. Which of the following statements is most likely *incorrect*?
   A. All debentures are secured bonds.
   B. Extendible bonds allow bondholders to extend the maturity date.
   C. Callable bonds give the bond issuer an option to buy back the bond at a predetermined price.
   D. Convertible bonds give the bondholders an option to convert into another security at a predetermined conversion ratio.

3. The bond quote of a 5-year, 7 percent, semi-annual coupon bond when the market rate is 8 percent is *closest* to:
   A. 95.94.   B. 96.01.   C. 100.00.   D. 100.84.

4. The bond quote of a 5 percent, semi-annual pay bond with 5 years to maturity and priced to yield 8 percent is *closest* to:

    A. 80.70.   B. 87.83.   C. 88.02.   D. 100.00.

5. Consider bonds A, B, C, and D, each with a par value of $100 million. Which of the following bond's price is most sensitive to market rate changes?

    A. Bond A: 5-year, 5 percent coupon rate, yield 5.5 percent

    B. Bond B: 3-year, 8 percent coupon rate, yield 5.6 percent

    C. Bond C: 7.5-year, 4.5 percent coupon rate, yield 5.5 percent

    D. Bond D: 10-year, 4.5 percent coupon rate, yield 5.5 percent

6. The yield to maturity on a 6-year, 7 percent, semi-annual coupon bond, which is now priced at 99.3, is *closest* to:

    A. 3.632 percent.   B. 7.089 percent.   C. 7.145 percent.   D. 7.148 percent.

7. Which of the following statements is *correct*?

    A. If a bond is selling at a discount, the coupon rate < current yield < YTM.

    B. The current yield is the ratio of the annual coupon payment divided by the par value.

    C. When the coupon rate is higher than the market rate, the bond is priced at a discount.

    D. When the market rate is higher than the coupon rate, the bond is priced at a premium.

8. Which statement is *incorrect*?

    A. A sovereign debt is a bond issued by a government.

    B. A debt rating of AAA is a worse rating than BB for S&P.

    C. The risk premium in the bond yield reflects default risk, liquidity risk, and issue-specific features.

9. The quoted price of a 182-day T-bill that has a face value of $10,000 and a bond equivalent yield of 5.5 percent is *closest* to:

    A. 94.7867.   B. 97.3307.   C. 99.7276.

10. Which of the following statements is *false*?

    A. TIPS provide protection against the effects of inflation.

    B. Zero-coupon bonds are priced at a discount from face value.

    C. Floating-rate bonds provide the investor protection against decreasing interest rates.

    D. Zero-coupon bonds are often created when cash flows are stripped from traditional bonds.

Practice Problems and Questions

6.1 The Basics of Bonds

11. Describe the cash flows associated with a bond in terms of amount and timing.

12. Distinguish between positive and negative bond covenants.

13. In a callable bond, which party—the issuer or the investor—has an option? Describe the option and what would make it more valuable.

14. Distinguish between a callable bond and a putable bond.

15. Explain the role of a bond indenture in protecting the bond investor.

16. Explain the role of credit ratings in evaluating a bond.

6.2 Bond Valuation

17. Describe the relationship between market rates and bond prices.

18. Calculate the price of the following bond: a face value of $1,000; a coupon rate of 8 percent, and coupons are paid semi-annually; the yield to maturity is 5 percent; the term to maturity is 10 years.

19. Calculate the value of a zero-coupon bond that has 5 years to maturity and is priced to yield 8 percent.

20. Consider a 10-year, $100 face value zero-coupon bond.
    A. If the yield is 14 percent, what is the value of this bond?
    B. If the price quote is 76, what is the yield to maturity on this bond?

21. Consider a bond that pays 6 percent interest in the first 2 years, 5 percent interest in the next 2 years, and 4 percent interest in the next 2 years. If this bond is priced to yield 5 percent, what is the value of the bond? Assume semi-annual compounding and 6 years remaining to maturity.

22. Complete the following table:

	Coupon Rate Paid Semi-annually	Yield to Maturity	Number of Years to Maturity	Face Value	Value
A.	5%	8%	10	$1,000	
B.	7%	8%	20	$1,000	
C.	5%	8%	7	$500	
D.	3%	3%	8	$1,000	
E.	9%	10%	10	$1,000	

23. At maturity, each of the following zero-coupon bonds (pure discount bonds) will be worth $1,000. For each bond, calculate the missing quantity in the following table.

Bond	Price	Maturity (Years)	Yield to Maturity
A	$409	30	
B	$127		7%
C		10	5%

24. Consider a bond that has 20 years to maturity, a coupon rate of 5 percent, and is currently priced at 7 percent.
    A. Calculate and graph the value of the bond until maturity if the yield to maturity remains the same until the bond matures.
    B. Describe the path of the bond's value until maturity.

25. Calculate, using both a calculator and a spreadsheet program, the value of a bond with a face value of $1,000, a coupon rate of 6 percent (paid semi-annually), and 3 years to maturity when the yield to maturity is:
    A. 5 percent.   B. 6 percent.   C. 7 percent.

26. Suppose that 1 year ago a company issued a 5-year semi-annual pay bond with a $1,000 face value and a 12 percent coupon.
    A. If the market yield is 11 percent when these bonds are issued, what was the price of the bonds at issuance?
    B. If the market yield is now 6.5 percent, what is the price of the bond that pays coupons semi-annually?
    C. Using a spreadsheet, calculate and graph the value of this bond for yields ranging from 0 percent to 15 percent in increments of 0.5 percent for both the original maturity and now.

6.3 Bond Yields

27. If a bond is trading at a discount from its face value, what is the relationship between the coupon rate and the yield to maturity?

28. What assumption is made about reinvesting coupons when we calculate the yield to maturity on a bond?

29. Complete the following table, indicating whether the bond will trade at a premium or a discount from its face value:

Bond	Coupon Rate	Yield to Maturity	Discount or Premium?
A	5%	4.5%	
B	6%	9%	
C	4%	8%	
D	9%	8%	
E	12%	15%	

30. Complete the following table:

Value	Coupon Rate Paid Semi-annually	Number of Years to Maturity	Face Value	Call Price	Number of Years until First Call	Yield to Maturity	Yield to Call	Lower of the Yield to Maturity and the Yield to Call
A. $1,000	6%	10	$1,000	101	4			
B. $1,100	9%	10	$1,000	101	4			
C. $990	5%	10	$1,000	101	4			
D. $800	4%	10	$1,000	101	4			
E. $1,025	3%	10	$1,000	101	4			

31. Consider a zero-coupon bond that has 10 years remaining to maturity and has bond quote of 75. What is the yield to maturity on this bond?

32. Complete the following table for these zero-coupon bonds:

Bond	Quote	Years Remaining to Maturity	Yield to Maturity
X	70	5	
Y	80	3	
Z	65	10	

33. Complete the following table for these zero-coupon bonds:

Bond	Quote	Years Remaining to Maturity	Yield to Maturity
M	60	6	
N	55	20	
O	70	5	

34. Complete the following table:

Bond	Value	Coupon Rate Paid Semi-annually	Number of Years to Maturity	Face Value	Yield to Maturity
A	$1,000	5%	10	$1,000	
B	$1,240	5%	15	$1,000	
C	$100	7%	5	$100	

35. You find the following data on two bonds at a time when the market yield is 7 percent:

Bond	Coupon Rate	Quote
A	6%	95.842
B	8%	104.158

These bonds are otherwise identical (5 years to maturity, semi-annual coupon payments). Which bond's price will change by more (and by how much) if the market yield increases by 100 basis points?

36. A 10-year bond has just been issued with its coupon rate set equal to the current market yield of 6 percent. How much would the price of the bond change (in percentage terms) if the market yield suddenly fell by 50 basis points? How much would the price change if the yield rose by 50 basis points?

37. Complete the following table:

	Coupon Rate	Quoted Price	Number of Years Remaining to Maturity	Yield to Maturity	Current Yield
A.	5%	78	5		
B.	8%	110	10		
C.	9.5%	98	20		
D.	2%	105	10		
E.	0%	75	5		

38. Consider a bond that has a 4.875 percent coupon, paid semiannually, 5 years remaining to maturity.

A. Using a spreadsheet program, calculate and graph the yield to maturity and the current yield for this bond for bond quotes from 80 to 120 in increments of 1. [Horizontal axis: bond quotes | Vertical axis: Yield to maturity and current yield]

B. Describe the relationship that you observe between the yield to maturity, the current yield, and the bond quotes.

6.4 Government Debt Obligations

39. Distinguish between a Treasury bill and a Treasury bond in terms of maturity and how yields are quoted.

40. Calculate the bank discount yield on a 92-day U.S. T-bill that is currently quoted at 98.0468.

41. Complete the following table for the following Treasury bills:

	Face Value	Number of Days to Maturity	Bond Equivalent Yield	Value of the Bill
A.	$100,000	90	3.00%	
B.	$100,000	60	2.50%	
C.	$1,000,000	30	1.75%	

42. Complete the following table for the following Treasury bills:

	Face Value	Number of Days to Maturity	Bond Equivalent Yield	Value of the Bill
A.	$100,000	25	1.60%	
B.	$100,000	55	2.00%	
C.	$1,000,000	25	1.00%	

43. Complete the following table for the following Treasury bills:

	Face Value	Price	Number of Days to Maturity	Bond Equivalent Yield	Bond Discount Yield
A.	$100,000	$99,000	60		
B.	$100,000	$99,500	30		
C.	$1,000,000	$999,000	90		

44. Complete the following table for the following Treasury bills:

	Face Value	Price	Number of Days to Maturity	Bond Equivalent Yield	Bond Discount Yield
A.	$100,000	$99,500	20		
B.	$100,000	$99,900	10		
C.	$1,000,000	$999,500	20		

45. Using both your calculator and a spreadsheet, complete the following table for the following Treasury bonds, calculating the yield to maturity:

Bond	Coupon Rate	Years to Maturity	Value	Yield to Maturity
A	5%	10	101	
B	6%	20	102	
C	4%	30	99	
D	5%	15	90	
E	6%	20	105	

46. Consider a 91-day Treasury bill

A. Calculate and graph the value of this security for bond-equivalent yields from 0 percent to 7 percent.

B. Describe the relationship between the bond-equivalent yields and the value of the bill.

6.5   Interest Rates

47. Describe what is meant by the "Fisher relationship."

48. Bo Ulder explained to you that the risk-free rate is 2%, which is the sum of the real rate of interest and the expected inflation rate. Is Bo correct? Explain.

49. Explain why we may observe different yields on bonds issued by the same company.

50. Consider two bonds issued by Avis Budget Car Rental LLC, both of which have a maturity date of January 15, 2019, and a coupon rate of 8.25 percent. One issue, CAR.AA, has a price of 101.464, and the other issue, CAR.GO, has a price of 104.750. What could explain the different values of these two bonds?

51. Complete the following table, calculating the risk-free rate of interest:

	Real Rate	Expected Inflation	Risk-free Rate
A.	3.00%	0.00%	
B.	2.00%	1.00%	
C.	1.00%	3.00%	
D.	1.50%	2.00%	
E.	2.00%	1.50%	

52. Complete the following table, calculating the risk-free rate of interest:

	Real Rate	Expected Inflation	Risk-free Rate
A.	1.50%	0.50%	
B.	1.00%	1.00%	
C.	1.20%	2.00%	
D.	0.50%	2.00%	
E.	1.00%	2.00%	

53. The two bonds below are identical (face value of $1,000, 8 percent coupon rate paid semi-annually), except that they mature at different times:

Bond	Time to Maturity	Quote
C	3 years	102.664
D	8 years	106.047

If the market yield, currently 7 percent, falls by 100 basis points, which bond's price will change more, and by how much? Why?

 54. Consider two bonds, Bond One and Bond Two, with the following characteristics:

Feature	Bond One	Bond Two
Maturity	3 years	8 years
Coupon rate	6%	5%
Coupon frequency	Semi-annual	Semi-annual

A. Calculate the value of each bond if the yield to maturity for each is 5.5 percent using the PRICE spreadsheet function.
B. Using a spreadsheet program, calculate the value of each bond for each yield to maturity from 0 percent to 15 percent.
C. Using a spreadsheet program, graph the values of each bond for yields to maturity ranging from 0 percent to 15 percent on one graph.
D. What conclusions can you draw regarding the sensitivity of the bonds' values to changes in the yield to maturity?

 55. Consider three bonds, Bond Three, Bond Four, and Bond Five, with the following characteristics:

Feature	Bond Three	Bond Four	Bond Five
Maturity	10 years	20 years	15 years
Coupon rate	8%	5%	0%
Coupon frequency	Semi-annual	Semi-annual	N/A

A. Calculate the value of each bond if the yield to maturity for each is 7 percent.
B. Using a spreadsheet program, calculate the value of each bond for each yield to maturity from 0 percent to 15 percent.
C. Using a spreadsheet program, graph the values of each bond for yields to maturity ranging from 0 percent to 15 percent on one graph.
D. What conclusions can you draw regarding the sensitivity of the bonds' values to changes in the yield to maturity?

Cases

Case 6.1 Slice & Dice

The Slice & Dice Investment Co. needs some help understanding the intricacies of bond pricing. It has observed the following prices for zero-coupon bonds that have no risk of default:

Number of Years to Maturity	Price per $1 Face Value
1 year	0.97
2 years	0.90
3 years	0.81

A. How much should Slice & Dice be willing to pay for a 3-year bond that pays a 6 percent coupon, assuming annual coupon payments start 1 year from now?

B. What is the yield to maturity of this 3-year coupon bond?

C. Suppose Slice & Dice purchases this coupon bond, and then "un-bundles" it into its four component cash flows: three coupon payments and the par value amount. At what price(s) can the company re-sell each of the first three cash flows (the coupon payments) today?

D. The remaining cash flow (the face value amount) is a "synthetic" 3-year zero-coupon bond. How much must this zero-coupon be sold for if Slice & Dice is to break even on the investment?

CHAPTER 7

EQUITY VALUATION

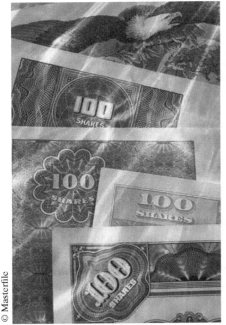

© Masterfile

What determines the value of stock? Old ideas are still new. We have long recognized that the value of the stock of a corporation is not likely the same as the value of the stock on the company's books. For example, for a company without any debt, it was recognized over one hundred years ago that:[1]

> If a company has special privileges or monopoly of any kind of business, its franchises may have a separate and independent value, and the value of the stock of the company may exceed largely the value of all the tangible property of the corporation. [p. 159]

The valuation of stock based on the future dividends of a company has also long been recognized. For example, Benjamin Graham and David Dodd, back in 1934, remarked:[2]

> the investor may look to future dividends or even to future enhancement of market value, instead of to the current dividend. [p. 320]

The many forces that influence the value of stock were recognized in the early 20th century and beyond. For example, Charles A. Conant wrote in 1905:[3]

> Among the influences which affect prospective earning power, are all the facts and rumors which indicate the economic future,—not only whether crops are to be large or small, but whether consumption is to be greater or less, whether given properties are managed well or ill; whether the rate of growth of population and wealth promises increased earning power in the future, or whether competitive establishments threaten to reduce the margin or profit; whether legislatures are disposed to grant new franchises and continue old ones, or to impose direct burdens to be paid out of dividends and indirect burdens, which gradually cripple the producing power and the initiative of the community. [p. 351]

In other words, it's complicated. But that is what makes the value of stock interesting and rewarding.

Learning Outcomes

After reading this chapter, you should be able to:

LO 7.1 Describe the basic characteristics of equity securities, and identify the primary factors that affect stock values.

LO 7.2 Estimate the value of these securities using the most common dividend discount models.

LO 7.3 Apply multiples to value stock, and relate valuation models to commonly used ratios or multiples.

---

[1] *The Pacific Reporter*, Volume 2, "Ryan v. Board County Commissioners Leavenworth Coal Co., and Others," Filed July 5, 1883, pp. 156–161.

[2] Benjamin Graham and David Dodd, *Security Analysis* (New York: McGraw-Hill, 1934), p. 320

[3] Charles A. Conant, "How the Stock-Market Reflects Values," *The North American Review*, Vol. 180, No. 580 (March 1905) pp. 347–359.

237

Chapter Preview In this chapter, we apply the time value of money principles and mathematics to value the equity of a company. We began by examining how to evaluate both preferred and common equity based on the present value of their expected future dividend stream. We proceed to show how this approach is related to the fundamental factors that affect stock prices, including future profitability, dividends, interest rates, and risk. We conclude with a discussion of relative valuation approaches and show how they too can be related to company fundamentals.

7.1 EQUITY SECURITIES

equity security ownership interest in an underlying entity, usually a corporation or a partnership

stock ownership interest in a company

share or **share of stock** security that represents a portion of the stock of a company

shareholder or **stockholder** owner of an equity security of a company

cash dividend payments to owners in the form of cash

common stock residual ownership of a corporation

A corporation will issue an **equity security**, which is a financial instrument that represents ownership in the corporation. We often refer to this financial instrument as the **stock** of the company. A unit of ownership is represented by a **share** or a **share of stock**, and an owner of a share is a **shareholder** or **stockholder**. Because a corporation has a perpetual life, the owners of these securities own a security that has no fixed maturity date. Companies that issue equity securities may choose to pay a **cash dividend**, which is paid from after-tax earnings. Unlike interest payments on debt obligations, dividends are not a tax-deductible expense to the paying corporation.[4]

A corporation, at a minimum, has **common stock**, but it may also choose to issue **preferred stock**. Preferred stock and common stock both represent ownership interest, or equity, but preferred shareholders, as the name implies, have a prior claim to income and assets of the company relative to common shareholders. Common shareholders are the residual claimants of the corporation, which means that they are entitled to income remaining only after all creditors and other, more senior claimants, including preferred shareholders, have been paid. Similarly, in the case of liquidation of the corporation, common shareholders are entitled to the remaining assets only after all other claims have been satisfied. As owners, they can exert control over the corporation through their power to vote, which allows them to elect the board of directors and vote on major issues, such as takeovers, corporate restructuring, and so on.

By far, the most common type of equity security is the common share, which represents a certificate of ownership in a corporation. A purchaser of 100 shares of common stock owns $100/n$ percent of the corporation, where n is the total number of shares of common stock outstanding. A publicly traded corporation may have millions or even billions of common shares outstanding at a point in time. For example, at their June 30, 2012, fiscal year end, Microsoft had 8.383 billion shares of stock outstanding.[5]

Preferred stock provides the owner with a claim to a fixed amount of equity that is established when the shares are first issued. Most preferred stockholders have preference over common stockholders with respect to income and assets (in the event of liquidation), but they rarely have any voting rights. Traditionally, preferred stock has no maturity date, but over the past 30 years preferred stock has been increasingly issued with a fixed maturity date, similar to a bond. The main difference between preferred stock and a bond is that the board of directors declares the dividends and until then, and unlike an interest payment, dividends are not a legal obligation of the company. Usually, no payments can be made to common shareholders until preferred shareholders have been paid the dividends they are due in entirety.

From the perspective of the company issuing the stock, dividends are not considered a cost of doing business, and therefore they are not deductible for tax purposes by the paying company. This is different than the interest paid by the company issuing bonds; interest is a deductible expense for tax purposes.[6] From the perspective of the investor

---

[4] Corporations that receive dividends from other corporations may be able to deduct some or all of these dividends from income and therefore reduce the burden of double taxation, as we described in Chapter 3.

[5] Source: Microsoft Corporation 10-K filing with the SEC, filed July 28, 2011.

[6] The U.S. Internal Revenue Code, a result of federal legislation, has always viewed interest as a necessary and ordinary cost of doing business and, hence, has allowed interest to be deducted; dividends were not viewed as necessary and ordinary costs of doing business and therefore are not deductible for tax purposes.

238

of bonds and stocks, we also see a difference in the tax treatment: Interest received on bonds is taxed as income of the bond investor, whereas the dividend received by a shareholder may be subject to special treatment. In the case of a corporation owning stock in another corporation, a portion or all of the dividend income may be deducted for tax purposes, hence escaping some or all taxation on this income.[7] For individual owners of stock, the dividend income may be taxed at a lower rate than other income, including interest income.[8] Because of the tax implications:

- from the perspective of the company issuing the securities, debt financing is a lower cost of financing because interest is deductible and dividends are not;
- from the perspective of the corporate investor, stock is preferred to bonds because the dividend income is, at most, partially taxable, whereas interest income is taxed fully; and
- from the perspective of the individual investor, a dollar of income from dividends is preferred to a dollar of income from bonds for tax purposes because dividends are taxed at a lower rate than interest income.

Apart from the tax implications, a dollar of income from debt is less risky than a dollar of income from equity for a given company because creditors have a claim to income and assets prior to shareholders. Therefore, an investor would need to consider the benefits that shares offer from a tax perspective with the additional risk.

The Basics of Valuing Equity

Equity securities may have cash flows in the form of cash dividends, which are paid at the discretion of the board of directors. Therefore, valuing equity is more challenging than, say, valuing bonds. This is because with bonds there is a legal commitment to paying interest and repaying the principal, but with equity there is no such commitment associated with dividends. Therefore, valuing equity requires estimating future dividends.

In the case of preferred stock, the dividends are generally fixed in terms of the payment frequency and the amount, but these still are paid at the discretion of the company's board of directors. Therefore, a company can choose not to pay preferred dividends, with the only consequence (technically) being that the company cannot pay dividends on common shares until the preferred dividends are paid. However, practically speaking, this would send a negative signal to the capital markets, which would likely have a negative effect on the value of the company's financial securities (i.e., bonds, preferred shares, and common shares). Hence, companies are generally reluctant to omit these dividends if at all possible. We refer to preferred stock with a fixed dividend, no maturity, and no embedded option as **straight preferred stock**. We do this to distinguish these from preferred stock with dividends that vary from period to period (as is the case of adjustable rate preferred stock), preferred stock that, essentially, matures, and preferred stock with an embedded option such as preferred stock convertible into common shares or preferred stock that is callable.

straight preferred stock preferred stock with no embedded option, for which the issuer promises to pay a fixed, periodic dividend

We generally value preferred stock using discounted cash flow methods, discounting the expected dividends at a discount rate that reflects the uncertainty associated with the payment of these dividends. In the case of straight preferred stock, the valuation is simply the present value of the perpetual stream of cash dividends.

Because common stock is the last in line in terms of the pecking order of claims on a company and because some companies simply reinvest earnings instead of paying them

---

[7] We reviewed this provision in more detail in an earlier chapter.

[8] There are various ways that dividend income received by individuals has gotten special treatment in the U.S., including a lower rate for dividends on stocks held a specified period (e.g., six months) and an exclusion of a specified dollar amount of dividends from taxation. The current law, set to expire in 2012, taxes dividend income that qualifies at either 15 percent or 0 percent, depending on the taxpayer's income level. Qualifying dividends under current law are dividends on stocks of U.S. companies held for 61 days around a dividend payment date.

out to shareholders, there are two common approaches to valuing common stock: the discounted cash flow approach, with its many variations, and the **method of multiples**, using the market's evaluation of the value of equity of similar companies to value the a company's equity. The discounted cash flow approach requires an estimate of the **required rate of return**, which is the minimum return that investors expect to earn on the investment in the stock. In the method of multiples, we approach valuation at a different angle: We estimate values based on the market's assessment of comparable companies.

method of multiples approach to valuing an entity or the equity of an entity by applying the market multiples of comparable companies

Discounted Cash Flow Approach

Method of Multiples

Why do we need two approaches to value common stock? Because unlike bonds and preferred stock, the future cash flows to owners are uncertain in both the amount and the timing. Also, because the cash flows depend on dividend policies and how the market values these dividends, one approach may be more appropriate for some types of companies, and the other approach may be more appropriate for other types of companies. Do analysts really use these models? Yes, as we show in Table 7-1. Analysts use both approaches, though there are many variations of each approach, as you will see in this chapter.

The Required Rate of Return

Key to the discount models used to value preferred and common stock is the required rate of return. The required rate of return becomes a benchmark for valuation: If a company returns more than required, the value of the stock rises; if a company returns less than required, the value of the stock falls. The difficulty is that we cannot observe this required rate of return directly. We can back into this return by looking at how the market values a company's stock, given a projection of dividends, but we cannot simply look up the required rate of return.

We generally think of the discount rate for equities as the sum of the risk-free rate of return—that is, the compensation for the time value of money—plus a premium for bearing risk:

$$r_e = r_f + \text{Risk premium} \qquad (7\text{-}1)$$

where r_e is the required return on an equity security and r_f is the risk-free rate of return. The risk-free rate comprises the real rate of return plus expected inflation, and we often use the

TABLE 7-1 **Common Share Valuation Approaches**

Method Used	*Percentage*
Price-earnings (P/E) approach	88.1
Discounted free cash flow approach	86.8
Enterprise value multiple	76.7
Price-to-book-value approach	59.0
Price-to-cash-flow approach	57.2
Price-to-sales approach	40.3
Dividend-to-price or price-to-dividend approaches	35.5
Dividend discount model	35.1

Source: *Model Selection from "Valuation Methods" Presentation, October 2007, produced by Tom Robinson, Ph.D., CFA, CPA, CFP®, Head, Educational Content, CFA Institute. Copyright 2007, CFA Institute. Reproduced and republished from* Valuation Methods *with permission from CFA Institute. All rights reserved.*

return on Treasury bonds to represent this rate of return.[9] The **risk premium** is based on an estimate of the risk associated with the security; the higher the risk, the higher the risk premium because investors require a higher return as compensation for bearing more risk.[10]

Irrational Exuberance I, II, and III | LESSONS LEARNED

One of the lessons of the recent financial crisis is that we don't always take these lessons to heart. Consider a few of the recent bubbles in our financial history. Alan Greenspan, former chairman of the Federal Reserve Bank of the U.S. noted in a speech in 1996:[11]

> Clearly, sustained low inflation implies less uncertainty about the future, and lower risk premiums imply higher prices of stocks and other earning assets. We can see that in the inverse relationship exhibited by price/earnings ratios and the rate of inflation in the past. But how do we know when irrational exuberance has unduly escalated asset values, which then become subject to unexpected and prolonged contractions as they have in Japan over the past decade?

His comments were followed by declines in the stock markets around the world.

Robert Shiller used the phrase "irrational exuberance" in describing the dot.com frenzy in markets around the world, with stocks with little or no earnings prospects having values that made little sense using almost any one of the valuation models. In his book *Irrational Exuberance*, published in 2000, he discussed speculative bubbles in general, but also the speculative bubble that is often referred to as the "dot.com" or "Internet Bubble."[12] The publication of this book preceded the bursting of the Internet bubble in 2001.

Shiller's second edition of his book, published in 2005, added an analysis of the real estate bubble.[13] He discussed the problems associated with personal bankruptcies leading to financial difficulties for financial institutions. The publication of this book preceded the subprime mortgage-fueled boom that went bust in 2007.

The challenge, as you can see, is that the participants in markets do not always learn and there is a psychological dimension to how market participants value stocks.

---

[9] Because stock is a long-term investment, we generally use the interest rate on a long-term security to proxy the risk-free rate using the rate on a default-free long-term security. You may see applications in which the rate on a Treasury bill is used, but this may understate the appropriate risk-free rate when there is a normal, upward-sloping yield curve.

[10] We discuss the factors affecting the risk premium and methods for estimating a discount rate for equities in later chapters.

[11] Greenspan, Alan. "The Challenge of Central Banking in a Democratic Society," speech to the American Enterprise Institute, December 5, 1996.

[12] Shiller, Robert, *Irrational Exuberance* (Princeton, NJ: Princeton University Press, March 2000).

[13] Shiller, Robert, *Irrational Exuberance* (Princeton, NJ: Princeton University Press, 2005).

Concept Review
Questions
1.   What distinguishes an equity security from a debt security that is relevant for valuation purposes?

2.   What is the relationship between the required rate of return and the risk of the security being valued?

7.2   DISCOUNTED CASH FLOW APPROACHES TO VALUING EQUITY

A commonly used approach for valuing equity securities follows the discounted cash flow approach used to estimate the value of bonds. In particular, we estimate the expected future cash flows associated with the security and then determine the discounted present value of those future cash flows, based on an appropriate discount rate (r_e).

Valuing Preferred Stock

As mentioned previously, traditional preferred stock has no maturity date and pays dividends of a fixed amount at regular intervals indefinitely (that is, to infinity, ∞), as we depict in Figure 7-1, where we represent the periodic dividend payment as D_p.

Because the payments are essentially fixed when the preferred shares are issued, they are often referred to as fixed-income investments. The payment of a fixed dividend amount at regular intervals indefinitely means we can view these investments as *perpetuities*. We can estimate the value of preferred shares using Equation 7-2, the equation that determines the present value of a perpetuity, where P_p is the present value of the preferred stock, D_p is the periodic dividend amounts (or payments), and r_p is the required rate of return on the preferred shares (or discount rate):

$$P_p = \frac{D_p}{r_p} \tag{7-2}$$

The amount of the dividend payments is usually based on a stated par (or face) value and a stated dividend rate, which is similar to the coupon rate on a bond. For example, a preferred share with a par value of $100 and an 8 percent dividend rate would pay an annual dividend of $8 per year. In practice, dividends are paid quarterly; however, for illustration purposes, we assume they are paid annually.[14] This assumption has little influence on the valuation because of the long time involved (i.e., assuming the dividends are paid to infinity).

Consider an example. Suppose a preferred stock has a par value of $50 per share and a dividend rate of 8 percent. If the required rate of return for this preferred stock is 6 percent, what is the value of a share of this stock? The dividend is $50 \times 0.08 = $4 per share, which we discount at the rate of 6 percent:[15]

$$P_p = \frac{\$50 \times 0.08}{0.06} = \frac{\$4}{0.06} = \$66.67$$

Time	0	1	2	3	...	∞
Cash Flow		D_p	D_p	D_p		D_p

FIGURE 7-1   **The Cash Flow Pattern for a Straight Preferred Stock**

[14] We will also assume annual dividends when valuing common shares, even though they also usually pay quarterly dividends.

[15] Another way of stating this is saying that we capitalize the $4 at 6 percent.

The stock trades at a premium to its face value. What if the required rate of return is 10 percent, instead of 6 percent?

$$P_p = \frac{\$50 \times 0.08}{0.10} = \frac{\$4}{0.10} = \$40$$

In this case, the stock trades at a discount to its face value. What if the required rate of return is 8 percent instead of 6 percent?

$$P_p = \frac{\$50 \times 0.08}{0.08} = \frac{\$4}{0.08} = \$50$$

In this case, the stock is valued at its par value. Notice that, similar to bonds, preferred shares will trade:

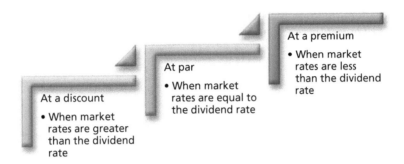

At a premium
• When market rates are less than the dividend rate

At par
• When market rates are equal to the dividend rate

At a discount
• When market rates are greater than the dividend rate

Also note that the market value of preferred shares increases when market rates decline, and vice versa.

PROBLEM

Determine the value of a $50 par value preferred share that pays annual dividends based on a 7 percent dividend rate, when the market yield is:

a. 7 percent.
b. 8 percent.
c. 6 percent.

Solution

First, calculate the expected dividend per year: $D_p = \$50 \times 0.07 = \$3.50$
Then, capitalize this dividend at the appropriate required rate of return:

a. $P_p = \dfrac{D_p}{r_p} = \dfrac{\$3.50}{0.07} = \$50$

b. $P_p = \dfrac{\$3.50}{0.08} = \$43.75$

c. $P_p = \dfrac{\$3.50}{0.06} = \$58.33$

EXAMPLE 7.1

Determining the Value of Preferred Stock

We can rearrange Equation 7-2 to determine the required rate of return on the preferred shares for a given market price, as follows:

$$r_p = \frac{D_p}{P_p} \qquad\qquad (7\text{-}3)$$

If a preferred stock that pays an annual dividend of $2 per share is selling at $25 per share, the required rate of return on this preferred stock is $2 ÷ $25 = 8 percent.

Consider Consolidated Edison Co.'s 4.65% Series C Cumulative Preferred Stock. Each share of this stock has a par value of $100, and the annual dividend, D_p, is $4.65. Because Consolidated Edison pays dividends on this stock every three months (January, April, July, and October), it pays $4.65 ÷ 4 = $1.1625 every three months. On October 26, 2011, this stock had a price of $99.50. We can infer that its required rate of return on this date was r_p = $4.65 ÷ $99.50 = 4.673 percent. Looking back to an earlier date, the stock traded at $90.35 per share on August 9, 2011, which means that the required rate of return was $4.65 ÷ $90.35 = 5.1467 percent.

EXAMPLE 7.2

Estimating the Required Rate of Return on Preferred Stock

PROBLEM

Determine the required rate of return on preferred shares that provide a $6 annual dividend if they are presently selling for $70.

Solution

$$r_p = \frac{D_p}{P_p} = \frac{\$6}{\$70} = 8.57\%$$

Valuing Common Stock

Valuing common shares involves several complications that arise with respect to the appropriate future cash flows that should be discounted. Which cash flows should be discounted? Dividends? Free cash flow? One of the most popular discounted cash flow valuation models, which we discuss next, uses dividends. However, unlike bonds or even preferred shares, there is no requirement that common shares pay dividends at all. In addition, the level of dividend payments is discretionary, which implies we must make *estimates* regarding the *amount* and *timing* of any dividend payments. So, you can see why valuing common stock is treacherous.

The basic dividend discount model

dividend discount model (DDM) model for valuing common shares that assumes common shares are valued according to the present value of their expected future dividends

In the **dividend discount model (DDM)** we assume that common shares are valued according to the present value of their expected future cash flows—specifically, dividends. Based on this premise, we estimate today's value, based on an n-year holding period:

$$P_0 = \frac{D_1}{(1 + r_e)^1} + \frac{D_2}{(1 + r_e)^2} + \ldots + \frac{D_n + P_n}{(1 + r_e)^n} \qquad (7\text{-}4)$$

where

P_0 = the value of a share of common stock today

D_t = the expected dividend at the end of year t

P_n = the expected share value after n years

r_e = the required return on the common shares

We diagram this in a time line on Figure 7-2. As you can see, there are two cash flows in the nth period: the expected dividend in that period, plus the expected value of the stock. You will notice that in the case of the value of a preferred share, we used a constant dividend amount (D_p), whereas for common shares we use a dividend that may be different each period (hence, we subscript the dividend in Equation 7-4 and Figure 7-2 to indicate the period). This is because most preferred shares have a stated, constant dividend, whereas common share dividends tend to change over time, at the discretion of the company's board of directors.

FIGURE 7-2 **The Cash Flow Pattern for a Share of Common Stock**

Consider a stock that is expected to pay $2 at the end of the first year and $3 at the end of the second year. If the stock is expected to have a value of $20 at the end of 2 years, what is the value of the stock today if the required rate of return is 8 percent?

$$P_0 = \frac{\$2}{(1 + 0.08)^1} + \frac{\$3}{(1 + 0.08)^2} + \frac{\$20}{(1 + 0.08)^2}$$

$$= \$1.8519 + \$2.5720 + \$17.1468$$

$$= \$21.5707$$

PROBLEM

An investor buys a common share and estimates she will receive an annual dividend of $0.50 per share in 1 year. She estimates she will be able to sell the share for $10.50. Estimate its value, assuming the investor requires a 10 percent rate of return.

Solution

$$P_0 = \frac{\$0.50 + \$10.50}{(1 + 0.10)^1} = \$10.00$$

EXAMPLE 7.3

Estimating the Value of a Share for a One-Year Holding Period

---

In the dividend discount model, the value at any point (say, time n) is equal to the present value of all the expected future dividends from period $n + 1$ to infinity. So the price next year, for example, is the present value of the expected dividend and share value for year 2. By repeatedly substituting for the future share value, we replace it with the present value of the dividend and share value expected the following year. As a result we remove P_n in Equation 7-4 and eventually get the following:

$$P_0 = \frac{D_1}{(1 + r_e)^1} + \frac{D_2}{(1 + r_e)^2} + \ldots + \frac{D_\infty}{(1 + r_e)^\infty} = \sum_{t=1}^{\infty} \frac{D_t}{(1 + r_e)^t} \qquad (7\text{-}5)$$

In other words, the value today is the present value of all future dividends to be received (i.e., from now to infinity).

Why use dividends? Well, if an investor buys a particular stock, the only cash flows that he or she will receive until the investor sells the stock will be the dividends. Although a company's residual earnings technically belong to the common shareholders, corporations generally do not pay out all their earnings as dividends. Of course, earnings are important too—without them the corporation could not sustain dividend payments for long. In fact, earnings receive more attention from investors than any other single variable. However, corporations typically reinvest a portion of their earnings to enhance future earnings and, ultimately, future dividends.

Equation 7-5 is the workhorse of share valuation because it says that the value of a share is the present value of expected future dividends. However, by repeatedly substituting for the share value, we are implicitly making a very important assumption: Investors are rational. We assume that at each time, investors react rationally and value the share based on what they rationally expect to receive the next year. This assumption specifically rules out "speculative bubbles," or what is colloquially known as the "bigger fool theorem."

Suppose, for example, a broker tells a client to buy XYZ at $30. The investor says, "No, it's only worth $25." The broker replies, "I know, but there is momentum behind it and

I am seeing a lot of interest. I think it will go to $40 by next year." The investor is a fool to pay $30 for something he or she thinks is worth $25, but it is not the fool theorem but the *bigger* fool theorem. If the investor does buy it, he or she *is* a fool, but he or she is also assuming that an even bigger fool will buy it in a year's time for $40.

This type of speculative bubble, in which prices keep increasing and become detached from reality, is specifically ruled out by the assumption of rational investors coolly calculating the present value of the expected cash flows at each time, so that prices never get detached from these fundamentals. Of course, there have been speculative bubbles when it has been very difficult to estimate these fundamental values.[16] However, we cannot build models based on irrationality, so we continue with the development of models based on fundamental cash flows.

Valuation with constant growth

growth rate rate of increase in an amount or value

It is impractical to estimate and discount *all* future dividends one by one, as required by Equation 7-5. Fortunately, we can simplify this equation into a usable formula by making the assumption that dividends grow at a constant rate (g) indefinitely. This **growth rate** represents the annual growth in dividends, ad infinitum.[17]

Once we make the assumption about constant growth, we can estimate all future dividends, assuming we know the most recent dividend paid (D_0):

$$D_1 = D_0(1 + g)$$

$$D_2 = D_1(1 + g) = D_0(1 + g)^2$$

$$D_3 = D_2(1 + g) = D_0(1 + g)^3$$

and so on.

Therefore, under the assumption of constant growth in dividends to infinity, Equation 7-5 reduces to the following expression:

$$P_0 = \frac{D_0(1 + g)^1}{(1 + r_e)^1} + \frac{D_0(1 + g)^2}{(1 + r_e)^2} + \ldots + \frac{D_0(1 + g)^\infty}{(1 + r_e)^\infty} \tag{7-6}$$

growing perpetuity stream of cash flows that grows at a constant rate, forever

constant growth DDM version of the dividend discount model for valuing common shares that assumes that dividends grow at a constant rate indefinitely

In Equation 7-6, we are, essentially, multiplying the dividend today, D_0, by a factor of $(1 + g) \div (1 + r_e)$ every period. This represents a **growing perpetuity**, which we can solve easily because it represents the sum of a geometric series. In fact, Equation 7-6 reduces to the following expression, which is the constant growth version of the dividend discount model, or simply the **constant growth DDM**:

$$P_0 = \frac{D_0(1 + g)}{r_e - g} = \frac{D_1}{r_e - g} \tag{7-7}$$

We should note a few features of Equation 7-7:

1. This relationship holds only when $r_e > g$. Otherwise, the answer is negative, which is uninformative.[18]

2. Only *future* estimated cash flows and estimated growth in these cash flows are relevant in the valuation.

---

[16] In Appendix 7A, we review the famous bubble involving the South Seas Company in 1720, in which Sir Isaac Newton almost bankrupted himself and then proclaimed, "I can calculate the motions of the heavenly bodies, but not the madness of people." The madness of people was the way in which the share price of the South Seas Company became completely detached from its fundamentals. The Internet bubble of the late 1990s, in which shares of Internet stocks rose without regard to fundamentals—and then crashed—indicates that the madness of people may not have changed much in almost 300 years.

[17] This growth rate is the same rate we looked at in our study of the time value of money, but forward looking instead of looking at the past. As a refresher, consider that if a company's dividend was $2 in 2007 and $4 in 2012, the average rate of growth in the dividend in these 5 years is 14.87 percent [$FV = 4$; $PV = 2$; $n = 5$; solve for i].

[18] The negative answer occurs because if $g > r$ in Equation 7-6, each future dividend is worth more than the previous one. The value never converges but increases to infinity.

3. The relationship holds only when growth in dividends is expected to occur *at the same rate indefinitely*.

4. If there is no growth (that is, $g = 0$ percent), this collapses to the value of a perpetuity.

Does the constant growth model actually fit companies? Consider the Hershey Foods Corporation. Hershey pays a dividend to its common stockholders each quarter, as we indicate in Figure 7-3. The dividends have grown at an average annual rate of 6.9939 percent, having grown from $0.092 per share to $1.28 per share over the period 1971 through 2010.[19] In Figure 7-3 we also compare the actual dividend growth with what dividends would have been if the growth had been perfectly constant. As you can see, Hershey's dividend growth is approximated well by assuming constant growth.

PROBLEM

Assume a company is currently paying $1.10 per share in common stock dividends. Investors expect dividends to grow at an annual rate of 4 percent indefinitely, and they require a 10 percent return on the shares. Determine the value of a share of this stock.

Solution

First, calculate the next period's dividend:

$$D_1 = D_0(1 + g) = \$1.10 \times (1 + 0.04) = \$1.144$$

Then, using next period's dividend, the required rate of return, and growth rate, calculate the value today:

$$P_0 = \frac{D_1}{r_e - g} = \frac{\$1.144}{0.10 - 0.04} = \$19.07$$

EXAMPLE 7.4

Using the Constant Growth Dividend Discount Model to Estimate a Share's Value

---

FIGURE 7-3 Hershey Foods Corporation Common Stock Dividends, 1971 Through 2010

Source: *Hershey Foods Corporation 10-K filings and annual reports, various years.*

---

[19] We adjusted the dividends for Hershey's stock splits. Because a stock split increases the number of shares proportionately, we adjusted the historical dividends downward to reflect a split. For example, Hershey split its stock 2 for 1 in 2004, doubling the number of shares outstanding. Hence, we divided the dividend in 2003 by two to put it on the same basis as 2004 dividends. We will cover stock splits in more detail in a later chapter.

Estimating the required rate of return

We can rearrange the constant growth dividend discount model to estimate the rate of return required by investors on a particular share, as follows:

$$r_e = \frac{D_1}{P_0} + g \tag{7-8}$$

capital gains yield or capital yield return in the form of the appreciation or depreciation in the value of an asset

The first term $(D_1 \div P_0)$ in Equation 7-8 is the expected **dividend yield** on the share. Therefore, we may view the second term, g, as the expected **capital gains yield** (or, simply, **capital yield**) because the total return must equal the dividend yield plus the capital gains yield. It is important to recognize that this equation provides an appropriate approximation for required return *only* if the conditions of the constant growth dividend discount model are met (i.e., in particular the assumption regarding constant growth in dividends to infinity must be satisfied).

Consider a common stock that has an annual dividend of $2 per share. If the value of a share of this stock is $20 and the expected growth rate is 4 percent, the dividend yield is $2 \div $20 = 10 percent, and the required rate of return is 10 percent + 4 percent = 14 percent.

Let's take another look at Hershey common stock. The current dividend yield on Hershey common stock is $1.28 \div $47.15 = 3.5764 percent. Combining this with the dividend growth rate of 6.9913 percent, we estimate Hershey's required rate of return of 3.5764 percent + 6.9913 percent = 10.5677 percent.

EXAMPLE 7.5

Estimating the Required Rate of Return Using the Dividend Discount Model

PROBLEM

The market value of a company's shares is $12 each, the estimated dividend at the end of this year, D_1, is $0.60, and the estimated long-term growth rate in dividends, g, is 4 percent. Estimate the implied required rate of return on these shares.

Solution

$$r_e = \frac{D_1}{P_0} + g = \frac{\$0.60}{\$12} + 0.04 = 0.05 + 0.04 = 0.09 = 9\%$$

This result suggests that the expected return on these shares comprises an expected dividend yield of 5 percent and an expected capital gains yield of 4 percent.

Estimating the Value of Growth Opportunities

The constant growth dividend discount model can also provide a useful assessment of the market's perception of growth opportunities available to a company, as reflected in its market value. Let's begin by assuming that a company that has no profitable growth opportunities should not reinvest residual profits in the company, but rather should pay out all its earnings as dividends. Under these conditions, we have no growth (that is, $g = 0$), EPS_1 represents the expected earnings per common share in the upcoming year, and earnings per share are equal to dividends, $D_1 = EPS_1$. Under these assumptions, the constant growth dividend discount model reduces to the following expression:

$$P_0 = \frac{EPS_1}{r_e} \tag{7-9}$$

It is unlikely to find a company that has exactly "zero" growth opportunities, but the point is that we can view the share value of any common stock (that satisfies the assumptions of the constant growth dividend discount model) as comprising two components: its no-growth component, and the remainder, which is attributable to the market's perception of the growth opportunities available to that company. We denote this as the **present value of growth opportunities (PVGO)**. Therefore, we get Equation 7-10:

$$P_0 = \frac{EPS_1}{r_e} + PVGO \qquad (7\text{-}10)$$

present value of growth opportunities (PVGO) amount of the value of an asset that is attributable to the expected growth opportunities of the asset's cash flows

If a company's common stock has a market value of $25, the expected earnings per share for next year is $1, and the required rate of return is 10 percent, the stock's present value of growth opportunities is $15:

$$\$25 = \frac{\$1}{0.10} + PVGO$$

Rearranging,

$$PVGO = \$25 - 10 = \$15$$

PROBLEM

A company's shares are selling for $20 each in the market. The company's EPS is expected to be $1.50 next year, and the required return on the shares is estimated to be 10 percent. Estimate the present value of growth opportunities per share.

Solution

We can solve this for PVGO by rearranging Equation 7-10:

$$PVGO = P_0 - \frac{EPS_1}{r_e} = \$20 - \frac{\$1.50}{0.10} = \$20 - \$15 = \$5.00$$

EXAMPLE 7.6

Estimating the Present Value of Growth Opportunities

Returning once again to Hershey Food's common stock, we observe the year-end stock price for 2010 as $47.15 per share, and its earnings per share for 2011 are expected to be $2.83 per share. Therefore, using the 10.5677 percent cost of equity, the present value of growth opportunities is $20.37:

$$PVGO_{Hershey} = \$47.15 - (\$2.83 \div 0.105677) = \$47.15 - 26.78 = \$20.37$$

Extending the Dividend Discount Model

The constant growth dividend discount model predicts that, all else remaining equal, the value of common shares (P_0) will *increase* as a result of:

- an increase in the dividend;
- an increase in the expected growth rate of dividends; or
- a decrease in the required rate of return.

This list illustrates the intuitive appeal of the dividend discount model because it links common share values to three important fundamentals: corporate profitability, the general level of interest rates, and risk. In particular, expected dividends are closely related to profitability, as is the growth rate of these dividends, whereas the required rate of return is affected by the base level of interest rates (r_f) and by risk (as reflected in the risk premium required by investors). In particular, all else being equal, the dividend discount model predicts that common share prices will be higher when profits are high (and expected to grow), when interest rates are lower, and when risk premiums are lower.

We can generally assume that current dividends (D_0) are given, so it is the movements in r_e and g that determine the value of a share (i.e., because $r_e - g$ is the denominator and because $D_0(1 + g)$ is the numerator). Suppose a company currently pays $2 per share each year in dividends, the expected rate of growth in dividends is 5 percent, and the required rate of return is 8 percent. The value of a share of this company's stock is $70:

$$P_0 = \frac{\$2(1 + 0.05)}{0.08 - 0.05} = \frac{\$2.10}{0.03} = \$70$$

But what happens if we vary the inputs? What if . . .

. . . the growth in dividends in 6 percent instead of 5 percent?

$$P_0 = \frac{\$2(1 + 0.06)}{0.08 - 0.06} = \frac{\$2.12}{0.02} = \$106$$

. . . the required rate of return is 9 percent instead of 8 percent?

$$P_0 = \frac{\$2(1 + 0.05)}{0.09 - 0.05} = \frac{\$2.10}{0.04} = \$52.50$$

We show what happens when we vary the growth rate and when we vary the required rate of return in Figure 7-4. As you can see in this figure, there is a positive relation between the growth rate and the value of the stock, and there is a negative relation between the required rate of return and the value of the stock.

EXAMPLE 7.7

Valuing Shares Using the Constant Growth Dividend Discount Model

PROBLEM

Consider a company that is currently paying $1.10 per share in dividends.

a. If investors expect annual growth in dividends to be 3 percent and the estimated required rate of return to be 10 percent, what is the value of these shares?
b. If investors expect annual growth in dividends to be 3 percent and the estimated required rate of return to be 11 percent, what is the value of these shares?

Solution

$$D_1 = \$1.10 \times (1 + 0.03) = \$1.133$$

a. $P_0 = \$1.133 \div (0.10 - 0.03) = \$16.1857$

b. $P_0 = \$1.133 \div (0.11 - 0.03) = \$14.1625$

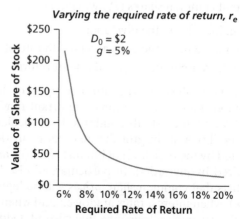

FIGURE 7-4 Comparison of the Value of Stock with Varying Growth Rates and Varying Required Rates of Return

Estimating the inputs into the constant growth dividend discount model generally requires a great deal of analysis and judgment. Assuming we know the most recent year's dividend payment, D_0, we need to estimate the required rate of return, r_e, and the expected growth in dividends, g, because $D_1 = D_0(1 + g)$. As discussed earlier, the required rate of return for equity will equal the risk-free rate of return plus a risk premium, as depicted in Equation 7-1.[20]

We can use several methods to estimate the expected annual growth rate in dividends. One of the most common approaches is to determine the company's **sustainable growth rate**, SGR, which can be estimated by using the following equation:

$$SGR = b \times ROE \tag{7-11}$$

where b is the company's earnings retention ratio and ROE is company's return on common equity (i.e., net income ÷ common equity).[21] The **retention ratio** is the complement of the dividend payout ratio; in other words, $b = 1 -$ dividend payout ratio. Another name for the retention ratio is the **plowback ratio**, named as such because these are the earnings that are *plowed back* into company.

From Equation 7-11 we see that growth in earnings (and dividends) is positively related to the proportion of each dollar of earnings reinvested in the company, b, as well as positively related to the company's return on equity. For example, a company that retains all its earnings and earns 10 percent on its equity would see its equity base grow by 10 percent per year. If the same company paid out all its earnings, then it would not grow. Similarly, a company that retained a portion, b, would earn 10 percent on that proportion, resulting in $g = b \times ROE$.[22]

> **sustainable growth rate (SGR)** earnings retention ratio multiplied by return on equity
>
> **retention ratio** or **plowback ratio** proportion of earnings reinvested in the company; the complement of the dividend payout ratio

---

PROMBLEM

A company has an ROE of 12 percent, and its dividend payout ratio is 30 percent. Use this information to determine the company's sustainable growth rate.

Solution

$$g = b \times ROE = (1 - 0.30) \times (0.12) = 0.70 \times 0.12 = 0.0840 = 8.40 \text{ percent}$$

> **EXAMPLE 7.8**
>
> **Estimating a Company's Sustainable Growth Rate**

We can use the DuPont system to decompose ROE into three factors, as we show in Equation 7-12:

$$ROE = (\text{Net income} \div \text{Revenues}) \times (\text{Revenues} \div \text{Total assets}) \times (\text{Total assets} \div \text{Equity})$$

or, equivalently,

$$ROE = \text{Net profit margin} \times \text{Turnover ratio} \times \text{Equity multiplier} \tag{7-12}$$

The ROE, and hence g, increases with higher profit margins, higher asset turnover, and higher debt (although higher debt implies higher risk and, therefore, higher r_e).

We should note, however, that companies' return on equity can be quite variable, so what we are looking for is really the long-term trend. Consider International Business Machines (IBM), a U.S. technology service provider. As we show in Figure 7-5, Panel A, IBM's return on equity was relatively constant until 1990, which marks IBM's

---

[20] We defer further discussion of estimating the discount rate for equities to later chapters in this text.

[21] You may notice that we refer to this equity as common equity, but we made no such distinction in prior chapters. Because common equity is the residual ownership of the company, the growth pertains to returns to common shareholders; the return to preferred shareholders is fixed.

[22] A major weakness of this approach is its reliance on accounting figures to determine ROE because it is based on book values and the accrual method of accounting. As a result, it may not represent the "true" return earned on reinvested funds.

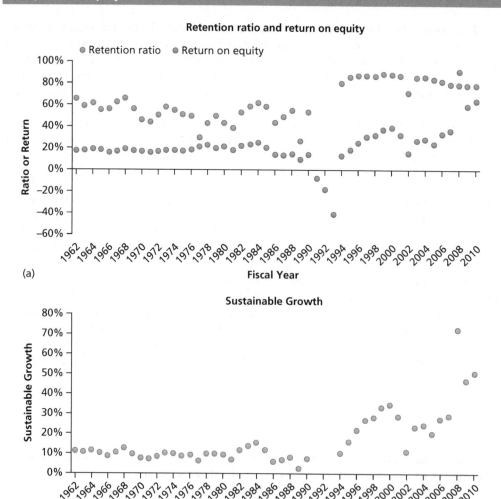

FIGURE 7-5 International Business Machines' Retention Ratio and Return on Capital, 1962 Through 2010

Source of data: *International Business Machines Annual Reports, various years, and 10-K filings.*

diversification from computers into technology services and consulting; this also marks when IBM's return on equity increased, in general, but also became more variable.[23]

Considering the variability of the return on equity and the retention ratio, as illustrated using IBM, we need to focus on the long-term trend, rather than a particular year's calculated SGR. For example, we might estimate IBM's retention ratio beyond 2011 to be around 80 percent and its return on equity as 35 percent, which typifies the 1994–2008 period. This implies a sustainable growth of IBM as 28 percent; however, in practice such a high rate of growth is not sustainable in the long run.

Another approach to estimating *g* is to examine historical rates of growth in dividends and earnings levels, including long-term trends in these growth rates for the company, the industry, and the economy as a whole. Predictions regarding future growth rates can be determined based on these past trends by using geometric or arithmetic averages or by using more involved statistical techniques, such as regression analysis. Finally, an important source of information regarding company growth, particularly for the near term, can be found in analyst estimates. Investors are often especially interested in "consensus" estimates because market values are often based to a large extent on these estimates.

---

[23] 1993 marks the beginning of a new phase in IBM's financial history as it defines its new business lines with a new CEO, Louis Gerstner, Jr. at the helm. IBM experienced losses in 1991, 1992, and 1993, but maintained its dividend; hence, its retention ratio and sustainable growth are not defined with losses.

PROBLEM

A company just paid an annual dividend of $1.00 per share and had earnings per share of $4. Its projected values for net profit margin, asset turnover, and the leverage ratio are 4 percent, 1.25 times, and 1.40, respectively. Estimate the company's sustainable growth rate.

EXAMPLE 7.9

Estimating a Company's Sustainable Growth Rate Using the DuPont System

Solution

Step 1: Calculate the return on equity

$$\text{ROE} = 0.04 \times 1.25 \times 1.40 = 0.07 = 7.00\%$$

Step 2: Calculate the retention rate

$$\text{Payout ratio} = \text{DPS} \div \text{EPS} = \$1 / \$4 = 0.25, \text{ so } b = 1 - 0.25 = 0.75$$

Step 3: Calculate the sustainable growth rate

$$g = b \times \text{ROE} = 0.75 \times 7.00\% = 5.25\%$$

It is important to remember in the application of any of these approaches that we are estimating future growth, and the inputs require judgment on the part of the analyst. If researchers believe past growth will be repeated in the future or want to eliminate period-to-period fluctuations in the plowback and return on equity, they may choose to use 3- to 5-year averages for these variables. Conversely, if the company has changed substantially, or analysts have good reason to believe the ratios for the most recent year are the best indicators of future sustainable growth, they will use these figures. In addition, an analysis of macroeconomic, industry, and company-specific factors may lead researchers to develop predicted values for these variables, independent of their historical levels.[24]

A key element in estimating future growth is to consider the company's ability to sustain growth. If the company has a competitive advantage that may be whittled away over time by its competitors, the best long-term growth rate may be the industry's growth rate, or even the long-term growth rate of the general economy. Therefore, the best estimate of growth may not be determined by the numbers, but by the application of judgment that considers not only the company's past, but also the many factors that affect its future.

Valuation With Multistage Growth

As we have noted, the constant growth dividend discount model relationship holds only when we are able to assume constant growth in dividends from now to infinity. In many situations it may be more appropriate to estimate dividends for the most immediate periods up to some point in time, after which it is assumed there will be constant growth in dividends to infinity. Several situations lend themselves to this structure. For example, it is reasonable to assume that competitive pressures and business cycle influences will prevent companies from maintaining extremely high growth in earnings for long periods. In addition, short-term earnings and dividend estimates should be much more reliable than those covering a longer period, which are often estimated by using some very general estimates of future economic, industry, and company conditions. To use the best information available at any point, it may make the most sense to estimate growth as precisely as possible in the short term, before assuming some long-term rate of growth. In practice, the discounted cash flow approach assuming multistage growth is used often by analysts.

---

[24] Some evidence indicates that using macroeconomic factors and company-specific factors, such as the independent auditor's opinion, are useful in predictions.

We can apply Equation 7-13 when steady growth in dividends to infinity does not begin until period t:

$$P_0 = \frac{D_1}{(1 + r_e)^1} + \frac{D_2}{(1 + r_e)^2} + \ldots + \frac{D_t + P_t}{(1 + r_e)^t} \qquad (7\text{-}13)$$

where $P_t = \dfrac{D_{t+1}}{r_e - g}$. Notice that this is Equation 7-4, with n replaced by t and with an estimate for the future share price, P_t.

In Figure 7-6 we depict the cash flows associated with this type of a valuation framework, but with one growth rate for a finite number of periods and another growth rate following in perpetuity. This well-known version of the multiple-growth dividend discount model is the **two-stage growth rate model**, which assumes growth at one rate for a certain period, g_1, followed by some steady growth rate to infinity at g_2. This model is applied often to start-up companies, in which growth for the first few years is expected to be high, but then slowing as the company, industry, or product matures. In the example in Figure 7-6, dividends grow at a rate g_1 for 4 years, and then beginning in the 5th year, dividends begin to grow at a rate of g_2. This means that the dividend in year 5, D_5, is affected by the growth rate for the first 4 years, as well as the growth rate in the 5th year:

$$D_5 = D_4(1 + g_2) = D_0(1 + g_1)^4(1 + g_2)$$

Essentially, whenever we use multiple period growth rates, we estimate dividends *up to the beginning* of the period in which it is reasonable to assume constant growth to infinity. In Figure 7-6, constant growth begins after the fourth period. Then we can use the constant growth dividend discount model to estimate of the market value of the share at that time; in the case of Figure 7-6, we estimate the value of a share at the end of the fourth period, which is the present value of the dividends from period 5 on, growing at a constant rate g_2:

$$P_4 = \frac{D_5}{(1 + r_e)^5} + \frac{D_6}{(1 + r_e)^6} + \frac{D_7}{(1 + r_e)^7} + \ldots + \frac{D_\infty}{(1 + r_e)^\infty} = \frac{D_4(1 + g_2)}{(r_e - g_2)} = \frac{D_5}{(r_e - g_2)}$$

two-stage growth rate model valuation model for equity in which there are two stages, each with a different growth rate

FIGURE 7-6 **The Cash Flow Pattern for Multiple Stage Growth in Dividends**

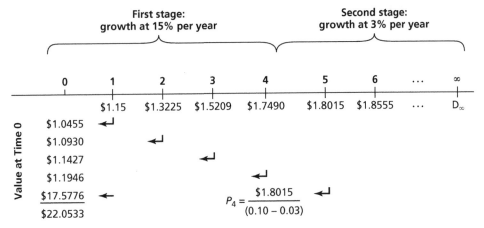

FIGURE 7-7 The Cash Flow Pattern for Multiple Stage Growth in Dividends

Finally, we discount all the estimated dividends up to the beginning of the constant growth period, as well as the estimated market value at that time.[25] This provides us with today's estimate of the share's market value.

Let's put some numbers to this problem. Assume that the current dividend is $1 and that dividends are expected to grow at a rate of 15 percent for the first 4 years, 3 percent thereafter. If the required rate of return is 10 percent, what is the value of share of stock today? As you can see in Figure 7-7, the value of the stock today is $22.0533, which is comprised of the present value of the first four dividends and the present value of the value of a share four years from today.

PROBLEM

A company is expected to pay a dividend of $1.00 at the end of this year, a $1.50 dividend at the end of year 2, and a $2.00 dividend at the end of year 3. It is estimated dividends will grow at a constant rate of 4 percent per year thereafter. Determine the market value of this company's common shares if the required rate of return is 11 percent.

Solution

First, estimate dividends up to the start of constant growth to infinity. In this example, they are all given, so no calculations are required:

$D_1 = \$1.00$

$D_2 = \$1.50$

$D_3 = \$2.00$

Second, estimate the value at the beginning of the constant growth to infinity period:

$$D_4 = \$2.00 \times (1 + 0.04) = \$2.08$$

$$P_3 = \frac{D_4}{r_e - g} = \frac{\$2.08}{0.11 - 0.04} = \$29.71$$

Third, discount back the relevant cash flows to time 0:

$$P_0 = \frac{1.00}{(1 + 0.11)} + \frac{1.50}{(1 + 0.11)^2} + \frac{2.00 + 29.71}{(1 + 0.11)^3} = 0.90 + 1.22 + 23.19 = \$25.31$$

EXAMPLE 7.10

Using the Multistage Dividend Discount Model

---

[25] Recall that P_t represents the present value of all the expected dividends from time $t + 1$ to infinity, so we are essentially discounting *all* the expected future dividends associated with the stock.

Using a financial calculator, enter the cash flows and interest rate, then solve for the NPV:

CF_t	1.0
CF_t	1.5
CF_t	31.71 ← 29 + 2.71
i	11

Solve for the NPV

Using a spreadsheet, type the cash flows in the appropriate cells and using the NPV function:

	A	B
1	1	
2	1.5	
3	31.71	
4		= NPV(.11, A1:A3)

Limitations of the Dividend Discount Model

Although the dividend discount model provides a great deal of insight into the factors that affect the valuation of common shares, it is based on several assumptions that are not met by a large number of companies. In particular, it is best suited for companies that (1) pay dividends based on a stable dividend payout history that they want to maintain in the future, and (2) are growing at a steady and sustainable rate. As such, the dividend discount model works reasonably well for large corporations in mature industries with stable profits and an established dividend policy.[26]

Not surprisingly, the dividend discount model does not work well for many resource-based companies, which are cyclical in nature and often display erratic growth in earnings and dividends. In addition, many of these companies (especially the smaller ones) do not distribute dividends to shareholders. Consider Hecla Mining, which mines for metals including silver, gold, lead, and zinc. Looking at Hecla's net income, you can see that its earnings were relatively stable until 1975, as we show in Figure 7-8, but the company paid dividends on and off until 1991; when net income became quite variable, dividends ceased.

The dividend discount model will also not work well for companies in distress, companies that are in the process of restructuring, companies involved in acquisitions, and private companies. Finally, if a company enters into substantial share-repurchase arrangements, we must adjust the model because share repurchases also represent a method of distributing wealth to shareholders.

Due to the limitations of the dividend discount model, and because common share valuation is a challenging process, involving, as it does, predictions for the future, analysts often use several approaches to value common shares. Aside from the relative valuation approaches discussed in the next section, another discounted cash flow approach—using the free cash flow instead of dividends—is used frequently. The free cash flow approach is implemented almost identically to the dividend discount model, except that instead of discounting estimated future dividends, you discount expected future free cash flows. The underlying rationale is that dividends are discretionary, and many firms may choose not to

---

[26] When we look at dividends for companies, we need to also consider the effects of severe economic environments. For example, many mature, steady-dividend-paying companies cut their dividends during the 2007–08 financial crisis, but have since resumed these dividends, albeit at lower rates. General Electric, with a history of steadily increasing dividends, cut its dividend in mid-2009 from $0.31 each quarter to $0.10 each quarter, but then resumed a pattern of steadily-increasing dividends in the quarters that followed.

FIGURE 7-8 Hecla Mining Net Income, 1960 Through 2010

Source of data: *Hecla Mining Annual Report and 10-K filings, various years.*

pay out the amount of dividends they could. Therefore, instead of using dividends, you use free cash flow, which is in some sense a measure of what a firm could pay out if it chose to.

We will not discuss this model in detail but will note that there are two variations of this approach:

1. using free cash flows to equity holders and discounting them using the required return to equity holders (as in the dividend discount model); and
2. using free cash flows to the firm, and discounting them using the firm's weighted average cost of capital. This approach is often more appropriate when firms do not pay out a significant portion of their earnings as dividends, or pay out well below their capacity.

BP and Its Dividend | ETHICS

BP PLC is a British limited company in the energy industry, with fiscal year 2009 revenues of $239 billion. From 2005 to 2009, the dividends on BP shares grew at an average rate of 17.4 percent per year, increasing each year despite the fact that the earnings to shareholders declined in 2009. BP had not reduced its dividends since 1992.

In April 2010, BP declared a dividend of $10 billion, with payment in June 2010. BP experienced a disaster with its Deepwater Horizon drilling operation, which exploded on April 20, 2010, resulting in a massive oil spill in the U.S. Gulf of Mexico. BP faced a dilemma regarding paying its dividend while still wrangling with the 2010 oil spill in the Gulf. The spill resulted in not only direct and future costs to BP, but also a problem: The company had committed to shareholders to pay the dividend, but there was pressure by politicians for BP to not pay the dividend. Should BP disappoint the pensions and other investors who depend on the dividend? Should BP consider the political fallout and cut the dividend?

In the first two quarters of 2010, BP took a $32.2 billion charge for current and anticipated spill-related costs. In the quarter ending June 30, 2010, BP had current assets of $77 billion, equity of $85 billion, cash flow from operations of $14 billion, but a loss after the spill charge, of $17 billion. For the fiscal year 2010 BP was expected to generate profits, and the charge for the spill was manageable considering the earnings of the company.

BP resolved this dilemma by canceling its dividend for 2010, but promised to consider paying a dividend in the future. By not paying a dividend, BP contributed to a fund to pay for spill-related costs, as well as pay down its debt. BP resumed its dividend in 2011.

Sources: Barr, Colin, "BP Slashes Dividend," *Fortune*, June 16, 2010; Herron, James, "BP Takes Heat from Two Sides on Dividend," *Wall Street Journal*, June 9, 2010; www.bp.com.

Concept Review
Questions

1. In what ways are preferred shares different from bonds, and how do these differences affect the valuation of preferred shares?

2. According to the dividend discount models used to value common stock, what factors are important in this valuation, and what relationship do they have to the value of a share of stock?

7.3   USING MULTIPLES TO VALUE EQUITY

We can use relative valuation to estimate the value of common shares by comparing the market values of similar companies, relative to a common variable, such as earnings, cash flow, book value, or sales. Because relative valuation relies on multiples, we refer to this methodology as the method of multiples. Conceptually, relative valuation appears simple to apply: All we need to do is find a group of comparable companies and then use their financial data and market values to infer the value of the company in question. However, finding comparable companies is difficult: What company is similar to Microsoft, for example? Even after we find a group of comparable companies, we have to estimate the appropriate multiple because values will differ even for comparable companies, so the exercise involves substantial analysis and judgment.

Using the Price-Earnings Ratio

We illustrate the approach by using the most commonly used relative valuation multiple: the **price-earnings (P/E) ratio**. The P/E ratio represents the number of times investors are willing to pay for a company's earnings, as expressed in the share price, or the share price divided by the earnings per share. The P/E approach is implemented by estimating the company's earnings per share (EPS) and multiplying it by a justifiable P/E multiple. The **justified P/E** is the multiple that is considered sustainable over the long term. The typical P/E formulation for valuation purposes uses estimated earnings per share (EPS_1) for the next 12 months. The basic valuation equation can then be expressed as shown in Equation 7-14:

justified P/E multiple that is considered sustainable over the long-term

$$P_0 = \text{Estimated } EPS_1 \times \text{Justified P/E} = EPS_1 \times (P_0/EPS_1) \qquad (7\text{-}14)$$

Notice that the P/E ratio used in Equation 7-14 is based on expected future earnings (Estimated EPS_1) and is therefore the *leading P/E ratio*. By comparison, when we analyze financial ratios, the reported P/E ratios are often based on earnings over the previous 12 months (EPS_0), resulting in *lagging P/E ratios*. For valuation purposes, we typically focus on the leading P/E ratio because market values are based on expectations about the future.

Using the P/E ratio is easy: If the company's forecast earnings per share are $2 and the P/E ratio for comparable companies is 20, we would arrive at a share value of $40 using the P/E approach. We can see from this example why this approach is also called "using multiples." In this case, the multiple of earnings is 20 times. In this sense the multiple is an example of a payback period. The higher the multiple, the longer the payback period and the more the investor is expecting earnings to increase. Alternatively, it could be that the shares are simply more expensive shares.

relative valuation valuing a company relative to other comparable companies

We can also see why the approach is commonly called **relative valuation**: We are valuing the company relative to other comparable companies. This means that if the comparable companies are all overvalued, using the P/E approach will overvalue the company

FIGURE 7-9 Price-Earnings Ratio for the S&P 500 Index, January 1881–November 2011

Source of data: *Robert Shiller, www.yale.edu.*

in question. What this means is that if the market is in a "speculative bubble," the P/E approach will not detect it directly. What is then needed is some yardstick or benchmark P/E. We can ballpark this by looking at the P/E ratio for the S&P 500 Composite Index, which we show in Figure 7-9.

The P/E is based on trailing or lagged earnings for the companies in the S&P 500 Index, and it vividly demonstrates the problems with the P/E ratio: Very low earnings cause the value of the P/E to skyrocket. In the early 1990s, the U.S. experienced a bubble in Internet stock, causing the average P/E ratio to increase to 45 times. Then during the slowdown in 2002 and the puncturing of the Internet bubble, price-earnings ratios fell, recovering slightly.

What we see in Figure 7-9 is the **Molodovsky effect**. This effect is named after Nicholas Molodovsky, who observed that P/E ratios are overstated in slow economic periods.[27] The numerator in the trailing P/E ratio is the current price, which reflects investors' expectations about future earnings and cash flows to investors, whereas the denominator reflects the most recent earnings experience. Because of the forward-looking nature of prices, the P/E ratios of cyclical stocks tend to have prices looking forward to better economic times, but earnings that reflect poor economic times. Therefore, high P/E ratios during recessions, for example, are likely overstated. On the other hand, if investors are forecasting declining earnings, a trailing P/E may be understated.

Molodovsky effect
trailing P/E ratios of cyclical companies are overstated during low points of the economic cycle

Recognizing these problems, we can see that typically the P/E is in the range of 15 to 20 times. When P/E ratios fall to the lower band of this range, we tend to think the stock market is undervalued; when the P/E creeps above 20, we take it as a warning signal that equities are overvalued. At the end of the 2007–2009 recession, both the stock market and earnings prospects fell, but in late 2009 investors priced stocks expecting that earnings would recover.[28]

The P/E ratio is an attractive (and commonly reported) statistic for investors and analysts for several reasons. First, it relates the price to the earnings owned by the shareholders. Second, it is easy to compute and as a result is commonly available. This makes

[27] Molodovsky, Nicholas, "Some Aspects of Price-Earnings Ratios," *Financial Analysts Journal*, May 1953, Vol. 9, No. 2, pp. 65–78.

[28] The National Bureau of Economic Research indicates that this recession began in December of 2007. The previous recession was from March 2001 through November 2001 [www.nbre.org/cycles/].

comparisons relatively straightforward. Third, it is intuitive, as it indicates the payback period and thus can be related to a number of other company characteristics, such as growth opportunities and risk.

We need two estimates to calculate Equation 7-14. Unfortunately, obtaining reasonable estimates requires a substantial amount of analysis and also an element of judgment. EPS_1 can be determined by using several approaches, which are similar to those described earlier for estimating future dividends. In particular, we can analyze historical earnings data, project trends, and the company's present situation and forecast future earnings.[29] In addition, the use of analyst estimates (and consensus estimates) may provide reasonable forecasts of EPS_1.

Estimating justifiable P/E ratios is even more involved, and there are several approaches we can use. One common approach is to find comparable companies and estimate an appropriate P/E ratio for the company being analyzed, based on a comparison of this company with the others, in terms of risk and growth opportunities. This approach often involves using an industry average P/E ratio, which is then scaled up or down, based on an assessment of whether or not the company is above or below average. Unfortunately, this approach involves a great deal of subjectivity regarding several company-specific characteristics, including risk, potential for growth, and the overall financial health of the company. Further, differences in accounting among companies may require some adjustments for comparability among companies. In addition, this approach may build market errors into the value estimation process. For example, even though a company may be average within its industry, the industry average P/E ratio may be too high if the industry's earnings are currently depressed (understating the denominator), but the market anticipates that earnings will recover for a particular industry at a particular time. Another commonly used approach is to examine historical averages for the company or the company's industry. However, using historical averages may be inappropriate if the company has changed substantially and as market and industry conditions change.

Potential problems are associated with the use of industry or historical averages to estimate the appropriate P/E ratio, so it is beneficial to obtain corroborating estimates based on economic, industry, and company fundamentals, if possible. Fortunately, we can estimate the P/E ratio by relating it to the fundamentals in the dividend discount model.[30] We illustrate this by using the simplest DDM model: the constant growth model:

$$P_0 = \frac{D_1}{r_e - g}$$

Dividing both sides of this equation by expected earnings (EPS_1), we get Equation 7-15:

$$\frac{P_0}{EPS_1} = \frac{D_1 / EPS_1}{r_e - g} \tag{7-15}$$

We are left with the P/E ratio on the left side of Equation 7-15 and the expected dividend payout, required rate of return, and growth rate on the right-hand side. Notice that it is *expected earnings*, not historical earnings, that are relevant. Also note that r_e and g are typically the most important factors in the determination of the P/E ratio because a small change in either can have a large effect on its value. Based on Equation 7-15, the following relationships should hold, all else being equal:

- The higher the expected payout ratio, the higher the P/E.
- The higher the expected growth rate, g, the higher the P/E.
- The higher the required rate of return, r_e, the lower the P/E.

---

[29] You can also refer to our discussion of forecasting financial statements in Chapter 4.

[30] Similar to the DDM, this approach for estimating P/E ratios will work best for companies with relatively stable dividend and growth patterns.

However, "all else being equal" is a brave assumption because many of these variables are interrelated. For example, raising the payout ratio and thus increasing the dividend seems to increase the P/E, but raising the payout may also reduce growth because one estimate of the growth rate is the sustainable growth rate, where $g = (1 - \text{Payout}) \times \text{ROE}$. We might also try to increase the growth rate by taking on risky investment projects that could increase future earnings and dividends, but this could also cause the required rate of return to increase (i.e., recall $r_e = r_f + \text{Risk premium}$). However, what we can say is that P/E ratios tend to be higher when future growth in earnings and dividends is also expected to be high and when interest rates or risk premiums are low (because they both affect r_e).

EXAMPLE 7.11

Using the P/E Ratio Approach

PROBLEM

Assume that a company has just reported an EPS of $2.00 and expects to maintain a 40 percent payout ratio. Estimate the company's P/E ratio and its market value, assuming its ROE is 10 percent and that investors require a 9 percent return on their shares.

Solution

First, estimate $g = (1 - \text{payout}) \times \text{ROE} = (1 - 0.40) \times 10\% = 6.00\%$.

Second, estimate $EPS_1 = (EPS_0)(1 + g) = (2.00 \times 1.06) = \$2.12$.

Third, estimate $\dfrac{P}{E} = \dfrac{D_1/EPS_1}{r_e - g} = \dfrac{0.40}{0.09 - 0.06} = 13.33$

Fourth, estimate $P_0 = EPS_1 \times P_0/EPS_1 = \$2.12 \times 13.33 = \$28.26$.

We assume that the payout ratio remains constant at 40 percent, but we vary the main subjective inputs, r_e and g, to assess the effect on the P/E ratio and on value.

EXAMPLE 7.12

Varying the Inputs of the P/E Ratio Approach

PROBLEM

Suppose a company has EPS of $2.00 and a payout ratio of 40 percent. Value a share of common stock assuming:

a. a growth rate of 5 percent and a required rate of return of 10 percent.
b. a growth rate of 7 percent and a required rate of return of 8 percent.

Solution

a. $EPS_1 = \$2.00 \times 1.05 = \$2.10$

$\dfrac{P}{E} = \dfrac{0.40}{0.10 - 0.05} = 8$

So, $P_0 = \$2.10 \times 8.00 = \$16.80$

b. $EPS_1 = \$2.00 \times 1.07 = \$2.14$

$\dfrac{P}{E} = \dfrac{0.40}{0.08 - 0.07} = 40$

So, $P_0 = \$2.14 \times 40.00 = \$85.60$

Notice the wide range of P/E and value estimates that arise for relatively small changes in our estimates of r_e and g.

Aside from the difficulties in estimating an appropriate P/E ratio and in estimating future EPS, there are several other practical concerns regarding the use of P/E ratios:

- The P/E ratio is uninformative when companies have negative or very small earnings.[31]
- The P/E ratio may be highly variable across an industry.
- The volatile nature of earnings implies a great deal of volatility in P/E multiples. For example, the earnings of cyclical companies fluctuate quite dramatically throughout a typical business cycle.
- Net income, and hence earnings per share, is susceptible to the influence of accounting choices and earnings management.

For these reasons, P/E ratios are often based on smoothed or normalized estimates of earnings for the forecast year. This is also the reason analysts use other, similar relative value approaches along with a P/E analysis.

LESSONS LEARNED | Low Price-Earnings Ratio

Are low-P/E stocks good buying opportunities? Some may refer to low-P/E stocks as "cheap," but cheap does not always mean it's a good deal. Here are a few reasons:

- A low P/E ratio may mean that the company is likely headed for trouble. Look at any company that is in financial distress, and you will see a falling share price and shrinking earnings—it may be that the share price, which is forward-looking—shrinks faster than reported earnings.
- Some argue that a stock with a low P/E may be undervalued. But isn't the value of the stock in the market

the value of the stock? Could the market—the millions of investors who watch the value of stocks—be so wrong as to make such a mistake in valuing a stock? Not likely so.

- A P/E may be low because of inflation. In periods of high inflation, the deductions for depreciation are based on historical costs, and the cost of goods sold may reflect historical, not replacement, costs. In this case, high inflation will result in overstated earnings, hence resulting in a low P/E.

Additional Multiples or Relative Value Ratios

The **market-to-book (M/B) ratio** is the market value per share divided by the book value per share. Equivalently, we can calculate the market-to-book ratio as the ratio of the market capitalization of the common stock divided by the book value of common equity. Recall that the book value per share equals the book value of equity (i.e., assets – liabilities) divided by the number of common shares outstanding. As such, valuing stocks relative to their M/B is an attractive approach for several reasons. Book value provides a relatively stable, intuitive measure of value relative to market values that can be easily compared with those of other companies, provided accounting standards do not vary greatly across the comparison group. It eliminates several of the problems arising from the use of P/E multiples because book values are rarely negative and do not exhibit the volatility associated with earnings levels. However, book values may be sensitive to accounting standards and may be uninformative for companies that do not have a large proportion of fixed assets (such as service companies) or that have negative equity.

The use of the M/B ratio fell out of favor in the 1980s and 1990s because of high rates of inflation that distorted the M/B ratio. This is because using historical cost accounting in an inflationary period results in understated carrying or book values. However, the low

---

[31] We can sometimes get very large or meaningless numbers for the P/E ratio, even when we aggregate across all companies. For a particular company, the possibility of these problems is much higher.

rate of inflation of the last 10 to 15 years has removed most of these problems, whereas changes in accounting standards have made the book value of equity more useful.[32]

The **price-to-sales (P/S) ratio** has several properties that make it attractive for valuation purposes. Similar to the P/E and M/B approaches, we implement it by multiplying a justifiable P/S ratio by the revenue per share. Unlike earnings and book values, sales (or revenues) are relatively insensitive to accounting decisions and are never negative.[33] Sales are not as volatile as earnings levels, hence P/S ratios are generally less volatile than P/E multiples. In addition, sales figures provide useful information about corporate decisions, such as pricing. However, sales do not provide information about expenses and profit margins, which are important determinants of company performance.

Another commonly used relative valuation ratio is the **price-to-cash-flow (P/CF) ratio**, where cash flow (CF) is often estimated as cash flow from operations.[34] By focusing on cash flow rather than on accounting income, this ratio alleviates some of the accounting concerns regarding measures of earnings.

We can form multiples using earnings before interest and taxes (EBIT) or earnings before interest, taxes, and depreciation and amortization (EBITDA) instead of net income to eliminate a significant proportion of volatility caused in EPS figures by the use of debt, and by depreciation and amortization (which are noncash expenses). Because EBIT and EBITDA are earnings to all suppliers of capital (that is, bondholders and shareholders), we often compare the value of the entity's capital with these earnings. The market value of an entity's capital, less cash and cash equivalents, is the entity's **enterprise value**. The enterprise value is often referred to as the takeover value of the company because this is what another entity would have to pay to purchase the company.[35] Comparing the enterprise value to these measures of earnings, the resultant ratios are **enterprise value to EBIT** and the **enterprise value to EBITDA ratio**. We use the enterprise value in the numerator to reflect the fact that EBIT and EBITDA represent income available to both debt and equity holders.[36]

However, although there are many different valuation ratios or "multiples," they are all related to the fundamental valuation drivers. Suppose an investor requires a 15 percent return on his or her shares, expects the company to pay a $1 dividend, and expects dividends and earnings to grow at 10 percent. In this case, we can use the constant growth model to value the shares at $20.

$$P_0 = \frac{\$1}{0.15 - 0.01} = \$20$$

If 0.5 million shares are outstanding, this company would have a total market value for the equity or equity market capitalization of $10 million.[37]

Suppose the XYZ Company has the forecast income statement and financial data we show Table 7-2. We can link all these valuation multiples using this data.

In valuing this company, one valuation metric is to simply compare dividend yields across other comparable companies. A high dividend yield relative to other companies

price-to-sales (P/S) ratio market price per share divided by sales per share

price-to-cash-flow (P/CF) ratio market price per share divided by per share cash flow

enterprise value market value of an entity's debt and equity, less cash and cash equivalents

enterprise value to EBIT ratio total market value of the company, less cash and cash equivalents, divided by earnings before interest and taxes

enterprise value to EBITDA ratio total market value of the company, less cash and cash equivalents, divided by earnings before interest, taxes, and depreciation and amortization

---

[32] At one point, companies were required to write off goodwill, and this seriously affected both earnings and the book value of equity. Now the goodwill arising from an acquisition is only written off when it is impaired by a drop in value. This is what caused the huge losses to Nortel and JDS Uniphase in 2002.

[33] We use the terms *revenues* and *sales* interchangeably. If we were to be fussy, we would use *sales* when referring to retail firms and *revenues* for all other types of firms.

[34] A number of estimates of cash flow are used in practice. For example, some analysts focus on free cash flow available to shareholders, which is estimated as net income, plus depreciation and deferred taxes, less capital expenditures, the change in net working capital, and net external debt financing.

[35] The reason that cash and cash equivalents are removed is that if the company is taken over the cash and cash equivalents can be used to offset the purchase price of the firm.

[36] Technically, what we would want to use for the market value of capital is the market value of equity, plus the market value of debt capital. Debt capital in this context is the interest-bearing obligations of the company.

[37] The market capitalization is sometimes referred to casually as the "market cap" or simply the "cap."

TABLE 7-2   Forecast Income Statement for XYZ Company

	(in millions)
Earnings before interest taxes, depreciation, and amortization (EBITDA)	$3.3
Less: Depreciation	0.8
Earnings before interest and taxes (EBIT)	$2.5
Less: Interest	0.5
Earnings before taxes (EBT)	$2.0
Less: Income tax (50 percent)	1.0
Net income	$1.0
Dividends	$0.5
Cash and cash equivalents	$1.0
Book value of equity	$5.0
Book value of debt	$6.0
Market value of debt	$5.0
Market value of equity	$10.0

might then indicate an undervalued stock. Another way of looking at the dividend yield is to take its reciprocal and look at the dividend multiple, that is, the market value divided by the dividend. In this case, XYZ's dividend yield is $0.5 ÷ $10.0 = 5 percent, and its stock is selling at 20 times its dividend.

In practice, we don't often talk about the value in terms of a multiple of the dividend because the dividend yield provides the same information, and yields on stocks are often compared directly with yields on income trusts, bonds, and other interest-earning securities. However, the fundamental problem with using dividend multiples is that many companies do not pay dividends.

An alternative to dividends is to examine earnings. In the case of XYZ, with a market value of equity of $10 million and $1 million in net income, the P/E ratio is 10 times. Immediately we can see that although many companies do not pay cash dividends, they should all expect to have some earnings. The problem here is that earnings are cyclical and industry specific, so let's move up the income statement a bit more.

The next item is the earnings before interest and tax (EBIT), which with our example is $2.5 million. The difference between the EBIT and the net income is that the EBIT does not belong to the shareholders because some flows through to the company's creditors and some to the government. This is why we usually calculate the total company value (or enterprise value), that is, the value of the debt plus the value of the equity for all the ratios "above" net income. For our example, this comes to $15 million.[38] The EBIT multiple is $15 million ÷ $2.5 million = 6 times.

However, as we know from our accounting discussion, depreciation is a noncash charge, so we go farther up the income statement and add back depreciation to get EBITDA. This adds back all the accounting items that do not involve cash.[39] Looking at our example once again, with a total enterprise value of $6 + 10 − 1 = $15 million, the EBITDA multiple is 4.5 times. The EBITDA multiple is the most commonly used multiple when companies look at acquiring other companies because it is a good proxy for the cash

---

[38] The debt market value is assumed to be the book value of $5 million.

[39] Depreciation of fixed assets is by far the largest component of these noncash adjustments, but there are also amortizations, such as issue costs attached to debt, as well as other noncash adjustments.

flow that the company generates that can be used by another company. Another useful metric is to look at the contribution generated by the company, which is the EBITDA with all the fixed costs added back. In our example, this is $5 million, giving a multiple of three times. This is useful for companies valuing other companies when they can consolidate operations and remove the fixed costs.

The final valuation multiple uses sales. In our case, the sales multiple is the $10 million in sales divided by $10 million in common equity, with a resulting multiple of 1.0. This multiple is useful if the entire sales of the company could be switched to another company and the existing plant and facilities closed down. Another variant on this is to look at the equity value per unit of sales, in our case, $10 million for 1 million unit sales means that the company's shares are selling for $10 per unit of sales.

If we use these valuation multiples, along with the market-to-book ratio, which in our case is $10 million ÷ $5 million = 2 times, and the company's return on equity (ROE) of 20 percent, we have a comprehensive list of key valuation ratios for the company, all flowing from the fundamental valuation model.

Now let's examine how multiples work with actual companies. Consider IBM and Microsoft. If we look at these two companies for fiscal years 2010 and 2009, as we show in Table 7-3, we see the following:

- IBM is a larger company than Microsoft, as measured by revenues, but slightly larger in size than Microsoft in terms of assets.
- The market assigns a higher multiple to IBM stock for earnings, book value, EBIT, and EBITDA.
- The market assigns a higher multiple to Microsoft for revenues, as indicated with the P/S multiple.

One of the advantages of using multiples is that it doesn't matter what currency you are using: The multiple simply relates the market's valuation to a financial statement item, no matter the currency. Consider Anheuser-Busch Inbev, which is a Belgium beverage firm. Its global competitors include the Japanese beverage companies Kirin Holdings Co. and Asahi Group Holdings, and the French company, Danone. We can compare how the markets value these companies by comparing the multiples of these companies in their home markets:[40]

	Multiple			
	As of October 2011			
Company	*P/E*	*P/S*	*M/B*	*P/CF*
Anheuser-Busch Inbev	18.81	2.41	2.46	9.46
Kirin Holdings Co	42.70	0.44	0.95	5.24
Asahi Group Holdings	14.23	0.54	1.23	6.70
Danone	16.25	1.78	2.74	12.61
Industry	21.50	5.21	1.42	6.61

Source: *Reuters.com.*

Whereas Kirin Holdings receives the highest multiple based on earnings, Anheuser-Busch Inbev has the highest based on sales, and Danone has the highest multiple based on cash flow and book value. In all four cases, however, the price-to-sales multiple is less than the industry average; this industry average may be affected by smaller, relatively young companies that have high sales growth yet do not generate earnings and are perceived as valuable due to their future prospects.

[40] We should note that cross-country comparisons may be affected by accounting standards, which may differ across countries.

TABLE 7-3 **IBM and Microsoft Multiples**

	IBM		Microsoft	
Fiscal year	*2010*	*2009*	*2010*	*2009*
In millions				
Revenues	$99,871	$95,759	$69,943	$62,484
Total assets	$113,452	$109,022	$108,704	$86,113
Cash and equivalents	$10,661	$12,183	$9,610	$5,505
Book value of debt	$28,624	$26,100	$11,921	$5,939
Book value equity	$23,046	$22,637	$57,083	$46,175
Cash flow from operations	$19,549	$20,773	$26,994	$24,073
EBIT	$18,150	$17,011	$27,161	$24,167
EBITDA	$21,807	$20,784	$29,927	$26,840
Net income	$14,833	$13,425	$23,150	$18,760
Number of shares outstanding	1,287	1,341	8,593	8,927
Per Share				
Price per share	$146.76	$130.90	$26.00	$23.01
Book value per share	$17.91	$16.88	$6.64	$5.17
Sales per share	$77.60	$71.41	$8.14	$7.00
Cash flow from operations per share	$15.19	$15.49	$3.14	$2.70
EBIT per share	$14.10	$12.69	$3.16	$2.71
EBITDA per share	$16.94	$15.50	$3.48	$3.01
Earnings per share	$11.53	$10.01	$2.69	$2.10
Multiple				
P/E	12.734	13.075	9.651	10.949
M/B	8.196	7.754	3.914	4.449
P/S	1.891	1.833	3.194	3.287
P/CF	9.662	8.450	8.277	8.533
EV/EBIT	9.819	9.603	7.872	8.272
EV/EBITDA	8.173	7.860	7.144	7.448

Source of data: *Microsoft Corporation's 2010 10-K filing, IBM Corporation's 2010 10-K filing, and Yahoo! Finance.*

Not all these ratios are equally useful for every company. Cable companies, for example, usually sell on a value per unit of output, in their case, a value per subscriber because the more subscribers a cable company has, the more revenue it can generate. "Old-line" manufacturing companies generally sell on a market-to-book or P/E ratio basis because they tend to have stable earnings. Growth companies tend to sell on EBITDA or sales multiples. However, in all cases, these valuation multiples are simply shortcuts for the fundamental discounted cash flow valuation.

In a Recession, Buy Revenues, Not Earnings

The price-to-sales ratio tells you how many dollars of revenues you are buying for each dollar you pay for a stock.

The price-to-earnings ratio is the most popular metric for getting a quick read on how investors are valuing an individual stock or the overall market. The Standard & Poor's 500 index, for example, sells for 18 times latest 12-month earnings and at 11 and 10 times the consensus forecast for 2008 and 2009, respectively. The P/E ratio, however, has its limitations, especially in sharp economic downturns.

For example, of the Standard & Poor's 500 companies, 60 have posted losses over the latest 12 months. According to consensus estimates tabulated by Thomson IBES, security analysts expect 27 S&P companies to deliver losses in their current fiscal year. Analysts tend to be optimistic, so the actual number of S&P companies reporting fiscal losses will likely be higher—possibly much higher. Keep in mind that, at the onset of a downturn, a low P/E can be a warning of an impending collapse in earnings, not a sign of a cheap stock. Once earnings slip into negative territory, the P/E becomes a nonmeaningful, useless statistic.

The price-to-sales ratio (stock price divided by sales per share, or PSR) does not suffer such limitations. *Forbes* columnist and investment manager Kenneth Fisher has been a long-time proponent of the PSR.

In short, the PSR tells you how many dollars of revenues you are buying for each dollar you pay for a stock. If a stock has a PSR of 0.5 it means you are buying two dollars of revenues for each dollar of stock price.

PSRs can also tell you a great deal about the earning power of company. Supermarkets, for example, only make a few pennies of net profit for each dollar of revenue. The median PSR for large supermarket chains is only 0.2. In contrast, a high-margined business such as software has a median PSR of 3.1

Revenues, too, are not immune from slippage during a business slump but they are usually more resilient than earnings. It does not matter, of course, how good a deal you get investing in corporate revenues if management is unable eventually to turn a corporate revenue stream into profits. The trick is to seek out companies selling for low PSRs relative to their long-term history and/or industry average, where management seems capable of improving margins or restoring a money-losing business to profitability.

Steve Kichen, "In a Recession, Buy Revenues, Not Earnings," *Forbes.com*, November 10, 2008.

Concept Review Questions

1. Why can the P/E ratio be viewed as a type of payback period?

2. What fundamental factors drive P/E ratios?

3. What other relative valuation multiples are useful in valuation?

SUMMARY

- A value of a share of stock is the future value of future cash flows to that share. In terms of preferred and common stock, the value of a share is the present value of expected future dividends.

- The valuation of preferred stock is rather straightforward; we typically use the present value of a perpetuity formula to estimate the value of a share of preferred stock.

- Because the dividend rate on common stock is not set, but rather the amount and timing of dividends is left to the discretion of the board of directors, the valuation of a share of common stock is more complicated than the value of preferred stock. A useful model is the dividend discount model, assuming a constant growth in dividends. This model can be modified to consider multiple stages of growth, and other patterns of future dividends.

- A value of a share of stock can also be estimated by looking at how the market values comparable companies. Using the multiples of the market value of comparable companies' stocks to these companies' respective earnings, cash flows, sales, or other measure of performance, we can then apply these multiples, such as the price-earnings ratio, to value a company's stock.

- The constant growth version of the DDM is related to the fundamentals that affect stock values (i.e., future profitability and dividends, interest rates, and risk), which we can then associate with multiples.

FORMULAS/EQUATIONS

(7-1) $r = r_f + \text{Risk premium}$

(7-2) $P_p = \dfrac{D_p}{r_p}$

(7-3) $r_p = \dfrac{D_p}{P_p}$

(7-4) $P_0 = \dfrac{D_1}{(1 + r_e)^1} + \dfrac{D_2}{(1 + r_e)^2} + \ldots + \dfrac{D_n + P_n}{(1 + r_e)^n}$

(7-5) $P_0 = \dfrac{D_1}{(1 + r_e)^1} + \dfrac{D_2}{(1 + r_e)^2} + \ldots + \dfrac{D_\infty}{(1 + r_e)^\infty} = \sum\limits_{t=1}^{\infty} \dfrac{D_t}{(1 + r_e)^t}$

(7-6) $P_0 = \dfrac{D_0(1 + g)^1}{(1 + r_e)^1} + \dfrac{D_0(1 + g)^2}{(1 + r_e)^2} + \ldots + \dfrac{D_0(1 + g)^\infty}{(1 + r_e)^\infty}$

(7-7) $P_0 = \dfrac{D_0(1 + g)}{r_e - g} = \dfrac{D_1}{r_e - g}$

(7-8) $r_e = \dfrac{D_1}{P_0} + g$

(7-9) $P_0 = \dfrac{EPS_1}{r_e}$

(7-10) $P_0 = \dfrac{EPS_1}{r_e} + PVGO$

(7-11) $SGR = b \times ROE$

(7-12) $ROE = \text{Net profit margin} \times \text{Turnover ratio} \times \text{Leverage ratio}$

(7-13) $P_0 = \dfrac{D_1}{(1 + r_e)^1} + \dfrac{D_2}{(1 + r_e)^2} + \ldots + \dfrac{D_t + P_t}{(1 + r_e)^t}$

(7-14) $P_0 = \text{Estimated } EPS_1 \times \text{Justified P/E} = EPS_1 \times (P_0 / EPS_1)$

(7-15) $\dfrac{P_0}{EPS_1} = \dfrac{P}{E} = \dfrac{D_1 / EPS_1}{r_e - g}$

QUESTIONS AND PROBLEMS

Multiple Choice

1. Which of the following is a correct characterization of the cash flows of a bond and a stock?

	Bond	*Stock*
A.	Discretionary	Discretionary
B.	Discretionary	Legal obligation
C.	Legal obligation	Discretionary
D.	Legal obligation	Legal obligation

2. Which of the following is a correct characterization of the tax deductibility of payments by a company paying interest and dividends?

	Bond	*Stock*
A.	Deductible	Deductible
B.	Deductible	Not deductible
C.	Not deductible	Deductible
D.	Not deductible	Not deductible

3. The government Treasury bond yield is 4 percent, and the risk premium of the Boise Company is 6.5 percent. Boise's common stock's required rate of return is *closest* to:

    A. 0.26 percent.   B. 2.5 percent.   C. 10.5 percent.   D. 17 percent.

4. Bismarck Inc. just paid a dividend of $2.00 per share, which is expected to grow at a constant rate of 4.5 percent, indefinitely. The T-bond rate is 3 percent, and the risk premium of Bismarck's common stock is 6.5 percent. Bismarck Inc.'s value of a share of its common stock is *closest* to:

    A. $1.80.   B. $40.00.   C. $41.80.   D. $42.60.

5. Bloomfield Holdings recently paid an annual dividend this year of $1.50 per share, and its estimated long-term growth rate in dividends is 4 percent. The current market price of each share is $26. The implied rate of return on the share for Bloomfield stock is *closest* to:

    A. 6 percent.   B. 9.77 percent.   C. 10 percent.   D. 10.24 percent.

6. Firestone Co. just paid a dividend of $1.50 per share, and its EPS is $9.00. Its book value per share is $36. Firestone's sustainable growth rate is *closest* to:

    A. 0.69 percent.   B. 4.17 percent.   C. 20.83 percent.   D. 25 percent.

7. The sustainable growth rate is *negatively* related to:

    A. payout ratio.   B. retention ratio.   C. net profit margin.   D. leverage ratio or equity multiplier.

8. Which of the following is *not* a workable assumption in the constant growth dividend discount model?

    A. Dividends do not grow.
    B. Dividends are expected to decline at a constant rate.
    C. The required rate of return is less than the growth rate.

9. Using the method of multiples to value the equity of a private company, you've concluded that the comparable companies had price-earnings ratios around 15. If the private company's earnings are $3 million, the value of the private company's equity is *closest* to:

    A. $0.2 million.   B. $5 million.   C. $15 million.   D. $45 million.

10. A company with a current dividend of $2 per share, an earnings per share of $5, expected dividend growth of 5 percent, and a required rate of return of 8 percent, is expected to have a price-earnings ratio *closest* to:

    A. 5.25 times.   B. 13.33 times.   C. 14.00 times.   D. 70.00 times.

Practice Questions and Problems

7.1   Equity Securities

11. Describe preferred stock in terms of seniority, maturity, and dividends.

12. Compare how dividend income is taxed in the U.S. compared to interest income. Which is likely taxed at a lower rate?

13. What distinguishes preferred stock from common stock?

14. Why is it more likely that you can use the formula for the present value of a perpetuity to value a share of preferred stock than it is for a share of common stock?

15. If a share of preferred stock has a face value of $50 and a dividend rate of 3 percent per year, what is the annual dividend on this stock?

7.2   Dividend Discount Valuation of Equity

16. State the relationship that the required rate of return, the expected growth rate, and expected dividends have with the market value of a share of stock according to the constant growth dividend discount model.

17. Describe how to estimate the present value of growth opportunities (PVGO) and what it represents.

18. The Alabama Power Company had 6.48 million shares of its 5.2% preferred stock outstanding as of the end of 2011. The stated par value of each share is $25.

   A. What is the amount of dividend paid on each share?
   B. If the stock is trading at $25.70, what is the required rate of return on this stock?
   C. If the required rate of return is 6 percent, what is the market value of this preferred stock per share?

19. Bayer AG paid the following dividend per share:

Year	Dividend
2004	€0.55
2005	€0.95
2006	€1.00
2007	€1.35
2008	€1.40
2009	€1.40
2010	€1.50

   A. What is the average annual growth rate of dividends from 2004 to 2010?
   B. What is the average annual growth rate of dividends from 2007 to 2010?

20. Fill in the missing information in the following table for preferred shares A through G:

Company	Value Per Share	Par Value	Required Rate of Return	Dividend Rate	Dividend
A		$100	8%	5%	$5.00
B	$33.33	$50	3%		
C	$90.00	$75			$4.50
D	$116.67	$50		14%	$7.00
E	$30.00	$30	7%		$2.10
F		$100	4%		$7.00
G			7%	9%	$9.00

21. Fill in the missing information in the following table pertaining to the value of common stocks using the constant growth dividend discount model:

Company	Value of a Share Today	Required Rate of Return	Dividend Growth	Current Dividend	Dividend Expected One Year from Today
A		15%		$4.50	$5.00
B	$600	3%	1%		
C	$70		5%		$8.00
D	$55			$10.00	$11.00
E		14%	6%	$9.50	
F		15%	0%		$18.00
G	$40	5%	–2%		

22. Determine the present value of growth opportunities for a company with a leading EPS of $1.85, a required rate of return of 8 percent, and a current stock price of $50.

23. The Ames Company's current dividend is $3.60. Dividends are expected to grow by 9 percent for years 1 to 3, by 6 percent for years 4 to 7, and by 2 percent thereafter. The required rate of return on the stock is 12 percent. What is the value of a share of stock today for the Ames Company?

24. The Charlotte Clothing Company's current dividend is $4.00. Dividends are expected to grow by 25 percent for years 1 to 3 and by 10 percent thereafter. The required rate of return on the stock is 15 percent. What is the current value of a share of stock of the Charlotte Clothing Company?

25. The Tallahassee Company's preferred shares have a par value of $50, and a dividend rate of 7 percent and trade at a price of $70. The St. Pete Company's preferred shares have a par value of $60 and a dividend rate of 4 percent and trade at a price of $45. Which company's preferred stock is riskier?

26. The Orono Company is expected to earn $10,000,000 next year. There are 2,000,000 shares outstanding, and the company uses a dividend payout ratio of 40 percent. The required rate of return for companies like the Orono Company is 8 percent. The current share price of Orono Company common stock is $75.
    A. What are the expected earnings per share for the Orono Company?
    B. What are the expected dividends per share for the Orono Company?
    C. What is the present value of growth opportunities for this company?

27. The Boulder Granite Company's most recent earnings were $300,000. From these earnings, it paid dividends on common equity totaling $175,000. There are 50,000 common shares outstanding. The ROE for Boulder is 12 percent. Determine the following:
    A. Earnings per share. Which can you calculate: leading or lagging EPS?
    B. Dividends per share
    C. Earnings retention ratio
    D. Sustainable growth rate

28. The Milliken Corporation has issued $1 million in preferred shares to investors with a 7.25 percent annual dividend rate on a par value of $100. Assuming the company pays dividends indefinitely and the required rate is 10.5 percent, calculate the value of the preferred stock.

29. The Tampa Company currently doesn't pay any dividends, but is expected to start paying dividends 5 years from today. The first dividend is expected to be $1.00 and to grow at 6 percent thereafter. The required rate of return for the company is 10 percent. What is the current value of a share of Tampa Company stock?

30. The Tucson Tomato Company's current dividend is $5. You expect the growth rate to be 0 percent for years 1 to 5, and 2 percent for years 6 to infinity. The required rate of return on this company's equity is 10 percent. Determine the following:

   A. The expected dividend at the end of year 5.

   B. The expected dividend at the end of year 6.

   C. The expected value of the stock at the end of year 5 (immediately after the year 5 dividend).

   D. The price of the stock today.

31. The Belvedere Butler Services, Inc.'s current dividend is $5. You expect the growth rate to be 8 percent for years 1 to 5, and 2 percent from years 6 to infinity. The required rate of return on this company's equity is 10 percent. Determine the following:

   A. The expected dividend at the end of year 5.

   B. The expected dividend at the end of year 6.

   C. The expected value of a share of the stock at the end of year 5 (immediately after the year 5 dividend).

   D. The value of a share of the stock today.

32. Victor Blazquez is interested in investing in the XML Software Company. XML's current dividend is $5.50, and XML shares are selling for $180. The required rate of return for companies like XML is 8 percent. Victor has conducted an extensive analysis of the company and believes that the dividend growth rate should be 5 percent.

   A. Should Victor buy the stock at $180? Why or why not?

   B. Do you expect the value of a share of the stock to stay at $180? Explain your answer.

 33. Consider a company that has common stock with a dividend this year of $1. The dividend is expected to grow at a rate of 10 percent per year for the next 5 years, and then grow at a rate of 3 percent per year thereafter. The required rate of return on this stock is 6 percent.

   A. Using a spreadsheet, calculate and graph the dividends on this stock for the current year and for each of the next 25 years.

   B. Using a spreadsheet, calculate and graph the value of the share of stock for the current year and for each of the next 25 years.

   C. Compare the graphs that you prepared for A and B. What is the relationship between these two graphs?

7.3   Using Multiples to Value Equity

34. What is the relationship between a company's sustainable growth rate and its return on equity?

35. What is the Molodovsky effect? What is the relevance of this effect on the interpretation of P/E ratios?

36. Consider a company with the following characteristics:

   • Book value per share of $4.00

   • Market value per share of $6.00

   • Number of shares of common stock outstanding of 5 million

   A. What is this company's market capitalization?

   B. What is this company's market-to-book ratio?

37. Consider a company that pays out 25 percent of its earnings in dividends, has dividends that are expected to grow at a rate of 5 percent per year, ad infinitum, and has a price-earnings ratio of 10 times. What is the required rate of return on this company's common stock?

38. Calculate the leading P/E ratio, given the following information: retention ratio = 0.6, required rate of return = 10 percent, and expected growth rate = 5 percent.

39. Athens, Inc. just paid a dividend of $4, and its current earnings per share is $5. The current Treasury bond rate is 3 percent, and Athens's risk premium is 12 percent. The net profit margin, asset turnover, and debt-to-equity ratio are 20 percent, 1.5 times, and 0.67, respectively. Calculate the sustainable growth rate for Athens, Inc.

40. The LMX Company is expected to pay a $2 dividend in one year. The required rate of return is 9 percent. The company uses a dividend payout ratio of 25 percent. Calculate the leading P/E ratio in the following cases:

A. Expected growth rate = 4 percent

B. Expected growth rate = 8 percent

C. If a company is expected to have a constant dividend growth rate, do you expect the P/E ratio to change over time? Explain your answer.

41. A financial analyst has completed a fundamental analysis of the PDP Company. PDP is a young company and expects to invest heavily in facilities and research and development during the next 5 years; it expects to reap the benefits of its research and development during years 6 to 10; however, it expects rivals to enter the market and margins and profitability to stabilize at a lower level after year 10. The details of the analysis are presented here:

Fundamental Analysis of the PDP Company

Period	Net Profit Margin	Turnover	Equity Multiplier	Dividend Payout Ratio
Years 1–5	1%	0.75	3.0	0.05
Years 6–10	15%	2.00	1.5	0.10
Years 11–?	5%	1.40	1.0	0.50

The current dividend for PDP is $3.00 and the required rate of return for this type of company is 15 percent. Determine the current stock value for a share of PDP stock.

Cases

Case 7.1 Big G Company

An analyst is concerned about the effect of errors in his estimates of the future dividend payout ratio for the Big G Company. Assume that the current dividend is $1, return on equity is fixed at 10 percent, and the required rate of return is 15 percent. Using a spreadsheet program, complete the following:

A. Calculate the value of a share of stock today for dividend payout ratios ranging between 5 percent and 75 percent in 5 percentage point increments.

B. Graph the relationship between the stock value and the dividend payout ratios.

C. Describe the relationship between the stock value and the payout ratios. Is the percentage change in the stock price for a 5 percentage point change in dividend payout ratio constant?

Case 7.2 The Denver Company

The Denver Company is expected to pay a $1.50 dividend next year. Dividends are expected to grow at 3 percent forever, and the required rate of return is 7 percent.

A. Calculate each of the following:

1) The value of a share of Denver stock today.

2) The expected dividend yield.

3) The expected capital gains yield.

B. In one year, immediately after the dividend is paid,

1) What is the value of a share of the stock?

2) What was the one-year holding period return?

3) Looking forward one year, what are the expected dividend and capital gains yields?

C. In year 10, immediately after the dividend is paid,

1) What is the value of a share of the stock?

2) What was the 1-year holding period return (year 9 to 10)?

3) Looking forward 1 year, what are the expected dividend and capital gains yields?

D. Using a spreadsheet,

   1) Calculate the dividends for years 1 through 30 into the future.

   2) Calculate the expected price at the end of years 1 through 30 into the future.

   3) Plot these dividends and prices starting today and extending through 30 years from today.

Case 7.3 Nova Lobster Company

The Nova Lobster Company (NLC) is a privately held lobster farming company. It has hired the Naslaan Consulting Company to help evaluate an offer for the company from Star Lobster Company. Currently NLC has a net income of $150,000 on sales of $350,000, and it processes 250,000 lobsters each year. The total assets are $2,500,000, and the book value of equity is $2,000,000. The company is the sole source of income for the owners, the Wong family, and consequently the dividend payout ratio is 65 percent. The risk-free rate is 2 percent, and the appropriate risk premium for this company is 5 percent.

A. There are three other publicly traded lobster farming companies. Summary data on those companies is presented here:

Company	SeaLobster	ToroLobster	AgriLobster
Price per share	$25	$10	$15
Number of shares outstanding	1,000	10,000	500,000
Market value of company per lobster processed	5	7	12
P/E	15	5	35

Given the data on these companies, determine the value of NLC. Discuss the strengths and weaknesses of the comparable companies' approach to valuation.

B. StarLobster believes that it can make several changes to the operations of NLC that will increase value. It believes that it can improve the net profit margins to 50 percent without changing the turnover ratio. It will also increase the equity multiplier (i.e., total assets divided by equity) to 1.50 and reduce the dividend payout ratio to 40 percent. What is the maximum price StarLobster should consider?

A Short Primer on Bubbles[41]

In 1711, the South Seas Company (SSC) was given a monopoly on all English trade to the South Seas, that is, South America.[42] Unfortunately, South America was largely under the control of Spain, and England was at war with Spain. Nevertheless, the hope was that in the ensuing peace, England would be able to dictate a freeing up of trade to the company's benefit. As it turns out, the peace would be to England's benefit, but not very much to the company's. Meanwhile, John Law, a Scottish promoter in France, had set up the Mississippi Company, which was draining investment from England to France. In response, the South Seas Company offered to have investors convert England's national debt into shares of the company. The company would pay a one-time fee to the government for this conversion and receive the fixed annual payments on the national debt. The certainty of receiving the interest payments would allow the company to borrow to fund its South Seas trade.

It was an audacious plan in an age of optimism and jubilation at England's defeat of both Spain and France. In April 1720, the government accepted the offer, and the stock price took off. It was clear that the plan could only be accepted if the stock price went up enough to encourage investors to convert their national debt into SSC equity. Consequently, the company issued shares on an installment basis. As the cash came in, the company lent it back so that investors could buy more shares. The stock took off and in doing so sucked in a whole group of neophyte investors.

It also spawned imitators. One of the most interesting of these declared that it was "a company for carrying on an undertaking of great advantage, but nobody was to know what it is." Prices soared, and small investors got in for fear of missing out. Sir Isaac Newton sold his stock in the SSC in April 1720 for a 100 percent gain. However, SSC's stock price rocketed up from 300 pounds to its peak of more than 1,000 pounds, and he bought back in. In August the bubble burst, and by September prices were back to 300 pounds. The *London Gazette* was full of bankruptcies, and Isaac Newton lost 20,000 pounds; philosophically, he made his famous statement, "I can calculate the motions of the heavenly bodies, but not the madness of people."

We have learned from this, haven't we? Leaving aside the Great Crash of 1929, there is the little matter of the Crash of 2000 and our recent experience with technology and Internet stocks. The most recent crashes stemmed from the high valuation of the equity market as a result of the long bull markets of the late 1990s.

Long bull markets pull in inexperienced investors who have unrealistic expectations. Over long periods, equity market average returns have exceeded 10 percent a year, which is not enough to get investors really excited. However, a couple of 25 percent plus years bring in the people who then come to expect 25 percent plus returns. Moreover, plenty of people are willing to tell them that they can get 25 percent returns and that this time it is different: It is a new world of investing with new metrics.[43]

---

[41] This appendix is based on Laurence Booth, "Investments, 'Alternative' Investments and Bubbles." *Advisor's Guide to New Investment Opportunities,* 2002, pp. 12–19.

[42] See Jim Harrison, "The Damn'd South Sea," *Harvard Magazine,* May–June 1999.

[43] The Ponzi scheme operated for 20 years by Bernard Madoff is an example of how people can be swayed to invest funds for outsized returns. A Ponzi scheme, basically, is paying returns to old investors with the funds of new investors. The Madoff scheme fell apart in December 2008, and Bernard Madoff was sentenced to prison for securities and mail fraud, among other felonies.

In the September 1999 issue of *Atlantic Monthly*, James Glassman and Kevin Hassett discussed the advice in their book that the Dow will go to 30,000. They stated (page 37), "Stocks were undervalued in the 1980s and 1990s and they are undervalued now. Stock prices could double, triple or even quadruple tomorrow and still not be too high." They went on to suggest (page 42), "A profound change has occurred in the attractiveness of stocks since the early 1980s, as investors have become more rational. The old limits of yields and P/Es do not apply anymore, if they ever did." And finally (page 56), "In truth there is no extra risk in stocks."[44]

It is a familiar refrain during times of speculative bubbles that this time it is different. After all, the little investors get in only after a run-up in prices, so it has to be "different this time," otherwise, they have missed the boat. On May 15, 1929, the *Outlook* and *Independent* remarked, "But apparently there has been a fundamental change in the criteria for judging security values. Widespread education of the public in the worth of equity securities has created a new demand." Similarly, before the correction in 1969, *Barron's* stated, "The failure of the general market to decline during the last three years despite its obvious vulnerability, as well as the emergence of new investment characteristics, has caused investors to believe that the U.S. has entered a new investment era to which old guidelines no longer apply."[45]

The fact is that "old guidelines" are perennial; the only thing that changes is that the old investors die off and a new generation has to learn the same old lessons. Does that 1720 English company that promised "carrying on of an undertaking of great advantage, but nobody to know what it is" sound familiar? It should. On January 25, 2000, Michael Lewis, the author of *Liar's Poker*, pointed out that an Internet company, NetJ.com, had filed statements with the U.S. Securities and Exchange Commission with the confession that "the company is not currently engaged in any substantial activity and has no plans to engage in any such activity in the foreseeable future." The company had $127,631 in accumulated losses and so little money on hand that the directors would have had to chip in to pay any filing costs to raise capital. The only snag was NetJ.com had a market capitalization of $22.9 million.

---

[44] They also go through an interesting valuation of Cisco (page 52), in which they state, "Using the standard formula for calculating a stock's present value according to the flow of cash it generates over time, we find that Cisco's PRP should be $399 a share. In other words, Cisco's price last June would need to sextuple. Its P/E would rise to 539 (No that's not a misprint)." As we read this, Cisco's price is $18.56. James Glassman and Kevin Hassett, "Dow 36,000," *Atlantic Monthly*, 284, no. 3 (September 1999).

[45] Quoted in Jim Stack, *The New Paradigm Era or Bubble* (Whitefish, MT: InvesTech Research, 1997).

PART 4

CAPITAL MARKET THEORY AND FINANCIAL MANAGEMENT

In this section of the text, we develop the key topics of risk, return, portfolio theory, asset pricing, and market efficiency. In Chapter 8, we discuss various measures of risk and methods for estimating the required rate of return for assets and portfolios. We provide a discussion of market efficiency and asset pricing in Chapter 9.

277

CHAPTER 8

RISK, RETURN, AND PORTFOLIO THEORY

Diversification One of the most important elements to come out of academic research for investment management, financial management, and even personal finance, is the idea of diversification. Diversification is the idea that you can reduce risk by investing in investments whose returns are not in perfect synch with one another. The basic idea has been around for a very long time: Don't put all your eggs in one basket.

To illustrate how this works, consider the investment of $1 at the end of 2000 in either small corporate stocks or long-term government bonds:

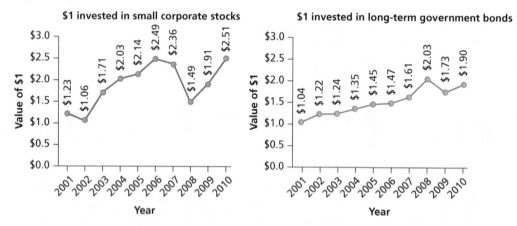

You would have more from the stock investment ($2.51 v. $1.90), but you would also have more variability in your portfolio's value. Now let's see what would you have had if you invested half your portfolio (that is, 50¢) in small corporate stocks and half in U.S. government bonds:

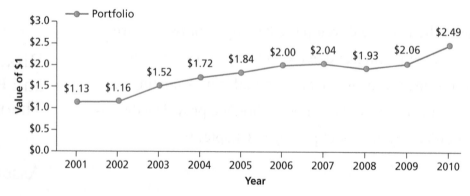

By investing in both stocks and bonds, you reduce the year-to-year fluctuations in your portfolio value because the returns on stocks and government bonds do not always move together. And, instead of $2.51, you wind up with $2.49, which is not much of a sacrifice to achieve less volatility. This is the beauty of diversification: *reduce risk without sacrificing much return.*

Source of data: *Morningstar.com* and *OnlyGold.com.*

278

After reading this chapter, you should be able to:

LO 8.1 Distinguish between ex post and ex ante returns and calculate ex post and ex ante returns.

LO 8.2 Estimate expected returns and risk for individual assets.

LO 8.3 Describe what happens to risk and return when assets are combined in a portfolio.

LO 8.4 Explain what is meant by an "efficient frontier."

LO 8.5 Justify the importance of diversification for financial managers and investors.

Chapter Preview Financial management requires making decisions now that have uncertain payoffs in the future. This uncertainty is pervasive throughout financial decision making, which means that the financial manager must identify, measure, and manage risk.

In this chapter we describe ways to measure, analyze, and manage risk. Although our goal is to put this in the context of decision making within a business entity, we introduce the concepts, mathematics, and methods using generic assets and securities. We develop the basic terminology and concepts and then establish the relationship between risk and return. We also demonstrate the benefit from diversification, whether what we are diversifying is a portfolio of stocks or a collection of products in a business entity.

8.1 MEASURING RETURNS

What is risk? One definition is that **risk** is the chance or possibility that outcomes may not turn out as expected.[1] Recognizing that we often are not concerned about making too much money, but rather are concerned about losses, a common definition of risk is the possibility of incurring harm or the chance of a loss.

risk chance that future outcomes may not turn out as expected

Up until now, we have measured returns in term of the percentage change in a value over a period, considering not only the change in the value of something, but any associated cash flows as well. And we were often measuring these returns over some past period. When we are making financial decisions, however, we are regularly faced with estimating returns for some future period, rather than simply looking back on what has occurred. Therefore, we must distinguish between returns measured in the past and those estimated for a future period.

Ex Post Versus Ex Ante Returns

Let's first distinguish between an **ex post return** and an **ex ante return**. Ex post means "after the fact," so ex post returns are past or historical returns. Ex ante means "before the fact," so ex ante returns are expected returns. Advertisements for mutual funds and other investments show historical or ex post returns, and then in smaller print have a disclaimer that past returns do not necessarily reflect future, or ex ante, returns. Of course, what investors are interested in are these future or expected returns, but their judgment in terms of what they can reasonably expect is informed by what has happened in the past.

ex post return past or historical, return

ex ante return future or expected return

So how can investors measure these ex post or historical returns? As we saw in previous chapters, the return on an investment consists of two components: the income yield and the capital gain (or loss) yield. The **income yield** is the return earned in the form of a

income yield return earned by investors as a periodic cash flow

---

[1] We could distinguish between uncertainty and risk. In common use, these two are used interchangeably. However, the term *risk* is used when we are able to estimate probabilities associated with possible future outcomes, whereas we use the term *uncertainty* when we cannot.

279

periodic cash flow received by the investors. These cash flows are interest payments from bonds and dividends from equities. When we refer to this yield for a security, there are two types of yield: the cash flow yield, which is the ratio of the periodic cash flow to the security's price, and the capital yield, which is the ratio of the price change to the share price.[2] We show this in Figure 8-1 for the S&P 500 over time.

$$\text{Income yield} = \frac{CF_1}{P_0} \tag{8-1}$$

where CF_1 is the expected cash flows to be received and P_0 is the purchase price today.

We provide the monthly dividend yield on the S&P Index in Figure 8-1 from 1871 through October 2011.[3] As you see in this figure, the dividend yields appear to have a cyclical pattern, but the trend in the last 30 years has been declining dividend yields.

The dividend yield may change for two reasons: (1) changes in the dividends per share, or (2) changes in the stock prices of the dividend-paying companies. The apparent increases in dividend yields in late 2008 and early 2009 are primarily from the decrease in the share prices—that is, the denominator in the dividend yield formula. But the dividend yield does not tell the whole story. The **capital gain** (or **capital loss**) component measures the appreciation (or depreciation) in the price of the asset from some starting price, usually the purchase price or the price at the beginning of the year. Dividing this gain or loss by the price produces the capital gain (or loss) yield or return, as expressed in Equation 8-2.

$$\text{Capital gain or loss return} = \frac{P_1 - P_0}{P_0} \tag{8-2}$$

where P_1 is the selling price 1 year from today.

Creating a generic equation for a return that we could apply to stocks, bonds, or any other asset, we add the income yield and the capital gain (or loss) yield together to get the

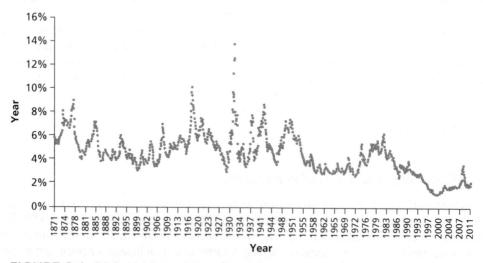

FIGURE 8-1   S&P 500 Monthly Dividend Income Yields, 1871 Through October 2011

Source of data: *Robert Shiller, www.yale.edu.*

---

[2] When we refer to this yield for a bond, there are several types of yields: the current yield, which is the ratio of the annual interest to the current bond price, the yield to maturity, which is the internal rate of return on the bond, and the yield to call, which is the internal rate of return on a callable bond assuming the bond is called at the first opportunity.

[3] The dividend yield depicted here is measured as D_0/P_0, i.e., using dividends paid over the last 12 months, not the expected dividends.

complete picture of the return from investing in bonds versus common shares. The **total return** is the sum of the income yield and the capital gain yield:

total return income yield plus the capital gain (or loss) yield

$$\text{Total return} = \text{Income yield} + \text{capital gain (or loss) yield}$$

$$\text{Total return} = \frac{CF_1}{P_0} + \frac{P_1 - P_0}{P_0} = \frac{CF_1 + P_1 - P_0}{P_0} \tag{8-3}$$

Suppose a stock was purchased a year ago for $25 and is currently worth $30. If the stock paid a dividend of $1 at the end of the year, then:

- the total return is ($30 − 25 + 1) ÷ $25 = 24 percent,
- the capital yield is ($30 − 25) ÷ $25 = 20 percent, and
- the income yield is $1 ÷ $25 = 4 percent.

Consider another example, using the stock price and dividends for IBM Corporation. At the end of 2009, IBM had a stock price of $130.90 and at the end of 2010 IBM had a stock price $146.76. During 2010, IBM paid four dividends, totaling $2.50. The return on IBM stock for 2010 is:

$$\text{Total return}_{2010} = \frac{\$2.50}{\$130.90} + \frac{\$146.76 - 130.90}{\$130.90} = 1.91\% + 12.12\% = 14.03\%$$

In other words, in 2010 IBM had a dividend yield of 1.91 percent and a capital yield of 12.12 percent, for a total return of 14.02 percent. During 2011, a share of IBM stock received a dividend of $2.90 and the closing price for 2011 was $183.88. Therefore, IBM's return for 2011 is:

$$\text{Total return}_{2011} = \frac{\$2.90}{\$146.76} + \frac{\$183.88 - 146.76}{\$146.76} = 1.98\% + 25.30\% = 27.28\%$$

We provide the total return, indicating the dividend and capital components, for the S&P 500 from 1970 through 2010 in Figure 8-2. As you can see in this graph, in most years the dividend component is a small part of the return on the S&P 500. However, in some years, such as 1994, the dividend yield is a substantial part of the return, and in other years, such as 2000–2002, and 2008, the dividend yield is a small offset of the large capital loss.

FIGURE 8-2 **Dividend and Capital Gain or Loss Components of the Return on the S&P 500 Index, 1970–2011**

Source of data: *Standard and Poor's, www.standardandpoors.com,* and *Robert Shiller, www.yale.edu.*

EXAMPLE 8.1

Calculating Returns

PROBLEM

Estimate the income yield, capital gain (or loss) yield, and total return for the following securities over the past year:

1. An investment in a security of $990 that is currently selling for $995 and provides a cash flow to the investor of $60 at the end of each year.
2. A stock that was purchased for $20, provided an annual dividend of $1 and is currently worth $19.50.

Solution

1. $CF_1 = 0.06 \times \$1,000 = \$60$; $P_0 = \$990$; $P_1 = \$995$

   Income yield $= \$60/\$990 = 0.0606 = 6.06\%$

   Capital gain return $= (\$995 - \$990) \div \$990 = 0.0051 = 0.51\%$

   Total return $= 6.06\% + 0.51\% = 6.57\%$

   Or, total return $= (\$60 + 995 - 990) \div \$990 = 0.0657 = \mathbf{6.57\%}$

2. $CF_1 = \$1.00$; $P_0 = \$20$; $P_1 = \$19.50$

   Income yield $= \$1/\$20 = 0.0500 = 5.00\%$

   Capital loss return $= (\$19.50 - 20.00) \div \$20 = -0.0250 = -2.50\%$

   Total return $= 5.00\% - 2.50\% = 2.50\%$

   Or, total return $= (\$1 + 19.50 - 20) \div \$20 = 0.0250 = \mathbf{2.50\%}$

When calculating a holding period return on a stock or a bond, it does not matter whether or not the stock or bond is sold in calculating the rate of return. This may seem obvious to most people, but psychologists have observed that people make different decisions if they own something than if they don't. For example, people will keep something for years because it cost $100 and is "valuable," even after they see the identical thing in a flea market selling for $1 and yet wouldn't buy it for $1. Owning assets includes an attachment effect, and with such an attitude, many people refuse to accept capital losses in the total return calculation until they actually sell the asset and realize them. Until then, people refer to them as a **paper loss**, with the implication that they are not real. This attitude is reinforced by the tax rules: Capital gains and losses are only taxable on realization.

A second important point is that whether or not we include paper gains and losses, in part, depends on our investment horizon. For example we can look at rates of return over daily, weekly, monthly, annual, or even longer periods. A **day trader** is someone who buys and sells based on intraday price movements. In that case, the total return for a day's trading includes the effect of capital gains and losses daily and sometimes over even shorter periods. In contrast, most people review their investments less frequently, perhaps quarterly or sometimes annually. For them the intraday price variability and total return are not as big a concern. What is of concern is the total return over, say, a quarter or a year. They are much less concerned about rates of return over shorter periods or the paper losses that are involved.[4]

paper loss capital loss that people do not accept as losses until they actually sell and realize them

day trader someone who buys and sells based on intraday price movements

---

[4] This brings to mind the philosophical question, Does a falling tree in a forest make a noise if there is no one there to hear it? Similarly, does a daily total return matter to an investor who only reviews his or her investments once a month?

The contrary view is that investors have to **mark to market** the prices of all financial securities over the relevant investment horizon. This means that investors always carry securities at the current market value regardless of whether they sell them. As a result, the total return includes the effect of paper gains and losses on securities not yet sold. This view is based on the basic opportunity cost argument: What is the alternative use for the funds tied up in the investment? Clearly, an investor cannot sell the security at its historical cost; he or she can sell at the current market value, and this is the value that can be reinvested elsewhere. We focus on the mark to market and consider the total return as including paper gains and paper losses over the relevant investment horizon because this reflects the economic value of past investment decisions.

Measuring Average Returns

How can we measure these ex post or historical returns? Two often-used statistical measures are the arithmetic mean and the geometric mean. The **arithmetic mean** or **arithmetic average** is commonly used to summarize data. We calculate the arithmetic mean return as the sum of all the returns divided by the total number of observations, as we express in Equation 8-4:

arithmetic mean or **arithmetic average** sum of all observations divided by the total number of observations

$$\text{Arithmetic mean return} = \frac{\sum_{i=1}^{n} r_i}{n} \tag{8-4}$$

where r_i is the individual returns for period i, and n is the total number of observations.

The **geometric mean**, in contrast, measures the average or compound growth rate over multiple periods. For investments, this is the growth rate in the value invested or equivalently the compound rate of return:

geometric mean average or compound growth rate over multiple time periods

$$\text{Geometric mean return} = \sqrt[n]{(1 + r_1) \times (1 + r_2) \times (1 + r_3) \times \ldots \times (1 + r_n)} - 1 \tag{8-5}$$

or, equivalently,

$$\text{Geometric mean return} = [(1 + r_1) \times (1 + r_2) \times (1 + r_3) \times \ldots \times (1 + r_n)]^{1/n} - 1$$

Consider a set of returns on two stocks:

Year	Stock 1	Stock 2
1	5%	5%
2	2%	−1%
3	3%	10%
4	2%	−3%
5	4%	5%

The arithmetic mean of both stocks' returns is 3.2%. The geometric mean return for Stock 1 is:

$$\text{Geometric mean return of Stock 1} = [1.05 \times 1.02 \times 1.03 \times 1.02 \times 1.04]^{1/5} - 1 = 3.193\%$$

The geometric mean return for Stock 2 is:

$$\text{Geometric mean return of Stock 2} = [1.05 \times 0.99 \times 1.10 \times 0.97 \times 1.05]^{1/5} - 1 = 3.095\%$$

Notice that the geometric mean is less than the arithmetic average. This will always be the case unless the returns are identical. The more the returns vary, the bigger the difference between the arithmetic and geometric means.

EXAMPLE 8.2

Calculating the Arithmetic Average and the Geometric Mean

PROBLEM

Estimate the arithmetic mean and the geometric mean for the following returns:

Observation	Return
1	4.3%
2	3.2%
3	5.6%
4	10.5%
5	−7.6%

Solution

Arithmetic mean $= (0.043 + 0.032 + 0.056 + 0.105 - 0.76) \div 5 = 16 \div 5 = \mathbf{3.20\%}$

Geometric mean $= [1.043 \times 1.032 \times 1.056 \times 1.105 \times 0.924]^{1/5} - 1$

$= (1.1605455)^{1/5} - 1$

$= 1.0302 - 1 = 0.0302 \text{ or } \mathbf{3.02\%}$

We report the arithmetic and geometric average annual rates of return on the S&P 500 over various intervals of time in Table 8-1. These returns assume that the investor buys and holds the security for each year, but using different starting points in time. Note that we provide the standard deviation of the annual returns in the last row of Table 8-1. The standard deviation measures the "typical" variation of the return: The larger the standard deviation, the more variable the return.[5] The squared standard deviation is the variance. Approximately, the difference between the arithmetic and geometric return is half this variance.

As we indicated before, the more variable the annual returns, the bigger the difference between the arithmetic and geometric measures of return. Looking again at Table 8-1, the biggest difference is for the more recent intervals of time. So when should we use the arithmetic mean to describe the average return from an investment? And when should we use the geometric mean to describe the average return from an investment? The answer depends on what we are trying to determine.

TABLE 8-1   Average and Standard Deviations of Monthly Returns, 20 Years Ending June 2010

	5 Years Ending June 2010	10 Years Ending June 2010	20 Years Ending June 2010
Arithmetic average monthly return	2.049%	1.673%	2.623%
Geometric average monthly return	0.964%	1.578%	2.548%
Standard deviation of monthly returns	4.725%	4.364%	3.877%

Source of data: *Robert Shiller, Yale University.*

[5] Remember from statistics that the standard deviation for a sample of observations is the square root of the variance. The variance is the sum of the squared deviations of each observation from the mean, divided by the number of observations less one.

The arithmetic mean is appropriate when we are trying to estimate the typical return for a given period, such as a year. So if we wanted to know the best estimate for the rate of return over the next year, we would use the arithmetic mean of the annual rates of return because, by definition, this measures the average annual rate of return. We use the geometric mean when we are interested in determining the "true" average rate of return over multiple periods, for instance, if we wanted to know how our investment (and wealth) will grow over time. We use the geometric mean because it measures the compound rate of growth in our investment value over multiple periods. In this sense, the difference between the arithmetic mean and geometric mean is dependent on the relevant investment horizon.

Consider an investment in a stock that pays no dividend. You purchase the stock initially for $20 per share, and the stock has the following values over the 3-year holding period:

Year	Price of the Stock
Initial	$20
1	$25
2	$26
3	$20

What is the return on this investment? Let's first calculate the return each year:

Year	Price of the Stock	Annual Return
Initial	$20	
1	$25	25.000%
2	$26	4.000%
3	$20	−23.077%

What is the average annual return on this stock? By comparing the initial value with the value at the end of 3 years, we see that there is no return—the stock is worth the same at the end of three years as initially. If we calculate the arithmetic average of the annual returns, we end up with 1.974 percent. If, on the other hand, we calculate the geometric mean return, we have 0 percent, which confirms our basic comparison of initial and at-the-end-of-3-years values:

Year	Price of the Stock	Annual Return	1 + Annual Return
Initial	$20		
1	$25	25.000%	1.25000
2	$26	4.000%	1.04000
3	$20	−23.077%	0.76923
		Sum = 5.923%	Product = 1.00000
		Arithmetic mean = 1.974%	Geometric mean = 0.000%

Why do the arithmetic mean return and the geometric mean return differ? The arithmetic mean simply averages the annual rates of return without taking into account that the amount invested varies across time. For this reason, the geometric mean is a better average return estimate when we are interested in the rate of return performance of an investment over time.

SPREADSHEET APPLICATION: MEANS

Spreadsheets have built-in functions for both the arithmetic mean and the geometric mean:

Arithmetic mean: = AVERAGE(values)

Geometric mean: = GEOMEAN(values)

When working geometric with returns, or any values less than 1.0, you have to take care to add one to the values; the spreadsheet function will not do this automatically.

Consider the case of calculating the mean for the following returns:

	A	B
1	*Observation*	*Return*
2	1	5%
3	2	1%
4	3	0%
5	4	−3%
6	5	5%

We calculate the arithmetic mean using = AVERAGE(B2:B6).

For the geometric mean, we first add one, then calculate the geometric mean, and then subtract one:

	A	B	C
1	*Observation*	*Return*	*Return + 1*
2	1	5%	1.05
3	2	1%	1.01
4	3	0%	1.00
5	4	−3%	0.97
6	5	5%	1.05

And we calculate the geometric mean using = GEOMEAN(C2:C6) − 1. Alternatively, we could use = (PRODUCT(C2:C6)^(1/5)) − 1.

Estimating Expected Returns

Although it is important to be able to estimate the ex post returns realized from past investments, financial managers are generally interested in the returns they expect to realize from an investment made today. In practice, the **expected return** is often estimated based on historical averages, but the problem is that there is no guarantee that

expected return
estimated future return

the past will repeat itself. For example, 1938 to 2009 included World War II (1939–45), a period of significant inflation (1970s and into the 1980s), a recession in the early 1990s that followed the 1987 stock market collapse and the savings and loan crisis, and the 2007–08 financial crisis. For investors interested in expected returns, such events as these can have unexpected effects.

An alternative approach is to use all available information to assess the most likely values under various future scenarios, and then attach probabilities to the likelihood of each occurring. When this approach is used, the expected value is estimated as the weighted average of the expected outcomes under each scenario, where the weights correspond to the probabilities of each scenario actually occurring:

$$\text{Expected value} = \sum_{i=1}^{n} (\text{outcome}_i \times \text{probability}_i) \qquad (8\text{-}6)$$

where outcome$_i$ is the likely outcome (in this case, the return on the investment) in scenario i, and probability$_i$ is the probability of state i occurring.[6]

Suppose you have two possible returns on an investment:

Scenario	Probability of Occurrence	Return on Investment
Outcome 1	60%	15%
Outcome 2	40%	−5%
	100%	

The expected return is the weighted average of the possible returns, where the weights are the probabilities:

Scenario	Probability of Occurrence	Return on Investment	Probability × Return on Investment
Outcome 1	60%	15%	0.09
Outcome 2	40%	−5%	−0.02
		Expected return, $E(r) = 0.07$	

We calculate the expected return by weighting the possible returns by the probabilities. Where do these probabilities come from? For example, economists might make estimates of different economic growth scenarios for the upcoming year, and then security analysts will estimate the prospects for each firm. Consider the distribution of the annual returns for the S&P 500, as we show in Figure 8-3. Though the past is not a precise forecaster of the future, an analyst could use this information on historical frequencies to formulate an estimate of the likelihood of monthly returns in the future.

---

[6] If we are dealing with returns, we often express this formula as $E(r) = \sum (r_i \times p_i)$, where $E(r)$ is the expected return and r_i is the return in scenario i.

EXAMPLE 8.3
Estimating Expected Values

PROBLEM

Consider the expected cash flows from a project, in millions of dollars:

Scenario	Probability	Possible Outcome (in millions)
High	10%	$100
Medium	60%	$50
Low	30%	$20

What is the expected cash flow for this project?

Solution

Scenario	Probability	Possible Outcome (in millions)	Probability-weighted Outcome
High	10%	$100	$10
Medium	60%	$50	30
Low	30%	$20	6
			Expected cash flow = $46

Therefore, the expected cash flow from this project is $46 million.

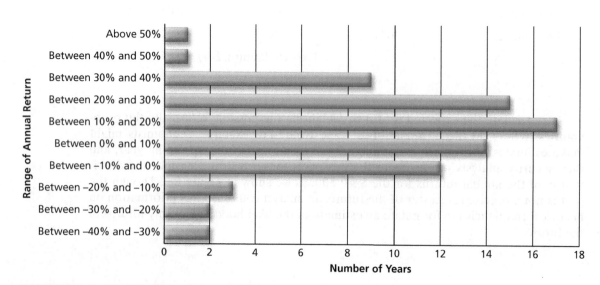

FIGURE 8-3 **Distribution of Annual Returns on the S&P 500 Index**

Source of data: *Standard and Poor's, www.standardandpoors.com*

There are pros and cons to each method for determining expected rates of return. For short-term forecasts the scenario-based approach makes more sense because where we are today has a huge bearing on what is likely to happen over a short period. However, for longer-run forecasts, the historical approach tends to be better because it reflects what actually happens even if it was not expected. In the next sections, we will use the scenario-based approach.

Concept Review Questions

1. What is the difference between ex ante and ex post returns?

2. Why does the income and capital gains component of the total return differ between common shares and bonds?

3. Why is the geometric mean return a better estimate of long-run investment performance than the arithmetic mean return?

8.2 MEASURING RISK

We have already touched on *risk* several times. Risk is the probability of incurring harm, and for financial managers harm generally means losing money or earning an inadequate rate of return. In the rest of this chapter, we use *risk* to mean the probability that the actual return from an investment is less than the expected return. This means that the more variable the possible return, the greater the risk. We normally see a trade-off between risk and return: Assets offering higher expected rates of return tend to be riskier than those offering a lower rate of return.

The Standard Deviation: Ex Post

Measuring risk requires capturing the variability or dispersion of possible outcomes. One measure of dispersion is the range. The **range** is the difference between the highest value and the lowest value, and therefore it does not capture the variability of returns *between* these two values. However, a more common measure of risk is the **standard deviation**, which uses all the observations and provides a measure of how disperse the observations are from the average. When we are dealing with a sample of observations using information that has occurred (that is, ex post), we can also refer to this standard deviation as the **ex post standard deviation**.

range measure of dispersion calculated as the difference between the maximum and minimum values

standard deviation measure of risk; measure of dispersion

We often look back on historical returns to gauge the risk to expect in the future. If σ is the standard deviation, $\bar{x}$ is the average return, x_i is the observation in year i, and N is the number of observations, we calculate the standard deviation for a series of historical or ex post returns or cash flows as:

ex post standard deviation measure of risk for a set of observations

$$\text{Ex post standard deviation} = \sqrt{\frac{\sum_{i=1}^{N}(x_i - \bar{x})^2}{N - 1}} \qquad (8\text{-}7)$$

This is the sample standard deviation, where the sample consists of N observations on returns, cash flows, or other measureable outcome. The term inside the square root sign in Equation 8-7 is the variance, which we denote as σ^2. Therefore, the standard deviation is the square root of the variance, and, conversely, the variance is the square of the standard deviation. We focus on the standard deviation because it is easier to interpret: The standard deviation for a return series is expressed in the same units as the returns, that is, as a percentage. In contrast, the variance is expressed in units of squared returns, which makes its interpretation less obvious.

variance standard deviation squared; denoted as σ^2 and expressed in units of squared units

EXAMPLE 8.4

Calculating the Ex Post Standard Deviation

PROBLEM

Consider the cash flows generated from each of the five divisions of Company X for this past fiscal year, in millions of dollars:

Division	Cash Flow (in millions)
1	$500
2	$100
3	$25
4	$400
5	$300

What is the standard deviation of these cash flows?

Solution

Division	Cash Flow (in millions)	Deviation from the Mean	Squared Deviation
1	$500	$235	55,225
2	100	−165	27,225
3	25	−240	57,600
4	400	135	18,225
5	300	35	1,225
Sum	$1,325		Sum = 159,500
Mean	$265		

The standard deviation is the square root of 159,500 / 4 or $199.6873.

SPREADSHEET APPLICATIONS: THE STANDARD DEVIATION

Spreadsheets make it easy to calculate the standard deviation. Consider the following observations:

	A	B
1	Observation	Return
2	1	5%
3	2	1%
4	3	0%
5	4	−3%
6	5	5%

We calculate the standard deviation using = STDEV(B2:B6), and the variance using = VAR(B2:B6).

The Standard Deviation: Ex Ante

Though an ex post standard deviation is useful in gauging risk, what we really need for decision making, if we can formulate expectations about the asset's future cash flows or returns, is an **ex ante standard deviation**; that is, a standard deviation that is formulated based on *expectations* about the future. We can use Equation 8-8 to estimate the scenario-based standard deviation.

$$\text{Ex ante standard deviation} = \sqrt{\sum_{i=1}^{n} p_i (r_i - E(r))^2} \qquad (8\text{-}8)$$

ex ante standard deviation weighted standard deviation, with the likelihood of each occurrence used as the weight applied to the squared deviation from the expected value; a forward-looking measure of risk

We refer to this as the ex ante measure because we are explicitly taking into account updated probabilities of future events happening. In this application, r_i is one of the possible outcomes and $E(r)$ is the calculated expected value of the possible outcomes. As you can see in this equation, the standard deviation is the result of weighting the squared deviations from the expected value by the likelihood of the outcome occurring.

Consider our previous example, with an expected return of 7 percent, which we calculated based on the possible outcomes and the likelihood of the possible outcomes:

Scenario	Probability of Occurrence	Return on Investment
Outcome 1	60%	15%
Outcome 2	40%	–5%
	100%	

We calculate the variance and standard deviation of the variance by applying Equation 8-8:

Scenario	Probability of Occurrence p_i	Possible Return on Investment r_i	Probability × Return $p_i \times r_i$	Deviation: Return less Expected Return $(r_i - E(r_i))$	Deviation Squared $(r_i - E(r_i))^2$	Deviation Squared, × Probability $p_i(r_i - E(r_i))^2$
Outcome 1	60%	15%	0.09000	0.08000	0.00640	0.00384
Outcome 2	40%	–5%	–0.02000	–0.12000	0.01440	0.00576
			Expected return, $E(r) = 0.07000$			Variance = 0.00960

Standard deviation = 0.09798

where the standard deviation is $\sqrt{0.0096} = 0.0978$.

SUMMARIZING: EX ANTE AND EX POST STANDARD DEVIATIONS

	Ex Post Standard Deviation	Ex Ante Standard Deviation
Perspective	Looking back on what has occurred.	Looking forward to what may happen.
Observations	Observations from the past.	Possible outcomes in the future.
Calculation of the variance	Average of the squared deviations of observations from the mean of the observations.	Weighted average of the squared deviations of possible outcomes from the expected outcome, where the weights are the probabilities.
Formula for the standard deviation (σ)	Ex post $\sigma = \sqrt{\dfrac{\sum_{i=1}^{N}(x_i - \bar{x})^2}{N - 1}}$	Ex ante $\sigma = \sqrt{\sum_{i=1}^{n}p_i(r_i - E(r))^2}$

EXAMPLE 8.5

Estimating the Ex Ante Standard Deviation

PROBLEM

Estimate the standard deviation of the possible cash flows of a company based on possible economic climates:

	Probability	Possible Cash Flow (in millions)
Good	25%	$1,250
Fair	55%	$1,000
Poor	20%	$750

Solution

	Probability	Possible Outcome (in millions)	Probability-weighted Outcome (in millions)	Deviation from Expected Cash Flow (in millions)	Squared Deviation	Probability-weighted Squared Deviation
Good	25%	$1,250	$313	$238	56,406	14,102
Fair	55%	$1,000	$550	–$13	156	86
Poor	20%	$750	$150	–$263	68,906	13,781
		Expected cash flow = $1,013				Variance = 27,969

Standard deviation $= \sqrt{27,969} = \$167.239$

Concept Review Questions

1. Why is the range sometimes a poor measure of risk?

2. What is the difference between a scenario-based (probability) estimate of risk versus a historical data-based estimate of risk?

3. Why would we sometimes want to use scenario-based risk measures rather than the standard deviation of actual returns over a long period?

8.3 EXPECTED RETURN AND RISK FOR PORTFOLIOS

A **portfolio** is a collection of assets that are combined and considered a single asset. In the case of securities, a portfolio is a collection of stocks, bonds, and other financial assets. In the case of a company, a portfolio is the collection of the products or services the company produces. A portfolio therefore may refer to the holdings of a single investor, as well as to holdings that are managed as a unit by one or more portfolio managers on behalf of their clients, or a corporation or other business entity.

portfolio collection of assets, such as stocks and bonds, that are combined and considered a single asset

It is a basic proposition in finance that assets should be managed within a portfolio rather than individually because risk-reduction gains are possible by combining assets into a portfolio. We will be using the statistical ideas that we have just discussed to explore portfolio theory and the implications for financial managers. The basic idea is as simple as the old adage "Don't put all your eggs in one basket": Investors should diversify their investments so that they are not unnecessarily exposed to a single negative event. Modern portfolio theory (MPT) takes this basic idea and shows how to form portfolios with the highest possible expected rate of return for any given level of risk. First, we examine how to calculate the expected return and risk of a portfolio.

Calculating a Portfolio's Return

The expected return on a portfolio is simply the weighted average of the expected returns on the individual assets in the portfolio. Let $E(r_p)$ represent the expected return on the portfolio, $E(r_i)$ the expected return on asset i, and w_i the portfolio weight of asset i.[7] The expected return on a portfolio is:

$$E(r_p) = \sum_{i=1}^{n} (w_i \times E(r_i)) \tag{8-9}$$

The portfolio weight of a particular asset is the percentage of the portfolio's total value that is invested in that asset. These weights sum to one because 100 percent of the portfolio must be invested in something, even if it is in cash.

Consider investments X and Y, which have three different possible outcomes: Good, OK, and Bad:

Scenario	Probability of Possible Outcome	Possible Return on Investment X	Possible Return on Investment Y
Good	35%	15.0%	4.0%
OK	55%	10.0%	6.0%
Bad	10%	–5.0%	8.0%

[7] Confused about $E(r)$ and $E(r_i)$? It's easy to get confused. Unfortunately, in the realm of portfolio theory and statistics we have many expected returns to contend with. Here is the difference: When we are dealing with a probability distribution, the expected value is the measure of central tendency (a type of weighted average) for that probability distribution. When we are dealing with portfolio returns, these are all expected returns for the individual assets (hence, the subscript i).

The expected return on both investments is the same, 10.5 percent:

Scenario	Probability of Possible Outcome	Possible Return on Investment X	Probability-weighted Return on Investment X	Possible Return on Investment Y	Probability-weighted Return on Investment Y
Good	35%	15.0%	5.25%	4.0%	1.40%
OK	55%	10.0%	5.50%	6.0%	3.30%
Bad	10%	−5.0%	−0.50%	8.0%	0.80%
	100.00%		$E(r_X) = 10.25\%$		$E(r_Y) = 5.50\%$

Now consider a portfolio that has these two investments, Investment X and Investment Y, with $150,000 and $250,000 invested, respectively:

Investment	Amount Invested	Expected Return
Investment X	$150,000	10.25%
Investment Y	250,000	5.50%
Total	$400,000	

The weights associated with each investment are:

Investment X: $150,000 ÷ 400,000 = 37.5%
Investment Y: $250,000 ÷ 400,000 = 62.5%

The expected return on the portfolio comprised of investments X and Y is therefore 7.281 percent:

Investment	Weight w_i	Expected Return $E(r_i)$	$w_i \times E(r_i)$
Investment X	37.5%	10.25%	0.03844
Investment Y	62.5%	5.50%	0.03438
	100.0%	$\sum_{i=1}^{2}[w_i \times E(r_i)] = 0.07282$	

We can simplify the expected return formula in the two-asset case to make it more informative. Let us define w as simply the weight placed on asset X, so that $(1 - w)$ is the weight placed on asset Y. The expected return on X is 10.25 percent and the expected return on Y is 5.5 percent. In this case, we can rearrange the expected return for a two-asset portfolio, $E(r_p)$:

$$E(r_p) = E(r_Y) + w[E(r_X) - E(r_Y)] \qquad (8\text{-}10)$$

For example, if we place a weight of 0 in X, then by definition 100 percent is invested in Y, and we expect to earn 5.5 percent, the expected return on Y. Conversely, if we invest 100 percent in X and nothing in Y, then we expect to earn 10.25 percent. Incrementally, as we increase w and put more money (weight) in X, then the return on the portfolio approaches 10.25 percent.

PROBLEM

Consider a company that has two divisions: Division One, with an expected return of 25 percent, and Division Two, with an expected return of 30 percent. The total value of the company is $500 billion, $300 billion attributed to Division One and $200 billion attributed to Division Two. What is the expected return on this company?

EXAMPLE 8.6

Estimating the Expected Portfolio Return

Solution

The company is a portfolio comprised of two divisions. The expected return on this company is the weighted average of the expected returns on the two divisions, or 27%:

Division	Value (in billions)	Weight	Expected Return	Weighted Expected Return
One	$300	60%	25%	15%
Two	200	40%	30%	12%
	$500		Portfolio return = 27%	

We graph this relationship between the weights and the expected return in Figure 8-4. Note that the graph sets the base return at 10.5 percent, where nothing invested in X, and then increases to 10.25 percent as we invest more and more in X.[8]

Regardless of the number of assets held in a portfolio or the portfolio weights, the expected return on the portfolio is *always* a weighted average of the expected return on each individual asset. However, this is *not* the case for the portfolio standard deviation because we must account for correlations, or comovements, among the individual asset returns included in the portfolio, which in turn affect the variability in total portfolio returns. Therefore, the standard deviation for a portfolio will reflect the weighted impact of the individual assets' standard deviations and the relationship among the comovements of the returns on those individual assets.

FIGURE 8-4 Expected Return on a Portfolio Comprising Investments X and Y

[8] For the purposes of this discussion, we have limited the investment weights to a range from 0 percent to 100 percent. However, if we are allowed to short sell either asset, then the weights can be less than 0 (i.e., negative) and more than 100 percent. Short selling means investors sell shares in a stock that they do not own. This can be done through a broker who "lends" investors shares that they can sell on the condition that the investors agree to "replace" these borrowed shares in the future (i.e., by buying them in the market). Thus, it provides investors with a way to profit from the belief that share prices will decrease. There are several technicalities associated with short selling that we will not discuss here. The main implication of short selling for our present discussion is that investors can maintain a negative position in one of the two stocks, so they can short sell A and use the proceeds to invest in B and vice versa.

We estimate the standard deviation of a two-asset portfolio using Equation 8-11. Notice that the first two terms inside the square root sign account for the weighted individual asset standard deviations (or variances), whereas the third term accounts for the weighted comovement of the returns on the two assets. We denote this as COV_{XY}, which is the **covariance** of the returns on X and Y. A covariance is simply a statistical measure of how two variables move together—how they covary. The covariance is in terms of squared units (e.g., squared returns, squared dollars, etc.). The standard deviation of the portfolio's returns, using the covariance of X and Y, is:

$$\sigma_p = \sqrt{w_X^2\, \sigma_X^2 + w_Y^2\, \sigma_Y^2 + 2\, w_X\, w_Y\, COV_{XY}} \tag{8-11}$$

where σ_P = the portfolio standard deviation.

We calculate the variances of the investments' returns as:[9]

Investment X

Scenario	Probability of Occurrence p_i	Return on Stock r_i	Probability × Return $p_i \times r_i$	Deviation: Return less Expected Return $(r_i - E(r_i))$	Deviation Squared $(r_i - E(r_i))^2$	Deviation Squared, × Probability $p_i(r_i - E(r_i))^2$
Good	35.00%	15.0%	5.25%	4.75%	0.002256	0.0007897
OK	55.00%	10.0%	5.50%	−0.25%	0.000006	0.0000034
Bad	10.00%	−5.0%	−0.50%	−15.25%	0.023256	0.0023256

Expected return, $E(r_X) = 10.250\%$
Variance = 0.0031188
Standard deviation = 0.0558458

Investment Y

Scenario	Probability of Occurrence p_i	Return on Stock r_i	Probability × Return $p_i \times r_i$	Deviation: Return less Expected Return $(r_i - E(r_i))$	Deviation Squared $(r_i - E(r_i))^2$	Deviation Squared, × Probability $p_i(r_i - E(r_i))^2$
Good	35.00%	4.0%	1.40%	−1.50%	0.000225	0.0000788
OK	55.00%	6.0%	3.30%	0.50%	0.000025	0.0000138
Bad	10.00%	8.0%	0.80%	2.50%	0.000625	0.0000625

Expected return, $E(r_Y) = 5.500\%$
Variance = 0.0001550
Standard deviation = 0.0124499

We see that Investment X has a higher expected return than Investment Y, but also a larger standard deviation.

We calculate the covariance of the returns on asset X and asset Y, COV_{XY}, as follows:

$$COV_{XY} = \sum_{i=1}^{n} p_i(r_{X,i} - \bar{r}_X)(r_{Y,i} - \bar{r}_Y) \tag{8-12}$$

[9] You may notice that (1) it is important to use many decimal places, and (2) there may be slight differences due to rounding.

where $r_{X,i}$ = the ith return on asset X. The covariance between investments X and Y is −0.0003625:

Possible Outcome	Probability of Possible Outcome	Return on Investment X	Return on Investment Y	Deviation for Investment X $(r_{X,i} - r_X)$	Deviation for Investment Y $(r_{Y,i} - r_Y)$	Product of the Probability and the Deviations $p_i(r_{X,i} - r_X)(r_{Y,i} - r_Y)$
Good	35.00%	15.0%	4.0%	4.75%	−1.50%	−0.0002494
OK	55.00%	10.0%	6.0%	−0.25%	0.50%	−0.0000069
Bad	10.00%	−5.0%	8.0%	−15.25%	2.50%	−0.0003813
	Expected return = 10.250%		5.50%		Covariance = −0.0006375	

This covariance indicates that the two returns tend to move in the opposite direction.

If we construct a portfolio comprising 37.5 percent of Investment X and 62.5 percent of Investment Y, the portfolio standard deviation is:

$$\sigma_p = \sqrt{w_X^2 \sigma_X^2 + w_Y^2 \sigma_Y^2 + 2\,w_X\,w_Y\,COV_{XY}}$$

$$= \sqrt{(0.375)^2(0.00311875) + (0.625)^2(0.00015500) + 2(0.375)(0.625)(-0.00063750)}$$

$$= \sqrt{0.00043857 + 0.00006055 - 0.0002988}$$

$$= \sqrt{0.000200293}$$

$$= 0.01415249 \; or \; 1.415249\%$$

Remember that the term σ_X^2 and σ_Y^2 are the variance of the possible returns on Investment X and Y, respectively. Notice that the portfolio standard deviation of 1.415 percent is *less than* the weighted average of the standard deviations of each individual asset, which is 2.8723 percent [that is, $(0.375 \times 0.05584577) + (0.625 \times 0.01244990)$]. This is always the case, except for one special situation, which we discuss momentarily.

What happens to the portfolio's standard deviation if we vary our investment in the riskier asset? We graph this in the case of the portfolio comprising Investments X and Y in Figure 8-5.

Notice that we start out with the standard deviation of the portfolio at 1.245 percent because all funds are in Y, and we finish up at 5.585 percent because all funds are in X, but

FIGURE 8-5 **Portfolio Risk as Weights in Assets Change**

EXAMPLE 8.7
Estimating a Covariance

PROBLEM

Consider the portfolio comprising two assets, Asset M and Asset N, with the following possible returns for two different scenarios, Up and Down:

Market Condition	Probability	Return on Asset M	Return on Asset N
Up	40%	10%	40%
Down	60%	–5%	–20%

What is the covariance of the returns on the two assets that comprise this portfolio?

Solution

First, we calculate the expected return for each asset:

Market Condition	Probability-weighted Outcome of Asset M	Probability-weighted Outcome of Asset N
Up	4.00%	16.00%
Down	–3.00%	–12.00%
	Expected return = 1.00%	Expected return = 4.00%

Then we calculate the deviation of the possible return from the respective expected return, and then probability weight the product of these deviations. This process produces a covariance of 0.02160:

Market Condition	Probability	Deviation for Asset M	Deviation for Asset N	Product of the Probability and the Deviations
Up	40%	9.00%	36.00%	0.01296
Down	60%	–6.00%	–24.00%	0.00864
				Covariance = 0.02160

in between it is not a straight line. In fact, the lowest standard deviation in Figure 8.5 is when there is 85 percent invested in Y and 15 percent invested in X. In this case, the standard deviation is 0.0443 percent. This is a clear win for the investor: an expected return of 6.21 percent (see Figure 8-4) and virtually no risk (see Figure 8-5).

Correlation Coefficient

correlation coefficient statistical measure that identifies how asset returns move in relation to one another; denoted by ρ

Although covariance provides a useful measure of the relationship of the comovements of returns on individual assets, it is difficult to interpret intuitively because, as was the case with the variance, the unit is percent squared. Fortunately, covariance is related to another statistical measure, the **correlation coefficient** (ρ_{AB}), which we can interpret more intuitively: The correlation coefficient ranges from –1 (perfect negative correlation) to +1 (perfect positive correlation). The correlation coefficient is related to covariance and individual standard deviations according to the relationship in Equation 8-13:

$$\rho_{XY} = \frac{COV_{XY}}{\sigma_X \sigma_Y} \tag{8-13}$$

We can also solve for covariance by rearranging this equation:

$$COV_{XY} = \rho_{XY}\, \sigma_X \sigma_Y \tag{8-14}$$

The correlation between the returns on Investment X and Y is close to 1.0:[10]

$$\rho_{XY} = \frac{COV_{XY}}{\sigma_X \sigma_Y} = \frac{0.0012}{0.02450 \times 0.04899} = 0.999992$$

Finally, we can replace the covariance term in Equation 8-11 to produce Equation 8-15, which is commonly used to estimate portfolio standard deviation when there are two assets:

$$\sigma_p = \sqrt{w_X^2 \sigma_Y^2 + w_Y^2 \sigma_Y^2 + \underbrace{2\, w_X\, w_Y\, \rho_{XY}\, \sigma_X \sigma_Y}_{\uparrow \; COV_{XY}}} \tag{8-15}$$

Using the values from our Investment X and Investment Y example,

$$\sigma_p = \sqrt{(0.375)^2(0.00311875) + (0.625)^2(0.00015500) + 2(0.375)(0.625)(-0.91690440)(0.05584577)(0.01244990)}$$

$$= \sqrt{0.00043857 + 0.00006055 - 0.00029883}$$

$$= \sqrt{0.000200293}$$

$$= 0.01415249 \text{ or } 1.415249\%$$

Notice that this is the same answer we got when we used the covariance, but we expect this because of the relation between the correlation coefficient and the covariance. We can now separate the standard deviation component from the correlation component. This is useful because we already have the standard deviation of both assets in the first two terms, so the correlation coefficient is the only *new* information.

	EXAMPLE 8.8
PROBLEM	**Estimating the Correlation of Returns**

Consider the portfolio comprised of two assets, Asset Three and Asset Four. What is the correlation between the returns on Asset Three and Asset Four, based on the following information?

Covariance of Three and Four	−0.00045
Standard deviation of the returns on Three	0.04
Standard deviation of the returns on Four	0.03

Solution

$$\text{Correlation} = -0.00045 \div (0.04 \times 0.03) = -0.375$$

---

[10] When we are dealing with only a couple or a few possible outcomes, the correlations tend to be either very high or very low. We see correlations more representative of what we see in practice when we allow for more possible returns—beyond three—for each asset.

The correlation coefficient measures how asset returns move in relation to one another. It is a relative measure that has a maximum value of +1.0, which denotes perfect positive correlation, and a minimum value of −1.0, which denotes perfect negative correlation. Positive correlation coefficients imply that the returns on asset A tend to move in the *same* direction as those on asset B. In other words, when the returns on asset B go up, the returns on asset A also tend to increase, and vice versa. It doesn't mean to say that they always go up together; if they did, they would be perfectly positively correlated. Negative correlation coefficients imply the opposite: The returns on asset A tend to move in the opposite direction to those on asset B. In other words, on average, when the returns on asset B go up, the returns on asset A tend to decrease, and vice versa.

The closer the absolute value of the correlation coefficient is to 1, the stronger the relationship between the returns on the two assets. In fact, when $\rho_{AB} = +1$, that is, perfect positive correlation, and if we know the return on one asset, we can predict the return on the other asset with certainty.[11] The same applies when we have $\rho_{AB} = -1$, that is, perfect negative correlation, which implies the returns have a perfect negative relationship with each other. When $\rho_{AB} = 0$ (i.e., zero correlation), there is no relationship between the returns on the two assets; therefore, knowing the return on one asset provides no useful information for predicting the return of the second asset. We illustrate correlation in Figure 8-6, including perfect positive and negative correlation, positive correlation, negative correlation, and no correlation. You can recognize perfect positive and perfect negative correlation right away because the pairwise observations of returns lie on a perfectly straight line.

Focusing on securities, the extreme correlation coefficient values described earlier do not occur for traditional common stock in practice because so many different factors influence stock returns. Generally, security returns display positive correlations with one another but these correlations are less than one. This is logical because most stocks tend to follow the movements of the overall market. As expected, the correlations tend to be higher among securities whose companies are similar in nature, for example, if they are in the same industry, are about the same size, and so on.

Correlation Coefficients and the Portfolio Standard Deviation

As we discussed earlier, the correlation between the returns on the two assets included in a portfolio affects the portfolio's standard deviation of returns. Holding the weights and the individual standard deviations constant, it is clear that the lower the correlation coefficient, the lower the portfolio's standard deviation.

We illustrate this in Figure 8-7, using a portfolio of two assets, with equal weights. The standard deviation of the monthly returns of the two assets is 5 percent and 2 percent, respectively. As you can see in this figure, the portfolio standard deviation is lowest when there is a negative correlation of −1.0, and highest when there is a positive correlation of 1.0. Also, the portfolio standard deviation is less than the weighted average of the individual assets portfolios, 3.5 percent, for all correlations except for when correlation is equal to 1.0.

We can learn a few things from this figure:

- As long as the correlation is not perfect, that is, correlation of 1.0, the portfolio's standard deviation is less than the weighted average of the two assets' standard deviation. *This result is very important because we have just shown the secret of modern portfolio theory: By combining assets into portfolios, we can reduce risk.*

---

[11] Technically, when $\rho = +1$ or -1 and we plot the returns of one asset on the x-axis and the returns on the other asset on the y-axis, we can draw a straight line through the points, and all of them will lie on the line. Such a line would be upward sloping when $\rho = +1$, and it would be downward sloping when $\rho = -1$.

- The slope of the relationship between the portfolio standard deviation and correlation is not linear.
- With perfect, negative correlation, the variability of the portfolio is reduced to almost zero, which means there is almost no risk. In fact, whenever the correlation coefficient equals −1, there exists one set of portfolio weights for the two assets such that we can eliminate risk completely.

This suggests that to discuss how the standard deviation and expected return of a portfolio varies as we change its composition, we can look at three special cases: when the correlation coefficient between the two assets is 0, +1, or −1.

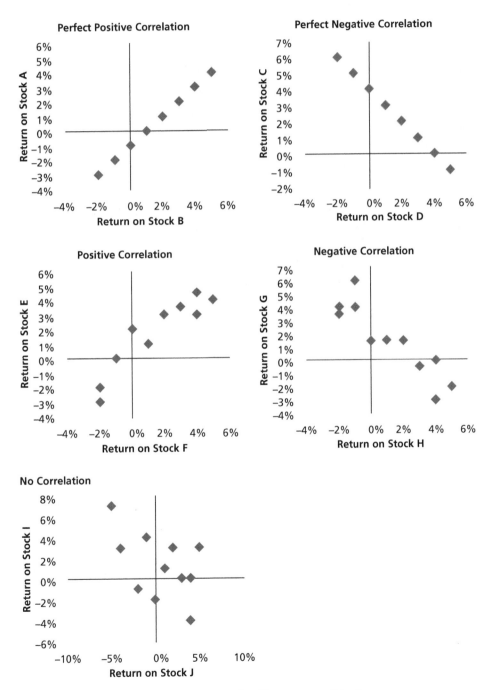

FIGURE 8-6 **Correlation between the Returns on Stocks**

SPREADSHEETS: CORRELATION

We can use spreadsheets to calculate the correlation between or among any series. Consider the annual returns for small stocks, long-term government bonds, and gold in the following spreadsheet:

	A	B	C	D
	Year	*Small Company Stocks*	*Long-term Government Bonds*	*Gold*
1				
2	2001	22.77%	3.70%	1.41%
3	2002	−13.28%	17.84%	23.96%
4	2003	60.70%	1.45%	21.74%
5	2004	18.39%	8.51%	4.40%
6	2005	5.69%	7.81%	17.77%
7	2006	16.17%	1.19%	23.92%
8	2007	−5.22%	9.88%	31.59%
9	2008	−36.72%	25.87%	3.97%
10	2009	28.09%	−14.90%	25.04%
11	2010	31.26%	10.14%	30.60%

We can calculate the correlation between the return on the small company stocks and long-term government bonds using the CORREL function: =CORREL(B2:B11,C2:C11). This results in a correlation of −0.71.

We can also use the spreadsheets' data analysis tools to calculate all of the pairwise correlations among the three investments: Data > Data Analysis > Correlation

The result is a correlation matrix:

G	H	I	J
	Small Company Stocks	*Long-term Government Bonds*	*Gold*
Small company stocks	1		
Long-term government bonds	−0.71171	1	
Gold	0.218616	−0.27263	1

This tells us that the returns on long-term government bonds are negatively correlated with the returns on both small company stocks and gold, and that the returns on small company stocks and gold are positively correlated.

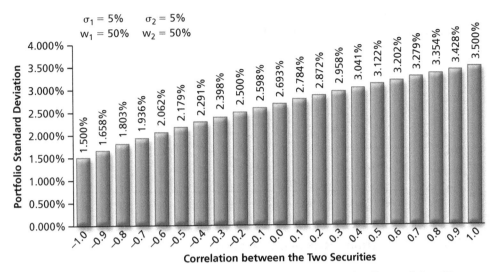

FIGURE 8-7 Portfolio Standard Deviation of a Portfolio Comprising Two Investments with Different Correlations

Let's go back to Equation 8-15, for the portfolio standard deviation of two assets, X and Y, which for ease of reference we repeat here.

$$\sigma_p = \sqrt{w_X^2 \sigma_X^2 + w_Y^2 \sigma_Y^2 + 2 w_X w_Y \rho_{XY} \sigma_X \sigma_Y}$$

The three special cases produce simplified versions of the standard deviation of the portfolio's return.

$$\text{If } \rho = +1 \; \sigma_p = \sqrt{w_X^2 \sigma_X^2 + w_Y^2 \sigma_Y^2 + 2 w_X w_Y \sigma_X \sigma_Y}$$

$$\text{If } \rho = 0 \; \sigma_p = \sqrt{w_X^2 \sigma_X^2 + w_Y^2 \sigma_Y^2}$$

$$\text{If } \rho = -1 \; \sigma_p = \sqrt{w_X^2 \sigma_X^2 + w_Y^2 \sigma_Y^2 - 2 w_X w_Y \sigma_X \sigma_Y}$$

The zero correlation coefficient case is obvious as the covariance term disappears. However, in the other two cases, the correlation coefficient also disappears because it is either +1 or −1.[12] This allows us to simplify the equation for the standard deviation of the portfolio return. We showed earlier how the portfolio risk (standard deviation) varied with the composition of the portfolio (i.e., for the weights invested in X and Y). Now we can consider how the variability changes with the portfolio composition for these three special cases—correlations of 1.0, 0.0 and −1.0. We show the results in Figure 8-8.

Note that with perfect positive correlation, the variability changes in a linear (straight line) fashion with the portfolio weights. As we discussed before, in this case the standard deviation of the portfolio is a weighted average of each asset's standard deviation. However, when the correlation is less than perfectly positive, the relationship is "bowed," and it gets more bowed as the correlation decreases until, with a perfect negative correlation, we can remove all risk. In this case, the bow becomes two straight lines that touch the horizontal axis. At this point in the $\rho = -1$ case, we can create a portfolio with a standard deviation of zero and no variability at all. In this example, if we invest 30 percent in Investment X, with the remainder in Investment Y, we have no portfolio risk when the correlation between the returns on X and Y is −1.0. In other words, we have to put *more* in the lower-variability Investment X to compensate for the fact that it does not move as much as Investment Y.

---

[12] We now get a perfect square: For a perfect positive correlation, think $(a + b)^2$, and for a perfect negative correlation, $(a - b)^2$, where a is the standard deviation of asset A times its portfolio weight (i.e., $w_X \sigma_X$) and b is the same for asset B (i.e., $w_Y \sigma_Y$).

Portfolio has two assets, Investments X and Y. Investment X has a standard deviation of 2.920%, and Investment Y has a standard deviation of 1.245%

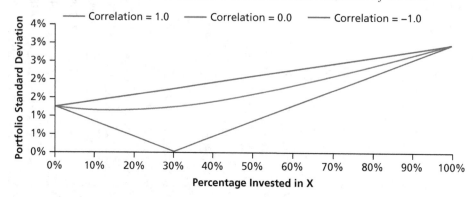

FIGURE 8-8   **Portfolio Risk and Composition**

hedging offsetting an investment position to reduce risk

The perfect negative correlation case is of great importance in managing risk, because it is the basis of **hedging**, which is to take an offsetting position to minimize risk. The principle of hedging helps us to understand the relationship between correlation and covariance. Note that although the two assets are perfectly negatively correlated, we do not create an equally weighted portfolio, investing the same amount in each asset.

GLOBAL PERSPECTIVE | The Linkage Between the U.S. and the European Union Economies

Financial markets in the United States have been buffeted by the European problems. Over the four-week period leading up to May 6, just prior to news that EU members would be meeting to craft the most recent package, broad U.S. stock price indexes declined and implied volatility on equities rose sharply, reflecting some increased aversion to risk. The flight to quality also showed through to U.S. Treasury yields and the foreign exchange value of the dollar, with the 10-year Treasury yield declining 50 basis points over the four-week period and the dollar climbing more than 6 percent against the euro. Following the announcement of the May 10 package, Treasury yields moved back up slightly and equity prices rebounded, but these moves were subsequently reversed and the dollar rose further against the euro.

These effects on U.S. markets underscore the high degree of integration of the U.S. and European economies and highlight the risks to the United States of renewed financial stresses in Europe. One avenue through which financial turmoil in Europe might affect the U.S. economy is by weakening the asset quality and capital positions of U.S. financial institutions. There are, to be sure, good reasons to believe that these institutions can withstand some fallout from European financial difficulties. In the past year, the Federal Reserve has pressed the largest financial institu-

tions to raise substantial additional capital. Moreover, the direct effect on U.S. banks of losses on exposure to one or more sovereigns in peripheral Europe—which, in the current context of sovereign debt concerns, is generally understood to mean Greece, Portugal, Spain, Ireland, and Italy—would be small. According to the Federal Financial Institutions Examination Council, almost all U.S. exposure to peripheral European sovereigns is held by 10 large U.S. bank holding companies, whose balance sheet exposure of $60 billion represents only 9 percent of their Tier 1 capital. However, if sovereign problems in peripheral Europe were to spill over to cause difficulties more broadly throughout Europe, U.S. banks would face larger losses on their considerable overall credit exposures, as the value of traded assets declined and loan delinquencies mounted. U.S. money market mutual funds and other institutions, which hold a large amount of commercial paper and certificates of deposit issued by European banks, would likely also be affected.

Extracted from Daniel K. Tarullo, Testimony on the International Response to European Debt Problems, Before the Subcommittee on International Monetary Policy and Trade and Subcommittee on Domestic Monetary Policy and Technology, Committee on Financial Services, U.S. House of Representatives, Washington, D.C., May 20, 2010.

The Financial Crisis and Risk Models | LESSONS LEARNED

The essential problem is that our models—both risk models and econometric models—as complex as they have become, are still too simple to capture the full array of governing variables that drive global economic reality. A model, of necessity, is an abstraction from the full detail of the real world. In line with the time-honored observation that diversification lowers risk, computers crunched reams of historical data in quest of negative correlations between prices of tradeable assets; correlations that could help insulate investment portfolios from the broad swings in an economy. When such asset prices, rather than offsetting each other's movements, fell in unison on and following August 9 last year, huge losses across virtually all risk-asset classes ensued.

The most credible explanation of why risk management based on state-of-the-art statistical models can per-

form so poorly is that the underlying data used to estimate a model's structure are drawn generally from both periods of euphoria and periods of fear, that is, from regimes with importantly different dynamics.

The contraction phase of credit and business cycles, driven by fear, have historically been far shorter and far more abrupt than the expansion phase, which is driven by a slow but cumulative build-up of euphoria. Over the past half-century, the American economy was in contraction only one-seventh of the time. But it is the onset of that one-seventh for which risk management must be most prepared. Negative correlations among asset classes, so evident during an expansion, can collapse as all asset prices fall together, undermining the strategy of improving risk/reward trade-offs through diversification.

Extracted from Alan Greenspan, "We Will Never Have a Perfect Model of Risk," *Financial Times*, March 16, 2008.

Concept Review Questions

1. What is the relationship between the returns on individual assets in a portfolio and the portfolio's expected return and standard deviation of returns?

2. What is the relationship between the covariance and the correlation coefficient?

3. Why can you always remove all risk in a two-asset portfolio if the assets are perfectly negatively correlated?

8.4 THE EFFICIENT FRONTIER

In the previous section, we examined the return and the standard deviation of a two-asset portfolio, where the two assets have different expected returns and standard deviations. We have shown how the expected return of a two-asset portfolio changes as we shift the proportion invested from the lower to the higher return asset. We have also shown how the portfolio standard deviation changes as we shift the weight from the lower risk to the higher risk asset. We also demonstrated the role of the correlation between the two assets' returns in the standard deviation of the portfolio: There is a mix of each asset that minimizes the portfolio's standard deviation.[13]

The Role of Correlation

Let's consider another example, this time involving Asset One and Asset Two:

Asset	Expected Return	Standard Deviation
One	15%	4%
Two	5%	1%

[13] We limited the investment in any one asset to the 0–100% range. Allowing short selling, that is, which would result in a negative weight for an asset, would, for lower return levels, create a greater standard deviation (and the graph would resemble a boomerang).

First, let's assume a correlation of 1.0. If we calculate the return and standard deviation of every two-asset portfolio comprised of One and Two, using the different possible weights, and plot these results with expected return on the vertical axis and standard deviation on the horizontal axis, we arrive at the relationship we depict in Panel A of Figure 8-9, which represents all possible portfolio combinations that can be constructed by varying the weights in our two assets, One and Two. As you can see, this is a straight line: If the returns of the two assets are perfectly correlated, the standard deviation is:

$$\sigma_p = \sqrt{w_{One}^2 \sigma_{One}^2 + w_{Two}^2 \sigma_{Two}^2 + 2\, w_{One}\, w_{Two}\, \sigma_{One}\, \sigma_{Two}}$$

Now let's assume that the correlation between the returns of Asset One and Asset Two is 0.5. This means that 0.5 is multiplied in the last of the terms in the square root:

$$\sigma_p = \sqrt{w_{One}^2 \sigma_{One}^2 + w_{Two}^2 \sigma_{Two}^2 + 2\, w_{One}\, w_{Two}\, \sigma_{One}\, \sigma_{Two} 0.5}$$

or, multiplying 2 and 0.5 and simplifying,

$$\sigma_p = \sqrt{w_{One}^2 \sigma_{One}^2 + w_{Two}^2 \sigma_{Two}^2 + w_{One}\, w_{Two}\, \sigma_{One}\, \sigma_{Two}}$$

Therefore the influence of the last term on the variance is one-half what it was when the correlation was 1.0. This means that except for the extremes when one of the weights is zero, the standard deviation will be less than when the correlation was perfectly 1.0. You can see this in Panel B of Figure 8-9.

What happens to the return-standard deviation relationship when the correlation between the returns of Asset A and Asset B is negative? This means that the influence of the last term in the standard deviation formula is negative, reducing the portfolio standard deviation:

$$\sigma_p = \sqrt{w_{One}^2 \sigma_{One}^2 + w_{Two}^2 \sigma_{Two}^2 - w_{One}\, w_{Two}\, \sigma_{One}\, \sigma_{Two}}$$

You can see the effect on the standard deviation in Panel C of Figure 8-9. What we show in Figure 8-9 is what is referred to as the "frontier," which is the possible set of portfolios that we can create based on the expected returns, standard deviations, and the correlation between the two assets. As long as the correlation coefficient is not close to either extreme value (i.e., −1 or +1), the parabola shape prevails, as we show in Panels B and C of this figure. Further, because risky assets tend to have positive correlation coefficients that are less than one, the frontier in Panel B is most representative of the return and standard deviation relationship for portfolios formed by using most assets.

Modern Portfolio Theory

modern portfolio theory set of theories that explain how rational investors, who are risk averse, can select a set of investments that maximize the expected return for a given level of risk

risk averse to dislike risk, and require compensation to assume additional risk

We can generalize from the two-asset to the *n*-asset case, for which the expected return is the weighted average of the expected returns on the individual assets, regardless of the number of assets in the portfolio. As a result, Equation 8-9 for estimating portfolio expected returns still applies, and the portfolio weights still must sum to 100 percent. However, calculating the standard deviation on a portfolio of more than two assets becomes cumbersome quite quickly as the number of assets increases, and we will leave that for your further studies in Finance. Harry Markowitz, who is considered the father of modern portfolio theory, was awarded the 1990 Nobel Prize in Economics as a result of his work in this field during the 1950s.[14] **Modern portfolio theory (MPT)**, in a nutshell, is the set of theories that explain how rational investors, who are risk averse, can select a set of investments that maximize the expected return for a given level of risk. A **risk-averse** investor is one that likes return but doesn't like risk; therefore, to be enticed to take on more risk requires a higher expected return.

[14] Harry Markowitz, "Portfolio Selection," *Journal of Finance*, Vol. 7, No. 1 (March 1952) pp. 77–91.

FIGURE 8-9 **Two-Asset Portfolios Formed Using Asset One and Asset Two**

One of Harry Markowitz's main contributions was to show investors how to diversify their portfolios optimally. His arguments are based on several assumptions, the most important of which are:

1. Investors are rational decision makers.
2. Investors are risk averse.
3. Investor preferences are based on a portfolio's expected return and risk (as measured by variance or standard deviation).

Based on these assumptions, Markowitz introduced the notion of an **efficient portfolio**, which dominates other portfolios that could be constructed from a given set of available assets. Efficient portfolios are those that offer the highest expected return for a given level of risk, or offer the lowest risk for a given expected return. Investors can identify efficient portfolios by specifying an expected portfolio return and minimizing the portfolio risk at this level of return, or by specifying a portfolio risk level they are willing to assume and maximizing the expected return given that level of risk.

The first step in the Markowitz analysis is to determine the expected return-risk combinations available to investors from a given set of assets, by allowing the portfolio

efficient portfolio collection of investments that offers the highest expected return for a given level of risk, or offers the lowest risk for a given expected return

FIGURE 8-10 **The Efficient Frontier**

minimum variance frontier curve in return–standard deviation space, produced when determining the expected return-risk combinations available to investors from a given set of assets by allowing the portfolio weights to vary

attainable portfolio collection of investments that may be constructed by combining the underlying assets and lies along the minimum variance frontier

weights to vary, just as we did in Figure 8-9 when we considered only two assets. The entire curve is referred to as the **minimum variance frontier**, which we illustrate in Figure 8-10. Although our discussion has focused on plotting expected return against standard deviation, remember that the variance is just the standard deviation squared.

Notice that the shape is virtually identical to the frontier we constructed using only two assets in Figure 8-9. However, although the shape is similar, by using all available assets, we will be able to generate a set of more efficient portfolios, in the sense of offering higher expected return for a given risk level, or lower risk for a given expected return level.

The other difference between Figures 8-9 and 8-10 is the five portfolios marked I through V that we include in Figure 8-10. We can create all the portfolios that lie along the efficient frontier, including II, IV, and V, by combining the underlying assets. A portfolio along the efficient frontier is an **attainable portfolio**. Portfolios I and III, conversely, which lie above and below the efficient frontier, respectively, are *not* attainable:

- Portfolio I is not attainable in the sense that there is no way that the underlying assets can be combined in such a way to achieve this combination of expected return and risk. It is simply impossible.

- Portfolio III is unattainable in a different sense: It can be attained only by deliberately wasting money—that is, by simply not investing some portion of wealth and leaving money to earn zero return. It means that the portfolio is not formed by efficient combinations of the underlying assets.

minimum variance portfolio (MVP) portfolio that lies on the efficient frontier and has the minimum amount of portfolio risk available from any possible combination of available assets

efficient frontier set of portfolios that offers the highest expected return for their given level of risk

This leaves us with portfolios II and V, which do lie on the minimum variance frontier. Here we can ignore portfolio IV because it is a *dominated* portfolio, even though it lies on the minimum variance frontier. Like portfolio III, which is inefficient (as well as dominated), portfolio IV offers a lower expected rate of return for the same risk as another portfolio on the upper half of the minimum variance frontier. We can see this by drawing a vertical line though IV. The point where it intersects the top part of the minimum variance frontier indicates a portfolio with the same standard deviation of return but a higher expected rate of return. Portfolio V is a special portfolio: it lies on the efficient frontier and also has the minimum amount of portfolio risk available from any possible combination of available assets. It is the **minimum variance portfolio (MVP)**.

The importance of the MVP is that portfolios that lie below it on the bottom segment of the minimum variance frontier are dominated by portfolios on the upper segment. The segment of the minimum variance frontier above the global minimum variance portfolio, therefore, offers the best risk-expected return combinations available to investors from this particular set of assets. This segment includes the set of efficient portfolios that comprise the **efficient frontier**. Rational, risk-averse investors are interested in holding only those portfolios, such as portfolio II, that offer the highest expected return for their given level of risk.[15] In this sense, these portfolios are not dominated by other attainable portfolios. In fact, the efficient frontier is the cornerstone of modern portfolio theory.

Finally, the particular portfolio chosen by an investor will depend on his or her risk preferences. A more aggressive (i.e., less risk averse) investor might choose Portfolio II in Figure 8-10, whereas a more conservative (i.e., more risk averse) investor might prefer Portfolio V (i.e., the MVP).

Concept Review Questions

1. How do you form the minimum variance frontier in the two-asset case?

2. What assumptions about investors underlie Markowitz's theories regarding efficient portfolios?

3. What are the implications of portfolio theory for the financial manager?

8.5 DIVERSIFICATION

We previously demonstrated that the expected portfolio return is *always* a weighted average of individual asset returns, and as long as the correlation between the two assets' returns is less than perfect, positive correlation, portfolio risk is always *less than* a weighted average of the risk of the two assets that comprise the portfolio. Therefore, there is a benefit to combining assets into portfolios. In other words, we can eliminate risk by investing our funds across several assets, or by "not putting all our eggs in one basket." This principle is **diversification**. We have already seen how Markowitz showed that efficient diversification leads investors to hold a portfolio along the efficient frontier, which is one of the cornerstones of modern portfolio theory. However, we have also seen that calculating all those correlation coefficients and generating the efficient frontier is not easy.

diversification reduction of risk by investing funds across several assets

Diversification and Risk

Let's first look at what happens if there is simply random or naïve diversification. **Random diversification** or **naïve diversification** refers to the act of randomly diversifying without regard to relevant investment characteristics, such as company size, industry classification, and so on.[16] That is, in the case of stocks, an investor randomly selects a relatively large number of stocks.[17] We can see this in Figure 8-11, in which we graph the average portfolio standard deviation against the number of assets in the portfolio.[18]

The benefits of random diversification do not continue indefinitely. As more and more assets are added, the marginal risk reduction per asset becomes extremely small, eventually producing an almost negligible effect on total portfolio risk. In the case of stocks, for example, going from 10 to 20 stocks eliminates an additional 7 percent of the monthly portfolio standard deviation, and going from 20 to 30 stocks eliminates only 3 percent of the monthly standard deviation. Thus, although a large number of securities is not required to achieve substantial diversification benefits, the monthly portfolio risk levels out as additional securities are added to the portfolio.

random diversification or **naïve diversification** randomly buying assets without regard to relevant investment characteristics

---

[15] We will talk more about risk aversion in the next chapter.

[16] This is commonly represented in cartoons as someone throwing darts into a dartboard to randomly pick stocks. Nowadays we do it with computers.

[17] When investors relied on stock quotes printed in the newspaper, this was referred to as choosing stocks using darts on the stock pages. With most investors using the Internet for stock quotes, this doesn't work too well.

[18] How do we create Figure 8-11? What this represents is the portfolio standard deviation for each size portfolio. The standard deviation that we graph is the average standard deviation for portfolios created by randomly drawing securities for a portfolio consisting of one stock, and then repeating this for a large number (e.g., 10,000) of random draws. This is repeated for portfolios consisting of two stocks, and so on.

FIGURE 8-11 **Portfolio Risk for Different Size Portfolios, Assuming Naïve Diversification**

ETHICS | Socially Responsible Investing and the Fiduciary Duty

The portfolio manager of a fund has a fiduciary duty to the beneficiaries of the fund to act "with the care, skill, prudence and diligence under the circumstances prevailing that a prudent man acting in a like capacity and familiar with such matters would use in the conduct of an enterprise of like character with like aims." ERISA Section 404(a)(1)(B).

So how does this fiduciary duty translate if the portfolio manager focuses on socially responsible investments (SRI)? If making decisions that are consistent with SRI do not lead to the risk and return that are possible without constraining the feasible set of investments to be consistent with SRI, is the portfolio manager being prudent?

If the set of feasible investments is limited, there is a possibility that SRI investing will not permit fund managers to take advantage of the reduction in risk through diversification. So far, the evidence with respect to how SRI funds perform relative to other funds is mixed; some studies find that SRI funds underperform other funds, whereas other studies find that there is no difference in performance.[19]

Decomposing Risk

unique risk or nonsystematic risk or diversifiable risk company-specific part of total risk that is eliminated by diversification

market risk or systematic risk or nondiversifiable risk systematic part of total risk that cannot be eliminated by diversification

The part of the total risk that *is* eliminated by diversification is the company-specific **unique risk**, which we sometimes refer to as **nonsystematic risk** or **diversifiable risk**. The part that is *not* eliminated by diversification is the **market risk**, which is also referred to as **systematic risk** or **nondiversifiable risk**. A portion of the risk cannot be eliminated because all the securities in the portfolio are directly influenced by overall movements in the general market or economy. We also refer to market risk as beta risk because we often measure this risk as the coefficient when we regress excess returns on a stock (that is, returns above and beyond the return on a risk-free asset) against the excess returns on the market. We show the total and market risk components in Figure 8-12.

$$\text{Total risk} = \text{Market risk} + \text{Unique risk} \quad (8\text{-}16)$$

or, equivalently,

$$\text{Total risk} = \text{Systematic risk} + \text{Nonsystematic risk}$$

[19] For an overview of the issues and evidence, see "Socially Responsible Investing: Is Your Fiduciary Duty at Risk?" by William Martin, *Journal of Business Ethics*, Vol. 90 (2009), pp. 549–560.

FIGURE 8-12 Total and Market Risk for Different Size Portfolios, Assuming Naïve Diversification

In the case of portfolios of securities, diversification can be achieved more efficiently when we take a more structured approach to forming portfolios by consciously selecting securities that can be expected to have lower correlations among their returns, that is, to choose them from different industries, countries, and so on. In the case of a company, diversification requires selecting products or projects whose cash flows are not highly correlated with one another.

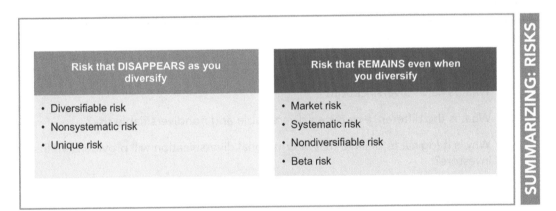

SUMMARIZING: RISKS

Everything That Falls Must Converge | **FINANCE in the News**

Assets have high correlations during stressful times, meaning diversification isn't the silver bullet it's touted as.

The writer Flannery O'Connor titled one of her stories "Everything That Rises Must Converge." And while it is unknown whether the markets have a sense of irony, it can be said that their recent behavior has inverted O'Connor's title quite neatly. For in the last quarter of 2008 most major asset classes converged, but on the way down.

In less highfalutin' terms, the end of 2008 was when the gospel of diversification was dealt a serious blow. Domestically the Russell 3000 and the Standard & Poor's

500 both collapsed. Globally major indexes like the FTSE 100 and the Nikkei 225 ended the year in the red. Indeed stocks all hung together, but not for the better.

It wasn't just stocks. The benchmark 10-year Treasury fell off a cliff, oil prices took a spill and even gold ended the quarter lower, although the metal's drop was relatively slight by comparison. Real estate, of course, continued to be a bloodbath. The S&P/Case-Shiller U.S. National Home Price Index recorded an 18.2% decline in the fourth quarter of 2008 vs. the fourth quarter of 2007, the largest in the series' 21-year history. Truly there was nowhere to run and nowhere to hide as everything converged.

These convergences are problematic because they show that diversification meant the least when it was needed the most. As investors, we are always told to not put all our eggs in one basket, but as 2008 closed out this strategy didn't perform as hoped. You could almost say that what this strategy yielded instead was simply more eggs in more baskets falling at the same time, and yet somehow still ending up on our faces.

The question then becomes whether diversification is merely a truism with little truth in it or whether investors are right to continue to try and parcel out their way to less volatility.

David Joy, chief market strategist at RiverSource Investments, says that while only time will give a clear answer to this question he believes the fourth quarter's close correlations were an aberration. The reason their asset classes moved in tandem is because hedge funds did all they could to dump any assets that had any liquidity at all. Noting this, he says that diversification should still have some value but that "alternative assets, with very low correlations to broad asset categories, are increasing in importance in the search for diversification."

For the wealthy, such alternative assets could include hedge funds and venture capital projects. For those with fewer riches, gold and other precious metals could be areas worth investigating.

Vahan Janjigian, chief investment strategist at Forbes, is more skeptical about the value of diversification. "When there are market panics and widespread selling, diversification does not do much good," he says. Which is not to say investors shouldn't diversify, he says, but investors should realize that it doesn't bullet-proof your portfolio. Like most pieces of inherited market wisdom, diversification offers no refuge from keeping a constant eye on your portfolio, and it should not offer false peace of mind.

Marc Lowlicht, the head of the wealth management division at Further Lane Asset Management, hopes that diversification works once again, or it will become increasingly hard to manage risk. But if diversification continues to proven ineffectual he forecasts having to use various hedging strategies in order to gain more upside on his client's investments.

Still, Lowlicht remains confident, at least for now, that once the great deleveraging is over that asset classes will start to diverge once again. Should the markets rise and converge, however, all bets are off.

Source: Serchuk, David, "Everything That Falls Must Converge," *Forbes*, May 14, 2009.

Reprinted with the permission of the author.

Concept Review Questions

1. What is naïve diversification?

2. What is the difference between diversifiable and nondiversifiable risk?

3. Why is it logical to believe that international diversification will provide benefits to investors?

8.6   A COMPREHENSIVE EXAMPLE

We demonstrate the measurement of risk and the concept of diversification with an example using two assets. Suppose you are given the following information for two investments, A and B, where the return on each varies with the state of the economy:

State of the Economy	Probability of Occurrence	Return on Investment A	Return on Investment B
High growth	10%	60%	5%
Moderate growth	20%	20%	25%
No growth	50%	10%	5%
Recession	20%	−25%	0%
	100%		

The Expected Return

We calculate the expected return for each investment using a weighted average of the possible outcomes, where the weights are the probabilities of each outcome:

$$E(r_A) = (0.10 \times 0.60) + (0.20 \times 0.20) + (0.50 \times 0.10) + (0.20 \times -0.25) = 10\%$$

$$E(r_B) = (0.10 \times 0.05) + (0.20 \times 0.25) + (0.50 \times 0.05) + (0.20 \times 0.00) = 8\%$$

Therefore, Investment A has a higher expected return than Investment B. You may find it easier to perform this calculation in table form. In this case the calculation is:

State of the Economy	Probability of Occurrence	Return on Investment A	Probability × Return on Investment A	Return on Investment B	Probability × Return on Investment B
High growth	10%	60%	0.06	5%	0.005
Moderate growth	20%	20%	0.04	25%	0.050
No growth	50%	10%	0.05	5%	0.025
Recession	20%	−25%	−0.05	0%	0.000
			$E(r_A) = 0.10$		$E(r_B) = 0.080$

The Standard Deviation

The expected return on Investment A is 10 percent and the expected return on Investment B is 8 percent. What is the standard deviation of each investment's possible returns? To calculate the standard deviation, we must first calculate the variance of each investment's possible returns, which requires:

1. comparing the possible outcomes with the expected value of the outcomes,
2. squaring this deviation from the expected value, and then
3. weighting the squared deviation by the probability associated with the possible outcome.

The calculation for each investment is:

$$\sigma_A^2 = 0.10(0.60 - 0.10)^2 + 0.20(0.20 - 0.10)^2 + 0.50(0.10 - 0.10)^2 + 0.20(-0.25 - 0.10)^2$$

$$\sigma_A^2 = 0.00515$$

$$\sigma_B^2 = 0.10(0.05 - 0.08)^2 + 0.20(0.25 - 0.08)^2 + 0.50(0.05 - 0.08)^2 + 0.20(0.0 - 0.08)^2$$

$$\sigma_B^2 = 0.00760384$$

In tabular form,

State of the Economy	Probability of Occurrence	Return on Investment A	Deviation from the Expected Return for Investment A	Squared Deviation for Investment A	Weighted Squared Deviation for Investment A
High growth	10%	60%	0.06	0.2500	0.02500
Moderate growth	20%	20%	0.04	0.0100	0.00200
No growth	50%	10%	0.05	0.0000	0.00000
Recession	20%	−25%	−0.05	0.1225	0.02450
					$\sigma_A^2 = 0.05150$

State of the Economy	Probability of Occurrence	Return on Investment B	Deviation from the Expected Return for Investment B	Squared Deviation for Investment B	Weighted Squared Deviation for Investment B
High growth	10%	5%	−0.03	0.0009	0.00009
Moderate growth	20%	25%	0.17	0.0289	0.00578
No growth	50%	5%	−0.03	0.0009	0.00045
Recession	20%	0%	−0.08	0.0064	0.00128
					$\sigma_B^2 = 0.00760$

The standard deviation of each investment's return is the square root of the respective variance:

$$\sigma_A^2 = \sqrt{0.00515} = 22.69\%$$
$$\sigma_B^2 = \sqrt{0.00760} = 8.72\%$$

Notice that Investment A has the higher standard deviation than Investment B; therefore, it appears to have the more risk, based on the variability of the forecast return around its expected return.

Suppose you create a portfolio that has 30 percent invested in Investment A and 70 percent invested in Investment B. What is the expected return on this portfolio? The expected return on this portfolio, $E(r_p)$, is the weighted average of the returns on the investments, 8.6 percent:

$$[w_A \times E(r_A)] + [w_B \times E(r_B)] = (0.30 \times 10\%) + (0.70 \times 8.0\%) = 8.6\%$$

Covariance

What is the covariance between the returns of Investment A and those of Investment B? We go back to the probability distribution of each investment's returns, calculate the probability-weighted return for each possible economic scenario, and then calculate the variance of these weighted returns. This variance is the covariance between the returns on Investment A and the returns on Investment B:

State of the Economy	p_i	Return on Investment A	Return on Investment B	Calculation	Result
High growth	10%	60%	5%	$0.10 \times (0.60 - 0.10) \times (0.05 - 0.08)$	−0.0015
Moderate growth	20%	20%	25%	$0.20 \times (0.20 - 0.10) \times (0.25 - 0.08)$	0.0034
No growth	50%	10%	5%	$0.50 \times (0.10 - 0.10) \times (0.05 - 0.08)$	0.0000
Recession	20%	−25%	0%	$0.20 \times (-0.25 - 0.10) \times (0.00 - 0.08)$	0.0056
					$COV_{A,B} = 0.0075$

Correlation

The correlation between the returns on Investments A and B is related to the investments' respective standard deviations. More specifically, the correlation is the ratio of the covariance of returns of the two investments, divided by the product of their respective standard deviations:

$$\rho_{AB} = \frac{COV_{AB}}{\sigma_A \sigma_B} = \frac{0.0075}{(0.22669)\,(0.0872)} = 0.379$$

The Portfolio's Risk

We use the following information to calculate the portfolio risk:

w_A = 30%   *The proportion invested in Investment A*

w_B = 70%   *The proportion invested in Investment B*

σ_A = 22.69%   *The standard deviation of the returns on Investment A*

σ_A = 8.72%   *The standard deviation of the returns on Investment B*

ρ_{AB} = 0.379   *The correlation between the returns of Investment A and Investment B*

Using Equation 8-11, we calculate a portfolio standard deviation of 10.73 percent:

$$\sigma_p = \sqrt{(0.30)^2(0.2269)^2 + (0.70)^2(0.0872)^2 + 2(0.30)(0.70)(0.0075)}$$

$$\sigma_p = \sqrt{0.0046335 + 0.003725 + 0.003149} = \sqrt{0.01151} = 10.73\%$$

Using Equation 8-15, we arrive at the same portfolio standard deviation:

$$\sigma_p = \sqrt{(0.30)^2(0.2269)^2 + (0.70)^2(0.0872)^2 + 2(0.30)(0.70)(0.379)(0.2269)(0.0872)}$$

$$\sigma_p = \sqrt{0.0046335 + 0.003725 + 0.003149} = \sqrt{0.01151} = 10.73\%$$

Sensitivity Analysis

The calculation of the standard deviation is based on a number of estimates about the future. We can perform sensitivity analysis on the portfolio's risk based on varying different parameters. Consider if we vary the proportions invested in Investment A and Investment B:

Scenario	Proportion Invested in Investment A	Proportion Invested in Investment B	Expected Return on the Portfolio	Standard Deviation of the Returns on the Portfolio
1	100%	0%	10.000%	22.69%
2	30%	70%	8.600%	10.73%
3	70%	30%	9.400%	17.05%
4	0%	100%	8.000%	8.72%

A few observations:

- If the entire portfolio is invested in Investment A (Scenario 1), the risk of the portfolio is the same as that of Investment A: 22.69 percent.
- If the entire portfolio is invested in Investment B (Scenario 4), the standard deviation of the portfolio is the same as that of Investment B.
- The greater the proportion of the portfolio invested in Investment A, the higher the portfolio risk, but also the higher the expected return.

If we vary the estimate of, say, the probabilities of the possible outcomes, we end up with different expected values and standard deviations. Consider a change in the probabilities associated with each state of the economy:

State of the Economy	Probability	Return on Investment A	Return on Investment B
High growth	20%	60%	5%
Moderate growth	20%	20%	25%
No growth	50%	10%	5%
Recession	10%	–25%	0%

If 30 percent is invested in Investment A and 70% in Investment B:

Statistic	Investment A	Investment B	Portfolio
Expected return	19%	9%	11.5%
Standard deviation	23.88%	8.38%	9.87%

Covariance of returns	0.002775	
Correlation of returns	0.138646	

The change in the probabilities associated with the different outcomes changes all of the parameters: expected returns, standard deviations, covariance, and correlation. As you can see from these examples, it is important to consider the sensitivity of the estimates used in the evaluation of a portfolio's expected return and risk.

Concept Review Questions

1. What is the relation between the covariance and the correlation of two assets' returns?

2. What is meant by stating that a portfolio lies on the efficient frontier?

3. What is the role of correlation in a portfolio's risk?

SUMMARY

- In financial decision making and analysis, we use both ex post and ex ante returns on investments: We use ex post returns when we look back at what has happened, and we use ex ante returns when we look forward, into the future.

- One measure of risk is the standard deviation, which is a measure of the dispersion of possible outcomes.

- When we invest in more than one investment, there may be some form of diversification, which is the reduction in risk from combining investments whose returns are not perfectly correlated.

- If we consider all possible investments and their respective expected return and risk, there are sets of investments that are better than others in terms of return and risk. These sets make up the efficient frontier.

- If we consider a company as a portfolio of investments, diversification plays a role in financial decision making. Financial managers need to consider not only what an investment looks like in terms of its return and risk as a stand-alone investment, but more important, how it fits into the company's portfolio of investments.

FORMULAS/EQUATIONS

(8-1)   Income yield $= \dfrac{CF_1}{P_0}$

(8-2)   Capital gain or loss return $= \dfrac{P_1 - P_0}{P_0}$

(8-3)   Total return $= \dfrac{CF_1 + P_1 - P_0}{P_0}$

(8-4)   Arithmetic mean $= \dfrac{\sum\limits_{i=1}^{n} r_i}{n}$

(8-5)   Geometric mean $= \sqrt[n]{(1 + r_1) \times (1 + r_2) \times (1 + r_3) \times \ldots \times (1 + r_n)} - 1$

(8-6)   Expected value $= \sum\limits_{i=1}^{n}(outcome_i \times probabilty_i)$

(8-7)   Ex post standard deviation $= \sqrt{\dfrac{\sum\limits_{i=1}^{N}(x_i - \bar{x})^2}{N - 1}}$

(8-8)   Ex ante standard deviation $= \sqrt{\sum\limits_{i=1}^{n} p_i (r_i - E(r_i))^2}$

(8-9) $E(r_p) = \sum\limits_{i=1}^{n}(w_i \times E(r_i))$

(8-10) $E(r_P) = E(r_Y) + w[E(r_X) - E(r_Y)]$

(8-11) $\sigma_p = \sqrt{w_X^2 \sigma_X^2 + w_Y^2 \sigma_Y^2 + 2 w_X w_Y COV_{XY}}$

(8-12) $COV_{XY} = \sum\limits_{i=1}^{n} p_i (r_{X,i} - \bar{r}_X)(r_{Y,i} - \bar{r}_Y)$

(8-13) $\rho_{XY} = \dfrac{COV_{XY}}{\sigma_X \sigma_Y}$

(8-14) $COV_{XY} = \rho_{XY} \sigma_X \sigma_Y$

(8-15) $\sigma_p = \sqrt{w_X^2 \sigma_X^2 + w_Y^2 \sigma_Y^2 + 2 w_X w_Y \rho_{XY} \sigma_X \sigma_Y}$

(8-16) Total risk $=$ Market risk $+$ Unique risk

QUESTIONS AND PROBLEMS

Multiple Choice

1. An investor purchased a company's stock at $25 1 year ago and it is now worth $24. The company paid a quarterly dividend of $1 per share during the year. The capital gain or loss return for this stock is closest to:

    A. –16 percent.   B. –4 percent.   C. 4 percent.   D. 12 percent.

2. An investor purchased a stock at $25 1 year ago and it is now worth $24. It paid a dividend of $4 per share at the end of the year. The total return for this stock is *closest* to:

    A. 0 percent.   B. 4 percent.   C. 16 percent.   D. 12 percent.

3. Which of the following is *incorrect*?

    A. The geometric mean of 50 percent and –50 percent is –13.4 percent.

    B. The arithmetic average is always less than the geometric mean of a series of returns.

    C. The income yield of an asset that has a $3 cash flow during a period with a beginning price of $15 is 20 percent.

    D. The greater the dispersion of a distribution, the greater the spread between the geometric mean and the arithmetic average.

4. The expected return on a stock that has a 30 percent probability of a 30 percent return, a 20 percent probability of a 40 percent return, and a 50 percent probability of a 15 percent return, is *closest* to:

    A. 15 percent.   B. 20 percent.   C. 24.5 percent.   D. 35.5 percent.

5. Consider a stock that has a 30 percent probability of a 30 percent return, a 20 percent probability of a 40 percent return, and a 50 percent probability of a 15 percent return. The standard deviation is *closest* to:

    A. 10.11 percent.   B. 10.25 percent.   C. 11.12 percent.   D. 12.00 percent.

6. Which of the following is *false*?

    A. Standard deviation is easier to interpret than variance as a measure of risk.

    B. Covariance measures the comovement between the returns of individual assets.

    C. The expected return of a portfolio is always the weighted average of the expected return of each asset in the portfolio.

    D. The standard deviation of a portfolio is always the weighted average of the standard deviations of individual assets in the portfolio.

7. The correlation coefficient:

    A. may be greater than +1.

    B. measures how asset returns move in relation to one another.

    C. equals covariance multiplied by the individual standard deviations.

    D. shows a stronger relationship between the returns of two assets when its absolute value is closer to 0.

8. The correlation coefficient between the returns on a portfolio and a potential investment of the portfolio that most likely will provide the greatest diversification benefits for a given portfolio is:

    A. −0.9.   B. 0.0.   C. 0.5.   D. 1.0.

9. Consider a portfolio consisting of two assets, A and B. The expected return on A is 5 percent, whereas the expected return on B is 10 percent. If the market value of A is €100 and the market value of B is €300, the expected return on this portfolio is *closest* to:

    A. 7.5%.   B. 8.75%.   C. 13.17%.

10. Which of the following statements is incorrect?

    A. Investors can reduce a portfolio's risk by diversifying.

    B. The portfolios that lie along the efficient frontier provide the greater expected return for a given level of risk.

    C. Portfolios that lie on the part of the efficient frontier that is below the minimum-variance portfolio are the most attractive portfolios for investors.

    D. Adding a security to a portfolio that has returns that are negatively correlated with the existing portfolio will result in a portfolio risk that is less than the weighted average of the individual securities' standard deviations.

Practice Questions and Problems

8.1   Measuring Returns

11. Distinguish between ex post and ex ante returns on investments. Which, if any, would a financial manager find useful in evaluating an investment?

12. Describe the circumstances in which a financial manager or analyst would use the arithmetic mean to describe a return series.

13. Describe the circumstances in which a financial manager or analyst would use the geometric mean to describe a return series.

14. Suppose a financial manager is evaluating the performance of the following investments made last year, all values in millions:

	Investment One	Investment Two	Investment Three
Initial investment	$10	$20	$15
Cash flow, year 1	$1	$2	$5
Value of investment, end of year 1	$10	$18	$12

What is the income yield, capital yield, and total yield for each investment?

15. An analyst's file on the daily performance of the Houston Company has been partially completed.
    A. Complete the table, filling in the missing data.

The Houston Company Stock Performance

Quarter	Opening Price	Dividend	Closing Price	Income Yield	Capital Yield	Total Return
1	$20	$1.00	$21	5.00%	5.00%	
2	$21		19	4.76%		–4.76%
3	$19	$0.50	21		10.53%	
4		$0.50	22	2.38%		

B. What is the geometric mean return for the year for the Houston Company stock?

16. Calculate the annual arithmetic mean and geometric mean return on the following security, and state which method is more appropriate for the situation: purchase price = $30; 1st-year dividend = $5; price after 1 year = $35; 2nd-year dividend = $8; selling price after 2 years = $28.

8.2 Measuring Risk

17. What is the difference between an ex ante standard deviation and an ex post standard deviation?

18. Why might a financial manager estimate and use the ex post standard deviations of a company's past capital investments when evaluating new capital projects?

19. You observed the following daily returns for two companies: ABC and DEF.

Daily Returns

	ABC	DEF
Monday	3%	2%
Tuesday	2%	8%
Wednesday	–8%	14%
Thursday	–10%	12%
Friday	7%	3%

Calculate, for each stock, the:
A. Geometric mean daily return
B. Arithmetic mean daily return
C. Standard deviation of daily returns

20. Calculate the expected return and the standard deviation of the returns for the following investment:

Conditions	Probability	Possible Return
Boom	15%	10%
Stable	60%	5%
Recession	25%	1%

21. Calculate the expected return and the standard deviation of the returns for the following asset:

Conditions	Probability	Possible Outcome
Best	20%	25%
OK	60%	15%
Lousy	20%	−5%

22. The analysts at Food Products Inc. have conducted an extensive analysis of the economy and have concluded that the probability of a recession next year is 25 percent, a boom is 15 percent, and a stable economy is 60 percent. The CFO has estimated that the earnings per share will be $1 if there is a recession, $2 if there is a boom, and $1.25 if the economy is stable.

A. What is the expected earnings per share for Food Products, based on the analysts' and CFO's expectations of the economy?

B. What is the standard deviation of the possible earnings per share?

23. You have observed the following returns:

Period	Return
1	10 percent
2	−8 percent
3	5 percent
4	2 percent
5	−20 percent

A. Calculate the geometric mean return.
B. Calculate the arithmetic mean return.
C. Calculate the variance and standard deviation of these returns.

24. On January 1, 2013, the Absent Minded Profs published the following forecasts for the economy:

State of the Economy	Probability	Forecasted Quarterly Return
Poor	20%	−3%
Average	50%	5%
Boom	30%	8%

During 2013, you observed quarterly returns of 2 percent, −5 percent, 3 percent, and 8 percent.

A. Calculate the ex ante expected quarterly return.
B. Calculate the ex ante standard deviation of quarterly returns.
C. Calculate the ex post average quarterly return.
D. Calculate the ex post standard deviation of quarterly returns.
E. Explain the difference between the ex ante and ex post returns.

 25. Calculate the ex post standard deviation of returns for the following:

Period	Return
1	50 percent
2	30 percent
3	20 percent
4	35 percent
5	55 percent

8.3   Expected Return and Risk of Portfolios

26. Distinguish between a correlation and a covariance.

27. Why would a financial manager be concerned about the correlation among a company's different products when making investment decisions?

28. Suppose you determine that the correlation between the returns on two products is 0.4. What does that mean?

29. Suppose a company has the following three products: peanut butter, toothpaste, and computers. What is likely to be the correlation (positive, negative, or zero) among the cash flows of these products? Explain.

30. Consider a portfolio consisting of two assets, A and B. The expected return on A is 5 percent, whereas the expected return on B is 10 percent. If the market value of A is £750 million and the market value of B is £250 million, calculate the expected return on this portfolio.

31. The managers of the Dayton Fund are exploring different portfolio allocations between two stocks. Complete the following table.

	Case 1	Case 2	Case 3	Case 4	Case 5
Amount invested in Stock 1	$500		$100	$200	
Amount invested in Stock 2	$500	$1,600	$5,000	$300	$900
Total invested	$1,000	$2,000	$5,100	$500	$1,000
Weight in Stock 1	50%		2%	40%	
Weight in Stock 2		80%			90%
Expected return of Stock 1	8%	3%	10%	5%	1%
Expected return of Stock 2		5%		6%	10%
Expected return on the portfolio	5.5%	4.6%	5.1%		

32. Your portfolio consists of two assets: Ice-T and Mr. B. The expected return for Ice-T is 8 percent, while for Mr. B it is 3 percent. The standard deviation is 4 percent for Ice-T and 14 percent for Mr. B. If 15 percent of the portfolio is invested in Ice-T, calculate the portfolio standard deviation if:

   A. the correlation between the stocks is 0.75.

   B. the correlation between the stocks is –0.75.

33. An investor owns a portfolio of $30,000 that contains $10,000 in Bluechip Inc. stock, with an expected return of 12 percent; $5,000 in bonds, with an expected return of 8 percent; and the rest in Redchip Inc. stock, with an expected return of 20 percent. Calculate the expected return of his portfolio.

34. The Diverse Funds are exploring the risk of different portfolio allocations between two stocks. Complete the following table.

	Case 1	Case 2
Weight in Stock 1		15%
Weight in Stock 2	25%	
Standard deviation of Stock 1	15%	2%
Standard deviation of Stock 2	3%	10%
Covariance between Stocks 1 and 2		
Correlation between Stocks 1 and 2	–0.20	0.40
Portfolio variance		
Portfolio standard deviation		

35. Analysts have reported the following return data on six stocks:

Day	XYZ	ABC	DEF	GHI	JKL	MNO
Monday	1%	–18%	3%	6%	7%	3%
Tuesday	2%	–15%	8%	3%	5%	–4%
Wednesday	3%	–12%	13%	1%	3%	8%
Thursday	4%	–9%	18%	3%	2%	–2%
Friday	5%	–6%	22%	–5%	0%	0%

A. Graph the returns of each stock (ABC, DEF, GHI, JKL, and MNO) over time.
B. Based on the five graphs, which stocks are positively correlated with XYZ?
C. Based on the five graphs, which stocks are negatively correlated with XYZ?
D. Based on the five graphs, which stocks are uncorrelated with XYZ?

8.4   The Efficient Frontier

36. What is an efficient frontier?

37. State three of the most important assumptions underlying Markowitz's notion of efficient portfolios.

38. What is the role of the decision maker's risk aversion in selecting a portfolio?

39. Complete the following table, indicating whether each of the following portfolios cannot lie on the efficient frontier?

Portfolio	Expected Return	Standard Deviation of Returns	Cannot Lie on the Efficient Frontier? Yes or No
A	6%	10%	
B	7%	12%	
C	5%	10%	
D	7%	11%	
E	6%	11%	

8.5   Diversification

40. Evaluate the following statement:
"Diversification can only exist when the assets' returns are negatively correlated."

41. For each of the following identify the risk:

Characteristic	Type of Risk
Risk that can be eliminated by diversifying	
Risk that remains after diversifying	
Unavoidable risk	

42. Some companies embark on acquisitions for the purposes of diversifying their business, arguing that by acquiring a company that operates in a different line of business, they are reducing the risk of the company as a whole.

A. What would be the benefit, if any, from this form of diversification to the financial management of the company? Explain.

B. Would this diversification benefit shareholders of the companies performing this type of diversification? Explain.

43. The New Bedford Analysts have recently published a study claiming that the benefits to diversification are constant. In other words, adding one more stock to a three-stock portfolio will have the same impact as adding one more stock to a 500-stock portfolio. Evaluate this claim.

44. Consider a portfolio that has five investments. The financial manager is considering adding a sixth investment to the portfolio. The possible candidates are:

Security	Expected Return	Standard Deviation of Returns	Correlation with the Company's Existing Investments
A	10%	10%	0.9
B	9%	9%	–0.2
C	9%	8%	–0.2
D	8%	8%	0.0

Which investment do you recommend, and why?

 45. A financial analyst with the Auburn Cat Supply Company has developed forecasts for a new cat food product, the Natural Tiger. The analyst is preparing a presentation on the return and risk of this new product and wants to be prepared for questions of how this product will fit into the current lineup of products. The analyst has gathered the following forecasts:

State of the Economy	Probability	Return on Auburn Cat Supply Company	Return on Natural Tiger
High growth	10%	20%	6%
Moderate growth	30%	10%	8%
No growth	50%	3%	12%
Recession	10%	–5%	15%

A. Calculate the expected return for both the company and the new product.
B. Calculate the standard deviation of returns for both the company and the new product.
C. Calculate the covariance and correlation between the returns for the company and the new product.
D. Assume that after investing the product, the company is comprised of 80 percent of products before Natural Tiger, and Natural Tiger is the remaining 20 percent. Should the analyst recommend the new product? Explain.
E. Assume that after investing the product, the company is comprised of 90 percent of products before Natural Tiger, and Natural Tiger is the remaining 10 percent. Should the analyst recommend the new product? Explain.
F. Using a spreadsheet, calculate and graph the expected return and standard deviation of the Auburn Cat Supply Company using different weights for Natural Tiger, ranging from investing such that Natural Tiger comprises 50 percent of the Auburn Cat Supply Company after investment, to 0 percent, in increments of 5 percent. What level of investment would you recommend, relative to the Auburn Cat Supply Company, based on your analysis? Why?

 46. Consider the returns on the following ex post returns on three investments:

Year	Investment 1	Investment 2	Investment 3
1	2%	10%	–3%
2	2%	7%	9%
3	3%	8%	–2%
4	4%	9%	12%
5	4%	6%	0%
6	3%	9%	15%
7	3%	10%	–1%
8	3%	5%	20%
9	2%	8%	12%
10	3%	8%	18%

A. What is the arithmetic mean annual return for each investment over these 10 years?

B. What is the geometric mean annual return for each investment over these 10 years?

C. What is the standard deviation of returns for each investment?

D. What is the correlation of returns among each pair of investments (that is, Investment 1 and 2, Investment 1 and 3, and Investment 2 and 3)?

E. If Investment 1 represents a company's existing investments and Investments 2 and 3 are possible investments, which investment, 2 or 3, offers the most diversification potential? Why?

Case

Case 8.1 The Boise Boyz Company

The Boise Boyz Company (BBC) currently has a single line of business, buoys. The company is considering the purchase of one of two companies, each in a different line of business: The Treasure Search Company (TSC) and the Old Lady Knitting Company (OLKC). BBC is four times as large as TSC and OLKC, each considered alone. The financial analysts of BBC have worked up some numbers to present to the CFO, Bobby Boyz, regarding returns on BBC and the two other companies for the next year. The analysts project the following:

Economic Environment	Probability	Returns		
		BBC	*TSC*	*OLKC*
Economic recovery	20%	15%	20%	11%
Stagnant economy	50%	8%	10%	10%
Recession	30%	1%	–10%	9%

Answer the following questions regarding the evaluation of the acquisition of TSC and OLKC, using a spreadsheet to perform the calculations:

A. What is the expected return and standard deviation of these returns for each company?

B. What is the expected return if BBC acquires TSC? OLKC?

C. What is the standard deviation of the portfolio consisting of BBC and TSC? BBC and OLKC?

D. Based on the expected return and the portfolio standard deviation, which acquisition is preferred: TSC or OLKC? Explain your reasoning.

CHAPTER 9

ASSET PRICING

Hither or Whither the Random Walk? Now in its tenth edition, the popularity of Burton Malkiel's book, *A Random Walk Down Wall Street,* has survived investors' fascination for small stocks, the Internet bubble, and the fervor and fury over mortgage-backed securities.[1] First published in 1973, it has stood the test of time and the market's ups and downs.

The basic message of the book is that the markets are efficient and that it is not possible to beat the market on a risk-adjusted basis. Burton Malkiel dispels the notion that you can earn abnormal returns—that is, those in excess of what you expect based on the amount of risk—using technical analysis or fundamental analysis.

Does this mean that you cannot earn profits when trading in stock? No, but don't expect to earn profits in excess of those adequate for the amount of risk on a consistent basis. Does this mean you should not analyze stocks? No, because fundamental analysis is useful in determining whether a stock fits in your portfolio in terms of returns and risk.

Learning Outcomes

After reading this chapter, you should be able to:

LO 9.1 Describe the importance of the efficient frontier in portfolio selection.

LO 9.2 Describe how the capital market line and returns are determined from modern portfolio theory, and explain the relationship between the capital asset pricing model's security market line and the capital market line.

LO 9.3 Discuss implications of the capital asset pricing model for risks that investors face.

LO 9.4 Describe the basics of models of asset pricing that are alternatives to the CAPM.

LO 9.5 Explain what is meant by market efficiency, and differentiate among different levels of efficiency.

LO 9.6 Discuss the implications of behavioral finance in financial decision making.

Chapter Preview Our focus in this chapter is on the asset pricing models, which help us understand the relation between return and risk and how assets are priced considering risk. We begin our discussion with an overview of the efficient frontier, which is the set of assets that offer the best opportunities in terms of risk and return. We then build on the idea of an efficient frontier, introducing the capital asset pricing model, which describes how assets are priced by market participants. We also look at alternative asset pricing models and then shift our focus to market efficiency. We conclude the chapter with a discussion of the behavior of financial decision makers that does not always match up with what our asset pricing models assume and learn how this behavior may affect decisions.

[1] Burton G. Malkiel, *A Random Walk Down Wall Street,* 10th ed. (New York: W. W. Norton & Company, 2011). **325**

9.1   THE EFFICIENT FRONTIER

Which would you rather have?

Receive $100 if a coin flip
produces a head   or   **$50**
Pay $100 if a coin flip produces a tail

This is a fair gamble because the expected payoff is $0, that is, the expected payoff is [$100 × 0.50] + [–$100 × 0.50] = $0. If someone turns down a fair gamble, he or she is likely risk averse. A risk-averse person prefers the risk-free situation—that is, not gambling on a risky situation where there is an equal probability of winning or losing the same amount of money. We assume that investors are risk averse when choosing among different investments: Investors are not willing to undertake fair gambles.

The Role of Risk

The corollary to turning down a fair gamble is that the risk-averse person requires a **risk premium** to enter into a risky situation. For example, someone might be willing to undertake a gamble if the head's payoff is $150 instead of $100. In this case, the expected payoff increases to $25, and it is no longer a fair gamble because there is a risk premium of $25. Another person may require that the head's payoff increases to $200 before undertaking the gamble, so the risk premium increases to $50. The second individual is more risk averse and requires a larger expected payoff or risk premium to get into the risky situation. Generally, investor behavior is consistent with risk aversion and the existence of risk premiums to induce individuals to bear risk. We can represent this risk aversion by the required risk premium per unit of risk, with higher risk premiums indicating greater risk aversion.

We can also reverse the situation and put the individual in a risky situation and ask how much he or she is willing to pay to get out of the risky situation. Suppose, for example, someone faces a fair gamble; how much would he or she pay to get out of it? A very risk averse individual would pay a large amount, say $25, to get out of the fair gamble with equally likely payoffs of +/–$100. In this case, instead of calling the increased payoff a risk premium, we refer to the payment to get out of a risky situation as an **insurance premium**.

insurance premium
payment to get out of a
risky situation

The Efficient Frontier with Risk-Free Borrowing and Lending

The existence of insurance markets indicates how risk aversion creates a demand to remove risk, whereas the existence of capital markets indicates how risk aversion generates risk premiums required to induce people to bear risk. We assume that investors are risk averse, that is, they require a risk premium to bear risk. We also assume that the more risk averse an investor, the higher the risk premium the investor requires. Further, we assume that we can represent risk by the standard deviation of the return on the portfolio.[2]

These assumptions lead to the result that investors choose only portfolios on the efficient frontier. The efficient frontier represents all portfolios of risky assets that have better risk-return situations than other portfolios of risky assets, which we represent in Figure 9-1.

---

[2] This is a simplification, but helps illustrates the point. The standard deviation assumes that the individual is just as concerned about making too little as making too much return on an investment. There are metrics that we could use to address this (e.g., semivariance), but this is beyond the scope of this book.

FIGURE 9-1 The Efficient Frontier

We can't say where a particular person's preference falls on the efficient frontier because individuals differ in terms of their risk aversion. But a very risk-averse individual may choose portfolio A, and a less risk-averse individual may choose portfolio B. Why do we know that the investor choosing A is more risk averse than the investor choosing B? The line going through A to the origin is steeper than the line through B and the origin. The slope of the line is the height (the expected return on the portfolio) divided by the length (the standard deviation of the portfolio). Because the line through A is steeper than the line through B, the individual who invests in A requires a higher expected rate of return per unit of risk—that is, he or she is more risk averse.

Many lines go through the origin and touch different points on the efficient frontier: the flatter the line, the less risk averse the investor. Investors choose a portfolio with a lower expected rate of return per unit of risk and gradually move out along the efficient frontier. Apart from knowing that investors differ in terms of their risk aversion, we know only that their preferred portfolio lies somewhere along the efficient frontier.[3]

The origin is the point with a zero expected rate of return and zero risk. Another way of describing a risk-free asset is that it has zero risk, such as a government's Treasury security, where the return on the asset is guaranteed with no possibility of earning more or less. We usually use a Treasury security as the risk-free asset simply because they are obligations of the government, which also has a monopoly on issuing government bank notes; Treasury securities are default free because investors generally believe that they will always be paid off in full.

Risk-Free Investing

Consider any point on the efficient frontier in Figure 9-1. Now, assume an investor places a portion w of his or her wealth in the risky portfolio X and the remainder $(1 - w)$ in the risk-free asset, a U.S. Treasury bond. Remember that the expected return on a portfolio is always a weighted average of the expected returns on the individual assets, so we can estimate the expected return on this portfolio as:

$$E(r_p) = r_f + w[E(r_X) - r_f] \tag{9-1}$$

where $E(r_p)$ is the expected return on the portfolio, r_f is the expected return on the risk-free asset, $E(r_X)$ is the expected return on the risky portfolio X, and w is the proportion of the portfolio invested in the risk portfolio.

Suppose the investor begins with a 100 percent investment in the risk-free asset; that is, $w = 0$. As the investor shifts the portfolio, adding more of the risky asset, w increases,

[3] The previous discussion may be a bit light for those with extensive economics training. We could represent each individual by his or her indifference curve, symbolizing his or her risk aversion and personal trade-off between risk and return. However, this adds little to our discussion.

so the investor increases the expected return on the portfolio, $E(r_p)$, at the cost of reducing the investment in the risk-free asset. As a result, the expected return on the portfolio increases by the difference: $E(r_X) - r_f$.

If the return on the risk-free asset is 3 percent and the return on the risky portfolio X is 11 percent, a portfolio consisting only of the risk-free asset has an expected return of 3 percent, whereas a portfolio consisting of only the risky portfolio X has an expected return of 11 percent. However, a portfolio consisting of equal parts of the risk-free and risky portfolio X has an expected return of:

$$E(r_p) = (0.50 \times 0.03) + (0.50 \times 0.11) = 0.07 \text{ or } 7\%$$

We can estimate the standard deviation on this portfolio as:[4]

$$\sigma_p = \sqrt{w_X^2 \sigma_X^2 + w_Y^2 \sigma_Y^2 + [2\, w_X\, w_Y\, \sigma_X\, \sigma_Y\, \rho_{XY}]}$$

where σ_X^2 and σ_Y^2 are the standard deviations of the returns on assets X and Y, respectively, w_X and w_Y are the proportions invested in X and Y, respectively, and ρ_{XY} is the correlation of returns between X and Y.

If we replace portfolio Y with the risk-free security, $(1 - w)$ for w_Y, we arrive at the following:

$$\sigma_p = \sqrt{w^2 \sigma_X^2 + (1 - w)^2 \sigma_{r_f}^2 + [2\,(1 - w)\, w\, \rho_{X,r_f}\, \sigma_X\, \sigma_{r_f}]}$$

We know exactly what we are going to get from the risk-free asset, so the standard deviation of its return is zero; that is, $\sigma_{r_f} = 0 = 0$. Because the return does not vary, the correlation between the return on the risk-free asset and that on the risky portfolio X is also zero. Therefore, the standard deviation with $\sigma_{rf} = 0$ and $\rho_{X,rf} = 0$ reduces to:

$$\sigma_p = \sqrt{w^2 \sigma_X^2}$$

Taking the square root of the final term leaves us with Equation 9-2:

$$\sigma_p = w \sigma_X \tag{9-2}$$

In other words, portfolio risk increases in direct proportion to the amount invested in the risky asset, w. Therefore, the higher the proportion of the portfolio allocated to the risky asset, the higher the portfolio risk.

If the standard deviation of the returns on risky portfolio X is 20 percent, a portfolio comprising equal parts of the risk-free asset and the risky portfolio X will have a standard deviation of:

$$\sigma_p = 0.5 \times 0.20 = 0.10 \text{ or } 10\%$$

If, on the other hand, only 25 percent of the portfolio is invested in the risk-free asset and 75 percent is invested in portfolio X, the portfolio's standard deviation is:

$$\sigma_p = 0.75 \times 0.20 = 0.15 \text{ or } 15\%$$

Because both the expected return and the standard deviation of a portfolio comprising any risky portfolio and a risk-free asset can be represented by a line that is based on the weights invested in r_f and in the risky asset, we can express all the expected returns and risks for various portfolio combinations as a straight line. We can show this by rearranging Equation 9-2 in terms of the portfolio weight:

$$w = \frac{\sigma_p}{\sigma_X}$$

and substituting for w in Equation 9-1, we can solve for the return on the portfolio, $E(r_p)$:

$$E(r_p) = r_f + \left(\frac{E(r_X) - r_f}{\sigma_X}\right)\sigma_p \tag{9-3}$$

[4] This equation was introduced in Chapter 8.

FIGURE 9-2 Portfolio of the Risk-Free Asset and Risky Assets

Equation 9-3 is the equation of a straight line when we graph the expected return against the portfolio standard deviation: The line intersects the vertical axis at the risk-free rate and then has a constant slope. The slope is the rise over the run, or the increased expected return divided by the increased risk. The increased expected return, as discussed, is the incremental return on the risky portfolio minus the lost return by taking money out of the risk-free asset. We represent this portfolio in Figure 9-2.

We interpret this figure the same as before: if $w = 0$, all the investment is in the risk-free asset (e.g., Treasury security), and the portfolio has no risk and earns r_f. As w increases, the expected return on the portfolio increases by $E(r_X) - r_f$ and its risk by σ_P, until $w = 100$ percent and the portfolio expected return is $E(r_X)$ and its risk is σ_X.

Consider portfolio T in Figure 9-3. All portfolios composed of risky portfolio T and the risk-free rate lie along the line from r_f to T and offer a higher expected rate of return for the same risk as do portfolios composed of the risk-free rate and risky portfolio X. Portfolio T is the **tangent portfolio**; graphically, it is the risky portfolio on the efficient frontier whose tangent line cuts the vertical axis at the risk-free rate. Portfolios composed of the risk-free asset and portfolio T offer the highest expected rate of return for any given level of risk and represent the **new efficient frontier** (or **super-efficient frontier**), which we depict in Figure 9-4.

Consider, for example, portfolio X, which was optimal for a very risk-averse investor before we considered investing in the risk-free asset. Now this investor could hold a portfolio of the risk-free asset and the risky portfolio T that offers a higher expected rate of return for the same risk as X. This is the new portfolio X+. What this demonstrates is that a portfolio partially invested in the risk-free asset reduces the portfolio risk but can achieve a higher expected rate of return than any portfolio on the efficient frontier of risky assets.

tangent portfolio risky portfolio on the efficient frontier whose tangent line cuts the vertical axis at the risk-free rate

new efficient frontier or **super-efficient frontier** portfolios composed of the risk-free rate and the tangent portfolio that offer the highest expected rate of return for any given level of risk

FIGURE 9-3 Efficient Portfolios

FIGURE 9-4 **The New Efficient Frontier**

EXAMPLE 9.1

Expected Return and Standard Deviation for a Two-Asset Portfolio That Includes Investment in a Risk-Free Asset

PROBLEM

Assume that a portfolio R has an expected return of 10 percent, with a standard deviation of 25 percent, and that the risk-free rate is 4.5 percent. Estimate the expected return and standard deviation for a portfolio that has 30 percent invested in the risk-free asset and 70 percent in R.

Solution

$$w = 0.70; (1 - w) = 0.30$$

Therefore,

$$E(r_p) = (0.30 \times 4.5\%) + (0.70 \times 10\%) = 1.35\% + 7.0\% = 8.35\%$$

and

$$\sigma_p = 0.70 \times 25\% = 17.50\%$$

Risk-Free Borrowing

Now consider a less risk-averse investor who held portfolio Z in Figure 9-4. That investor could now hold portfolio Z+ and also get a higher expected rate of return for the same level of risk as Z. However, getting to portfolio Z+ involves having more than 100 percent invested in the risky portfolio T ($w > 100$ percent) and thus a negative or **short position** in the risk-free asset.

short position negative position in an investment

We create a short position in the risk-free asset by borrowing. One way to do this is to buy stocks on margin, which means the investor can borrow part of the purchase price from a broker.[5] For example, some stocks have margin requirements as low as 30 percent, indicating an investor could buy $1,000 worth of stocks by investing only $300 and borrowing the remaining $700 from the broker. In this case, the portfolio weights are $w = 1,000 \div 300$ or 333 percent in the risky asset and –233 percent in the risk-free asset. Of course, investors must pay interest on the borrowed money. For simplicity, we assume that they can also borrow at the risk-free rate.[6]

---

[5] In the case of an interest-bearing debt instrument, if you invest in the debt instrument and receive income, you have a *long* position; if you are on the other side of the transaction, the borrower, you have a *short* position.
[6] Although borrowing rates are generally higher than the risk-free rate in practice, this assumption can be relaxed without greatly affecting our key results.

Consider an investor who invests $10,000 in a portfolio of risky assets, portfolio V. Portfolio V has an expected return of 12 percent and a standard deviation of returns of 25 percent. If, in addition, the investor borrows $5,000 at the risk-free rate of 3 percent and invests it in portfolio V, the total invested in portfolio V increases to $15,000. What is the expected return on this investment? The expected return calculation requires us to first calculate the weights:

$$w = \$15,000 \div \$10,000 = 1.5$$
$$(1 - w) = 1 - 1.5 = -0.5$$

In other words, there is a short position, borrowing at the risk-free rate. The expected return on the portfolio is therefore:

$$E(r_p) = (-0.50 \times 0.03) + (1.50 \times 0.12) = -0.015 + 0.18 = 0.165 \text{ or } 16.5\%$$

The standard deviation of the investor's investment, considering both the investment in the risky portfolio V and the borrowing, is the weight invested in the risky portfolio (150 percent, in this example), multiplied by the standard deviation of the returns on the risky asset (the 25 percent):

$$\sigma_P = w\sigma_X = 1.50 \times 0.25 = 0.375 \text{ or } 37.5\%$$

PROPBLEM

PROBLEM

Assume that an investor invests all her wealth, $1,000, in a portfolio that has an expected return of 10 percent and a standard deviation of 25 percent. She borrows an additional $700 at the risk-free rate of 4.5 percent, which she also invests in the portfolio. Estimate the expected return and standard deviation for this portfolio.

Solution

$$w = 1,700 \div 1,000 = 1.70;$$

$$(1 - w) = 1 - 1.70 = -0.70$$

Therefore,

$$E(r_p) = (-0.70 \times 0.045) + (1.70 \times 0.10) = -0.0315 + 0.17 = 0.1385 \text{ or } 13.85\%$$

$$\sigma(r_p) = 1.70 \times 0.25\% = 0.425 \text{ or } 42.50\%$$

EXAMPLE 9.2

Expected Return and Standard Deviation for a Two-Asset Portfolio That Includes Borrowing at the Risk-Free Rate

---

The Separation Theorem

We showed earlier that any point along the tangent line from the risk-free rate is attainable by either investing or borrowing at r_f and then investing all remaining proceeds in the risky portfolio T. From Figure 9-4, we see that all the portfolios along this line dominate all the portfolios on the efficient frontier, except for point T. As we showed, X+ is better than X and Z+ is better than Z. Therefore, allowing for the possibility of risk-free investing and borrowing expands the efficient set and provides investors with *more* portfolios from which to choose. This line is the new (or super) efficient frontier. The efficient frontier that we started with is the *efficient frontier of risky portfolios*, which distinguishes it from the efficient frontier of the risk-free asset and the tangent portfolio.

Investors can achieve any point on this new efficient frontier by borrowing or investing desired amounts at the risk-free rate and investing the remainder in one portfolio of risky assets, which is the tangent portfolio T. Therefore, each investor can choose the point on this line that suits his or her personal risk preferences: More risk-averse investors can choose portfolios, like X+, that are heavily invested in the risk-free asset, whereas more aggressive investors can choose portfolios, like Z+, that involve borrowing.

FIGURE 9-5 **Separation Theorem**

Suppose investors all agree on the expected rates of return and the risk attached to each security. In that case, the efficient frontier of risky assets is the same for all investors. This would occur, for example, if the investors were clients of an investment company that estimated all these values and then discussed the best portfolio for a particular client. It would no longer be necessary to match each investor's risk preferences with a specific risky portfolio. Instead, the investment company would recommend the same tangent portfolio to all its clients. It might then refer to this portfolio as its model portfolio, and some investors would invest in this and the risk-free asset, whereas others would borrow to invest in the model portfolio.

Suppose further that all investment companies agreed on the set of expected returns and the risk attached to the securities. In that case, the tangent or model portfolio would also be the same. This result provides the basis for the **separation theorem**, which is that the investment decision (that is, how to construct the portfolio of risky assets) is separate from the financing decision (that is, how much should be invested or borrowed in the risk-free asset). In other words, the tangent portfolio T is optimal for every investor regardless of his or her degree of risk aversion. Further, if everyone holds the same portfolio, it must be the **market portfolio** of all risky securities, which we represent as M, as we show in Figure 9-5, because every security has to be held by someone. This is an equilibrium condition because supply equals demand for all the risky securities, and we replace T with M, which is not just the tangent portfolio but also the market portfolio. This hypothesis is the basis for the most common model we use in finance to price securities, which we discuss in the next section.

separation theorem theory that the investment decision (how to construct the portfolio of risky assets) is separate from the financing decision (how much should be invested or borrowed in the risk-free asset)

market portfolio portfolio that contains all risky securities in the market

---

Concept Review Questions

1. What is risk aversion, and how do we know investors are risk averse?

2. What is the risk of a portfolio consisting of a risk-free asset and a risky security?

3. Why is the tangent portfolio so important?

4. How do we generate a portfolio with a higher expected rate of return than that of the tangent portfolio?

9.2 THE CAPITAL ASSET PRICING MODEL

capital asset pricing model (CAPM) pricing model that describes the expected return as the sum of the risk-free rate of interest and a premium for bearing market risk

William Sharpe and John Lintner are credited for developing the **capital asset pricing model (CAPM)**, which is a model that describes expected returns in terms of the risk-free rate of interest and a premium for bearing market risk.[7] The initial development of the CAPM is based on a number of assumptions that we have already briefly discussed:

---

[7] William F. Sharpe ["Capital Asset Prices: A Theory of Market Equilibrium under Conditions of Risk," *Journal of Finance*, Vol. 19 (1964): 425–442] and John Lintner ["The Valuation of Risk Assets and Selection of Risky Investments in Stock Portfolios and Capital Budgets," *Review of Economics and Statistics*, Vol. 47 (1965): 13–37]. William Sharpe won the Nobel prize for developing the best-known equilibrium asset pricing model, which relates expected returns to risk.

1. All investors have identical expectations about expected returns, standard deviations, and correlation coefficients for all securities.
2. All investors have the same one-period time horizon.
3. All investors can borrow or lend money at the risk-free rate of return (r_f).
4. There are no transaction costs.
5. There are no personal income taxes so that investors are indifferent between capital gains and dividends.
6. There are many investors, and no single investor can affect the price of a stock through his or her buying and selling decisions. Therefore, investors are price takers.
7. Capital markets are in equilibrium.

These assumptions may appear unrealistic at first. For example, we need the assumption of identical expectations so that the efficient frontier of risky portfolios is the same for all investors. However, not all investors have the same impact in the market; the most important are the big institutions that invest most of the money. They all have access to the same information, and they all have expert analysts analyzing the data. Similarly, borrowing rates differ from lending rates for small investors, but for large institutional investors, the difference is not material. The same applies to transaction costs. The result is that most of the assumptions can be relaxed without significantly affecting the CAPM or its main implications. However, before discussing the CAPM, we discuss what happens to the overall capital market.

The Market Portfolio and the Capital Market Line

The assumptions for the CAPM listed earlier give rise to the following very important implications, which we discussed previously:

1. The "optimal" risky portfolio is the one that is tangent to the efficient frontier on a line that is drawn from the risk-free rate, as we show in Figure 9-4. This portfolio is the same for all investors.
2. This optimal risky portfolio is the market portfolio that contains all risky securities. The value of this portfolio is the aggregate of the market values of all the individual assets in the portfolio. Therefore, the weights of these assets in the market portfolio are their proportionate weight in its total value.

As we have discussed, the second implication results from our assumption that market equilibrium exists. This implies that supply equals demand—in other words, all assets are assumed to be bought and sold at the equilibrium price established by supply and demand. Because all assets trade, it must mean that they are correctly priced to adequately compensate investors for the associated risks. For example, if an asset is priced too high, and therefore the expected rate of return is too low, demand for it would fall, as would its price. Market clearing implies that the price would eventually fall to an equilibrium level. Because the market consists of all available assets, and all these assets are assumed to be priced correctly to reflect adequate compensation for the associated risk, the market portfolio is the most efficient (or optimal) portfolio, with respect to the weights attached to the individual securities in the market portfolio.

Theoretically, the market portfolio should contain all risky assets worldwide, including stocks, bonds, options, futures, gold, real estate, and so on, in their proper proportions. Such a portfolio, if it could be constructed, is completely diversified. However, in practice, the market portfolio is unobservable, so we use proxies to measure its behavior. It is common to use stock market indexes, such as the S&P 500 Composite Index in the United States.

We graph the relationship between expected return and standard deviation implied by the capital asset pricing model in Figure 9-6. This graph is similar to Figure 9-4, but we do not include the efficient frontier portion, and the only portfolio is M, the tangent portfolio, because the market portfolio (M) is the optimal portfolio of risky securities that is combined with the risk-free asset. Recall that this line produces the highest attainable expected return for any given risk level; therefore, it includes only efficient portfolios.

FIGURE 9-6 **The Capital Market Line**

capital market line (CML) line depicting the highest attainable expected return for any given risk level that includes only efficient portfolios

Further, all rational, risk-averse investors will seek to be on this line. In Figure 9-6, this line is the **capital market line (CML)**.

We can see from Figure 9-6 that the CML has an intercept of r_f, just as with any portfolio consisting of the risk-free asset and a risky portfolio. But the risky portfolio is not arbitrary: Now it is the market portfolio. So we have a special version of Equation 9-3:

$$\text{Slope of the CML} = \frac{E(r_M) - r_f}{\sigma_M} \tag{9-4}$$

market price of risk incremental expected return divided by the incremental risk; indicates the additional expected return that the market demands for an increase in risk

As in Equation 9-3, the slope of the capital market line is the incremental expected return divided by the incremental risk. This special trade-off of risk and return is the **market price of risk** for efficient portfolios; in other words, this is the equilibrium price of risk in the capital market. It indicates the additional expected return that the market demands for an increase in a portfolio's risk. Adding the risk-free rate, r_f, gives the CML as

$$E(r_p) = r_f + \left[\frac{E(r_M) - r_f}{\sigma_M}\right]\sigma_p \tag{9-5}$$

$E(r_M)$ = the expected return on the market portfolio M;

σ_M = the standard deviation of returns on the market portfolio; and

σ_p = the standard deviation of returns on the efficient portfolio being considered.

The CML is a special version of Equation 9-3 in another important way. The CML indicates an expected rate of return, yet we have made enough assumptions to identify the portfolio as the market portfolio and as an equilibrium condition in the capital market, where supply equals demand. As a result, the CML describes not just an expected rate of return but also the appropriate return for the risk, which is the **required rate of return**, that we denote as $E(r_p)$.

Having defined the CML, we can focus on the difference between expected and required rates of return. Consider the CML that we show in Figure 9-7, and we are looking at three portfolios: D, E, and F.

- Only portfolio E lies on the CML. For this portfolio, the expected rate of return is the same as the required rate of return, so the portfolio is fairly priced.
- The expected return on Portfolio F is higher than that of E. However, this portfolio is below the CML, which indicates that the required rate of return is higher than this expected rate of return. If we look at just the expected rate of return, F would seem to be a good buy, but this is wrong because it is a very risky portfolio. Given its risk, it is a bad buy, and its price would drop, forcing up its expected rate of return until it was fairly priced and the expected and required rates of return were the same.

PROBLEM

EXAMPLE 9.3
Using the CML

Assume the expected risk-free rate is 4.5 percent. The expected return on the market is 10 percent, and it has a standard deviation of 20 percent. Determine the expected return necessary for investors to hold an efficient portfolio with a standard deviation of 25 percent.

Solution

$$E(r_p) = E(r_f) + \left[\frac{E(r_M) - E(r_f)}{\sigma_M} \right] \sigma_p$$

$$= 0.045 + \left[\frac{0.10 - 0.045}{0.20} \right] \times 0.25$$

$$= 0.045 + (0.275 \times 0.25)$$

$$= 0.045 + 0.06875 = 11.375\%$$

Notice that the required return on the portfolio is greater than that expected for the market portfolio because it has a higher standard deviation.

- Portfolio D presents the opposite situation: It has a high expected rate of return and relatively low risk. In this case, the expected rate of return exceeds the required rate of return, and investors would bid up its price and cause its expected rate of return to fall until it lies on the CML.

    It is also important to recognize that:

1. The CML must always be *upward sloping* because the risk premium always be positive with risk averse investors, and
2. The CML predicts *required* returns.

As a result, risk-averse investors will not invest unless they expect compensation for bearing risk. The greater the risk, the greater the required rate of return.

However, there is a big difference between ex post and ex ante returns. After the fact (ex post) returns can be, and often have been, less than the Treasury rate. If this were never the case, investing in the equity market would have no risk, and no one would hold Treasury securities. The observation of ex post poor returns on risky securities does not negate the validity of the CML, however; it merely indicates that returns actually realized

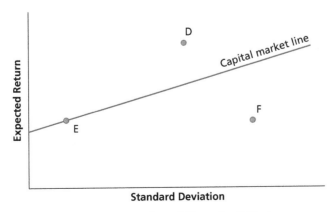

FIGURE 9-7 **Expected and Required Rates of Return**

differed from those that were expected. Another way of saying this is that investors sometimes get it wrong, and they do not get what they expected. Of course, if investors were never wrong, there would be no risk in the equity market.

The ideas that we have just described are a critical part of the evaluation of investment performance in a financial system. Consider the slope of the CML. In equilibrium, all portfolios should lie along the CML, investors will bid up those offering higher expected returns than the required rate of return, and investors will bid down those offering lower returns than the required rates of return. The CML is based on expected rates of return, so it is ex ante. However, if expectations are realized (that is, on average the actual return is what was expected), we can use the CML to judge the performance of different portfolios ex post, that is, actual portfolio performance.

FINANCE in the News | Efficient Frontier

The true challenge to investment professionals today is to find an investment solution that can assemble non-correlated asset classes that are liquid, transparent and still appropriate for individual investor's risk profiles wherein the Efficient Frontier meets the client's "indifference curve."

A security's real risk is the variability of its returns that cannot be diversified away, called systematic beta risk. Systematic beta risk has increased significantly on many traditional strategic asset allocation models, causing considerable damage to account values and in some cases, panic by clients. Non-correlation is the major influence in this increased systematic beta risk crisis challenging the efficacy of strategic investment portfolios, and investment professionals are desperate to find alternative solutions.

Excerpt from "The Dubious Efficiency of the Efficient Frontier," by Andrew Hanlon, *Forbes*, April 9, 2009.

Risk-Adjusted Performance and the Sharpe Ratio

When the ideas underlying the CML are used in this way, it leads to the **Sharpe ratio,** the ratio of *ex post* excess returns to risk[8]:

$$\text{Sharpe ratio} = \frac{r_p - r_f}{\sigma_p} \tag{9-6}$$

Sharpe ratio or **reward-to-variability ratio** or **reward-to-risk ratio** measure of portfolio performance that describes how well an asset's return compensates investors for the risk taken

We also refer to the Sharpe ratio as the **reward-to-variability ratio** or the **reward-to-risk ratio** because this ratio is a comparison of the return, in excess of the risk-free rate, to risk. This measure is commonly used to evaluate the historical (that is, ex post) performance of portfolio managers. When comparing two investments, the investment with the higher Sharpe ratio is preferred because the investment with the higher Sharpe ratio provides the greater reward per unit of risk. The ex ante Sharpe ratio of the market portfolio is the slope of the CML.

Suppose a portfolio has an expected return of 5 percent and a standard deviation of returns of 8 percent. If the risk-free rate of interest is 3 percent, the Sharpe ratio is:

$$\text{Sharpe ratio} = \frac{0.05 - 0.03}{0.08} = 0.25$$

We have derived the Sharpe ratio in terms of "expected" (i.e., ex ante) returns in our discussion. However, in practice, it is a commonly used measure of ex post (i.e., realized) returns, where we replace expected returns with historic realized returns. For example, a

[8] This ratio is named after William Sharpe of Stanford University, who developed it and first applied it to assessing portfolio performance.

PROBLEM

EXAMPLE 9.4

Sharpe Ratios

a. Calculate the Sharpe ratio for each of the following securities, assuming a risk-free rate of 3 percent:

Security	Expected Return	Standard Deviation of Returns
A	4%	3%
B	5%	5%
C	4.5%	7%
D	3.5%	2%

b. Which security has the best reward-to-risk ratio?

Solution

a.

Security	Sharpe Ratio
A	0.33
B	0.40
C	0.21
D	0.33

b. Security B has the highest Sharpe ratio.

stock has return of 6 percent and a standard deviation of returns of 7 percent. If the return on the risk-free security is 2 percent, the Sharpe ratio of the stock is 0.571:

$$\text{Sharpe ratio} = \frac{0.06 - 0.02}{0.07} = 0.5714$$

1. What is the market price of risk according to the CML?

2. If the expected return on a diversified portfolio lies above the CML, should an investor buy or sell it?

3. When is the expected return equal to the required return?

4. Why is the Sharpe ratio frequently referred to as a "risk-adjusted" measure of performance?

Concept Review Questions

9.3 THE CAPM AND MARKET RISK

The CML provides a method of estimating the required return on equity assets relative to their risk, but it applies only to efficient portfolios and not to individual securities. In addition, the risk premium is based on portfolio risk, as measured by the standard deviation of the return on the portfolio. In financial management, we are usually concerned with the risk associated with individual firms and the required return for investing in them. From the principles of diversification, we know that as the number of securities included

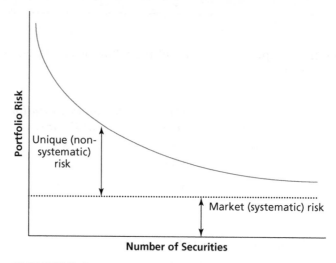

FIGURE 9-8   **Portfolio Risk and Diversification**

in a portfolio increases, unique (nonsystematic or diversifiable) risk is eliminated, and only market (systematic or nondiversifiable) risk remains. We depict this relationship in Figure 9-8.

We show the average risk of an individual security in Figure 9-8, where the curve gets very close to the vertical axis, that is, a one-stock portfolio. Therefore, by randomly building diversified portfolios, the risk of a portfolio falls until it reaches a baseline, and we cannot reduce risk below this market level. What this means is that part of an asset's risk is diversifiable. Further, if it can be diversified away by holding a portfolio of more than, say, 20 different assets, it is not important to rational investors. This is the key insight of the CAPM.

GLOBAL PERSPECTIVE | Is There Still a Benefit from International Diversification?

The implication of modern portfolio theory and the capital asset pricing model is that investors can benefit from holding a well-diversified portfolio. Investing internationally has been seen as one way to enhance diversification, reducing the level of market risk below the level available domestically. This is because different countries have different economic growth and different timing and extent of expansions and contractions in their business cycle.

But is this still true? With market integration on a global scale, increased international trade and flow of funds, and increased cooperation among central banks in times of economic stress, is there still diversification benefit from investing internationally?

Much of the evidence suggests that there is a little benefit from international diversification in developed markets, but some diversification benefit remaining in emerging markets, where an emerging market is a market in an economy in which there is low to middle per capita income.[9] Therefore, an investor in the U.S. is not likely to achieve much diversification by investing in Germany or Japan. But a U.S. investor may achieve diversification by investing in Morocco or Indonesia.

So, yes, it is possible to reduce risk by investing internationally, but the benefit depends on which country.

[9] Peterson Christoffersen, Vihang R. Errunca, Kris Jacos, and Xisong Jin, "Is the Potential for International Diversification Disappearing?" working paper, March 16, 2010, Available at SSRN: ssrn.com/abstract=1573345.

Beta

In the CAPM, rational investors are not compensated for unique or diversifiable risk because it can be eliminated through diversification. This implies that market risk is the appropriate measure of risk to determine the risk premium required by investors for holding a risky security. We now introduce a new term, **beta (β_i)**, which is a commonly used measure of market risk that relates to the extent to which the return on an asset moves with that on the overall market.

We typically estimate beta by first plotting the returns on an individual security on the vertical axis relative to the returns for the market, which we plot along the horizontal axis, and then fitting a line through the observations, as we show in Figure 9-9. The line is the **characteristic line**, and we determine it by using a statistical technique called regression analysis. Regression is a statistical method of determining the best fitting line that depicts the relationship between two variables; in this case, between the return on an asset and the return on the market portfolio. The slope of the line is the asset's beta coefficient. For example, in Figure 9-7, the slope coefficient is 0.85, which indicates that if the return on the market portfolio goes up or down by 1.0 percent, the return on this asset is expected to go up or down by 0.85 percent, respectively; that is, it changes by 0.85 of the return on the market.[10]

Estimating beta coefficients is tricky because we are interested in the extent that an asset's returns move with the market over a future period. We typically estimate beta coefficients by using historical data, which assumes that what has happened in the past is a good predictor for the future. Typically, betas for securities are estimated by using 60 months of monthly returns, but sometimes 52 weekly returns are used. Betas change through time as the risk of the underlying asset or portfolio changes. This is particularly important for individual securities, for which betas can change quite dramatically over relatively short periods. Conversely, betas estimated for large portfolios or for industries are much more stable because of averaging over many assets. Therefore, estimates of portfolio betas show less change from period to period and are much more reliable than are the estimates for individual assets.

beta (β_i) measure of market risk, or performance volatility, that relates the extent to which the return on an asset moves with that on the overall market; the covariance between an investment and the market divided by variance of the market

characteristic line line of best fit through the returns on an individual asset, plotted on the vertical axis, relative to the returns for the market, plotted along the horizontal axis

Market Return

FIGURE 9-9 **The Characteristic Line for Security A**

[10] The characteristic line is also often estimated by using excess returns. The excess return is calculated by subtracting the risk-free rate from both the return on the stock and the return on the market. In excess return form, the same analysis applies.

Under some common statistical assumptions, we can estimate betas by using Equation 9-7:[11]

$$\beta_i = \frac{\text{Covariance of returns in security } i}{\text{Variance of the market portfolio's returns}} = \frac{COV_{i,M}}{\sigma_M^2} = \frac{\rho_{i,M}\sigma_i}{\sigma_M} \tag{9-7}$$

In Equation 9-7, we can see that the beta of an individual asset is the ratio of the covariance of that asset's return with the market, compared to the total variance of the market portfolio's returns.

Beta is a measure of the risk of an individual asset, stock, or portfolio relative to the market portfolio. A beta of 1 implies that if the market return increased (or decreased) by 1 percent, the return on the security (or portfolio) would, on average, increase (decrease) by 1 percent. Therefore, the market portfolio, by definition, has a beta of 1. An asset with a beta of 1.2 has returns that are 1.2 times as volatile as market returns, both up and down. In other words, if the market increased 10 percent, that security's returns would increase by 12 percent, and so on.[12]

Consider an example. Stock One has a beta of 0.8, whereas Stock Two has a beta of 1.2. If the returns on the market increase by 3 percent, we expect:

- Stock One returns to increase by $0.8 \times 0.03 = 0.024$ or 2.4%
- Stock Two returns to increase by $1.2 \times 0.03 = 0.036$ or 3.6%

If the returns on the market decline by 3 percent, we expect:

- Stock One returns to decline by $0.8 \times 0.03 = 0.024$ or 2.4%
- Stock Two returns to decline by $1.2 \times 0.03 = 0.036$ or 3.6%

SUMMARIZING: BETAS AND MARKET RISK

Beta		*Market Risk*
Greater than 1.0	$\beta_i > 1$	More market risk than the average security in the market
Equal to 1.0	$\beta_i = 1$	Market risk the same as the average security in the market
Less than 1.0	$\beta_i < 1$	Less market risk than the average security in the market
0	$\beta_i = 0$	No market risk (e.g., risk-free security)
Less than 0.0	$\beta_i < 0$	Negative correlation with the market return[13]

[11] The characteristic line is also often estimated by using excess returns. The excess return is calculated by subtracting the risk-free rate from both the return on the stock and the return on the market. In excess return form, the same analysis applies.

[12] You may notice that beta is an elasticity measure: It captures the sensitivity of the return on the stock to changes in the return on the market.

[13] According to Equation 9-7, negative betas can only occur if an asset has a negative correlation coefficient with market returns, which is uncommon. This is the only way a negative beta is possible because the standard deviation terms in Equation 9-7 are always positive. Gold stocks have sometimes had negative betas because the price of gold tended to go in the opposite direction of the market; investors would invest in gold when they were nervous about future market movements. However, this relationship is not as strong as it used to be, and negative betas rarely occur, even for gold stocks.

EXAMPLE 9.5

Estimating Beta

PROBLEM

The returns on stock X have a standard deviation of 25 percent and a correlation coefficient of 0.70 with market returns, which have a standard deviation of 20 percent. Estimate the beta for stock X.

Solution

$$\beta_x = \frac{\rho_{x,M}\sigma_x}{\sigma_M} = \frac{0.70 \times 0.25}{0.20} = 0.875$$

Notice that even though stock X has a higher standard deviation than the market, its beta is less than one because of the correlation coefficient of 0.70.

Consider how we would estimate a beta using historical stock returns. We would need a large number of monthly, weekly, or daily returns on the stock, along with the same number of monthly, weekly, or daily returns on a market index. Using this data, we can then use statistical packages or spreadsheets to estimate the regression line; the slope of the line is the estimate of the security's beta.

Let's see how this works using Microsoft Corporate common stock.

1. We collect monthly returns (including dividends), on Microsoft common stock (MSFT) from January 2006 through December 2010.[14]

2. We collect monthly returns on the Standard & Poor's 500 Index (S&P 500) for the same months.[15]

3. We put both time-series in a workbook and regress the returns on Microsoft stock against the returns on the S&P 500.

	A	B	C
		Return on	*Return on*
1	*Month*	*MSFT*	*S&P 500*
2	Jan-06	7.65%	2.55%
3	Feb-06	−4.23%	0.05%
4	Mar-06	1.27%	1.11%
5	Apr-06	−11.25%	1.22%
6	May-06	−5.84%	−3.09%

4. We use the spreadsheet SLOPE function to estimate the beta:

=SLOPE(B2:B61,C2:C61)

which produces a beta estimate of 1.0719. We can see this graphically when we see the scatterplot of the returns on MSFT and those on the S&P 500 (see next page).

The slope of the line, which represents the average relationship between the returns on MSFT and the S&P 500, is 1.0719.

[14] Sources of the data needed to calculate these returns include Yahoo! Finance and Google Finance. Don't forget to include dividends in your calculation of the monthly return.

[15] Sources of the data needed to calculate these returns include Robert Shiller (available at his web site at www.econ.yale.edu/~shiller/data.htm; however, the dividends on the S&P 500 have been smoothed in his spreadsheet), Yahoo! Finance, YCharts.com, and many other financial sites. You may find slight differences in returns due to different assumptions regarding when to include dividends: during the month at which the dividend is ex-dividend (that is, no longer trades with the stock), or the month the dividend is payable.

Betas tend to vary a great deal across companies in different industries because they possess different risk profiles. Although betas tend to be more similar for companies operating in the same industry, they can still vary substantially because even companies within the same industry can differ substantially across various dimensions, such as financial risk, size, and so on. Betas also may change over time; for example, high-growth companies tend to have betas much larger than 1.0, but over time, as the company matures and growth slows, the beta approaches 1.0. We provide examples of betas in Table 9-1.

Unlike portfolio standard deviations, portfolio betas are weighted averages of the betas for the individual securities in the portfolio. Therefore, we can estimate the beta for an n-security portfolio by using Equation 9-8:

$$\beta_p = w_A\beta_A + w_B\beta_B + \ldots + w_n\beta_n \tag{9-8}$$

Consider a portfolio with one-quarter of its investment in Lockheed Martin and the remainder invested in Big Lots. Using the data in Table 9-2, the beta for this portfolio is 1.165:

$$\beta_p = (0.25 \times 1.09) + (0.75 \times 1.19) = 1.165$$

TABLE 9-1   Estimated Betas for U.S. Companies

Company	Ticker	Industry	Beta
Boeing Company	BA	Aircraft manufacturing	1.24
Lockheed Martin	LMT	Aircraft manufacturing	1.09
Coca-Cola Company	KO	Beverages	0.60
Pepsico, Inc.	PEP	Beverages	0.54
Celanese Corporation	CE	Chemicals	2.78
Eastman Chemical Corporation	EMN	Chemicals	1.84
Johnson & Johnson	JNJ	Consumer products	0.53
Procter & Gamble Company	PG	Consumer products	0.57
Big Lots	BIG	Discount retail	1.19
Family Dollar Stores	FDO	Discount retail	0.17
International Business Machines	IBM	Information technology	0.79
Microsoft	MSFT	Information technology	1.01
Target Corporation	TFT	Retail	1.16
Wal-Mart Stores	WMT	Retail	0.20
PPG Industries	PPG	Specialty chemicals	1.16
Valspar Corporation	VAL	Specialty chemicals	0.97

Source: *Yahoo! Finance.*

We can see from this result why diversified portfolios end up with only market risk. First, the beta on the market portfolio, by definition, is 1.0. We can see this from Equation 9-7 by substituting M for the standard deviation of the security and noting that an asset is perfectly correlated with itself! So, if the average beta is 1.0, as we randomly add securities to a portfolio, we eventually end up with an average risk portfolio with a beta of 1.0, composed of all market risk. This is also why most large portfolios made up of a large number of securities are essentially the same as the market portfolio and earn the same rate of return.[16]

EXAMPLE 9.6

Estimating a Portfolio Beta

PROBLEM

An investor has a portfolio that consists of $10,000 invested in stock B, which has a beta of 1.2; $20,000 in stock C, which has a beta of 0.8; and $20,000 in stock D, which has a beta of 1.3. Estimate the beta of this portfolio.

Solution

$$w_B = \frac{10,000}{(10,000 + 20,000 + 20,000)} = 0.20; \; w_c = \frac{20,000}{50,000} = 0.40; \; w_D = \frac{20,000}{50,000} = 0.40$$

$$\begin{aligned} \beta_p &= w_B\beta_B + w_C\beta_C + w_D\beta_D \\ &= (0.20 \times 1.2) + (0.40 \times 0.8) + (0.40 \times 1.3) \\ &= 0.24 + 0.32 + 0.52 \\ &= 1.08 \end{aligned}$$

The Security Market Line

An important result of the capital asset pricing model is that investors should be compensated for market risk, as measured by beta. Though we will leave the derivation to investments texts, we can use the capital market line to derive the **security market line (SML)**:[17]

$$E(r_i) = r_f + [E(r_M) - r_f]\beta_i \tag{9-9}$$

where $E(r_i)$ is the expected return on the asset (or portfolio) i. The term $E(r_M) - r_f$ is the expected **market risk premium** and is also a function of market conditions. When we multiply an asset's beta by the market risk premium, we get an asset's risk premium. Adding the asset's risk premium to the risk-free rate gives us the required rate of return on the asset.

Suppose the risk-free rate is 3 percent and the expected return on the market is 9 percent. If an asset's beta is 1.2, the expected return on this asset is 9.2 percent:

$$\begin{aligned} E(r_i) &= 0.03 + [(0.09 - 0.03) \times 1.2] \\ &= 0.03 + [0.06 \times 1.2] = 0.02 + 0.072 = 0.092 \text{ or } 9.2\% \end{aligned}$$

The market risk premium in this case is 6 percent, and the risk premium for this asset is 7.2 percent.

The SML is the most widely used contribution of the CAPM, and we depict this graphically in Figure 9-10. The SML represents the trade-off between market risk and the required rate of return for any risky asset, whether it is an individual asset or a portfolio.

security market line (SML) relationship between market risk and the required rate of return for any risky security, whether an individual asset or a portfolio

market risk premium risk premium as a function of market conditions; the expected return on the market minus the risk-free rate

---

[16] This is what is commonly referred to as closet indexing because although they charge large fees, most mutual funds have similar performance.

[17] For a formal derivation of the SML from the CML, refer to almost any investment textbook. To avoid confusing the SML and the CML, remember that the CML is a depiction of the relationship between expected return and total risk, whereas the SML is a depiction of the relationship between expected return and market risk.

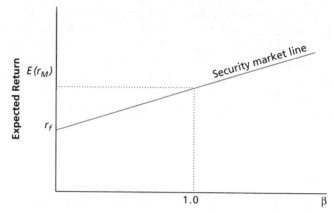

FIGURE 9-10 **The Security Market Line**

The SML is upward sloping, which indicates that investors require a higher expected return on higher-beta assets. In essence, the SML formalizes the notion we discussed before: The required rate of return on an asset equals the risk-free rate plus a risk premium. The size of the risk premium varies directly with an asset's market risk, as measured by beta, in the SML.

According to the SML, assets or portfolios with betas greater than the market beta of 1.0 will have larger risk premiums than the "average" asset and will therefore have higher required rates of return. Conversely, assets with betas less than that of the market are less risky and will have lower required rates of return.

EXAMPLE 9.7

Using the SML

PROBLEM

Given an expected return on the market of 10 percent and a risk-free rate of 4.5 percent, estimate:

a. the market risk premium.
b. the required return for Security X that has a beta of 0.875.
c. the required return for a portfolio that has a beta of 1.08.

Solution

a. $E(r_M) - r_f = 0.10 - 0.045 = 5.5\%$

b. $E(r_X) = r_f + (E(r_M) - r_f)\beta_X = 0.045 + (0.055 \times 0.875)$
$= 0.045 + 0.04813 = 9.313\%$

Notice that the required return for X is *less* than the expected market return because its beta is *less* than one.

c. $E(r_p) = r_f + (E(r_M) - r_f)\beta_p = 0.045 + (0.055 \times 1.08) = 0.045 + 0.0594 = 10.44\%$

Notice that the required return for this portfolio is greater than the expected market return because its beta is greater than one.

The SML and Security Valuation

In equilibrium, the expected return on all properly-priced assets will lie *on* the SML, just as the expected return on all portfolios will lie on the CML. As with the CML, when investors expect a return equal to the required return, the asset is correctly priced. However, at any given time, some assets may be temporarily mispriced according to CAPM.

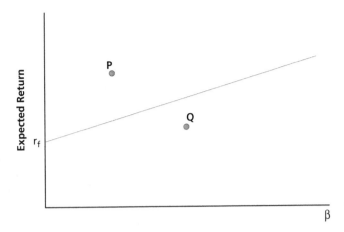

FIGURE 9-11 **The SML and Security Valuation**

Whenever analysis suggests that the expected return on an asset differs from its required rate of return according to CAPM, that asset is considered undervalued or overvalued. Assets or portfolios that have expected returns greater than their required rate of return are undervalued because they provide investors with an expected return that is higher than the return required given their risk. Similar to the CML, undervalued securities will lie *above* the SML, reflecting the fact that the expected return exceeds the required return, which is the return along the SML that corresponds to the beta coefficient. Asset P in Figure 9-11 represents an example of an undervalued security. Similarly, assets or portfolios whose expected returns are less than their required rate of return, such as Q in Figure 9-11, are overvalued and will lie below the SML.

If markets are efficient, we would expect prices to be correct. Therefore, whenever rational investors observe an undervalued asset, such as P, they will rush to purchase it because it offers a higher expected return than its required return. As a result of this increase in demand for asset P, its price will increase until it eventually equals the price level at which its expected return equals the required return according to the SML. In other words, asset P's price will adjust until it lies along the SML. In similar fashion, selling pressure for asset Q (which is overvalued) would increase, causing Q's price to decline until it too lies along the SML.

This discussion of the security market line is very similar to the discussion of the capital market line. The primary difference is the measure of risk: For individual assets, the measure of risk is beta, whereas for diversified portfolios, it is the standard deviation.

Using the SML to Estimate Long-Term Discount Rates

Technically, the CAPM is a one-period model, and some analysts will use Treasury bill rates instead of the government Treasury bond rate as the appropriate risk-free rate.[18] However, financial analysts often use the CAPM to estimate the required return on common shares over many periods, such as when they are trying to estimate the share price using the dividend discount model or free cash flow models. In these applications, which are the most common for financial managers, the rate on a Treasury note or bond would be most appropriate as the rate on a risk-free security. These models require the discounting of expected cash flows that occur over many periods in the future. It is also common to use the CAPM to estimate the cost of a firm's common equity financing component when estimating the firm's overall cost of capital. This cost of capital is then used to discount the expected future cash flows associated with capital expenditure decisions.

[18] The Treasury bill rate is sometimes used for the risk-free rate in the CAPM because this rate provides a better one-period rate of return. However, short-term rates tend to fluctuate widely.

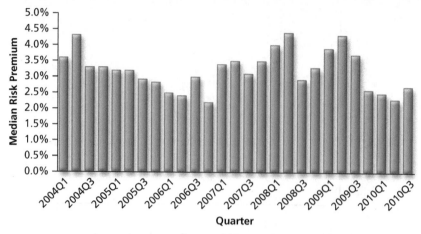

FIGURE 9-12 Estimated Market Risk Premiums
Source of data: *John R. Graham and Campbell R. Harvey, "The Equity Risk Premium in 2010," Working paper, Duke University, ssrn.com/abstract=1654026, Table 1.*

Estimates of the market risk premium are sensitive to the period used in estimating this premium, as well as the method of estimation. For example, if you are using ex post data, you are using an observation that occurred, rather than the whole spectrum of possible returns that investors considered in pricing assets at that time. Ex post measures of market risk premiums in the U.S. range from 6 percent to close to 13 percent, depending on the time period considered.[19] However, several researchers have argued that these ex post estimates overestimate the ex ante market risk premium.[20] Researchers estimating the ex ante market risk premium, which is what is relevant in asset pricing, observe values for the U.S. that are much less than ex post estimates.[21]

We show the expected market risk premiums according to a recent survey of CEOs by John R. Graham and Campbell R. Harvey in Figure 9-12.[22] Notice that (1) risk premiums are variable, and (2) risk premiums have declined since their peak in 2009, and in mid-2010 they were around 2.5 to 3 percent. The risk premiums cited in the Graham and Harvey study are less than those reported by Pablo Fernandez in his survey of professors, analysts, and companies. Fernandez finds that the risk premiums estimated in 2011 were around 5 to 5.5 percent in the U.S. and in the range of 4.5 to 6 percent in most developed nations.[23]

Concept Review Questions

1. Why is beta a measure of market risk for an asset?

2. If an asset's correlation with the market return increases, will its beta increase or decrease?

3. What is a characteristic line, and why is it useful?

4. If the market risk premium increases, will securities become overvalued or undervalued?

---

[19] E. Scott Mayfield, "Estimating the Market Risk Premium," *Journal of Financial Economics*, Vol. 73, No. 3 (September 2004): 465–496, Table 5.

[20] Eugene F. Fama and Kenneth R. French, "The Equity Premium," *Journal of Finance*, Vol. 57, Issue 2 (2002): 637–659.

[21] Fama and French (2002) estimate market risk premiums of 2.55–4.32% for the 1951–2000 period.

[22] John R. Graham and Campbell R. Harvey, "The Equity Risk Premium in 2010," Working paper, Duke University, ssrn.com/abstract=1654026.

[23] Pablo Fernandez, Javier Aguirreamalloa, and Luis Corres, "Market Risk Premium Used in 56 Countries in 2011: A Survey with 6,014 Answers," Working paper, IESE Business School, University of Navarra, May 2011.

9.4 ALTERNATIVE ASSET PRICING MODELS

The CAPM is a "single-factor" model because it suggests that the required return on capital assets—that is, stocks—is determined by only one risk factor: market risk. CAPM is often criticized because it is based on several assumptions, many of which are called into question in the real world. In addition, a substantial amount of empirical evidence finds that the CAPM does not hold well in practice. In particular, although empirical estimates of the ex post SML suggest that it is, indeed, an upward-sloping straight line, the ex ante y-intercept has been found to be higher than $E(r_f)$, and the slope of the SML is less than that predicted by theory—that is, it is "flatter" than it should be. Although this research remains very controversial, a 1992 study of U.S. stock returns by Fama and French concluded that beta, the sole risk factor in the CAPM, possessed no explanatory power for predicting stock returns.[24] In addition, they found that two other factors (discussed in the next subsection) do a much better job of explaining common stock returns.

Richard Roll in 1976 identified an important theoretical problem associated with tests of the CAPM, and this identification is commonly referred to as Roll's critique.[25] Roll argued that the CAPM cannot be tested empirically because we cannot observe the market portfolio, which consists of all risky assets. Therefore, researchers are forced to use market proxies, which may or may not be the optimal mean-variance efficient portfolio. In effect, Roll argued that tests of the CAPM are actually tests of the mean-variance efficiency of the chosen market portfolio. He showed that the basic CAPM results hold whenever the chosen proxy is mean-variance efficient and do not hold if the converse is true. As a result the empirical tests have no power.

Despite the criticisms of the CAPM, it remains a commonly used method of estimating the required rate of return on individual assets used by both academics and practitioners. One of the main reasons for its staying power is its intuitive appeal for assessing the trade-off between risk and expected return and the observation that individuals hold diversified portfolios. Further, the other options have had at least as much difficulty generating statistical support as has the CAPM. However, in response to some of the problems associated with the CAPM, alternative asset pricing models have been developed, and we discuss two of the better-known alternatives in the next section. In contrast to the CAPM, both of these models are multifactor models because they assume that more than one factor affects asset returns.

Fama and French Model

Professors Eugene Fama and Kenneth French examined a large number of companies' security returns and financial statement data and found that two factors affected stock returns in addition to market returns. Based on this discovery, they developed a three-factor pricing model. Like the CAPM, their model includes an overall market factor; however, it also includes the market value of equity and the ratio of the book value of equity to the market value of equity.[26]

The **Fama–French model** became popular because some believe that it does a better job than the CAPM of explaining ex ante stock returns. For example, Ibbotson Associates, Inc., a major provider of financial information, now gives estimates of the required return

Fama–French model pricing model that uses three factors (a market factor, the market value of a firm's common equity, and the ratio of a firm's book equity value to its market value of equity) to relate expected returns to risk

[24] See E. Fama and K. French, "The Cross Section of Expected Stock Returns," *Journal of Finance, 47* (1992): 427–65.

[25] See R. Roll, "A Critique of the Asset Pricing Theory's Tests; Part I: On Past and Potential Testability of the Theory," *Journal of Financial Economics, 4* (1976): 129–76.

[26] See Eugene Fama and Kenneth French, "Size and Book-to-Market Factors in Earnings and Returns," *Journal of Finance, 50* (1995): 131–55.

LESSONS LEARNED | Debunking Beta

It's time to delete the CAPM from business school textbooks. The theory has done more harm than good for investors. Ever since the 1980s CAPM has been widely accepted by almost all sophisticated trading and money management firms practicing Modern Portfolio Theory to price stocks. It's baked into most Wall Street computer models. Indeed, most of the big firms and their chief risk officers focus on beta but—at least until recently—have ignored most other types of risks. Little things like leverage and liquidity. I believe that this contributed to the severity of at least three major crashes since the 1980s: the Crash of 1987, Long-Term Capital in 1998 and the subprime debacle we are still working through.

In the years leading up to the 2007–08 crash, leverage and liquidity were not considered risky on subprime bonds. After all, the beta of these bonds was relatively low,

despite the garbage they were holding and the leverage they piled on. When housing prices fell, the markets collapsed.

The low-beta ABX.HE.BBB investment-grade mortgage bond index, for example, sank into a black hole. Most investment banks, banks and many hedge funds were heavily margined in bonds of this type, anywhere from 25-to-1 to 40-to-1. At 30-to-1 leverage it takes a drop of only 3.3% to wipe out invested capital.

But the ABX mortgage index did not decline 3.3%; it dropped 98%. The loss was a stunning—2,940%. Banks lost billions and buyers disappeared. That's why Bear Stearns, Lehman and Washington Mutual no longer exist. Thank you, CAPM.

Extracted from David Dreman, "Debunking Beta," *Forbes*, September 27, 2010.

---

on equity for companies based on this model, in addition to estimates determined by the more widely recognized CAPM. However, the FF model has been criticized because it is not based on sound economic fundamentals, whereas the CAPM is based on economic reasoning and fundamentals. Further, many believe that the FF model is simply an example of data mining, in which the data have been examined so many times that eventually some variables are bound to be discovered that explain returns better than the CAPM does.[27]

Arbitrage Pricing Theory

arbitrage pricing theory (APT) pricing model that uses multiple factors to relate expected returns to risk by assuming that asset returns are linearly related to a set of indexes, which are proxy risk factors that influence asset returns

arbitrage process of taking advantage of different pricing for the same item in different markets

no-arbitrage principle rule that two otherwise identical assets cannot sell at different prices

Another well-known multifactor asset-pricing model is the **arbitrage pricing theory (APT)**. The APT requires very few assumptions, unlike the CAPM. In particular, the APT does not depend on the existence of an underlying market portfolio, and it allows for the possibility that several types of risk may affect asset returns. **Arbitrage** is the process of taking advantage of different pricing for the same item in different markets; if this different pricing exists, you would buy the item in the market with the cheaper price and sell it in the market where it has a higher price, making a profit from simple buying and selling. In fact, APT is based on the **no-arbitrage principle**, which states that two otherwise identical assets cannot sell at different prices.

Development of the formal APT assumes, as we have noted, that asset returns are linearly related to a set of indexes, which are proxy risk factors that influence asset returns. The underlying risk factors in the APT represent broad economic forces, which are unpredictable. We express the APT in Equation 9-10:

$$E(r_i) = a_0 + b_{i1} F_1 + b_{i2} F_2 + \ldots + b_{in} F_n \tag{9-10}$$

---

[27] This reminds us of the quote from economist Ronald Coase: "If you torture the data long enough, it will confess" [from a 1960s talk to the University of Virginia]. The Fama–French model is derived from the examination of the historical relation between a large number of financial statement data and stock returns, with a few of these financial statement items bubbling to the top in terms related to returns. This is always a risky approach to model building because what happened in the past does not always happen in the future.

where $E(r_i)$ = the expected return on asset i

a_0 = the expected return on a asset with zero systematic risk

b_i = the sensitivity of asset i to a given risk factor

F_i = the risk premium for a given risk factor

In Equation 9-10, you can see that an asset's risk is based on its sensitivity to basic economic factors, and the expected return increases proportionate to this risk. The sensitivity measures (b_i) have a similar interpretation to beta in the CAPM because they measure the relative sensitivity of a asset's return to a particular risk premium. In fact, the APT is equivalent to the CAPM if there were only one risk factor—that is, market returns—influencing asset returns.

The main problem with the APT is that the factors are not specified ahead of time. In fact, APT does not even specify the number of risk factors that exist or state which factors are the most important. As a result, these factors, as well as their relative importance, must be identified empirically.

Most empirical evidence suggests that three to five factors influence asset returns and are priced in the market. For example, Roll and Ross identify the following five systematic factors:[28]

1. Changes in expected inflation
2. Unanticipated changes in inflation
3. Unanticipated changes in industrial production
4. Unanticipated changes in the default-risk premium[29]
5. Unanticipated changes in the term structure of interest rates

The key is that these factors represent surprises because what is expected is already built in to the current price of an asset.[30] In other words, surprises drive returns because it is the new information—the surprise—that causes participants to revalue assets and, hence, generate returns.

A challenge in using the APT in financial decision making is that identifying these factors can be criticized as data mining and as such may be hazardous. Factors or their importance may change over time, making it difficult to use these factors in forward-looking decision making.

Summary of Alternatives

So, if these alternative models all have warts, and the CAPM has its warts, which model should you use, if any? The problem is that none of these models will help you earn abnormal returns on your investments. These models were developed to understand better how investors price assets. In addition to helping us understand what is important in the pricing of securities (risk and return), these models also rationalize what moves market prices (surprises).

Concept Review Questions

1. Why do we refer to the CAPM as a single-factor model?

2. Describe some of the criticisms of the CAPM, including Roll's critique.

3. Briefly describe the strengths and weaknesses of the Fama–French model and the APT.

---

[28] Richard Roll and Stephen Ross, "An Empirical Investigation of the Arbitrage Pricing Theory," *Journal of Finance, 35*, no. 5 (December 1980): 1073–1103.

[29] This variable is commonly defined as the yield on long-term corporate bonds minus the yield on long-term government bonds.

[30] And because they are surprises, there is no way to anticipate these.

9.5   MARKET EFFICIENCY

Financial managers need to know what investors want when they make investments, whether these investments are bonds, stocks, land, or plant and equipment. Financial managers also must know the required rates of return for different investments to make informed decisions. Once financial managers know what investors require, they can then make decisions that enhance shareholder value. Never forget that financial managers have a responsibility, as well as a legal obligation, to act in the owners' best interests. Correctly estimating discount rates is only part of the problem. A second important element is whether or not market prices correctly reflect the actions of managers. This brings up the question of market efficiency.

Defining Market Efficiency

efficient market market in which prices reacts quickly and relatively accurately to new information

An **efficient market** is one in which the prices of all assets accurately reflect all relevant and available information about the assets. This definition implies that asset prices in efficient capital markets are "correct." In other words, the current price of a common share reflects all known information, both past and present, about the corporation, including information about a company's earnings, financial strength, management strengths and weaknesses, and future plans as announced through press releases and the management discussion and analysis (MD&A) in its financial statements. Prices reflect rational expectations about what is expected to happen in the future and therefore mirror today's beliefs about future interest rate changes, future profits, potential mergers, and so on. Events that cause these beliefs about the future to change will have a corresponding impact on today's prices.

efficient market hypothesis (EMH) theory that markets are efficient and therefore, in its strictest sense, implies that prices accurately reflect all available information at any given time

The **efficient market hypothesis (EMH)** formalized the concept of an efficient market into a theory that markets are efficient, and therefore, in its strictest sense, it implies that prices accurately reflect all information at any point in time. Because the strictest form of the EMH represents such a high hurdle, we commonly break the EMH down into three different, and cumulative, levels based on the extent that prices reflect different types of available information: the weak form, semi-strong form, and strong form. For example, because of the cumulative nature of the definition, a market that is strong form efficient is also weak form and semi-strong form efficient.

Weak form of market efficiency

weak-form efficient characteristic of a market in which asset prices fully reflect all market data, which refers to all past price and volume trading information

If a market is **weak-form efficient**, asset prices fully reflect all market data, which refers to all past price and volume trading information. If markets are weak-form efficient, historical trading data is already reflected in current prices and should be of no value in predicting future price changes. In other words, it is not possible to generate an **abnormal profit**, a profit in excess of that expected for the asset's level of risk on a consistent basis.

abnormal profit profit in excess of those expected for the asset's level of risk

random walk hypothesis theory that prices follow a random walk, with price changes over time being independent of one another

If a market is weak-form efficient, current market prices reflect all historical trading data. Therefore, past price changes (and total returns) should be unrelated to future price changes. This idea is related to the **random walk hypothesis**, in which prices follow a random walk, with price changes over time being independent of one another. This hypothesis is logical if information arrives randomly, as it should, and if investors react to it immediately.

technical analysis study of historical trading information to identify patterns in trading data that can be used to invest successfully

Technical analysis involves the analysis of historical trading information to attempt to identify patterns in trading data that can be used to invest successfully. Most of the empirical evidence regarding the profitability of technical analysis in U.S. stock markets and markets in other developed countries suggests that technical trading rules, on average, have not been able to outperform a simple buy-and-hold strategy once we consider risk and trading costs. This is not to say that there are no opportunities in emerging markets; evidence suggests that emerging markets such as China, Bangladesh, and Turkey are not considered weak-form efficient and that technical analysis may provide abnormal returns. [31]

In addition to tests of specific technical trading rules, there is research that examines market anomalies based on the calendar (so-called calendar anomalies), which are patterns, such as the day-of-the-week or month-of-the-year that may produce profitable trading strategies. For example, there was evidence beginning in 1980 that Friday returns are larger than Monday returns, providing a profitable trading opportunity.[32] However, over time this "anomaly" disappeared.[33] Though these patterns are interesting to note, it would be difficult and very risky to attempt to exploit them because the evidence refers to averages that are observed in the past, which means (1) they do not occur all the time, and (2) anyone attempting to exploit these anomalies would incur trading costs that likely offset any potential profit. However, there is evidence that using some strategies, such as trading based on the day of the week, is profitable in some developing markets.[34] The bottom line is that securities markets in developed countries are weak-form efficient, but there remain inefficiencies in developing nations' markets.

Semi-strong form of market efficiency

In a market that is **semi-strong-form efficient**, asset prices reflect all publicly known and available information. For stock markets this includes information about earnings, dividends, corporate investments, management changes, and so on. This also includes market data, which are publicly available. Therefore, this version of the EMH encompasses the weak form. In other words, if a market is semi-strong efficient, then it must also be weak-form efficient.

A market that quickly incorporates all publicly available information into its prices is semi-strong efficient. In such a market, it would be futile to act on publicly available information, such as earnings announcements, merger announcements, and so on, in an attempt to consistently generate abnormal profits.[35]

One way of testing for semi-strong market efficiency is to examine the speed of adjustment of stock prices to announcements of significant new information. In a semi-strong efficient market, prices would adjust quickly and accurately to this new information so that investors could not act on it after its announcement and earn abnormally high risk-adjusted returns. In contrast, if the market overreacts or underreacts, or if time lags exist in stock price adjustments, and investors could exploit these flaws, then the market is not semi-strong efficient.

Most of the tests of semi-strong-form efficiency in securities markets take the form of an **event study**: Researchers examine stock returns to determine the impact of a particular event on stock prices. The vast majority of these studies support the notion that the market adjusts to new public information rapidly and accurately, and that investors could not earn abnormal profits based on inefficient market reactions to significant information

semi-strong-form efficient characteristic of a market in which all publicly known and available information is reflected in security prices

event study statistical examination of stock returns to determine the effect of a particular event on stock prices

[31] See, for example, Suzanne Fifield, David Power, and C. Donald Sinclair ["An Analysis of Trading Strategies in Eleven European Stock Markets," *European Journal of Finance*, Vol. 11, No. 6 (2005), 531–548] and Asma Mobarek, A. Sabur Mollah, and Rafiqul Bhuyan ["Market Efficiency in Emerging Stock Market," *Journal of Emerging Market Finance*, Vol. 7, No. 1 (January 2008): 17–41], and Kong-Jun Chen and Xiao-Ming Li ["Is Technical Analysis Useful for Stock Traders in China? Evidence from the Szse Component A-Share Index," *Pacific Economic Review*, Vol. 11, No. 4 (2006): 477–488].

[32] Kenneth R. French, "Stock Returns and the Weekend Effect," *Journal of Financial Economics*, Volume 8, Issue 1 (March 1980): 55–69.

[33] See, for example, Seyed Mehdian and Mark J. Perry ["The Reversal of the Monday Effect: New Evidence from US Equity Markets," *Journal of Business Finance & Accounting*, Vol. 28, No. 7 (September/October 2001): 1043–1065].

[34] See, for example, Francesco Guidi, Rakesh Gupta, and Suneel Mahesdhwari ["Weak-Form Market Efficiency and Calendar Anomalies for Eastern Europe Equity Markets," *Journal of Emerging Market Finance*, Vol. 10, No. 3 (December 2011): 337–389].

[35] Does this mean that financial analysis is fruitless? No, because analysts use information to formulate valuation estimates and to measure the risk of an asset. The measurement of risk and return is crucial to the formation and maintenance of security portfolios.

announcements.[36] Consider, for example, the market reaction to a surprise in earnings. If earnings are a surprise—better than expected or worse than expected—the earnings announcement provides information to the market. In an efficient market, we expect the share price to react quickly to this information. Early studies claimed that there was a quick reaction, but that some of the reaction lingered for days, supporting the idea that markets were not semi-strong efficient. However, subsequent evidence indicates that much of what was viewed as a delayed reaction could be explained once we control for transactions costs and risk. [37]

The other common test of semi-strong efficiency is to examine strategies that earn abnormal risk-adjusted returns over the long term. Perhaps the strongest evidence of semi-strong market efficiency is the fact that professional fund managers, with all of their training, expertise, technological capability, and access to data, do not outperform the market on a risk-adjusted basis, on average. In fact, most studies indicate the performance of the average active portfolio manager, after expenses, is actually worse than the performance of their passive benchmarks. Some studies suggest they may underperform their benchmarks by as much as 50 to 200 basis points (that is, 0.5% to 2%). Adding further support for capital markets as semi-strong efficient, evidence also suggests that pension fund managers consistently underperform their benchmarks.

Strong form of efficient markets

strong-form efficient characteristic of a market in which stock prices fully reflect all information, which includes both public and private information

If a market is **strong-form efficient**, asset prices fully reflect all information, which includes both public and private information. Public information is any information that is readily available to investors, whereas private information is any information not available, which we generally think of as inside information.[38] This would include, for example, an acquisition that is being planned yet has not yet been disclosed. It is obviously the most stringent form of market efficiency, and it encompasses both the weak and semi-strong versions because market data and all other publicly available information must be reflected in prices, as well as any private information that is possessed by some market participants but not by all. In such a market, no investor could take advantage of the possession of superior information or the superior processing of information to identify mispriced securities because the prices would already properly reflect all information. Obviously, this is a very strong assertion. For example, it asserts that insiders could not profit from private inside information.

If a market is strong-form efficient, this suggests that insiders cannot profit from inside information that is not known to the public because prices would already reflect this information. However, it seems impossible that prices could reflect information that is not yet publicly available. Strong-form market efficiency tests examine whether any group of investors has information (public or private) that allows them to earn abnormal profits consistently. Therefore, it is common to examine the performance of groups that are thought to have access to "private" information, such as insiders. Given their access to privileged information, it is not surprising that several studies have found that they have consistently earned abnormal returns on their stock transactions, which refutes strong-form efficiency. However, some studies have found that they perform only slightly better than average. It should be noted that the trading activity of insiders is restricted to protect the general investing public. Therefore, their potential to exploit this insider knowledge is quite limited. We can conclude that it is not surprising that, on balance, the evidence does not support this version of the EMH.

---

[36] Usually, abnormal returns are defined as those that exceed the expected return on a stock according to a model of stock returns, such as the CAPM.

[37] Dongcheol Kim and Myungsun Kim, "A Multifactor Explanation of Post-Earnings Announcement Drift," *Journal of Financial and Quantitative Analysis*, Vol. 38, No. 2 (June 2003): 383–398.

[38] Several definitions exist for "insiders." We suggest the use of a broad definition that includes any party that has access to private information about an asset as a result of a special relationship with the underlying entity. For example, this would include anyone who sat on the board of directors for a corporation, as well as that company's officers, lawyers, bankers, and so on.

Strong form	• Public and private information
Semi-strong form	• Publicly available information
Weak Form	• Past prices, volume, and other market information

Trading on Private Information | ETHICS

If a market is strong-form efficient, it would not pay for someone to trade on inside information because this information would already be reflected in asset prices. However, we know that individuals have traded on private information, made profits, and been caught.

In 2010, the Securities and Exchange Commission focused on hedge funds and the potential for insider trading. The heart of the issue is the following:

1. If markets are efficient, then hedge funds should not be able to earn abnormal profits.

2. If hedge funds have an advantage regarding information on publicly traded companies, this provides an unfair advantage to this group of investors.

One of the more recent large cases involved a hedge fund advisory firm, Galleon Management LP. Not only was Galleon and the hedge fund's manager charged, but also

the individuals supplying the insider information were.[39] For example, Rajat K. Gupta was charged in October 2011 for illegally tipping Raj Rajaratnam, providing information from his serving on boards of Goldman Sachs and Proctor & Gamble.

Not to be outdone by hedge funds, some members of the U.S. Congress have traded on insider information and profited nicely. Though members of Congress are not insiders in the sense of a CEO or a CFO, they are privy to information that is nonpublic, but profitable to trade on. As exposed in Peter Schweizer's 2011 book *Throw Them All Out*, the insider trading laws that forbid trading on material, nonpublic information—at least up until the book exposed the issue—were not enforced with respect to the trading by members of Congress and their families.[40] In response to this exposure, the Stop Trading on Congressional Knowledge Act (or the STOCK Act), was signed in to law in April, 2012.[41]

Market Efficiency Assumptions

For prices to be correct, the market must react quickly and accurately to new information. Several conditions must exist before markets can operate efficiently. One critical piece of this puzzle is that all market participants are treated fairly; that is, the market is a level playing field. This requirement is the reason that such a heavy emphasis is placed on **disclosure**; that is, the revelation of all material facts so that everyone in the market is buying and selling based on the same disclosed material facts about the firm.

A lack of disclosure is one reason that smaller, more loosely regulated markets tend to be less efficient, and that the prices in these markets do not accurately reflect available information. In this case, information is either not disclosed, is disclosed late, or is disclosed in such a way that not all market participants are aware of what is going on. Information disclosure is a very important part of **securities law**, and significant attention is

disclosure revelation of all material facts so that everyone in the market is buying and selling based on the same material facts about the firm

securities law body of law that ensures, through capital market regulations, that all investors have equal access to, and an equal opportunity to react to, new and relevant information and that governs the buying and selling of assets

---

[39] *SEC v. Galleon Management, LP, Raj Rajaratnam, Rajiv Goel, Anil Kumar, Danielle Chiesi, Mark Kurland, Robert Moffat and New Castle LLC* Civil Action No. 09-CV-8811.

[40] Peters Schweizer, *Throw Them All Out* (New York: Houghton Mifflin Harcourt Publishing Company, 2011).

[41] Public Law 112-05, signed into law April 4, 2012.

devoted to the maintenance and enforcement of these capital market regulations designed to ensure that all investors have equal access to, and an equal opportunity to react to, new and relevant information. For example, insider trading laws prevent insiders from acting on private information before that information is made public.

The technical definition of market efficiency suggests that market prices are *always* correct, which requires instantaneous and perfect price adjustments in response to the arrival of new information in the marketplace. This type of efficiency is not a practical reality; however, efficient markets do react quickly and relatively accurately to new information, and therefore prices are correct on average. We can expand on this logic and note that market efficiency is a matter of degree. In other words, more efficient markets process information faster and more accurately than do inefficient ones; therefore, the prices in these efficient markets are closer to the true values.

The following assumptions underlie the existence of efficient markets:

1. A large number of rational, profit-maximizing investors exist, who actively participate in the market by analyzing, valuing, and trading assets. The markets are assumed to be competitive, which means that no one investor can significantly affect the price of an asset.

2. Information is costless and widely available to market participants at the same time.

3. Information arrives randomly, and therefore announcements are not related to one another.

4. Investors react quickly and fully to the new information, which is reflected in stock prices.

Though these conditions are stringent and are not met in the strictest sense in the real world, they are not unreasonable today. A large number of market participants actively follow the prices of securities trading in the market and devour information that may affect these prices. For example, all the major investment banks have securities analysts whose job is to monitor companies and regularly report on their value through earnings forecasts and buy/sell/hold recommendations. We refer to this type of analyst as a **sell-side analyst** because they work for the investment banks that underwrite and sell assets to the public. Many institutions invest in assets, such as insurance companies, mutual funds, and pension funds. For example, CNA Financial, an insurance holding company, had over $55 billion of assets at the end of 2010, $42.6 billion of which are investments in fixed-income securities, equity securities, and short-term investments, among other investments. These institutions also employ assets analysts to evaluate the research and recommendations produced by the sell-side analysts. Because these institutions buy assets, we refer to this type of analyst as a **buy-side analyst**.

With all these analysts following publicly traded companies, we might expect prices to be rational and based on available information and economic fundamentals. In addition, an abundance of free or inexpensive information is available about most actively traded securities, and some would even argue that an overabundance of such information makes it difficult to "separate the wheat from the chaff." This information generally arrives randomly and is not predictable; if it were predictable, the prices would already reflect the information. Therefore, it is reasonable to assume that markets *could* be efficient. However, whether they are efficient or not is another matter because the analysts and market participants are human and may not process this information efficiently.

sell-side analyst person whose job it is to monitor companies and regularly report on their value through earnings forecasts and buy/sell/hold recommendations; employed by the investment banks that underwrite and sell securities to the public

buy-side analyst person whose job it is to evaluate the publicly available information for institutions in the capital market that invest in securities

Anomalies

Researchers have documented numerous anomalies in security pricing over the past few decades. An **anomaly** is a mispricing of an asset such that the pricing of the asset is not consistent with efficient markets. In other words, the pricing of an asset is not associated with relevant information about the asset that is known to all market participants. The presence of an anomaly would permit an investor to consistently earn abnormal profits

anomaly mispricing of an asset such that the pricing of the asset is not consistent with efficient markets from using a strategy to exploit an anomaly. Therefore, if you do some data snooping and discover that there is a relationship, say, between a company's stock price and the first letter of the company's name, such that you could make money by buying the stock of companies whose name starts with M and selling companies' stock whose name begins with P, this may be present for the time period of your study. But there are three questions to ask:

1. Could you make a profit after considering transactions costs for your trades?
2. Could you make a profit after adjusting for the market risk of the stocks?
3. Could you make a profit consistently in any other time period (especially going forward) using this strategy?

The answer is, "Probably not."

What are the types of anomalies that researchers have found? We list a few of these in Table 9-2. Consider a few of these:

- The size effect is that small capitalization stocks outperform large capitalization stocks, which indicates that the market is not weak-form efficient.
- The January effect is that returns in January are higher than the rest of the year. This indicates that the market is not weak-form efficient.
- The earnings surprise anomaly is that when earnings are released by a company and there is an unexpected portion, the market not only reacts immediately, but also continues to react for some days following the earnings announcement. This is evidence against semi-strong market efficiency.
- The value anomaly is that value stocks (that is, low market/book ratios) outperform other securities, which would indicate that the market is not semi-strong-form efficient.

Though these anomalies are documented as statistically significant in some periods, the issue becomes one of whether these anomalies are economically significant, that is, they are not profitable on a risk-adjusted basis after considering transactions costs.

While we will not go into detail on the evidence regarding these, the general conclusions are the following:

- Some anomalies, such as the size, the January, or day-of-the-week effects, do not persist over time. This may be due to either the anomaly being time specific or to the anomaly disappearing because investors have exploited the anomaly and therefore the stocks then become correctly priced.
- Some anomalies, such as momentum, can be explained by rational behavior or a factor that is not accounted for in pricing models. What appears to be an anomaly may, in fact, be a rational response to information that is disseminated slowly.
- Some anomalies, such as the value and small firm effect, may be attributed to the use of the CAPM in the analysis, but these anomalies most likely are not apparent if a more robust model, such as the Fama–French model, were used in developing expected returns and asset pricing.

TABLE 9-2 Examples of Anomalies Documented by Researchers

Cross-Sectional Anomalies	Time-Based Anomalies	Other Anomalies
• Book-to-market ratio	• January	• Earnings surprise
• P/E ratio	• Day-of-the-week	• Initial public offerings
• Value	• Weekend	
• Small firm	• Time-of-day	
• Size	• Momentum	
	• Overreaction	

- Some anomalies, such as earnings surprise and initial public offerings, do not exist once transactions costs and risk are adequately accounted for in the analysis.
- Some anomalies, such as the overreaction anomaly and the initial public offering effect, may be explained by investor behavior that is not captured in pricing models. However, it may not be possible to earn abnormal returns once transactions costs and risk are properly considered.

The late Professor Fischer Black, who summed up anomalies succinctly in his discussion of expected returns, remarked that "so called 'anomalies' don't seem anomalous to me at all. They seem like nuggets from a gold mine, found by one of the thousands of miners all over the world."[42]

LESSONS LEARNED | Wacky Indicators

In addition to the technical analysis and calendar-based anomalies that investors have used to chase abnormal returns, a number of indicators fall into the category of superstitious indicators:

Super Bowl winners	If a former member of the American Football League wins, the stock market will experience a down year.
Butter production in Bangladesh	The return on the S&P Index will be twice that of the change in butter production in Bangladesh.
Triple Crown	If a horse wins the Triple Crown (that is, wins the Kentucky Derby, the Belmont Stakes, and the Preakness Stakes), the stock market will have a bad year.
Hemlines of women's dresses	There is a positive relationship between movement in the market and hemlines: if hemlines get shorter, prices go up, and vice versa.
Sports Illustrated Swimsuit Model	The market does well when the swimsuit model chosen for the cover is of U.S. nationality.

If you plan to start trading based on any of these, please note that they have been, largely, debunked.

Implications

Overall, based on the available empirical evidence with regard to capital markets of the United States and most developed markets, these markets are weak-form and semi-strong-form efficient, but not strong-form efficient.

[42] Fischer Black, "Estimating Expected Return," *Financial Analysts Journal*, September/October 1993, p. 37.

The EMH states that security prices fully and accurately reflect all available information at any given time. The evidence suggests that market efficiency does hold. The implications for investors and for corporate officers include:

1. Technical analysis is not likely to be rewarded in the form of abnormal returns because markets appear to be weak-form efficient.
2. Fundamental analysis, based on the use of various forms of publicly available information, is likely to be unsuccessful at generating abnormal profits. The implication is that to benefit from the use of such data, the analysis must be of superior and consistent quality.

In light of items 1 and 2 just listed, active trading strategies are unlikely to outperform passive portfolio management strategies on a consistent basis. An **active trading strategy** includes trading based on timing the market, trends, or other criteria. A **passive investment strategy** involves buy-and-hold strategies and the purchase of such products as index mutual funds or exchange-traded funds (ETFs) that replicate the performance of a market index. The lack of success for active strategies is partially attributable to the extra costs associated with collecting and processing information, as well as to the additional trading costs associated with active strategies. These extra costs can be justified only if the approach generates sufficient additional returns to compensate for them. Passive strategies minimize these costs.

Two of the most important implications of efficient markets for financial managers are as follows:

1. The timing of security issues or repurchases is unimportant in an efficient market because prices will be correct on average. In other words, prices will not become inflated, so there is no optimal time to sell new securities, and securities will not be undervalued, so there is no optimal time to repurchase outstanding securities.
2. If short-run momentum and overreaction continue, we would expect the opposite: that corporations issue equity after a price run-up and repurchase shares after a price decline. Therefore, managers should monitor the price of the company's securities and see whether price changes reflect new information or short-run momentum and/or overreaction.

active trading strategy trading based on timing the market, trends, or other criteria

passive investment strategy buy-and-hold strategies and the purchase of such products as index mutual funds or exchange-traded funds (ETFs) that replicate the performance of a market index

Market Efficiency Around the World | GLOBAL PERSPECTIVE

The International Monetary Fund has promoted the distribution and transparency of economic and financial data in capital markets to encourage the efficiency of capital markets around the world. The IMF's program includes the Special Data Dissemination Standard (SDDS) in 1996 and the General Data Dissemination Initiative in 1997.

As of 2010, 153 of the IMF's 185 member nations participate. The data available include economic data such as the consumer price index, trade data, demographic data, and national accounts. Market data include exchange rates, interest rates, and stock market indices.

Data on any of these 153 nations can be accessed through www.imf.org.

Concept Review Questions

1. Define market efficiency in terms of information.
2. Discuss the reasonableness of the assumptions underlying market efficiency.
3. What are the main implications of the efficient markets hypothesis for financial managers?
4. If someone discovers that stock returns for stocks with a ticker symbol of one character are higher than stock returns for stocks with a ticker symbol of three characters, what would you want to know before putting your money into this strategy?

9.6 BEHAVIORAL FINANCE AND FINANCIAL MANAGEMENT

behavioral finance study of how human behavior affects economic decision making

Behavioral finance is the study of how human behavior affects economic decision making. While we devise theories that depend on rational, risk-averse investors, there is always the possibility that financial managers do not act this way and, in fact, make decisions that are biased. Why look at behavioral finance? Because decisions are not made by computers; no matter how much decisions depend on formulas and models, there is always a human element somewhere along the way, either through the inputs to the formulas and models or through the interpretation of the results of the formulas and models.

Cognitive Biases

Individuals' behaviors enter into decision making, whether intentional or subconsciously. Asset pricing models, in particular, make certain assumptions about behavior (e.g., risk averse, rational). But what happens if these assumptions are not true? What can be done to ensure that personal biases do not enter into decision making? An important step is to understand psychology and the cognitive biases that may exist.

cognitive bias mistake in decision making that results from one's own preferences and beliefs

A **cognitive bias** is a mistake in decision making that results from one's own preferences and beliefs. These biases result in decisions that are not consistent with pure scientific or statistical reasoning. The many sources of bias include overconfidence, loss aversion, the disposition effect, representativeness, anchoring, framing, and mental accounting. Though this is not a complete list of such biases, by discussing a few of these biases briefly, you can get an idea of how behavior may affect financial decision making and the need for monitoring and mechanisms to minimize the effects of these biases.

Overconfidence

People, including and perhaps even more so financial professionals, are generally overconfident about their abilities. There are many ways that this becomes apparent when we observe behavior. For example, a decision maker who has a good understanding of the role of diversification may nevertheless choose an investment portfolio without adequate diversification because of overconfidence in his or her ability to select investments.

One result of this overconfidence in the stock market is that individuals who are more overconfident tend to trade more often than others, generally to the detriment of the value of their portfolio. Overoptimism is quite common in speculative bubbles in markets.

Overoptimism also affects the outlook of companies' top management. In the Duke/CFO Magazine Optimism Index, CFOs are generally more optimistic about their own company's prospects compared to how they perceive the economy in general.[43] Overconfidence can lead to subconsciously biasing investment project choices toward projects that the financial manager believes are more profitable. How could this be possible? Many subjective inputs contribute to capital investment decisions, as you will see in later chapters, which a manager can use to manage the outcome of the analysis, making a project appear more profitable or less risky. And this does not have to be intentional; this could be subconscious.

People tend to differ in the degree of overconfidence, with men more overconfident than women and entrepreneurs more overconfident than other persons in the business. But this is not necessarily a bad thing because this optimism is what helps individuals take on outsized risk related to new businesses, inventions, and new products.

BOTTOM LINE: Overconfidence may lead to poor or risky decision making.

---

[43] The average of CFO's assessments of prospects should coincide with the average assessment of the economy as a whole, but it does not.

Loss aversion

In asset pricing models, we base the theories on risk aversion. However, loss aversion has different implications for pricing. **Prospect theory** is the area of study of how individuals make choices given information about probabilities. According to prospect theory, individuals tend to be risk averse when there are gains, but tend not to be risk averse—and, in fact, are risk seekers—when considering losses.[44] The different type of risk preference for gains and losses arises from **loss aversion**, which is a willingness to avoid losses that is disproportionate to the willingness to seek similar-sized gains.

The basic idea is the following: Individuals do not weigh probabilities as we would expect based on probabilities. Consider the following choice:[45]

prospect theory the area of study of how individuals make choices given information about probabilities and outcomes

loss aversion willingness to avoid losses that is disproportionate to the willingness to seek similar-sized gains

Choice 1	*Choice 2*
50 percent chance to win $1,000	$450 for sure
50 percent chance to win nothing	

Which would you prefer? If you apply the expected value calculations that we covered in an earlier chapter, you would see that Choice 1 has an expected value of $500. However, as this problem is framed, many will choose Choice 2, letting certainty outweigh the expected value.

What are the implications for financial management? Loss aversion implies that decision makers may give more weight to certainty and therefore not think in terms of the statistical expected value. Loss aversion also implies that managers may focus too much on what has already been spent—a sunk cost—in making decisions.

Closely related to loss aversion is the disposition effect. The **disposition effect** is the behavior of individuals in which they avoid realizing any paper losses, but tend to realize paper gains. In other words, people tend to hang onto losers longer than they should. We can see this in any stock market: In a bull market, in which stock prices are climbing, there is increased trading volume; in a bear market, in which stock prices are declining, there is decreased trading volume.

disposition effect behavior of individuals in which they avoid realizing any paper losses, but tend to realize paper gains

This may explain why markets may not react to news as quickly as we would expect in an efficient market because some investors will hesitate in selling when there is bad news, hence perpetuating a drop in a stock's price, and will sell quickly when the price rises, hence dampening the initial response to good news.

BOTTOM LINE: Financial managers may not be willing to abandon an investment project that is not turning out as expected.

Representativeness and anchoring

Representativeness is the tendency for people to judge something, such as an investment, by the degree to which this something resembles something else in the person's experience. In other words, an individual will overweight most recent events, giving less weight to long-term averages. For example, when the market falls significantly, it is this fall that most investors consider, not the rise before that fall.

It is all too often that employees invest in the employer's own stock. An example may be an employee of a food processor selecting food processor stocks in his or her personal investment portfolio, despite the heavy investment in food processing of his total portfolio in the form of in-human capital investment through the employee's career. The familiarity with the employer or the industry may deter an investor from fully diversifying a portfolio.

representativeness tendency for people to judge something, such as an investment, by the degree to which this something resembles something else in the person's experience

---

[44] Prospect theory was developed by Daneil Kaheman and Amos Tversky, "Prospect Theory: An Analysis of Decision Under Risk," *Econometrica*, No. 37 (1979): 264–291.

[45] This example is modeled from the A–B choice in Kahneman and Tversky, ibid.

anchoring tendency
to use inappropriate
or irrelevant factors in
decision making

Closely related to representativeness is anchoring. **Anchoring** is the tendency to use inappropriate or irrelevant factors in decision making. Consider forecasting a time series. If individuals are asked to forecast the following:

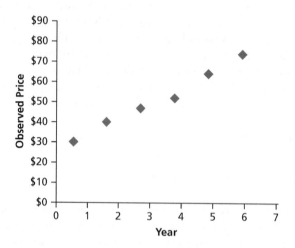

people tend to underestimate the seventh observation due to anchoring, predicting the observed price lower than the statistical trend line:

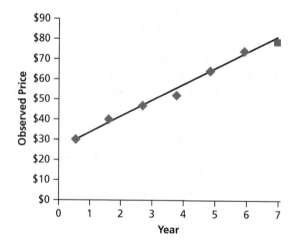

If a decision is anchored, this means that the decision is influenced by how something is presented. Consider two series of numbers:

Series A:	44	48	63	72	88
Series B:	101	81	50	43	40

Without resorting to your calculator, which series has the highest mean? If you chose Series B, you are likely anchoring your answer on the first few observations of each series. Although the average is the same for both series—63—there is a tendency to let the first observations in the series influence the choice. Related to this is the investment in projects for which the manager has the most familiarity, rather than those projects that offer the most diversification.

BOTTOM LINE: Past experiences, especially the most recent past, may unduly affect the forecasts that are made for capital projects or investments made today.

Framing

Framing is the manner in which something is presented, which may influence how someone feels about this something. Consider the classic example of specials. Most of the time you see "happy hour" specials with some type of discount (e.g., two for one) during certain hours, corresponding to the period of time in which there is the slowest bar traffic. Therefore, by arriving during happy hour, the individual believes that they are getting a deal. Now let's turn this around and have the same exact pricing, but a different advertisement, or framing. What if the advertisement were, instead, that you pay full price during happy hour, but pay more than full price when it is not happy hour? The way this is framed, you may come away feeling that you would not like to visit the bar during any time but happy hour because you would have been taken advantage of otherwise. You may no longer feel that happy about happy hour; rather, you may feel quite negative about the bar from this advertisement. Your attitude is shaped by this framing.

BOTTOM LINE: How an investment opportunity or project is presented and evaluated may influence its acceptability.

framing manner in which something is presented, which may influence how someone feels about this something

Mental accounting

Mental accounting is the process of investors separating money into different accounts in their thought process, which affects decision making. For example, a financial manager may view funds generated internally as free or low-cost capital and treat funds raised from a stock issue as costly, even though they are—with the exception of flotation costs—the same cost.[46] Another example of mental accounting is evaluating investments in a company as separate "silos," instead of taking the companywide perspective.

BOTTOM LINE: Mental categorization of funds may not be optimal when making decisions to maximize shareholder wealth.

mental accounting process of investors separating money into different accounts in their thought process

Implications of Behavior in Financial Decision Making

Most asset pricing models assume that investors are rational, and the value of an asset reflects rational decision making. We also assume that investors are risk averse but are willing to take on risk if compensated for this risk in the form of higher expected returns. So what if these assumptions are not true? What are the implications?

Despite the long list of assumptions, and despite the role of human behavior in decision making that may not be rational or risk averse, the CAPM model has generally withstood a barrage of attacks. This is because the basic conclusion of expected returns determined by the time value of money and a premium for bearing market risk still stands. Therefore, using the CAPM in determining the cost of funds, one of the more prominent uses in financial management, is still acceptable.

Another implication of human behavior in decision making is that any system of governance should build in protections against behaviors that may be detrimental to the goal of the firm. Policies and procedures can be developed that guard against overconfidence, disposition effect, mental accounting issues, and framing.

1. How does loss aversion affect decision making?

2. Can a financial manager be ethical and still be overconfident?

3. If not all investors are risk averse, can the CAPM still hold true? Explain.

Concept Review Questions

---

[46] This is similar to the mental accounting mistake that many individuals make when looking at tax refunds. A tax refund is simply what was overpaid to the government over a period, but many individuals treat the refund as "found money."

SUMMARY

- The efficient frontier is the set of portfolios that provides the best return for a given level of risk (or, similarly, the lowest risk for a given level of return). If we combine borrowing or lending at the risk-free rate of interest, the set of investment opportunities improves.

- The capital market line depicts the required return for efficient portfolios based on their standard deviations, whereas the security market line depicts the relation between the required return and market risk, as measured by beta.

- An efficient market is a market in which asset prices reflect available information quickly and accurately. The EMH is commonly broken down into three forms that are based on the extent to which prices reflect different types of available information. The weak-form EMH states that security prices reflect all market data; the semi-strong form states that prices reflect all publicly known and available information; and the strong form states that prices reflect all public and private information

- An implication of the capital asset pricing model for financial decision making is that return on an investment is consistent with the amount of market risk of the investment, not on the investment's total or stand-alone risk. The implications of market efficiency for financial decision making include the (1) inability to time security offerings and (2) the expectation of returns commensurate with market risk.

- Behavioral finance is an area of study that examines how human behaviors can enter into decision making. Cognitive biases can enter into decision making, resulting in decisions that are not in the best interest of owners.

FORMULAS/EQUATIONS

(9-1) $E(r_p) = r_f + w[E(r_X) - r_f]$

(9-2) $\sigma_p = w\sigma_X$

(9-3) $E(r_p) = r_f + \left(\dfrac{E(r_X) - r_f}{\sigma_X}\right)\sigma_p$

(9-4)   Slope of the capital market line $= \dfrac{E(r_M) - r_f}{\sigma_M}$

(9-5) $E(r_p) = r_f + \left[\dfrac{E(r_M) - r_f}{\sigma_M}\right]\sigma_p$

(9-6) $\beta_i = \dfrac{COV_{i,M}}{\sigma_M^2} = \dfrac{\rho_{i,M}\sigma_i}{\sigma_M}$

(9-7)   Sharpe ratio $= \dfrac{r_p - r_f}{\sigma_p}$

(9-8) $\beta_p = w_A\beta_A + w_B\beta_B + \ldots + w_n\beta_n$

(9-9) $E(r_i) = r_f + (E(r_M) - r_f)\beta_i$

(9-10) $E(r_i) = a_0 + b_{i1}F_1 + b_{i2}F_2 + \ldots + b_{in}F_n$

QUESTIONS AND PROBLEMS

Multiple Choice

1. Which of the following statements is *false*?
   A. The standard deviation of a risk-free asset is zero.
   B. The covariance of any combination of a risky security and a risk-free asset is zero.
   C. Portfolios on the efficient frontier dominate all other attainable portfolios for a given risk or return.
   D. The risk measurement associated with the security market line (SML) is the standard deviation of the portfolio.

2. If Portfolio A lies above the security market line, Portfolio A is:

   A. overvalued.

   B. undervalued.

   C. undetermined.

   D. properly valued.

3. The expected return and standard deviation of a portfolio consisting of $2,000 invested in the risk-free asset with an 8 percent rate of return, and $8,000 invested in the risky security with a 20 percent rate of return and a 25 percent standard deviation, is *closest* to:

Expected Return	*Standard Deviation*
A. 5 percent	10.4 percent
B. 10.4 percent	5 percent
C. 17.6 percent	20 percent
D. 20 percent	17.6 percent

4. Which of the following statements is *false*?

   A. The market portfolio is observable.

   B. Systematic risk cannot be diversified away.

   C. The *y*-intercept of both the SML and the CML is the risk-free rate of interest.

   D. The market portfolio includes all risky assets, including stocks, bonds, real estate, derivatives, and so on.

5. Systematic risk:

   A. is also called unique risk.

   B. does not change throughout time.

   C. equals total risk divided by nonsystematic risk.

   D. measures of portfolios are more stable than those of individual assets.

6. Which of the following statements about an efficient market is false?

   A. Prices reflect all relevant and available information.

   B. Prices react to new information quickly and correctly.

   C. Price changes follow predictable patterns through time.

   D. Prices reflect such information as a company's financial strength and earnings.

7. Which of the following is *useful* in attempting to identify mispriced securities if a market is semi-strong efficient, yet not strong-form efficient?

   A. Earnings expectations

   B. Past stock price changes

   C. Relevant insider information

   D. Past and current published trading volumes

8. Which of the following statements is true?

   A. The weak form of the efficient market hypothesis encompasses the semi-strong form.

   B. The strong form of the efficient market hypothesis encompasses the semi-strong form.

   C. The semi-strong form of the efficient market hypothesis encompasses the strong form.

   D. The strong form of the efficient market hypothesis does not encompass the weak form.

9. An event study is most often used to evaluate:

   A. whether a market is weak-form efficient.

   B. whether there is insider trading for a stock.

   C. the effect of information as it reaches market participants.

10. A portfolio manager who believes that markets are semi-strong efficient would most likely use:
    A. active trading strategy.
    B. passive investment strategy.

Practice Questions and Problems

9.1   The Efficient Frontier

11. What does the efficient frontier represent?

12. If a portfolio does not lie on the efficient frontier, what does this mean about this portfolio?

13. Determine if you are risk averse or risk loving. For the following decisions, indicate if they are consistent with risk aversion or risk loving:
    A. Buying a lottery ticket
    B. Buying fire insurance for your house
    C. Backing up your computer

14. The Mason Consulting firm has been hired to conduct an investigation of the advice the Sketchy Broker-age Company has been giving its clients, and the investigation might result in a lawsuit. Mason observes that clients have been placed in the following portfolios:

Investor	Portfolio	Expected Return	Standard Deviation
A	A	2.0%	0.40%
B	B	4.0%	0.60%
C	C	5.0%	0.30%
D	D	7.0%	0.50%
E	E	9.0%	0.45%
F	F	10.0%	0.70%

Evaluate the advice the broker has been giving his clients (assume that investors can only invest in one of the six portfolios).
    A. Which investors are holding inefficient portfolios?
    B. What changes would you make to their investments—how will this improve their portfolio?
    C. Mr. Al Locate, the broker under investigation, argues that these portfolios are appropriate because these investors are risk loving. Are inefficient portfolios appropriate for risk-loving investors?
    D. Of the investors who are holding efficient portfolios, who is:
       i) The most risk averse
       ii) The least risk averse

15. Suppose that an investor invests all his wealth, $10,000, in a portfolio that has an expected return of 10 percent and a standard deviation of 20 percent. He borrows an additional $5,000 at the risk-free rate of 3 percent, which he also invests in this portfolio. What is the estimated expected return and standard deviation for this portfolio?

9.2   The Capital Asset Pricing Model

16. According to the CAPM, what are the primary determinants of an asset's return?

17. Why might a financial manager care about the CAPM and a company's beta?

18. Calculate the missing values for the following four efficient portfolios. The expected return on the market is 8 percent, with a standard deviation of 5 percent, and the risk-free rate is 2 percent.

Investor	Weight in Risk-free Asset	Expected Portfolio Return	Portfolio Standard Deviation
Charles	25%		
Fritz	40%		
Eddy	50%		
Nellie	75%		

19. Jackie borrowed $800 at the risk-free rate of 8 percent. She invested the borrowed money and $1,000 in a portfolio with a 15 percent rate of return and a 30 percent standard deviation. What is the expected return and standard deviation of her portfolio?

20. Stock FM has a standard deviation of 30 percent. It has a correlation coefficient of 0.75 with market returns. The standard deviation of market return is 20 percent, and the expected return is 16 percent. The risk-free rate is 6.5 percent. What is the required rate of return of Stock FM? Compare FM's required return to the expected market return.

21. Three investors are having an argument about investments and have come to you for advice. The set of possible investments are A, B, and C:

Risky Portfolio	Expected Return	Standard Deviation
A	7%	5%
B	13%	7%
C	17%	11%

Assume you cannot mix risky investments. Investor 1 says that they should all invest in portfolio A because it has the lowest risk. Investor 2 says that they should all invest in portfolio C because it has the highest return. Investor 3 is just confused.

A. If there is no risk-free asset, can you recommend the same portfolio for each of the friends? Why or why not?

B. If the expected risk-free rate is 2 percent, can you recommend the same set of risky assets for each of the friends? Why or why not?

C. Does the existence of a risk-free asset make the friends better off? Explain your reasoning.

9.3 The CAPM and Market Risk

22. What does beta in the CAPM represent?

23. What is the beta of the:
    A. risk-free asset?
    B. market portfolio?

24. Which of the following are examples of systematic and unsystematic risks:
    A. Inflation risk
    B. CFO's fraudulent activities
    C. Changes in interest rates
    D. Product tampering
    E. Political risk
    F. CEO's aversion to working on Fridays

25. You are on the board of directors of the BY Company. The stock price of BY has suddenly increased by 20 percent, and the CEO has come to the board asking for a substantial pay increase. The CEO argues that the company's prospects have dramatically improved—after all, why else would the stock price increase? Do you feel that the CEO should receive a large pay increase?

26. The manager of the Mountaineer Company is puzzled. Analysts are saying that the future prospects for his company are poor because the stock price has dropped 5 percent.

    A. Explain to the manager the relationship between stock prices and market expectations.

    B. Would you be as concerned about the company's future prospects if the company had a beta of 1.5 and the market has fallen 4 percent?

27. Which security, A, B, or C, will provide the greatest return per unit of risk when combined with the risk-free asset with a 5 percent rate of return?

Security	Expected Return	Standard Deviation of Returns
A	20%	5%
B	17%	11%
C	28%	20%

28. Determine the beta of a company's stock based on the following information:

Market expected return	8 percent
Standard deviation	3 percent
Risk-free rate	3 percent
Current dividend	$4.50
Dividend growth rate	5 percent
Current stock price	$25

29. Using the relationship between individual security betas and the portfolio beta, complete the following table:

	Security 1 Beta	Security 2 Beta	Weight in Security 1	Portfolio Beta
Case 1	0.40	1.50	0.60	
Case 2		0.45	0.80	0.49
Case 3	1.10	1.90		1.50
Case 4	1.25	0.40	0.75	
Case 5	1.30		0.15	1.895

30. Estimate the beta of a stock with the following characteristics:

    • market risk premium is 20 percent;

    • risk-free rate of interest is 10 percent;

    • the current stock price per share is $10;

    • expected dividend at the end of the year is $2.50; and

    • expected price per share in one year is $12.50.

Assume the market is in equilibrium.

31. Suppose you have a portfolio now that has $100 in Stock A with a beta of 0.9, $400 in Stock B with a beta of 1.2, and $300 in the risk-free asset. You have another $200 to invest and wish to achieve a beta of your portfolio that is the same as the market beta. What would the beta of the stock added to your portfolio do to achieve this goal?

32. The Redrock Consulting firm is valuing the Vancouver Rain-Making Company (VRMC) and needs to calculate the following:

A. The required rate of return of the VRMC, assuming the market risk premium is 8 percent, the risk-free rate is 2 percent, and its common stock's beta is 1.2.

B. The price of VRMC based on the current dividend of $1.25 and a dividend growth rate of 3 percent.

33. The Wise Advisers are following five different stocks and need to issue a recommendation (buy, hold, or sell) to their customers. The market return is 7 percent with a standard deviation of 4 percent. The risk-free rate is 3 percent. The CAPM is assumed to hold.

Security	Expected Return	Standard Deviation	Beta	Recommendation
ABC	5%	9%	1.50	
DEF	10%	3%	1.10	
GHI	6%	10%	.95	
JKL	9%	4%	.75	
MNO	14%	6%	1.25	

To determine the recommendations, begin by calculating the required returns for each security using the capital asset pricing model. Comparing the expected and required returns will indicate which securities are under, over, or correctly priced.

9.4 Alternative Asset Pricing Models

34. Describe and provide an example of an arbitrage opportunity.

35. What type of factors drive returns in the arbitrage pricing theory?

36. Consider two analysts, Joe and Jane. Joe is convinced that the only relevant factor in explaining stock returns is the market return. Jane believes that surprises drive returns. Classify each analyst according to the asset pricing model that is most consistent with their beliefs.

37. Consider two portfolios, A and B. Portfolio A has a beta of 1.0 and an expected return of 15 percent. Portfolio B has a beta of 0.8 and an expected return of 12 percent. If the risk-free rate of return is 5 percent, how can you take advantage of this arbitrage opportunity according to the arbitrage pricing theory?

9.5 Market Efficiency

38. What distinguishes a weak-form efficient market from a semi-strong-form efficient market?

39. What distinguishes a semi-strong-form efficient market from a strong-form efficient market?

40. Why would a financial manager of a corporation be interested in whether financial markets are efficient?

41. If insiders can make abnormal profits by trading in the company's stock,
A. what does this say about the efficiency of the stock market?
B. would this activity be legal? Explain.

42. If a mutual fund claims that it can "beat the market on a risk-adjusted basis," what does this say about the efficiency of the market if this statement is true?

43. If a trader uses technical analysis and claims that she can "beat the market on a risk-adjusted basis," what does this say about the efficiency of the market if true?

44. The CEO of the Yucca Diet Pill Company has hired IB Consulting to advise her on issuing new stock. Her company will need to issue more stock soon to finance the development of a new product—the Yucca Hair Growth formula. The CEO has noticed that, on average, the stock price of diet pill companies is higher in the

spring than the rest of the year. She would like to issue the Yucca stock in the spring to obtain the highest price possible. Given your understanding of the efficiency of the market, what advice do you have for this CEO regarding the timing of the new stock issue of the Yucca Diet Pill Company?

45. On the morning of March 15, the Ames Company announced that it will pay its first dividend of $5 this year. The ex-dividend date will be July 3.

   A. If the announcement is a complete surprise to the market, what do you expect will happen to the stock price on March 15?

   B. If the announcement has been forecasted by the financial analysts, what do you expect to happen to the stock price on March 15?

   C. What do you expect to happen to the price of Ames stock on July 3?

46. On Monday evening, the East Tennessee Steam Engine Company announced that it would be restating its financial statements for the last 5 years, and the CFO was also arrested for fraud. Interpret the following Tuesday stock reactions:

   A. Stock price drops

   B. Stock price does not change

9.6   Behavioral Finance and Financial Management

47. Is loss aversion the same thing as risk aversion? Explain.

48. If a financial manager is interested in maximizing owners' wealth, how could the manager be overconfident and still be honest?

49. If a person gives too much weight to recent information, rather than long-term averages, what type of behavior does this exhibit? Explain.

50. A financial manager refuses to abandon an unprofitable project and believes that if the company sticks with this project it will be profitable. The manager is most likely exhibiting what type of behavior?

Cases

Case 9.1 Morgantown Company Stock

On Monday, February 18, the stock of the Morgantown Company was trading at $25 per share. The CEO was satisfied with this price, as it reflected the prospects of Morgantown in terms of the future dividend growth and required rate of return. The company's scientists worked all Monday night to complete a project, which will dramatically improve the quality of Morgantown's products and result in a huge increase in sales for the next 10 years.

   A. If markets are efficient and reflect available information, explain why the stock price of Morgantown should or should not reflect the top-secret project's prospects on Monday, February 18, and on Tuesday, February 19.

   B. The CEO of Morgantown has been watching the company's stock price and noticed that the stock price increased during trading on Tuesday, even though the market, in general, was flat. Why might the stock price be increasing on Tuesday, February 19, even though the company has not made any announcements regarding the top-secret project?

   C. The U.S. Securities and Exchange Commission's Regulation FD requires that companies disclose information to all investors at the same time.[47] To avoid any problems with this regulation, the management of Morgantown decides to issue a press release about the top-secret project on Wednesday, February 20. What, if anything, do you expect to happen to the stock price of Morgantown once this press release is issued? Why?

---

[47] 17 Code of Federal Regulation Parts 240, 243, and 249, RIN 3235-AH82, effective October 23, 2000.

Case 9.2 JPMorgan Chase's Sinking Profit

On Saturday, January 14, 2012, JPMorgan Chase (ticker symbol JPM), announced a drop in profit of 23 percent for the fourth quarter of 2011, compared to the same quarter a year earlier. This drop in profit is attributed to a drop in investment banking activity, but it was offset somewhat by a reduction in defaults on mortgages and credit-card debt.

A. What do you believe should have happened to JPMorgan's common stock on Friday, January 13, 2012? Why?

B. What do you believe should have happened to JPMorgan's common stock on Tuesday, January 17, 2012, which is the first trading day following this announcement? Why?

C. Download daily stock prices for JPM for the ten trading days before and after this announcement, and calculate the return for each trading day. Do the same for the S&P 500. Using a beta of 1.35, estimate the expected return on JPM stock for each day based on the security market line.

D. Using the analysis in C, estimate the abnormal return for each trading day:

$$\text{Abnormal return} = \text{Actual return} - \text{return expected using the SML}$$

Relate your findings to the earnings announcement.

PART 5

LONG-TERM INVESTMENT DECISIONS

The long-term, capital decisions of a company are important for the sustainability of a company. Without new capital investments and assessment of existing investments, a company will not grow and create value. In Part 5, we focus on decision making involving the investment in long-term assets. We discuss different evaluation techniques in Chapter 10 and then focus on estimating future cash flows from a project in Chapter 11.

371

CHAPTER 10

CAPITAL BUDGETING DECISIONS

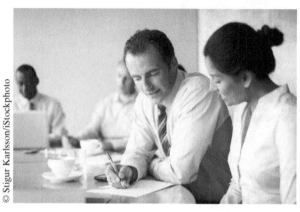

Many working business professionals consider returning to school to earn an MBA. But is it worth it? It depends. Antony Davies and Thomas Cline considered the cost and potential earning power from individuals who pursued an MBA in the years 1993–2000, and found:

- The return on investment in an MBA was better than Treasury Bills, the return on triple-A rated bonds, and the Dow Jones Industrial Average.

- The payback period, in years to recover tuition and fees, is 8–10 years.

- The NPV—the present value of the benefits from increased salary and benefits, less the present value of the costs of tuition and fees—ranges from $360,000 (in 1993) to around $700,000 in 1998, with the NPV in 2001 of $550,000.

They also observed that there is variation in the benefits from an MBA. In other words, your experience may differ from that of the "average."

Source: *Antony Davies and Thomas Cline, "The ROI on the MBA,* BizEd, *January/February 2005, pp. 42–45.*

Learning Outcomes

After reading this chapter, you should be able to:

LO 10.1 Describe the process of basic capital budgeting.

LO 10.2 Compare and apply capital budgeting techniques used to evaluate long-term investments, including the net present value and internal rate of return techniques.

LO 10.3 Reconcile the approach to capital budgeting that is consistent with value maximization with the capital budgeting techniques used in practice.

Chapter Preview In this chapter, we discuss long-term investment decisions made by companies; that is, investments in real assets, such as plants and equipment. In previous chapters, we have seen that a company's investment decisions are critical to its value because market values are based on the expected future growth in company earnings, dividends, and distributable cash flows.

We revisit several concepts that we discussed when describing how to value bonds and shares. In particular, we emphasize that the basic techniques are similar: estimate future cash flows from the investment, determine appropriate discount rates, convert those expected future cash flows into their corresponding present values, and compare these present values with the cost of the investment. The essential difference between valuing shares and valuing projects or companies is not in the approach, but rather in the judgment necessary because of the differing quality of the inputs.

372

10.1 THE CAPITAL BUDGETING PROCESS

A **capital expenditure** is a company's investment in long-lived assets, which may be tangible assets, such as property, plants, and equipment, or intangible assets, such as research and development, copyrights, brand names, and franchise agreements. Tangible assets are hard, physical assets, whereas intangible ones are more abstract; it is easier for a company to borrow against tangible assets than against intangible ones.[1]

capital expenditure investment in long-lived assets, which may be tangible or intangible

What Is Capital Budgeting?

Long-term investment decisions determine a company's future direction and may be viewed as the most important decisions a company makes because its capital expenditures usually involve large amounts of money, and the decisions are frequently irrevocable. For example, Buckeye Partners, L.P., owns 5,400 miles of pipelines for petroleum products in the U.S. Once these pipeline assets are in place, they are largely unique to that application and have very little alternative use. It is therefore important that the decision to make capital investments is made on sound financial and economic grounds. The irrevocable and unique nature of real investments has its parallel in investments in intangible assets, where a decision to bring out a new soft drink, for example, with the attendant product development costs and marketing campaign, is also irrevocable. In this case, it is almost impossible to get back the investment costs of a failed new product launch.

The importance of capital investment decisions lies in their ability to affect the risk of the company. In some cases, the very survival of the company depends on the success of a new product produced from prior investment decisions. Apple Computer (AAPL), for example, was revived in the 2000s when it brought out the iPod, and later iTunes, the iPhone, and the iPad.[2] New products can also provide a much-needed boost to maintain competitiveness or increase market share. For instance, McDonald's (MCD) had a resurgence of sales when it introduced espresso-based coffee, McCafe, in 2009, which allows McDonald's to compete with coffee chains, such as Starbucks.

Capital budgeting refers to the process through which a company makes capital expenditure decisions:

capital budgeting process through which a company makes capital expenditure decisions by identifying investment alternatives, evaluating these alternatives, implementing the chosen investment decisions, and monitoring and evaluating the implemented decisions

---

[1] Under U.S. and International Financial Reporting Standards (IFRS), most spending to generate intangible assets, such as research and development (R&D) and advertising, is expensed rather than capitalized. Therefore, these items do not generally appear on the balance sheet as an asset. As a result, most intangible assets that appear on the balance sheet result from a company taking over another at a premium to its book value. The acquiring company allocates this premium among identifiable intangible assets, with any not otherwise allocated premium ending up in the account referred to as goodwill.

[2] See "Apple's Remarkable Comeback Story," Amanda Cantrell, *CNNMoney.com,* March 29, 2006.

We focus most of our discussion on the general framework that should be used to evaluate various investment alternatives because the remaining decisions are company specific. First, we briefly discuss the goals of this process.

Where Does Value Come From?

A company that does not invest effectively will find itself at a competitive disadvantage, which in the extreme will affect its long-term survival. In the short run, poor investment decisions will make a company less attractive than those that have better prepared themselves for the future. This will manifest itself in the market price of its debt and equity securities, which will decline and hence increase its cost of capital.

To fully understand where value comes from, we need to apply basic economic principles. Recall from economics that to earn more than a "normal" profit, a company must have some type of comparative or competitive advantage. A **normal profit** is the return on an investment that compensates the investor for explicit and implicit costs, where implicit costs include the opportunity cost of the investor's capital. **Economic profit**, on the other hand, is the return on an investment *in excess* of the normal profit. This is the essence of creating value: generating economic profits through capital investment.

A **comparative advantage** is the ability of a company to produce a product at a lower cost than its competitors. This includes the innate advantage that a company has over other companies due to access to resources, inputs, or markets. Examples of such access include ownership of oil fields, mines, chemicals, land, or production of inputs.[3]

A **competitive advantage** is any strategy or company action that reduces the competition that the company experiences. These advantages include patents, copyrights, and trademarks, which may keep competitors at bay, or at least slow down imitations of products. Another competitive advantage is economies of scale; if a particular good can produce a lower cost if the scale of production is increased, this will discourage competitors from entering the market because it would be difficult for any entrant to compete against an existing, larger producer. Still another example of a competitive advantage is when a government grants a monopoly to a company, such as a cable company or an electric utility, which then creates a barrier keeping any other potential competitors out of the market.[4,5]

Michael Porter, a professor at Harvard Business School, reframed these basic economic principles by identifying five critical factors that determine the attractiveness of an industry in terms of the ability to generate economic profit:

1. entry barriers,
2. the threat of substitutes,
3. the bargaining power of buyers,
4. the bargaining power of suppliers, and
5. rivalry among existing competitors.[6]

These are often referred to as the **five forces**. Porter argues that, after inception, companies have little immediate control over the attractiveness of their industry. This implies that industry structure is a significant input into every company's investment decisions and

normal profit return on an investment that compensates the investor with the explicit and implicit costs, where implicit costs include the opportunity cost of the investor's capital

comparative advantage innate advantage that a company has over other companies due to access to resources, inputs, or markets

competitive advantage any strategy or feature that reduces the competition that the company experiences

five forces based on the work of Michael Porter, the five critical factors that determine the profitability and, hence, attractiveness of investing an industry: entry barriers, the threat of substitutes, the bargaining power of buyers, the bargaining power of suppliers, and rivalry among existing competitors

---

[3] The idea of comparative advantage is not new. It was first discussed by economist David Ricardo in 1817 [*On the Principles of Political Economy and Taxation*, London: John Murray, 1817].

[4] For a discussion of the cable monopolies, see Clint Bollick, "Cable Television: An Unnatural Monopoly," Cato Policy Analysis, No. 34, Cato Institute, March 13, 1984.

[5] We can distinguish comparative and competitive advantages by noting that comparative advantages are static, whereas competitive advantages are created by the company and, hence, are dynamic. That is, a company could overcome the comparative advantage of a competitor with a competitive advantage. For example, suppose a company owns all oil fields, which would be a comparative advantage; another company could innovate by creating lower-cost synthetic oil that could compete against the company with the oil fields.

[6] Michael E. Porter, "The Five Competitive Forces That Shape Strategy," *Harvard Business Review*, January 2008.

profitability. However, Porter points out that a company *may* exert control over the manner in which it strives to create a competitive advantage within their industry. Obviously, these decisions are also closely related to a company's long-term investment decisions.

Michael Porter argues that companies can create competitive or comparative advantages for themselves by adopting one of the following strategies:

1. *Cost leadership: strive to be a low-cost producer.* This strategy is viable for companies that are able to take advantage of economies of scale, proprietary technology, or privileged or superior access to raw materials. Investment outlays should be made in accordance with a company's potential advantage. For example, if economies of scale or technological advantages are possible, companies should invest in a manner that will enable them to exploit these opportunities.

2. *Differentiation: offer "differentiated" products.* Companies may provide products that are differentiated from others in several ways. The most obvious is to have a product that is itself unique by virtue of its physical or technological characteristics. However, companies may also differentiate their products by providing customers with unique delivery alternatives or by establishing a marketing approach that distinguishes their products from those of their potential competitors.

Either of these strategies can be applied with a broad, industrywide focus, or with a narrow, industry-segment focus, and both have their corollary in capital investment decisions. As we will discuss, cost leadership usually follows from replacement decisions, when companies are constantly striving to use the latest technology to lower the costs of production. Product differentiation usually follows from new product development decisions, such as the launch of a new soft drink or a new model of a car.

SUMMARIZING: STRATEGIES FOR COMPETITIVE AND COMPARATIVE ADVANTAGES

Basic economic principles, echoed by Michael Porter, suggest that it is difficult to sustain a competitive advantage once one has been created. This is particularly true in industries where competition is heated or there are low barriers to entry. Therefore, companies must continually plan (and invest) strategically. This brings up the question: What is the relationship between corporate strategy and the capital investment decision?

A Perspective on Capital Budgeting Decision Making

It is a basic premise of finance that when a senior executive justifies a project on nonfinancial grounds, either the analysis is not rigorous enough, with the advantages not fully developed, or it is a pet project and should not be pursued. Every project is amenable to the analytical techniques that we discuss later—the only difference is that the inputs are more qualitative the more strategic the analysis. However, this does bring up a basic distinction—the difference between bottom-up and top-down analysis.

Bottom-up analysis is based on the idea that a company is simply a set or portfolio of capital investment decisions. Equipment replacement is a typical bottom-up analysis, in which an engineer estimates the savings in terms of labor hours, power, material costs, and so on, from replacing one piece of equipment with another. A financial analyst then translates these savings into financial parameters to see whether the replacement savings are worth the cost of the equipment. However, at no point does either the engineer or the financial analyst consider whether the company should continue in this business. An analogy might be the engineer on the *Titanic* deciding to replace some equipment just after the ship struck the iceberg! In isolation, it might be a good decision, but obviously it is irrelevant on a larger scale.

bottom-up analysis investment strategy in which capital investment decisions are considered in isolation, without regard for whether the company should continue in this business or for general industry and economic trends

top-down analysis
investment strategy that
focuses on strategic
decisions, such as which
industries or products
the company should be
involved in, looking at the
overall economic picture

In contrast, **top-down analysis** focuses on the strategic decisions about which industries or products the company should be involved in. It is the basic decision of whether Ford should produce passenger cars or trucks, rather than of which passenger cars should be developed. The auto industry has undergone drastic changes that include splitting off divisions and product lines, through closures, sale, or spin-offs. For example, shortly before declaring bankruptcy in June 2009, General Motors discontinued its Pontiac brand.

Top-down: Start with strategy and find profitable investments that fit this strategy

Bottom-up: Start with the most profitable, potential investments

In looking at bottom-up versus top-down analysis, the capital budgeting framework is identical. What is different is the quality of the estimates. In replacement decisions, it may be easier to specify the degree of risk because the analyst can estimate the cost savings with more clearly defined probabilities. It may be possible, for example, to estimate that that there is a 30 percent chance of saving $5 million and a 70 percent chance of saving $100 million per year. In this way, replacement decisions are similar to the evaluation of equity investments for which there is a long price history, and means, variances, and so on can be estimated to say there is a 50 percent chance of a share going up 15 percent in price and a 50 percent chance of it going down 5 percent.

In contrast, top-down or strategic decisions often involve a situation of uncertainty, in which it is almost impossible to place probabilities on the possible outcomes.[7] In these situations, it is important for the analysis to involve different scenarios, so that the company can better assess the risk of a project.[8] This flexibility in top-down decision making is an application of the theory of option pricing to capital investment decisions, **real option valuation (ROV)**. ROV, in a nutshell, is the valuation of a capital investment considering the value of all the options that the investment provides, such as the option to expand, abandon, or delay.[9] ROV is very difficult to implement, but it is important in financial management because many capital investment decisions involve one or more of these options.

real option valuation (ROV) valuation of a capital investment considering the value of all the options that the investment provides, such as the option to expand, abandon, or wait

Discounted Cash Flow and Maximizing Owners' Wealth

The goal of the company should be to maximize owners' wealth, and many techniques are available for making capital investment decisions that are consistent with this over-riding objective. These techniques are **discounted cash flow (DCF)** methodologies, and as their name suggests, they are the capital investment analogues to the DCF valuation techniques discussed earlier. DCF valuation involves estimating future cash flows and comparing their discounted values with investment outlays required today. In this way, they are technically identical to the approaches used to evaluate bonds and stock.

discounted cash flow (DCF) determining a value today by estimating future cash flows and comparing their discounted values with the cash outlay today

---

[7] This distinction between risk and uncertainty is attributed to Frank Knight, *Risk, Uncertainty, and Profit* (Boston: Hart Schaffner & Marx; Houghton Mifflin Co., 1921).

[8] We discuss scenario analysis in Chapter 11.

[9] We discuss real options and real options valuation in Appendix 11B.

The only practical difference is that whereas the cash flows are fixed in valuing bonds and shares in the sense that the analyst cannot change them, in making capital investment decisions the analyst can change the underling cash flows by changing the structure of the project. For example, the company can decide to defer a project for a year or, after the analysis, decide to change the form of a product. If it is a new car development, for example, some parts may become optional extras to hit a target price point, or a substitute sweetener may be used in a new soft drink. As a result, the application of DCF valuation techniques in capital investment decisions is, by nature, more of an iterative process than a one-time decision.

In this chapter, we focus on the application of the approaches themselves and discuss their relative advantages, assuming that we already know the expected cash flows. In this way we can focus on the capital budgeting framework and techniques that we may use to evaluate project cash flows.[10]

---

1. Contrast top-down versus bottom-up analysis.

2. In what ways are discounted cash flow methods used in capital investment analysis similar to methods for valuing common shares, and in what ways are they different?

10.2 EVALUATING INVESTMENT PROJECTS

A financial manager can use a number of approaches to evaluate an investment. These approaches include measures of an investment's contribution to the company's value, measures of the return on the investment, and measures of the time it takes to recover the original investment.

The Net Present Value Method

The **net present value (NPV)** of an investment is the estimated value added of a project, which we calculate as the sum of the present value of all future after-tax incremental cash flows generated by an initial cash outlay, less the present value of the investment outlays. In other words, the NPV is the present value of the expected cash flows net of the costs needed to generate them. We depict this process graphically in Figure 10-1, where, for simplicity, there is a single outlay at time zero, each cash flow is represented by CF and a subscript indicating the period end, and the final cash flow occurs at the end of period n.[11] Each of these cash flows are incremental cash flow related to a project. Put another way, these cash flows represent how a business entity's cash flows change if they were to take on this project.[12]

net present value (NPV) added value from a capital project; sum of the present value of all future cash flows generated by an initial cash outlay, less the present value of the investment outlays

---

[10] We discuss the estimation of cash flows in detail in Chapter 11.

[11] We've simplified the project's cash flows to assume that all the project's cash outflows occur immediately (today, which we designate as time 0). If the project's cash outflows occur over time, we would discount these to the present.

[12] We discuss the calculation of cash flows in Chapter 11. Though covered in this later chapter, the basic idea is that this cash flow includes any relevant cash flow, including taxes.

where

CF_t = the estimated cash flow at time t; and
CF_0 = the initial cash outlay, which is a negative cash flow.

FIGURE 10-1 The Cash Flow Pattern for a Traditional Capital Expenditure

We use the project's cost of capital, which is the cost of capital that reflects the riskiness of the project's cash flows: the greater the riskiness of a project's future cash flows, the greater the cost of capital. We represent the NPV of an n-year project as Equation 10-1:

$$NPV = \frac{CF_0}{(1+i)^0} + \frac{CF_1}{(1+i)^1} + \frac{CF_2}{(1+i)^2} + \frac{CF_3}{(1+i)^3} + \cdots + \frac{CF_n}{(1+i)^n} \qquad (10\text{-}1)$$

where CF_t is the estimated incremental cash flow at time t;
        CF_0 is the initial incremental cash outlay; and
        i is the project's cost of capital.

Therefore, the project's cost of capital is the discount rate applied to the project's cash flows. We can rewrite the formula for the NPV as simply:

$$NPV = \sum_{t=0}^{n} \frac{CF_t}{(1+i)^t} \qquad (10\text{-}2)$$

risk-adjusted discount rate discount rate that reflects the overall riskiness of the project

We have discussed previously that the market value of any company in an efficient market is the present value of its expected incremental cash flows, discounted at an appropriate **risk-adjusted discount rate**, which is based on the overall riskiness of the project. In other words, the risk-adjusted discount rate is the project's cost of capital. Therefore, we can say that projects that have a positive net present value add value to the company and should be accepted: A positive NPV implies that the present value of the expected future cash flows exceeds the cash outlay today—that is, it increases the value of the company. Because the company's creditors have a fixed claim on the company's income, regardless of the value of the project, this NPV trickles down to the shareholders and increases the market value of the company's common shares. In this way, accepting positive NPV projects maximizes the company's market value and creates shareholder value. In contrast, accepting negative NPV projects destroys company value and should be rejected because, by definition, the destruction of shareholder value is not in the best interest of the shareholders.

We would expect positive NPVs to arise only in situations in which a company has a competitive advantage. Because of the competitive nature of today's business environment, we would not expect to see an abundance of such opportunities, nor would we expect them to persist for very long. Therefore, projects that produce an NPV of $0 will be the norm where companies operate in competitive markets. These projects should be accepted because they provide the appropriate return required to compensate for the financing costs (and risks) associated with the investment.

Let's consider an example. Suppose the Duke Company has an investment that requires a $12 million cash outlay today. It estimates that the expected incremental cash flows associated with this investment are $5 million at the end of years 1 and 2 and $8 million at the end of year 3. Using a 15 percent discount rate, what is this project's NPV? One way to approach this is that we could lay out all the cash flows in a timeline and then discount each cash flow back to the present, summing the present values. Using 0 to indicate today and then laying out the end-of-year cash flows:

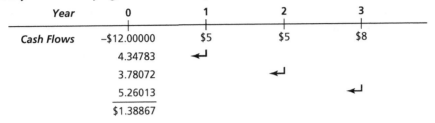

Year	0	1	2	3
Cash Flows	−$12.00000	$5	$5	$8
	4.34783			
	3.78072			
	5.26013			
	$1.38867			

Using Equation [10-2]:

$$NPV = CF_0 + \frac{CF_1}{(1 + i)^1} + \frac{CF_2}{(1 + i)^2} + \frac{CF_3}{(1 + i)^3}$$

$$NPV = \left[\frac{-\$12}{(1 + 0.15)^0} \frac{\$5}{(1 + 0.15)^1} + \frac{\$5}{(1 + 0.15)^2} + \frac{\$8}{(1 + 0.15)^3}\right]$$

$$NPV = -\$12 + 4.34783 + 3.78072 + 5.26013$$

$$NPV = \$1.38867 \text{ million}$$

Therefore, the Duke Company should accept this project because it has a positive NPV and would increase company value by $1.38867 million.

CALCULATOR TOOLS: SOLVE FOR THE NPV

Consider the set of cash flow from the Duke Company example. The calculator program requires that you enter the cash flows in sequence.

TI BA II Plus	HP10B	HP12C	TI-83/84
CF 2nd CLR WORK	CLEAR ALL	f REG	{5,5,8}
−12 Enter ↓	+/− 12 CF	12 CHS CF_0	STO L1
5 Enter ↓ ↓	5 CF	5 CF_j	Apps Finance 7
5 Enter ↓ ↓	5 CF	5 CF_j	NPV(.15, −12, L1)
8 Enter ↓	8 CF	8 CF_j	ENTER
NPV 15 Enter ↓	15 I/YR	15 i	
CPT	NPV	f NPV	

SPREADSHEET APPLICATIONS: SOLVE FOR THE NPV

Consider the set of cash flow from the Duke Company example. The NPV function in a spreadsheet requires you to enter the cash flows in order, starting with the *first* year's cash flow and then subtracting the initial cash outlay, which is $12 million in this example. You can simply type in:

$$= NPV(0.15, 5, 5, 8) - 12$$

or you can include the data in cells and use cell-referencing:

	A
1	.15
2	−12
3	5
4	5
5	8
6	=NPV(A1,A3:A5)+A2

EXAMPLE 10.1

Calculating the NPV

PROBLEM

Consider an investment that requires an outlay of $5 million initially, with expected cash flows of $1 million, $0, and $5 million, respectively, for the following 3 years.

a. What is the net present value of this investment if the discount rate is 5 percent?

b. What is the net present value of this investment if the discount rate is 8 percent?

Solution

a. NPV = −$5 + 0.95238 + 4.31919 = $0.27157 million
b. NPV = −$5 + 0.92593 + 3.96916 = −$0.10491 million

The Internal Rate of Return

The **internal rate of return (IRR)** is the discount rate that makes the NPV equal to zero for a given set of cash flows.[13] This implies that it is the discount rate that sets the present value of future cash flows equal to the initial cash outlay. Or, in other words, the NPV is equal to zero. In this way, it is a rate of return that is internal to this particular set of cash flows; for this reason, we often refer to it as the economic rate of return of a given project. Consider Equation 10-1 once again:

$$\text{NPV} = \frac{CF_0}{(1 + IRR)^0} + \frac{CF_1}{(1 + IRR)^1} + \frac{CF_2}{(1 + IRR)^2} + \frac{CF_3}{(1 + IRR)^3} + \cdots + \frac{CF_n}{(1 + IRR)^n}$$

Setting the NPV to zero and simplifying,

$$0 = \frac{\sum_{t=0}^{n} CF_t}{(1 + IRR)^t} \qquad (10\text{-}3)$$

The general rule for IRR evaluation criteria is that a company should accept a project whenever the IRR is greater than the appropriate risk-adjusted discount rate, which is the project's cost of capital. Just like NPV, the IRR represents a discounted cash flow approach; in general, it will lead to the same accept/reject decisions as NPV. The project's cost of capital, when used in conjunction with the IRR, becomes a **hurdle rate**; the IRR must exceed the project's cost of capital or hurdle to be acceptable. In other words, the project's cost of capital is the minimum acceptable return on the project.

hurdle rate minimum acceptable return on an investment project

An issue with the IRR is that you cannot solve directly for the IRR.[14] There is no finite solution for the IRR when solving Equation 10-3; this means that solving for the IRR requires trial and error. Fortunately, financial calculators and spreadsheets make this process very manageable.

We illustrate the calculation process using the example with a $12 million outlay and end-of-year cash flows of $5, $5, and $8. The IRR is the value that solves the following expression:

$$\left[\frac{\$5}{(1 + IRR)^1} + \frac{\$5}{(1 + IRR)^2} + \frac{\$8}{(1 + IRR)^3}\right] = \$12$$

Solving by trial and error is very complicated, even for this simple three-period problem. We know from our earlier calculation that the project's NPV is positive at the discount

---

[13] The IRR is the same as the yield to maturity (YTM) for a bond that we estimated earlier. In fact, the yield to maturity is the IRR of a bond for a given purchase price.

[14] Looking at Equation 10-3, we can see this if we multiply through by $(1 + IRR)^n$; it then becomes clear that in finding the IRR, we are solving for the roots of an nth order polynomial.

rate of 15 percent. Therefore, we know that the NPV will be zero at some discount rate greater than 15 percent. Trying different discount rates, we see that the NPV changes from positive to negative between the discount rate of 21 percent and 22 percent. Therefore, we know that the IRR is between 21 percent and 22 percent:

Discount Rate	NPV
20%	$ 0.27
21%	$ 0.06
22%	$ (0.14)
23%	$ (0.33)

> NPV is $0 between 21% and 22%

This is one case for which it is worthwhile to use a financial calculator or spreadsheet—and this is only a three-period project; imagine if it were a 20-year project.

SPREADSHEET APPLICATIONS: THE IRR

We can also calculate the IRR using a calculator or spreadsheet, using the IRR function and the following data:

	A	B
1	CF_0	−30
2	CF_1	5
3	CF_2	5
4	CF_3	5

The IRR function in this case, using cell-referencing, is =IRR(B1:B4).

Notice that the IRR of 21.31 percent exceeded the company's cost of capital of 15 percent, which implies that the project increases shareholder value and should be accepted. This will always be the case when the NPV is positive, as it is in this case. In fact, this should be obvious when we look at Equations 10-1 and 10-2, because the NPV will equal zero when the IRR = i. Therefore, when IRR exceeds the project's cost of capital, the NPV will be positive because the NPV will be higher when we use a *lower* discount rate than it will when we use the *higher* discount rate (i.e., IRR). This is very intuitive: A positive NPV implies that a project earns a return (IRR) that is higher than the cost of funds. Similarly, we can say that a negative NPV implies that IRR is less than the project's cost of capital, and vice versa. We can see this in Figure 10-2, where we graph the NPV of this project on the vertical axis, against the discount rate on the horizontal axis. We refer to this illustration as the project's **net present value profile** (or **NPV profile**). The IRR is the rate at which the curve representing the NPVs crosses the horizontal axis.[15]

An issue with the IRR is that the IRR is not meaningful if there is more than one sign change in cash flows. Every time the sign of the polynomial changes (that is, the cash flows change from positive to negative or negative to positive), there is a root, so for complex cash flow streams we often find that there is more than one IRR, or more than one root.[16]

net present value profile or **NPV profile** graph of a project's net present value against the discount rate

---

[15] Another name for a graph of this relationship is the *investment profile*.

[16] As previously mentioned, this will not be true if we pick the wrong IRR when there are multiple reversals in the signs of the cash flows. This does not happen often in normal projects, but it does happen sometimes, to the surprise of analysts who forget this fact.

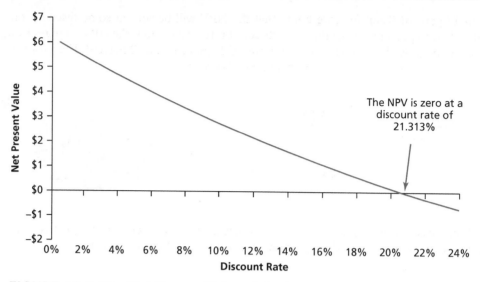

FIGURE 10-2 **The Net Present Value of the Duke Company Project for Different Discount Rates**

EXAMPLE 10.2	PROBLEM

Calculating the IRR

Consider an investment that requires an outlay of $5 million initially, with expected end-of-year cash flows of $1 million, $0, and $5 million, respectively, for the end of the following 3 years. What is the internal rate of return of this investment?

Solution

The NPV is positive when the discount rate is 5 percent, but negative when the discount rate is 8 percent. Therefore, we know that the IRR falls between 5 percent and 8 percent. Through trial and error, we find:

Discount Rate	NPV (in millions)
5%	$0.27157
6%	$0.14149
7%	$0.01607
8%	−$0.10491

Therefore, we can conclude that the IRR is between 7 percent and 8 percent. Using a financial calculator or a spreadsheet program, we find the precise IRR of 7.1308 percent.

A Comparison of NPV and IRR

We can see the relation between the NPV and the IRR using the NPV profile, such as the one we show in Figure 10-3 for two separate projects. NPV profiles depict the NPV of a project for various discount rates.

Consider the cash flows for Project A and Project B:

	End of Period Cash Flows	
Period	Project A	Project B
0	−£1,000	−£1,000
1	£500	£0
2	£500	£0
3	£500	£1,700

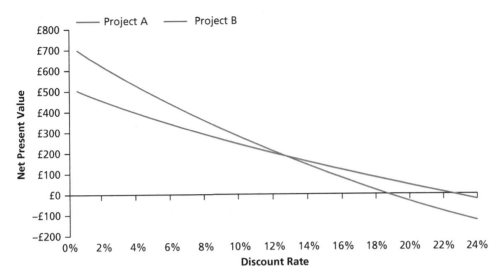

FIGURE 10-3 **NPV Profiles for Two Projects, A and B**

In Figure 10-3, we graph the NPV against the discount rate for both projects. As you can see, the NPV depends critically on the appropriate discount rate, obvious from Equation 10-2. As the discount rate increases, the NPV decreases and eventually becomes negative for higher discount rates. By definition, we know that the IRR occurs at the discount rate that makes the NPV = £0. This corresponds to the point at which the NPV curve crosses the *x*-axis in Figure 10-3. For project A, the IRR is 23.375 percent, whereas for project B, the IRR is 19.348 percent. The diagram shows that whenever the discount rate exceeds the IRR, we have a negative NPV, and whenever the discount rate is less than the IRR, we have a positive NPV. Recall that we have previously noted these relationships between NPV and IRR.

Whether or not the projects should be accepted depends on the discount rate. We can make several useful observations from Figure 10-3:

- Project A should be accepted if the **project cost of capital** is less than 23.375 percent because the NPV will be positive for these discount rates and because IRR is greater than the project cost of capital.

- If the project cost of capital is greater than 23.375 percent, Project A should be rejected, because the NPV will be negative, and IRR is less than the project's cost of capital.

- Project B should be accepted if the project's cost of capital is less than 19.348 percent, and it should be rejected if the project's cost of capital is greater than 19.348 percent.

So, if we are independently evaluating a project by using either the NPV or IRR evaluation criteria, we should arrive at the same conclusion.

In Figure 10-3 we also see that we can rank projects differently by using NPV versus using IRR. Suppose, for example, these two were **mutually exclusive projects**, meaning that a company has to decide between them and can accept only one. Because the IRR of project B is 19.348 percent, whereas the IRR of project A is 23.375 percent, project A will always appear to be superior according to the IRR approach. However, by using the NPV approach, we arrive at different rankings depending on the project's cost of capital (*i*), because in this example the NPV profiles cross over and have the same NPV at one special discount rate, which is the **crossover rate**. If *i* is greater than the crossover rate of 12.788 percent, then project A is preferable to project B because it generates a higher NPV, whereas if *i* is less than 12.788 percent, then project B is preferred. As a result, the NPV rule can rank projects differently from the IRR rule, so which one is better?

To answer this question, we have to understand why the slopes of the two NPV profiles differ: The slope reflects the change in the NPV as the discount rate changes. If a project has cash flows that are far in the future, then changes in the discount rate have a big impact on the NPV of the project. In this case project B has cash flows that are farther

project cost of capital discount rate that reflects the return suppliers of capital require considering the project's risk

mutually exclusive projects projects for which the acceptance of one precludes the acceptance of one or more of the alternative projects

crossover rate discount rate at which the net present value profiles of two projects cross away, so at high discount rates these cash flows are valued less, and the NPV falls by more than the NPV of project A. As a result, beyond the crossover point, A is preferred to B, because B's far-off cash flows are worth less, whereas at lower discount rates, the reverse happens, and B is preferred to A.

How do we determine this crossover rate? We can guesstimate from the graph, which would mean that the crossover rate is between 12 and 13 percent, or we can use this simple procedure:

1. Calculate the difference in cash flows between the projects for each period; and
2. Calculate the IRR of these differences.[17]

In the example with Project A and Project B,

	End-of-year Cash Flows		
Period	*Project A*	*Project B*	*Difference*
0	–£1,000	–£1,000	£0
1	£500	£0	£500
2	£500	£0	£500
3	£500	£1,700	–£1,200

The IRR of the differences is 12.788 percent. Therefore, the crossover rate is 12.788 percent, and this is the discount rate at which our preference changes: Below 12.788 percent, we prefer Project B; above 12.788 percent we prefer project A; at 12.788 percent, we are indifferent between the two projects because they have the same NPV.

In addition to the timing of cash flows, another source of differences between NPV and IRR is the scale factor. The internal rate of return does not consider the scale or size of the project, whereas the NPV does. Consider the example of two projects, Small and Big, each with a project cost of capital of 5 percent:

	End-of-year Cash Flow	
Year	*Small*	*Big*
0	–$10,000	–$50,000
1	$0	$0
2	$0	$0
3	$12,500	$62,500

The projects have similar timing of cash flows, but the scale is different: Big's cash flows are five times those of Small. Both projects have a positive NPV ($797.97 and $3,989.85, respectively) at the project cost of capital, and the IRR of both projects is 7.72 percent. If these projects are independent, we would choose both projects. However, if these projects are mutually exclusive, using the IRR would not be best because the IRR considers both projects to return the same 7.72 percent. Using the net present value approach, we would choose Big because it provides the greater added value.[18] The bottom line is that the IRR does not consider the scale or size of the project.

Further, the fact that the NPV decision depends on the discount rate, whereas the IRR decision does not, is very important and relates to the different reinvestment rate assumptions of the two techniques:

[17] It will not matter whether you subtract A's cash flows from B's, or vice versa—as long as you are consistent for all periods.

[18] If there is a limit to the capital budget, as we discuss later in this chapter, we would need to look at the total net present value of possible projects that fit into the budget, which may imply choosing Small or Big, depending on the budget and the profitability of the other projects under consideration.

- The NPV assumes that all cash flows are reinvested at one consistent discount rate (i.e., the cost of capital).
- The IRR assumes instead that all cash flows are reinvested at the IRR. In other words, the cash flows are reinvested in similar yielding investments.

If we remember that most projects will have low or zero NPV in a competitive market and that the discount rate reflects the opportunity cost or the all-in required return of the company's investors, it is clear that the NPV assumption is more realistic. To put it another way, if an executive estimates an IRR of, say, 30 percent because he or she finds a wonderful project, the executive is then implicitly assuming that the cash flows generated by this wonderful project can be reinvested in another similarly wonderful project. This means that the executive is assuming that he or she has many wonderful projects, which is not normally a very realistic assumption.

Issue	NPV	IRR
1. Future cash flows change sign	It still works the same for both accept/reject and ranking decisions.	Multiple IRRs may result—in this case, the IRR cannot be used for either accept/reject or ranking decisions.
2. Ranking projects	Higher NPV implies greater contribution to company wealth—it is an *absolute* measure of wealth.	The higher IRR project may have a lower NPV, and vice versa, depending on the appropriate discount rate and the size of the project.[19]
3. Reinvestment rate assumed for future cash flows received	Assumes all future cash flows are reinvested at the discount rate.	Assumes cash flows from each project are reinvested at that project's IRR.

SUMMARIZING: NPV VERSUS IRR

CALCULATOR TOOLS: SOLVE FOR THE IRR

Consider a project that has a $5 million cash outlay today, but is expected to produce end-of-year cash flows of $4, $1, and $2 in the succeeding years. What is the internal rate of return for this project? Answer: 22.808%

TI BA II Plus	HP10B	HP12C	TI 83/84
CF 2nd CLR WORK	CLEAR ALL	f REG	{4,1,2}
−5 Enter ↓	+/− 5 CF	5 CHS CF$_0$	STO L1
4 Enter ↓ ↓	4 CF	4 CF$_j$	Apps Finance IRR
1 Enter ↓ ↓	1 CF	1 CF$_j$	IRR(−5, L1)
1 Enter ↓ ↓	2 CF	2 CF$_j$	ENTER
IRR ↓	IRR	f IRR	
CPT			

[19] For example, would analysts prefer an IRR of 100 percent on $1,000 or 20 percent on $1 million?

SPREADSHEET APPLICATIONS: SOLVE FOR THE IRR

	A	B
1	0	−5
2	1	4
3	2	1
4	3	2
5	IRR	=IRR(B1:B4)

Answer: 22.808%

The Modified Internal Rate of Return

The assumption built into the internal rate of return mathematics that all cash inflows are reinvested at the internal rate of return may be too aggressive an assumption to make. We can modify this assumption by calculating the return on the project with a more realistic assumption regarding the reinvestment of cash inflows. The result is the **modified internal rate of return (MIRR)**. The accept/reject criteria for the MIRR is similar to that of the IRR: If a project has a MIRR greater than its cost of capital, it is acceptable; if a project has a MIRR less than its cost of capital, it is not acceptable.

Let's start with a Project X that has a project cost of capital of 10 percent and the following cash flows:

Year	End-of-year Cash Flow
0	−$10,000
1	4,200
2	4,200
3	4,200

The IRR of Project X is 12.51 percent, and the NPV is $444.78. To illustrate the role of reinvestment, let's assume that the company has no other projects in which to reinvest any of these cash flows. We calculate the return on Project X in this situation by comparing the investment of $10,000 with what is available at the end of the project. If each cash flow that comes in is deposited in an account that earns no interest, the company will have $12,600 at the end of 3 years. Therefore,

PV = $10,000
FV = $12,600
N = 3
Solve for $i \rightarrow i = 8.01\%$

Given no other use of the cash, the company has a return, which is the MIRR, of 8.01 percent. Under these circumstances, Project X is not acceptable.

Now let's assume that the company has other investment opportunities available that earn 5 percent. We can represent this in a diagram, indicating the cash flows and how they "grow" when reinvested at 5 percent:

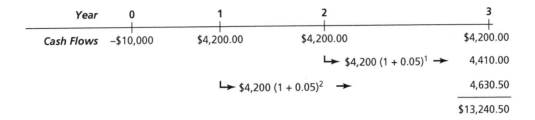

In table form, we have:

Year	End-of-year Cash Flow	Future Value of Reinvested Cash Flows, End of Period 3
0	–$10,000.00	
1	$4,200.00	$4,630.50
2	$4,200.00	4,410.00
3	$4,200.00	4,200.00
Total		$13,240.50

The future value of the reinvested cash flows, FV, is $13,240.50, and therefore the MIRR is 9.81 percent:

PV = $10,000

FV = $13,240.50

N = 3

Solve for $i \rightarrow i = 9.81\%$

Again, the project is not acceptable because the return on the project is less than the project's cost of capital.

A common assumption for reinvestment opportunities is to use the company's cost of capital, which is the return on the typical or average project of the company. The reasoning is simple: If the company has cash flows from a project, they are most likely reinvested in a typical project for the company. If the company's cost of capital is, say, 9 percent, the MIRR becomes 11.25 percent.[20] In this case, the project is acceptable because the MIRR of 11.25 percent exceeds the project's cost of capital of 10 percent.

The MIRR is sensitive to the reinvestment assumption, as we show in Figure 10-4, where we graph the MIRR against the reinvestment rate for Project X; the better the reinvestment opportunities, the better the return on the project, as measured by MIRR.[21]

Payback Period and Discounted Payback Period

Companies often use a measure of time to screen or evaluate projects. Conceptually and mathematically easier than the net present value, the internal rate of return, and the modified internal rate of return, the **payback period** is the number of years required to fully

payback period number of years required to fully recover the initial cash outlay associated with a capital expenditure

---

[20] If you are checking this calculation, the future value of the cash flows, considering reinvestment at 9 percent, is $13,768.02.

[21] Using Microsoft's Excel Solver function, we can solve for the reinvestment rate at which the MIRR is equal to the project's cost of capital. We do this by setting the goal of the MIRR equal to 10 percent and then solve for the reinvestment rate that is applied against the project's cash inflows. For Project X, the project is acceptable as long as the return on reinvested cash flows is equal to or greater than 5.5329 percent.

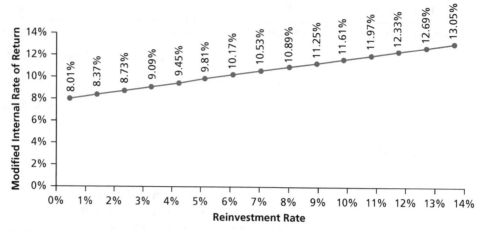

FIGURE 10-4 **Modified Internal Rate of Return for Project X**

EXAMPLE 10.3

The Modified Internal Rate of Return

PROBLEM

Consider a project with the following cash flows:

Year	End-of-year Cash Flow
0	–$1,000.00
1	$500.00
2	$0.00
3	$800.00

If the project's cost of capital is 11 percent and the reinvestment rate for its cash flows is 9 percent, is this project acceptable based on the modified internal rate of return?

Solution

Year	Future Value of Reinvested Cash Flows, End of Period 3
1	$594.05
2	0.00
3	800.00
	$1,394.05

$PV = \$1,000$

$FV = \$1,394.05$

$N = 3$

Solve for $i \rightarrow i = 11.71$ percent.

Therefore, the project is acceptable because the MIRR exceeds the project's cost of capital of 11 percent.

---

recover the initial cash outlay associated with the capital expenditure. Shorter payback periods are better, and usually this decision criterion is implemented by choosing a cutoff date and rejecting projects whose payback period is longer than the cutoff period.

SPREADSHEET APPLICATIONS: THE MIRR

You can calculate the modified internal rate of return using the built-in function, MIRR. The function has three arguments:

1. the cells indicating the set of cash flows,
2. the financing rate (that is, the project's cost of capital), and
3. the reinvestment rate.

Consider the example of

	A	B
	Year	End-of-year Cash Flow
1		
2	0	–$1,000.00
3	1	$200.00
4	2	$300.00
5	3	$400.00
6	4	$500.00

Suppose the project's cost of capital is 10 percent, but the reinvestment rate is 5 percent. You calculate the MIRR using:

=MIRR(B2:B6,0.1,0.05)

to arrive at the MIRR of 10.34 percent.

What is the payback period for our example with an outlay of $12 million and subsequent cash inflows of $5, $5, and $8 million, respectively? We determine this by calculating the cumulative cash flows over time:

Year	End-of-year Cash Flow	Cumulative, Recovered Cash Flows
1	$5	$5
2	$5	$10
3	$8	$18

If the cash flows are received evenly throughout the year, the payback period is 2 + (2/8) = 2.25 years.[22] With a $12 million cash outlay, $10 million is recovered in 2 years, and then the additional $2,000 is recovered one-quarter of the way through the 3rd year, assuming that the cash flows are evenly spaced throughout the year.

The payback period provides a useful intuitive measure of how long it takes to recover an investment, and it is sometimes used as an informal measure of project risk, especially for short-lived projects. This is because in some sense the quicker a company recovers its investment outlay, the less risky the project. However, the payback period has some important drawbacks. In particular, it disregards the time and risk value of money because it treats a dollar of cash flow received in year 3 the same as those received

---

[22] If the cash flows are period-end cash flows, the payback period is a full 3 years because it is not until the third period, when cash flows are received, that the initial outlay of $12 million is recovered.

EXAMPLE 10.4

Calculating the Payback Period

PROBLEM

Consider an investment that requires an outlay of $5 million initially, with expected end-of-year cash flows of $1 million, $0, and $5 million, respectively, for the following 3 years. What is the payback period on this investment?

Solution

Year	End-of-year Cash Flow (in millions)	Cumulative Cash Flows Recovered (in millions)
1	$1	$1
2	$0	$1
3	$5	$6

If the cash flows are received evenly throughout the year, the payback period is 3 years.[23]

in year 1, and so on. In addition, the payback period does not account for the cash flows received after the cutoff date, which could be substantial for some long-lived projects. Finally, the choice of the cutoff date is somewhat arbitrary and may vary from one company to the next.

discounted payback period number of years required to fully recover the initial cash outlay associated with a capital expenditure, in terms of discounted cash flows

The **discounted payback period** alleviates the first shortcoming of the payback period by accounting for the time value of money. It is defined as the number of years required to fully recover the initial cash outlay in terms of discounted cash flows. Shorter periods are better, and projects with discounted payback periods before the cutoff date will be accepted. Unfortunately, just as was the case for the payback period criterion, the discounted payback period ignores cash flows beyond the cutoff date, and the cutoff date is somewhat arbitrary.

What is the discounted payback period for our example with an outlay of $12 million and subsequent end-of-year cash inflows of $5, $5, and $8 million, respectively, if the discount rate is 15 percent? We determine this by calculating the cumulative discounted cash flows over time:

Year	End-of-year Cash Flow (in millions)	Calculation	Accumulated Discounted Cash Flows (in millions)
1	$5	$5 \div 1.15 =$	$4.34783
2	$5	$4.3473 + [\$5 \div (1.15)^2] =$	$8.12854
3	$8	$8.12854 + [\$8 \div (1.15)^3] =$	$13.38867 ← $12 million recovered

The discounted payback period is 3 years.

The discounted payback period is either the same or longer than for the simple payback period; the future cash flows are worth less because they have been discounted for time and risk. If a company is going to use discounting, it might as well discount all the future cash flows and calculate the NPV. For this reason, the discounted payback period is a sort of compromise between the payback period and the NPV.

[23] If the cash flows are period-end cash flows, the payback period is a full 3 years because it is not until the third period, when cash flows are received, that the initial outlay of $5 million is recovered.

PROBLEM

Consider an investment that requires an outlay of $5 million initially, with expected end-of-year cash flows of $1 million, $0, and $5 million, respectively, for the following 3 years. What is the discounted payback period on this investment if the discount rate is 5 percent?

EXAMPLE 10.5

Calculating the Discounted Payback Period

Solution

Year	End-of-year Cash Flow (in millions)	Accumulated Discounted Cash Flow
1	$1	$0.95238
2	$0	$0.95238
3	$5	$5.27157

The discounted payback period is 3 years.

The Profitability Index

The **profitability index (PI)** is another DCF approach used to evaluate capital expenditure decisions. Like the IRR, the PI is a relative measure of project attractiveness. It is defined as the ratio of a project's discounted net incremental after-tax cash inflows divided by the discounted cash outflows, which is usually the initial after-tax cash outlay. We calculate the PI as:

profitability index (PI) discounted cash flow approach used to evaluate capital expenditure decisions; the ratio of a project's discounted net incremental cash inflows over the discounted cash outflows

$$PI = \frac{PV(\text{cash inflows})}{PV(\text{cash outflows})} \qquad (10\text{-}4)$$

It should be obvious from Equation 10-4 that projects with ratios greater than 1 should be accepted because, by definition, they have positive NPVs, whereas projects with ratios less than 1 should be rejected. It is also obvious that larger ratios are favored because their NPVs are higher. The discount rate to be used is the same as the one used for calculating the NPV, and it is usually the project's cost of capital. Therefore, we observe the following relationship between NPV and PI:

If NPV > 0 then PI > 1
If NPV < 0 then PI < 0

What is the profitability index for our example with an outlay of $12 million and subsequent end-of-year cash inflows of $5, $5, and $8 million, respectively, if the discount rate is 15 percent?

Present value of cash inflows = $4.34783 + 3.78072 + 5.26013 = $13.38867 million
Present value of cash outflows = $12 million

and therefore:

PI = $13.38867 million ÷ 12 million = 1.11572 million

We show the relation between the PI and the NPV in Figure 10-5, with the NPV on the left vertical axis and the PI on the right vertical axis. You'll notice that when the NPV is negative, the PI is less than 1.0.

As discussed earlier, the PI produces the same accept/reject decisions as do the NPV and the IRR approaches in the case of independent projects. In addition, the PI does not suffer from two of the weaknesses of the IRR approach because it uses one consistent and reasonable discount rate and because it works even when future cash flows change signs.

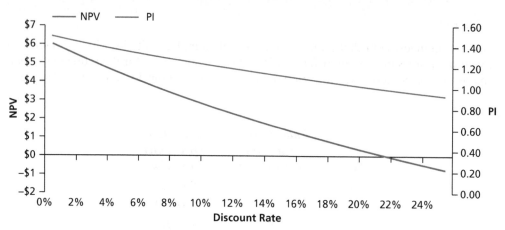

FIGURE 10-5   **NPV and PI for the Duke Company Project**

EXAMPLE 10.6	PROBLEM

Calculating the PI

Consider an investment that requires an outlay of $5 million initially, with expected end-of-year cash flows of $1 million, $0, and $5 million, respectively, for the following 3 years. What is the profitability index on this investment if the discount rate is 5 percent?

Solution

$$PI = \frac{PV(\text{cash inflows})}{PV(\text{cash outflows})} = \frac{\frac{\$1}{(1.05)^1} + \frac{\$5}{(1.05)^3}}{\$5} = \frac{\$5.27157}{\$5} = 1.0543$$

Therefore, the project should be accepted because the PI > 1.

Like the IRR, the PI is attractive because it can be expressed as a percentage, so a PI of 1.116 could be restated as +11.6 percent.

One weakness that the PI measure shares with IRR is that it is a relative measure and not an absolute measure of wealth, like NPV. Although it is useful as a starting point for ranking projects when some projects must be rejected, final decisions should be based on which projects maximize the total NPV for the company.[24] In this case, the PI is often used when companies are capital constrained, as we discuss later.

A Comprehensive Example

Let's review the different methods of evaluating capital projects by applying these methods to another example. Consider two projects:

	End-of-year Cash Flows (in millions)	
Year	Project M	Project N
2011	–$100	–$100
2012	$0	$55
2013	$0	$55
2014	$0	$55
2015	$240	$55

---

[24] We will elaborate on this point later in this chapter, when we discuss capital rationing.

Suppose the appropriate cost of capital for each project is 8 percent. What is each project's:

- net present value?
- internal rate of return?
- profitability index?
- payback period?
- discounted payback period?

We can discount each cash flow and then calculate the net present value:

	Present Value of Cash Flows (in millions)	
	Project M	Project N
1	$0.00	$50.93
2	0.00	$47.15
3	0.00	$43.66
4	$176.41	$40.43
Present value of inflows	$176.41	$182.17
Present value of outflows	−100.00	−100.00
Net present value	$76.41	$82.17

The net present value of both projects is positive; in other words, both projects would enhance the company's value. We could also use a calculator or a spreadsheet to calculate the net present value:

CALCULATOR TOOLS: THE NPV

Project M			Project N		
TI BA II Plus	HP10B	TI 83/84	TI BA II Plus	HP10B	TI 83/84[25]
CF 2nd CLR	CLEAR ALL	{0,0,0,240}	CF 2nd CLR	CLEAR ALL	{55,55,55,55}
WORK	+/− 100 CF	STO L1	WORK	+/− 100 CF	STO L2
−100 Enter ↓	0 CF	Apps Finance 7	−100 Enter ↓	55 CF	Apps Finance 7
0 Enter ↓ ↓	0 CF	NPV(8, −100, L1)	55 Enter ↓ ↓	55 CF	NPV(8, −100, L2)
0 Enter ↓ ↓	0 CF	ENTER	55 Enter ↓ ↓	55 CF	ENTER
0 Enter ↓ ↓	240 CF		55 Enter ↓ ↓	55 CF	
240 Enter ↓ ↓	8 I/YR		NPV 8 Enter ↓	8 I/YR	
NPV 8 Enter ↓	NPV		CPT	NPV	
CPT					

The internal rate of return is the rate that equates the present value of the future cash flows with the $100 million investment. Because the net present value of both projects is positive using a discount rate of 8 percent, we know that the internal rate of return of each project is greater than 8 percent. Using a calculator or a spreadsheet, we find the internal rates of return of 24.467 percent and 41.140 percent for Project M and Project N, respectively.

[25] We can use any of the storage locations for the array (L1, L2, etc.). By storing each project's cash flows in a different stored array, we can then use this same array (without having to retype it) when we calculate the IRR for each.

SPREADSHEET APPLICATIONS: THE NPV

	A	B	C
1	**Year**	**Project M**	**Project N**
2	2011	–$100	–$100
3	2012	$0	$55
4	2013	$0	$55
5	2014	$0	$55
6	2015	$240	$55
7			
8	NPV	=NPV(0.08,B3:B6)+B2	=NPV(0.08,C3:C6)+C2

CALCULATOR TOOLS: THE IRR

	Project M				**Project N**	
TI BA II Plus	*HP10B*	*TI 83/84*		*TI BA II Plus*	*HP10B*	*TI 83/84*
CF 2nd CLR	CLEAR ALL	{0,0,0,240}		CF 2nd CLR	CLEAR ALL	{55,55,55,55}
WORK	+/– 100 CF	STO L1		WORK	+/– 100 CF	STO L2
–100 Enter ↓	0 CF	Apps Finance 8		–100 Enter ↓	55 CF	Apps Finance 8
0 Enter ↓ ↓	0 CF	IRR(–100, L1)		55 Enter ↓ ↓	55 CF	IRR(–100, L2)
0 Enter ↓ ↓	0 CF	ENTER		55 Enter ↓ ↓	55 CF	ENTER
0 Enter ↓ ↓	240 CF			55 Enter ↓ ↓	IRR	
240 Enter ↓ ↓	IRR			IRR Enter ↓		
IRR Enter ↓				CPT		
CPT						

SPREADSHEET APPLICATIONS: THE IRR

	A	B	C
1	**Year**	**Project M**	**Project N**
2	2011	–$100	–$100
3	2012	$0	$55
4	2013	$0	$55
5	2014	$0	$55
6	2015	$240	$55
7			
8	IRR	=IRR(B2:B6)	=IRR(C2:C6)

The profitability index for both is the ratio of the present value of the cash inflows to the $100 million investment. Therefore:

$$\text{Profitability index of Project M} = \frac{\$176.41 \text{ million}}{\$100 \text{ million}} = 1.7641$$

$$\text{Profitability index of Project N} = \frac{\$182.17 \text{ million}}{\$100 \text{ million}} = 1.8217$$

The payback period for Project M is 4 years because there are no cash flows until the 4th year, and that cash flow is sufficient to "pay back" the $100 investment. The payback period for Project N is 2 periods: At the end of the first period, there are $55 million of cash flows, whereas at the end of the second period, the project produces a total of $55 + 55 = $110 cash flows.

We use the discounted cash flows to determine the discounted payback period:

	Discounted Cash Flows (in millions)		Accumulated Discounted Cash Flows (in millions)	
Year	Project M	Project N	Project M	Project N
2012	$0.00	$50.93	$0.00	$50.93
2013	$0.00	$47.15	$0.00	$98.08
2014	$0.00	$43.66	$0.00	$141.74
2015	$176.41	$40.43	$176.41	$182.17

Project M pays back by the end of 2015, so its discounted payback period is 4 years. Project N, on the other hand, does not accumulate $100 million of cash flows until the 3rd year, so its discounted payback period is 3 years.[26]

We can see the comparison between the two projects by graphing the projects' net present value profiles, as we show in Figure 10-6. The crossover discount rate, the discount rate at which our decision changes between projects, is 5.83 percent. If the discount rate is below 5.83 percent, the best project is Project M; if the discount rate is above 5.83 percent, the best project is Project N.

Summarizing,

Method	Project M	Project N
Net present value (in millions)	$76.41	$82.17
Internal rate of return	24.461%	41.140%
Profitability index	1.764	1.822
Payback period	4 years	2 years
Discounted payback period	4 years	3 years

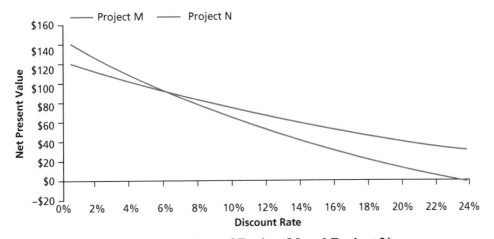

FIGURE 10-6 **The NPV Profiles of Project M and Project N**

[26] If the cash flows occur evenly throughout each year, we would calculate a fractional payback period. However, because we have assumed end-of-period cash flows for the net present value, internal rate of return, and profitability index, we would have a payback period in whole years.

Based on the net present values and the internal rates of return, both projects are acceptable. If the company must choose between these projects, Project N is preferred because it would add more value to the company when compared to Project M.

What Methods Do Companies Really Use?

John Graham and Campbell Harvey surveyed the chief financial officers (CFOs) of major U.S. companies on how they conducted their capital budgeting.[27] We report their basic results in Figure 10-7. What is clear is that despite the limitations of the IRR method, it is very widely used in practice and just nudges out the NPV as the most important criterion. This is because, in most cases, the IRR gives the "correct" accept/reject decision, and most of the criticisms of the IRR do not often appear in practical applications.

More important, the IRR holds intuitive appeal because it provides a rate of return on particular investment projects that can be compared with the company's financing costs. However, as we pointed out earlier, using this approach can cause problems for the analyst who is unaware of its shortcomings.[28]

GLOBAL PERSPECTIVE | Factoring in Political Risk

Two researchers, Martin Holmen and Bengt Pramborg, surveyed companies regarding the capital budgeting techniques they use when they are making investments in foreign countries.* Investments in foreign countries expose the investor to political risk, which is the risk a company faces that a change in political climate may involve losses (such as expropriation).

They found that in cases in which there is substantial political risk, companies tend to use a method such as the payback period; in cases in which there is little political risk, companies tend to use the net present value method.

* Martin Holmen and Bengt Pramborg, "Capital Budgeting and Political Risk: Empirical Evidence," *Journal of International Financial Management and Accounting*, 20, Issue 2 (Summer 2009): 105–134.

FIGURE 10-7 **Evaluation Criteria Used by Companies**
Source: *Data from Table 2 of John R. Graham and Campbell R. Harvey, "The Theory and Practice of Corporate Finance: Evidence from the Field,"* Journal of Financial Economics, *60 (2001): 187–243.*

[27] John R. Graham and Campbell R. Harvey, "The Theory and Practice of Corporate Finance: Evidence from the Field," *Journal of Financial Economics*, 60 (2001): 187–243.

[28] We have sometimes been approached by former students when they have problems with their analysis. Often, these problems occur because they have forgotten the problems with the use of the IRR.

Concept Review Questions

1. What discount rate do we use to determine the NPV of a project, and why?

2. What are the reinvestment rate assumptions underlying NPV and IRR?

3. What is the crossover rate?

4. Is the PI rule consistent with the NPV rule?

10.3 SPECIAL ISSUES

Independent and Interdependent Projects

Two or more **independent projects** have no relationship with one another. A company's decision to accept one project (e.g., purchase a new computerized accounting system) has no impact on the company's decision to accept another project that is independent of the first one (e.g., replace an aging piece of machinery that is used in the production process). As long as there are no capital spending restrictions, the decision rule is to accept projects that generate a positive NPV (or an IRR > i, or a PI > 1), and reject those that don't.[29] However, many projects are interrelated.

independent projects projects that have no relationship with one another; accepting one project has no impact on the decision to accept another project

The Trouble with IRR | LESSONS LEARNED

Assumptions about reinvestment based on internal rate of return can lead to major capital budget distortions.

Practitioners often interpret internal rate of return as the annual equivalent return on a given investment; this easy analogy is the source of its intuitive appeal. But in fact, IRR is a true indication of a project's annual return on investment only when the project generates no interim cash flows — or when those interim cash flows really can be invested at the actual IRR.

When the calculated IRR is higher than the true reinvestment rate for interim cash flows, the measure will overestimate—sometimes very significantly—the annual equivalent return from the project. The formula assumes that the company has additional projects, with equally attractive prospects, in which to invest the interim cash flows. In this case, the calculation implicitly takes credit for these additional projects. Calculations of net present value (NPV), by contrast, generally assume only that a company can earn its cost of capital on interim cash flows, leaving any future incremental project value with those future projects.

IRR's assumptions about reinvestment can lead to major capital budget distortions. Consider a hypothetical assessment of two different, mutually exclusive projects, A and B, with identical cash flows, risk levels, and durations— as well as identical IRR values of 41 percent. Using IRR as the decision yardstick, an executive would feel confidence

in being indifferent toward choosing between the two projects. However, it would be a mistake to select either project without examining the relevant reinvestment rate for interim cash flows. Suppose that Project B's interim cash flows could be redeployed only at a typical 8 percent cost of capital, while Project A's cash flows could be invested in an attractive follow-on project expected to generate a 41 percent annual return. In that case, Project A is unambiguously preferable.

Even if the interim cash flows really could be reinvested at the IRR, very few practitioners would argue that the value of future investments should be commingled with the value of the project being evaluated. Most practitioners would agree that a company's cost of capital—by definition, the return available elsewhere to its shareholders on a similarly risky investment—is a clearer and more logical rate to assume for reinvestments of interim project cash flows.

When the cost of capital is used, a project's true annual equivalent yield can fall significantly—again, especially so with projects that posted high initial IRRs. Of course, when executives review projects with IRRs that are close to a company's cost of capital, the IRR is less distorted by the reinvestment-rate assumption. But when they evaluate projects that claim IRRs of 10 percent or more above their company's cost of capital, these may well be significantly distorted. Ironically, unadjusted IRRs

---

[29] This issue is discussed in the next section.

are particularly treacherous because the reinvestment-rate distortion is most egregious precisely when managers tend to think their projects are most attractive. And since this amplification is not felt evenly across all projects, managers can't simply correct for it by adjusting every IRR by a standard amount. (The amplification effect grows as a project's fundamental health improves, as measured by NPV, and it varies depending on the unique timing of a project's cash flows.)

How large is the potential impact of a flawed reinvestment-rate assumption? Managers at one large industrial company approved 23 major capital projects over five years on the basis of IRRs that averaged 77 percent. Recently, however, when we conducted an analysis with the reinvestment rate adjusted to the company's cost of capital, the true average return fell to just 16 percent. The order of the most attractive projects also changed considerably. The top-ranked project based on IRR dropped to the tenth-most-attractive project. Most striking, the company's highest-rated projects—showing IRRs of 800, 150, and 130 percent—dropped to just 15, 23, and 22 percent, respectively, once a realistic reinvestment rate was considered. Unfortunately, these investment decisions had already been made. Of course, IRRs this extreme are somewhat unusual. Yet even if a project's IRR drops from 25 percent to 15 percent, the impact is considerable.

John C. Kelleher and Justin J. MacCormack, "Internal Rate of Return: A Cautionary Tale," *The McKinsey Quarterly*, McKinsey & Co., August 2004.

---

contingent projects projects for which the acceptance of one requires the acceptance of another, either beforehand or simultaneously

Capital expenditures can represent **contingent projects**. For example, if a company can implement investment A (e.g., purchase the newest accounting software package) only if it also undertakes investment B (e.g., change the operating system to Microsoft Windows), investment A is contingent on investment B. In other words, one project is feasible only if another project is undertaken either beforehand or simultaneously. For these types of investment projects, the rule is to estimate the total NPV of *all* contingent projects and accept them if this total NPV is positive. In such a situation, it is possible that a project on which others are contingent (e.g., the updating of operating system) can be accepted even if it does not generate a positive NPV on its own. In fact, this is often the case with operating systems. This could occur if the benefits provided by the contingent projects more than offset the losses generated by the initial project.

Mutually exclusive projects, as defined earlier, imply that a company must choose among two or more alternatives. In other words, if a company is considering replacing an old computer system with either system A or system B, it would never buy both, even if the analysis suggested that they both generated positive NPVs.[30] In such a case, the company must decide which project is best. Recall from our previous discussion on IRR versus NPV that whenever a company has to rank projects, NPV is superior.

Capital Rationing

capital rationing allotting investment capital among available investment projects

investment opportunity schedule (IOS) internal rate of return expected on each potential investment opportunity, ranked in descending order

Theoretically, companies should accept all independent projects that generate positive NPVs, which enhance company value. However, in practice, companies often face capital budget constraints, which may force them to turn down attractive projects. Theoretically, these constraints should not exist in efficient markets because companies should always be able to source new financing to take advantage of investment opportunities that generate returns that exceed the cost of raising the required investment funds. However, constraints may arise because of market inefficiencies, which restrict the company's ability to raise funds in the capital markets, or because they are imposed internally (i.e., management sets certain budget limits that cannot be exceeded). When companies face capital budget constraints, it is common to say that **capital rationing** prevails—that is, investment capital must be rationed among available investment projects.

In Figure 10-8 we depict a company's investment decision environment. The company has $25 million of available projects, which are ranked by internal rate of return and plotted in this graph along the **investment opportunity schedule (IOS)**. A company should invest in opportunities along its IOS until the IRR equals its weighted average cost of

---

[30] If A and B are independent projects that generated positive NPVs, a company would accept both projects.

FIGURE 10-8 **The Investment Opportunity Schedule and Optimal Investing**

capital (WACC)—or equivalently until the last project accepted has an NPV of zero. This would mean that the optimal amount it should invest is $12 million, even though it has $25 million of available projects. However, suppose the company had only $5 million of internal funds; it could not accept all its projects and would be capital rationed, unless it issued new debt or equity.

The important point about capital rationing is that the cost of capital is no longer the appropriate opportunity cost. Now, cash flows generated by a project can be reinvested at a rate higher than assumed by the cost of capital because the company is leaving some positive NPV projects on the table, due to lack of financing. The reinvestment rate assumption underlying the IRR has more validity because the company can reinvest the cash flows from a project at the IRR of the marginal project, rather than at its cost of capital. The problem is that the IOS schedule is rarely a nice smooth downward-sloping function, like the one we show in Figure 10-8.

When companies have to choose among discrete, lumpy projects with limited funds, they have to consider the cost of the investment because this is constrained by the capital budget. In this case, we can first estimate the NPVs and the IRRs, but we can't fully rely on either of them as a criterion because they ignore the cost of the investment and the capital constraint. The PI is often a useful starting point because it gives the highest present value relative to the initial cash outlay, which is constrained. However, the final decision should be based on which combination of projects generates the highest total NPV while satisfying the capital budget constraint. This is because the PI, like the IRR, may lead to incorrect decisions; it is a relative measure.

Consider a company that is evaluating the following independent investments, A through F:

Project	Initial Cash Outlay (CF_0)	NPV	PI
A	€100,000	€13,646	1.136
B	€50,000	−€3,342	0.934
C	€80,000	€10,558	1.132
D	€60,000	€4,320	1.072
E	€75,000	€10,825	1.144
F	€90,000	€7,225	1.080

In the absence of capital rationing, which projects should be selected? If we look at projects ranked by NPV and PI, we see the following rankings:

Rank	Rank Based on NPV	Rank Based on PI
1	A	E
2	E	A
3	C	C
4	F	F
5	D	D
6	B	B

Why do they differ? Because the NPV is in monetary terms, and PI is in relative terms (benefit/cost ratio).

The company should select projects A, C, D, E, and F because they all have positive NPVs and are assumed to be independent. Therefore, the capital spending is €100,000 + 80,000 + 60,000 + 75,000 + 90,000 = €405,000, and the expected value added from this set of projects is €13,646 + 10,558 + 4,320 + 10,825 + 7,225 = €46,574.

Now suppose a capital budget constraint of €250,000 is placed on new investments. Which projects should be selected? The company should take on the combination of positive NPV projects that maximizes total NPV, within the given budget constraints. Possible combinations of projects are the following:

Projects selected	Total NPV	Capital Spending Required	Within the Budget?
A, C, D	€28,524	€240,000	Yes
A, C, E	€35,029	€255,000	No
A, C, F	€42,254	€345,000	No
A, D, E	€28,791	€235,000	Yes
C, E, F	€28,608	€245,000	Yes

If the capital budget constraint is fixed €250,000, the company should select only projects A, D, and E.[31] Why? Because the spending fits in the budget, and this is the set of projects within the budget that has the highest total NPV. What if the budget is €200,000? The company should select projects A and E, requiring an investment of €175,000, with an expected added value of €24,471.

If the company could invest in all projects that have positive NPV, the total investment would be €405,000, and the value added—the sum of the NPVs of these projects— is €46,574. With a budget constrained to €250,000, the total NPV is now only €28,791 under capital rationing, and the "loss" to the company = €46,574 − €28,791 = €17,783. Notice that the loss of €17,783 is the sum of the NPVs of the two forgone positive NPV projects (i.e., C and F). This is detrimental to company value, as it is forced to turn down two "good" positive NPV investments because the company lacks the capital to proceed with them.

Although we have come up with the maximum NPV given the budget constraint, in reality the company would conduct further analysis. For example, the company would forecast its budget for the following year and look at the deferral possibilities. It may be, for example, that E can be deferred, and it is better to go with A and C this year and roll over the excess in the budget to take on E and other projects next year.

---

[31] If there was €5,000 "slack" in the constraint, then the combination of A, C, and E would generate the highest NPV; however, it requires a €255,000 outlay, which exceeds the $250,000 constraint.

Overconfidence and Capital Budgeting | ETHICS

Capital budgeting decisions are, ultimately, made by people, not machines. Though we have tools to quantify the analysis, most of what we are doing is working with estimates: estimates of the initial investment, estimates of future cash flows resulting from the investment, and estimates of the risk associated with the project. Because of the human element, there is a potential for biases in recommending or promoting capital budgets within a company, especially if there is rationed capital. Overconfidence may be reflected in a number of ways, including forecasted cash flows that are too rosy or risk that is understated, and be motivated by compensation formulas, empire building, or simply hubris.

Studies have shown that there is a relationship between a company's CEO overconfidence and investment decisions.[32] Particular to one type of capital budgeting decision, mergers and acquisitions, studies document that the CEO's overconfidence is related to the premium the company pays to acquire other companies: the more overconfident, the higher the premium paid.

Companies can mitigate some of the biases in their capital budgeting processes by requiring specific analyses and data for each capital project, along with supporting assumptions.

The Appropriate Discount Rate

As mentioned earlier, it is usually appropriate to use the project's cost of capital as the discount rate to evaluate a long-term investment project. However, it is often the case that the company's weighted average cost of capital (WACC) is used as the project's cost of capital. The WACC is the after-tax cost of a dollar of additional long-term financing to the company, and we assume that companies will finance long-term investments by using long-term financing. This is appropriate if the project under consideration is an "average" risk investment project for the company—in other words, if it is a typical investment and will not substantially change the asset mix of the company.

However, if a company is considering a project that is atypical, in the sense that it is either more or less risky than the average investment for that company, this fact should be reflected in the discount rate used to evaluate that project. For example, a company could be considering introducing a new product line that entails greater (or lower) risks than its traditional offerings. Under these circumstances, a higher discount rate should be used for projects that possess above-average risk, and a lower discount rate should be used for projects that possess below-average risk. If a company does not adjust the discount rate under these circumstances and merely uses a constant WACC to select investment projects, it will make inappropriate decisions. In particular, this could lead the company to reject positive NPV low-risk projects that appear unattractive if evaluated by using a discount rate that is too high. It could also lead the company to accept negative NPV high-risk projects that appear attractive if evaluated by using a discount rate that is too low.

A good example of this problem was USX Company (USX). For a time, the company comprised two divisions: Marathon Oil Company and U.S. Steel.[33] Suppose, for example, the oil company's WACC was 8 percent and the steel company's was 12 percent, and the overall company was composed of 50 percent of each division, so the company WACC was 10 percent. Applying the company WACC of 10 percent to capital projects would cause some of the steel division's projects with IRRs of 11 percent to be accepted, even if stand-alone steel companies were rejecting similar projects. Likewise, desirable oil projects earning 9 percent would be rejected, even if they were being accepted by

---

[32] See, for example, David J. Ravenscraft and F. M. Scherer, "Life after Takeover," *Journal of Industrial Economics*, 36, no. 2 (1987): 147–156; Mathew L. A. Hayward and Donald C. Hambrick, "Explaining the Premiums Paid for Large Acquisitions: Evidence of CEO Hubris," *Administrative Science Quarterly*, 42, no. 1 (1997): 103–127.

[33] The two companies ultimately became independent companies, each with its own stock ownership, in 2002. The steel business is now known as United States Steel Company (X) and the oil business Marathon Oil Company (MRO).

EXAMPLE 10.7

Applying the Company's Cost of Capital to All Projects

PROBLEM

Consider a company that has two projects under consideration with the following characteristics:

	End-of-Period Cash Flows	
Year	Project P	Project Q
0	–$10,000	–$10,000
1	$3,000	$4,000
2	$3,000	$3,000
3	$3,000	$2,000
4	$2,000	$3,000

Project P's cost of capital is 3 percent, and Project Q's cost of capital is 9 percent. The cost of capital for the company is 6 percent.

What happens when we use a single cost of capital for both projects and can only invest in one of these projects?

Solution

We may draw an incorrect conclusion regarding whether the projects add value:

	Project P	Project Q
Net present value based on company's cost of capital	–$396.78	$499.09
Decision	Reject	Accept
Net present value based on project's cost of capital	$262.81	–$135.59
Decision	Accept	Reject

equivalent oil companies. If Marathon Oil did this over time, it would gradually become a less valuable oil company, rejecting many opportunities that other oil companies would have accepted.

The common response to the Marathon Oil problem is to estimate risk-adjusted discount rates by adjusting the cost of capital up or down based on the risk level and financing of a specific project under consideration. Marathon Oil would use a discount rate of 8 percent in its oil division and 12 percent in its steel division. Estimating these different discount rates involves estimating betas and the risk associated with the investment and the optimal financing. One method of doing this is the **pure play approach**. This approach involves estimating the weighted average cost of capital of companies in a line of business associated with the project, adjusting for the difference in capital structures between the pure play and the company. Another approach is to estimate beta for the project by regressing the return on assets of the project against that of the market index. Similar techniques can be used to estimate the appropriate project cost of debt and then to estimate the appropriate overall cost of capital.

Several practical difficulties are associated with estimating a project's cost of capital. For example, it may be difficult to find an appropriate company to use as a pure play, and the regression of project return on an index return on assets may lead to an inaccurate beta measure. In addition, intuitive adjustments that are made by managers are subjective in nature and prone to error, but this may be no more prevalent here than in other techniques. However, despite the associated difficulties, estimating risk-adjusted discount rates is preferable to blindly applying one constant discount rate to all projects, regardless of their individual risk characteristics.

pure play approach estimating betas and the risk associated with an investment and the optimal financing by estimating the weighted average cost of capital of companies in an industry associated with the project

Comparing Evaluation Techniques

The net present value, internal rate of return, modified internal rate of return, and profitability index techniques offer objective criteria when evaluating projects:

| | | Decision Criteria | | |
| | | (i is the project cost of capital) | | |
Evaluation Technique	Metric	Accept	Indifferent	Reject
Net present value	Monetary amount	NPV > 0	NPV = 0	NPV < 0
Internal rate of return	Rate of return	IRR > i	IRR = i	IRR < i
Modified internal rate of return	Rate of return	MIRR > i	MIRR = i	MIRR < i
Profitability index	Index	PI > 1.0	PI = 1.0	PI < 1.0

These methods will generally offer the same accept/reject decisions when evaluating a set of independent projects and when there is no limit on the capital budget. However, when we look at situations in which there are mutually exclusive projects, capital rationing, or different project sizes, we need to take more care in selecting the evaluation technique.

Each technique has its advantages and disadvantages, which we summarize in Table 10-1. As you can see, the net present value technique tends to dominate in terms of consistency with the objective of this decision making, which is to maximize the value of the owners' value.

TABLE 10-1 Comparing Techniques

	Advantages	Disadvantages
Net Present Values	• Considers the time value of money through the discount rate. • Considers all of the project's cash flows. • Has an objective criterion (i.e., accept if NPV is positive).	• Result is in monetary terms, not as the more familiar return. • Sensitive to the project's cost of capital.
Internal Rate of Return	• Considers the time value of money through the hurdle rate. • Considers all the project's cash flows. • Has an objective criterion (i.e., accept if IRR is greater than the project's cost of capital).	• Should not be used when deciding among mutually exclusive projects. • Cannot be used when the signs of cash flows change more than once. • Should not use when the capital budget is limited.
Modified Internal Rate of Return	• Considers the time value of money through the hurdle rate. • Considers all of the project's cash flows. • Indicates the return on the project considering a realistic reinvestment of the project's cash inflows. • Has an objective criterion (i.e., accept if MIRR exceeds the project's cost of capital).	• Should not be used when deciding among mutually exclusive projects. • Should not use when the capital budget is limited.

(Continued)

TABLE 10-1 *(Continued)*

	Advantages	*Disadvantages*
Payback Period	• Easy to calculate. • A useful initial screening technique. • Measures the liquidity of a project (i.e., how fast cash inflows occur).	• Does not consider the time value of money. • Ignores cash flows beyond the payback period. • Has no objective criterion for what is a good payback period.
Discounted Payback Period	• Indicates whether a project will ever pay back. • Considers the time value of money of the project cash flows.	• Ignores cash flows beyond the payback period. • Has no objective criterion for what is a good discounted payback period.
Profitability Index	• Considers the time value of money through the discount rate. • Considers all the project's cash flows. • Has an objective criterion (i.e., accept if PI is greater than one). • Useful in ranking projects in terms of benefit/cost.	• Should not be used when deciding among mutually exclusive projects.

Concept Review Questions

1. What complications arise when companies are rationed in terms of their available capital budget?

2. Explain how companies should decide which projects to accept and which to reject when capital rationing exists.

3. Distinguish between a project's cost of capital and the company's weighted cost of capital.

SUMMARY

- There are alternative approaches to evaluating capital investment projects. These approaches include the net present value, the internal rate of return, the modified internal rate of return, the profitability index, the payback period, and the discounted payback period.

- The net present value method requires the calculation of the value added from the project, which is the difference between the present value of the cash inflows from a project and the present value of the project's cash outflows, where all cash flows are discounted at the project's cost of capital. A positive net present value indicates that the investment is expected to enhance the value of the company.

- The internal rate of return is the yield on the project, which we derive by solving for the discount rate resulting in a zero net present value. In many cases, a project with an internal rate of return greater than the project's cost of capital is attractive because the project earns more than what the supplier of capital requires considering the project's risk.

- One of the drawbacks of the internal rate of return is that the reinvestment assumption applied to cash flows is the internal rate of return. We can use the modified internal rate of return, with its more realistic reinvestment rate assumption, to overcome this problem. In addition, we should not use the internal rate of return when deciding among mutually exclusive projects or evaluating projects with different initial investments. Another drawback of the internal rate of return is that the internal rate of return should not be used when the sign of the cash flow changes more than once during the life of the project.

- The profitability index is related to the net present value; instead of the difference between the present value of the inflows and outflows, the profitability index is the ratio of these two present values.

- The payback period and the discounted payback period are measures of how long it takes to recover a project's cash outlay in cash inflows and discounted cash inflows, respectively.

- The net present value method is the preferred method because it is consistent with the maximization of shareholder wealth and is not complicated by issues that may cause the internal rate of return to provide misleading results, with respect to mutually exclusive projects, mathematical issues, and an aggressive reinvestment rate.

- If capital is rationed—that is, there is a limit on the capital budget—the focus should be in selecting projects that best enhance shareholder wealth, which means selecting the set of projects that provides the greatest sum of net present values with a sum of initial investments that fit within the budget.

FORMULAS/EQUATIONS

(10-1) $NPV = \dfrac{CF_0}{(1 + i)^0} + \dfrac{CF_1}{(1 + i)^1} + \dfrac{CF_2}{(1 + i)^2} + \dfrac{CF_3}{(1 + i)^3} + \cdots + \dfrac{CF_n}{(1 + i)^n}$

(10-2) $NPV = \dfrac{\sum\limits_{t=0}^{n} CF_t}{(1 + i)^t}$

(10-3) $0 = \dfrac{\sum\limits_{t=0}^{n} CF_t}{(1 + IRR)^t}$

(10-4) $PI = \dfrac{PV(\text{cash inflows})}{PV(\text{cash outflows})}$

QUESTIONS AND PROBLEMS

Multiple Choice Questions

1. Consider an investment that requires a $10 million initial investment and has a net present value of $6 million. Which of the following statements is *not* correct regarding this investment?

   A. The profitability index is 0.6.

   B. The investment pays back in terms of its discounted cash flows.

   C. The internal rate of return of the project is greater than the project's cost of capital.

   D. Making this investment is expected to increase the value of the company by $6 million.

2. Which of the following is *not* a critical factor that Porter identified in determining industry attractiveness?

    A. Entry barriers

    B. Rivalry among competitors

    C. Bargaining power of suppliers

    D. Bargaining power of government

3. The NPV for a project with an after-tax initial investment of $17,000, five equal annual cash flows of $8,000 at the start of each year, beginning with the 3rd year, and a discount rate of 20 percent, is *closest* to:

    A. −$385.49.   B. $1,998.35.   C. $2,937.41.   D. $6,924.90.

4. Which of the following statements about IRR and NPV is *incorrect*?

    A. NPV and IRR yield the same ranking when evaluating projects.

    B. NPV assumes that cash flows are reinvested at the cost of capital of the company.

    C. IRR may have multiple IRRs when the sign of cash flow changes more than once.

    D. IRR is the discount rate that, when applied to a project's cash flows, results in an NPV equal to zero.

5. When evaluating two mutually exclusive projects with a crossover rate of 5 percent and $IRR_A < IRR_B$, we prefer project A when the discount rate is:

    A. less than 5 percent.   B. equal to 5 percent.   C. greater than 5 percent.

6. Consider the following end-of-year cash flows for Projects X and Y:

    Project X: $CF_0 = -\$2,000$ $CF_1 = \$1,000$ $CF_2 = \$1,000$ $CF_3 = \$1,000$
    Project Y: $CF_0 = -\$2,000$ $CF_1 = \$0$ $CF_2 = \$500$ $CF_3 = \$3,000$

    If the discount rate is 15 percent, the decision regarding projects X and Y should be to accept:

	Independent	*Mutually Exclusive*
A.	Both	X
B.	Neither	Y
C.	Both	Y
D.	Neither	X

7. Consider a project with an after-tax initial investment of $6,000 and expected cash flows of $CF_1 = \$2,500$; $CF_2 = \$4,000$; $CF_3 = \$5,000$, and a discount rate of 20 percent. The IRR is *closest* to:

    A. 15 percent.   B. 25.65 percent.   C. 35.87 percent.

8. Which of the following would *not* happen if a company uses the company's weighted average cost of capital for all projects, regardless of the individual risks of the projects?

    A. Reject a low-risk project with positive NPV

    B. Reject a high-risk project with positive NPV

    C. Accept a high-risk project with negative NPV

    D. Accept an average-risk project with positive NPV

9. To estimate risk-adjusted discount rates, a company could use all of the following methods, *except* the:

    A. pure play approach.

    B. cost of capital ± risk premium.

    C. regression of the ROA of the project on the ROA of the whole company.

    D. regression of the return on assets (ROA) of the project on the ROA of market index.

10. We should *reject* a project if:

    A. PI < 1.   B. NPV > 0.   C. IRR > project's cost of capital.   D. MIRR > project's cost of capital.

Practice Questions and Problems

10.1 The Capital Budgeting Process

11. What are capital expenditures?

12. How can an investment project add value to a company?

13. Is the net present value technique consistent with the maximization of owners' equity? Explain.

14. Provide an example of a company that uses cost leadership to give it a comparative or competitive advantage.

15. Provide an example of a company that uses product differentiation to give it a comparative or competitive advantage.

16. Analysts often assume that a company's return on assets will eventually "regress toward the mean," approaching the typical growth in gross domestic product. Is this consistent with Porter's model and basic economic theory? Explain.

10.2 Evaluating Investment Projects

17. For each of the following, describe the basis of accept/reject of a capital project:
    A. Net present value
    B. Internal rate of return
    C. Modified internal rate of return
    D. Profitability index

18. Which of the following techniques is consistent with the maximization of owners' equity? Explain why or why not.
    A. Payback period
    B. Discounted payback period
    C. Net present value
    D. Internal rate of return
    E. Modified internal rate of return

19. List and describe briefly the drawbacks of payback period and discounted payback period.

20. Regarding the net present value profile,
    A. What are the values on the horizontal axis?
    B. What are the values on the vertical axis?
    C. How do you determine the intersection of the profile with the vertical axis?
    D. How do you determine the intersection of the profile with the horizontal axis?
    E. How do you calculate the intersection of any two profiles?

21. If you calculate a project's net present value of $1 million, what is the interpretation of this value?

22. Suppose you are evaluating two mutually exclusive projects, and you calculate the crossover rate as 8 percent. What is the meaning of this rate?

23. If a project has a positive net present value using a discount rate of 5 percent, is the project's internal rate of return greater than or less than 5 percent? Explain.

24. If a project has a positive net present value, is the project's profitability index greater than or less than 1.0? Explain.

25. If a project has a positive net present value, does this project pay back in terms of discounted cash flows? Explain.

26. Consider a project with the following:
    - An after-tax initial investment of $66,777
    - After-tax cash flows at each following six year ends of $20,000 each
    - A year-end cash flow at year 7 of $40,000
    - A discount rate of 10 percent

    A. Draw a time-line of the cash flows for today through period 7.
    B. Is the decision the same using NPV and IRR? Why?

27. Suppose a project has cash inflows following its initial outlay, an NPV of $5,090, and the after-tax initial investment is $10,050.

    A. What is the project's PI?
    B. Should the company accept the project?
    C. Does PI yield the same decision as NPV?

28. Complete the following table by calculating each project's profitability index:

Project	Initial Outlay	Net Present Value	Profitability Index
A	$100,000	$15,000	
B	$10,000	$1,000	
C	$32,000	–$1,000	
D	$40,000	$5,000	

29. Consider a project with the following cash flows:

Year	End-of-year Cash Flow
0	–$100,000
1	$0
2	$90,000
3	$40,000
4	$5,000

    A. Draw a timeline, indicating both the period and the cash flow.
    B. Calculate the project's NPV if the project's cost of capital is 10 percent.
    C. Calculate the project's IRR.
    D. Calculate the MIRR, assuming a reinvestment rate of 10 percent.
    E. Using a spreadsheet, illustrate the project's net present value profile, labeling the axes and indicating the project's internal rate of return on this profile.

30. Consider the following project's cash flows:

Year	End-of-year Cash Flow
0	–$1,000
1	–$2,000
2	$2,000
3	$1,500

A. What is this project's net present value if the discount rate is 6 percent?

B. What is this project's internal rate of return?

C. What is this project's modified internal rate of return if the reinvestment rate is 5 percent?

D. What is this project's modified internal rate of return if the reinvestment rate is 6 percent?

31. SK Inc. has two projects as follows:

| | End-of-year Cash Flows | | | | |
Project	Year 0	Year 1	Year 2	Year 3	Year 4
E	−€2,500	€800	€1,200	€900	€2,000
F	−€3,000	€750	€1,500	€1,000	€4,000

A. Which project(s) will be selected if it uses the *discounted* payback period method and a discount rate of 12 percent? Explain.

B. What is each project's net present value if the cost of capital for each project is 12 percent?

32. Consider a project with the following cash flows:

Year	End-of-year Cash Flow
0	−$100,000
1	$0
2	$0
3	$0
4	$115,000

A. Draw a time line, indicating both the period and the cash flow.

B. Calculate the project's NPV if the project's cost of capital is 10 percent.

C. Calculate the project's IRR.

D. Using a spreadsheet, illustrate the project's net present value profile, labeling the axes and indicating the project's internal rate of return on this profile.

33. Consider the following end-of-year cash flows for Project C and Project D:

Projects	Today	Year 1	Year 2	Year 3
C	−$22,000	$6,000	$9,000	$15,000
D	−$20,000	$4,000	$8,000	$15,000

A. What is the internal rate of return for each project?

B. Graph the net present value profiles for each project on a single chart, indicating each project's internal rates of return.

C. What is the crossover rate for Projects C and D?

D. If the discount rate for both projects is 10 percent, which project, if any, should be selected?

10.3 Special Issues

34. What is capital rationing?

35. Is capital rationing consistent with the maximization of owners' value? Explain.

36. If two projects are mutually exclusive, which technique(s) should you use?

37. If a project has cash flows that consist of an initial cash outlay, positive cash flows for 5 years, and then a negative cash flow in the final year, what techniques should you use in evaluating this project?

38. Suppose a project has the following cash flows:

Year	End-of-year Cash Flow
20X0	−$100,000
20X1	$0
20X2	$0
20X3	$120,000
20X4	−$2,000

A. If the discount rate is 5 percent, should this project be accepted?
B. If the discount rate is 6 percent, should this project be accepted?
C. What is the internal rate of return for this project?

39. Consider the cash flows for the projects A through D:

	Project End-of-year Cash Flows (in millions)			
Year	A	B	C	D
Initial	−$10	−$10	−$10	−$10
1	$2	$0	$0	$5
2	$2	$0	$0	$0
3	$2	$0	$6	$2
4	$2	$0	$0	$0
5	$4	$13	$6	$5

The cost of capital for each project is 5 percent.
A. Calculate the IRR for each project.
B. Calculate the NPV for each project.
C. If the projects are independent, which project or projects should be accepted?
D. If the projects are mutually exclusive, which project or projects should be accepted?

 40. Consider two mutually exclusive projects, named for their planned locations of Corvalis and Portland:

	End-of-year Cash Flow	
Year	Corvalis	Portland
0	−$9,500	−$9,500
1	$0	$3,000
2	$0	$3,000
3	$0	$3,000
4	$12,000	$2,000

A. If the project discount rate for both projects is 5 percent, what is the appropriate decision?
B. If the project discount rate for both projects is 6 percent, what is the appropriate decision?
C. If the project discount rate for both projects is 7 percent, what is the appropriate decision?
D. Draw the net present value profile for these projects on one graph.

41. Consider the results of the analysis of the following projects:

Project	Initial Outlay	Net Present Value	Internal Rate of Return	Payback Period
A	$10,000,000	$500,000	10%	5 years
B	$5,000,000	−$40,000	9%	4 years
C	$11,000,000	$1,000,000	13%	3 years
D	$2,000,000	$40,000	9%	5 years
E	$3,000,000	−$20,000	12%	4 years
F	$4,000,000	$70,000	7%	3 years
G	$9,000,000	$60,000	3%	5 years

A. If the capital budget is limited to $12 million, which projects, if any, should be selected? Explain.
B. If the capital budget is limited to $20 million, which projects, if any, should be selected? Explain.
C. If the capital budget is limited to $25 million, which projects, if any, should be selected? Explain.

42. Consider the following projects and cash flows:

Dollar Amounts (in millions)	A	B	C	D
Initial cash outlay	−$5	−$15	−$10	−$10
Cash flow, end of period 1	$0	$0	$2	$0
Cash flow, end of period 2	$2	$0	$3	$0
Cash flow, end of period 3	$2	$0	$4	$0
Cash flow, end of period 4	$2	$18	$4	$15
Project discount rate	5%	6%	7%	8%

A. If these projects are independent and there is no capital rationing, which project(s) should you invest in?
B. If these projects are mutually exclusive and there is no capital rationing, which project(s) should you invest in?
C. If these projects are independent and there is a limit on the capital budget of $25 million, which project(s) should you invest in?
D. Draw the net present value profile for each project on a single chart, identifying the internal rate of return of each project.

 43. Consider the cash flows for the projects E through H:

Project End-of-year Cash Flows
(in millions)

Year	E	F	G	H
Initial	−$10	−$10	−$10	−$10
1	$2	$0	$0	$0
2	$2	$0	$0	$0
3	$2	$0	$6	$0
4	$2	$0	$0	$0
5	$4	$13	$6	$13

The cost of capital for each project is 4 percent.

A. Using a spreadsheet program, calculate the IRR for each project.
B. Using a spreadsheet program, calculate the NPV for each project.
C. If the projects are independent, which project or projects should be accepted?
D. If the projects are mutually exclusive, which project or projects should be accepted?
E. What is the crossover rate for Projects E and F?
F. What is the crossover rate for Projects G and H?
G. Using a spreadsheet program, graph the net present value profiles of Projects E and F on the same chart, indicating the crossover point and internal rates of return.
H. Using a spreadsheet program, graph the net present value profiles of Projects G and H on the same chart, indicating the crossover point and internal rates of return.

Case

Case 10.1 The Austin Saddle Company Expansion

The Austin Saddle Company (ASC) is considering expanding its tannery facilities, increasing its production capacity by 20 percent. The ASC has brought in the marketing, production management, procurement, capital investment, and accounting departments to formulate estimates of the initial cost of the expansion, as well as future cash flow that can be used to evaluate this expansion. The procurement and capital management teams expect that the expansion will require $10 million initially, with the first year's operating cash flows of $2 million. The operating cash flows are expected to grow at a rate of 5 percent each year for 3 years, but then to slow to a 3 percent growth thereafter.

The ASC has a cost of capital of 8 percent, and the expansion project is expected to have risk similar to ASC's typical project.

A. Should ASC expand? Explain your reasoning.
B. If ASC's cost of capital increased to 10 percent, would your recommendation change?
C. At what cost of capital, if any, would your recommendation change? Indicate your decision on a net present value profile of this investment decision.
D. If the growth rate were to be 3 percent, ad infinitum, would your decision change? Explain.

DEALING WITH UNEQUAL LIVES

We have simplified the world in this chapter by assuming that any projects that we are comparing have the same lives. Why is this important? Because if the projects have different useful lives, we would need to make adjustments to make the projects comparable.

Suppose a company is evaluating equipment to use in the new production line. The company can only use one piece of equipment, but the problem is that the two eligible pieces of equipment have different useful lives; Equipment 1 has a useful life of 5 years, and Equipment 2 has a useful life of 4 years:

	End-of-year Cash Flows	
Year	Equipment 1	Equipment 2
0	−$10,000	−$10,000
1	$1,000	$2,000
2	$2,000	$3,500
3	$4,000	$4,500
4	$5,000	$4,000
5	$3,000	

The company expects to have the need for equipment to perform the particular function in the production process for the foreseeable future. To keeps things simple, let's assume that the project cost of capital is 10 percent for each project.

Because these projects are mutually exclusive, we would use the net present value to select the most profitable project, which would be Equipment 1:

	Equipment 1	Equipment 2
NPV	$845.07	$823.71

The issue, however, is that we face the proverbial conundrum of comparing "apples with oranges": These projects are not directly comparable because they provide benefits over different numbers of years.

10A.1 THE COMMON LIFE APPROACH

One way to adjust for this problem is to consider that replacements could be made for each project such that they would have the same useful life. The **common life approach** assumes a finite number of replacements such that each project being compared has the same useful life, the **common life**. The common life for these two projects is 20 years: three replacements of Equipment 1 is equivalent to four replacements of Equipment 2. This is how it works: You invest today in Equipment 1. At the end of 5 years, you invest in Equipment 1 again, with a present value of $845.07. You repeat this at the end of the 10th year and the 15th year. You do likewise for Equipment 2: replace at the end of the 4th, 8th, 12th, and 16th years. This way we have all 20 years covered, as shown in Table 10A-1.

common life approach method of comparing mutually exclusive projects with different useful lives, assuming a finite number of replacements for each project, consistent with the projects' common life

common life revised useful life of projects considering a finite number of replacements such that the projects being compared have the same useful life

TABLE 10A-1 **Net Present Values for Reinvestment in Equipment 1 and Equipment 2**

Year	Equipment 1	Equipment 2
0	$845.07	$823.71
1		
2		
3		
4		$823.71
5	$845.07	
6		
7		
8		$823.71
9		
10	$845.07	
11		
12		$823.71
13		
14		
15	$845.07	
16		$823.71
17		
18		
19		
20		

The next step is to calculate the net present value of the series of values and then compare these for the two projects:

	Equipment 1	Equipment 2
NPV	$2,946.63	$3,434.76

The value added by Equipment 2 is higher than that provided by Equipment 1. Therefore, we prefer Equipment 1.

10A.2 EQUIVALENT ANNUAL ANNUITY

equivalent annual annuity approach method of comparing mutually exclusive projects that have different useful lives, assuming reinvestment in each in perpetuity

An alternative method of dealing with the unequal lives is to consider reinvestment in each project in perpetuity. Using this approach, which we refer to as the **equivalent annual annuity approach**, we assume that at the end of each project the company will reinvest in the same project, ad infinitum. Although it may appear daunting to consider the mathematics of reinvesting in, say, Equipment 1 every 5 years, forever, there is a simple approach: First calculate the annual annuity amount that is equivalent to the project's net present value, and then assume this annual stream ad infinitum.

For example, the net present value of Equipment 1's cash flows is $845.07. What is this equivalent to in terms of an annuity? Use the NPV as the present value, use the project's life as the number of years, and use the project's cost of capital as the discount rate:

$$PV = \$845.07$$
$$N = 5$$
$$i = 10\%$$
$$\text{Solve for PMT} \rightarrow \text{PMT} = \$222.93$$

We often refer to this annuity amount as the **equivalent annual annuity** because it is the annuity stream that is equivalent to the net present value of the project.

> **equivalent annual annuity** amount of the annuity that is equivalent to the net present value of a project

With this annual payment, assuming this in perpetuity, we can calculate the present value of the perpetuity:

$$\text{Present value of Equipment 1 in perpetuity} = \frac{\$222.93}{0.10} = \$2{,}229.28$$

Repeating this for Equipment 2, using $823.71 for the present value and four for the number of years, produces an annuity of $259.86 and a present value of Equipment 2 in perpetuity of $2,598.58.[35] Summarizing,

	Equipment 1	Equipment 2
NPV	$846.09	$824.73
EAA	$222.93	$259.86
Present value of perpetuity	$2,229.28	$2,598.58

The two methods—valuing the projects using a common life and using the equivalent annual annuity—can be used in any situation in which the net present value is used.

PRACTICE QUESTIONS AND PROBLEMS

1. Distinguish the use of the common life approach to investment decision making with unequal lives with that of the equivalent annual annuity approach. Be sure to identify the assumptions of each.

2. Suppose you are evaluating three projects, with lives of 5, 6, and 7 years, respectively. What is the common life for these projects?

3. Consider two mutually exclusive projects, Project 1 and Project 2, that have the following cash flows:

	End-of-year Cash Flow	
Year	Project 1	Project 2
0	−$10,000	−$10,000
1	$1,000	$4,500
2	$2,000	$4,500
3	$4,000	$4,500
4	$5,000	
5	$3,000	
Cost of capital	8%	7%

---

[35] It looks like we could have come to the same conclusion if we had stopped at the amount of the annual annuity. However, if the project cost of capital is different for the two projects, we need to continue on and calculate the present value of the annuity.

A. What is the common life for these projects?

B. What is the net present value of each project?

C. Using the equivalent annual annuity approach, which project is preferred? Explain.

4. Consider three mutually exclusive projects, Projects A, B, and C, that have the following cash flows:

	End-of-year Cash Flow		
Year	*Project A*	*Project B*	*Project C*
0	−$100,000	−$100,000	−$100,000
1	$24,000	$37,000	$0
2	$24,000	$37,000	$0
3	$24,000	$37,000	$0
4	$24,000		$132,500
5	$24,000		
Cost of capital	6%	5%	7%

A. What is the common life for these projects?

B. What is the net present value of each project?

C. Using the equivalent annual annuity approach, which project is preferred? Explain.

CHAPTER 11

CAPITAL BUDGETING: CASH FLOWS AND RISK

Capital spending in the U.S. is cyclical, with less spending during recessionary periods. You can see this over time, using data from the Annual Capital Expenditures Survey (ACES), produced by the U.S. Census Bureau:*

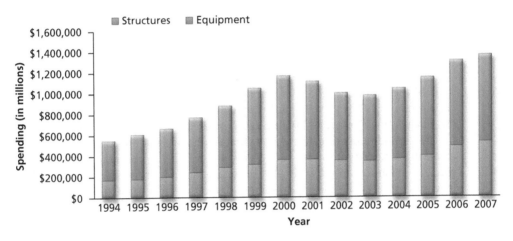

According to the National Bureau of Economic Research, the U.S. economy was in a recession from March 2001 through November 2001.** Capital spending in the U.S. declined in 2001 and continued its decline in 2002 and 2003.

The recession that began December 2007 was expected to have a dampening effect on capital spending in 2008 and beyond. Not only was capital spending affected by lower consumer spending, but companies also found it difficult to raise capital in the financial markets in 2008 and 2009.***

Learning Outcomes

After reading this chapter, you should be able to:

LO 11.1 Identify the relevant cash flows for a capital budgeting analysis.

LO 11.2 Estimate the investment cash flows, operating cash flows, and terminal cash flows of an investment project.

LO 11.3 Conduct a sensitivity analysis to examine the sensitivity of capital investment decisions to the estimates of cash flows.

LO 11.4 Estimate cash flows for a replacement decision.

LO 11.5 Evaluate the effects of inflation on capital budgeting decisions.

* Annual Capital Expenditures Survey, U.S. Census Bureau, Historical Data. 2007 is the most recent year available, as of January 2012.

** National Bureau of Economic Research, Business Cycle Expansions and Contractions, www.nber.org/cycles.htm.

*** David Wyss and Beth Ann Bovino, "A Deep and Long Recession," *Business Week*, January 23, 2009.

417

Chapter Preview In the previous chapter, we discussed capital budgeting techniques used to evaluate capital projects, including the net present value and internal rate of return. We took it for granted in that chapter that we already knew the inputs to the analysis: the net cash flows for each year of the project's useful life. All these methods require an estimate of the present cash outlay, as well as estimates of the future cash flows associated with the investment opportunity. In this chapter, we discuss how to incorporate these inputs into the evaluation process. We need to draw on our previous coverage regarding the company's financial statements, as well as the depreciation for tax purposes.

We begin our discussion by laying out the basic principles of relevant cash flows. We then describe and demonstrate how to estimate the individual cash flows that contribute to a project's net cash flows. Following this, we illustrate how sensitivity analysis can be used to evaluate how the effects of uncertain elements in a capital project can be analyzed. We wrap up the chapter covering specific issues that arise when dealing with replacement decisions and inflation. To provide an additional example of the cash flow determination for a capital project, we provide an integrative problem in Appendix 11A.

11.1 IDENTIFYING RELEVANT CASH FLOWS

One of the most, or perhaps the most, challenging task in capital budgeting is estimating a project's cash flows. We begin by providing some general guidelines for identifying relevant cash flows associated with capital expenditure decisions, along with examples.

In capital budgeting, we need to first determine the appropriate time horizon for the project. We need to know how long a project is likely to continue before it is economically wise to finish or replace it. In this sense, abandonment decisions have to be considered because projects are finished when it is economic to do so and not when the engineer says the assets are no longer functioning.

What Are the Relevant Cash Flows?

The key to determining relevant cash flows is identifying how cash flows of the business change if the business goes ahead with a project:

What are cash flows if the company goes ahead with the project?

What are cash flows if the company does not go ahead with the project?

What is the difference in these cash flows?

marginal or **incremental cash flow** the additional cash flow that results from a capital budgeting decision, generated by a new project

In other words, we need to determine each **marginal** or **incremental cash flow** arising from capital budgeting decisions. For example, suppose a company is purchasing equipment that replaces existing equipment. Not only do we consider the cost of the new equipment, but we also consider any cash flows when we dispose of the existing equipment.

What about taxes?

When a company introduces a new product, when it replaces equipment with more efficient equipment, or when it buys physical assets that it will sell at some future point in

418

time, there are likely to be effects of these decisions on the taxable income of the company. Because changes in taxable income result in changes in taxes and, hence cash flows, we need to estimate any and all tax implications for a project's cash flows.

There is also the possibility that tax credits are available for specific capital projects. Periodically throughout the past 50 years, tax credits on investments in capital projects have been available to companies for U.S. federal tax purposes. An investment tax credit is a direct reduction of the company's tax bill at the time the investment is made, which can significantly affect the initial cash outlay for a project.[1]

Using Tax Credits to Compete | GLOBAL PERSPECTIVE

European countries compete for companies to locate within their boundaries. For example, France offers a reimbursement of research and depreciation expenses (through a tax credit) of 40 percent the first year, 35 percent the second year, and 30 percent thereafter up to €100 million, with the possibility of doubling the credit for public-sector research.[2] The goal is to garner jobs and share of investment in Europe by companies in other countries, notably India and China.[3]

Therefore, we when we estimate cash flows, we do this considering any effect on taxes; hence, our goal is to estimate the project's after-tax cash flows. What happens when we apply the net present value or the internal rate of return techniques to analyze these cash flows? We use the project's cost of capital which is on an after-tax basis.[4]

BOTTOM LINE: Any taxes arising from a project are included in the project's cash flows.

What about any effect on other products of the company?

Consider a company that is thinking about introducing a new product line that is expected to generate $100,000 per year in additional after-tax cash flows. The introduction of this new product line, however, will likely affect the sales of another product of the same company; more precisely, introducing the new product will cost the company $40,000 in after-tax cash flows as a result of lost sales for an existing product. The $40,000 is the result of cannibalization; **cannibalization** is when a new product competes with, and therefore affects, the sales of another product of the same company. In this example, the incremental cash flows that we use in evaluating the new product line are $60,000 per year (i.e., $100,000 – $40,000).

BOTTOM LINE: If a proposed capital project would affect the cash flows of other products of the company, the effect on these other products must be considered as part of the determination of the relevant cash flows.

cannibalization competition of a new product with an existing product of the same company, resulting in diminished sales of the existing product

What if the project affects levels of working capital?

Working capital consists of the short-term assets and liabilities that support the day-to-day operations of a company, including cash, accounts receivable, inventory, or accounts payable. Many capital projects require adjustments in a company's working capital. For example, consider a company that is evaluating a new production process. The process requires the company to hold additional inventory on hand, which would tie up more funds and is reflected in the company's level of working capital. This represents a drain of cash that

[1] In 2011, these credits were limited, for the most part, to alternative fuel production, employment of targeted groups, and research and development. Historically, however, the U.S. has had in place, at different points in time, tax credits for capital spending up to 10 percent of the investment.

[2] Source: *Innovation Comes First*, www.invest-in-france.org.

[3] 2010 Report Job-Creating Foreign Investment in France, investinfrance.org.

[4] We discuss this in more detail later in the chapter.

should be considered in the capital budgeting decision because any funds that are tied up have an associated cost. Of course, another company could be considering a process that requires the company to hold lower amounts of inventory on hand, and this would represent a source of funds for the company, which should also be considered in evaluating the implementation of that process.

The change in working capital affects cash flows: Increases in working capital are decreases in cash flows, and vice versa. A capital project could result in the increase or decrease in any of the working capital accounts. Manufacturing a new product may require having more raw materials on hand (hence, a larger investment in inventory), but replacing existing production line equipment with more efficient machinery may result in having less work-in-process (hence, lowering the investment in inventory). An expansion involving more retail outlets may increase the company's need for cash on hand, as well as inventory on the shelves.

Another reason why we adjust for working capital changes is that we need to adjust for the actual flow of funds. To see how this works, consider a sale to a customer on credit. When the sale is made, there is no effect on cash; cash is not affected until the account is collected:

Event	Balance Sheet Effect		Income Statement Effect			Cash
	Inventory	Accounts Receivable	Sales	Cost of Goods Sold	Net Profit	
Sale of goods on account	↓	↑	↑	↑	↑	No effect
Collect on account		↓				↑

By adjusting for the change in the working capital accounts, we are adjusting for the effect on cash: When the accounts receivable decreases, cash comes into the business from the sale, but not before that time. Considering the different working capital accounts, the adjustment we make in the analysis depends on whether the account is an asset or a liability:

Working Capital Account	Effect on Cash Flow of an ...	
	... Increase in the Account	... Decrease in the Account
Cash	−	+
Accounts receivable	−	+
Inventory	−	+
Accounts payable	+	−

A particularly tricky aspect of dealing with working capital changes is that we always return the company's working capital to the original levels by the end of the project's life. Again, this harks back to the idea that we are looking at how different cash flows are with and without the project. If a project has a useful life of 5 years, this means that after 5 years, the working capital levels should return to the preproject levels.

We often simplify the world when we devise capital budgeting problems that involve working capital changes; we assume that working capital increases abruptly at the beginning of the life of the project and then returns to its preproject levels just as abruptly at the end of the life of the project. A more realistic situation is that working capital changes gradually over the project's life.

BOTTOM LINE: *We need to adjust cash flows, particularly the investment cash flow and the terminal cash flow at the end of the estimated project life, to reflect any additional working capital requirements that are associated with the project.*

What about sunk costs?

If the company has made an expenditure prior to the decision of whether to invest in a capital project, this expenditure is not relevant to the investment decision; it is a sunk cost. A **sunk cost** is any cost that has been incurred prior to the capital project decision, and these sunk costs are not included in the capital project decision.

sunk costs costs that have already been incurred, cannot be recovered, and should not influence current capital budgeting decisions

You also should ignore sunk costs because the focus of capital budgeting is with *future* cash flows. Suppose a company has spent $50,000 to try to get a project up and running. If something happens to make the project undesirable, the company should not proceed any further; otherwise, it will simply be "throwing good money after bad." In other words, it should accept the $50,000 loss, which makes more sense than losing another $100,000 on the project. Obviously, this is easier said than done.

Other examples of sunk costs include research and development, marketing research, and engineering costs that result in the product idea or develop the estimates for the analysis of the capital project. But what about the use of assets, such as land and buildings, that a company already owns? Suppose, for example, the company bought land 10 years ago for $10 million and has no other use for it. If the company then wants to use this land for a capital project, this $10 million is a sunk cost and therefore does not enter the cash flow analysis for the capital project.

BOTTOM LINE: *If the expenditure has already been made, we do not consider this in the cash flow analysis for a capital project.*

What about foregone opportunities?

Although sunk costs are irrelevant, we do need to factor **opportunity costs** into cash flow estimates. Opportunity costs represent cash flows that must be forgone as a result of an investment decision. We use the following example to distinguish between sunk costs and opportunity costs. Consider a company that purchased a piece of land several years ago for $150,000. Today, the company is deciding whether or not to use the land as the location for a new storage facility. In this situation, the original outlay of $150,000 is a sunk cost and should be ignored. However, the land cannot be considered "free" because the company always has the option of using it for another purpose or selling it. Assuming the company could sell this land today at a market price of $200,000, this would represent the opportunity cost of using the land for the storage facility; as such, it should be included in the cost of the project.

opportunity costs cash flow that must be forgone as a result of an investment decision

Consider another example. Suppose a company has a building that it purchased 5 years ago for $500 million. And suppose that the company has decided to use a third of this building for the processing of its food product. If the company has no other use for this portion of the building, the cost of the building is a sunk cost and not part of the analysis of the new food product. However, if the company could have rented out that portion of the building for, say, $50 million per year, this $50 million is a foregone cash flow and must be included in the analysis of the new food product.

BOTTOM LINE: *Opportunity costs that represent foregone cash flows should be included in the cash flow analysis of a capital project.*

What about financing costs?

We do not include associated interest and dividend payments in estimated project cash flows because we account for these in the project's cost of capital; to affect cash flows with these costs would result in double-counting these costs.

When evaluating a project using the net present value, the project's cost of capital is the discount rate applied to the project's cash flows; in the case of evaluating a project using the internal rate of return, the costs of financing the project are captured in the project's cost of capital, which is used as a hurdle rate when compared to the project's internal rate of return.

BOTTOM LINE: Financing costs do not affect the cash flows of a project.

What about benefit or harm to unrelated, third parties?

externalities
consequences that result from an investment that may benefit or harm unrelated third parties

Also to be ignored are **externalities**. Externalities are the consequences that often result from an investment that may benefit or harm unrelated third parties. An example is a project that generates employment in a depressed region. Although there are intangible benefits for the community and the company, we do not include these in the project's cash flows. Another example is any environmental damage that may occur as a result of a capital project. Any direct costs, such as the cost of mitigation or pollution control devices, would be included in the cash flows of the project because they would be necessary costs related to the investment. In this case, they are not externalities, but rather are costs of the project. Intangible effects, however, would be difficult, if not impossible, to estimate and are not included in the cash flow estimates.

BOTTOM LINE: Costs related to externalities are not considered in a project's cash flows.

What else?

Capital project analysis is challenging primarily because each capital project is unique. Therefore, financial managers must be on the watch for any other cash flow and value effects from a particular capital project.

For example, consider the effect of all project interdependencies on cash flow estimates. If a company is considering projects that are mutually exclusive, the decision to accept one of the projects precludes the acceptance of any other in the set of projects. The other extreme is that projects may be independent; that is, accepting one project would not affect any other project's cash flows. But more realistic situations often include interdependencies.

Consider that companies are, basically, portfolios of projects. A consumer product company, for example, may have many products that are related and may affect each other. If the company has toothpaste products, it also may have floss and mouthwash products. The promotion and sharing of brands and promotions will cause new products to potentially affect existing products, producing cannibalization, as we discussed earlier. But there is also the potential for contingent projects, in which one project's cash flows depend on another project. This includes such contingencies as tie-ins for toys and movies and software and apps for specific operating systems.

real option opportunity associated with a real asset, such as the opportunity to delay, abandon, or expand

Another consideration is that most projects have real options. A **real option** is an opportunity associated with a real asset. Like any other option, a real option is the right, but not the obligation, to undertake an action. Examples of real options include the option to delay a project, the option to abandon a project, or the option to expand a project. For example, the option to delay or wait on a project may provide time for some uncertainties in the economy or regulation to be resolved, providing more certainty in the amount and timing of a project's cash flows. Though difficult to estimate their contribution to a project's value (much of which is beyond the scope of this book), these options are valuable. Our goal in this chapter is to discuss and demonstrate how financial managers estimate cash flows for a project. We reserve the discussion of real options to Appendix 11B.

BOTTOM LINE: Each capital project is unique.

Concept Review Questions

1. Why do we not deduct interest costs from the cash flows to be discounted?

2. Distinguish between a sunk cost and an opportunity cost. What is an example of each?

11.2 ESTIMATING CASH FLOWS

Sometimes it is convenient to distinguish among three different categories of cash flows and estimate each type of cash flow separately. We discuss each category of cash flow next: the investment cash flow, operating cash flows, and terminal after-tax cash flows.

Considering the cash flows for a project in broad terms, we diagram these in Figure 11-1. We start with the initial investment at the beginning of the project, generate operating cash flows throughout the life of the project, and may have terminal cash flows as we close out the project. The sum of these cash flows for any given year is the net cash flow. Our goal is to estimate the net cash flow for each year in the project's life.[5]

> Working capital changes are important to include in the analysis because they help us adjust for the timing of cash receipts, but also capture the opportunity cost of investing in working capital.
>
> Whether you include the cash flow effects from working capital changes in investment cash flows, operating cash flows, and/or terminal cash flows depends on the individual project's scenario. For example, if working capital changes only at the beginning and end of a project, it is easiest to collect these with the investment and terminal cash flows. If, however, working capital changes along with the changes in operations during the life of the project, it is probably easiest to group these with the operating cash flows. The key is not how you classify cash flows from changes in working capital, but rather getting the amount and timing correct.

The Investment Cash Flow

The **investment cash flow** is the total cash outlay that is required to initiate an investment project. Because the investment cash flow often occurs at the beginning of the project, we also refer to this as the **initial cash flow** or **initial cash outlay**. It is the cost of the plant

investment cash flow or **initial cash flow** or **initial cash outlay** total cash outlay required to initiate an investment project, including the change in net working capital and associated opportunity costs

FIGURE 11-1 **Typical Project Cash Flows**

[5] We simplify things by assuming that the cash flows only occur at the end of each year. The reason we do this in explaining capital budgeting is to illustrate the approach and techniques. A more realistic analysis would likely involve monthly cash flows and would require more complexity in analyzing the cash flows using the techniques of net present value and internal rate of return, for example.

capital cost cost incurred to make an investment operational, such as machinery installation expenses, land-clearing costs, and so on

or equipment associated with the project, which we call the **capital cost** of an investment, and includes all costs incurred to make an investment operational, such as machinery installation expenses, land-clearing costs, and so on. In most cases, the capital costs are depreciated for tax purposes.

The initial after-tax cash flow includes other cash flows, such as the change in net working capital and any other associated opportunity costs or cash flows. Each capital project has its own specific cash flows at the beginning of the investment decision, but we can generalize these based on a new project and a replacement project:

	New Project	Replacement project
	Capital cost	Capital cost
Less	Change in working capital	Change in working capital
Less	Opportunity costs	Opportunity costs
Plus	Tax credits	Tax credits
Plus		Proceeds from sale of replaced equipment
Less		Taxes related to sale of replaced equipment
Equals	Investment cash flow	Investment cash flow

The key to the estimation of the investment cash flow is to make sure that you are consistent in the signs of the flows. Consider an example. The Brennan Co. is evaluating the proposed acquisition of a new milling machine. The machine's base price is $625,000, and it would cost another $25,000 to modify it for special use by the company. The company will need to maintain additional raw materials inventory of $100,000 to use the machine. Brennan Co.'s marginal tax rate is 35 percent. What is the company's associated after-tax cash outlay?

$$\text{Capital cost} = \$625,000 + 25,000 = \$650,000$$

$$\text{Investment cash flow} = -\$650,000 - 100,000 + 0 = -\$750,000$$

Note that the cost of the capital asset is not just the $625,000 purchase price, but also all other cash outlays that are needed to get the equipment operational. In this case, the $25,000 in modifications must be capitalized and then depreciated over the life of the machine because, just like the equipment, these modifications generate benefits over the life of the equipment. Generally, in any analysis, costs have to be divided into capitalized costs and expenses. In most tax systems, anything that generates future benefits is capitalized, and then the value is expensed through depreciation expenses over future periods. In contrast, costs that generate no future benefits can be expensed immediately and so are immediately tax deductible.

EXAMPLE 11.1

Investment Cash Flows

PROBLEM

Consider an investment that requires the purchase of equipment for $1 million and decreases working capital by $0.2 million. The company must spend $0.1 million to install the equipment. What is the investment cash flow for this investment?

Solution

Investment cash flow = –$1 million + $0.2 million – $0.1 million = –$0.9 million.

---

operating cash flows cash flows that are estimated to occur as a result of the investment decision, comprising the associated expected incremental increase in after-tax operating cash flow

Operating Cash Flows

The **operating cash flow** in a given period t is the incremental operating cash flow, attributed to the operations of the project's investments. In other words, these are the after-tax operating cash flows associated with the project. These cash flows comprise the associated expected incremental increase in after-tax operating income (i.e., the operating cash flows), as well as any incremental tax savings or additional taxes paid in future years that result from the initial investment outlay. The tax savings are associated with the additional depreciation expenses that may be charged for tax purposes as a result of the initial investment.

The amount of depreciation charged for tax purposes is prescribed by U.S. tax law according to the rates prescribed in the **Modified Accelerated Cost Recovery System (MACRS)** for the asset's classified life. There are two important aspects of MACRS. First, the depreciable life of an asset for tax purposes is determined by reference to the tax code; the company does not choose the depreciable life, but rather looks it up. The possible depreciable lives are 3, 5, 7, 10, 15, or 20 years for most property other than real estate. For example, if the company buys a truck, it is classified as 5-year property for tax purposes no matter how long it will be depreciated for financial reporting purposes. Second, MACRS consists of a set of rates applied against the depreciable basis (that is, the capital cost) that are based on declining balance methods 200 percent declining balance for 3-, 5-, 7-, and 10-year assets and 150 percent declining balance for 15- and 20-year assets. Real property is depreciated over 27.5 years or 39 years straight-line depreciation under MACRS, depending on the type, though land is never depreciated.

We summarize the MACRS rates in Table 11-1 for the MACRS lives up to 15 years.[6] Because of the use of a half-year convention, the asset is not fully depreciated—that is, its book value for tax purposes is equal to zero—after 1 year beyond its classified life.[7] For example, if the asset is a 3-year asset, it is fully depreciated after 4 years.

TABLE 11-1 MACRS Rates

Tax rates are effective rate, which are applied against the original cost of the asset

Year	3-year	5-year	Classified Life 7-year	10-year	15-year
1	33.33%	20.00%	14.29%	10.00%	5.00%
2	44.45%	32.00%	24.49%	18.00%	9.50%
3	14.81%	19.20%	17.49%	14.40%	8.55%
4	7.41%	11.52%	12.49%	11.52%	7.70%
5		11.52%	8.93%	9.22%	6.93%
6		5.76%	8.92%	7.37%	6.23%
7			8.93%	6.55%	5.90%
8			4.46%	6.55%	5.90%
9				6.56%	5.91%
10				6.55%	5.90%
11				3.28%	5.91%
12					5.90%
13					5.91%
14					5.90%
15					5.91%
16					2.95%

Rates are those assuming the half-year convention is applied.

[6] The MACRS depreciation is sometimes referred to as the capital cost allowance or cost recovery. See Department of the Treasury, Internal Revenue Service's *Publication 946: How to Depreciate Property* for details on the MACRS system.

[7] For tax purposes, a company may also use a midquarter convention. However, in the interest of keeping the tax depreciation explanation as simple as possible, we are demonstrating MACRS depreciation using the more common half-year convention.

Because depreciation is a noncash expense and we are trying to estimate cash flows, we have two ways to deal with it. The first approach is to deduct the change in depreciation from the change in operating income, then deduct the associated taxes, and finally add the change in depreciation expense back because it is a noncash expense. The second approach is to recognize that depreciation creates tax savings for the company in the amount of the change in depreciation multiplied by the company's marginal tax rate. We refer to this tax savings as the **depreciation tax shield** because the deduction of depreciation to arrive at taxable income shields some income from taxation. We then add this amount to the change in after-tax operating income, which is determined by deducting the taxes associated with the company's before-tax operating income.

We show these two approaches in Table 11-2. This may look complicated on the surface, but Approach 1 is, basically, the income statement for the incremental cash flows, with the noncash charge of depreciation added back to the incremental income to arrive at the cash flow. Approach 2 isolates the depreciation effect by separating the effects of a change in operating income and changes in depreciation. Does it matter which approach you use? Not at all. Which is easier to use? It depends on the problem at hand.

depreciation tax shield tax savings associated with the depreciation deduction for tax purposes, which is the amount of the depreciation expense multiplied by the marginal tax rate

TABLE 11-2 **Two Ways to Determine Cash Flows**

Approach 1		*Approach 2*	
	Change in revenues		Change in revenues
Less	Change in expenses	*Less*	Change in expenses
Less	Change in depreciation	*Equals*	Change in EBITDA
Equals	Change in taxable income	*Less*	Change in taxes payable
Less	Change in taxes	*Equals*	Change in after-tax operating income
Equals	Change in after-tax income	*Plus*	Change in depreciation tax shield
Plus	Change in depreciation	*Equals*	Operating cash flow
Equals	Operating cash flow		

With respect to the milling machine purchase that Brennan Co. is considering, the company's production department anticipates the machine will generate an additional $525,000 per year in annual operating revenue, whereas the associated annual operating expenses are projected to be $325,000 per year. The economic life of the machine is expected to be 5 years. What is the annual after-tax cash flow for each year?

For each of the 5 years, the change in operating income before depreciation is equal to the change in revenues less the change in operating expenses, or $525,000 − $325,000 = $200,000. The change in operating income before depreciation is the change in EBITDA—earnings before interest, taxes, depreciation, and amortization. Under MACRS, the depreciation for each year is generally different for each year because the tax systems allow the use of an accelerated depreciation system. For example, in the U.S. tax system, the rates for most assets are based on a 200DB system with a half-year convention. The details do not really matter—other than knowing that the rates are different for each year and are applied against the original cost—because the rates prescribed and presented in the tax code are the effective depreciation rates.[8]

---

[8] Consider depreciation that is based on 200DB, with a half-year convention, for a 5-year MACRS asset. 200DB indicates that the annual rate applied to the carrying value (original cost less accumulated depreciation) is what it would be under straight-line, multiplied by 2. The depreciation rate for the second year based on 200DB would be 20% x 2 = 40% of the asset's carrying value. The carrying value is 1 − 0.20, or 80% of the original cost. Therefore, the effective rate is 0.40 x 0.80 = 32%. The 32% is what is reported in the tax cost and is applied against the original cost of the asset.

Looking up the rates for a 5-year asset, and applying these rates to the asset cost of $650,000, we estimate the 5 years of depreciation and the book value of the assets for tax purposes:

Year	Asset Cost	MACRS Rate	Depreciation Expense	Book Value for Tax Purposes
1	$650,000	20.00%	$130,000	$520,000
2	$650,000	32.00%	$208,000	$312,000
3	$650,000	19.20%	$124,800	$187,200
4	$650,000	11.52%	$74,880	$112,320
5	$650,000	11.52%	$74,880	$37,440

We estimate the book value of the asset for tax purposes (that is, the undepreciated cost of the asset) because if the company sells the asset at any time before it is fully depreciated, this book or carrying value is used to compute any gain or loss.

Combining these estimates with the company's tax rate of 35 percent, we can estimate the project's operating cash flow for each year as follows:

Approach 1		Year 1	Year 2	Year 3	Year 4	Year 5
	Change in revenues	$525,000	$525,000	$525,000	$525,000	$525,000
Less	Change in expenses	325,000	325,000	325,000	325,000	325,000
Less	Change in depreciation	130,000	208,000	124,800	74,880	74,880
Equals	Change in taxable income	$70,000	$8,000	$75,200	$125,120	$125,120
Less	Change in taxes	24,500	2,800	26,320	43,792	43,792
Equal:	Change in after-tax income	$45,500	$5,200	$48,880	$81,328	$81,328
Plus	Change in depreciation	130,000	208,000	124,800	74,880	74,880
Equals	Operating cash flow	$175,500	$202,800	$173,680	$156,208	$156,208

Approach 2		Year 1	Year 2	Year 3	Year 4	Year 5
	Change in revenues	$525,000	$525,000	$525,000	$525,000	$525,000
Less	Change in expenses	325,000	325,000	325,000	325,000	325,000
Equals	Change in EBITDA	$200,000	$200,000	$200,000	$200,000	$200,000
Less	Change in taxes payable	70,000	70,000	$70,000	$70,000	$70,000
Equals:	Change in after-tax operating income	$130,000	$130,000	$130,000	$130,000	$130,000
Plus:	Change in depreciation tax shield	45,500	72,800	43,680	26,208	26,208
Equals:	Operating cash flow	$175,500	$202,800	$173,680	$156,208	$156,208

A few observations from this analysis:

1. The use of a declining balance method for depreciation with a half-year convention means that the asset is not fully depreciated at the end of its useful life, which is 5 years in this example. Therefore, in this example, if the company disposes of the asset at the end of 5 years, the asset will have a book value of 5.76% of $650,000 or $37,440, which must be considered when calculating terminal cash flows.

2. Depreciation expense is lower in Year 1 because of the half-year rule, then is the highest in Year 2 and declines thereafter.

3. No matter which of the approaches you use, you get the same operating cash flows.

In this example, we estimated the future cash flows without considering what happens to the machine at the end of its useful economic life. There are often cash flows in the last year that relate to selling or disposing of the asset and returning working capital to its preproject level. In some cases, there may also be expenses related to mitigating the site because of the environmental impact of the project.

EXAMPLE 11.2

Depreciation Tax Shield

PROBLEM

Suppose an asset is classified as a 3-year asset for tax purposes, but has a useful life of 5 years. If the asset has an initial cost of $1 million, what is the depreciation tax shield for each year in the asset's useful life if the tax rate is 40 percent?

Solution

	Year 1	Year 2	Year 3	Year 4	Year 5
MACRS rate	33.33%	44.45%	14.81%	7.41%	0%
Deprecation	$333,300	$444,500	$148,100	$74,100	$0
Tax rate	40%	40%	40%	40%	40%
Deprecation tax shield	$133,320	$177,800	$59,240	$29,640	$0

EXAMPLE 11.3

Operating Cash Flows

PROBLEM

Consider an investment in equipment that does not affect revenues, but reduces expenses. The equipment costs $5 million and is classified as a 3-year asset for tax purposes. The investment does not affect working capital, but it is expected to reduce expenses by $1 million for each of the next 5 years. Once the 5 years are up, the equipment will be worthless and will be scrapped at no cost to the company. If the company's tax rate is 40 percent, what is the operating cash flow for each year of this asset's life?

Solution

Without Effect of Depreciation		Year 1	Year 2	Year 3	Year 4	Year 5
	Change in expenses	$1.00	$1.00	$1.00	$1.00	$1.00
Less	Change in taxes	$0.40	$0.40	$0.40	$0.40	$0.40
Equals	Change in after-tax income	$0.60	$0.60	$0.60	$0.60	$0.60

Effect of Depreciation						
	Change in depreciation	$1.67	$2.22	$0.74	$0.37	$0.00
Multiplied by	Tax rate	40%	40%	40%	40%	40%
Equals	Change in depreciation tax shield	$0.67	$0.89	$0.30	$0.15	$0.00
Summing the change in after-tax income and the change in the depreciation tax shield						
Equals	Operating cash flow	$1.49	$0.90	$0.75	$0.60	$0.60

Terminal Cash Flows

The **terminal cash flow** or **ending cash flow** is the project's cash flow expected in the terminal year of a project, aside from that year's operating cash flow, as determined earlier. It comprises the estimated selling or **salvage value** of the asset.[9]

The salvage value is the estimate of the value of the asset at the end of its useful life; it is, in effect, the estimate of the selling price of the asset at the end of the project. The sale of an asset at the end of the project's life may have tax consequences. First, if the selling price is greater than the original capital cost, a capital gain arises, which is taxable. If a depreciable capital asset is sold below its book value for tax purposes, it generates a capital loss.

Aside from capital gains and losses, additional tax consequences can arise. In particular, depreciation recapture may be generated by the sale of an asset. Under this scenario, the company would have to pay additional taxes on "excess" depreciation charged against the asset or assets if the salvage value is greater than the ending tax book value of the asset. The amount by which the salvage value exceeds the book or carrying value is fully taxable as ordinary income.[10] However, if the salvage value is less than the ending book value, the amount by which the book value exceeds the salvage value is called a terminal loss, which is fully tax deductible.[11] Finally, depreciation recapture may occur if an asset is sold for more than its book value of that asset for tax purposes.

terminal (or ending) cash flow total cash flow expected to be generated in the terminal year of a project, aside from that year's operating cash flow

salvage value estimated sale price of an asset at the end of its useful life

Sell the Asset ...	*Capital Gain or Loss*	*Recapture of Depreciation*
for more than the original cost	Salvage value − Original cost _____ Gain	Original cost − Book value _____ Recapture
for less than the original cost, but more than the book value	None	Salvage value − Book value _____ Recapture
for less than the book value	Carrying value − Salvage value _____ Loss	None

SUMMARIZING: GAIN, LOSS, OR RECAPTURE ON THE SALE OF AN ASSET

Generally, capital gains are rare for depreciable capital assets because these assets typically cannot be sold for more than their original cost after they are put in use. The recapture of depreciation, however, is common because the MACRS rates are likely more accelerated than the actual deterioration of the asset.

[9] In financial accounting, the salvage value is important in the calculation of the depreciation. For tax accounting purposes, salvage value is ignored in the calculation of depreciation. We do not ignore salvage value in the analysis of cash flow for a capital project because this is our best guess of what the company can sell the asset for at the end of the project.

[10] In other words, it is viewed as if the firm charged too much depreciation because the asset is sold for more than its depreciated book value for tax purposes. Therefore, the firm must pay back the amount of taxes it saved by charging too much depreciation.

[11] In this instance, the firm did not charge enough depreciation because the asset was sold below its book value for tax purposes. Therefore, it is permitted to depreciate the asset to its selling price and deduct this charge for tax purposes.

In addition to the salvage value and all the associated tax complications, the working capital associated with the project will be returned to preproject levels, which may represent a cash inflow or outflow. This means that the people to whom you have extended credit will pay off the debts once the project is finished, and all inventory on hand will be sold, so that the net amount after the company has paid its suppliers is available to finance other projects.

We can estimate the ending cash flow with tax implications:

	Estimated selling price of the asset
Less	Taxes on sale
Plus	Change in working capital
Equals	Terminal cash flow

Regarding the project being considered by Brennan Co., the production department estimated that the $100,000 in additional net working capital requirements will be released after the economic life of the machine; therefore, the change in working capital is −$100,000, and the cash flow from this change is +$100,000.[12] Management estimates that at the end of 5 years, the milling machine can be sold for $37,440. What are the terminal cash flow and the present value of this ending cash flow?

Notice in this example that there are no capital gains and no depreciation recapture because the asset is sold for its carrying value of $37,440. Therefore, we can estimate the terminal cash flows as:

$$\text{Terminal cash flow} = \$37,440 + \$100,000 = \$137,440$$

EXAMPLE 11.4

Disposition of an Asset

PROBLEM

Suppose a company has equipment that had an original cost of $10 million, and it sells this equipment 6 years later for $2 million. If the carrying value of this equipment for tax purposes is $1 million, what is the cash flow associated with the sale of this equipment? The company's marginal tax rate is 35 percent.

Solution

Cash flows:
Sale price of $2 million
Tax on recapture of depreciation: $0.35 \times (\$2 - 1) = \$0.35$ million
Cash flow associated with the sale = $\$2 - 0.35 = \$1.65$ million

---

Assembling the Pieces

There are three basic pieces that we have to fit together to evaluate a project:

1. Investment cash flow
2. Operating cash flows
3. Terminal cash flow

The investment cash flow is an outlay that may occur at the beginning of the project or may be spread over several periods, depending on the project. For example, if a company is building a new plant, the outlays may span 2 or 3 years. What is important is to make sure to get the timing of these cash flows correct.

The operating cash flows may be positive or negative, but when we are working with a typical project, these are often positive. When might operating cash flows be

---

[12] This means that the change in working capital provides a cash inflow of +$100,000 as this working capital is reduced.

negative? Examples include when there is a lag between the start-up of the project and revenues, when there are operating expenses that are larger in the beginning of the life of the project that diminish as learning occurs, and when competitors enter the market and the revenues for the product diminish significantly, but operating expenses do not.

The terminal cash flow may be positive or negative. If assets are sold at the end of the project, there is often a positive cash flow after considering taxes on any gain. If remediation of a site is necessary to satisfy environmental laws and regulations, for example, a company may have a significant negative cash flow in the final year.

For each period in a project's life, we sum the cash flows to produce the net cash flow for each period in the life of the project. What are the net cash flows associated with Brennan Co.'s project? Let's assemble the cash flows that we have estimated.

	Initially	*Year 1*	*Year 2*	*Year 3*	*Year 4*	*Year 5*
Investment cash flow	−$750,000					
Operating cash flow		$175,500	$202,800	$173,680	$156,208	$156,208
Terminal cash flow						137,440
Net cash flow	−$750,000	$175,500	$202,800	$173,680	$156,208	$293,648

Should Brennan accept or reject this project? This is where the capital budgeting techniques, such as the net present value and internal rate of return, enter the analysis.

Once you have calculated the net cash flow for each year of a project's life, you can apply the capital budgeting techniques to these cash flows to evaluate whether a project is acceptable. Let's apply several of the techniques from Chapter 10 to the Brennan example, assuming a project cost of capital of 9 percent.

Net present value	$17,327.44
Internal rate of return	9.84%
Profitability index	1.02
Payback period	5 years
Discounted payback period	5 years

Therefore, Brennan's capital project is acceptable: It is expected to add value, as indicated by the net present value, and its return exceeds what is required for the project's level of risk (that is, 9 percent).

SUMMARIZING: CONNECTING THE CASH FLOWS WITH THE CAPITAL BUDGETING TECHNIQUES

Because we are working with estimates of what may happen next year, the year after, and on until the expected end of the life of the project, we may want examine the sensitivity of the project's cash flows to the inputs, as we discuss in the next section.

---

1. Why does the investment cash flow often exceed the purchase price of an asset?

2. How do taxes affect the annual cash flows and terminal cash flows of an investment project?

3. If a project is expected to increase the level of inventories, how does this affect cash flows?

Concept Review Questions

LESSONS LEARNED | Tax Breaks Don't Boost Investment: Study

From 2001 to 2003, 25 companies with big tax breaks cut their capital investments by 22 percent, advocacy group finds.

In an ideal world, tax breaks provide an incentive to companies to plow large sums of money into new plants, equipment, research, people and other things that could spur growth in their businesses and the economy at large.

Alas, it doesn't work out so neatly. Or so a study of 275 profitable Fortune 500 companies by the Citizens for Tax Justice (CTJ) and the Institute on Taxation and Economic Policy (ITEP) suggests. Large tax breaks don't necessarily move corporations to invest more, the report's authors contend.

The study found that 82 companies paid no federal income tax in at least one year during the first three years of the current Bush administration. Indeed, the companies generated so much in the way of excess tax breaks that they received outright federal tax rebates totaling $12.6 billion. In other words, they made more after taxes than before taxes in those no-tax years, the report's authors note.

Further, in 2002 and 2003, the 275 companies sheltered more than half of their profits from tax, according to the report. (The Web site of CTJ, a 501(c)(4) advocacy group, lists "closing corporate tax loopholes" as one of its goals; ITEP refers to itself as "a non-profit, non-partisan research and education organization that works on government taxation and spending policy issues.")

Did companies at least use these enormous tax breaks to invest in their businesses and boost their long-term prospects? Not really, the study suggests. Just seven of the 25 companies with the largest total tax breaks from all sources over the three years increased capital investment from 2001 to 2003, according to the report.

Indeed, the 25 companies in the survey with the biggest total tax breaks cut their capital investments from 2001 to 2003 by 22 percent, on average. In contrast, the remaining 250 companies in the survey reduced their investments by 13 percent.

What's more, just seven of the 25 companies with the largest tax breaks hiked investment over the three-year period—Citigroup, ExxonMobil, Pfizer, Altria, Wachovia, Viacom, and American Express.

The study's authors also point out that tax laws adopted in 2002 and 2003 greatly increased corporate write-offs for accelerated depreciation and made it easier for corporations to use excess tax subsidies to trigger tax rebates, at a three-year cost of $175 billion.

Although backers of such incentives argued that they would spur corporate investment in plant and equipment, "they failed to do so," the study's authors note. For example, the 25 companies that reported the largest tax savings from accelerated depreciation cut their total property and plant and equipment investments by 27 percent from 2001 to 2003, according to the report. The investments of the remaining 250 companies, on the other hand, dipped by only 8 percent.

"We do not mean to imply in our report that corporate tax breaks actively discourage capital investments," said Robert S. McIntyre, director of CTJ and co-author of the report with T.D. Coo Nguyen of ITEP. "But the evidence shows, as it has so often in the past, that business investment decisions are primarily driven by supply and demand, not by government attempts to micro-manage the economy."

The study also found that 28 companies enjoyed negative federal income tax rates over the entire 2001–03 period. Those with large negative tax rates included Pepco Holdings (–59.6 percent), Prudential Financial (–46.2 percent), ITT Industries (–22.3 percent) and Boeing (–18.8 percent).

Half of the $87.1 billion in total tax-breaks over the three years in the companies studied went to just 25 corporations, with each garnering more than $1.5 billion.

Topping the list was General Electric, with $9.5 billion in tax breaks over the three years. It was followed by SBC Communications at $9 billion and Citigroup, IBM, Microsoft, and AT&T, each with about $4.6 billion.

Stephen Taub, "Tax Breaks Don't Boost Investment: Study," CFO.com, September 24, 2004.

11.3 SENSITIVITY TO INPUTS

Much of what goes into the cash flows in the analysis are estimates. Recognizing that estimates are simply that, we may want to perform a *sensitivity analysis*, examining whether the investment is still attractive under varying conditions.

Sensitivity Analysis

Financial analysts use **sensitivity analysis** to examine how an investment's cash flows change as the value of one input is changed. This type of analysis allows companies to determine which of their estimates are the most critical in the final decision, but also provides information for risk management. Obviously, the most critical estimates require the greatest amount of scrutiny on the part of the company.

sensitivity analysis examination of how an investment's value changes as one input at a time is changed

When we use sensitivity analysis, we can examine the cash flows and decision considering one input at a time. Consider the following "what-ifs" of inputs on the Brennan project.

What if:

1. The annual operating income before depreciation is $190,000 instead of $200,000?
   This would affect the operating cash flows and, hence, net cash flows, decreasing them by $10,000 \times (1 - 0.35) = $6,500 each year:

	Initially	Year 1	Year 2	Year 3	Year 4	Year 5
Investment cash flow	−$750,000					
Operating cash flows		$169,000	$196,300	$167,180	$149,708	$149,708
Terminal cash flow						137,440
Net cash flow	−$750,000	$169,000	$196,300	$167,180	$149,708	$287,148

2. What if the asset sold for $100,000 at the end of 5 years, instead of $37,440?
   This would affect the terminal cash flow. Instead of $137,440, the cash flow would be:

$$\text{Terminal cash flows} = \$100,000 - \underbrace{0.35\,(100,000 - 37,440)}_{\text{recapture of depreciation}} + 100,000$$

$$= \$100,000 - 21,896 + 100,000$$
$$= \$178,104$$

   This change would change the Year 5 cash flow by $40,664, from $293,648 to $334,312.

3. What if the tax rate were 25 percent instead of 35 percent?
   This would affect the net operating cash flows each period:

	Initially	Year 1	Year 2	Year 3	Year 4	Year 5
Investment cash flow	−$750,000					
Operating cash flows		$182,500	$202,000	$181,200	$168,720	$168,720
Terminal cash flow						137,440
Net cash flow	−$750,000	$182,500	$202,000	$181,200	$168,720	$306,160

4. What if there is an additional change in working capital investment?
   In our initial problem, we estimated that inventory would increase by $100,000, which is then restored at the end of the project's life. What if the project requires an additional $40,000 of inventory at the end of the first year of operations, when the project is up and running? In this case, there would be an addition investment cash flow in Year 1, and the working capital recoupment in Year 5 would increase from $100,000 to $140,000, increasing the terminal cash flow to $177,440:

	Initially	Year 1	Year 2	Year 3	Year 4	Year 5
Investment cash flow	−$750,000	−$40,000				
Operating cash flow		175,500	$202,800	$173,680	$156,208	$156,208
Terminal cash flow						177,440
Net cash flow	−$750,000	$135,500	$202,800	$173,680	$156,208	$333,648

SUMMARIZING: SENSITIVITY TO ACCEPTABILITY OF PROJECT TO "WHAT-IFS"

We can use the "what-ifs" to examine the acceptability of a project. Consider Brennan's capital project, using a 9 percent project cost of capital, and the four "what-ifs" that we discuss briefly:

	Base Case	Change in Operating Income	Change in Asset Selling Price	Change in Tax Rate	Change in Working Capital
Net present value	$17,327.44	−$7,955.29	$43,756.25	$45,878.69	$6,627.45
Internal rate of return	9.84%	8.61%	11.05%	11.18%	9.30%
Profitability index	1.02	0.99	1.06	1.06	1.01
Acceptable?	Yes	No	Yes	Yes	Yes

As you can see, "what-ifs" can change the acceptability of the project.

It is also informative to vary the discount rate used in the NPV calculations because this variable is hard to estimate precisely and can change substantially through time as market, industry, and company conditions change. Consider the Brennan example. We can look at the sensitivity of the project's net present value—and hence the project's acceptability—for different discount rates, as we show in Figure 11-2. The project is not acceptable at rates greater than the project's internal rate of return of 9.836 percent.

FIGURE 11-2 The Net Present Value of the Project for Different Discount Rates

Scenario Analysis

In practice, companies are dealing with estimates of future cash flows, discount rates, and so on. Because any estimate of the future is subject to error, it is often useful to examine the effect on the attractiveness of a project if one or more inputs turns out different than expected. In other words, companies may want to evaluate the acceptability of projects by using a range of estimates.

Scenario analysis is the examination of how an investment's net cash flows change in response to differing scenarios with respect to the values of one or more estimates, such as sales or costs. It often makes sense to vary more than one input variable at a time because it allows us to account for interactions among the variables and for the fact that many variables can be related to external variables, such as the overall health of the economy or the company's industry. For example, if interest rates decline, it is reasonable to assume that a company's discount rate may decline, and if the product it sells is sensitive to interest rates, it is also reasonable to assume that the operating cash flows associated with a particular capital expenditure could increase under this favorable scenario. Similarly, if the price of oil declines, this may reduce the expected operating cash flows from an investment for an oil producer. The decline in oil prices could also cause the market price of the oil producer's common shares to decline, which could increase its cost of capital.

scenario analysis examination of how an investment's cash flows change in response to varying more than one input variable at a time

Scenario analysis is often conducted in the form of a "what-if" analysis, but the scenarios generally involve more than one variable input. These alternatives may reflect, for example, different economic, competitive, or regulatory environments. In practice, it is common to produce a wide variety of what-if scenarios, which can be easily handled through the use of a spreadsheet program, such as Excel.

PROBLEM

A company has a project that requires an initial after-tax cash outlay of $100,000, which is also equal to the capital cost of the assets that are purchased to get the project up and running. The asset will be depreciated as a 5-year asset according to MACRS. The company's effective tax rate is 35 percent. The company makes the following estimates.

EXAMPLE 11.5

Scenario Analysis

	Worst Case	*Base Case*	*Best Case*
Project life	10 years	10 years	10 years
Discount rate	12%	10%	8%
Salvage value	$30,000	$40,000	$60,000
Operating cash flow	$10,000	$15,000	$20,000

Determine the NPV for each scenario.

Solution

Because the asset is a 5-year MACRS asset, its book value at the end of the 10th year is zero. Therefore, the salvage value represents the amount of depreciation recaptured. For example, the cash flow at the end of year 10 for the worst scenario is calculated as $10,000 + $30,000 - (0.35 \times $30,000) = $29,500$. The 10th year's cash flows for the other two scenarios are calculated in a like manner.

	Cash Flows		
Year	*Worst*	*Base*	*Best*
0	-$100,000	-$100,000	-$100,000
1	$10,000	$15,000	$20,000
2	$10,000	$15,000	$20,000

3	$10,000	$15,000	$20,000
4	$10,000	$15,000	$20,000
5	$10,000	$15,000	$20,000
6	$10,000	$15,000	$20,000
7	$10,000	$15,000	$20,000
8	$10,000	$15,000	$20,000
9	$10,000	$15,000	$20,000
10	$29,500	$41,000	$59,000
Discount rate	12%	10%	8%
NPV	−$37,219	$2,193	$52,266

Examining these three scenarios tells the company that although the project seems attractive and has significant upside, it could also turn out to be a losing proposition and is not without risk.

Suppose we are performing sensitivity analysis and assume that a project's incremental revenues are a lot less than originally anticipated, and yet we assume everything else remains the same. Let us also agree that it is unrealistic if the company does not change anything in response to this decline in revenues; a company would not stand by and watch a project deteriorate without doing anything. In practice, companies respond to changing circumstances. That is, they exercise their ability to terminate, adjust, or expand a project—all options—once the project has begun. The option to adjust a real project is a real option. A **real option** is the opportunity, but not the obligation, to undertake an action that changes the capital project. Most capital projects have one or more real options associated with them. We discuss real options in Appendix 11A, though because the mathematics and analytics are beyond the scope of this text, we only scratch the surface of real options in this appendix.

FINANCE in the News | Gas Drillers' Painful Growth Paradox

Growing, growing, gone? America's oil and gas exploration-and-production industry faces a shakeout.

The E&P sector is addicted to high growth. That is expensive: E&P capital expenditure has outstripped cash flow pretty consistently over the past decade, estimates James Murchie, founder of Energy Income Partners LLC. In contrast, Exxon Mobil, consistent winner in terms of return on capital, has reinvested just 41% in that time.

In turn, E&P capex leaves little for dividends and buybacks, meaning investors demand more growth, meaning . . . you get the idea. The model works when commodity prices are rising and capital is plentiful. But the price of natural gas—the fuel that constitutes more than two-thirds of the sector's reserves and production—has slumped on oversupply. That is what happens when every company needs superior growth rates.

Bob Gillon of consultancy IHS Herold points to a structural disadvantage as well. E&P companies' appetite for growth, especially when energy prices are rising, leaves them "having the most amount of money to spend when costs are the highest; the least to spend when costs are the lowest."

A growing realization of the challenge should curtail access to capital. Bank credit lines, predicated on the value of reserves, are being renegotiated.

Consolidation, resisted at the trough of the market, also should pick up. That would help in an industry where the largest company accounts for only 3% of production. That is one reason why U.S. natural gas is so cheap compared with OPEC-influenced oil.

Larger, better-capitalized companies would be better placed to develop America's vast gas reserves without relying on an intravenous drip of capital to fund it. Investors, in turn, could look forward to more sustainable rewards.

Liam Denning, "Gas Drillers' Painful Growth Paradox," *Wall Street Journal*, September 25, 2009.

Simulation Analysis

When examining the role of risk in a project, it is often necessary to apply statistical procedures to analyze the distribution of net cash flows when many inputs are uncertain. This form of the analysis helps us better understand the risk of a project. Let's consider the Brennan project, but look at what happens when just the EBITDA for each year is uncertain.

Suppose that the EBITDA each year has an expected value of $200,000, but is uncertain, normally distributed with a standard deviation of $25,000. To simulate the cash flows and returns on this project, we can use a spreadsheet to draw different values of EBITDA using a random number generator consistent with the distribution. Let's draw 1,000 random EBITDA for each of the 5 years. So what do we get? We get 1,000 sets of net cash flows, from which we can then calculate 1,000 different returns. We show the possible Year 1 net cash flows in Figure 11-3.

As you can see, this appears to be approximately normally distributed; if we were to draw more observations, say, 10,000, the distribution would appear even more bell shaped. With this simulation, we have a distribution of EBITDA and can then calculate a distribution of operating cash flows for each year. With this information, along with the investment and terminal cash flows, we can then estimate the net cash flows for each of the 1,000 draws. From this, we can then calculate the possible returns on this project using the internal rate of return method, as we show in Figure 11-4.

This information can then be used in evaluating the risk of the project and evaluated within the context of a company's risk tolerance. Why didn't we calculate the net present value for each draw? The net present value requires using a cost of capital that reflects the risk of the project. If we are still examining the risk of the project, we cannot determine the project cost of capital. The use of the internal rate of return provides information on the sensitivity of the project's return to the inputs and hence provides information on the project's risk.

---

1. What insights can be gained by using sensitivity analysis, scenario analysis, and simulation analysis?

2. How can a financial manager assess a project's risk using simulation analysis?

Concept Review Questions

FIGURE 11-3 Distribution of Year 1 Cash Flows for 1,000 Random Draws of EBITDA

FIGURE 11-4 Distribution of Internal Rate of Returns for 1,000 Random Draws of EBITDA for Each Year

11.4 REPLACEMENT DECISIONS

Earlier in this chapter, we introduced guidelines for estimating cash flows and stated that we should focus on marginal or incremental cash flows that arise as a result of a capital budgeting decision. This refers to the additional cash flows that will be generated for the company. So far, this has been relatively easy to deal with because we have been considering **expansion projects**—that is, projects that would add something extra to the company in terms of additional sales or cost savings. For these types of projects, the new cash flows that arise from the investment decision represent incremental cash flows.

Replacement projects, as their name suggests, involve the replacement of an existing asset (or assets) with a new one. We deal with these types of decisions in the same manner as we deal with expansion problems, except that we must be more aware of focusing on incremental cash flows.

expansion projects projects that add something extra to the company in terms of sales or cost savings

replacement projects projects that involve the replacement of an existing asset with a new one

An Example

Suppose the Raleigh Company is considering the purchase of a new machine priced at $350,000 to replace an existing machine. The present market value of the existing machine is $50,000, and it is expected to have a salvage value of $15,000 at the end of 8 years. The existing machine was purchased 3 years ago for $300,000. Management estimates that the company will benefit from the new machine by reducing annual operating expenses by $50,000 over the life of the project, which is expected to be 8 years. This new machine is expected to have a salvage value of $100,000 at the end of 8 years. The company's marginal tax rate is 40 percent. Both machines qualify as 5-year assets for MACRS purposes. What is the NPV of replacement? Should the company replace the existing machine?

We must first estimate the incremental capital cost, which is the difference between the purchase price of the new machine and the salvage price of the old machine. The incremental capital cost also represents a component of the company's incremental initial after-tax cash outlay (ΔCF_0).

The new machine costs $350,000, but we also must consider the sale of the old machine. The old machine was purchased 3 years ago at $300,000. Therefore, the book value of the old machine after 3 years of its life is $86,400:

Year in the Life of the Old Machine	Depreciable Cost of the Old Machine	Depreciation Rate	Depreciation	End-of-period Book Value of the Old Machine
1	$300,000	20.00%	$60,000	$240,000
2	$300,000	32.00%	$96,000	$144,000
3	$300,000	19.20%	$57,600	$86,400
4	$300,000	11.52%	$34,560	$51,840
5	$300,000	11.52%	$34,560	$17,280
6	$300,000	5.76%	$17,280	$0
7	$300,000	0.00%	$0	$0
8	$300,000	0.00%	$0	$0

We therefore need to consider the gain on the sale of the old machine in our analysis. The gain is $13,600, which results in a tax on that gain of $13,600 × 0.40 = $5,440. In this example, there is no mention of opportunity costs arising or of additional working capital being tied up. Putting all this together results in an initial outlay of $255,440:

Purchase of new machine
Initial cost of new machine   −$350,000

Sale of old machine
Proceeds from sale of the old machine	$100,000	100,000
Less: Book value of the old machine	86,400	
Equals: Gain on the sale of the old machine	$13,600	
Tax on sale of old machine @ 40%		−5,440
Investment cash flow		−$255,440

Now we need to estimate the operating cash flows for each year. This requires us to estimate the change in the depreciation; that is, how is depreciation different once the new machine replaces the old machine? If depreciation is greater, this provides an increase in the depreciation tax shield; if depreciation is less, this reduces the tax shield.

The old machine is not fully depreciated, so we must compare the depreciation on the new and old machines:

	Year 1	Year 2	Year 3	Year 4	Year 5	Year 6	Year 7	Year 8
Depreciation rate—new	20.00%	32.00%	19.20%	11.52%	11.52%	5.76%	0.00%	0.00%
Depreciation rate—old	11.52%	11.52%	5.76%	0.00%	0.00%	0.00%	0.00%	0.00%

Applying these rates against the original costs of each asset, we can then calculate the change in depreciation:

	Year 1	Year 2	Year 3	Year 4	Year 5	Year 6	Year 7	Year 8
Depreciation—new	$70,000	$112,000	$67,200	$40,320	$40,320	$20,160	$0	$0
Depreciation—old	$34,560	$34,560	$17,280	$0	$0	$0	$0	$0
Change in depreciation	$35,440	$77,440	$49,920	$40,320	$40,320	$20,160	$0	$0

Considering the change in operating income and the change in depreciation, we can then calculate the operating cash flows for Raleigh's replacement project, as we show in Table 11-3.

TABLE 11-3 Operating Cash Flows for the Raleigh Replacement Decision

		Year 1	Year 2	Year 3	Year 4	Year 5	Year 6	Year 7	Year 8
	Change in EBITDA	$50,000	$50,000	$50,000	$50,000	$50,000	$50,000	$50,000	$50,000
Less:	Change in depreciation expense	35,440	77,440	49,920	40,320	40,320	20,160	0	0
Equals	Change in taxable income	$14,560	–$27,440	$80	$9,680	$9,680	$29,840	$50,000	$50,000
Less:	Change in taxes	5,824	–10,976	32	3,872	3,872	11,936	20,000	20,000
Equals	Change in after-tax income	$8,736	–$16,464	$48	$5,808	$5,808	$17,904	$30,000	$30,000
Plus:	Change in depreciation expense	35,440	77,440	49,920	40,320	40,320	20,160	0	0
Equals:	Operating cash flow	$44,176	$60,976	$49,968	$46,128	$46,128	$38,064	$30,000	$30,000

TABLE 11-4 Net Cash Flows Associated for the Raleigh Replacement Decision

		Initially	Year 1	Year 2	Year 3	Year 4	Year 5	Year 6	Year 7	Year 8
	Investment cash flow	–$255,440								
	Terminal cash flow									$21,000
	Change in EBITDA		$50,000	$50,000	$50,000	$50,000	$50,000	$50,000	$50,000	$50,000
Less	Change in depreciation		35,440	77,440	49,920	40,320	40,320	20,160	0	0
Equals	Change in taxable income		$14,560	–$27,440	$80	$9,680	$9,680	$29,840	$50,000	$50,000
Less	Change in taxes		5,824	–10,976	32	3,872	3,872	11,936	20,000	20,000
Equals	Change in after-tax income		$8,736	–$16,464	$48	$5,808	$5,808	$17,904	$30,000	$30,000
Plus	Change in depreciation		35,440	77,440	49,920	40,320	40,320	20,160	0	0
Equals	Operating cash flow		$44,176	$60,976	$49,968	$46,128	$46,128	$38,064	$30,000	$30,000
	Net cash flow	–$255,440	$44,176	$60,976	$49,968	$46,128	$46,128	$38,064	$30,000	$51,000

Next, we need to estimate the incremental ending cash flow associated with the replacement decision as follows:

	Sale of new machine	$50,000	
Less:	Tax on sale	20,000	
	Net cash flow from sale of new machine		$30,000
	Foregone sale of old machine	$15,000	
	Foregone tax on sale of old machine	6,000	
Less:	Forgone cash flow from sale of old machine, after tax		9,000
	Ending cash flow, net of foregone opportunity		$21,000

We can then combine these results to determine the NPV of the replacement decision, as we show in Table 11-4. Once we have the net cash flows, we can evaluate these cash flows using the net present value, the internal rate of return, or one of the other evaluation techniques.[13]

Concept Review Questions

1. Discuss any differences in the evaluation of a replacement decision versus an expansion decision.

2. List the cash flows to consider in the investment cash flow associated with a replacement decision.

11.5 INFLATION AND CAPITAL BUDGETING

Because capital expenditures typically involve the estimation of cash flows several years in the future, inflation can play an important role in determining these estimates because it will affect future levels of sales and expenses. In addition, inflation alters the level of interest rates and therefore affects the company's cost of capital that is to be used in discounting these future cash flows.

Nominal Versus Real Cash Flows

Earlier in this chapter, we said that we need to treat inflation consistently. So far, we have been estimating future cash flows on a nominal basis (i.e., estimating the actual cash flow that will result in year 2, etc., without making adjustments for inflation). As a result, we have been discounting these cash flows by using nominal (or actual) discount rates. This approach treats inflation consistently.

An alternative is to estimate future real (that is, inflation-adjusted) cash flows and discount these real cash flows by using real discount rates. However, one difficulty with this approach is that the depreciation tax savings estimates represent the actual amount of depreciation that can be charged in a given year. Therefore, the easiest way to proceed is usually to estimate the nominal cash flows and discount them by using nominal discount rates.

---

[13] We calculate the NPV by discounting the net cash flows. If the project's cost of capital is 10 percent, the net present value of this project's cash flows is −$1,320. Because the net present value is negative, the company should not go ahead with this replacement project.

It is important for companies to consider the effect that inflation will have on both sales and expenses, as well as the discount rate. Although it is often reasonable to assume that sales and expenses will be equally affected by inflation, this will not be the case for all companies or all situations. Much depends on the industry a company is in and on the products it sells. For example, sometimes inflation will have a greater impact on selling prices than it will on expenses, and sometimes the opposite will hold.[14]

Consider a company that has a 3-year project with the following:

- Unit sales are expected to be level at 10,000 units each year for the entire 3 years. The real sales price is expected to be $10 per unit, but the expected sales price inflation is expected to be 4 percent per year.
- Real expenses are expected to be $6 per unit produced and sold, but the expense inflation is expected to be 4 percent per year.
- The initial cost of the asset is $1 million, and there is no salvage value expected.
- Depreciation is calculated using the 3-year MACRS depreciation.
- The company's marginal tax rate is 35 percent.
- The nominal cost of capital for this project is 8 percent.

The net present value of this project is $58,684, as we detail in Table 11-5.

TABLE 11-5 Cash Flows and the Net Present Value with Inflation at 4 Percent Per Year

		Initially	Year 1	Year 2	Year 3
	Unit sales		80,000	80,000	80,000
	Sale price per unit		$21.00	$21.84	$22.71
	Operating expense per unit		$15.00	$15.60	$16.22
	Investment cash flow	−$1,000,000			
	Salvage value				$0
	Tax benefit from loss on disposal				−$74,100
	Terminal cash flow		$0	$0	−$74,100
	Change in revenues		$1,680,000	$1,747,200	$1,817,088
Less	Change in expenses		1,200,000	1,248,000	1,297,920
Less	Change in depreciation		333,300	444,500	148,100
Equals	Change in taxable income		$146,700	$54,700	$371,068
Less	Change in taxes		51,345	19,145	129,874
Equals	Change in income after tax		$95,355	$35,555	$241,194
Plus	Change in depreciation		333,300	444,500	148,100
	Operating cash flow		$428,655	$480,055	$389,294
	Net cash flow	−$1,000,000	$428,655	$480,055	$315,194
	Net present value	$58,584			

[14] For example, from October 2010 to October 2011, the price of wheat increased 9.6 percent, yet the price of flour products rose only 7.4 percent; therefore, a wheat processor was not able to pass along the entire increase in its raw materials to its customers.

TABLE 11-6 Cash Flows and the Net Present Value with Different Inflation Expectations

		Year 0	Year 1	Year 2	Year 3
	Unit sales		80,000	80,000	80,000
	Sale price per unit		$21.00	$22.26	$23.60
	Operating expense per unit		$15.00	$16.20	$17.50
	Investment cash flow	−$1,000,000			
	Salvage value				$0
	Tax benefit from loss on disposal				−$74,100
	Terminal cash flow				−$74,100
	Change in revenues		$1,680,000	$1,780,800	$1,887,648
Less	Change in expenses		1,200,000	1,296,000	1,399,680
Less	Change in depreciation		333,300	444,500	148,100
Equals	Change in taxable income		$146,700	$40,300	$339,868
Less	Change in taxes		51,345	14,105	118,954
Equals	Change in income after tax		$95,355	$26,195	$220,914
Plus	Change in depreciation		333,300	444,500	148,100
	Operating cash flow		$428,655	$470,695	$369,014
	Net cash flow	−$1,000,000	$428,655	$470,695	$294,914
	Net present value	$34,560			

If the inflation expectations change, so that the rate of inflation of revenues differs from that of expenses, we have a different outcome. For example, if the rate of inflation on units sold results in an increase of the sale price by 6 percent per year, and if the rate of inflation on operating expenses per unit is 8 percent each year, we arrive at a net present value of $34,560, as we show in Table 11-6.

Comparing the two analyses, you can see that the depreciation remains the same, but the operating cash flows differ due to the differing inflation rates for revenues and expenses. The difference in rates of inflation can change an acceptable project into an unacceptable project. For example, if the rate of inflation in expenses is 10 percent instead of 5 percent, the net present value of the project is −$5,811, which therefore makes this project unacceptable.

Can there be such disparate inflation rates? Most definitely. Consider the U.S. producer price index (PPI), which is an index of all goods from the perspective of businesses. A nonchocolate confectionary producer in 2010 would have experienced an increase in the price of sugar, a key input, of 21.1 percent, but an increase in the price of its product of only 0.5 percent.[15]

1. What is the problem with using a nominal discount rate and nominal cash flows to adjust for inflation?

2. If inflation is expected to increase in the future, how would this affect the profitability of a project? Explain.

Concept Review Questions

[15] U.S. Bureau of Labor Statistics, Producer Price Index, Industry Data.

SUMMARY

- A challenging element of capital budgeting analysis is the estimation of the incremental cash flows of a project. These cash flows include the investment cash flow, operating cash flows, and terminal cash flows. The key is to identify how a company's cash flows change if the company invests in a project.

- Depreciation affects cash flows because the deduction of this noncash expense reduces a company's tax bill; hence, depreciation results in a positive cash flow. We quantify the effect of depreciation with the calculation of the depreciation tax shield.

- Financial managers can use sensitivity analysis and scenario analysis, among other tools, to determine how variations in estimates can affect the attractiveness of project evaluations. Because the inputs to the capital budgeting analysis are estimates, it is important to analyze the sensitivity of capital budgeting decisions to the estimates.

- Inflation may affect the capital budgeting decision. Inflation affects the different elements of a project's cash flows, except for depreciation, which is fixed in amount. Inflation also affects the discount rate. In most analyses, it is easiest to work with nominal cash flows and the nominal discount rate because depreciation is fixed, and its effect in real terms is more challenging to estimate.

QUESTIONS AND PROBLEMS

Multiple Choice Questions

1. When making capital expenditure decisions, companies should not consider which of the following?
   A. Sunk costs
   B. Opportunity costs
   C. After-tax incremental cash flows
   D. Additional working capital requirements

2. If the change in depreciation for a given year of a project is $30,000 and the marginal tax rate is 30 percent, the depreciation tax shield is *closest* to:
   A. $9,000.   B. $27,000.   C. $30,000.

3. If a project is expected to generate annual revenue of $50,000, while incurring an annual cost of $18,000, the effect of the change in revenue and costs on the annual cash flow if the marginal tax rate is 40 percent, is *closest* to:
   A. $12,800.   B. $19,200.   C. $32,000.

4. A company is planning to purchase new, faster printers to replace its existing printers. The capital cost of the new printers = $300,000. The current market price of the old printers = $50,000. The applicable depreciation rate for the first year is 20 percent, the tax rate is 40 percent, and the project's cost of capital is 20 percent. It is estimated that the new printers could last for 5 years. The depreciation tax shield for the first year of operations is *closest* to:
   A. $24,000.   B. $60,000.   C. $120,000.

5. Which of the following items is not included in the calculation of the terminal cash flow?
   A. Salvage value
   B. Operating cash flows
   C. The change in inventory levels
   D. The change in accounts receivable levels

6. The depreciation tax shield is best described as the:

   A. incremental depreciation expense.

   B. depreciation expense on the new asset.

   C. amount of tax savings from deducting depreciation for tax purposes.

7. Which of the following completions is incorrect? An asset that is classified as a 3-year asset for MACRS purposes has:

   A. a zero book value at the end of the 3rd year.

   B. a positive book value at the end of the 3rd year.

   C. been fully depreciated by the end of the 4th year.

8. Suppose a company has an asset that had an original cost of $100,000, that it has depreciated using MACRS as a 3-year asset. If the company sells this asset at the end of the 4th year for $20,000 and has a marginal tax rate of 35 percent, the cash flow from this sale is *closest* to:

   A. $7,000.   B. $13,000.   C. $20,000.   D. $27,000.

9. Consider a project with the following information:

   - Initial cost = $400,050
   - Research and development costs associated with the project = $10,000
   - Associated opportunity costs = $90,000
   - Decrease in inventory = $15,000
   - Installation costs = $5,000

   The investment cash flow is *closest* to:

   A. $480,050.   B. $490,050.   C. $510,050.   D. $520,050.

10. You are given the following information regarding the acquisition of a new machine:

    - The new machine will replace an older machine.
    - The old machine has a book value of $65,000.
    - The purchase cost of the new machine (including shipping and handling) is $120,000.
    - The old machine cost $120,000 and can be sold for $75,000.
    - The company's marginal tax rate is 40 percent.

    The initial investment cash flow is *closest* to:

    A. –$120,000.   B. –$75,000.   C. –$49,000.   D. –$45,000.

Practice Questions and Problems

11.1 Identifying Relevant Cash Flows

11. What is meant by a sunk cost? Provide an example of a sunk cost.

12. Why would you use the marginal tax rate of a company in evaluating a project instead of the company's average tax rate? Explain your answer.

13. Describe how taxes may affect the cash flows from a capital investment project.

14. Two analysts, Arturo and Victor, are in disagreement about how to treat research and development in capital project analysis. Arturo believes that these are sunk costs, and therefore should never be included in an analysis. Victor believes that if the decision involves whether or not to invest in research and development, the research and development expenses should affect the investment decision. Who, if anyone, is correct? Explain.

15. Suppose a company is evaluating a project that would require converting an existing building to house the new project. Which of the following costs or expenses should be considered in the new project's cash flows? For each item, provide an explanation.

A. The cost of the building

B. The cost of repairs to the heating system of the building to bring the building up to code

C. The cost of new lighting necessary for the new project's production process

16. Complete the following, identifying each of the following as a sunk cost, externality, or an opportunity cost:

Item		Sunk Cost	Externality	Opportunity Cost
A.	The cost of research and development to develop a new arthritis drug			
B.	The rent that the company could have received if it did not use the building for a new production line			
C.	The reduction in the revenues for a similar product of the company			
D.	The depreciation expense on a machine if replaced with another machine			
E.	The cost of equipment that is currently idle that could be used for the new product			
F.	The increased efficiency of the company due to synergies in the production of the new product			

11.2 Estimating Cash Flows

17. Consider a company that has a marginal tax rate of 40 percent. For each of the following, estimate the effect on cash flow, indicating inflows as positive values and outflows as negative values:

A. Increase inventory by $30,000

B. Decrease accounts payable by $20,000

C. Sale of an asset that had an original cost of $10,000 and a $0 book value for $2,000

D. Purchase of equipment for $40,000 and incurring $3,000 to install the equipment

E. Increase accounts receivable by $5,000

18. Consider an asset that has an initial cost of $500,000 and a useful life of 6 years. The company's marginal tax rate is 30 percent.

A. What is the depreciation tax shield for each year if the asset is classified as a 3-year asset for MACRS purposes?

B. What is the depreciation tax shield for each year if the asset is classified as a 5-year asset for MACRS purposes?

19. If the U.S. Congress were to lower tax rates for corporations across the board, would this affect capital investment decisions? If so, in what way, and would this encourage or discourage investment activity?

20. Consider the depreciation of an asset that costs a company $1 million and is classified as a 5-year asset for MACRS purposes. Complete the following table, assuming a marginal tax rate of 40 percent:

Year	Depreciation Expense	Depreciation Tax Shield
1		
2		
3		
4		
5		

21. Consider a company that expects the following working capital accounts associated with a 4-year project:

	Initial	Year 1	Year 2	Year 3	Year 4
Inventory	$10,000	$12,000	$12,000	$14,000	$10,000
Accounts receivable	$12,000	$11,000	$12,000	$13,000	$12,000
Accounts payable	$8,000	$9,000	$9,000	$7,000	$8,000

For each year, indicate the cash flow effects of the changes in the working capital accounts.

22. Consider a project that has the following features:
- Requires an investment cash flow of $50,000 for equipment and installation.
- The assets are classified as 3-year MACRS assets.
- There is no expected salvage value for the assets, but the company will have to pay $3,000 at the end of the 3rd year to dispose of the assets to meet local and federal environmental mitigation requirements. The disposal costs are a tax deductible expense.
- Inventory needs will be reduced by $5,000 for the duration of the project.
- The project will increase revenues by $25,000 each year, but will also increase operating expenses by $12,000.
- The marginal tax rate is 35 percent.

Complete the following table:

		Initial	Year 1	Year 2	Year 3
	Cost of equipment				
Less	Disposal costs and any related taxes from disposal				
Less	Change in working capital				
Equals	Nonoperating cash flows				

		Initial	Year 1	Year 2	Year 3
	Change in revenues				
Less	Change in operating expenses				
Less	Change in depreciation				
Equals	Change in taxable income				
Less	Change in taxes				
Equals	Change in income after tax				
Plus	Change in depreciation				
Equals	Change in operating cash flow				

	Initial	Year 1	Year 2	Year 3
Net cash flow				

23. Oxford Inc. has a project that requires purchases of capital assets costing $40,000 and additional raw material inventory of $2,000. Shipping and installation costs are $1,500. Oxford Inc.'s management estimated that the project would generate annual operating cash flows of $5,600 for each of 6 years. At the end of 6 years, the assets can be sold for $4,000, whereas the additional inventory that was tied up will be released. The assets are classified as 3-year assets for MACRS purposes. The tax rate = 40 percent, and the assets' cost of capital is 15 percent.

A. What are the cash flows for each of the 6 years of the project's useful life?
B. What is the net present value of the project?
C. Should Oxford Inc. accept the project? Explain your reasoning.

24. What is the present value of the operating cash flows if the revenue of a project grows at 5 percent, while expense grows at 4 percent, given that revenues in the first year are $15,000 and expenses in the first year are $7,000? Assume the project's cost of capital is 8 percent and the marginal tax rate is 40 percent. The project has an expected useful life of 8 years.

11.3   Sensitivity to Inputs

25. The U.S. government provided bonus depreciation rules for small businesses in the 2008, 2009, and 2010 stimulus legislation. The bonus depreciation rules allow businesses to deduct an additional 50 percent of an asset's cost in the first year for federal tax purposes, along with the regular depreciation based on MACRS applied to the other 50 percent of the asset's cost.

    A. How would this affect the analysis of the cash flows of a project that has depreciable assets?

    B. Would this make projects more or less profitable in terms of value to the owners?

26. Santa Fe Company is considering a project. The initial cost is $60,000, and the company will use $2,000 less in raw material inventory with this project. The project would generate annual revenue of $70,000 and annual costs of $40,000 for 6 years. At the end of the project, the equipment could be sold for $10,000, and the additional raw materials inventory will be released. The equipment is a 3-year asset for MACRS purposes. The tax rate is 40 percent.

    A. What are the cash flows for each of the 6 years of the project's useful life?

    B. What is the NPV of this project if the project's cost of capital is 15 percent?

    C. What is the NPV of this project if the project's cost of capital is 12 percent?

    D. What is project's internal rate of return?

27. The Evansville Egg Company (EEC) is evaluating a new product line. To create this new product line, the company will spend $500,000 for the new equipment. EEC's financial managers are using a 4-year horizon for this new product line and do not expect to be able to sell the equipment, which qualifies as a 3-year asset in MACRS, at the end of the useful life. EEC's financial managers estimate the product line's cost of capital to be 10 percent. The financial managers of EEC are not confident that they can produce a single estimate of revenues and expenses, but with the help of accounting, manufacturing, and marketing management, they can detail three possible scenarios:

	Worst Case	Most Likely	Best Case
Change in revenues per year	$200,000	$250,000	$350,000
Change in expenses per year	$160,000	$190,000	$210,000
Anticipated tax rate	45 percent	38 percent	35 percent

    A. What is the net present value of the new product line under each scenario?

    B. From this information, what do you conclude regarding the acceptability of the new product line?

    C. How important is the depreciation tax shield to the acceptability of the new product line?

11.4   Replacement Decisions

28. Why does the financial analyst need to consider the depreciation of the replaced equipment in the analysis of cash flows of a replacement project?

29. Suppose new equipment costs $100,000, and it replaces equipment that has no resale value. The change in depreciation is the following:

	Year 1	Year 2	Year 3	Year 4
Old equipment	$8,886	$8,886		
New equipment	$33,330	$44,450	$14,810	$7,410

    If the discount rate on this replacement project is 8 percent and the company's marginal tax rate is 40 percent, what is the contribution of the change in depreciation to the value of the replacement decision?

30. Suppose a company is evaluating the replacement of the equipment in its production line. The old equipment was considered a 3-year MACRS asset and was purchased 3 years ago for $100,000. The company's management estimates that the old equipment can be sold for $10,000. What is the cash flow associated with the old equipment if replaced?

31. The Ames Corp. Inc. is now considering replacing some old equipment. The old equipment was bought 5 years ago for $50,000, and Ames's management believes that the equipment could be sold today for $15,000. The new equipment will cost $100,000 and could be sold at the end of 5 years for $30,000. An additional $4,000 in working capital is required and will be released at the end of 5 years. The new equipment is estimated to reduce operating expenses by $20,000 each year. Assume that the marginal tax rate is 40 percent and the project's cost of capital is 10 percent. Both the new and old equipment are classified as 5-year assets under MACRS.

   A. What are the cash flows for each of the 5 years of the project's life?

   B. What is the replacement project's NPV?

   C. Should Ames make this replacement? Explain your answer.

11.5   Inflation and Capital Budgeting

32. If the revenues, expenses, and discount rate of a project are nominal amounts, how can inflation affect the capital budgeting decision?

33. The Richmond Company has a project that requires the purchase of equipment costing $90,000 and additional raw material inventory of $2,000. Richmond's management estimated that the project would generate revenues of $58,000 and operating expenses of $30,000 each year. At the end of 6 years, the equipment will be worthless, and the company will need to pay $5,000 for its disposal. Any additional inventory that was tied up will be released at the end of the project's life. The equipment is classified as a 3-year asset for MACRS purposes. The tax rate = 40 percent, and the project's cost of capital is 15 percent.

   A. What is the NPV of the project?

   B. If the revenues and operating expenses increase at a rate of 4 percent each year, what is the net present value of this project? Does your answer differ from your answer to A above? If so, why?

   C. If the revenues increase at a rate of 3 percent per year and the operating expenses increase at a rate of 5 percent each year, what is the net present value of this project?

   D. Should Richmond accept the project? Explain.

34. The Morgantown Company (MC) has a project that requires the purchase of production equipment that costs $800,000 initially. MC's management estimated that the project would generate revenues of $440,000 and operating expenses of $250,000 each year. At the end of 5 years, the equipment will be sold for $300,000. The equipment is classified as a 3-year asset for MACRS purposes. The tax rate = 35 percent, and the project's cost of capital is 10 percent.

   A. What is the NPV of the project?

   B. If the revenues and operating expenses increase at a rate of 3 percent each year, what is the net present value of this project? Does your answer differ from your answer to A above? If so, why?

   C. If the revenues increase at a rate of 3 percent per year and the operating expenses increase at a rate of 2 percent each year, what is the net present value of this project?

   D. Should MC accept the project? Explain.

Cases

Case 11.1 The Jam Music Company

The Jam Music Company is considering expanding its production line to satisfy the demand for more CDs. The company has commissioned consultant studies for the expansion, spending $200,000 for these studies. The results of the studies indicate that the firm must spend $900,000 on a new building and $300,000 on production equipment if it wants to have state-of-the-art production. The consultants' report predicts that the company can increase its revenues by $400,000 each year, while incurring an increase of $160,000 in expenses. The consultants expect rivals to step up production within 5 years, reducing benefits from the expansion to Jam after 5 years. Therefore, a 5-year time horizon is assumed for this expansion project. The expansion would require that the company increase its current assets by $100,000 initially, but these asset accounts will be returned to previous levels at the end of the project.

Assume that the building is depreciated as a 10-year MACRS asset and that it can be sold at the end of 5 years for $800,000. Further assume that the equipment is depreciated using MACRS over a 5-year period and that it can be sold at the end of 5 years for $150,000. The marginal tax rate of Jam is 40 percent, and the cost of capital for this project is 10 percent.

Requirements

A. Should Jam invest in this project? Explain.

B. What is the internal rate of return on this project?

C. If the increase in revenues is only $350,000 per year, should Jam invest in this project? Explain your answer.

D. If the revenues start at $600,000 for the first year and decline each year by 25 percent, but expenses do not change, should Jam invest in this project? Explain why or why not.

Case 11.2 Can Tax Credits Make Solar Panels Profitable?

Consider the cost of a solar panel system that is intended to replace 25 percent of a home's electricity use.[16] A system that would fit on the roof of a typical home and would reduce electricity usage by 25 percent costs $37,496.36 before any government tax incentives. Currently, the U.S. government provides a 30 percent tax credit in the year of the solar panel acquisition, and the system is exempt from state and local property taxes.[17] The average monthly electrical bill is $200 per month.

The cost of borrowing for a solar panel system through the FHA's Energy Efficient Mortgage (EEM) program, available for energy efficient home improvements, is an APR of 3.35%.[18] The amount of the mortgage is the cost of the panel system, less any federal incentive. The interest on the EEM is tax deductible, but electricity costs are not deductible for the individual homeowner.

Assume that the homeowner has a marginal tax rate of 38 percent and that the installation is at the end of the current year, but the panels are not used until the first month of the coming year. Further, assume that the solar panels have a useful life of 30 years and that at the end of the life of the panels the homeowner must pay a $500 for removal and disposal of the panels at the local dump.

Requirements

A. What is the payback period for a solar panel system?

B. What is the added value of investing in solar panels on a net present value basis?

C. If energy costs were to increase at a rate of 0.25 percent each month, would this affect the attractiveness of the panels? If so, why?

D. What is the minimum percent tax credit necessary to make the solar system attractive to homeowners on a net present value basis, assuming that energy costs do not escalate?

---

[16] Data for the costs and savings are drawn from CoolPlanetBioFuels.com.

[17] See Internal Revenue Service *Form 5695 Residential Energy Credits* for all the current credits.

[18] Based on 2011 rates.

INTEGRATIVE PROBLEM: DAZZLE

We demonstrate the principles of estimating cash flows using a capital budgeting decision involving a consumer products company that is evaluating a new product. We first introduce the capital budgeting problem and then pick the problem apart to find the relevant information for the cash flow analysis.

11A.1 THE PROJECT

Consider the Smile Toothpaste Company (STC), which has a line of successful dental products that are sold in retail outlets across the country. These products include toothpastes, flosses, and rinses. The financial managers of STC are considering the production of a new toothpaste that their research and development team has determined is an improvement over its existing whitening toothpaste. STC's marketing research has concluded that introducing the new toothpaste, Dazzle, next year would be appropriate, and that projected sales, in millions of units, would be the following:

Year	*Estimated Units Produced and Sold*
2014	750
2015	1,000
2016	1,500
2017	1,250
2018	250

The marketing managers estimate that each tube of Dazzle should sell for $3, and production management has estimated that the cost of each tube is $1.50. Marketing also estimates that advertising and other promotions will cost $200 million in 2014 and 2015, but then fall to $100 million in 2016 and then $50 million each year following.

The marketing research indicates that sales of Dazzle will reduce sales of its other whitening tooth paste, Brilliant, at a pace of approximately 400 million in the first year, 300 in the second year, and then 200 million units per year thereafter. Brilliant sells for $2.5 per tube and costs $1 per tube for manufacturing. STC will need to stock an additional $500 million of raw materials for the paste and tube production at the end of 2013, maintain this level through 2015, then reduce it to $400 million by the end of 2016, $200 million at the end of 2017, and then $0 at the end of 2018.

The company would be able to use vacant space in another production facility to produce Dazzle. This other production facility was built 10 years ago at a cost of $200 million and is being depreciated as a 20-year MACRS asset. Dazzle's production will take up approximately one-quarter of the floor space of this facility. The production equipment to manufacture the Dazzle toothpaste and tube will cost $20 million and will be depreciated as a 7-year MACRS asset. STC expects to be able to sell this equipment at the end of 5 years for $5 million. The equipment will be acquired December 31, 2013, and production begins in January 2014.

The purchasing managers have alerted the capital project's manager that there is uncertainty regarding the input prices for the abrasives, fluorides, and surfactants used in both Dazzle and Brilliant. Though their initial projections are the most likely costs, it is possible that due to potential fluctuations in the raw materials markets in the near-term that the costs may be 20 percent less than or greater than projected for both Dazzle and Brilliant toothpastes. However, due to competition in the consumer market, it is unlikely that STC can pass along any added costs in the sales price.

STC's marginal tax rate is 35 percent, and this project's cost of capital is 10 percent. Based on all this information, should STC go ahead with Dazzle?

11A.2 ANALYSIS OF THE FACTS

We will analyze the facts, picking out the relevant facts for the calculation of the cash flows.

Dissecting the Problem

Capital project analysis is usually quite detailed, and each problem is unique. Therefore, it is important to address all information about the project, assess whether the information is relevant to the analysis, and determine the implications for cash flows. We demonstrate this by taking apart the Dazzle project information.

Consider the Smile Toothpaste Company (STC), which has a line of successful dental products that are sold in retail outlets across the country. These products include toothpastes, flosses, and rinses. The financial managers of STC are considering the production of a new toothpaste that their research and development team has determined is an improvement over its existing whitening toothpaste.

Relevance: This tells us that though this is a new product, it may cannibalize the company's existing products.

STC's marketing research has concluded that introducing the new toothpaste, Dazzle, next year would be appropriate, and that that projected sales, in millions of units, would be the following:

Year	Estimated Units Produced and Sold
2014	750
2015	1,000
2016	1,500
2017	1,250
2018	250

Relevance: We can now sketch out potential sales for the relevant years of 2014 through 2018.

	2014	2015	2016	2017	2018
Expected sales of Dazzle (in millions of units)	750	1,000	1,500	1,250	250

The marketing managers estimate that each tube of Dazzle should sell for $3, and production management has estimated that the cost of each tube is $1.25. Marketing also estimates that advertising and other promotions will cost $200 million in 2014 and 2015, but then fall to $100 million in 2016 and then $50 million each year following.

Relevance: When we put this together with the projected sales volume, we can now estimate the revenues and expenses for Dazzle.

		2014	2015	2016	2017	2018
Dazzle dollar sales	(in millions)	$2,250	$3,000	$4,500	$3,750	$750
Dazzle dollar costs	(in millions)	$1,125	$1,500	$2,250	$1,875	$375
Marketing and promotion	(in millions)	$200	$200	$100	$50	$50

The marketing research indicates that sales of Dazzle will reduce sales of its other whitening toothpaste, Brilliant, at a pace of approximately 200 million units per year. Brilliant sells for $2.5 per tube and costs $1 per tube for manufacturing.

Relevance: This is the information we need to evaluate the cannibalization, and then the incremental revenues and expenses for Dazzle.

		2014	*2015*	*2016*	*2017*	*2018*
Brilliant sales price	(per unit)	$2.50	$2.50	$2.50	$2.50	$2.50
Brilliant cost per unit	(per unit)	$1.00	$1.00	$1.00	$1.00	$1.00
Change in Brilliant sales	(in millions of units)	−400	−300	−200	−200	−200
Change in Brilliant's dollar sales	(in millions)	−$1,000	−$750	−$500	−$500	−$500
Change in Brilliant's dollar costs	(in millions)	−$400	−$300	−$200	−$200	−$200
Dazzle dollar sales	(in millions)	$2,250	$3,000	$4,500	$3,750	$750
Dazzle dollar costs	(in millions)	$1,125	$1,500	$2,250	$1,875	$375
Change in revenues	(in millions)	$1,250	$2,250	$4,000	$3,250	$250
Change in operating costs	(in millions)	$725	$1,200	$2,050	$1,675	$175
Marketing and promotion	(in millions)	$200	$200	$100	$50	$50

It is easy to get tangled up in figuring out changes when there is cannibalization. Consider the effects for one year, 2014:

	With Dazzle Only	*Without Dazzle*	*Change*
Revenues	$2,250	$1,000	$1,250
Operating costs	1,125	400	725
Revenues less operating costs	$1,125	$600	$525

STC will need to stock an additional $500 million of raw materials for the paste and tube production at the end of 2013, maintain this level through 2015, then reduce it to $400 million by the end of 2016, $200 million at the end of 2017, and then $0 at the end of 2018.

Relevance: We use this information to determine the cash flows from the change in working capital.

(in millions)	*2013*	*2014*	*2015*	*2016*	*2017*	*2018*
Working capital level	$500	$500	$500	$400	$200	$0
Change in working capital	+$500	$0	$0	−$100	−$200	−$200
Cash flow from change in working capital	−$500	$0	$0	$100	$200	$200

The company would be able to use vacant space in another production facility to produce Dazzle. This other production facility was built 10 years ago at a cost of $200 million and is being depreciated as a 20-year MACRS asset. Dazzle's production will take up approximately one-quarter of the floor space of this facility.

Relevance: This is a sunk cost and is therefore not relevant for the Dazzle capital budgeting decision.

The production equipment to manufacture the Dazzle toothpaste and tube will cost $3 billion and will be depreciated as a 7-year MACRS asset. STC expects to be able to sell this equipment at the end of 5 years for $0.5 billion. The equipment will be acquired December 31, 2013, and production begins in January 2014.

This provides what we need for the depreciation expense for each year and provides information on the investment cash flow related to the sale of the equipment at the end of the project's life.

		2014	2015	2016	2017	2018
Depreciation rate for equipment	(percent of cost)	10.00%	18.00%	14.00%	12.00%	9.00%
Depreciation expense	(in millions)	$300	$540	$420	$360	$270

If the company sells the equipment at the end of 5 years, this defines the project's useful life for us. This also tells us that because it is a 7-year MACRS asset, selling it at the end of the 5th year means that the equipment has a positive carrying value at that point in time, which we need to know to calculate any gain or loss at the time of this sale.

(in millions)	2014	2015	2016	2017	2018
Book value of equipment	$2,700	$2,160	$1,740	$1,380	$1,110

This means that the company has an expected loss on the equipment of $500 − 1,110 = $610 million. This loss will result in a tax benefit.

The purchasing managers have alerted the capital project's manager that there is uncertainty regarding the input prices for the abrasives, fluorides, and surfactants used in both Dazzle and Brilliant. Though their initial projections are the most likely costs, it is possible that due to potential fluctuations in the raw materials markets in the near-term that the costs may be 20 percent less than or greater than projected for both Dazzle and Brilliant toothpastes. However, due to competition in the consumer market, it is unlikely that STC can pass along any added costs in the sales price.

Relevance: This will give us something to check in sensitivity analysis.

STC's marginal tax rate is 35 percent, and this project's cost of capital is 10 percent. Based on all this information, should STC go ahead with Dazzle?

Relevance: These are the last pieces that we need to put the puzzle together. This will allow us to calculate the tax on the change in taxable income.

	2014	2015	2016	2017	2018
Change in revenues	$1,250	$2,250	$4,000	$3,250	$250
Change in operating costs	725	1,200	2,050	1,675	175
Marketing and promotion	200	200	100	50	50
Depreciation	300	540	420	360	270
Change in taxable income	$25	$310	$1,430	$1,165	−$245
Tax	9	109	501	408	−86
Change in income after tax	$16	$202	$930	$757	−$159

Knowing the tax rate also allows us to calculate the tax benefit from selling the equipment at a loss:

	Sale price	$500
Less	Carrying value for tax purposes	1,110
Equals	Loss on sale	−$600
Multiply	Tax rate	0.35
Equals	Tax benefit from the loss on sale	$214

Assembling the Pieces

We assemble the pieces in Table 11A-1 for the base case of this analysis. Based on the positive net present value and internal rate of return, Dazzle is a profitable project when we use the base analysis: a positive net present value and a rate of return that exceeds the project cost of capital.

TABLE 11A-1 The Dazzle Analysis

		2013	2014	2015	2016	2017	2018
	Purchase of equipment	−$3,000					
Plus	Sale of equipment						$500
Plus	Tax benefit on loss on sale						214
Equals	Investment cash flows	−$3,000	$0	$0	$0	$0	$714
	Change in working capital	−$500	$0	$0	$100	$200	$200
	Change in revenues		$1,250	$2,250	$4,000	$3,250	$250
Less	Change in operating costs		725	1,200	2,050	1,675	175
Less	Change in marketing and promotion		200	200	100	50	50
Less	Change in depreciation		300	540	420	360	270
Equals	Change in taxable income		$25	$310	$1,430	$1,165	−$245
Less	Change in tax		9	109	501	408	−86
Equals	Change in income after tax		$16	$202	$930	$757	−$159
Plus	Change in depreciation		300	540	420	360	270
Equals	Change in operating cash flow		$316	$742	$1,350	$1,117	$111
Sum	Net cash flow	−$3,500	$316	$742	$1,450	$1,317	$1,024
	Net present value	$25.02					
	Internal rate of return	10.24%					
	Payback period	4 years					

Scenario Analysis

The primary uncertainty mentioned in Dazzle's project description is that costs may be 20 percent more or less than expected, and we can infer that these costs adjustments would occur immediately if they did. Let us consider the 20 percent increase in costs as the worst-case scenario and consider the 20 percent decrease as the best-case scenario.

When we look at the worst-case and best-case scenarios, with costs 20 percent more or less, respectively, for both Dazzle and Brilliant, the decision would be different:

	Net Cash Flows						Net Present	Internal Rate
Scenario	2013	2014	2015	2016	2017	2018	Value	of Return
Best case	−$3,500	$411	$898	$1,716	$1,535	$1,047	$602.70	15.64%
Base case	−$3,500	$316	$742	$1,450	$1,317	$1,024	$351.81	14.14%
Worst case	−$3,500	$222	$586	$1,183	$1,100	$1,002	−$552.67	4.59%

We would reject the Dazzle project if the costs were 20 percent more, but in the base-case and the best-case scenarios, the project is profitable. These conclusions present an issue for risk management: Is it worth the risk for an unprofitable project? What is the likelihood that the worst-case scenario will occur?

Simulation Analysis

We can extend this, performing a simulation assuming that the price changes of inputs are normally distributed with a mean of 0 percent and a standard deviation of 10 percent.[19] To make this simulation manageable for this example, we assume that that price change, which we draw from a random number generator, is the same for all years.[20]

We draw 1,000 observations from this distribution, which we use to recalculate each year's cash flow given the price change. For example, we show the 2014 cash flow in Figure 11A-1. How do we interpret this chart? First, the mean price change is 0 percent, so the mean of this distribution will have the same net cash flows as our base case.[21] Second, the distribution of these cash flows is wide ranging, from $190 to $480, but it is concentrated around the mean.

The result of performing this simulation for all years is that we generate 1,000 different internal rates of return, as we show in Figure 11A-2. How do we interpret this? This tells us that the project's returns can vary between 2 percent and 19 percent, depending on the price changes for the inputs, but that the return on the project is likely to be centered around 10–11 percent. The issue facing STC, therefore, is whether this project is consistent with the company's risk tolerance.

FIGURE 11A-1 **Distribution of the Year 2014 Cash Flows Based on 1,000 Different Price Changes**

FIGURE 11A-2 **Distribution of Internal Rates of Return for the Dazzle Project Based on 1,000 Different Price Changes**

---

[19] Therefore, we expect 95 percent of draws from this distribution to be plus or minor two standard deviations (that is, 20 percent) from the base case assumption.

[20] In Microsoft's Excel, we use the Data Analysis tools, specifically the Random Number Generator.

[21] Actually, it is close, but not precisely equal, to the base case. If we had drawn 10,000 observations, the mean would be extremely close to the base case.

CHAPTER 14

COST OF CAPITAL

How low can it go? The efforts of the Federal Reserve both before, during, and after the financial crisis of 2007–2008 to keep interest rates low has resulted in historically low costs of capital for companies in the U.S. in 2010 and 2011. The interest rates that corporations are seeing when they issue debt reminds everyone of the 1960s. For example, the yield on AAA-rated bonds was 9.05 percent in 1990, but 4.87 percent in 2010. The result of these low interest rates is that companies are issuing bonds. The cost of equity is also lower, and companies are issuing common and preferred stock. However, the memories of the 2007–2008 financial crisis are fresh, so the investors are being selective; it's *careful money*.

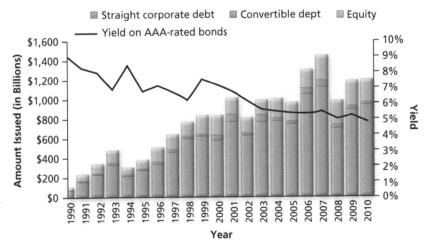

Source of data: *SIFMA.org*

Learning Outcomes

After reading this chapter, you should be able to:

LO 14.1	Explain how the return on equity and the required return by common equity investors are related to a company's growth opportunities.
LO 14.2	List, describe, and apply the steps in estimating a company's weighted average cost of capital, including how to estimate the market values of the various components of capital and how to estimate the various costs of these components.
LO 14.3	Explain how operating and financial leverage affect companies.
LO 14.4	Detail the advantages and limitations of using growth models and/or risk models to estimate the cost of common equity.

509

14.1 THE MARGINAL COST OF CAPITAL SCHEDULE

cost of capital the return the investor requires

The cost of capital is one of the most basic pieces of information a company needs in investment decision making because this cost is often used as the basis for determining an investment project's hurdle rate or discount rate in making decisions. In investment decision making, the **cost of capital** is the return the investor requires; hence, we refer to the cost of capital as the required rate of return from the perspective of the suppliers of funds (that is, the creditor or owner). Further, the cost of capital is often used in valuing a company, a subsidiary, or any asset, whereby future cash flows are discounted at the cost of capital to estimate a value.

In this chapter we focus on the meaning of the cost of capital, how to calculate it, and the challenges a financial decision maker faces in estimating the cost of capital. You will notice that during this process, we use many of the valuation approaches that you learned in earlier chapters, but we now look at these models from a different perspective: determining the required rate of return, instead of the value.

When a company is making an investment decision, it is determining whether the benefits of the investment (that is, future cash flows) exceed the cost of the investment in terms of not only the outlay, but also the cost of employing capital. When a financial manager evaluates an investment project, the focus is on the incremental cash flows; in other words, the marginal benefit of the project. Consistently, the cost of capital is a marginal cost, the cost of raising an additional dollar of financing. We calculate this marginal cost of capital as the **weighted average cost of capital**, or **WACC**, where:

weighted average cost of capital (WACC) the marginal cost of raising an additional dollar of capital

- the weights are the proportions of capital the company uses when it raises new capital; and
- the costs are the marginal cost for each source of capital.

It may be the case that the component costs change for different levels of financing. Therefore, the WACC would be different for different levels of financing. We often depict this graphically with the **marginal cost of capital schedule**, with the WACC for different levels of financing graphed against the level of financing, as we illustrate in Figure 14-1.

The WACC: The Basics

The basic equation for the WACC is:

$$\text{WACC} = \left(\begin{array}{c} \text{Proportion of} \\ \text{debt financing} \end{array} \times \begin{array}{c} \text{After-tax} \\ \text{cost of debt} \end{array} \right) + \left(\begin{array}{c} \text{Proportion of} \\ \text{preferred stock} \\ \text{financing} \end{array} \times \begin{array}{c} \text{Cost of} \\ \text{preferred equity} \end{array} \right)$$

$$+ \left(\begin{array}{c} \text{Proportion of} \\ \text{common stock} \\ \text{financing} \end{array} \times \begin{array}{c} \text{Cost of} \\ \text{common equity} \end{array} \right)$$

In other words, the costs of the different sources of capital are weighted by the proportion that the source represents in the cost of capital. We can represent this in notation form as:

$$\text{WACC} = \frac{D}{V} r_d^* + \frac{P}{V} r_p + \frac{E}{V} r_e$$

V represents the total value of the company' capital, D represents the value of debt, P represents the value of preferred stock, E represents the value of common equity, and r_d^*, r_p, and r_e represent the marginal costs of capital for debt, preferred equity, and common

FIGURE 14-1 **The Marginal Cost of Capital Schedule**

equity, respectively. We can simplify this using the notation for the weights of the different sources of capital, the w_i, as:

$$\text{WACC} = w_d r_d^* + w_p r_p + w_e r_e \tag{14-1}$$

The reason we designate the cost of debt different than the costs of preferred and common equity (that is, with an " * ") is that the relevant cost of debt is the after-tax cost because of the tax deductibility of interest. Therefore, for every dollar of interest paid, the company only bears a portion of that dollar. In the case of equity, dividends paid to shareholders are not a deductible expense for the paying corporation.

The WACC is the average of the required rates of return on all long-term sources of financing. But because each of the costs is a marginal cost, the WACC is also a marginal cost.

We illustrate the steps in estimating the cost of capital in Figure 14-2 and detail the estimation approach in the sections that follow. In the next section we look at how we determine the weights, and then we look at how we estimate the costs of the different sources of capital. Following the estimation of costs, we show how to put all the pieces together to arrive at a weighted average cost of capital.

FIGURE 14-2 **Steps in Calculating the Weighted Average Cost of Capital**

1. Why is the weighted average cost of capital so important?

2. Why do we say that the weighted average cost of capital is a marginal cost of capital?

14.2   ESTIMATING THE WEIGHTS

When calculating the cost of capital, we weight the component costs of capital by the proportion of capital that each source of capital represents when the company raises additional capital. We must first establish what we mean by capital, and then we will deal with the appropriate proportions.

What Is Capital?

Let's begin with a simple balance sheet, as we show in Table 14-1. On the asset side, we have current or short-term assets consisting of cash and marketable securities, accounts receivable, and inventory, plus there are usually some accounting items, such as prepaid expenses. When the current assets are added to the net fixed assets (i.e., gross fixed assets less accumulated depreciation) and any intangibles, we have total assets. On the other side of the balance sheet in Table 14-1, we see how the company finances its total assets.

capital sum of the interest-bearing debt and the equity of a company

The simple definition of **capital** is that it is the sum of the interest-bearing debt and the equity of a company. Debt capital consists of the interest-bearing obligations of the company, whereas equity capital is the sum of the capital of preferred and common shareholders.

Which liabilities do we include in debt capital? Only those that represent long-term sources of financing. We generally consider all interest-bearing debt obligations as debt capital. For example, many accruals are strictly accounting items required to prepare the statements according to generally accepted accounting principles (GAAP). As such, they do not represent a decision on the part of an investor or creditor to finance the company and therefore do not represent debt capital. For example, as long as a company's credit is good, accounts payable arise as a result of a telephone or computerized order, where the invoice arrives with the order. In most cases the supplier is not explicitly thinking of the value of its shipment as an investment in the company.[1] It is simply the way business is done between companies. The only debt capital items in current liabilities are typically bank debt, other short-term interest-bearing debt, and the current portion of any long-term debt that is due within a year. In other words, the debt capital in current liabilities consists of the interest-bearing obligations.

It is important to note that not all long-term liabilities are considered debt capital. Companies report the value of benefits owing to workers that is not fully funded with pension plan assets as a pension liability. Also, there are often deferred income taxes; deferred income taxes are taxes that the company expects to pay in the future. An argument can be made in the financial analysis of a company to include these as a liability (if it is expected that the taxes will be paid) or as equity (if it is expected that the company will always

TABLE 14-1 The Balance Sheet

Cash and marketable securities	
Accounts receivable	Accruals
Inventory	Accounts payable
Prepaid expenses	Short-term debt
Current assets	Current liabilities
Net fixed assets	Long-term debt
Intangible assets	Shareholders' equity
Total assets	Total liabilities and shareholders' equity

[1] Note that this is not always the case. For companies in serious financial trouble, a shipment may be seen as an investment with an explicit interest charge.

have this level of deferred taxes). However, deferred taxes are not considered debt capital because no funds are provided. In almost all cases, these "nondebt" accounting items are ignored in estimating company debt capital.

Another item excluded from debt capital is minority interest because this reflects the amount of shareholders' equity of a subsidiary that is not owned by the shareholders of the parent company.[2] Minority interest is best classified as equity because it is an allocation of ownership, but it does not represent contributed capital. Therefore, we do not consider minority interest as debt or equity capital.

A company's **financial structure** is the entire set of liabilities and equity accounts, whereas the **capital structure** of the company is how this invested capital is financed by debt and equity capital.[3] Therefore, the distinction we are making between a company's financial and capital structure is that the financial structure includes all liability and equity, whereas the capital structure includes only invested capital. **Invested capital** is the sum of the debt capital and equity capital.

We now take as an example the simplified balance sheet in Table 14-2.

- The financial structure is $2,000, consisting of $1,000 of liabilities and $1,000 of equity.
- The capital structure consists of invested capital and is $1,700: $1,000 in shareholders' equity, and $700 of interest-bearing debt (i.e., $50 + $650).

This capital structure results in a debt-to-equity ratio of $700 ÷ $1,000 = 0.70 and a debt-to-invested-capital ratio of $700 ÷ $1,700 = 0.41. This hypothetical capital structure is typical.

The numbers in Table 14-2 come from the company's financial statements and represent historical book values. We can convert them to market values if we have market information.[4] Suppose that the company's equity is selling for 2.5 times its book value, so that its **market-to-book (M/B) ratio** is 2.5. For this example, assuming that the book value of debt is the same as its market value, the total market value of the equity would then be $1,000 × 2.5 = $2,500, and the total market value of the company would be $700 + $2,500 = $3,200. Therefore, the company's market valued debt-to-equity ratio is $700 ÷ $2,500 = 0.28, and the debt to invested capital is $700 ÷ $3,200 = 0.22.

If the company's operating profit after taxes is $500, its **return on invested capital (ROIC)**, defined as operating profit after taxes divided by the book value of invested capital, is 29.31 percent. The company's **return on equity (ROE)**, defined as net income divided by the book value of equity, is $300 ÷ $1,000 = 30 percent.

financial structure liabilities and equity of a company

capital structure how a company finances its invested capital, consisting of debt capital and equity capital

return on invested capital (ROIC) earnings before interest and taxes divided by the book value of invested capital

TABLE 14-2 A Sample Balance Sheet

Cash and marketable securities	$50	Accruals	$100
Accounts receivable	200	Accounts payable	200
Inventory	250	Short-term debt	50
Prepaid expenses	0	Current liabilities	$350
Current assets	$500	Long-term debt	650
Net fixed assets	1,400	Shareholders' equity	1,000
Intangibles	100	Total liabilities and	
Total assets	$2,000	shareholders' equity	$2,000

[2] Minority interest arises when a company reports consolidated financial statements. GAAP requires consolidated statements even when a subsidiary is not 100 percent owned (usually more than 50 percent). As a result, all the subsidiary's debt and assets are included on the consolidated statements, and the part of the subsidiary's equity that is not owned is shown as minority interest.

[3] How the company arrives at these decisions is the focus of another chapter.

[4] Recall that long-term debt will usually be issued at coupon rates that are approximately equal to prevailing market rates so that they are sold at close to their face value. If the interest rates do not change very much, then the market value of such debt will remain close to the book value.

EXAMPLE 14.1

Estimating Debt Capital

PROBLEM

Using the following data from the balance sheet of Microsoft for fiscal year ending June 30, 2010, calculate the total liabilities and the debt for Microsoft:

	(in millions)
Accounts payable	$4,025
Short-term debt	$1,000
Accrued compensation	$3,283
Income taxes	$1,074
Short-term unearned revenue	$13,652
Securities lending payable	$182
Other	$2,931
Long-term debt	$4,939
Long-term unearned revenue	$1,178
Deferred income taxes	$229
Other long-term liabilities	$7,445

Solution

Total liabilities = $4,025 + 1,000 + 3,283 + 1,074 + 13,652 + 182 + 2,931 +

4,939 + 1,178 + 229 + 7,445 = $39,938 million

Note: Assuming the deferred taxes will persist through time and are therefore are most similar to equity, total liabilities = $39,709.

Debt = $1,000 + 4,939 = $5,939 million

Which Weights?

We estimate the proportions of the different sources of capital in the company's capital structure by estimating the proportions that the company uses when it raises new capital. Theoretically, we would like to use the proportions that represent the company's target capital structure, that is, the capital structure that the company aims for over time. However, we cannot observe this target capital structure. As a next-best alternative to the target capital structure, absent other information that may indicate otherwise, we use a company's present capital structure as the best estimate of the target capital structure.

But do we use the book values of the different capital or the market values? We generally use the market values of the capital that the company uses because we assume that the financial decision making of a company is based on market values of capital, rather than on the book values.

Estimating Market Values

Estimating the market value of a company's common equity is quite straightforward whenever a company has shares that are traded publicly. We simply use the market capitalization, which is the product of the company's market price per common share and the number of shares outstanding.[5] If the equity is not publicly traded, we need to use an approach such as the method of multiples to estimate the value based on market multiples of comparable, but publicly traded companies.

[5] Notice that in the preceding example we accomplished the same result by multiplying the company's book value of common equity figure by its M/B ratio.

Estimating the market value of a company's preferred shares is also quite straightforward if they are publicly traded. In the event that the company's preferred shares are not actively traded, we can estimate the market value of the preferred shares by using the present value of a perpetuity equation, where P_p is the price per share, D_p is the dividend per share, and r_p is the required rate of return on preferred shares:

$$P_p = D_p \div r_p \qquad (14\text{-}2)$$

This valuation assumes, of course, that we have an estimate of the required rate of return.

Estimating the market value of a company's debt can be somewhat more complicated. As mentioned earlier, if interest rates have not changed too much since the debt was first issued by the company, then the book value of the company's long-term debt is close to its market value, so we can use the book value. When a company has bonds outstanding, we can be more precise and use the following bond valuation equation to estimate the market value of those bonds:

$$PV = \left(\sum_{t=1}^{N} \frac{C}{(1 + r_d)^t} \right) + \frac{FV}{(1 + r_d)^N} \qquad (14\text{-}3)$$

where

PV is the bond value;

C is the interest (or coupon) payment;

r_d is the discount rate (or market rate);

N is the term-to-maturity; and

FV is the face (par) value of the bond.

If the bond pays interest semi-annually, which is the case for most U.S. bonds, the coupon is the coupon paid every 6 months, the discount rate is the 6-month rate, and the term to maturity is in terms of the number of 6-month periods.

If the company has more than one series of bonds or other types of long-term debt issues outstanding, we can repeat this process and add up all the calculated market values to determine the total market value of the company's debt outstanding.

Suppose the financial manager of Company BCD gathers the following information:

	Book value *(in millions)*
Debt: 8% coupon rate, semi-annual coupons 10 years to maturity	$1.0
Preferred shares: 10% dividend rate	1.0
Common stock: 100,000 shares (originally issued at $15 per share)	1.5
Retained earnings	0.5
Total capital	$4.0

Assume the marginal tax rate is 40 percent. Present market conditions are such that:

- The present market rate on similar risk 10-year bonds is 6 percent.
- Similar risk preferred shares are providing yields of 8 percent.
- The common share price is currently $25.

We first need to estimate the market value proportions of these components assuming the company wants to raise new funds to maintain its present capital structure based on these market value proportions. For long-term debt, the value of debt is:

$$PV = \left(\sum_{t=1}^{20} \frac{4}{(1 + 0.03)} \right) + \frac{100}{(1 + 0.03)^{20}} = 114.8775$$

Or we could use a calculator or spreadsheet program with:

$$FV = 100$$
$$PMT = 4$$
$$i = 3\%$$
$$N = 20$$

The value of debt is 114.8775 percent of its $1,000,000 face value, or $1,148,775.

The value of the preferred shares is the dividend of 10 percent $\times$ $1,000,000 = $100,000, divided by the market rate of 8 percent:

$$P_p = \frac{D_p}{r_p} = \frac{\$100,000}{0.08} = \$1,250,000$$

The value of common equity is the market value per share multiplied by the number of shares, or $25 $\times$ 100,000 = $2,500,000.

Putting these pieces together, we have the market value of the capital of Company BCD as:

Capital Source	Notation	Market Value	Proportion
Debt	D	$1,148,775	23.45%
Preferred equity	P	1,250,000	25.52%
Common equity	E	2,500,000	51.03%
Market value of invested capital	V	$4,898,775	100.00%

EXAMPLE 14.2

Calculating the Market Value of Debt

PROBLEM

Consider a company that has $100 million face value of debt outstanding. The debt consists of 20-year bonds with a coupon rate of 5 percent. These bonds have a yield to maturity of 6 percent, paid semi-annually. What is the market value of the company's debt?

Solution

The value of the debt [FV = 100; N = 40; PMT = 25; i = 3%] is 88.4426. Therefore, the market value of the company's debt is 0.884426 $\times$ $100 million = $88.4426 million.

Concept Review
Questions

1. What is meant by the capital structure of a company?

2. How can we estimate the market value of common equity, preferred equity, and long-term debt?

14.3   ESTIMATING THE COSTS OF CAPITAL

marginal cost of capital
cost of raising one more dollar of capital

Our objective is to estimate what it would cost the company to raise additional capital — specifically one more dollar of capital. This is the marginal cost of capital. The **marginal cost of capital** is the cost of raising one more dollar of capital. To this end, we need to estimate the marginal costs of each of the sources of capital the company uses.

The Cost of Debt

The cost of debt is the yield or interest on debt if the company borrows one more dollar. If the company has publicly traded debt, you can look at sources such as FINRA for yields.[6] And although that may seem simple, it is more complicated than that because most large companies have many issues of debt outstanding.

Consider the case of Archer-Daniels-Midland, ADM. In October 2009 it had fifteen publicly traded debt issues with remaining maturities ranging from 1 year to 88 years. Though most of these debt issues are debentures with fixed coupon rates, the coupon rates varied depending on when the debt was issued, and some of the issues are callable. Therefore it is not a simple matter to simply revalue the debt at current or expected yields. The current yields vary, depending on the maturity and features, but they generally range between 5.44 percent to 5.74 percent for noncallable debentures with maturities greater than 5 years. Let's use the midpoint of 5.59 percent.

We can estimate ADM's tax rate by looking at its tax footnote in its financial statements. In Note 12 of its June 30, 2009, fiscal year-end report, ADM reports that its effective tax rate is 32.6 percent. It is reasonable that, going forward, future income will be taxed at 32.6 percent.[7]

Putting the before-tax cost of debt of 5.59 percent on an after-tax basis produces a cost of debt of:

$$r_d^* = r_d(1 - T) = 0.0559 \times (1 - 0.326) = 0.03768 \text{ or } 3.768\%$$

PROBLEM

Suppose company ABC can issue new 10-year bonds, with 6 percent, paid semi-annually. Assume a tax rate of 40 percent.

a. What is the company's before- and after-tax cost of debt if these bonds are issued at par value?

b. What is the company's before- and after-tax cost of debt if these bonds are issued at 98?

Solution

a. If the bonds are issued at par, the present value is the same as the par value. Therefore, the yield to maturity is equal to the coupon rate of 6 percent. The after tax cost is $0.06 \times (1 - 0.4) = 0.06 \times 0.6 = 3.6$ percent.

b. If the bonds are issued at 98, the yield to maturity is 6.2723% [FV = 100; PMT = 3; N = 20; PV = 98 → 3.1361% per six months]. The after-tax cost of this debt is 6.2723 percent $\times (1 - 0.4) = 3.7634\%$ percent.

EXAMPLE 14.3

Determining the Cost of Debt

The Cost of Preferred Equity

We estimate the cost of preferred shares, r_p, at the ratio of the dividend to the current value of a share:

$$r_p = D_p \div P_p \tag{14-4}$$

For example, Company BCD has a 6.2% perpetual, noncumulative preferred stock that has a market value of $21.26 per share and a par value of $25. This implies an annual dividend of $25 \times 0.062 = \$1.55$. Therefore, the cost of this preferred stock to Company BCD is:

$$r_p = \$1.55 \div \$21.26 = 7.29\%$$

---

[6] The Financial Industry Regulatory Authority (FINRA) is a self-regulator for all securities firms in the U.S. You can find FINRA on the web at www.FINRA.org.

[7] ADM's tax rate is around 31 to 32 percent for most recent fiscal year ends.

EXAMPLE 14.4

Determining the Cost of Preferred Equity

PROBLEM

Suppose a company can issue new preferred shares with a par value of $100 at $98. This preferred stock issue has annual dividends at an 8 percent rate. Estimate the company's cost of preferred equity.

Solution

Based on their $100 par value, we get the following values:

$$D_p = \$8$$

$$P_p = \$98$$

So we have $r_p = D_p \div P_p = \$8 \div \$98 = 8.16\%$

The Cost of Common Equity

When we talk of adjusting for growth, we are referring to forecasting a company's future earnings and dividends. One way of assessing the importance of a company's growth prospects is to look at the stock market's time horizon and estimate the value of the company's current dividend when viewed as a perpetuity, and then compare this value with the stock price. If the values are significantly different, then it means that the stock market is valuing something other than the company's current earnings and dividends.

The value of a common share is the present value of its future dividends. We impose some assumptions to make the valuation workable; otherwise we would be forced into discounting dividends to infinity because common shares have no maturity date.

Growth models and the cost of common equity

The **dividend discount model (DDM)** represents the value of a share of stock today as the present value of all future dividends, discounted at the stock's required rate of return. A special case of the DDM is the constant growth version of the dividend discount model (DDM), which represents the value of a share of stock as the present value of a *growing* perpetuity. The dividend discount model with constant growth is commonly referred to as the **Gordon model** after economist Professor Myron Gordon.

Gordon model model of the value of a share of stock that assumes that dividends are a growing perpetuity

The basic valuation equation with constant growth is:

$$P_0 = \frac{D_1}{r_e - g} \tag{14-5}$$

where the price of a share, P_0 equals the expected next period's dividend, D_1, divided by the return required by common share investors, r_e, minus the forecast long-run growth rate, g, in dividends and earnings, or:

$$\text{Price of a share of stock today} = \frac{\text{Next period's dividend}}{\text{Required rate of return} - \text{Growth rate of dividends}}$$

We can rearrange this equation to estimate the common equity investors' discount rate or required rate of return. This process is the discounted cash flow method for estimating the investors' required rate of return. The equation for doing so is:

$$r_e = \frac{D_1}{P_0} + g \tag{14-6}$$

In this equation, the required rate of return is composed of the expected dividend yield, $D_1 \div P_0$, plus the expected long-run growth rate, g. The long-run growth rate is then the estimate of the increase in the share price and the investors' capital gain. As discussed previously, this is the appropriate cost of equity capital for the company when the company can raise the required funds internally (i.e., using reinvested profits).

Consider a company that has a current dividend of $1 per share and a current share price of $20. If the dividends are expected to grow at a rate of 5 percent per year, what is the required rate of return for this stock? We are given:

$D_0 = \$1$

$P_0 = \$20$

$g = 5\%$

The current dividend is $1, so next period's dividend, D_1, is $\$1 \times (1 + 0.05) = \$1.05$. We use Equation 14-6 to solve for the required rate of return, r_e:

$$r_e = \frac{\$1.05}{\$20} + 0.05 = 0.0525 + 0.05 = 0.1025 \text{ or } 10.25\%$$

PROBLEM

Assume a company paid a dividend per share this year of $1.00, which is expected to grow at 5 percent per year indefinitely. If its share price is $25, what is the cost of common equity?

Solution

First, we need to find D_1:

$$D_1 = D_0(1 + g) = \$1.00(1.05) = \$1.05$$

Now we estimate r_e:

$$r_e = \frac{D_1}{P_0} + g = \frac{\$1.05}{\$25} + 0.05 = 0.042 + 0.05 = 0.0920 \text{ or } 9.20\%$$

EXAMPLE 14.5

Determining the Cost of Common Equity

Sustainable growth, retention, and the return on equity

One of the issues we face in estimating the value of a share of stock is how to estimate the growth rate. Although the actual growth rate of the value of a share of stock may change from year to year, what we are most concerned with in valuing a stock today is the long-term growth of the stock's value. We can estimate this long-term growth using the sustainable growth rate. **Sustainable growth rate** is the growth we expect a company to be able to sustain in the future. We estimate sustainable growth as the product of the company's retention rate, b, multiplied by forecasted return on equity (ROE):

$$g = b \times \text{ROE} \tag{14-7}$$

Even if the company retains all its profits and reinvests them within the company, it is not plausible that it can earn a 20 percent ROE on this investment forever. Such an assumption would imply that no other company can enter the industry and compete with the company to also earn these high ROEs. If other companies can enter the market, which will normally be the case, then these high ROEs will be reduced to normal levels due to competitive pressures.

What has to be remembered is that Professor Gordon developed his model for use in public utility regulation where the allowed ROEs should be reasonable, and we do not get the problem of rapid growth rates. Further, it is a product of regulation that all common equity earns virtually the same regulated ROE. In this case, the average and marginal ROE is exactly the same, and every dollar the company retains earns the same ROE. In contrast, many extremely profitable companies cannot reinvest at the same ROE because they cannot find opportunities as good as their existing ones. In determining the growth rate, the ROE is the future growth rate on incremental investment, and this may be greater or smaller than what the company is currently earning.

However, let's return to the constant growth dividend discount model with the assumption of a constant ROE for the time being. Substituting the sustainable growth rate as expressed in Equation 14-7 into the constant growth dividend discount model in place of g, we get:

$$P_0 = \frac{D_1}{r_e - (b \times \text{ROE})}$$

Further, we can then recognize that the expected dividend per share, D_1, is the expected earnings per share in the next period, EPS_1, multiplied by the dividend payout rate (i.e., one minus the retention rate). This is reasonable because a dollar can either be paid out or retained and reinvested within the company. Making this substitution for D_1 we get:

$$P_0 = \frac{\text{EPS}_1(1 - b)}{r_e - (b \times \text{ROE})}$$

We can see in this equation that the price per share is determined by the company's forecast earnings per share, its dividend payout $(1 - b)$, its ROE, and the required return by common equity shareholders, r_e.

<table>
<tr><td colspan="5" style="writing-mode: vertical-lr">SUMMARIZING: SHARE PRICE AND ITS DETERMINANTS</td></tr>
</table>

SUMMARIZING: SHARE PRICE AND ITS DETERMINANTS

Based on the relationship in:

$$P_0 = \frac{\text{EPS}_1(1 - b)}{r_e - (b \times \text{ROE})}$$

we see that:

Variable		Relationship with Share Price	
Earnings per share	EPS_1	Positive	An increase in earnings per share increases share price
Retention rate of earnings	b	Depends on ROE	If ROE is positive, the greater the portion of earnings retained, the greater the share price
Return on equity	ROE	Positive	The greater the return on equity, the greater the share price
Required rate of return	r_e	Negative	The higher the required rate of return, the lower the share price

One important use of this equation is to see how growth and the company's ROE affects its share price. Suppose, for example, that the company's retention rate is 50 percent, its cost of equity capital is 12 percent, and its forecasted earnings per share are $2. If the company's ROE is 12 percent, then the forecast growth rate is 6 percent (i.e., 0.12×0.5) and the forecast dividend per share is $1 using the 50 percent payout ratio. In this case, the shares are worth $16.67.

Now suppose instead of a 12 percent ROE, the company is expected to earn 10 percent or 14 percent. At a 10 percent ROE, the company's forecast growth rate drops to 5 percent, and its share price is only $14.29:

$$P_0 = \frac{\text{EPS}_1(1 - b)}{r_e - (b \times \text{ROE})} = \frac{\$2 \times 0.50}{0.12 - (0.5 \times 0.10)} = \frac{\$1}{0.07} = \$14.29$$

whereas at a 14 percent ROE, the company's growth rate is 7 percent, and its shares are worth $20:

$$P_0 = \frac{\text{EPS}_1(1 - b)}{r_e - (b \times \text{ROE})} = \frac{\$2 \times 0.50}{0.12 - (0.5 \times 0.14)} = \frac{\$1}{0.05} = \$20$$

What this example illustrates is that the higher the growth rate, the higher the share price, as we show in Figure 14-3. This is because with a higher expected growth rate, investors will forecast larger future dividends and earnings.

Starting with the dividend discount equation for the price of a share of stock,

$$r_e = \frac{D_1}{P_0} + g$$

and rearranging, substituting $\text{EPS}_1(1 - b)$ for dividends and $b \times \text{ROE}$ for the growth rate:

$$r_e = \frac{\text{EPS}_1(1 - b)}{P_0} + (b \times \text{ROE})$$

In this equation, the first term is the forecast dividend yield and the second is the sustainable growth rate.

However, note what happens when we use this equation to estimate the cost of equity capital for our three growth scenarios, as we depict in Table 14-3. Because the shares were valued using a constant 12 percent discount rate, when we "reverse engineer" from the share price, we get the same 12 percent back as the estimate of the cost of equity capital. In this case, the higher forecast growth rate leads to a higher market price and a lower dividend yield. Generally, companies with high dividend yields have

FIGURE 14-3 **Return on Equity and Share Price**

TABLE 14-3 **Growth and r_e**

ROE	P_0	Expected Dividend Yield	Sustainable Growth Rate	r_e
10%	$14.29	7%	5%	12%
12%	$16.67	6%	6%	12%
14%	$20.00	5%	7%	12%

lower forecast growth rates and vice versa. However, there is no reason for the cost of equity capital to be the same because the composition of the return between dividends and growth changes.[8]

Note that the company's retention rate, and thus its dividend payout ratio, is reflected in the constant growth DDM as "*b*." In Figure 14-4 we present the share price if this retention rate changes under the three scenarios where the company's ROE is 10, 12, and 14 percent for a wide range of retention rates.

Let's look at the case when the return on equity is 10 percent in Figure 14-4. We already saw that at a 50 percent retention rate, its share price was $14.29, but now we see that its share price *decreases* as the company retains more money and reinvests within the company. In contrast, when the return on equity is 14 percent, the share price increases as the company retains more, whereas for the 12 percent return on equity, the share price is independent of the retention rate.

The reason for these results is that when the company's return on equity is 10 percent, it is less than the investors' required rate of return of 12 percent. As a result, as the company invests more by increasing its retention rate, the shareholders are unhappy. Why would they invest in a company where they require a 12 percent rate of return and be happy with the company returning at 10 percent? In this case, the share valuation model is telling the company's management to reduce investment and return the funds saved as a larger dividend. The shareholders can then take these funds and invest them elsewhere to earn their 12 percent required rate of return. Conversely, where the company is expected to earn 14 percent, the shareholders are saying the opposite: "Don't give us a dividend because we can only earn 12 percent elsewhere, please reinvest more and earn 14 percent." As a result, the share price increases as the company invests more. Finally, for the 12 percent return on equity case, the shareholders are saying: "We don't care what you do

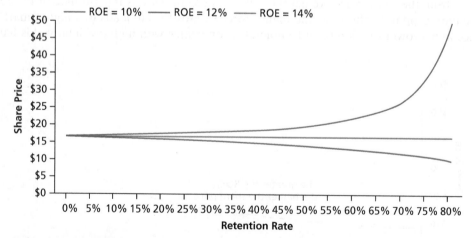

FIGURE 14-4 **Share Prices for Different Retention Rates and for Returns on Equity of 10%, 12%, and 14%**

___
[8] This is a question of the company's dividend policy, which will be discussed in a later chapter.

because you are not doing anything for us whether you invest or give us a dividend." As a result, there is no impact on the share price.

This example is very important in finance. For a long time it was felt this result was due to the company's dividend policy because the company's retention rate and dividend payout are changing. However, this is not true. What is really changing is the amount of investment the company is making, and the stock market is valuing whether the company is creating or destroying value. When the return on equity is greater than the cost of equity, the company is creating value when it reinvests, and when the return on equity is less than the cost of equity, it is destroying value. This result is independent of how much the company decides to pay out as a dividend because it can always raise money to pay a dividend. This indicates another aspect to the cost of capital: not only is it important to value the company's shares, but it is also a **hurdle rate** for making investment decisions. This is the meaning of the phrase *required return*: Unless an investment jumps this hurdle, it destroys value and should not be undertaken. We discuss this more at the end of the chapter.

The example with the different ROEs and different retention rates also emphasizes another key point: There is a big difference between a *growing* company and a *growth* company. When the return on equity is equal to the cost of equity, the share price was independent of how much the company reinvested. If the company paid out all its earnings and did not grow at all ($b = 0$), the share price is $16.67, whereas if it reinvests all its earnings ($b = 1$) and grows at 12 percent per year, the share price is still $16.67. This is an example of a growing company where if it simply reinvests at its cost of capital, it is "not doing anything" for the shareholders, and they don't care whether it is growing or not. Note also that the earnings yield for this growing company at a 50 percent retention rate is 12 percent, which equals its forecast earnings per share divided by its stock price (i.e., $2 ÷ $16.67). So for growing companies, the earnings yield is a good estimate of their cost of equity capital.

On the other hand, when the return on equity is greater than the cost of equity, the company is doing something that the shareholders cannot do, which is reinvest at 14 percent. We refer to these companies as growth companies and say they have growth opportunities. In this case, note that the earnings yield is $2 ÷ $20 or 10 percent, which underestimates the required return by common shareholders. Finally, some companies destroy shareholder value by investing where $ROE < r_e$. For these companies, the earnings yield is $2 ÷ $14.29 = 14 percent, which overestimates their cost of internal equity. What can a shareholder do if the company does not return what is required? They simply sell their shares (the proverbial "vote with their feet").

Multi-stage growth models

Another version of the dividend discount model to consider is the **multi-stage growth dividend discount model.** In practice there is no limit to the extent of the growth stages, but let's consider a simple case in which the company has some investment today, which we assume equals the company's book value per share (BVPS), which is earning a return (ROE_1) in perpetuity.[9] The company is expected to invest a similar amount next year (Inv), which will earn a return (ROE_2) in perpetuity. This particular version of the multi-stage model can be expressed as:

> **multi-stage growth dividend discount model** version of the dividend discount model that accounts for different levels of growth in earnings and dividends

$$P_0 = \frac{\text{Present value of}}{\text{cash flows of existing assets}} + \frac{\text{Present value of}}{\text{growth opportunities}}$$

or, using notation,

$$P_0 = \frac{ROE_1 \times BVPS}{r_e} + \frac{\dfrac{Inv_1}{(1 + r_e)}ROE_2 - r_e}{r_e} \tag{14-8}$$

[9] Notice that this will equal EPS_1, which means the value of existing opportunities $= EPS_1 ÷ r$.

present value of existing opportunities (PVEO) value today of the company's current operations assuming no new investment

present value of growth opportunities (PVEO) amount of the value of an asset that is attributable to the expected growth opportunities of the asset's cash flows; value today of the company's future investments

The first term in this equation is the present value of the current earnings, as we discussed previously, where the company is expected to earn an ROE_1. The second term represents further investment (Inv_1), which we assume is invested at ROE_2, and is discounted back one period because it is one period further off in the future, but adds a perpetual amount represented by the difference between the company's ROE on this investment of ROE_2 minus r_e. If $ROE_2 = r_e$, then this future investment adds nothing to the value of the company because it does not create value, and the second term is equal zero. However, if $ROE_2 > r_e$, this future investment adds value, with the amount of value depending on the amount of investment (Inv_1) that can be invested at this rate, and by how much ROE_2 exceeds r_e. Equation 14-8 is a basic approach to valuation that breaks out the value of shares into the **present value of existing opportunities (PVEO)**, the first term, and the **present value of growth opportunities (PVGO)**, the second term.

Although these equations make everything seem precise and quite scientific, the financial decision maker must understand the company and the assumptions behind all the parameters in the model before mechanically applying the valuation formulas.

Risk-based models and the cost of common equity

The previous section showed that the dividend discount model could be rearranged to estimate the investors' required return on a company's common shares. However, we also discussed how the model performs poorly when applied to growth stocks, which pay low dividends and/or display high growth rates. In these situations, it makes sense to rely more heavily on **risk-based models**. The most important risk-based model is the **capital asset pricing model (CAPM)**, which states that the expected return on a stock is the sum of the expected risk-free rate of interest and a premium for bearing market risk, specifically the stock's beta multiplied by the difference between the expected return on the market and the risk-free rate of interest.

risk-based models models that estimate costs based on the associated risks

We can represent the central equation of the CAPM, the security market line (SML), as follows:

$$E(r_i) = r_f + [E(r_M) - r_f]\beta_i \tag{14.9}$$

In this equation, the required return by common shareholders (r_e) is composed of three terms:

expected risk-free rate of return compensation, in the form of a return, for the time value of money

1. The **expected risk-free rate of return,** r_f, which represents compensation for the time value of money.
2. The expected **market risk premium** $[E(r_M) - r_f]$, which is compensation for assuming the risk of the market portfolio; r_M is the expected return on the market.

beta coefficient or beta measure of a company's systematic or market risk

3. The **beta coefficient** (or simply **beta**), β_i, for the company's common shares, which measures the company's systematic or market risk, and which represents the contribution that this security makes to the risk of a well-diversified portfolio.

The CAPM is derived as a single-period model, but just what is meant by a single period is an unresolved issue because investment horizons differ across investors. In testing the CAPM, it is common use a 30-day time horizon, and yet in making corporate finance decisions, such a short time horizon is rarely useful. In fact, when we talked about the characteristics of common equity, one of the most important is the absence of a maturity date. Although an individual investor may invest for 30 days, at that time, he or she will sell the shares to another investor, so the security is still outstanding. In addition, as we will see when we discuss corporate investment decisions, the cost of capital or WACC is used to evaluate long-term investment decisions made by the company. For this reason, the risk-free rate used in corporate applications of the CAPM is usually the yield on the longest maturity Treasury bond, which is currently the 30-year bond.

We generally use long-run averages supplemented by knowledge of the prevailing economic scenario to estimate the market risk premium. The basic idea is that over long periods, what people expect to happen should eventually be realized, otherwise they are biased in forming their expectations. In contrast, over short periods, it is unlikely that expectations are realized. It's like tossing a die: You may get three consecutive ones, but if you throw it enough times, eventually one-sixth of the time you will get ones, one-sixth of the time you will get twos, and so on. Similarly, we can consider the performance of the S&P 500 Index over the 1988 to 2010 period, as we report in Figure 14-5.

Clearly it is difficult to argue that in any one particular year, the performance of the S&P 500 Index was what had been expected. For example, nobody would have held shares in either 2001 or 2002 if they expected the stock market to go down! So what do we use for the expected market risk premium? A reasonable estimate, derived from academic research, is to use an estimate in the range of 3.5 to 4 percent.[10]

The final piece of information needed to use the SML to estimate required returns is the beta coefficient, which adjusts the risk of the market to the risk of an individual security, so it is an absolute number like 0.50 for a low-risk security and 1.5 for a high-risk security. The beta coefficient measures the degree to which securities move in relation to market movements: The more they move together, the less diversification gains there are and the riskier the security. Betas are normally estimated using the prior 5 years' monthly return data, but it is important to realize that if nothing happened during this period, then that is be reflected in the estimate. Conversely, if something special happened during this period, the beta will

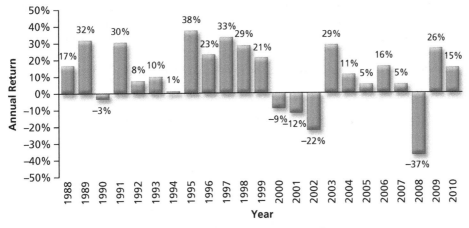

FIGURE 14-5 Annual Returns on the S&P 500 Index

Source of data: *Standard & Poor's.*

[10] In surveys of CFOs, John R. Graham and Campbell R. Harvey found that the average, 10-year risk premium is 3.46 percent; though during a recession it tends toward 3.97 percent and is lower, around 3.37 percent, in nonrecessionary periods ["The Equity Risk Premium amid a Global Financial Crisis," working paper, May 14, 2009]. These premiums are similar to what Graham and Harvey had found in their earlier surveys and studies. Eugene F. Fama and Kenneth R. French, in their study of the equity risk premium from 1951 to 2000, find a premium in the range of 2.55 percent to 4.32 percent ["The Equity Premium," *Journal of Finance,* 57, no. 2(2002): 637–659].

reflect it.[11] For this reason, we tend to go back over long periods and again analyze what happened during the estimation period. Consider the common stock of IBM. If we calculate the beta of IBM's stock using the 60 months of returns for the period 2006 through 2010, which includes the financial crisis of 2007–08, we estimate a beta of 0.70. If we calculate the beta over the broader period of 2001 through 2010, which includes a more "normal" market for most of the estimation period, we estimate a beta of 1.04.

As discussed in a previous chapter, if we sum up all the beta coefficients of individual companies, their value-weighted average has to equal 1.0, which is the beta of the market as a whole. For an individual company these may be quite different than 1.0. Consider the examples that we provide in Table 14-4.

The betas that we show in Table 14-4 are wide ranging, from a low of 0.36 for Wal-Mart Stores to a high of 2.42 for U.S. Steel. These betas are calculated using data that span the recent recession, so we need to consider them with the caveat that these may not be representative betas for other economic environments. However, you can see that these betas do tend to differentiate the firms in terms of risk—both operating and financial risk.

EXAMPLE 14.6

Determining the Cost of Common Equity Using CAPM

PROBLEM

Assume the beta for a company's stock is 1.15, that the risk-free rate is 4.5 percent, and the market risk premium is 4.5 percent. Estimate the company's cost of equity for internal funds using CAPM.

Solution

$$r_e = 4.5 + (4.5 \times 1.15) = 9.68\%$$

Flotation costs and the marginal cost of capital

In the example in the previous section, we were given the cost of equity, as well as the before-tax cost of debt, which we can adjust to determine the after-tax cost of debt. One complication that arises with respect to all sources of capital, except for internally generated funds, is that the company incurs **issuing costs** or **flotation costs** when new securities are issued. These include any fees paid to the investment dealer and/or any discounts provided to investors to entice them to purchase the securities. As a result, the cost of issuing new securities will be *higher* than the return required by investors because the net proceeds to the company from any security issue will be lower than that security's market price.

issuing costs or flotation costs costs incurred by a company when it issues new securities

TABLE 14-4 Betas for a Sample of Companies, December 2011

Company	*Ticker*	*Industry*	*Beta*
Goldman Sachs	GS	Diversified investments	1.39
Intel Corporation	INTC	Semiconductor	1.08
Johnson & Johnson	JNJ	Consumer products	0.54
Microsoft Corporation	MSFT	Software	0.98
Ryder Systems, Inc.	R	Rental and Leasing Services	1.62
United States Steel	X	Metal fabrication	2.42
Wal-Mart Stores, Inc.	WMT	Discount retail stores	0.36

Source of data: *Yahoo! Finance.*

---

[11] Edward Yardeni, "US Stock Valuation Models," Deutsche Bank, October 4, 2000.

Being aware of this fact is particularly important when we consider the cost of common equity to the company. In particular, remember that there are two sources of common equity financing: reinvested earnings, which show up on the company's balance sheet in retained earnings, and new common share issues. When the common equity portion of financing comes entirely from reinvested earnings, the company's cost of equity is equal the return required by its shareholders. However, when the company issues new common shares, it must pay flotation costs for issuing these shares, so the cost to the company is higher than the cost of using internally generated funds.

Adjusting for flotation costs: Two schools of thought

There are two different schools of thought regarding flotation costs. The first school of thought replaces the share price or present value with the proceeds after paying the flotation costs. Therefore, in using the dividend discount model, instead of:

$$r_e = \frac{D_1}{P_0} + g$$

we would use the P_0 less the flotation costs in the denominator of the first term. If we represent the price per share less flotation costs as $P_{0,f}$, we would then have a cost of equity that is slightly higher:

$$r_e = \frac{D_1}{P_{0,f}} + g \tag{14-10}$$

In the case of debt, if the proceeds of the debt issue are not the face value, but rather are P_f, the cost of debt before taxes is the value of r_d that solves the following:

$$P_f = \left(\sum_{t=1}^{N} \frac{C}{(1 + r_d)^t} \right) + \frac{FV}{(1 + r_d)^N} \tag{14-11}$$

What About Companies That Do Business Globally?

GLOBAL PERSPECTIVE

When we calculate the cost of capital in this chapter, we are focusing on the cost of capital for investments made in the same country as the investment, whether that country is the U.S., Canada, France, China, or any other country. This cost of capital represents the marginal cost of capital for a company's average project.

However, when making investments outside a company's home country, it is preferable to use a cost of capital that reflects the country in which the investment is made and the cost of capital appropriate for that country. This international cost of capital is often the starting point for estimating an international project's cost of capital.

How do we estimate an international cost of capital? There are several approaches available, including an international version of the CAPM; however, there is no consensus on the best model. In fact, the most appropriate model may depend on whether the economy is developed or emerging.

What is different in the international cost of capital estimation? One of the primary differences is that the

international cost of capital generally includes a country risk premium, which captures financial, political, and economic risks specific to a country. For example, Duff and Phelps note that Greece has a ratio of government debt to GDP of 115 percent in 2010, which increases both the political and economic risks of investing in that country.

Another factor to consider is that investing in other countries may offer some diversification, hence lowering a company's cost of capital. For example, Duff and Phelps estimate the correlation between return in the U.S. with those of emerging markets and find a correlation of 0.78; therefore, there is some diversification benefit from investing in these countries, and this lowers the cost of equity, and, hence, the weighted average cost of capital.

Sources: Duff & Phelps, *Cost of Capital Estimation in Emerging Markets*, September 30, 2010; Campbell Harvey, "12 Ways to Calculate the International Cost of Capital," working paper, National Bureau of Economic Research, Cambridge Massachusetts, October 11, 2005.

The effect of using the net proceeds instead of the current price or value is to have a higher cost of capital for the respective source.

The other school of thought is to leave the costs as we have calculated them, but then treat the cash flows for the flotation costs as an initial period cash outflow. The argument for this approach is that if we adjust the cost of capital, as in the first approach, we are representing what is a lump sum cash flow as something that affects the costs throughout the life of the project. This is not accurate and does not reflect the realities of the cash flows.

Concept Review Questions

1. Explain the relationship among ROE, retention rates, and company growth.

2. Explain how we can use the CAPM to estimate the cost of common equity.

14.4 ASSEMBLING THE PIECES

Once we have the weights and the costs of the different sources of capital, we calculate the weighted average cost of capital using Equation 14-1 that we introduced earlier:

$$r_a = w_d r_d^* + w_p r_p + w_e r_e$$

Gathering the Information

A financial analyst with the Dozer Company would like to estimate Dozer's cost of capital. He has gathered the following capital structure information using Dozer's most recent balance sheet:

	(in millions)
Current portion of long-term debt	$100
8% bonds	900
Total interest-bearing debt	$1,000
Preferred stock, 1 million $100 par value 7% perpetual preferred shares outstanding	$100
Common stock, 50 million shares outstanding	5
Additional paid-in capital	20
Retained earnings	1,400
Total shareholders' equity	$1,525
Total liabilities and equity	$2,625

Other information that the analyst has gathered:

- Dozer's tax rate is 35 percent.
- The bonds are due in 10 years, pay interest semi-annually, and have a current yield to maturity of 6 percent.
- The preferred stock has a current market value of $110 per share.
- The common stock has a current market value of $80 per share.
- The beta on Dozer's stock is 1.2.
- The expected market risk premium is 4 percent.

- The expected risk-free rate of interest is 2 percent.
- The current dividend on Dozer's common stock is $4 per share, and this dividend is expected to grow at a rate of 3 percent per year.

Calculations

Step 1: Calculate the proportions of capital

The first step in estimating Dozer's cost of capital is to calculate the capital structure proportions. Using book value weights, the capital structure is 39.6 percent debt and 60.4 percent equity: 4 percent preferred and 56.4 percent common. However, we have data available to calculate the market values components, which is the favored approach. We calculate the market value of the components as:

Capital Source	Calculation	(in millions)	Proportion of Total Capital
Debt	FV = 100; N = 20; i = 3%; PMT = 4; → PV = 114.877		
	114.877 × $1,000 face = $1,148.77	$1,149	21.85%
Preferred stock	$110 × 1 = $110	110	2.09%
Common stock	$80 × 50 = $4,000	4,000	76.06%
Total capital		$5,259	100.00%

Step 2: Estimate the costs of capital

The cost of debt is rather simple because we are given the current yield to maturity on Dozer's debt, 6 percent. The before-tax cost of debt is 6 percent, so therefore the after-tax cost of debt is $0.06(1 - 0.35) = 0.039$ or 3.9%.

We can infer the cost of preferred stock from the current market value and the dividend stream. We know that the current market value is $110 per share. With a dividend of 7 percent, the dividend per share is $7. Comparing the dividend to the price, we see that the required rate of return on the preferred stock is $7 ÷ $110 = 0.0636 or 6.36%.

The cost of equity is a bit more challenging because we have two different ways of estimating the cost. Applying the dividend valuation model, we use the following information:

$D_0 = \$4$

$g = 3\%$

$P_0 = \$80$

Given the current dividend of $4 and the growth rate, we know that the expected dividend for next period, D_1, is $4.12. Putting this together, we see that the cost of equity is 8.15 percent:

$$r_e = (\$4.12 \div \$80) + 0.03 = 0.0515 + 0.03 = 0.0815 \text{ or } 8.15\%$$

If we instead use the CAPM, we have:

$r_f = 2\%$

$E(r_M) - r_f = 4\%$

$\beta = 1.2$

Applying the formula for the security market line,

$$r_e = 0.02 + (1.2 \times 0.04) = 0.02 + 0.048 = 0.068 \text{ or } 6.8\%$$

We arrive at different costs of equity using the DDM and the CAPM. This is to be expected because these models are based on different assumptions and use different elements in the calculation; the DDM focuses on dividend and dividend growth, whereas the

CAPM focuses on risk premiums, the risk-free rate, and beta. Which is correct? We cannot say; all we can say is that these are two plausible estimates. If a company pays dividends and these dividends grow at a constant rate, the DDM may be most appropriate. If a company does not pay dividends, but its stock returns are best explained by the return on the market, the CAPM may be most appropriate.

Step 3: Assemble the pieces

Summarizing, we have the following "pieces" to the cost of capital puzzle:

Piece of the Puzzle		*Estimate*
w_d	proportion of debt	21.85%
w_p	proportion of preferred equity	2.09%
w_e	proportion of common equity	76.06%
r_d^*	after-tax cost of debt	3.90%
r_p	cost of preferred equity	6.36%
r_e	cost of common equity: DDM	8.15%
r_e	cost of common equity: CAPM	6.80%

Assembling the pieces, if we estimate a cost of capital using the dividend discount model for the cost of equity, assuming constant growth, we arrive at an estimate of 7.184 percent:

$$\text{WACC} = (0.2185 \times 0.039) + (0.0209 \times 0.0636) + (0.7606 \times 0.0815)$$
$$= 0.07184 \text{ or } 7.184\%$$

If, on the other hand, we use the CAPM for the cost of equity estimate, we estimate a cost of capital of 6.1572%:

$$\text{WACC} = (0.2185 \times 0.039) + (0.0209 \times 0.0636) + (0.7606 \times 0.068)$$
$$= 0.061572 \text{ or } 6.1572\%$$

We can state that the cost of capital for Dozer is likely close to the range from 6.1572% to 7.184%.

LESSONS LEARNED | A Losing Formula

Volatile financial markets can wreak havoc with your cost-of-capital calculations—and possibly skew your investment decisions and financial results.

You could always say this about your company's cost-of-capital calculation: however complex it might be, you generally had to do it only once. If only life were still so simple.

Thanks to volatile financial markets and a harsh economy, calculating a weighted average cost of capital that makes sense has become significantly more complex, and carries a far greater margin of error. At least one CFO has resorted to calculating two metrics, one for assessing short-term investment opportunities and another for vetting long-term projects.

Extraordinary times, it seems, demand extraordinary measurements—and hold the potential for extraordinary risks. Underestimate your capital cost and you might take on investments that are not, in fact, economically justifiable. Overestimate and you could wind up not taking on worthy projects.

You could tarnish today's financials, too. Setting your cost of capital too high will artificially boost the cost of your equity-compensation programs this year, and could inflate any impairment charges you must take on goodwill. A botched calculation also could affect the amount of incentive compensation awarded to any employees measured against your company's performance relative to its cost of capital.

The math behind all these calculations hasn't changed, of course, but the integrity of the inputs has. Treasury bond yields—a key component in reckoning the cost of equity, which is one part of a company's weighted average cost of capital—have fallen to historic and, some argue, unsustainable lows. That, warns Roger Grabowski, managing director at financial advisory and investment banking firm Duff & Phelps, could mask the business risks some companies face in this severely depressed economy. "At the very time you would expect that your risk, and therefore your cost of capital, should be higher," he says, "the beginning point of your cost-of-capital estimate is actually very low."

At the same time, Grabowski notes, stock prices have fallen dramatically, but not uniformly, with shares of financial firms and highly leveraged companies falling the hardest. Because stock volatility relative to the broader market is another component of the cost-of-capital calculation, any company whose stock was less volatile than the broader market might also come up with a misleadingly low calculation. Their risk may have declined relative to, say, bank stocks, Grabowski reasons, but not necessarily to the economy.

Of course, for companies that have seen their stocks brutalized and their access to affordable long-term debt choked off, this issue cuts in the other direction. They must worry whether their cost of capital is being artificially inflated. And layered over all of this is the question of whether any of these extreme cost-of-capital inputs are short-term aberrations that should be discounted.

Extracted from Randy Myers, " A Losing Formula," *CFO Magazine*, May 1, 2009.

A Case Study

We provide an example of the estimation of the cost of capital for an actual company so that you can see how all these equations work with actual values. In this example, we estimate the cost of capital of Archer-Daniels-Midland, as of the end of fiscal year 2009. We provide Archer-Daniels-Midland's capital structure, based on carrying values provided in its annual reports in Table 14-5.

U.S. generally accepted accounting principles require a company to report the market value of its liabilities, if it can be reasonably estimated, in footnotes to the financial statements. ADM provides in its debt footnote the amount by which the fair values of its liabilities exceed the carrying value. Using this information, we can calculate the market value of debt.

TABLE 14-5 Archer-Daniels-Midland Capital Structure, for Fiscal Years Ending June 30, 2006, Through June 30, 2009

(in millions)	Fiscal Year End, June 30			
	2009	2008	2007	2006
Interest-bearing short-term debt	$356	$3,123	$468	$549
Current portion of long-term debt	48	232	65	80
Long-term debt	7,800	7,690	4,752	4,050
Total debt capital	$8,204	$11,045	$5,285	$4,680
Shareholders' equity	$13,499	$13,490	$11,253	$9,807
Total capital	$21,703	$24,535	$16,538	$14,486
Debt-to-equity ratio	0.608	0.819	0.470	0.477
Debt to total assets ratio	0.378	0.450	0.320	0.323
Proportion of debt capital	37.8%	45.0%	32.0%	32.3%
Proportion of common equity capital	62.2%	55.0%	68.0%	67.7%

TABLE 14-6 **Market Value Capital Structure of ADM, for Fiscal Years Ending June 30, 2006, Though June 30, 2009**

(in millions)	Fiscal Year End, June 30			
	2009	*2008*	*2007*	*2006*
Market value of debt[12]	$8,103	$7,789	$4,862	$4,937
Market price per share	$26.77	$33.75	$33.09	$41.28
Number of shares of stock outstanding	643	644	651	654
Market value of equity	$13,499	$13,490	$11,253	$9,807
Total capital	$21,703	$24,535	$16,538	$14,486
Debt-to-equity ratio	0.608	0.819	0.470	0.477
Debt to total assets ratio	0.378	0.450	0.320	0.323
Proportion of debt capital	32.0%	26.4%	18.4%	15.5%
Proportion of common equity capital	68.0%	73.6%	81.6%	84.5%

With respect to the market value of equity, ADM reports the number of shares of common stock it has outstanding in the annual report each year and provides historical share price information on its Investors' Relations portion of its web site. Using these two pieces of information for each year, we can estimate the market value of equity. Based on the market value information in its annual reports, we estimate Archer-Daniels-Midland's market value capital structure, as we show in Table 14-6.

Using the information on the proportions of capital, we need to make an assumption regarding ADM's target capital structure. ADM's use of debt financing has increased slightly over the 4-year period. Though we cannot observe ADM's target capital structure, nor its intentions, we can assume that the most recent capital structure, in market value terms, is the most representative for this company.

With respect to the costs of the individual components, we calculated the after-tax cost of debt in an earlier section as 3.768 percent. This leaves us to calculate the cost of equity. Using the current dividend of $0.56 per share, and expecting this dividend to increase by the historical rate of 7 percent, we therefore expect next period's dividend to be $0.6328 per share. The current market price of ADM stock is $30.66 per share, and the expected long-term growth rate in dividends is 7 percent.[13] Putting this information in the dividend discount model, we have:[14]

$$r_e = (\$0.6328 \div \$30.66) + 0.07 = 0.02064 + 0.07 = 0.09064 \text{ or } 9.064\%$$

Estimating the WACC for ADM, we have:

$$\text{WACC} = (0.32 \times 0.03768) + (0.68 \times 0.09064) = 0.073693 \text{ or } 7.3693\%$$

Although we have used numbers to the fifth decimal place, you should remember that despite looking accurate, these are estimates: Each value in the WACC equation is an estimate, so the final result—in this case a cost of capital of 7.3693 percent—although seemingly precise, is just an estimate.

---

[12] Provided by the company in Note 6 of the respective annual reports.

[13] Per *Value Line Investment Survey*, July 31, 2009.

[14] If we estimate the cost of equity using the CAPM model, using a risk-free rate of 1.5 percent, a market risk premium of 4 percent, and a beta of 0.33, the cost of equity is: $r_e = 0.015 + (0.96 \times 0.04) = 0.0534$ or 5.34%.

SUMMARY

- The WACC is a market value weighted average of the marginal costs of the different sources of capital. If the company earns its WACC, then its present market values are supported; if it is expected to earn less than its WACC, then its market value will fall, and if it is expected to earn more than its WACC, then its market value will increase.

- The weights in the WACC are the proportions that each source of capital represents when the company raises new capital. If we assume that the company is at its target capital structure, then we use the current capital structure as the target capital structure. When calculating the proportions, it is important to use the market value of the different sources of capital, not the book or carrying values.

- A proxy for the before-tax cost of debt is the yield on the company's current debt. We can proxy the cost of preferred equity in a similar manner, looking at how the market currently prices the company's preferred stock.

- The most challenging estimate in the WACC is that for the cost of common equity capital. In estimating this, the financial decision maker can use the dividend discount model (or variants) of this model, or the capital asset pricing model.

- We use the proportions and the costs of each source of capital to estimate the weighted cost of capital. This weighted cost of capital is a marginal cost because each of the component costs is a marginal cost.

FORMULAS/EQUATIONS

(14-1) $r_a = w_d r_d^* + w_p r_p + w_e r_e$

(14-2) $P_p = D_p \div r_p$

(14-3) $PV = \left(\sum_{t=1}^{N} \frac{C}{(1 + r_d)^t} \right) + \frac{FV}{(1 + r_d)^N}$

(14-4) $r_p = D_p \div P_p$

(14-5) $P_0 = \dfrac{D_1}{r_e - g}$

(14-6) $r_e = \dfrac{D_1}{P_0} + g$

(14-7) $g = b \times ROE$

(14-8) $P_0 = \dfrac{ROE_1 \times BVPS}{r_e} + \dfrac{\frac{Inv_1}{(1 + r_e)} ROE_2 - r_e}{r_e}$

(14-9) $r_i = r_f + (r_M - r_f)\beta_i$

(14-10) $r_e = \dfrac{D_1}{P_{0,f}} + g$

(14-11) $P_f = \left(\sum_{t=1}^{N} \frac{C}{(1 + r_d)^t} \right) + \frac{FV}{(1 + r_d)^N}$

QUESTIONS AND PROBLEMS

Multiple Choice

1. If an all-equity company is expected to earn and pay out a $5.50 dividend forever (in perpetuity), the value of the company's stock given a cost of equity of 15 percent is *closest* to:

   A. $36.   B. $37.   C. $38.   D. $40.

2. The earnings yield given a $40,000 net income, a $10 market price per share, and 10,000 shares outstanding is *closest* to:

   A. 0.3.   B. 0.4.   C. 0.5.   D. 4,000.

3. What does the company have to earn, based on the following?
   - Market value of debt = $40,000
   - Market value of equity = $69,000

- $r_e = 12.5\%$
- $r_d = 7\%$
- Tax rate $= 35\%$

A. $2,800   B. $8,625   C. $10,099   D. $11,425

4.   Which of the following statements is *true*?

A. When ROE $< r_e$, management is adding value to the company.

B. When ROE $> r_e$, management is decreasing the company's value.

C. When ROE $> r_e$, the market price goes above the book value of the investment.

D. When ROE $= r_e$, the market price goes above the book value of the investment.

5.   Which of the following is *not* an input in the calculation of the WACC?

A. Cost of equity

B. Corporate tax rate

C. Book values of equity and debt

D. Market values of equity and debt

6.   To increase the stock price of a company that is assumed to grow at a constant rate g:

A. increase the cost of equity.

B. increase the retention ratio.

C. decrease the dividend payout ratio.

7.   Star Inc. just paid a $9.50 dividend, which is expected to grow at a constant rate. Recent EPS is $10.50 and net income is $550,000. Total book equity is $1,100,000, and the cost of equity is 12 percent. The market price per share is *closest* to:

A. $129.90.

B. $130.90.

C. $137.50.

D. $142.50.

8.   Which of the following companies is a growth company?

A. ROE $> r_e$

B. ROE $< r_e$

C. ROE $= r_e$

D. Net income $= r_e$

9.   A company with accounts payable of $1 million, current portion of long-term debt of $2 million, bonds of $3 million, and deferred taxes of $0.5 million has debt capital *closest* to:

A. $5.0 million.

B. $5.5 million.

C. $6.0 million.

D. $6.5 million.

10.   A company's financial analyst has gathered the following information in estimating the company's cost of capital:

- If the company issues debt, the analyst expects the yield on this debt to be 7 percent.
- The company's current dividend on its common stock is $1.5 per share, and the company intends on continuing its policy of increasing this dividend 4 percent each year.
- The current price of its common stock is $20 per share.
- The company has no preferred stock and does not intend on issuing any.
- The company's current capital structure is 35 percent debt and 65 percent equity, but its target capital structure is 40 percent debt, 60 percent equity.
- The company's marginal tax rate is 40 percent.

The company's weighted average cost of capital is closest to:

A. 8 percent.

B. 8.2 percent.

C. 8.7 percent.

D. 8.8 percent.

E. 9.2 percent.

Practice Questions and Problems

14.1 The Marginal Cost of Capital

11. Why is the weighted average cost of capital considered a *marginal* cost of capital?

12. What is the marginal cost of capital schedule?

13. A company is going to finance a new project 100 percent with debt, through a new bond issue. Because the company is using only debt to finance the project, the NPV of the project should be calculated using the cost of debt as the discount rate. Is this statement true? Explain your reasoning.

14. Tony Young has decided to estimate a company's cost of debt as the interest rate on the company's existing debt. He intends to use this interest rate as the before-tax cost of debt. Under what circumstances, if any, would this approach be appropriate?

14.2 Estimating the Weights

15. What is the difference, if any, between debt and liabilities?

16. Why would a company prefer to use market value weights in calculating its cost of capital instead of book value weights?

17. Consider a company that has $1 million face value bonds that are trading at 0.98. What is the market value of the company's debt?

18. If a company has a book value of equity of $20 million and a market-to-book ratio of 1.15, what is the market value of its equity?

19. For each of the following, classify the account as debt capital, equity, or other:

	Debt Capital	Equity Capital	Neither
Accounts payable			
Bank loan			
Bonds payable			
Common stock			
Current portion of long-term debt			
Deferred income taxes			
Notes payable			
Pension liability			
Preferred stock			
Retained earnings			
Taxes payable			
Wages payable			

20. Consider the following:

Book value of debt	$12 million
Book value of equity	$15 million
Market value of debt	$13 million
Market value of equity	$25 million

    What are the weights that this company should use in estimating its cost of capital? Explain your choice.

21. Consider the following information from the balance sheet of Procter & Gamble for the fiscal year 2009 [*Source: Procter & Gamble 10-K for fiscal year 2009*]:

Accounts payable	$7,251
Accrued and other liabilities	8,559
Debt due within one year	8,472
Long-term debt	21,360
Deferred income taxes	10,902
Other noncurrent liabilities (including pensions)	10,189
Total liabilities	$66,733

    What is Proctor & Gamble's debt capital for 2009?

22. Consider the 2010 financial data for ADM (for fiscal year end June 30, 2010):

(in millions)	*2010*
Interest-bearing short-term debt	$1,875
Current portion of long-term debt	$178
Long-term debt	$8,266
Shareholders' equity	$18,808

    A. Complete the following table:

Total debt capital	
Total capital	
Debt-to-equity ratio	
Debt to total assets ratio	
Proportion of debt capital	
Proportion of common equity capital	

    B. Compare the 2010 capital structure with ADM's 2009 and 2008 capital structure (Table 14-5). In what way, if any, did ADM's capital structure change?

14.3 Estimating the Costs of Capital

23. Why do we adjust the cost of debt for taxes, yet we do not adjust the cost of preferred equity or the cost of common equity for taxes?

24. Will the estimate of the cost of equity using the dividend discount model be the same as that determined using the capital asset pricing model? Explain.

25. What is the relationship between the retention rate and the cost of common equity?

26. If a company's yield on its debt increases, what do you expect to happen to the company's cost of debt and weighted average cost of capital? Explain.

27. The Dayton Poultry Equipment Company has been generating a return on equity around 15 percent. If this company increases the portion of earnings that it retains, what do you expect to happen to its stock price? Explain.

28. Consider a company whose stock currently trades for $190 per share. If the current dividend is $2.90 per share and is expected to grow at a rate of 3.44 percent per year, what is the cost of equity for this company based on the constant growth dividend discount model?

29. I. M. Grow Inc. just announced its earnings per share of $3. Its retention ratio is 70 percent. The earnings are expected to grow at 10 percent for 1 year and then grow at 4 percent indefinitely. Given that the cost of equity is 15 percent, what is the market price per share of stock?

30. Calculate the cost of issuing new equity for a company assuming: issue costs are 5 percent of the share price after taxes, market price per share is $20, current dividend per share is $3.50, and the growth rate of dividends is 5 percent.

31. A company has common shares outstanding with a market capitalization rate of 12 percent. The current market price is $13.80, and dividend payments for this year are expected to be $0.28. What is the implied growth rate?

32. Calculate present value of growth opportunities and present value of existing opportunities given the following information:

    Return on equity of existing opportunities = 20%
    Return on equity of future opportunities = 25%
    Further investment = $50
    Book value per share = $10
    Cost of equity = 15%

33. Consider the following information for a company: current dividend is $2.50, the payout ratio is 70 percent (assuming it is not changing), the return on equity is 15 percent, and the current market price of the stock is $11.50 per share.

    A. What is the cost of equity using a constant growth dividend discount model?

    B. Based on this information, is the current management adding to or reducing the shareholders' value?

34. A company's earnings and dividends are expected to grow at a constant rate indefinitely, and it is expected to pay a dividend of $9.20 per share next year. Expected earnings per share and book value per share next year are $10.50 and $30, respectively. The cost of equity is 12 percent and there are 10,000 shares outstanding. Calculate the company's value assuming that the retention ratio stays the same and the market value of debt is $500,000.

14.4 Assembling the Pieces

35. Consider a company with market values of equity and debt that are $500,000 and $600,000, respectively. The before-tax cost of debt is 6 percent, the risk-free rate of interest is 4 percent, the stock's beta is 1.5, the market risk premium is 10 percent, and the marginal tax rate is 40 percent. What is this company's cost of capital?

36. Consider a company with the following financial statement information:

Balance Sheet

Cash	$140,000	Accounts payable	$200,000
Marketable securities	200,000	Wages payable	100,000
Accounts receivable	40,000	Short-term debt	250,000
Inventory	1,000,000	Long-term debt	690,000
Fixed assets	900,000	Total liabilities	$1,240,000
		Common stock	950,000
		Retained earnings	90,000
Total assets	$2,280,000	Total equity & liabilities	$2,280,000

Income Statement

Sales	$1,200,000
Cost of goods sold	$400,000
Amortization	$90,000
Interest	$56,400
Earnings before taxes	$653,600
Taxes	$261,440
Net income	$392,160
Shares outstanding	300,000

A. What is the cost of equity given a risk-free rate of 5 percent, a beta of 1.2, and an expected market return of 10 percent?

B. What is the market price and market-to-book ratio, assuming the company's stock is a perpetuity and the retention ratio is zero?

C. What is the invested capital and before-tax return on investment for this company?

37. A company has the following capital structure based on market values: equity is 65 percent and debt is 35 percent. The current yield on government T-bonds is 10 percent, the expected return on the market portfolio is 15 percent, and the company's beta is approximated at 0.85. The company's common shares are trading at $25, and the current dividend level of $3 per share is expected to grow at an annual rate of 3.5 percent. The company can issue debt at a 2 percent premium over the current risk-free rate. The company's tax rate is 40 percent, and the company is considering a project to be funded out of internally generated funds that will not alter the company's overall risk. This project requires an initial investment of $11.5 million and promises to generate net annual after-tax cash flows of $1.4 million perpetually. Should this project be undertaken? Explain.

38. A company has the following balance sheet items:

Common stock: 300,000 shares at $8 each	$2,400,000
Retained earnings	$900,000
Debt: 15% coupon, 15 years to maturity	$1,800,000
Preferred shares: 12% dividend	$1,200,000

The before-tax interest cost on new 15-year debt would be 10 percent, and each $1,000 bond would net the company $975 after issuing costs. Common shares could be sold to net the company $8 per share, a 12 percent discount from the current market price. Current shareholders expect a 15 percent return on their investment. Preferred shares could be sold at par to provide a yield of 9 percent, with after-tax issuing and underwriting expenses amounting to 5 percent of par value. The company's tax rate is 45 percent, and internally generated funds are insufficient to finance anticipated new capital projects. Compute the company's marginal cost of capital using the method in which flotation costs are imbedded in the individual costs of capital.

39. A company can issue new 20-year bonds at par that pay 10 percent annual coupons. The net proceeds to the company (after taxes) will be 95 percent of par value. Management estimates that new preferred shares providing a $2 annual dividend could be issued to investors at $25 per share. The company has a beta of 1.20, and present market conditions are such that the risk-free rate is 6 percent, whereas the expected return on the market index is 12 percent. The company's common shares presently trade for $30. The company's tax rate is 40 percent.

A. Determine the company's cost of long-term debt, preferred shares, and common equity financing under the conditions given, using the method in which flotation costs are imbedded in the individual costs of capital.

B. Based on your answer to A, what is the company's weighted average cost of capital assuming that it has a "target" capital structure consisting of 30 percent debt, 10 percent preferred equity, and 60 percent common equity?

C. Suppose everything remains as given, except that the company decides it needs $5 million in total financing. Calculate the company's marginal cost of capital.

D. What is the company's cost of capital, assuming its target capital structure as noted in B, if you use the method in which the costs of flotation do not affect the individual costs of capital?

40. The Laredo Lounge, Inc., plans to issue 20-year bonds with a 12.80 percent coupon rate, with coupons paid semi-annually and a par value of $1,000. The company's tax rate is 50 percent.

A. What is the company's effective annual after-tax cost of debt?

B. Laredo Lounge plans to issue $50 par preferred shares with annual dividends of $6 (i.e., a 12 percent dividend yield). Find the company's cost of preferred stock.

C. Laredo Lounge wishes to make a new issue of common shares. The current market price is $25, next period's dividend is $1.75 (expected dividend at the end of this year), the risk-free rate is 11 percent, the expected return on the market is 18 percent, and the beta is 0.95. The growth rate is 9 percent per year, indefinitely. Calculate the company's cost of issuing new common shares using the:

   (a) dividend valuation approach.

   (b) CAPM.

D. Find the WACC if the company wishes to raise funds in the following proportions: 30 percent debt, 20 percent preferred stock, and 50 percent common equity. Assume the cost of equity is best estimated using the CAPM.

 41. Consider the example of Archer-Daniels-Midland (ADM) that we used in Section 14.3, but also consider the information for fiscal years 2010 and 2011 from ADM's financial statements:

	2011	*2010*
Interest-bearing short-term debt	$1,875	$374
Current portion of long-term debt	$178	$344
Long-term debt	$8,266	$6,830
Shareholders' equity	$18,808	$14,609

A. What is the total capital for ADM for 2010 and 2011 in book value terms?

   (1) Calculate the debt-to-equity ratio and the debt to total assets ratio for both years.

   (2) What are the proportions of debt and equity capital in book value terms?

B. Using additional sources, complete the following:

	2011	*2010*
Market value of debt		
Market price per share		
Number of shares of stock outstanding		
Market value of equity		
Total capital		
Debt-to-equity ratio		
Debt to total assets ratio		
Proportion of debt capital		
Proportion of common equity capital		

C. Describe how the capital structure has changed in 2010 and 2011, compared to the years 2007 through 2009.

D. What weights would you use in determining ADM's weighted average cost of capital? Why?

Cases

Case 14.1 The Lazquez Company

Suppose you are the assistant to the CFO of the Lazquez Company and are responsible for evaluating how its cost of capital is calculated. The Lazquez Company has the following financial structure:

	(in millions)
Accounts payable	$1.0
Wages payable	$0.5
Bank loans	$2.0
Long-term bonds	$10.0
Pension liability	$3.5
Minority interest	$2.0
Common stock (1.5 million shares outstanding)	$1.5
Retained earnings	$10.0
Accumulated comprehensive income or loss	$1.5
Treasury stock	$1

Additional information:
- The market price per share of stock is $20.
- The outstanding bonds have a coupon rate of 6 percent and mature in 10 years.
- The outstanding bonds are currently priced at 110.
- The beta of its common stock is 1.2.
- The expected risk-free rate of interest is 3 percent.
- The expected market risk premium is 4.5 percent.
- The marginal tax rate is 35 percent.

The Lazquez Company currently uses 10 percent as its cost of capital and has been doing so for the past 10 years.

A. Using Excel, prepare an analysis of the cost of capital for the Lazquez Company, detailing your calculations of the weights and the costs of the different sources of capital. Be sure to note your assumptions and address the sensitivity of your recommendation to the various inputs.

B. Based on your estimate, what are the implications of the Lazquez Company continuing to use a 10 percent cost of capital?

C. If Congress lowers the tax rates for corporations, what is the effect on the Lazquez Company's cost of capital? Demonstrate this using your spreadsheet analysis.

Case 14.2 The Cost of Capital of Merck & Co.

You have been assigned to estimate the cost of capital of Merck & Co. based solely on publicly available information. Merck is a pharmaceutical company that develops, manufactures, and markets medicines, therapies, and consumer and animal products. For the fiscal year end December 31, 2009, Merck had the following balance sheet information:

	(in millions)
Loans payable and current portion of long-term debt	$1,379.20
Trade accounts payable	2,236.90
Income tax payable	9,453.80
Dividends payable	1,189.00
6% mandatory convertible preferred stock, $1 par	206.6
Total current liabilities	$15,750.70
Long-term debt	16,074.90
Deferred income taxes and noncurrent liabilities	18,771.50

	(in millions)
Common stock, $0.50 par value	1,781.30
Other paid-in capital	39,682.60
Retained earnings	41,404.90
Accumulated other comprehensive loss	–2,766.50
Stockholders' equity before deduction for treasury	$80,102.30
Treasury stock	21,044.30
Total stockholders' equity	$59,058.00

Source: *Merck & Co. 10-K for fiscal year 2009.*

Other information:

- The market value per share of Merck common stock is $36.20 at the end of 2010.
- The beta of the common stock of Merck is 0.66.
- Merck debt is rated AA by Standard and Poor's and Aa3 by Moody's.
- The yield on Merck's long-term debt at the end of 2010 ranges from 4.099 to 5.243 percent. Merck's long-term debt trades for values ranging from 98.165 to 118.660.
- At the end of 2010, the rate on a 10-year Treasury bond is 3.48 percent.
- The expected market risk premium is in the range of 2.5 to 4 percent.
- The anticipated dividend for 2011 is $1.52 per share.
- The retention rate for Merck is typically 50 percent.
- The annual return on equity for 2010 and 2011 is anticipated to be 20 percent.

A. Using fiscal year 2009 balance sheet information for your best guide to the company's target capital structure for future years, estimate Merck's weighted average cost of capital as of the end of 2010. Be sure to list your assumptions and support your choices.

B. Look up Merck's 2010 and 2011 financial statement from the company's web site, and look up the 10-year Treasury bond rate for 2010 and 2011, as well as the beta and the market value of Merck stock at the end of 2010 and 2011.

   1. If you used the 2009 weights to estimate those for 2010 and 2011, how accurate was this? How has Merck's capital structure changed since 2009?

   2. Based on Merck's information for 2010 and 2011 that you looked up, how accurate were the assumptions that went into the estimate of the cost of capital for 2010?

ANSWERS TO MULTIPLE CHOICE QUESTIONS

CHAPTER 1
1 B
2 D
3 A
4 C
5 B
6 B
7 C
8 C
9 B
10 A

CHAPTER 2
1 A
2 C
3 A
4 A
5 B
6 C
7 B
8 C
9 B
10 B

CHAPTER 3
1 B
2 B
3 A
4 D
5 B
6 B
7 B
8 D Depreciation first year = $300,000 \times 0.20$
$= \$60,000$
9 B
10 D

CHAPTER 4
1 A Debt ratio $= 2,000,000 \div \$5,630,000 = 35.524\%$
2 B Debt-equity ratio $= \$2,000,000 \div \$2,890,000$
$= 69.2042\%$
Times interest earned
$= (\$360,000 + 150,000) \div \$150,000 = 3.4$

3 D Gross profit margin
$= (\$1,090,000 - 380,000) \div \$1,090,000$
$= 65.1376\%$
Operating margin
$= (\$1,090,000 - 380,000 - 200,000) \div \$1,090,000$
$= 46.789\%$
4 A DSI $= \$250,000 \div (\$380,000 \div 365) = 240$ days
5 C Working capital ratio
$= (\$400,000 + 500,000 + 250,000) \div \$5,630,000$
$= 20.426\%$
6 C Invested capital $= \$2,000,000 + 2,890,000$
$= \$4,890,000$
7 B ROE $= 0.05 \times (\$100 \div 50) = 10\%$
8 B
9 D ROA $= 10\% \times 5 = 50\%$
10 D

CHAPTER 5
1 D FV $= \$1,000 (1 + 0.05)^{10} = \$1,628.89$
2 D A: €1,800; B: €1,600; C: €1,838.46; D: €1,850.93
3 A Interest on interest $= \$12,166.53 - 12,000$
$= \$166.53$
4 B PV $= ¥10$ million $\div (1 + 0.15)^{45}$
$= ¥0.185608$ million or ¥18,561
5 C $i = \sqrt[8]{£17,000 / £10,000} - 1 = 6.8578\%$
6 B $n = \dfrac{\ln 3 - \ln 1}{\ln(1 + 0.09)} = 12.7482$
7 C N = 20; PMT = $2,000; i
$= 10\% \Rightarrow$ Solve for FV $\Rightarrow$ FV $= \$114,550$
8 B A: 10.2397%; B: 10.3618%; C: 10.1860%;
D: 10.2934%
9 B PV $= €1,500 \div 0.12 = €12,500$
10 B 2nd payment: $199,800.9 \times (0.06 \div 12)$
$= \$999.00$ interest, $1,199.10 - 999$
$= \$200.10$ principal

CHAPTER 6
1 A
2 A
3 A N = 10; i = 4%; PMT = 3.5 $\Rightarrow$ PV = 95.9445
4 B N = 10; i = 4%; PMT = 2.5 $\Rightarrow$ PV = 87.8337
5 D
6 C PV = 99.3; N = 12; PMT = 3.5 $\Rightarrow$ i
$= 3.57275\% \Rightarrow$ YTM $= 7.1455\%$

7 A

8 B

9 B $5.5\% = [(\$10,000 - P) \div P] \times [365 \div 182];$
$P = \$9,733.07$

10 C

CHAPTER 7

1 C

2 B

3 C Required rate of return = $0.04 + 0.065 = 10.5\%$

4 C Required rate of return

$= 0.03 + 0.065 = 0.095 \Rightarrow P = \dfrac{\$2(1 + 0.045)}{0.095 - 0.045}$

$= \dfrac{\$2.09}{0.05} = \$41.8$

5 C Required rate of return

$= \dfrac{\$1.5(1 + 0.04)}{\$26} + 0.04 = 0.10 \text{ or } 10\%$

6 C ROE = $\$9 \div \$36 = 25\%$ | Retention ratio
$= \$7.50 \div \$9.00 = 83.33\%$
Sustainable growth $= 83.33\% \times 25\% = 20.83\%$

7 A

8 C

9 D Value = $15 \times \$3$ million = $\$15$ million

10 B $\dfrac{P_0}{EPS_1} = \dfrac{D_1/EPS_1}{r_e - g} \quad \dfrac{P_0}{EPS_1}$

$= \dfrac{\$2/\$5}{0.08 - 0.05} \quad \dfrac{P_0}{EPS_1} = \dfrac{0.40}{0.03} = 13.33$

CHAPTER 8

1 B Capital gain or loss $= \dfrac{\$24-25}{25} = -0.04 \text{ or } 4\%$

2 D Total return $= \dfrac{\$24-25 + 4}{25} = 0.12 \text{ or } 12\%$

3 B The geometric mean is less than the arithmetic mean

4 C Expected return
$= (0.3 \times 0.30)+(0.2 \times 0.4)+(0.5 \times 0.15)$
$= 0.09 + 0.08 + 0.075 = 24.5\%$

5 A

Probability	Possible return	Probability x return	Probability weighted squared deviations
30%	30%	0.090	0.0009075
20%	40%	0.080	0.0048050
50%	15%	0.075	0.0045125
		0.245	0.010225
	Standard deviation		**10.11%**

6 D

7 B

8 A

9 B Expected return on the portfolio
$= (0.25 \times 0.05) + (0.75 \times 0.1)$
$= 0.0125 + 0.075 = 8.75\%$

10 C

CHAPTER 9

1 D

2 B More return for the level of risk as predicted by the CAPM; therefore it is undervalued (when the price corrects, there will be an abnormally higher return)

3 C Expected return = $(0.2 \times 0.08) + (0.8 \times 0.2)$
$= 0.016 + 0.16 = 0.176$ or 17.6%

Standard deviation
$= \sqrt{(0.2^2 \times 0^2) + (0.8^2 \times 0.25^2) + 0}$
$= \sqrt{0.04} = 20\%$

4 A

5 D

6 C

7 C

8 B

9 C

10 B

CHAPTER 10

1 A PI = $(\$10+6) \div \$10 = 1.6$

2 D

3 A

Period	End of period cash flow
0	$17,000
1	$0
2	$0
3	$8,000
4	$8,000
5	$8,000
6	$8,000
7	$8,000
NPV	−$385.49

4 A

5 A

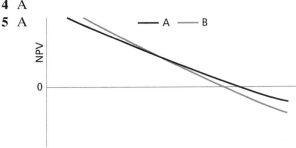

6 C $NPV_X = \$283; NPV_Y = \$351$

7 C IRR = 35.87%. Note: the discount rate is not relevant for the calculation of the IRR.

8 B The discount rate will be understated for high-risk projects.

9 C

10 A This would be equivalent to a negative NPV project.

CHAPTER 11

1 A

2 A Depreciation tax shield = $0.3 \times \$30,000 = \$9,000$

3 B Change in annual cash flow
= $(\$50,000 - 18,000) \times (1-0.4) = \$19,200$

4 A Depreciation tax shield
= $(\$300,000 \times 0.20) \times 0.40 = \$24,000$

5 B

6 C

7 A There will be a zero book value at the end of the fourth year.

8 B Cash flow = $\$20,000 - (\$20,000 \times 0.35)$
= $\$13,000$

9 A Investment cash flow
= $-\$400,050 - 90,000 + 15,000 - 5000 = \$480,050$

10 C Investment cash flow
= $-\$120,000 + 75,000 - [0.4 \times (\$75,000 - 65,000)]$
= $-\$49,000$

CHAPTER 12

1 D

2 B After-tax cost of debt = $0.08 \times (1 - 0.4) = 4.8\%$

3 B

4 C

5 D

6 D

7 B

8 D Conversion value of the bond = $30 \times \$40$
= $\$1,200$

9 B Bond equivalent yield
= $[(\$100 - 98) \div \$98] \times (360 \div 270) = 2.721\%$

10 C After-tax cost of debt = $0.06 \times (1 - 0.38)$
= 3.72%

CHAPTER 13

1 A

2 B

3 D

4 A

5 A

6 C

7 D Book value of equity = $\$1,000 + 50 + 100 = \$1,150$

8 A Book value per share
= $\$500$ million $\div 100$ million shares = $\$5$

9 A Dividend yield = $\$1 \div \$30 = 3.33\%$

10 B

CHAPTER 14

1 B Value of stock = $\$5.50 \div 0.15 = \$36.67$ per share

2 B Earnings yield = $\$40,000 \div (\$10 \times 10,000)$
= 40%

3 B Required return in dollar terms
= $0.125 \times \$69,000 = \$8,625$

4 C

5 C

6 C

7 C

8 A

9 A Debt capital = $\$2$ million + 3 million
= $\$5$ million

10 D WACC = $[0.07 \times (1 - 0.40) \times 0.40]$
$+ [(((\$1.5 \times 1.04) \div \$20) + 0.04) \times 0.60]$
= $0.0168 + 0.0708 = 8.76\%$

CHAPTER 15

1 A BE = $\$20,000 \div \$4 = 5,000$ units

2 B DOL = $(\$30,000 - 20,000)$
$\div (\$30,000 - 20,000 - 1,000) = 1.1$

3 C DTL = $1.5 \times 2 = 3.0$

4 D

5 A

6 D

7 B

8 D

9 C

10 C

CHAPTER 16

1 A

2 C

3 C

4 B

5 B Share price = $\$20 \times (1 + g) \Rightarrow$ Solve for
g: $\$20 = \$2 \div (0.10 - g) \Rightarrow g = 0\%$

6 C

7 C

8 C DPO = $\$0.6$ million $\div \$3$ million = 20%

9 A Dividend yield = $\$2 \div \$20 = 10\%$

10 D

CHAPTER 17

1 C

2 B

3 B

4 D

5 C

6 B Sustainable growth = $0.20 \times (1 - 0.3) = 14\%$

7 C

8 C

9 D

10 A

CHAPTER 18

1 C
2 A Time value = $20 – 12.50 = $7.50
3 D
4 A
5 B
6 C
7 C
8 D
9 A
10 D

CHAPTER 19

1 C
2 C Current ratio = $3,103,000 ÷ $900,000
    = 3.448 times
    Quick ratio = $1,900,500 ÷ 900,000
    = 2.1117 times
3 C DSO = $600,000 ÷ ($1,287,555 ÷ 365)
    = 170.0898 days
4 D DSI = $1,203,000 ÷ ($550,000 ÷ 365) = 798.3545
    Operating cycle = 180.0898 + 798.3545
    = 968.444 days
5 B
6 C
7 B
8 A

9 B
10 C

CHAPTER 20

1 C
2 C
3 B
4 A
5 B
6 A
7 C N = 5; PMT = $5,000; i
    = 8%; Annuity due ⇒ $21,560.63
8 D
9 D
10 D

CHAPTER 21

1 C
2 C
3 A
4 D
5 D
6 D Market value of equity = $550,000 × 4.5
    = $2,475,000
7 A
8 A
9 B
10 A

GLOSSARY

4 Cs of credit factors that affect credit: capacity, character, collateral, and conditions

ABC approach division of inventory into several categories based on the value of the inventory items, their overall level of importance to the company's operations, and their profitability, to determine the time and effort devoted to their management

abnormal profit profit in excess of those expected for the asset's level of risk

absolute priority rule rule that any assets of the company in liquidation are distributed to creditors, in order of seniority, and, if anything remains, to shareholders

acid test ratio See *quick ratio*

acceptance fee See *stamping fee*

account manager financial professional who manages a bank's relationships with companies, extending credit, helping to manage receivables and cash, and directing them to the bank's more specialized services

accounting identity relationship resulting from double-entry bookkeeping such that assets are equal to the sum of liabilities and equity

accounts receivable turnover See *receivables turnover*

accounts payable amounts owed the suppliers of the business

accrual basis reporting convention in which revenues and expenses are recorded when a transaction occurs, regardless of when cash changes hands

accrued expenses amounts owed from transactions that have occurred but for which payment is not due

accumulated comprehensive income or loss income or loss that bypasses the income statement, going directly to equity

acquisition purchase of one company by another

active trading strategy trading based on timing the market, trends, or other criteria

activity ratios See *productivity ratios*

adjustable rate convertible subordinated security (ARCS) security that has fixed principal and maturity, and interest that normally comprises a fixed interest rate and some function of the dividend paid in the previous six months; typically convertible into common shares

adjustable rate preferred stock (ARPS) equity security issue for which the dividend yield is pegged to a specific interest rate

adverse opinion audit opinion when the financial statements do not represent fairly the financial position, results of operation, or the change in financial position in accordance with generally accepted accounting principles

affirmative covenant promise that the issuer makes regarding the debt obligation, such as the timely payment of interest

after-tax cost of debt net cost of the company using debt, calculated as the before-tax interest cost of the company's debt multiplied by one minus the corporate tax rate

agency costs costs associated with agency problems that arise from the inherent conflicts of interest between managers, owners, and creditors

agency problem issue or conflict that arises due to potential divergence of interest between managers, shareholders, and creditors

agency relationship relationship that occurs when managers work on behalf of the shareholders

Altman Z score predictive measure of the likelihood of a company filing for bankruptcy, based on a company's financial ratios

American option option that can be exercised at any time up to and including the expiration date

amortization expense deduction from income that reflects the reduction in the value of tangible assets over a period of time

amortization process of determining how much of each payment is interest and principal repayment; reduction in value of a long-lived intangible asset over a specified period of time

amortization schedule breakdown of each payment of an amortized loan into interest and principal components

amortize determine the repayment of a loan in which regular payments consist of both interest and principal

analyst entry-level job in a financial institution

anchoring tendency to use inappropriate or irrelevant factors in decision making

annual percentage rate (APR) stated rate of interest, calculated as the product of the interest rate per compounding period and the number of compounding periods

annuity due annuity for which the payments are made at the beginning of each period

annuity regular payments from an investment that are for the same amount and are paid at regular intervals of time

anomaly mispricing of an asset such that the pricing of the asset is not consistent with efficient markets

arb See *arbitrageur*

arbitrage pricing theory (APT) pricing model that uses multiple factors to relate expected returns to risk by assuming that asset returns are linearly related to a set of indexes, which are proxy risk factors that influence asset returns

arbitrage process of taking advantage of different pricing for the same item in different markets

arbitrageur specialist who predicts what happens in takeovers and buys and sells shares in target companies

arithmetic mean or **arithmetic average** sum of all observations divided by the total number of observations

articles of incorporation rules of the governance of the corporation that are filed with the state of incorporation

assessment bond security backed by the property taxes of a government entity

asset purchase purchase of the company's assets rather than the company itself

asset turnover See *total asset turnover ratio*

asset utilization ratios See *productivity ratios*

asset-backed commercial paper (ABCP) short-term debt instrument backed by the cash flows of specific securities, generally held in a special purpose vehicle

asset-backed note or **asset-backed bond** debt obligation that has a specific asset, a group of assets, or a set of future cash flows as collateral

asset-based lending financing that is tied directly to a particular asset

associate second-level job in a financial institution; it requires an MBA or a professional designation (e.g., CFA)

at the money situation in which the value of the underlying asset of an option is equal to the option's strike price

attainable portfolio collection of investments that may be constructed by combining the underlying assets and lies along the minimum variance frontier

auction market See *exchange market*

available-for-sale method of accounting for marketable securities is one in which unrealized gains or losses are reported as part of accumulated other comprehensive income

average collection period See *days sales outstanding*

balance sheet snapshot of the financial position of a company, listing assets on the left and liabilities and owner's equity on the right

balloon payment payment that represents repayment of some amount of the principal of loan above and beyond what is paid as part of the amortized loan payments

balloon principal See *bullet payment*

bank discount method convention for specifying the interest on a security that compares the amount of the discount with the face value of the security

bank discount yield method of stating interest rates that compares the discount with the face value of the security, annualized by 360 divided by the maturity of the security

bankers' acceptance (BA) short-term paper sold by an issuer to a bank, which guarantees or accepts it, obligating the bank to pay off the debt instrument at maturity if the issuer defaults

banking associate financial professional who generates reports on companies, prepares industry reports, and performs background checks on credit applicants

bankruptcy legal status of a company that permits the company to deal with debt problems

basic earnings per share (basic EPS) earnings per share of common stock based on the weighted average of the number of shares outstanding during the fiscal period

basis point one one-hundredths of 1 percent

behavioral finance study of how human behavior affects economic decision making

best price rule requirement that the bidder of a tender offer pay all security holders that tender shares the highest price paid in the tender offer

beta (β_i) measure of market risk, or performance volatility, that relates the extent to which the return on an asset moves with that on the overall market; the covariance between an investment and the market divided by variance of the market

beta coefficient measure of a company's systematic or market risk

bill short-term debt instruments with an initial maturity of less than 1 year

bird in the hand argument notion that a cash dividend is worth more than an equivalent capital gain

bond equivalent method convention that specifies the yield on a security by comparing the discount to the C value of the security, and then annualizing

bond equivalent yield (BEY) yield for a short-term, discount security that is based on comparing the discount with the present value of the security, then annualizing

bond indenture legal document that specifies the payment requirements and all other salient matters relating to a particular bond issue, held and administered by a trust company

bond long-term debt instrument in which the borrower promises repayment, usually with interest, with an initial maturity longer than 7 years

bondholder party that lends funds by buying a bond issued by another party

book value per share shareholders' equity divided by the number of shares outstanding

bottom-up analysis investment strategy in which capital investment decisions are considered in isolation, without regard for whether the company should continue in this business or for general industry and economic trends

break fee See *termination fee*

break-up fee See *termination fee*

broker a market intermediary, who facilitates exchanges in a market.

bullet payment payment (partial or full) paid at maturity of a loan

business finance financing decision making within a business entity

business risk uncertainty regarding the operating earnings, which is influenced by both the sales risk and the operating risk of a company

buy-side analyst person whose job it is to evaluate the publicly available information for institutions in the capital market that invest in securities

C corporation business taxed as a corporation according to Subsection C of the Internal Revenue Code

call option right but not the obligation to buy an underlying asset at a fixed price within or at a specified time

call price price at which an issuer can buy back a bond from an investor of a callable bond

call protection provision that prohibits the issuer to call a bond for a specific length of time

call schedule series of call prices and applicable dates

callable bond debt obligation that give the issuer the option to repurchase outstanding bonds at predetermined prices at specified times

cannibalization competition of a new product with an existing product of the same company, resulting in diminished sales of the existing product

capacity customer's ability to pay

capital asset pricing model (CAPM) pricing model that describes the expected return on an asset as the sum of the risk-free rate of interest and compensation or a premium for bearing market risk

capital budgeting framework for analyzing investment or asset decisions; process through which a company makes capital expenditure decisions by identifying investment alternatives, evaluating these alternatives, implementing the chosen investment decisions, and monitoring and evaluating the implemented decisions

capital cost cost incurred to make an investment operational, such as machinery installation expenses, land-clearing costs, and so on

capital expenditure investment in long-lived assets, which may be tangible or intangible

capital expenditure analysis See *capital budgeting*

capital gain appreciation in the price of an asset from some starting point in time; in determining taxes, the taxable gain incurred when an asset is sold at a price greater than its original cost

capital gains yield return in the form of the appreciation or depreciation in the value of an asset

capital leases long-term rental agreements that are considered liabilities

capital loss depreciation in the price of an asset from some starting point in time; in determining taxes, the tax deductible loss generated when a nondepreciable asset is sold at a price lower than its original cost

capital market line (CML) line depicting the highest attainable expected return for any given risk level that includes only efficient portfolios

capital market security debt security with a maturity of greater than one year

capital rationing allotting investment capital among available investment projects

capital structure how a company finances its invested capital, consisting of debt capital and equity capital; mix of debt and equity used to finance an enterprise

capital yield See *capital gains yield*

capital sum of the interest-bearing debt and the equity of a company

captive finance company (CFC) company that finances companies that are divisions of major manufacturers to provide loans to purchase or lease their products

carrying value book value of an asset, which for a depreciable asset is the cost less accumulated depreciation

cash budget cash flow statement for each period

cash conversion cycle (CCC) estimate of the average time between when a company pays cash for its inventory purchases and when it receives cash for its sales

cash dividend payments to owners in the form of cash

cash flow bond debt obligation that has the same objectives as do income bonds

cash flow for/from financing (CFF) cash flow, on net, from financing activities

cash flow for/from investing (CFI) cash flow, on net, from investing activities

cash flow for/from operations (CFO) cash flow from the day-to-day operations of the business; the result of subtracting the increase in net working capital from traditional cash flow

cash flow statement See *statement of cash flows*

cash flow to debt ratio how long it takes to pay off a company's debt from its cash flow from operations; cash flow from operations divided by debt

cash flows actual cash generated from an investment

cash management bills short-term obligations of the U.S. government issued to meet temporary cash needs of the government

cash price the actual price paid for a debt obligation that considers the amount of accrued interest on the security

character how willing the company is to pay and how reliable and trustworthy the company is

characteristic line line of best fit through the returns on an individual asset, plotted on the vertical axis, relative to the returns for the market, plotted along the horizontal axis

chief financial officer (CFO) top financial manager in a company

clean price bond quote that does not consider the accrued interest

clearinghouse company that has the responsibility for reducing the credit risk and making sure that delivery takes place for futures contracts and option contracts

cognitive bias mistake in decision making that results from one's own preferences and beliefs

collateral the real estate, investments, and other property of the borrower; assets that are pledged to support a loan; assets that can serve as security for the bond in case of default

collateral trust bond bond secured by a pledge of other financial assets, such as common shares, bonds, or treasury bills

commercial paper (CP) short-term debt instruments, usually unsecured, issued by companies

commodity bond bond whose interest or principal is tied to the price of an underlying commodity, such as gold

commodity swap exchange of a fixed price for the floating price of a commodity

common life approach method of comparing mutually exclusive projects with different useful lives, assuming a finite number of replacements for each project, consistent with the projects' common life

common life revised useful life of projects considering a finite number of replacements such that the projects being compared have the same useful life

common share certificate of ownership in a corporation

common stock equity security that represents part ownership in a company and usually gives voting rights on major decisions affecting the company; residual ownership of a corporation

comparative advantage innate advantage that a company has over other companies due to access to resources, inputs, or markets

competitive advantage any strategy or feature that reduces the competition that the company experiences

compound factor amount that reflects the interest rate and the number of periods, which, when multiplied by a current or present value, results in the equivalent future value

compound interest arrangement in which interest is earned on the principal amount invested *and* on any accrued interest

compounding increase in value over time due to interest on both the principal amount and any interest earned up to that point in time

conditions state of the economy

confidentiality agreement document signed by a potential buyer guaranteeing it will keep confidential any information it sees in the data room about a target company

conglomerate merger merger in which two companies in unrelated businesses combine

constant growth DDM version of the dividend discount model for valuing common shares that assumes that dividends grow at a constant rate indefinitely

consultant See *corporate finance associate*

contingent interest interest on a debt security that is paid based on cash flows or earnings

contingent projects projects for which the acceptance of one requires the acceptance of another, either beforehand or simultaneously

continuously compounded interest or **continuous compounding** interest is instantaneous, compounded an infinite number of times

contribution margin portion of each dollar of sales that is available to cover fixed costs, after first satisfying variable costs; difference between the sales price per unit and the variable cost per unit

controller one of the two main finance jobs in a nonfinancial company; focuses on the accounting side: compliance, tax management, systems/MIS, internal audit, accounting, and budgeting

conversion premium difference between the value of a convertible security and the market value of the security into which it is convertible

conversion ratio number of common shares of the other security for which a convertible preferred share may be exchanged

conversion value value of the security the investor receives if he or she converts the security

convertible bond debt instrument that can be exchanged for a specified number of units of another security at a predetermined conversion price at the investor's option

convertible preferred stock preferred stock that can be exchanged for a specified number of units of another security

corporate finance associate finance professional who advises on restructuring, small-scale M&A, and corporate financing

corporate finance financial management of assets and financing decisions in a corporate enterprise

corporate governance set of processes and procedures established to manage the organization in the best interests of its owners

corporation business organized as a separate legal entity under corporation law, with ownership divided into transferable shares

correlation coefficient statistical measure that identifies how asset returns move in relation to one another; denoted by ρ

cost of capital the return the investor requires

costs of financial distress direct costs, opportunity costs, and losses to a company prior to declaring bankruptcy

counterparty party on the other side of a forward contract

counterparty risk See *credit risk*

coupon interest payment from a note or bond

coupon equivalent method See *bond equivalent method*

coupon rate percentage of a bond or note's face value that is paid in interest each year

covariance statistical measure of the the degree to which two or more series move together, or covary

covenant promise or restriction in a contract

credit analysis process designed to assess the risk of non-payment by potential customers

credit crunch lack of available loans for businesses

credit default swap (CDS) exchange of a payment or series of payments for a payoff in the event that the specified, underlying credit instrument (e.g., a bond) defaults; contract in which one party pays another party to assume a specified risk

credit enhancement action taken to reduce credit risk, such as requiring collateral, insurance, or other agreements

credit policy decisions on how a company grants, monitors, and collects payment for outstanding accounts receivable

credit risk uncertainty that a borrower will not repay what is owed or does not have the required payment

credit squeeze See *credit crunch*

credit watch status applied to a company by a rating agency when it is monitoring the company

creditor a party lending funds through a loan arrangement

creeping takeover acquisition of a target company over time by the gradual accumulation of its shares

crossover rate discount rate at which the net present value profiles of two projects cross

cumulative provision stipulation that no dividends can be paid on common shares until preferred share dividends, both current and arrears, are paid in full

currency future See *foreign currency future*

currency swap exchange of one currency for another to mitigate risk associated with specific assets or liabilities

current assets assets (cash and equivalents, short-term investments, accounts receivable, inventories, prepaid expenses) that are expected to be converted into cash within a year

current cost what it would cost to replace the asset or settle the liability

current liabilities short-term obligations

current ratio or **bankers' ratio** current assets divided by current liabilities

current yield (CY) the ratio of the annual coupon interest divided by the current market price

daily resettlement marking to market and adjusting investors' equity positions

data room place where a target company keeps confidential information about itself for serious potential buyers to consult

date of record See *record date*

day trader someone who buys and sells based on intraday price movements

days payables outstanding (DPO) number of days of purchases represented by the balance in accounts payable

days sales in inventory (DSI) average length of time between acquiring and selling inventory; number of days of sales represented by the amount in inventory

days sales outstanding (DSO) number of days, on average, that accounts receivable accounts are outstanding; number of days of sales represented by accounts receivable

dealer market secondary market that does not have a physical location and consists of a network of dealers who trade directly with one another

debenture debt instrument secured by a general claim on the issuer's unencumbered assets; debt obligation secured by the general credit of the issuer

debt capital interest-bearing obligations of an enterprise

debt contract between a lender and a borrower that stipulates the terms of repayment of a loan; promise by the borrower to repay the amount borrowed, plus interest

debt instrument legal obligation to repay borrowed funds at a specified maturity date and to provide interim interest payments

debt rating evaluation by professional debt-rating services after detailed analyses of bond issuers to determine their ability to make the required interest and principal payments

debt ratio total debt divided by total assets

debt-equity (D/E) ratio debt to shareholders' equity

debtor-in-possession (DIP) financing financing specifically for companies in financial distress that provides creditors more seniority than most existing claims of the distressed company

declaration date date on which the board of directors decides that the company will pay a dividend.

declining balance depreciation allocation of an asset's cost, less salvage value, over the life of the asset, with a rate applied against the declining carrying value of the asset

default free no risk of nonpayment

default risk uncertainty associated with the bond issuer and its ability to pay

default spread difference in yields attributed to the difference in default risk of the securities

deferred annuity annuity that begins two or more periods from the present

deferred income tax taxes that are anticipated to be paid in future years

deferred tax liability taxes that the company reasonably expects to pay in the future

degree of financial leverage (DFL) sensitivity of net income to changes in operating earnings, influenced by the use debt, relative to equity, as a source of capital

degree of operating leverage (DOL) measure of the sensitivity of the operating earnings to changes in the number of units produced and sold

degree of total leverage (DTL) sensitivity of net income to changes in unit sales, affected by the company's operating and financial leverage

demand line of credit See *operating*

depreciation expense deduction from income that reflects the reduction in the value of tangible assets over a period of time

depreciation recapture amount by which the salvage value (sale price) of an asset exceeds the asset's book or carrying value

depreciation reduction in value of a long-lived, tangible asset over a specified period of time

depreciation tax shield tax savings associated with the depreciation deduction for tax purposes, which is the amount of the depreciation expense multiplied by the marginal tax rate

derivative contract whose value depends on or is derived from a specified asset or variable

detachable warrant warrant that can be sold to investors apart from the security with which it was originally issued

diluted earnings per share (diluted EPS) net income divided by the total possible number of common shares that could be outstanding if all potentially dilutive securities outstanding were converted into common shares

direct financing lease contractual agreement in which the party owning the asset records a lease receivable for the promised lease payments, as well as earning interest on the financing

dirty price See *cash price*

disclaimer of opinion audit opinion in which the auditors cannot form an opinion on the business entity's financial statements

disclosure revelation of all material facts so that everyone in the market is buying and selling based on the same material facts about the firm

discount amount by which a bond's value is below its face value

discount factor value that, when multiplied by the future value, results in the present value of this future value

discount yield (DY) method See *bank discount method*

discounted cash flow (DCF) determining a value today by estimating future cash flows and comparing their discounted values with the cash outlay today

discounted payback period number of years required to fully recover the initial cash outlay associated with a capital expenditure, in terms of discounted cash flows

discounting calculating the present value of a future value, considering the time value of money

discrete compounding compound interest in which interest that is paid at specified intervals of time, such as quarterly or annually

disposition effect behavior of individuals in which they avoid realizing any paper losses, but tend to realize paper gains

diversifiable risk See *unique risk*

diversification reduction of risk by investing funds across several assets

dividend coverage ratio ratio of earnings to dividends for a fiscal period

dividend discount model (DDM) model for valuing common shares that assumes common shares are valued according to the present value of their expected future dividends

dividend payout ratio or **dividend payout** portion of earnings paid out in dividends to owners

dividend per share amount of a cash dividend paid by a company

dividend reinvestment plan (DRIP or DRP) plan allowing the use of cash dividends to be reinvested to buy new shares

dividend yield return on a stock in the form of cash dividends; the ratio of the dividend per share to the value of the stock

dividends received deduction amount of the dividends a corporation receives from another corporation that may be deducted from income for tax purposes

double declining balance method allocation of an asset's cost, less salvage value, over the life of the asset, with a rate applied against the declining carrying value of the asset at twice the straight-line rate

due diligence process of evaluating a target company by a potential buyer

DuPont System method of analyzing return ratios by breaking down these ratios into their components

duration measure of interest rate risk that incorporates several factors

Dutch auction bidding process that accepts the bids necessary to sell the intended amount; in the auction of interest-bearing securities, the rate on the securities is set at the rate that is necessary to sell the desired quantity of securities

Dutch auction tender offer method of repurchasing shares that requests shareholders to submit bids for the price they are willing to sell their shares, and then the company will pay the minimum price necessary to acquire the stated number of shares

earnings before interest and taxes (EBIT) earnings before interest and before taxes for nonoperating income and expenses

earnings before interest, taxes, depreciation, and amortization (EBITDA) operating earnings before depreciation and amortization

economic order quantity (EOQ) model approach that defines and determines the optimal inventory level as the level that minimizes the total of shortage costs and carrying costs

economic profit difference between revenue and expenses, after considering the opportunity cost of funds; return on an investment *in excess* of the normal profit

EE/E Savings bond debt obligation of the U.S. Treasury with a maturity of 20 or 30 years, with a fixed interest rate and accrued interest and paid at maturity

effective annual rate (EAR) rate at which a dollar invested grows over a given period; usually stated in percentage terms based on an annual period

efficiency ratio measure of how efficiently a dollar of sales is turned into profits

efficient frontier set of portfolios that offers the highest expected return for their given level of risk

efficient market hypothesis (EMH) theory that markets are efficient and therefore, in its strictest sense, implies that prices accurately reflect all available information at any given time

efficient market market in which prices reacts quickly and relatively accurately to new information

efficient portfolio collection of investments that offers the highest expected return for a given level of risk, or offers the lowest risk for a given expected return

enterprise risk management (ERM) process of identifying and managing risks throughout a business enterprise

enterprise value market value of an entity's debt and equity, less cash and cash equivalents

enterprise value to EBIT ratio total market value of the company, less cash and cash equivalents, divided by earnings before interest and taxes

enterprise value to EBITDA ratio total market value of the company, less cash and cash equivalents, divided by earnings before interest, taxes, and depreciation and amortization

EPS indifference point the EBIT level at which two financing alternatives generate the same EPS

equity trader See *fixed income*

equipment trust certificate type of debt instrument secured by equipment, such as the rolling stock of a railway

equity capital ownership interest of an enterprise

equity instrument or **equity security** ownership stake in a company

equity multiplier financial leverage ratio that is the ratio of total assets to shareholders' equity

equity security ownership interest in an underlying entity, usually a corporation or a partnership

equity swap exchange of a fixed cash flow stream for one based on the return on a stock portfolio

equivalent annual annuity amount of the annuity that is equivalent to the net present value of a project

equivalent annual annuity approach method of comparing mutually exclusive projects that have different useful lives, assuming reinvestment in each in perpetuity

European option option that can be exercised only at maturity

event study statistical examination of stock returns to determine the effect of a particular event on stock prices

ex ante return future or expected return

ex ante standard deviation weighted standard deviation, with the likelihood of each occurrences used as the weights applied to the squared deviations from the expected value; a forward-looking measure of risk

ex post return past or historical, return

ex post standard deviation measure of risk for a set of observations

exchange market secondary market that involves a bidding process that takes place in a specific location

ex-dividend date date on which shares trade without the right to receive a dividend

exercise price the price at which an investor can buy the underlying asset

exercise use the rights of options by buying (in the case of a call option) or selling (in the case of a put option)

expansion projects projects that add something extra to the company in terms of sales or cost savings; their new cash flows are incremental cash flows

expected return estimated future return

expiration date the last date on which options can be converted or exercised

extendible bond debt obligation that allows the bond-holder to extend the bonds' maturity dates

external financing requirements (EFR) funds that a company must raise using borrowing or selling equity interests

externalities consequences that result from an investment that may benefit or harm unrelated third parties

face value promised fixed amount in a note or bond agreement

factor financial company that buys receivables and collects on these accounts

factoring arrangement sale of a company's receivables, at a discount, to a financial company specializing in collections; outsourcing of the collections to a factor

fair market value (FMV) highest price obtainable in an open and unrestricted market by parties who are informed and trading freely, without coercion

fair value amount reasonably expected to be received for an asset, or settled in the case of a liability, between knowledgeable, willing parties to the transaction, which may be based on present value or market valuations

fairness opinion appraisal by an independent party of the value of the shares

Fama–French model pricing model that uses three factors (a market factor, the market value of a firm's common equity, and the ratio of a firm's book equity value to its market value of equity) to relate expected returns to risk

Federal Insurance Office (FIO) federal agency responsible for monitoring and advising regulators about insurance companies' risk and solvency

Federal Open Market Committee (FOMC) twelve-member committee that affects the monetary policy of the U.S.

Federal Reserve System (the Fed) central bank of the U.S., consisting of the Board of Governors and twelve district banks

finance motive holding cash in anticipation of major outlays, such as lump-sum loan repayments and dividend payments

finance study of how and under what terms funds are allocated between those with excess funds and those who need funds

Financial Accounting Standards Board (FASB) organization that establishes the accounting principles for U.S. financial reporting

financial analyst finance professional who performs research, conducts detailed analyses of individual investments, and makes recommendations on overall financial strategy

financial break-even point return on investment or quantity produced or sold at which a company's ROE is zero

financial derivative investment whose value is based on some other investment

financial distress state of business failing where bankruptcy seems imminent if dramatic action is not taken

Financial Industry Regulatory Authority (FINRA) self-regulatory organization that monitors and regulates brokerage firms, brokers, and market intermediaries

financial institution entity that serves as an intermediary in the financial system, and includes banks, credit unions, and financing companies

financial instrument legal agreement that represents an ownership interest, a debt obligation, or other claim on assets or income

financial intermediary entity that transforms the nature of securities in a market

financial lease lease agreement in which essentially all the benefits of ownership transfer to the lessee

financial leverage use of debt, rather than equity, to finance a company

financial management management of the financial resources of a business or government entity, where financial resources include both the investments of the entity, but also how the entity finances these assets

financial planning dynamic system that includes forecasting revenues, forecasting expenses, planning capital expenditures, managing funding needs, and managing risk

financial risk uncertainty regarding the earnings to owners, influenced by the degree to which assets are financed by debt (relative to equity)

financial structure liabilities and equity of a company

financial system environment in which households provide funds to businesses and government

financing sources of money for a company, including using debt or equity, retaining earnings or issuing equity, going public, using bank debt or bonds, and using the short-term money market or borrowing from a bank

five forces based on the work of Michael Porter, the five critical factors that determine the profitability and, hence, attractiveness of investing an industry: entry barriers, the threat of substitutes, the bargaining power of buyers, the bargaining power of suppliers, and rivalry among existing competitors

fixed asset turnover revenues divided by net fixed assets

fixed contractual commitment requirement that the parties involved adhere to specific requirements, such as a specified payment made on a specified date

fixed income finance professional who implements investment strategies and either buys or sells the securities of companies

float funds due a company that are not yet received due to mail and processing delays

float time length of time that elapses between the time the paying company initiates payment, and the time the funds are available for use by the receiving company

flotation costs See *issuing costs*

floating interest rate interest rate that changes regularly

floating rate preferred stock equity security that has a long maturity date and every 3 or 6 months has its dividend reset by an auction mechanism so that the dividend yield is in line with market interest rates

floating-rate bond (floater) debt obligation that has adjustable coupons that are usually tied to some variable short-term rate

flow-through taxation income flows directly to the owners as taxable income and is not taxed at the business entity level

foreign currency future contract to exchange two specified currencies at a specified rate at a specified point of time in the future

forward contract or **forward** agreement in which parties to contract today for an exchange to take place sometime in the future

forward P/E ratio share price divided by the expected earnings per share

forward-rate agreement (FRA) a contract for an exchange based on the interest calculated on a notional amount based on the difference between specified fixed and floating interest rates

fourth market trading of securities directly between investors without the involvement of brokers or dealers

framing manner in which something is presented, which may influence how someone feels about this something

free cash flow (FCF) funds available to the business, calculated as operating cash flows less capital expenditures

free cash flow of equity (FCFE) funds available to owners, calculated as cash flow from operations, less capital expenditures, plus net borrowing

friendly acquisition acquisition of a target company that is willing to be taken over

full payout lease See *financial lease*

future value annuity factor sum of the individual periods' future value compound factors that, when multiplied by the amount of an annuity, provides the future value of the annuity

future value interest factor See *compound factor*

futures contracts or **futures** standardized forward contract

general obligation bond debt security backed by the general credit of the issuer

general partnership form of business in which all partners share in the management and the profits of the business, and the income and losses from the business are reflected on the individual owners' tax returns

generally accepted accounting principles (GAAP) set of basic principles and conventions that are applied in the preparation of financial statements

geometric mean average or compound growth rate over multiple time periods

going private transaction special form of acquisition where a publicly traded company is taken private

goodwill excess amount of a target company's purchase price over the fair market value of its equity; intangible asset that is the difference between what is paid for another business entity and the value of the acquired business entity's assets

Gordon model model of the value of a share of stock that assumes that dividends are a growing perpetuity

government-sponsored entity (GSEs) financial service corporations that are created by the government to perform a service, such as buying mortgages

gross profit margin revenues minus the cost of goods sold, divided by revenues

gross property, plant, and equipment sum of book values of all physical long-lived assets

growing perpetuity stream of cash flows that grows at a constant rate, forever

growth rate rate of increase in an amount or value

half-year convention use of half of a year's depreciation in the first year of depreciating an asset

hedge position formulated to reduce or eliminate an exposure to risk, generally by taking a position opposite a position that the investor has already assumed; transaction designed to reduce the chance of a loss

hedging offsetting an investment position to reduce risk

held-to-maturity method of accounting is used when marketable debt securities are reported at cost

hierarchy principle theory based on the fact that rating agencies rate debt issues and not companies; rating agencies rate each class of debt lower than the previous class, unless there is very little of the higher-ranked debt outstanding

high-yield debt See *speculative debt*

historical cost amount paid for an asset when it is purchased

holder of record person who officially owns a share or shares on a given date

horizontal merger merger in which two companies in the same industry combine

hostile takeover takeover in which the target has no desire to be acquired and actively rebuffs the acquirer and refuses to provide any confidential information

hurdle rate minimum acceptable return on an investment project; return on an investment required to create value; below this rate, an investment would destroy value

hybrid security security that is part debt and part equity

I Savings bond debt obligation of the U.S. Treasury that protects the investor against inflation

implied volatility estimate of the price volatility of the underlying asset based on observed option prices

in the money option would generate a positive payoff if generated today

income bond debt obligation issued after a reorganization with the interest tied to some cash flow level for the company and with quite long maturity dates

income statement or **statement of earnings** summary of the company's performance over a period of time, typically a fiscal quarter or a fiscal year

income yield return earned by investors as a periodic cash flow

indenture agreement legal agreement that binds the issuer of a security to specified requirements, minimum financial conditions, or prohibitions

independent director member of the company's board of directors who is not employed by the company

independent projects projects that have no relationship with one another; accepting one project has no impact on the decision to accept another project

indifference point the quantity produced and sold or return on investment at which two financing strategies provide the same return on equity

indenture agreement See *bond indenture*

initial cash flow See *investment cash flow*

initial cash outlay See *investment cash flow*

initial margin relatively small deposit made with the clearinghouse, usually between 2 and 10 percent of the value of the contract

initial public offering (IPO) first sale of equity interests to the public

insurance contract between two parties in which one party assumes the risk of the other party and receives compensation in the form of an insurance premium

insurance premium payment made to transfer risk from one party to another

intangible asset asset that does not have a physical presence

interest compensation for the time value of money

interest payment or **coupon** amount paid on a bond at regular intervals

interest rate risk sensitivity of bond prices to changes in interest rates

interest rate swap exchange of interest payments on a principal amount in which borrowers switch loan rates

interest-bearing debt obligations that require the payment of interest

interest-on-interest interest earned on previously accumulated interest

intermediate-term bond debt obligation with a maturity between 4 and 10 years

intermediation transfer of funds from lenders to borrowers

internal rate of return (IRR) discount rate that makes the present value of all project cash flows equal to zero; return implicit in a set of cash flows, assuming reinvestment of cash flows in a similar-yielding investment

International Accounting Standards Board (IASB) organization that establishes the accounting principles for business entities in the European Economic Community

International Financial Reporting Standards (IFRS) accounting standards promulgated by the International Accounting Standards Board (IASB)

intrinsic value value of an option at expiration; it is positive when the option is in the money and zero when it is out of the money

inventory policy decisions on the levels of inventory to hold

inventory turnover cost of goods sold divided by inventory

invested capital sum of owners' equity and short- and long-term interest-bearing debt

investment analyst See *financial analyst*

investment cash flow total cash outlay required to initiate an investment project, including the change in net working capital and associated opportunity costs

investment grade bond rating that means the issuer is likely to meet payment obligations

investment opportunity schedule (IOS) internal rate of return expected on each potential investment opportunity, ranked in descending order

investment yield method See *bond equivalent method*

investment-grade debt debt obligation with a credit rating of AAA, AA, A or BBB (or Aaa, Aa, A, Baa)

investments deals with financial markets and securities, including stocks, bonds, and options.

issuer party that receives funds in exchange for a security, such as a bond

issue-specific premium additional yield, relative to straight, option-free bonds, required by investors when bonds have features that cause them to be more or less attractive to investors

issuing costs costs incurred by a company when it issues new securities

junior debt debt that ranks behind other securities in terms of the issuer's capitalization

junk bond speculative bonds with ratings below investment grade; often called high-yield bonds

justified P/E multiple that is considered sustainable over the long-term

just-in-time (JIT) inventory system inventory management approach that fine-tunes the receipt of raw materials so that they arrive exactly when they are required in the production process and thereby reduce inventory to its lowest possible level

lessee person or company that leases an item, paying a periodic amount in exchange for the use of the item

lessor owner of the asset; conveys the right to use in return for payment

letter of intent letter signed by an acquiring company scoping out the terms of agreement of its acquisition, including legal terms

leveraged buyout (LBO) See *management buyout (MBO)*

leveraged lease three-way agreement among the lessee, lessor, and a third-party lender in which the lessor buys the asset with only a small down payment, and the lender supplies the remaining financing

limited liability company (LLC) business organized as a separate legal entity in which owners have limited liability, but the income is passed through to the owners for tax purposes

limited liability limit on the financial responsibility of owners of a business entity to the amount of their investment

limited partnership or **limited liability partnership (LLP)** form of business in which there are both general and limited partners, with general partners making management decisions and having unlimited liability, and the limited partners being passive investors with limited liability

line of credit borrowing arrangement that permits a company to borrow up to a predetermined amount at a specified rate of interest

liquidity how quickly something can be converted into cash

liquidity premium additional yield offered on bonds that are less liquid than others

liquidity support ensuring money is available to pay off a debt, often in the form of a dedicated backup line of credit from a bank that ensures companies have money to pay off commercial paper if the companies cannot roll it over by selling to new investors

loan contract in which the borrower uses the funds of the lender, and, in exchange, repays the amount borrowed plus compensation for the use of the funds

loan-to-value ratio ratio of the amount of a loan to the value of the collateral used as security on the loan

lock-box system arrangement of local post office boxes for customers to mail their payments to and authorizing the local bank to empty these boxes and deposit the checks into the company's account

London Interbank Offering Rate (LIBOR) average of the lending rates of selected European banks to their best customers

long call position investment in the right to buy an asset

long hedge commitment to buy a commodity by buying a futures contract

loss aversion willingness to avoid losses that is disproportionate to the willingness to seek similar-sized gains

low-grade debt See *speculative debt*

maintenance margin minimum amount that must be maintained in a margin account

management buyout (MBO) a purchase of a company in which the purchasers are a company's managers; usually involves high levels of debt financing

mandatory convertible preferred stock preferred equity security that must be converted to common shares at or before a specified date

mandatory redeemable preferred stock or **mandatorily redeemable preferred stock** security that an issuer is obligated to repurchase at a specified price at a specified point in time or event

margin call requirement to add money and increase an equity position to a minimum level

margin good faith deposit with the clearinghouse by both the buyer and the seller to ensure they complete the transaction

marginal cost of capital cost of raising one more dollar of capital

marginal or **incremental cash flow** the additional cash flow that result from a capital budgeting decision, generated by a new project

marked to market position valuation that considers all unrealized profits and losses

market capitalization total value of the company's shares outstanding, calculated as the product the market price per share of stock and the number of shares of stock outstanding.

market conversion price value of a share of stock that, considering the conversion ratio of the convertible bond, is equivalent to the value of the bond

market intermediary entity that facilitates the working of markets and helps provide direct intermediation but does not change the nature of the transaction; also called a *broker*

market portfolio portfolio that contains all risky securities in the market

market price of risk incremental expected return divided by the incremental risk; indicates the additional expected return that the market demands for an increase in risk

market rate of interest See *yield to maturity (YTM)*

market risk systematic part of total risk that cannot be eliminated by diversification

market risk premium compensation, in the form of expected return, for assuming the risk of the market portfolio; conditions; expected return on the market minus the risk-free rate

market-to-book value ratio or **market-to-book ratio (M/B)** market price per share divided by the book value per share; alternatively, the market capitalization divided by the book value of shareholders' equity

mark-to-market writing the value of an asset up or down, depending on its current market value

master limited partnership form of business in which there are general and limited partners, with limited partner interests traded in the public market

materials requirement planning (MRP) detailed computerized system that orders inventory in conjunction with production schedules to determine the level of raw materials and work-in-process that must be on hand to meet finished goods demand

maturity point in time at which the borrower repays the amount borrowed

maturity value See *face value*

medium of exchange something that provides a way to buy goods and services but has no value in and of itself

medium-term note (MTN) debt obligation that matures in 1 to 30 years

mental accounting process of investors separating money into different accounts in their thought process

merger combination of two companies into a new legal entity

method of multiples approach to valuing an entity or the equity of an entity by applying the market multiples of comparable companies

minimum variance frontier curve in return–standard deviation space, produced when determining the expected return-risk combinations available to investors from a given set of assets by allowing the portfolio weights to vary

minimum variance portfolio (MVP) portfolio that lies on the efficient frontier and has the minimum amount of portfolio risk available from any possible combination of available assets

minority freeze-out acquisition of the remaining interest by a controlling shareholder

minority interest represents the interest in a company that is not owned by the controlling parent company

modern portfolio theory set of theories that explain how rational investors, who are risk averse, can select a set of investments that maximize the expected return for a given level of risk

Modified Accelerated Cost Recovery System (MACRS) system of depreciation prescribed in the U.S. tax code that requires first identifying the asset's MACRS life and then applying the appropriate rate of cost recovery

Molodovsky effect trailing P/E ratios of cyclical companies are overstated during low points of the economic cycle

money market instrument security with less than 1 year in maturity that trades in markets or can be privately placed

money market security short-term debt instrument

moneyness status of whether the option is in, at, or out of the money

mortgage bond debt obligation that is secured, or backed, by specified real estate as collateral

mortgage loan, usually for real estate, that involves level, periodic payments consisting of interest and principal repayment over a specified payment period

mortgage-backed securities claims on the cash flows of a pool of mortgages

multi-stage growth dividend discount model version of the dividend discount model that accounts for different levels of growth in earnings and dividends

mutually exclusive projects projects for which the acceptance of one precludes the acceptance of one or more of the alternative projects

naïve diversification See *random diversification*

naked warrant warrant that is issued without being attached to another security issue of the issuer

Nationally Recognized Statistical Rating Organizations (NRSROs) credit rating firms that are registered with the U.S. Securities and Exchange Commission

negative covenant provision in the indenture agreement that prohibits issuers from taking certain actions

net operating cycle length of time it takes to convert the investment of cash in inventory back into cash, considering that purchases are acquired using trade credit

net operating loss (NOL) loss generated when a company's tax deductions are greater than its taxable income

net payment payment representing the difference between the fixed and floating rates, multiplied by the notional amount of the contract

net present value (NPV) added value from a capital project; sum of the present value of all future cash flows generated by an initial cash outlay, less the present value of the investment outlays

net present value profile or **NPV profile** graph of a project's net present value against the discount rate

net profit margin net income divided by revenues

net property, plant, and equipment difference between the gross property, plant, and equipment and accumulated depreciation

net realizable value amount the company would reasonably get for the asset if it had to dispose of it in an orderly sale, or the settlement value for a liability

net working capital (NWC) difference between a company's current assets and its current liabilities

new efficient frontier or **super-efficient frontier** portfolios composed of the risk-free rate and the tangent portfolio that offer the highest expected rate of return for any given level of risk

no-arbitrage principle rule that two otherwise identical assets cannot sell at different prices

nominal interest rate rate charged for lending today's dollars in return for getting dollars back in the future, without taking into account the purchasing power of those future dollars

nominal rate See *annual percentage rate (APR)*

nondiversifiable risk See *market risk*

nonsystematic risk See *unique risk*

nontax lease contractual arrangement in which the lease is considered a purchase for tax purposes

nonvoting shares common shares that have no voting rights

normal profit return on an investment that compensates the investor with the explicit and implicit costs, where implicit costs include the opportunity cost of the investor's capital

no-shop clause clause in a letter of intent stating that the target agrees not to look for another buyer, demonstrating its commitment to close the transaction

note debt instrument that takes the form of a security, generally with a maturity between one and ten years

notional amount or **notional value** base amount used to determine a position in a futures or options contract

number of days of inventory See *days sales in inventory (DPO)*

NYSE Euronext world's largest stock market

off-balance-sheet financing financing arrangement that does not appear in a company's balance sheet, but only in the notes to the financial statements

offering memorandum description of a security's terms, used for private placements of securities; document describing a target company's important features to potential buyers

offsetting cancelling a futures position by making an equivalent but opposite transaction

open account basis credit in which the collateral is the assets sold to the customer

open interest number of contracts outstanding; the true amount of futures market activity

open market repurchase method of repurchasing shares in the market through brokers

operating assets short-lived assets that support the company's long-term investments

operating break-even level of sales at which the company covers all its variable and fixed operating costs

operating cash flows cash flows that are estimated to occur as a result of the investment decision, comprising the associated expected incremental increase in after-tax operating cash flow

operating cycle or **days working capital (DWC)** average time that is required for a company to acquire inventory, sell it, and collect the proceeds; length of time it takes for the company's investment of cash in inventory to be converted into cash in the form of collected accounts

operating income or **operating profit** earnings before interest and before taxes for nonoperating income and expenses

operating lease rental agreement in which some of the benefits of ownership do not transfer to the lessee, remaining with the lessor

operating leverage volatility in operating income from changes in units produced and sold as a result of the relation between fixed and variable operating costs

operating margin operating income divided by revenues

operating or **demand line of credit** lending facility that is made available by the bank for the company's operating purposes and that generally cannot be used to back up a commercial paper program; these demand loans can be cancelled at any time

operating profit margin See *operating margin*

operating risk uncertainty regarding operating earnings based on the mix of fixed and variable operating costs

operational liabilities obligations of a company that arise from normal operations

opportunity costs cash flow that must be forgone as a result of an investment decision

optimal cash balance amount of cash that balances the risks of illiquidity against the sacrifice in expected return that is associated with maintaining cash

option buyer party who buys an option

option premium value of the option

option right, but not the obligation, to buy or sell a specific asset at a specific price, within a specified period of time or on a specific date

option writer party who sells an option

ordinary annuity equal payments from an investment over a fixed number of years, with the payments made at the end of each period

over-the-counter (OTC) market See *dealer market*

out of the money option would generate a negative payoff if exercised today

paper See *bill*

paper loss capital loss that people do not accept as losses until they actually sell and realize them

par value or **face value** or **maturity value** amount paid at maturity for traditional bonds

participating preferred stock equity issue in which a fixed dividend is supplemented with an additional dividend if the issuer's common stock dividend exceeds a specified threshold

partnership business owned and operated by two or more people

passive investment strategy buy-and-hold strategies and the purchase of such products as index mutual funds or exchange-traded funds (ETFs) that replicate the performance of a market index

payback period number of years required to fully recover the initial cash outlay associated with a capital expenditure

payment date or **payable date** actual date the dividend is paid to shareholders

payment policy decisions on how quickly the company pays its bills

payoff proceeds that would be generated from the option if today was the expiration date

pecking order order in which companies prefer to raise financing, starting with internal cash flow and then debt, and finally issuing common equity

percentage of sales method approach to forecasting balance sheet and income statement accounts that uses a fixed percentage of sales from the previous period to determine amounts in a future period

perpetuity annuity that provides periodic payments forever

plain vanilla swap "fixed for floating" interest rate swap; the simplest and most commonly used type of swap

plowback ratio proportion of earnings reinvested in a company

poison pill See *shareholder rights plan*

portfolio collection of assets, such as stocks and bonds, that are combined and considered a single asset

portfolio manager professional in charge of the overall management of a portfolio

positive covenant clause in a bond indenture that requires specific actions by the issuer

precautionary motive holding cash to take care of unanticipated required outlays of cash, such as unexpected repairs on equipment

pre-emptive right right of shareholders to maintain proportional ownership in a company when new shares are issued

preferred share certificate of ownership of a fixed claim on the equity of a corporation

preferred stock equity security that usually entitles the owner to fixed dividend payments that must be made before any dividends are paid to common shareholders; ownership of a corporation that has preference over common stock

premium amount by which a bond's value is above its face value

prepayment the payment of a debt before its due date

present value annuity factor sum of the discount factors that, when multiplied by the amount of an annuity payment, results in the present value of the annuity

present value of existing opportunities (PVEO) value today of the company's current operations assuming no new investment

present value of growth opportunities (PVGO) amount of the value of an asset that is attributable to the expected growth opportunities of the asset's cash flows; value today of the company's future investments

present value sum of the discounted expected future cash flows arising from the asset or expected to be paid in the case of a liability

price earnings (P/E) ratio share price divided by the earnings per share

price-to-cash-flow (P/CF) ratio: market price per share divided by per share cash flow

price-to-sales (P/S) ratio market price per share divided by sales per share

primary market market that involves the issue of new securities by the borrower in return for cash from investors (or lenders)

prime lending rate standard cost of the operating line; the interest rate banks use to calculate their other interest rates

principal amount loaned or the amount of the investment

productivity ratios measurements of how productive the company is in generating revenues from its assets

profitability index (PI) discounted cash flow approach used to evaluate capital expenditure decisions; the ratio of a project's discounted net incremental cash inflows over the discounted cash outflows

profitability ratio See *efficiency ratio*

project cost of capital discount rate that reflects the return suppliers of capital require considering the project's risk

promised yield quoted interest rate received if the issuer does not default and the investor is paid off on time, as promised

promissory note written promise to pay back a loan

prospect theory is the area of study of how individuals make choices given information about probabilities and outcomes

prospectus detailed document that describes the security offering, which is required by the Securities and Exchange Commission for all public offerings

protective covenant clause in a bond indenture that restrict the actions of the issuer; covenants can be positive or negative

purchase fund provisions requirements that the repurchase of a certain amount of debt can occur only if it can be repurchased at or below a given price

purchase method method of accounting for business combinations where one company assumes the fair market value of all of the assets and liabilities of the other (target) company and all operating results included from the date of acquisition going forward

pure play approach estimating betas and the risk associated with an investment by estimating the weighted average cost of capital of single line of business companies with a line of business similar to the project being evaluated

put option right, but not the obligation, to sell an underlying asset at a fixed price within or at a specified time

putable bond debt obligation that allows the bondholder to sell the bonds back to the issuer at predetermined prices at specified times earlier than the maturity date

qualified dividend cash dividends from a stock held more than 60 days during the 121-day period beginning before the ex-dividend date

qualified opinion audit opinion in which the auditors find that the financial statements are presented fairly in accordance with generally accepted accounting principles except for a matter of qualification

quick ratio or **acid test ratio** cash, plus marketable securities and accounts receivable, divided by current liabilities

random diversification randomly buying assets without regard to relevant investment characteristics

random walk hypothesis theory that prices follow a random walk, with price changes over time being independent of one another

range measure of dispersion calculated as the difference between the maximum and minimum values

real option opportunity to take an action that changes a capital project, such as expansion, abandonment, contraction, and delaying of a project, in which this option adds value to the project

real option valuation (ROV) valuation of a capital investment considering the value of all the options that the investment provides, such as the option to expand, abandon, or wait

receivables turnover or **accounts receivable turnover** revenues divided by accounts receivables

record date or **date of record** date that determines the holder of record; the date that determines who receives the forthcoming dividend, as declared by the board of directors

redeemable preferred stock See *retractable preferred stock*

relative valuation valuing a company relative to other comparable companies

replacement projects projects that involve the replacement of an existing asset with a new one

representativeness tendency for people to judge something, such as an investment, by the degree to which this something resembles something else in the person's experience

required rate of return or **discount rate** market interest rate or the investor's opportunity cost; minimum return that investors expect to earn on the investment in the stock; rate of return investors need to tempt them to invest in an asset

residual owner equity owner who receive any remaining cash flows or property (on the dissolution of the business) after all other commitments have been satisfied

residual theory of dividends theory that the dividends paid out should be the residual cash flow that remains after the company has taken care of all of its investment requirements

retail broker and **private banker** financial professional who helps clients, usually people who have small to medium-sized accounts, manage their personal wealth

retention ratio proportion of earnings reinvested in the company; the complement of the dividend payout ratio

retractable bond See *putable bond*

retractable preferred stock equity interest that gives the investor the right to sell it back to the issuer, thus creating an early maturity date

return on assets (ROA) net income divided by total assets

return on equity (ROE) net income divided by shareholders' equity; net income divided by the book value of equity

return on invested capital (ROI or ROIC) ratio of operating income to invested capital

revenue bond debt obligation backed by a specific revenue stream

reverse stock split reduction in shares outstanding by exchanging fewer shares for existing outstanding shares

revolving line of credit See *term line of credit*

reward-to-risk ratio See *Sharpe ratio*

reward-to-variablility ratio See *Sharpe ratio*

rights offering issuance of the opportunity to purchase new shares of stock of a company

risk appetite specification of how much risk a company will tolerate

risk averse to dislike risk, and require compensation to assume additional risk

risk chance that future outcomes may not turn out as expected

risk premium difference in yield that compensates the investor for the assumption of additional risks; expected payoff to get into a risky situation; compensation for bearing risk

risk-adjusted discount rate discount rate that reflects the overall riskiness of the projects

risk-based models models that estimate costs based on the associated risks

risk-free rate (r_f) compensation for the time value of money

risk-free rate of return compensation, in the form of a return, for the time value of money

sales and trading activity that involves executing trades on behalf of the clients and conducting proprietary trading for the dealer itself by using the bank's own capital

sales risk uncertainty regarding the price and quantity of goods and services sold

sale-type lease or **sale and leaseback (SLB) agreement** or **sale-leaseback agreement** an agreement in which the owner of an asset sells it to another party and then leases the asset back

salvage value estimated sale price of an asset at the end of its useful life

Sarbanes-Oxley Act (SOX) law passed in 2002 in response to accounting scandals intended to restore confidence in corporate governance and public accounting

scenario analysis examination of how an investment's cash flows change in response to varying more than one input variable at a time estimates at the same time, such as sales or costs

seasoned bond issues actively traded bond issues that have been outstanding for some time

secondary market trading (or market) environment that permits investors to buy and sell existing securities

secured debt debt obligation backed with collateral

secured financing financing that is based on an underlying asset that serves as collateral in the event of a default

Securities and Exchange Commission (SEC) U.S. agency responsible for ensuring that financial markets are fair, orderly, and efficient

securities law body of law that ensures, through capital market regulations, that all investors have equal access to, and an equal opportunity to react to, new and relevant information and that governs the buying and selling of assets

securitization process of packaging loans and/or receivables together to create new securities that have rights to specific cash flows from this pool

security analyst financial professional who monitors the valuations of the companies and makes recommendations to buy and sell a company's shares

security market line (SML) relationship between market risk and the required rate of return for any risky security, whether an individual asset or a portfolio

security negotiable financial instrument that is evidence of indebtedness or ownership

self-regulatory organization (SRO) organization that oversees and monitors its members and member organizations

selling the crown jewels sale of a target company's key assets that the acquiring company is most interested in to make it less attractive for takeover

sell-side analyst person whose job it is to monitor companies and regularly report on their value through earnings forecasts and buy/sell/hold recommendations; employed by the investment banks that underwrite and sell securities to the public

semi-strong-form efficient characteristic of a market in which that all publicly known and available information is reflected in security prices

senior debt debt that has preference over other debt obligations in terms of the issuer's capitalization

senior vice-president of finance in some companies functions as the CFO

sensitivity analysis examination of how an investment's NPV changes as the value of one input at a time is changed

separation theorem theory that the investment decision (how to construct the portfolio of risky assets) is separate from the financing decision (how much should be invested or borrowed in the risk-free asset)

settlement price price used to settle futures contracts; usually the daily closing price

share or **share of stock** security that represents a portion of the stock of a company

shareholder or **stockholder** owner of an equity security of a company

shareholder rights plan plan by a target company that allows its shareholders to buy more shares at a discount price in the event of a takeover, to make it less attractive

shareholder value at risk (SVAR) measure of the value that is at risk for a party to a merger or acquisition

shareholders' equity ownership interest of the corporation, as represented on the balance sheet

Sharpe ratio measure of portfolio performance that describes how well an asset's return compensates investors for the risk taken

short hedge commitment to sell a commodity by selling a futures contract

short position negative position in an investment; the position taken by the option writer

short-form merger merger that takes place without shareholder approval that follows an acquisition of over 89.5 percent of the target company's shares

simple cash flow net income plus depreciation, amortization, and depletion

simple interest interest paid or received on only the initial investment

sinking fund call repurchase of bonds that have a sinking fund provision permitting the issuer to buy back the bonds

sinking fund provision requirement that the issuer set aside funds each year to be used to pay off the debt at maturity

small and medium-sized enterprise (SME) business that generally has fewer than 50 employees

soft-retractable preferred shares equity interest that gives the issuer the choice of redeeming the stock for cash or in its common shares

sole proprietorship business owned and operated by one person

sovereign debt obligation of a national government that is denominated in a currency other than that of the issuing government

special dividend cash dividend paid in addition to the regular dividend

special purpose vehicle (SPV) or **special purpose entity (SPE)** entity created to issue securities and hold assets, often the assets provided by the parent company creating the entity

speculative debt debt that is not investment grade; debt rated below BBB or Baa

speculative motive holding cash to take advantage of "bargains," such as the opportunity to purchase raw materials very cheaply

spontaneous liabilities accruals and payables that arise during the normal course of business

spot contract agreement for the immediate purchase of an asset

spot price price that is established today for immediate delivery

spread difference in yields, generally expressed in basis points

stable rating philosophy ratings based on structural and not on cyclical factors; changes in ratings are made not based on temporary changes in the economy but on clear structural changes in a company's credit

stakeholder any party affected by the decisions and actions of an entity

stamping fee fee paid to the financial institution accepting a bankers' acceptance

standard deviation measure of risk; measure of dispersion

stated rate See *annual percentage rate (APR)*

statement of cash flows summary of a company's cash receipts and disbursements over a specified period

statement of financial condition See *balance sheet*

static trade-off theory theory where a company uses debt to maximize its tax advantages up to the point where these benefits are outweighed by the associated estimated costs of financial distress and bankruptcy

stock dividend dividend paid in additional shares rather than cash

stock ownership interest in a company

stock split proportionate distribution of shares outstanding, typically involving an increase in shares outstanding of more than 25 percent

straight bond or **straight coupon bond** debt obligation that commits the issuer to pay a fixed amount of interest periodically, and then repay the principal amount at maturity

straight preferred share preferred share that has no maturity date and pays a fixed dividend at regular intervals, usually quarterly

straight preferred stock preferred stock with no embedded option, for which the issuer promises to pay a fixed, periodic dividend

straight value value of a convertible bond without considering the conversion feature of the bond

straight-line depreciation allocation of an asset's cost, less salvage value, over the life of the asset, with an equal portion allocated to each period

strategy is the direction that the entity intends on moving in the long-term

stress test scenario-based evaluation of a company's solvency, where the scenario is the worst-case scenario

stress testing evaluation of outcomes based on economic downturns or particular stresses, generally with extreme risk exposures

stress tests "what-if" examinations of the value of an asset or business entity under challenging conditions, such as an increase in interest rates or a decline in economic conditions

strike price See *exercise price*

strong-form efficient characteristic of a market in which stock prices fully reflect all information, which includes both public and private information

Sub S corporation corporation that elects to be taxed as a partnership

subordinated debt unsecured debt that ranks behind other debt of the issuer

subprime mortgage home loan to a borrower with poor credit who would not otherwise qualify for a conventional mortgage

sunk costs costs that have already been incurred, cannot be recovered, and should not influence current capital budgeting decisions

sustainable growth expected growth rate of a business entity considering the entity's return on equity and its earnings retention

sustainable growth rate (SGR) earnings retention ratio multiplied by return on equity; growth rate that the business entity is expected to sustain into the future

swap contract or **swap** an agreement between two parties to exchange cash flows in the future

synergy value created from economies of integrating a target and acquiring company; the amount by which the value of the combined company exceeds the sum value of the two individual companies

systemic risk uncertainty that affects the larger economy

takeover transfer of control from one ownership group to another

tangent portfolio risky portfolio on the efficient frontier whose tangent line cuts the vertical axis at the risk-free rate

tax clienteles different preferences for receiving dividend income as a result of investors having different tax situations

tax lease contractual arrangement in which the owner of the asset receives the benefits of depreciation, and the party that rents or leases the asset incurs a tax deductible expense

taxes payable amounts that are owed to federal, state, or local governments

technical analysis study of historical trading information to identify patterns in trading data that can be used to invest successfully

tender offer offer made directly to shareholders to purchase shares of stock

tender to sign an authorization accepting a takeover bid made to target company shareholders

Term Asset-Backed Securities Loan Facility (TALF) U.S. government program to inject capital in the financial system by lending funds to investors of specific high-quality asset-backed securities

term line of credit line of credit extended by a bank to a company for a specific amount that automatically adjusts as payments are made or received

term loan borrowing to finance longer-term requirements, such as equipment purchases, which have a fixed maturity and require repayment to be made on a fixed schedule

term preferred share See *retractable preferred stock*

term structure of interest rates relationship between interest rates and the term to maturity on underlying debt instruments

term to maturity time remaining to the maturity date

terminal (or ending) cash flow total cash flow expected to be generated in the terminal year of a project, aside from that year's operating cash flow

termination fee fee paid to an acquirer or target should the other party terminate the acquisition, often stated as a percent of the value of the transaction

terms of credit due date, discount date, and discount amount, where applicable, offered to customers

third market trading of securities that are listed on organized exchanges in the OTC market

time to expiration or **time to expiry** time remaining for an option before it expires

time value difference between the option premium and the intrinsic value

time value of money idea that money invested today has more value than the same amount invested later

times interest earned (TIE) or **interest coverage ratio** earnings before interest and taxes divided by interest expense

top-down analysis investment strategy that focuses on strategic decisions, such as which industries or products the company should be involved in, looking at the overall economic picture

total asset turnover ratio (or **total asset turnover**) sales or revenues divided by total assets

total return income yield plus the capital gain (or loss) yield

trade credit financing provided to customers for the purchase of a product or service

trade payables See *accounts payable*

trading securities method of accounting for marketable securities occurs when unrealized gains or losses are reported in net income

traditional cash flow cash flow measure that is equal to net income plus noncash expenses such as depreciation and deferred taxes

trailing P/E ratio share price divided by the most recent year's earnings per share

transactions motive holding cash to pay for normal operations, such as bills

treasurer one of the two main finance jobs in a nonfinancial company; focuses on the finance side: forecasting, pension management, capital budgeting, cash management, credit management, financing, risk management

Treasury bill (T-bill) obligation of the federal government with maturities up to one year that are sold at a discount from face value

Treasury Inflation-Protected Securities (TIPS) bonds issued by the U.S. government that provide investors with protection against inflation

Treasury security obligation of a national government

treasury shares shares of stock bought back by the issuer

Troubled Asset Relief Program (TARP) U.S. government program to infuse capital in the financial system by purchasing assets and equity from troubled financial institutions

true lease See *tax lease*

trust preferred security preferred equity security issued by a trust created by a company; the company backs the obligations of the preferred security

two-stage growth rate model valuation model for equity in which there are two stages, each with a different growth rate

U.S. Treasury bond obligation of the U.S. government that has a maturity of 30 years and that pays interest semi-annually

U.S. Treasury note obligation of the U.S. government that has a maturity of 2, 3, 5, 7, or 10 years and pays interest semi-annually

underlying or **underlying asset** variable or asset on which derivative is based

unique risk company-specific part of total risk that is eliminated by diversification

unlimited liability responsibility for obligations of a business that extends beyond the original investment, including personal assets

unqualified opinion audit opinion in which the auditors find that the financial statements are presented fairly in accordance with generally accepted accounting principles

unsubordinated debt unsecured debt that ranks first with the company; no other unsecured debt ranks ahead of it

value at risk (VaR) tool for evaluating the risk of a loss over a specified period of time

variance standard deviation squared; denoted as σ^2 and expressed in units of squared units

vertical merger combination of two or more companies in which one company acquires a supplier or another company that is closer to its existing customers

wages payable amounts that are owed the employees of the business

warrant securities that provide the investor with the option to convert or exchange the warrant into another security, such as a common stock

weak-form efficient characteristic of a market in which asset prices fully reflect all market data, which refers to all past price and volume trading information

weighted average cost of capital (WACC) marginal cost of raising an additional dollar of capital

white knight entity that rescues a target company from a hostile takeover by making a counterbid

working capital assets used in the day-to-day operation of a business; current, operating assets of a company; also known as operating assets

working capital management manner in which a company manages both its current assets (cash and marketable securities, accounts receivable, and inventories) and its current liabilities (accounts payable, notes payables, and short term borrowing arrangements)

working capital ratio current assets divided by total assets

yield curve graphical representation of the term structure of interest rates, based on debt instruments that are from the same issuer

yield spread difference between the yield on one debt instrument and the yield on another

yield to call (YTC) return on a callable bond, assuming that the bond is called away before maturity

yield to maturity (YTM) discount rate used to value the cash flows of a debt obligation

zero-coupon bond or **zero-coupon note** (or **zero**) debt obligation issued at a discount from its face value, pays no coupons, and repays the face value at the maturity date

INDEX